The Best Families

The Best Families

THE *TOWN* & *COUNTRY*
SOCIAL DIRECTORY, 1846–1996

BY JERRY E. PATTERSON

EDITED BY

ANTHONY T. MAZZOLA AND FRANK ZACHARY

HARRY N. ABRAMS, INC., PUBLISHERS
IN ASSOCIATION WITH HEARST MAGAZINES

For Hearst Magazines:
ANTHONY T. MAZZOLA & FRANK ZACHARY
Editorial Directors

KATHLEEN MADDEN
Editor

SAMUEL N. ANTUPIT
Design Director

MICHELE MORGAN MAZZOLA
Special Projects Editor

HEATHER CLARK, ELIZABETH CULLY
Assistants to the Editors

ANNE BREZA, VICTORIA GEIBEL, PAGE STARZINGER
Research

MARGRET FRAME, CATHERINE JONES
Research Assistants

LIZ TROVATO
Designer

For Harry N. Abrams, Inc.:
ROBERT MORTON
Project Manager

Library of Congress Cataloging-in-Publication Data

The best families: the Town & country social directory, 1846–1996 /
edited by Anthony T. Mazzola and Frank Zachary; texts by Jerry
Patterson.
p.   cm.
ISBN 0–8109–3890–1 (clothbound)
1. Upper class families—United States—Biography.   2. Upper class
families—United States—Quotations, maxims, etc.   3. United States—
Biography.   4. Social registers—United States.   I. Mazzola,
Anthony T.   II. Zachary, Frank.   III. Patterson, Jerry E.   IV. Town
& country (New York, N.Y.)
CT215.B38   1996
920.073—dc20
[B]   96–5529

Pages 2 and 3: Members of the Newport colony in 1890. *Seated, bottom step:* George Barclay, Mrs. George Barclay, Ferdinand Yznaga, Duncan Elliott, Mrs. Douglas Gill, Mrs. E.C. Potter, Count Sierstorpff. *Second row:* J.F.D. Lanier, Mrs. DeLancey Kountz, Mrs. Victor Sorchan, Mrs. Louis Rutherford, Mrs. Havemeyer, Mrs. S.D. Ripley, Floyd Warren, Mrs. J. B. Harriman, Mrs. Yznaga, Mrs. J. J. Astor. *Top row:* Mrs. Blair Fairchild, Victor Sorchan, Baron Fallon, Baron Leghais, Miss Anna Sands. *Page 5:* In 1907, Mr. and Mrs. Alfred Gwynne Vanderbilt take to the streets of New York. *Overleaf:* Supervised by the family chauffeur, the Gould children go driving. *From left:* Kingdon, Marjorie, George Jay, Jr., Jay, and Vivian.

CONTENTS

FOREWORD

Long before there ever was a *Social Register* (in 1887) and before Mrs. Astor named her Four Hundred five years later, there was *Town & Country*. Begun in 1846 (as a weekly publication called *The Home Journal*), *Town & Country* has chronicled, since its inception, the doings of the rich, the social, and the celebrated. The names of people included in this volume constitute American Society (with a capital "S") over the last century and a half. "Society" in America is a complex blend of bloodlines, old wealth, new wealth, genuine achievement, frivolity, and responsibility, and this book reflects that intriguing composition. Here are clubmen, sportsmen, hostesses, clothes horses, and dancing debs, also men and women of real accomplishment—statesmen, educators, titans of business, inventors, philanthropists, architects, writers, musicians, painters, explorers, suffragettes, scientists, soldiers, and missionaries. These were the men and women who constructed the American social landscape. If you want to know how the upper crust lived, worked, married, partied, and exercised, there is no better source than *Town & Country*.

In celebration of the magazine's 150th anniversary this year, this volume has been compiled: it is a listing of more than 2,000 key names in American Society that have appeared in *Town & Country* and *The Home Journal*. The abbreviated entries that accompany each name are direct quotations from stories about these men and women as they appeared at the time. Reading each issue turned up a treasure of buried information about prominent Americans.

Simply assembling the 5,195 issues of *The Home Journal* and *Town & Country* was not an easy job. The earliest issues were donated a number of years ago by the Hearst Corpora-

Opposite page: In 1923, at Belmont Park, horse-racing fans Marshall Field and Marshall Field, Jr.

tion to the American Antiquarian Society in Worcester, Massachusetts: I thank that generous institution for allowing me to borrow them back for this project. During its fifty-four-year run, pages of *The Home Journal* were considerably larger than newspapers of today, densely printed in tiny type, and without illustrations or photographs. But subscribers got a wealth of reading matter each week for their ten cents. Dust-covered and fragile today, the volumes had to be treated with care. Issues from the period after 1900 were located in forgotten bins in a Hearst warehouse in the Bronx, New York. Still others had to be sought from secondhand dealers.

Once a complete set was assembled, the real work began; the project was labor-intensive. The earliest issues had to be protected carefully from the sunlight in order to prevent fading; I read them with an electric magnifying glass in a darkened room while entering excerpts on an NEC computer. Bound issues after 1900 were still oversized and heavy to handle; the present page size, reached in the 1970s, makes *T & C* much easier to hold and hence much more readable.

Town & Country always had its favorites. Some families were chronicled by the magazine with almost biblical fidelity: hundreds of entries for the Vanderbilt family, for instance, could be included in this volume. In such cases, I have chosen references to give a sense of the style of those persons, their interests and accomplishments. I have tried for a chronological and regional mixture, but clearly the East Coast and the early ethnic groups of America are emphasized, as they were in the nineteenth century.

Telling details bring these lives into focus. The men and women on these pages led American taste in behavior, clothes, resorts, clubs, decor, and entertaining; they are the people who have been copied. They came from a class that could afford eccentrics, and there are some delightful ones here: Robert Collier, who hunted foxes from his low-flying private "aeroplane" in New Jersey; James Hobart Moore, who traveled cross-country with an orchestra in his private railroad car; the irascible Harry Worcester Smith, who summoned his butler by hurling saltcellars from the dinner table. Miss Eleonora Sears often walked from Boston to Providence merely for the exercise and bracing air.

These pages are also meant, in varying ways, to reflect American social history. The manners of our ancestors are endlessly fascinating; today we sometimes find them hilarious. I have tried to catch the spirit of America's eras throughout the anecdotes on these pages.

The beginnings of social coverage in the nineteenth-century were quite modest, for the very good reason that it took a long time for America's elite to become accustomed to press coverage, even reports as accurately detailed and dignified as those in *The Home Journal*. News of public receptions and private parties, quite brief, began in January 1851 under the title "New York Society," with a listing of prominent weddings—then, now, and ever the magazine's favorite function. (In 1996, *T & C* is still reporting about weddings, but today it's called "Tying the Knot." What's remarkable is how little has changed: the groomsmen may today sport sunglasses but they're still in cutaway coats or black tie.)

"Social Intelligence" became a regular feature in *The Home Journal* in 1867 and broadened the magazine's focus to include details of balls, dinners (with lists of invited guests), teas, and lavish children's parties. Obituaries were also a regular feature: the very first "Social Intelligence" on January 23, 1867, carried news of the death of Nathaniel Parker Willis, *The Home Journal*'s founding editor.

In later years, *T & C* printed millions of words about Society and its doings. In the late nineteenth century and the early part of this century, the wellborn and well-heeled were given as much attention as today's rock stars. New York activities were covered in detail every week; Chicago, Boston, Washington, San Francisco, Minneapolis, Buffalo, and other cities took their turns. The magazine, like the social set it reported, had a special fondness for certain summer and winter resorts: life was carefully detailed in Newport, Saratoga, Aiken, and Lenox. Faithful stringers filed from all over America; their reports often ran to hundreds of words.

The front pages of each issue until the 1930s also included "Social and Travel Notes" that provided a calendar of social and sporting events occurring across the country at the time of the issue's publication. "Travel," in this context, was not tips on hotels and restaurants but rather a record of who was sailing on what ship to Europe and who was booked into which resort hotel. This section included obituaries, often of great length, and, occasionally, the last testaments of the very rich (*T & C* published the complete will of J. P. Morgan in 1913), the very distinguished, or the very odd: Miss Anna T. Jeanes, for example, left a large legacy to Swarthmore College only if the school agreed to prohibit intercollegiate sports in the future.

In the 1920s and 1930s, "Letters" from Washington, London, Paris, and Berlin offered political observations from abroad but also contained news of expatriates under such rubrics as "the leading American hostesses in Paris." Always, American heiresses' marriages to titled Continentals proved a source of fascination—and gentle skepticism. The editors were slightly less suspicious of English bridegrooms. An illustrated section called "People We Know" provided more serious news from the worlds of politics, economics, and literature; many of the individuals in this book appeared on those pages.

Columns signed by Earl Blackwell, Cleveland Amory, Elsa Maxwell, and other social commentators kept readers in the 1940s and 1950s up to date on the doings of the happy few. In specific "city" issues, writers and photographers took *T & C* readers to major American cities, interviewing the leading citizens, visiting historic houses, photographing families and clubs. Society news began to be integrated into longer stories—often, a visit to a fashionable resort and the naming of who was seen there. Prominent women modeled designer clothes with aplomb—and quotable observations.

The rich are sports-minded. For years, "Dogs and Their Owners" was a regular feature of the magazine, and "Post and Paddock" gave exhaustive accounts of foxhunting and polo events, listing who were the sportsmen, who were the animals, who were the observers, and, usually, how each was dressed.

Specific charity functions are longtime *Town & Country* favorites: New York City's Purim Ball, given by the old German-Jewish families and attended by all of the best names; the St. Louis Veiled Prophet debutante party; the 1880s Patriarchs' Balls, organized by social arbiter Ward McAllister. The Charity Ball, "the oldest and one of the most outstanding social events held each year," as the magazine called it in 1933, held for the benefit of the "Nursery for the Children of Poor Women in New York City," was faithfully described from

1857 on. After New York City's Metropolitan Opera opened in 1883, it became customary for the magazine to give an account, box by box, of opera attendees and, equally important, what they were wearing. Imagine the diligence and keen eyesight of the reporters who had to scan each of the Met's thirty-six boxes and enumerate all "the glass hats"—as tiaras were once irreverently known.

From these more than 5,000 issues, I have also chosen twenty-three great American families to describe and illustrate in more detail. By and large, these families have been not only social presences but movers and shakers in each generation. And what a diverse lot they are: Boston Brahmins such as the Adamses from Massachusetts and nineteenth-century German beer barons (Busch), families such as the Freylinghuysens and Livingstons, who have achieved fame and fortune for generations, and still others, like the Belmonts, who have risen in the span of a single lifetime. Some family members have been wastrels, but more have carefully preserved their heritage. Most of these dynasties, some of them now in their fourth century in America, are still prominent; there is more continuity in American social history than one might suppose from the tag "Shirt sleeves to shirt sleeves in three generations."

So here they are, the 2,000 men and women, and, occasionally, the children, who have constituted Society in the pages of *Town & Country*. A note on arrangement: individuals and married couples are listed in alphabetical order by the name under which they appeared in the magazine, followed by the date of that story. Text is quoted as it originally ran, but in most cases has been shortened to eliminate repetitions and digressions. To the names of married couples I have added the maiden names of women when they could be found: a handful have eluded diligent search. In the case of those who had been married more than once, I have used the married name a woman carried at the time of the story, followed by her maiden name, then by the last names from previous marriages set off by dashes.

Jerry E. Patterson

A

ACHESON, DEAN GOODERHAM, the new Under Secretary of State, is doing a fine job as Jimmy Byrnes's top man. This fifty-two-year-old lawyer, former Under Secretary of the Treasury, and recently Assistant Secretary of State, has done much work on foreign policy and lend-lease. He was one of the first to announce his belief in defending America by aiding the Allies many months before the war. *October, 1946*

ADAIR, MRS. (CORNELIA WADSWORTH)—RITCHIE, is a member of the noted family of the Genesee Valley, New York. Mrs. Adair's first husband, Mr. Ritchie, and her father, General Wadsworth, were killed in battle on the same day in the Civil War. Mrs. Adair's ranch in Texas was bequeathed to her by her second husband, a wealthy Irishman. *April 13, 1907*

ADAMS, MR. AND MRS. ARTHUR (MARGERY LEE)—SARGENT After all football games in the Harvard stadium, there are celebrations in the various clubs. But the function staged in the Varsity Club was certainly unusual. The class of 1899 made it the occasion to present to Mr. Arthur Adams, a member of the class, and his bride a wedding present. A request went forth, all over the country, to each of the 1899 men, to contribute the sum of ninety-nine cents, no more and no less, for a wedding present. *November 20, 1921*

ADAMS, CATHERINE The wedding of Miss Catherine Adams and Mr. Henry Sturgis Morgan carries high distinction. The bride-elect's father is Mr. Charles Francis Adams, the noted yachtsman of international fame, and she is a lineal descendant of John Adams, second President of these United States, and of John Quincy Adams. Mr. Morgan graduates from Harvard with the 1923 class. He is the second son of Mr. and Mrs. J. Pierpont Morgan. His mother was Jane Grew, daughter of the Henry S. Grews of Beacon Street, Boston. *June 1, 1923*

ADAMS, CHARLES FRANCIS From his earliest childhood, Charles Francis Adams, known to his intimates as the Deacon, inherited the family passion for the sea. By the time Charles Francis Adams was twelve years old, he was sailing his own boat in races of the Quincy Yacht Club. In 1914, he was acclaimed throughout the country as the triumphant skipper of the *Resolute* in her victories over the *Shamrock*. That he still is entitled to his position as the premier skipper of the country is proved by his continued successes this year with Mr. Harry Payne Whitney's schooner, *Vanitie*. *September 15, 1926*

ADAMS, CYRUS HALL was a grandson of Robert McCormick and a nephew of the first Cyrus H. McCormick. In 1871, he became a member of the firm of McCormick, Adams, and Company. He was a leader in many philanthropic enterprises and a trustee of McCormick Theological Seminary. *June 1, 1923*

ADAMS, EDWARD D. is a man of wide interests. He has a summer home at Seabright and has done much in a public-spirited way for the neighborhood. He probably has memberships in more clubs and societies than any other man in New York. He is interested, for instance, in medals and belongs to numismatic associations in Germany and in France. He is Vice President of the Germanistic Society of America. Archaeology, art, natural history, sculpture, all have his support. *December 11, 1909*

ADAMS, F. DOUGLAS, an architect and member of the town-planning board of Lincoln, Massachusetts, finds inspiration in small-town government and is working to preserve land once owned by the family of John Adams' wife, Abigail Smith. *October, 1986*

ADAMS, FREDERICK T. The nomination of Mr. Adams for the position of Commodore of the Larchmont Yacht Club has caused general satisfaction. Five years ago, he was a flag officer of the Atlantic Yacht Club, serving as Vice Commodore for three years. Commodore Adams' flagship of the Larchmont Club will be the schooner yacht *Sachem*. *January 10, 1901*

AGASSIZ, MRS. LOUIS (ELIZABETH CARY) was the widow of the naturalist. In 1865, she accompanied her husband to Brazil. In 1871, the coast-survey, having occasion to send the new war steamship *Hassler* round Cape Horn to operate on the Pacific Coast, extended to Professor Agassiz an invitation to make the voyage in the interest of science. Mrs. Agassiz also accompanied her husband on this voyage. Mrs. Agassiz was the honorary President of Radcliffe College. *July 9, 1907*

AITKEN, RUSSELL of Cleveland may usually be found in association with animals. When he is not playing polo at White Sulphur, he is either making pottery beasts for exhibition, flying, shooting, fencing, or skiing. He is also an honorary Indian. *December, 1935*

AKELEY, HEALY CADY was one of the pioneer lumbermen of the Northwest and amassed a fortune from the pine lands of Wisconsin and Minnesota. He gave up the practice of law to go into the lumber business and removed to Minneapolis in 1887. Mr. Akeley was much interested in philanthropic work among the old soldiers and erected a memorial building to the soldiers of Vermont in Stowe, his birthplace. It is now used as a soldiers' home. *August 17, 1912*

ALDEN, HENRY MILLS was editor of *Harper's* magazine for the last half century. He was a direct descendant of John and Priscilla Alden, of *Mayflower* fame. He worked his way through Williams College. Mr. Alden began his literary career while at Andover Theological Seminary. On his graduation, he continued to write and to fill vacant pulpits. Soon began his connection with the publishing house of Harper Brothers. *November 1, 1919*

ALDEN, JOHN G. is a yacht designer, many of whose boats have won ocean races. The last *Lloyd's Register of American Yachts* lists 543 Alden boats—more than those of the next three designers combined. Direct descendant of the pair you have in mind, John Alden was born in Troy, New York. At twenty five, after an eight-year apprenticeship under the famous B. B. Crowninshield, he hung out his own drawing board. His boats have won four of the eight Bermuda races. *June, 1938*

ALDIS, MR. AND MRS. ARTHUR (MARY DUNCAN REYNOLDS) of Chicago, on their grounds at Lake Forest, Illinois, have a private theater that was originally an old farmhouse. To convert it into a theater, they tore out the partitions, ceiled the four walls, built in a miniature stage, sent for decorators and scenic painters who produced forthwith the "dearest little set of playhouse scenery" . . . and then bid their friends enter for an opening performance. *July 29, 1911*

ALDRICH, CHARLES FROST Charlie and Talbot Aldrich are twin sons and only children of Thomas Bailey Aldrich. Mr. and Mrs. Aldrich (Lillian Woodman) have one of the finest town mansions on historic Mount Vernon Street in Boston, just back of the State House. It is a sumptuous house, and the entertainments in it are characterized by a rare and elegant hospitality. The twin brothers have been inseparable companions from their infancy, and with their parents have been round the world twice. *December 20, 1900*

ALDRICH, NELSON WINTHROP began his career in the political world as a member of the Common Council of Providence. In 1875, he was elected to the Rhode Island Assembly. In 1879, he was sent to Congress, and at the end of two sessions he went to the Senate. He was re-elected four times. *May 1, 1915*

ALDRICH, RICHARD STODDARD Even before he entered the class of '25 at Harvard, he joined two fellow Bostonians in the firm of Hart, Brown & Aldrich to produce revues at the Nonquitt summer colony. After graduation, he camped about New England with the Jitney Players. After his marriage to Helen Beals, Dick Aldrich went to the Guaranty Trust Company but returned to the fold with MacGowan & Reed. *April 1, 1933*

ALDRICH, STUART MORGAN is a son of Senator Nelson Winthrop Aldrich. Mr. Aldrich is a clever young man, and his father's beautiful home at Warwick Neck, Providence, has architectural features that display his skill. He designed the tea house and planned the pathways, lawns, and flower gardens that make the estate so attractive. Senator Aldrich's daughter, Miss Abby Green Aldrich, became the wife of Mr. John D. Rockefeller, Jr., in October, 1901. *October 3, 1903*

ALDRICH, MR. AND MRS. WINTHROP (HARRIET ALEXANDER), of New York, have been the guests of her uncle and aunt, Mr. and Mrs. William Crocker, in Burlingame. Mr. Aldrich has been at the Bohemian Grove for the greater part of his stay. He came west at this time for the particular purpose of attending the annual High Jinks of this club. *September 1, 1923*

ALEXANDER, DR. AND MRS. ALEXANDER JOHN AITCHESON (JEAN PRESTON) "Woodburn House," in Woodford County, has been the country seat of one of the most distinguished of Kentucky families, the Alexanders, since 1791. Woodburn, of Georgian architecture, is a storehouse of treasures, especially noted for its family portraits and Troye paintings of Alexander horses, cattle, and sheep. General William Preston, Mrs. Alexander's great-

ADAMS

Charles Francis Adams, Jr. and Sr., in 1928.

Presidents and patriots, diplomats and diarists, savorers of history and signers of the Declaration of Independence: the Adams family, in the opinion of many historians, is America's most distinguished dynasty. Though the first Adams arrived in Massachusetts from England in 1636, it was a full five generations later that Sam Adams and his cousin John, the son of a farmer and shoemaker, brought the family name to public prominence. Political shrewdness and intellectual brilliance, not money and social clout, were their family tools: when eighteenth-century Harvard College listed its students in order of social position, John ranked fifteenth in a class of twenty-four (and that high only because his mother belonged to the established Boylston family).

A leader in the American Revolution and a signer of the Declaration of Independence, John Adams was sent to Europe as diplomatic representative of the new republic. He returned to become the second president of the United States in 1797. His wife, Abigail Smith, achieved fame for her own wit and political shrewdness. Their son, John Quincy Adams, acted as his father's diplomatic secretary and the first American minister to Russia before, in 1825, becoming president himself for one uneasy term. In 1831, as a congressman from Massachusetts, he returned to Washington—where he remained until in 1848 he collapsed in the House of Representatives and died in the Capitol two days later.

While both Adams presidents were respected for their knowledge and statecraft, their chilly personalities kept them from being truly popular. Adams family members have long

paired New England virtues of learning, diligence, and thrift with a blunt and outspoken manner. They also have a decided sense of their place in America's past. In 1976, the airing on television of *The Adams Chronicles* brought together dozens of descendants. "It was scary," an invited nonfamily member said. "They nodded and joked about everything Abigail Adams said on the tube as if they were going to lunch with her the next day."

In each generation, it seems, there are Adams writers: the two presidents penned diaries, letters, and political tracts; brothers Charles Francis, Henry, and Brooks Adams, grandsons of John Quincy, were all historians. In more recent years, Thomas Boylston Adams has been a noted columnist for the *Sunday Boston Globe* (and also president of the Massachusetts Historical Society). Abigail Adams Homans published charming memoirs of her Boston childhood.

Although they have given up politics on a national scale, the Adams family has continued, into the fourth century, to play an active role in Boston life. Charles Francis Adams III, who died in 1954, was secretary of the Navy, an intrepid yachtsman who defended the *America*'s Cup, the treasurer of Harvard University, director of nearly one hundred companies, and, by common acclaim, the First Citizen of Boston. His son Charles Francis IV served as chairman of Raytheon, the electronics giant. Throughout, the Adamses have retained their independent way of thinking. As Thomas Boylston Adams said, in 1986: "There will always be the establishment and the rebels. I hope our family will always be on the side of the rebels."

The Adams family, in the twentieth century:
left, Abigail Adams Homans, 1968;
below, F. Douglas Adams and his father, Thomas Boylston Adams, in 1986.

grandfather, served as Minister to Spain prior to the War for Southern Independence (as Southerners prefer to speak of the conflict between the states). *May, 1950*

ALEXANDER, MRS. EDWARD (GLORIA BAKER)—TOPPING was the first nationally recognized Glamour Girl. "Mimi" was the daughter of Mrs. Margaret Emerson, and her father was a former director of the U.S. Mint. She earned her share of the limelight, and at fourteen and fifteen was being admitted to nightclubs by intimidated doormen who didn't dare to question her age. However, Mimi escaped the deb tragedy and settled down (after only one unhappy marriage, to Bob Topping) as the wife of Brigadier General Edward Alexander. *June, 1962*

ALEXANDER, REV. DR. MAITLAND occupies a unique position in Pittsburgh. As pastor of the First Presbyterian Church, he has a wide influence and has accomplished much toward the organizing of boys' clubs and industrial organizations. At the same time, he takes a very active part in the social life of Pittsburgh—plays golf, rides, and participates in every pleasure. *November 7, 1903*

ALEXANDRE, J. HENRY was the youngest son of the late Mr. Francis Alexandre, the founder and chief owner of the Alexandre steamship line. He was an enthusiastic follower of horse racing, and as a boy rode horses on the track of Jerome Park. *July 13, 1912*

ALGER, LUCILE When the Red Brook Kennels were started at Great Neck, Long Island, by Miss Lucile Alger in 1899 for the breeding of French poodles, there were already several good individual dogs and one large kennel in the country. Miss Alger, having lived many years abroad, had studied carefully the characteristics of the breed, and when she launched her enterprise she possessed a good knowledge of the French poodle. Her desire to improve the breed and her love for this variety of dogs were incentives for the building of the kennels and exercising yards on her beautiful North Shore estate. *September 19, 1902*

ALLEN, DR. ALFRED REGINALD gave Gilbert and Sullivan's comic opera *Trial by Jury* at the Merion Cricket Club. This was the beginning of an effort to form a company to study and present Gilbert and Sullivan and was most successful. The cast included most of the more prominent young people on the Main Line. *May 11, 1901*

ALLEN, COLONEL ETHAN, lawyer and writer, was a collateral descendant of the Ethan Allen of the Revolution. He managed Greeley's campaign for the Presidency and was one of the founders of the Cuban League of American Sympathizers. *December 16, 1911*

ALLEN, INMAN Scion of the Atlanta pioneers, both sides of the family, his father is Mayor of Atlanta. Hunting is his chief diversion: quail and duck at home; lions, leopards, and other big cats on African safaris. What to expect: A life of charm in the true Old South tradition, and eventually high-finance interests. *June, 1967*

HE WAS VERY HUNGRY

Annie Russell Allen of St. Louis, who recently married the Italian Duke of Montefeltro, is the same young woman who, six months or more ago, broke her engagement with Count Paul Festetics of Hungary when she discovered that that nobleman had been conducting a quiet but very thorough inquiry as to the extent of her fortune. *November 1, 1899*

ALLEN, MR. AND MRS. PHILIP DILLON (ELISABETH H. FELL) In 1928, Clarence Dillon had Cross and Cross design "Dunwalke," a splendid Georgian manor house in Far Hills, New Jersey. Today, his nephew lives, not far away, in a house patterned after it and close to the Essex hunt club (he hunts twice a week). The scale is majestic. "We do have black-tie dinners once in a while," says his wife Betsy, "with the Chinese armorial porcelain, the Baccarat crystal, and, best of all, a 1945 Haut Brion, a Bordeaux from the French château owned by Philip's first cousin, the Duc de Mouchy." *June, 1986*

ALLEN, SUZANNE CORTELYOU was married to Mr. Henry Lloyd Herbert, of New York. Mr. and Mrs. Herbert are both descended from Long Island families. Mrs. Herbert is a granddaughter of Adrian Cortelyou, a descendant of Jacques Cortelyou, a Huguenot who came to this country from Holland in 1652. The homestead of the family is still standing on the Long Island battlefield. Mr. Herbert descends from the Earls of Pembroke, through a branch that settled in New Jersey in 1665. *October 4, 1900*

ALSOP, MRS. JOSEPH W. (CORINNE DOUGLAS ROBINSON) She has all of the dynamic energy of her uncle, former President of the United States Theodore Roosevelt. She was recently active in the ratification of the federal suffrage amendment by the Connecticut legislature and is now Chairman of the Republican Women's Organization of the state of Connecticut. *October 10, 1920*

ALTEMUS, ELIZABETH Another young horsewoman who is quickly winning recognition in Philadelphia is Miss Elizabeth Altemus, who is still in the schoolroom. Her prowess in the saddle comes naturally, and she is but taking her place in another generation of the famous Dobson hunting set. *September 1, 1922*

AMES, MRS. ADELBERT (BLANCHE BUTLER), a daughter of General Benjamin F. Butler and wife of Brigadier General Adelbert Ames, is having the historic schooner yacht *America,* first winner of the international cup, put into commission for the purpose of taking a cruise to Cuba to see her husband and her son, Lieutenant Butler Ames, both of whom are now under arms in the island. *August 3, 1898*

AMES, AMYAS is Chairman of the Board of New York's Lincoln Center and the New York Philharmonic. Like scores of other mainlanders who have come to Martha's Vineyard for decades, Ames has found a way to hide in the

island's hinterland. He is proud of his oversized blueberries and the publication of his book about deer, raccoons, and birds, *Private Lives of Our Natural Neighbors.* Ames, the naturalist, daily watches a nearby osprey's nest through binoculars and prowls his beach in pursuit of colorful pebbles. *July, 1981*

AMORY, MR. AND MRS. HARCOURT, JR. (JEAN D. MOORE)—TRUDEAU have been dedicated for a long time to East Hampton. This year, they have rented the big house and are living in the carriage house. Next year, they plan to give up the East Hampton life completely. Said Jean Amory, "We find, somehow, we've got completely away from going clamming and even swimming. What we really want is something closer to nature." *August, 1966*

ANDERSON, MR. AND MRS. LARZ (ISABEL WELD PERKINS) Born in Paris in 1866, while his parents were visiting there, Mr. Anderson was a member of all the best clubs at Harvard. After two years of foreign travel, he took a course at the Harvard Law School. He has been Assistant Secretary at the United States Embassies in London and in Rome. Married to Isabel Weld Perkins, daughter of Commodore George H. Perkins, U.S.N., in 1897, Mr. Anderson enlisted as a Captain in the Spanish War and returned with the rank of Adjutant General. *April 30, 1910*

ANDERSON, MONROE D. In 1939, Monroe D. Anderson, cotton merchant whose Anderson Clayton Co. has spread to the far reaches of the globe, died and left the bulk of his estate in an Anderson Foundation. Today, its worth is in excess of twenty five million dollars. Its major project has been the conception, planning, and support of the already great Texas Medical Center. *March, 1954*

ANDREWS, MARY LORD Historical tableaux were given at Continental Hall, the home of the Daughters of the American Revolution in Washington. President and Mrs. Taft were present at the tableaux, which indeed made the past live in the present, with the lineal descendants of distinguished folk of yore appearing in the roles. A youthful Pocahontas was Miss Mary Lord Andrews, the artist. Little Miss Andrews is a direct descendant of the Indian maiden through her mother, who was Miss Marrietta Minnigerode, of Alexandria, Virginia. *April 16, 1910*

ANGELL, JAMES B., President of the University of Chicago, was born in Rhode Island, and in early manhood had a chair at Brown University. His wife is a daughter of Dr. Alexis Caswel, who was President of the university. Since 1871, Mr. Angell has been President of the University of Michigan, though he was absent while Minister to China and Minister to Turkey. *October 12, 1907*

ANTHON, MRS. WILLIAM HENRY (SARAH MEERT) was the mother of Mrs. Stuyvesant Fish. Mr. Anthon was a member of the New York Assembly and during the Civil War served as Judge Advocate General on the staff of Governor E. D. Morgan. *April 22, 1911*

ANTHONY, MRS. ROSCOE TATE (WINIFRED ORMSBY CLARKE) Her father, Louis Clarke, inventor of the shaft-driven car, was an original Palm Beach settler. He purchased in 1891 the land Mrs. Anthony still lives on. She is known as "The Saint of Bethesda" for her decades of devotion to the Episcopal church, where she taught Sunday school until her eighty-fifth year. *March, 1979*

APPLETON, DANIEL was unanimously elected Colonel of the Seventh Regiment of the National Guard, in place of General Clark, who for twenty five years has so successfully led the Seventh to victories in camp and in the social field. Colonel Appleton has every requisite to fill the position, being a man of fine presence, high social position and wealth, and a member of the well-known publishing house of D. Appleton & Co. *July 24, 1889*

APPLETON, CAPTAIN DANIEL SIDNEY, is a direct descendant of the first dean of Harvard University and grandson of Daniel Appleton, founder of the Appleton Publishing House. He married Miss Caroline Dawes in 1916, her great-great-grandfather the founder of Northwestern University. *December 1, 1924*

APPLETON, JAMES WALDINGFIELD, JR. is the Master of the Myopia Hounds and one of the leading sportsmen of America. He is President of the National Beagle Club, which held its annual field trials in Virginia. *December 1, 1923*

APPLETON, R. M. was a former Master of Myopia, having the hounds from 1893 to 1900. The first Appleton who came to America left two great inheritances, the lovely rolling acres and the love of sport, which all his descendants inherit. Appleton Farms has been in the undisturbed possession of the Appleton family since 1635, a great sporting estate where foxes abound and where sports reign. *December 1, 1923*

ARCHBOLD, MRS. ANNE "Hillandale," an estate bordering Georgetown, with the highest tax assessment of any private residence in Washington, was built by Standard Oil heiress Anne Archbold in 1910. She designed the Italian country-style house, furnished it with antiques, including many Renaissance pieces, and went on safari often enough for her friends to claim, "There is not a rug on the floor that Anne didn't shoot." She was married to an Englishman but resumed the Archbold name after her divorce and gave it to her four children. *September, 1975*

ARLEN, MR. AND MRS. MICHAEL were seen leaving the Russian Church in Cannes after a ceremony which created as much excitement in sophisticated circles as the advent of Mr. Arlen's first novel, *The Green Hat*. Mrs. Arlen was Countess Mercati, the daughter of Count Mercati and granddaughter of Princess Kara-Georgevitch, formerly Mrs. Pratt of Cleveland. *June 1, 1928*

ARMOUR, ALLISON V., who is a widower, is considered the most desirable among the eligible men of Chicago. He is very good looking, tall, broad-shouldered, and blond, and besides being a social favorite, is greatly interested in science. He has led more than one expedition into the interior of South America in search of geological or botanical specimens. *April 5, 1902*

ARMOUR, PHILIP DANFORTH was born a poor boy in Stockbridge, New York, in 1832. He went to the Pacific coast in the gold fever of 1849 and reappeared in Milwaukee in 1859, in the packing business. The Civil War gave him his start. In 1870, with two brothers, Armour & Co. was started in Chicago, where Philip Danforth Armour died in 1901. Retaining always the meat industry as a basis, Armour & Co. has, step by step, so utilized the principle of converting by-products and waste products into profit that today the name of Armour appears on the labels of some three thousand products. *February 20, 1919*

HOW THE WEST WAS WON

We find the Astor estate to be the result of the traffic of John Jacob Astor with the Indian tribes through some half a century. Mr. Astor, buying his furs cheap, took them, or sent them, to Europe and China and sold them dear. He bought teas and other productions cheap, and those he sold again—as dear as he could. In due time, he had money to invest, and then his sagacious, money-making faculty told him that New York was destined to become a great commercial city, and that real estate, judiciously bought, must increase in value. He bought, and he bought largely. This appetite for accumulating millions grew with what it fed on, and the power to do it grew vastly with the growing millions; and thus it went on for sixty five years, until, in 1848, he was gathered to his fathers, leaving an estate to his son estimated at twenty millions. *May 6, 1868*

ARMOUR, MRS. PHILIP DANFORTH, JR. (MAY LESTER) The summer home of Mrs. Armour, at Oconomowoc, Wisconsin, is one of the best-known places on Lac La Belle. "Danforth Lodge" is situated on a stretch of land high above the lake. The grounds cover about three hundred acres. It is said that the cost of keeping up Danforth Lodge amounts to something like $40,000 a year. *November 23, 1901*

ARMSTRONG, DAVID MAITLAND had a varied career as diplomatist, lawyer, and artist both here and in Europe. At home, he assisted in founding the Metropolitan Museum of Art and became a life fellow of the museum. The French government made him a Chevalier of the Legion of Honor in appreciation of his efforts in spreading knowledge of American art there. *June 10, 1918*

ARMSTRONG, HENRY BEEKMAN died at his home at Red Hook, Dutchess County, New York. Mr. Armstrong was the son of Lieutenant Colonel Henry B. Armstrong, an 1812 veteran, and the grandson of General John Armstrong, Minister to France and Secretary of War in 1812. Mr. Armstrong was a bachelor. He kept an excellent stable, and spent much time experimenting in scientific farming. *September 14, 1912*

ARMSTRONG, MR. AND MRS. THOMAS N. III (V. WHITNEY BREWSTER) "The National Horse Show is the one time of the year that you get to see everyone you know in the horse world and on the committee," says Mrs. Armstrong, wife of the President of the Whitney Museum and Co-chairman of the ladies' committee. "When I got married, I told my husband there was only one thing I wanted to do all year and that was the horse show. It's part of our marriage contract." *October, 1983*

ASTOR, ALICE Of interest to a wide circle is the recent announcement of Alice Astor's betrothal to Prince Serge Obolensky Meletsky of Russia. Miss Astor is the daughter of Lady Ribblesdale and the sister of Mr. Vincent Astor. She has been educated almost wholly abroad and has paid only infrequent visits to her native New York since the death of her father, Mr. John Jacob Astor. Prince Serge is a member of an ancient Russian family, tracing his ancestry back to Rurik, who established the Russian monarchy. *August 1, 1924*

ASTOR, MRS. JOHN JACOB III (CHARLOTTE AUGUSTA GIBBES) In commemoration of the marriage of her son, Mrs. John Jacob Astor has made to the Children's Aid Society a donation of $1,500 for the purpose of finding good and permanent homes in the West for one hundred of the destitute boys of New York. Mr. Charles Loring Brace started with his hundred wards for St. Louis. Before starting, the boys were informed of the circumstances under which they were going, and as the train left the station they made the depot ring with three hearty cheers for Mrs. Astor, Mr. Astor, and Miss Paul. *June 12, 1878*

ASTOR, MRS. JOHN JACOB IV (AVA WILLING) There is such a thing nowadays as "fashionable mourning," and it consists of just so much entertaining—no more. For instance, Mrs. John Jacob Astor gives small dinners and small luncheons; that is, she does not give dinners, but a few friends are asked to dine or to lunch. Everything is served with as much ceremony as though it were the largest and most formal affair of the season, but it is not recorded in the papers, and therefore doesn't count. This is considered the very art of entertaining when one is in deep mourning in Newport. *August 29, 1903*

ASTOR, JOHN JACOB VI has shown a more than regal disregard for his obligations ever since he told reporters that college was "a waste of time." Mr. Astor later accepted a desk downtown, but he rapidly retired from business at the age of twenty-four. Having given the International Mercantile Marine a chance to show what it could offer him, Mr. Astor coldly announced, "I liked the ships and piers, but I didn't care for office work. I didn't get through until five o'clock, which meant that it was six o'clock before I got uptown. Also, I had to get up early." *December, 1940*

ASTOR, MRS. JOHN JACOB VI (ELLEN TUCK FRENCH) is the daughter of Francis O. French and the present Mrs. James Lenox Banks. She and her husband live well in a house in Newport, an apartment at the St. Regis, and the recently-bought "Foxhollow"

ASTOR

John Jacob Astor IV in 1903.

The Astors were New York City's landlords. No family has ever owned so much of Manhattan: all of the west side of the island lying between 42nd and 51st streets, including what is now Times Square; hundreds of acres on the Lower East Side, the Upper West Side, and Harlem. Most all of it was on twenty-one-year leases, all building and repairs at the tenant's expense. "The Astors lease but do not sell," *Town & Country* observed in 1911, when the family's real estate was thought to be worth at least $100 million.

Beaver skins were the earliest foundation of Astor wealth. The first John Jacob Astor, who arrived from Germany in 1784, sold musical instruments, then traveled in upstate New York and Canada buying beaver skins—then universally used in making men's hats—from the Indians. At first, he and his wife tanned the furs themselves, but within a few years Astor was president of the vast American Fur Company. He was also one of the founders of American trade with China. Profits were channeled into New York City real estate; Astor's only regret in later years, as the city expanded around him, was that he hadn't bought more. When he died in 1848, his estate of $20 million was about ten times larger than any other American's.

John Jacob's heir was his son, William B. When *Town & Country*'s precursor, *The Home Journal,* compiled its first list of millionaires in New York in 1857 (there were only thirteen), the name of William B. Astor led all others. Concentrated among only a few heirs, the Astor fortune continued to grow through the years. When John Jacob III died, he left an estate of $150 million; William B., Jr., handed on an additional $75 million.

The second William Astor's wife, Caroline Webster Schermerhorn, has gone down in history as *the* Mrs. Astor. Over-dressed and notoriously without conversation, she had few obvious attractions as a hostess. But determination, backed by the Astor fortune, made her queen of American society. The guest list for her January 1892 ball comprised the original Four Hundred. *Town & Country* mourned her at her death in 1908 as "the last real society leader" and wrote respectfully of her "famous ball, an invitation to which established beyond dispute one's social status."

Her nephew-in-law, William Waldorf Astor, feuded bitterly over social rank with his imperious aunt, annoying her by building a busy hotel next to Mrs. Astor's Fifth Avenue mansion. She, in turn, tore down her own house and built another hotel in its place. The two eventually merged into the first Waldorf-Astoria. William Waldorf (the second name was that of the German village from which John Jacob had come) could not endure the American press, which criticized his wealth and haughty manners. Declaring "America was not fit for a gentleman to live in," he moved to Britain, became a British viscount, and established the British branch of the Astor family.

The Mrs. Astor's son, John Jacob IV, was an inventor, the author of an early science fiction novel, and the builder of the St. Regis Hotel. When he went down on the *Titanic* in 1912, he left his two sons an estate of $87 million.

The elder of these, W. Vincent Astor, was a yachtsman who gave his yacht, the *Nourmahal* ("Light of the Harem"), one of the biggest in the world, to the U.S. government for use as a destroyer in World War II. Childless, he left the Vincent Astor Foundation more than $100 million. Under the direction of his third wife and widow, Brooke Russell Astor, the foundation has devoted most of its grants to cultural and medical institutions in New York City—the place where, for two centuries, the Astors derived their fortune.

A merica's landlords: *clockwise from top left*, Princess Serge Obolensky (Alice Muriel Astor); John Jacob Astor III; Mrs. William Astor (Caroline Schermerhorn), whose ballroom accommodated the first Four Hundred; John Jacob Astor VI in 1919; William B. Astor; Mrs. John Jacob Astor IV (Ava Willing).

in Dutchess County near Ferncliffe, the Astor family estate. They often appear at nightclubs and entertain a good deal, but are not society leaders like their grandparents. *April, 1939*

ASTOR, W. VINCENT During the past fortnight, general attention has been naturally drawn to Mr. Vincent Astor, the heir of Colonel John Jacob Astor and the representative of one branch of the Astor family in this country. For the last three years, father and son have been constant companions and the greatest and best of chums. They were both fond of the theater and other amusements. From an early age, Vincent has evinced marked aptitude for practical mechanics and not only knows more about motors and aeroplanes than most young men in his set, but also than many professional and expert mechanics. *May 4, 1912*

ASTOR, MRS. W. VINCENT (BROOKE RUSSELL)— KUSER—MARSHALL Brooke Astor's own life sounds like a novel, so it's not surprising that, from time to time, she has turned to fiction to write about her experiences. The daughter of a commandant of the Marines, she lived in China, returned to Washington and married at seventeen, was divorced within a decade and wrote a play about it. In addition to two novels, she has written short stories, articles for magazines (including *Town & Country* in the 1930s), and two autobiographies. *March, 1993*

ASTOR, WILLIAM The steel steam yacht *Nourmahal* is about to be launched. The *Nourmahal* will be a veritable queen of yachts. Her length on deck is two hundred and thirty-five feet. The main saloon, ladies' cabin, state-rooms, passageways, bath-rooms, and other rooms will be finished in solid hard wood. Electric bells will be fitted from all rooms and electric lights arranged throughout the vessel. *May 7, 1884*

ASTOR, WILLIAM B. The tax to be paid by Mr. William B. Astor to the city government this year will amount to forty thousand dollars, a sum considerably larger than is expended for the same purpose by any other individual. *August 20, 1853*

ASTOR, MRS. WILLIAM B. (CAROLINE WEBSTER SCHERMERHORN) gave a "small dance" which in size and elegance was really a ball. The two houses occupied by Mrs. Astor and her son and his wife were thrown into one for the purpose, the ballroom being common to both houses. Mrs. Astor wore a Worth gown of pale French gray satin, brocaded with long sheaves of wheat. Her jewels included a tiara of diamonds and pearls, a necklace to match, and the famous large bowknot of diamonds which originally formed part of the crown jewels of Louis XIV. *January 19, 1898*

ATHERTON, HENRY LEE has of late years made his residence in California, but he will be remembered by New Yorkers as the head of the Riverdale-Arthur family. Years ago he owned most of Riverdale-on-the-Hudson. He owns a vast quantity of real estate, ten thousand acres of land near Galveston, Texas, being only a part of his property. *June 17, 1896*

ATHERTON, MRS. RAY (CONSTANCE COOLIDGE), of the Boston Coolidges, went to Chicago to live after her marriage, where she held a court of admirers—some of whom called her "the most beautiful woman in Chicago." Her husband is now second secretary to the American Legation at Peking, China. *August 10, 1921*

AUCHINCLOSS, HUGH D., a Georgetown resident whose family has been prominent in U.S. society for generations, came to Washington in 1926, "looking for a job in the State Department." He got it, after a stint at the Department of Commerce. He married Nina Gore Vidal, daughter of the famous blind senator from Oklahoma, Thomas P. Gore, and the mother of author Gore Vidal. Later, Hugh married Janet Lee Bouvier, the mother of two daughters, Jacqueline and Caroline Lee. "It was O.K. with old Washington when Hudie married Janet, because of who she was—her parents were the James T. Lees, of East Hampton and New York," recalls a third-generation Washingtonian. "But when Jackie married Jack Kennedy, everyone thought she was marrying beneath her." *September, 1975*

AUCHINCLOSS, MRS. JOHN (ELIZABETH BUCK) was one of the society leaders of other days, and one of the first New Yorkers to establish a home at Newport. In fact, she was considered one of the discoverers of "The City by the Sea," having made her first visit there in 1851. She was a daughter of Gurdon Buck, a merchant, who built the house on Liberty Street (in which she was born) in the latter half of the eighteenth century. John Auchincloss, her husband, was at the time of his death in 1876 the oldest merchant in the city. *January 19, 1907*

AUCHINCLOSS, LOUIS "When I was a child, I was taken down to Wall Street by my father and, although he never told me so, I believed this is where a man belongs." Today Auchincloss is a brilliant Wall Street lawyer himself, also prexy of the Museum of the City of New York, but most widely known as a best-selling novelist with a sharp eye for social detail. "I deplore the loss of class structure," he says, "but only as a novelist, not as a human being. It used to be a great source for material." *September, 1967*

AULT, MR. AND MRS. LEE Their supper party at "Milleroche" on the East Hill, Cincinnati, delighted one hundred guests. The night was perfect, the moon at its best, and the supper "a carte blanche creation" of the St. Nicholas. Milleroche is a modern gray stone mansion built into one of the cliffs that picturesquely border the Ohio River. The lower terrace is a most fascinating place, its three great stone arches looking south and commanding a superb view of the river and the Kentucky shore. The terrace was gay with brilliant Chinese lanterns of very odd shapes. The whole scene was like a Belasco stage setting. *July 6, 1907*

AVERY, MR. AND MRS. SAMUEL PUTNAM (MARY OGDEN) With her husband, she founded and endowed the Avery Architectural Library at Columbia University in memory of their son, Henry Ogden Avery. She was interested in the uplift of the colored race and endowed several free beds in New York hospitals. Her husband was at one time the President of the Grolier Club, the Vice President of the Sculpture Society, and one of the founders of the Metropolitan Museum of Art. *May 6, 1911*

AYER, COMMODORE AND MRS. NATHANIEL (HELEN DRAPER TAFT) of the Eastern Yacht Club were hosts aboard the *Queen Mab* at New London for the Harvard-Yale regatta. Immediately afterward, the *Commodore* won for the third time the New London–Marblehead run for the Harold S. Vanderbilt gold cup. *July 15, 1924*

AYMAR, ELIZABETH was the daughter of the late John Q. Aymar, one of the old-time merchants of New York. She was one of the owners of the Aymar property recently sold and the residences demolished on Fifth Avenue. *August 26, 1911*

AYRES, LIEUTENANT HENRY FAIRFAX graduated from West Point in the class of 1908. He comes of the oldest and one of the most distinguished military families in the United States. He represents the sixth generation in his father's family of soldiers. His great-great-grandfather was General Henry Dearborn, who was on Washington's staff, Secretary of War under Jefferson for eight years, and General-in-Chief of the Army of 1812. It was the grandfather of Lieutenant Ayres, Major General Romeyn B. Ayres, who held Little Round Top, the key of the position at Gettysburg. *October 16, 1909*

B

BACON, ROBERT It is said he owes his appointment as Assistant Secretary of State to the strong recommendation of Mr. J. P. Morgan, as well as to his personal friendship with President Theodore Roosevelt, whose classmate he was at Harvard. The appointment is regarded as significant, too, of the role which American interests, especially those of Morgan & Co., are to play in the new conditions which the State Department must face in the Far East. Mr. Bacon has not only the confidence of Wall Street but also an intimate knowledge of its plans in the transformation of China. *September 16, 1905*

BACON, MRS. ROBERT LOW (VIRGINIA MURRAY) has been a permanent pillar of Washington society for more than half a century. She holds court in a four-story red-brick Federal house just two blocks from the White House. She moved there from Long Island's North Shore after her Republican husband was elected to Congress in 1922. Since then, she has been one of the capital's great party givers. "I don't want my home to become a museum or a historic site," she says in her soft aristocratic voice. "The house has always been connected with the government in some way or another. It demands people. The house itself wants to live." *September, 1975*

BAILEY, JAMES MUHLENBERG spent many years in Sicily, studying its ancient history. Born to large fortune, Mr. Bailey never entered business life and, though a member of the Union Club, preferred the quiet of his extensive library. It is surmised that he has left his art treasures, valuable books, and bibelots to the Metropolitan Museum of Art. Mr. Bailey was related by birth or marriage to nearly all the old Knickerbocker families. *March 10, 1897*

BAILEY, NATHALIE is of interest to even those old gallants, stiff of knee, who sit in club corners. She is a granddaughter, on her mother's side, of Dominick Lynch, whom Ward McAllister dubbed "the prince of dinner givers" and who is often referred to as having first brought the opera to New York. Miss Bailey's great-great-grandfather, who came to this country prior to the Revolution, had a great deal to do with the development of the Mohawk [Valley], much of the Lynch property being located near Utica and Rome. Her father, the late J. Muhlenberg Bailey, was a man well-known in the art world as a collector of engravings and books. *December 22, 1906*

BAILEY, MRS. PEARCE continues her work for the Equal Franchise Society. Mrs. Bailey is at Mt. Kisco but comes into the city personally to superintend the work that is so bravely planned for the summer. During the winter, there were dances on Saturday nights for the young people of the different settlements in New York, and boys and girls had a jolly dance following a short talk on equal suffrage. The society aims to do sociological work in connection with its labors in behalf of votes for women. *July 27, 1912*

BAKER, GEORGE F. The recent gift of a million dollars in Liberty Bonds by George F. Baker to the Metropolitan Museum of Art in New York serves to direct attention to the magnificent, though not generally known, philanthropies which the Chairman of the board of directors of the First National Bank has bestowed. Among other recent gifts are included one of seven hundred thousand dollars to Columbia University for the acquisition of a stadium in the Dyckman tract section of New York. *September 15, 1922*

BAKER, MR. AND MRS. GEORGE F., JR. (KIM KENDALL) George, apart from being a director of First National City Bank, has a line in performing whales—he's the founder of Marine Land of the Pacific. The Bakers have a summer house at Oyster Bay, where Kim messes about in the family yacht. Of course, she may be breaking a leg (or two) at their ski lodge in Vail, Colorado. *September, 1967*

BAKER, MARY LANDON is the daughter of Mr. and Mrs. Alfred Landon Baker of Chicago and Lake Forest, and her fiancé, Allister McCormick, is the son of Mr. and Mrs. L. Hamilton McCormick. Thus two of Chicago's old families are intermarrying. Mrs. Alfred Baker was a Corwith, which means much in Chicago. Allister McCormick's grandfather was Leander McCormick, of the well-known Chicago family. *March 1, 1921*

BALDWIN, MRS. H. C. is emulating the Countess of Warwick in putting into practice principles of higher socialism. A number of settees have been placed in front of her estate, "Snug Harbor," Newport, and here the public—and even the excursionists—will be allowed to rest. The other cottagers make every effort to keep the people off their estates. Mrs. Baldwin believes, no doubt, that familiarity with the celebrities of society will make the public less inquisitive in peering into the lives of well-known people. *August 6, 1904*

BALDWIN, MARIE is a daughter of the late Henry Porter Baldwin, Governor of Michigan from 1869 to 1873 and United States Senator from Michigan from 1879 to 1881. While Governor, Mr. Baldwin obtained appropriations for the enlargement of the University of Michigan and projected the state capitol at Lansing. *March 2, 1907*

BALL, MR. AND MRS. THOMAS R. (MARY C. GOODSELL) Dullness apparently reigns at Water Mill, yet no complaints emanate from the cottagers. They are a driving and automobiling colony, and in this way they entertain their houseguests. In "High Toynton," Mr. and Mrs. Thomas R. Ball have so beautiful an estate that the average guest would be satisfied to merely loiter away the days amidst its gardens and groves, or from its broad verandas watch the sun set over Mecox Bay. *July 20, 1907*

BALTZELL, FRANCIS DREXEL Because he is a court tennis player (captain of the Van Alen Cup team that beat the British), handsome Frank Baltzell lives in the exclusive Philadelphia Racquet Club. Founded by two of his forefathers, it is one of the nine places in America where he can practice the medieval game. "Court tennis is a game with the restraint of golf, the stamina of tennis, and the strategy of chess," he says. *November, 1984*

BANCROFT, CATHERINE is the fiancée of Mr. William David Haviland. Miss Bancroft made her debut at the Bancroft mansion in Cambridge. "Shawfieldmont," the home at Groton, on property bought by Dr. Amos Bancroft in 1812, is the summer residence of the Bancrofts. The Bancroft family lived in Groton for six generations. Major General W. A. Bancroft, Miss Bancroft's father, was a Groton boy, and at Harvard was famous as captain and stroke oarsman of the crews of '77, '78, and '79. Mr. Haviland is a son of Mr. Theodore Haviland, the manufacturer of the famous china. The Haviland home is in Limoges, France; but young Mr. Haviland was a classmate of Mr. Guy Bancroft, Harvard, '02. *December 3, 1904*

BANCROFT, EDGAR ADDISON was recently named by President Coolidge Ambassador-designate to Japan. Mr. Bancroft is descended from a family that settled in what is now New England in 1640 and has since produced many men prominent in the civil and military life of the country. Among these were Aaron Bancroft, biographer of Washington, and George Bancroft, diplomat and historian. *September 15, 1924*

BANCROFT, GEORGE, United States Minister to Prussia, is a man of considerable wealth, having a fine town residence in Twenty First Street and a villa at Newport. He has sent from Berlin two thousand dollars to found a scholarship at Phillips Exeter Academy, with the message that "A schoolboy is forgotten in the place of his haunts, but, for himself, he can never forget them." He entered Phillips Academy in 1811. *September 21, 1870*

BANCROFT, MR. AND MRS. THOMAS M., JR. (BARBARA H. SYMMERS)—WIEDEMANN Barbara Bancroft is an ebullient hostess with a flair for lively, informal dinner parties at the North Shore home, "Harrow Hill," decorated by Mark Hampton. Her husband, Thomas Bancroft, Jr., is a lifelong resident of the North Shore. Both Barbara and Tommy are horse enthusiasts. Tommy is co-owner of the Pen-y-bryn Farm, a breeding and racing stable, and recently became President of the New York Racing Association. *June, 1983*

BANCROFT, GENERAL WILLIAM A., who is President of the Boston Elevated Railway Company, has also been prominent in his stand for good government. He is one of the men of "old family," of the sort now coming forward in politics. He has been the Mayor of Cambridge and has been chosen to preside over Republican conventions. *July 20, 1907*

BARCLAY, SIR GEORGE AND LADY (BEATRIX JAY CHAPMAN) The announcement that Sir George Barclay has been made Minister to Persia delighted many of the old friends of Lady Barclay, whose marriage is more often referred to as a love-match rather than as an international alliance. When she became engaged to Mr. Barclay, now Sir George Barclay, he was the third secretary of the legation in Washington. Since then, he has had diplomatic posts at Madrid, Constantinople, and Japan. Lady Barclay, who is a granddaughter of the late John Jay, Minister to England, is a favorite with King Edward and Queen Alexandra. *October 31, 1908*

BARNARD, GEORGE G., of the Supreme Court of New York City, is said to be one of the quickest and clearest of our judicial lights, and also one of the most industrious students upon the cases submitted to him for decision. He frequently devotes eighteen hours out of twenty four to the study necessary for correct decisions. Few jurists are so accurate and few possess so many warm and devoted friends as this legal scholar. *July 6, 1870*

BARNES, MRS. COURTLANDT D., JR. is related to all the Hannas and McCormicks, and as a vivid individualist has spent considerable time in discreetly achieving the dramatic. At an early age, she took a cotton dress off the back of an Austrian peasant and ever since has had Muriel King working on adaptations of it. Most of the King versions have wide pleated sleeves and full free skirts; all of them are in deep, rich colors. Over these, Mrs. Barnes throws designer King's new fur madness, a cape made out of an ordinary little animal curried to look like chinchilla. *December, 1937*

BARNEY, MR. AND MRS. CHARLES TRACY (LILLIAN WHITNEY) Their dinner will be a sixteenth-century costume affair. There are to be tables representing the English, French, Italian, and Spanish of that period; and at these, the quaint guests, attired in costume, will partake of the food and wines of the sixteenth century, served by servitors in the costume worn by servitors of that time. Each card of invitation indicates the style of costume the guest is expected to wear, and in this way the French courtiers will not outnumber those from the courts of Spain, Italy, and England. *February 17, 1906*

BARNEY, J. STEWART, of New York and Newport, came to White Sulphur Spring and took one of "The Greenbriar" cottages. Mr. Barney brought with him his painting outfit and intends to take back with him a dozen or more canvases of this section of the Alleghenies to be shown at his exhibition in New York. With a versatility which has enabled him since the war to turn from architecture to landscape painting, and even to try his hand at novel writing, Mr. Barney is unique among American artists. *May 1, 1925*

BARRETT, DR. JUAN DE LA GUERRA Y NORIEGA Among his distinguished relatives were one grandfather who was a President of Dartmouth College and one who was a German baron. His father was Ambassador to Spain, Brazil, and Argentina. His mother's second husband was Lord Ashdown. And Dr. Barrett himself has served as Ambassador to the Council of the Americas. *December, 1985*

BARTLETT, COLONEL FRANKLIN One cannot pass the list of the officers of the Union Club without mentioning Colonel Franklin Bartlett, who for so many years has been its efficient Secretary. Colonel Bartlett is one of the most popular men in New York. He is a well-known lawyer, descended from a legal family. Colonel Bartlett, besides being a military man, is also a conspicuous figure in society. He was one of the cotillon leaders who were the choice of the late Ward McAllister. *October 22, 1904*

BARTON, OTIS is going to Nassau to make undersea movies with a new camera of his own invention. Recently, when observed by several corpulent nudes, he was nearly thrown out of the Harvard Club for trying his camera out from the bottom of their pool. In the course of subsequent explanations, the astonished members were forced to recognize a cousin of President Lowell, whose mother was of the sacrosanct Coolidges. *February 1, 1933*

BASS, MR. AND MRS. SID (ANNE HENDRICKS) Like all the Basses, Sid and Anne actively collect twentieth-century art. "They're not just collecting major people," says E. A. Carmean, Jr., Director of the Fort Worth Art Museum. "They're collecting major pictures by major people." *November, 1986*

BATCHELLER, MRS. FRANCIS (TRYPHOSA BATES) A very good illustration of the accomplishments and serious purpose of which a society woman may be capable is Mrs. Francis Batcheller of Boston, who, as a singer, is only an amateur in the Old French meaning of the word—an amateur in her love for music and a professional in her ability. She is a Radcliffe girl and speaks French, German, and Italian fluently. This winter, in Rome, Mrs. Batcheller was presented at court, and at the court ball Queen Helena stopped to converse with her when she made a tour of the ballroom. *July 22, 1905*

BATES, MRS. WILLIAM MAFFITT, JR. (ANNE DESLOGE)—WERNER If you were to pick a reigning monarch for St. Louis's horsey set, it would be "Queen Anne." Whether she's atop a horse in hunt regalia or wearing the egret-plumed crown of a former Veiled Prophet Queen at the annual ball, Mrs. Bates is a larger-than-life figure. Always a great beauty, she was reared at "Vouziers," her family's estate in St. Louis County, and has been identified in the minds of St. Louisans with flamboyant fashion and equally flamboyant lifestyle. *October, 1980*

BAYARD, KATE The sudden death of Miss Bayard has deeply affected the society of the capital. Miss Bayard had received with her parents the preceding evening. Having been up very late at the reception, she had requested her maid not to waken her until two o'clock, when she would prepare for Miss Cleveland's reception. Her sister, going to her room, found her dead. It is reported that her physician had warned Miss Kate Bayard that she was not sufficiently strong to endure the many social duties which evolved upon her as eldest daughter of an invalid mother. *January 20, 1886*

BAYARD, THOMAS FRANCIS A gigantic loving cup, fashioned to represent a pumpkin, was presented to Mr. Bayard, our retiring Ambassador to England, at a farewell public banquet in London last week. The lid of the cup is surmounted by a portrait bust of Mr. Bayard, modeled from life, and on either side stand the figures of Columbia and Britannia clasping hands. The cup cost over $2,000. *May 12, 1897*

BAYLIS, MRS. HENRY, the wife of a New York merchant, has left a home of affluence and ease and is now devoting her whole time and energies to the relief of the sick and wounded soldiers at Yorktown. She has not only volunteered to endure the privations and discharge the disagreeable duties of hospital life, but has studied the profession of surgeon and nurse so that she can care for a wounded limb equal to any of the surgeons of the army. *November 1, 1862*

BEACH, ETHEL HOLBROOK is a granddaughter of Moses Yale Beach, who, in 1835, acquired an interest in *The Sun,* of which he was later sole proprietor. Her father, Mr. Frederick Converse Beach, is well known as an editor and is the Publisher of *The Scientific American* and *American Homes and Gardens.* Among his minor achievements, he founded the Society of Amateur Photographers, now known as The Camera Club. *February 20, 1909*

BEACH, LIZZIE The novelty thus far this season at Newport is a Neapolitan harness, in which the pony of Miss Lizzie Beach is dressed. It is complete in every particular, even to the purple-and-green pompom on the highest point of the head-stall. The harness, which was bought in Naples, is covered with brass studs, which glitter in the bright sunlight, and the mounting makes a merry sound, as the pony passes by. *July 2, 1879*

BEADLESTON, MRS. WILLIAM (PRINCESS MARINA ROMANOFF), whose husband is a noted art collector, lives in a five-story Manhattan brownstone enhanced by a Renoir, Léger, and Manet. In addition, the house is packed with Romanoff memorabilia. "I want my children to know that along with a chance for a great future they also possess a great past," she says. "By that, I mean the American Dream in relation to families such as the Romanoffs who once knew immense wealth, who lost everything, and just like all the other impoverished immigrants of this century had to start from point zero. We tell our children how their imperial grandparents climbed the American ladder step by step, just like everyone else." *March, 1984*

BEALE, MRS. TRUXTUN (MARIE OGE), who lives in the historic Decatur house on Jackson Place where Commodore Decatur died after his duel with Commodore Barron, always holds one of the best jigs of the year, a full-dress supper after the diplomatic reception at the White House. The handsome inlaid floors of Decatur house gleam in the candlelight (no electric light bulb or even a gas jet has ever been allowed under the roof), shirt fronts shine with medals and ribbons, Mrs. Beale blazes in white satin spattered with diamonds. *January, 1939*

BEAUX, CECILIA, of Philadelphia, is making Boston her temporary home. For the second tea at the Monet exhibition, Miss Beaux poured, having for her vis-à-vis Mrs. Winthrop Sargent, one of the handsomest married women in Boston. Miss Beaux is being widely congratulated on her portrait of Mrs. Larz Anderson, now being exhibited in Philadelphia at the Academy of Fine Arts. *March 25, 1905*

BECK, MRS. H. BROOKS (EMILY M. MORISON), daughter of the legendary sailor-historian Admiral Samuel Eliot Morison, is another who grew up in Northeast Harbor, Maine, and has followed in her family's footsteps. Long a noted editor for *Bartlett's Familiar Quotations,* she also edited her father's book *Sailor Historian: The Best of Samuel Eliot Morison.* *July, 1985*

BEEBE, LUCIUS From the studious quiet of the *Herald-Tribune* editorial rooms, let Beebe, the drama assistant, speak for himself: "I am only one of a number of Stanley Walker's bright young gentlemen reporters. We pride ourselves on a literate and personable staff and sneer rudely at down-at-the-heel ruffians and picture snatchers. When I first came here, the editorial staff included Cabot Lodge, a German count, myself, and four Rhodes scholars. There were two copy boys, believe it or not, who were in the *Social Register. Trib* men, to the disgust and amazement of the other leg men of the town, dress for evening assign-

BELMONT

August Belmont II, horseman and banker, in 1904.

In the 1850s, August Belmont's house on Fifth Avenue and 18th Street was the scene of the most glorious balls ever held in New York. The carriages of guests would back up for three blocks along Fifth Avenue; two hundred ate comfortably at table on New York City society's first gold dinner service. An art gallery built onto the house for Belmont's collection of French paintings was often opened to the public.

But August was really more a connoisseur of horseflesh than paint and canvas. A German-Jewish emigrant, he arrived in New York City in 1837 at age twenty-one to represent the Rothschild bank. Within ten years, he had become one of America's leading bankers and made a great deal of money. Mad about horses, August Belmont rode in gleaming carriages, and his four-in-hand driving was much admired. For two decades, he presided over the American Jockey Club, an astonishing social success for an immigrant—even one who had married into an aristocratic American family. His wife, Caroline Slidell Perry, was the daughter of Admiral Matthew Calbraith Perry, who opened isolationist Japan to the West, and niece of Oliver Hazard Perry ("We have met the enemy, and they are ours"), naval hero of the War of 1812.

August Belmont's three sons were never as active in bank-ing as their father, but they became leading figures in the horse world: Oliver Hazard Perry Belmont (O. H. P.) built stables at Newport that were almost as elaborate as his mansion. (The horses were rumored to have satin sheets in their stalls.) His brother, August Belmont, Jr., owned Man O'War, considered by many the greatest racehorse ever bred in America. In 1905, he opened a new racetrack named Belmont Park in Queens, New York, which he called "my legacy to the American turf." In 1920, *Town & Country* said of August Belmont, Jr., he "is unquestionably entitled to the position of the foremost and most intelligent breeder of thoroughbreds in America and one of the leading breeders of the world." A third brother, Perry, lived to be ninety-seven years old; for many years, he was one of the leading clubmen of Newport.

Two of the Belmont brothers made notable marriages: O. H. P.'s second wife, Alva Smith, previously the wife of William K. Vanderbilt, became a suffragette, wrote an opera about women's rights, and even, to the horror of her relatives, marched on Fifth Avenue in a great Women's Vote Parade. August Jr.'s, second wife, English actress Eleanor Robson, was founder of the Metropolitan Opera Guild and famed for her encouragement of opera in America.

ments uptown. There is a copy of Horace somewhere in the city desk. You can see it is a very *bon ton* newspaper office." *November 15, 1932*

BEECKMAN, ROBERT LIVINGSTON All Rhode Island is quite pleased with itself over the recent inauguration of Livvy Beeckman as Governor. Governor Beeckman first acquired fame in that part of Rhode Island where the tennis court is, and at the age of twenty won the All-Comers championship at Newport. This may really be considered the beginning of his public career, which, since then, has passed through the various progressive stages of American sport from polo to politics, attaining finally the highest reward from the people of his state. *February 1, 1915*

BEEKMAN, JAMES W. Before the Revolution, the Beekman mansion at the corner of Fiftieth Street and First Avenue, New York, was the farmhouse or "bouwerie" of the Beekmans, then well-to-do merchants. Sumptuous as was the old house in its time, with its carved mantels, further adorned with pictured tiles, its spacious rooms, and leather-covered furniture, it is hardly equal to the demands of modern luxury. The Beekmans live there no longer, but they preserve it with all natural fondness. *September 25, 1872*

BEHR, MRS. MAX H. is the daughter of Mr. and Mrs. Grant B. Schley of New York and a niece of Mr. and Mrs. George F. Baker. At Far Hills, New Jersey, she has a country home that was a wedding gift from her father, whose idea it was to have the house span a stream flowing below the library. Mr. Schley is well known as a patron of art and for his liberality in furthering the interests of charity. *December 4, 1909*

BELIN, CAPTAIN AND MRS. PETER (MAY E. D. COATES) "Evermay," built in 1792 and one of the most exquisite houses in Georgetown, still is the setting for beautifully planned, stimulating parties. The Belin family (heirs to the Jermyn Coal fortune and du Pont wealth) has owned Evermay for more than fifty years; Captain Belin inherited from his father, a former Ambassador to Poland. *September, 1975*

BELL, MR. AND MRS. JAMES F. (LOUISE HEFFELFINGER) Mrs. James F. Bell went to New York to meet her husband on his return from a hunting trip in Newfoundland that was a scientific expedition. Mr. Bell organized it at his own expense to secure specimens of the rapidly disappearing wild animals of North America for the Museum of the University of Minnesota. The hunters brought back, among other trophies, ten caribou that will be mounted for the university. A journey of three hundred miles into the trackless wilds of Newfoundland was made. *December 11, 1909*

BELMONT, AUGUST Mr. August Belmont's stylish stagecoach, propelled by four blood bays, with two "tigers" seated behind, with folded arms, is rolling about Newport, to the edification of everybody. *August 5, 1868*

BELMONT, MRS. AUGUST (ELEANOR ROBSON), the beloved and popular star of *Salomy Jane, The Dawn of Tomorrow,* and the darling of London as well as New York, on becoming Mrs. August Belmont closed her meteoric stage career with the finality that Mr. Ibsen's Nora slammed the famous door on her exit from *A Doll's House.* The stage lost a beguiling actress, and it turned out that opera was to gain an ardent fan, supporter, and later a great organizer. *May, 1955*

BELMONT, OLIVER HAZARD PERRY was a son of the late Mr. and Mrs. August Belmont, the latter a daughter of Commodore Matthew Calbraith Perry, who opened Japan to the commerce of the world. Mr. Belmont was a graduate of the United States Naval Academy. He was a member of the banking firm of August Belmont & Co. until 1899, when he retired. He then published a weekly paper, *The Verdict*, devoted to the interests of politics. From 1901 to 1903, he was a representative in Congress from the Thirteenth District. He was an ardent supporter of William Jennings Bryan, who was his guest at a dinner given in his Fifth Avenue home in January 1900. *June 20, 1908*

HOUDINI ON THE BEACH

Houdini was the performer at the garden party given on Wednesday of last week by Mrs. August Belmont, at the old Belmont estate "By-the-Sea." The musicians were stationed on the piazza. For Houdini, there was a golden tent for a dressing room, and the audience gathered around him seated on chairs under the trees. When the time for the last trick arrived, all the guests hurried across the lawn. Houdini was rowed out to the *Scout*, and the big box with two hundred pounds of iron lashed to it was taken over in another boat. Houdini waved farewell to those on shore before he was boxed up. He escaped from the trunk, swam for a distance while those on the cliffs applauded. When Houdini, with his hair dripping wet from his swim in the sea, made his returning climb to the cliff walk, Mrs. Belmont, her violet scarf fluttering, ran to meet him. First clasping, then clapping her hands in front of her, she said with her pretty sparkle and animation, "Mr. Houdini, that was splendid! I don't see how you have strength." *August 31, 1912*

BELMONT, MRS. OLIVER HAZARD PERRY (ALVA SMITH)—VANDERBILT has leased a floor in the building at 505 Fifth Avenue. This floor is to be arranged as a club for women suffragists. Mrs. Belmont, who never does anything by halves, has gone heart and soul into the suffrage movement. Her daughter, the Duchess of Marlborough, will come over later and join her mother in this new venture. *July 24, 1909*

BELMONT, MRS. PERRY (JESSIE ROBBINS), always appropriately gowned as a Frenchwoman, was conspicuous for this reason in her box at the races at the Coney Island Jockey Club. In pale blue, Mrs. Belmont wore a large black hat, laden with white plumes. This season, at the afternoon weddings, she had a preference for soft-toned gowns, gold-brown velvet in winter, and grays when the springtime came. At the opera, where her emeralds, set in quaint designs, attracted a great deal of scrutiny from the glasses of the orchestra occupants, she wore a series of truly Parisian-like frocks, several having butterfly appendages of soft tulle that were wing-like in effect. *June 25, 1904*

BELMONT, RAYMOND, the second son of Mr. August Belmont, is coming rapidly to the front as a crack polo player; in fact, he is a veteran, having been on the field ever since he was a little over twelve years old. He is an enthusiastic yachtsman, a follower of motor boating and all outdoor sports. All three of Mr. Belmont's sons are interested in the banking business. *July 20, 1912*

BENEDICT, COMMODORE ELIAS CORNELIUS sailed last week on board the *Oneida* for a six weeks' trip to South America, where he will travel a distance of ten thousand miles. This is the Commodore's fifth trip to South America. He has sailed for a considerable distance up the Amazon. The log of the *Oneida* contains the names of Presidents, Governors, and notables of this and other lands. Commodore Benedict was an intimate friend of the late Grover Cleveland and is in close personal relations with President Wilson. *May 3, 1913*

BENJAMIN, BEATRICE W., is a granddaughter, on the maternal side, of Mr. H. H. Rogers, Sr. She is a granddaughter of Park Benjamin, the poet, famous as the author of "The Nautilus," and a niece of John Lothrop Motley, the historian and diplomat, who was Minister to Austria and also to England, and whose daughter married Lord Harcourt. *February 20, 1909*

BENJAMIN, MRS. GEORGE HILLIARD (GRACE H. TREMAINE) At the Thursday afternoon meetings of the roller-skating class, the leader of which is Mrs. George Hilliard Benjamin, there are happy New Yorkers skating as though never tired and eager for a partner every time the band begins to play. They are all, with few exceptions, women who follow the social program of the week with pleasure. The tea table at the side of the rink is sought for the sake of sociability rather than stimulant, and until time to rush home for dinner and dancing the floor is crowded. *February 8, 1913*

BENNETT, MRS. JAMES GORDON (HENRIETTA AGNES CREAN) The most elegant and *recherché* turn-out at Saratoga this season is that of Mrs. Bennett, the wife of the editor of the *New York Herald:* a pony phaeton, evidently built in Paris. She drives her pair-in-hand herself, carrying jauntily her parasol, attached to a delicate ivory whip, which is thus made to serve, very gracefully indeed, a double purpose. She drives carefully, and there are few teams there that can pass her ponies when she fancies to put them on their mettle. *August 25, 1860*

BERGH, HENRY Twenty years ago Henry Bergh, in company with other eminent citizens, founded the Society for the Prevention of Cruelty to Animals at the Astor Place Opera House. Today, three-fourths of the states of the union have similar societies, and Mr. Bergh holds in his hands wills bequesting at least half a million dollars. *January 27, 1886*

BERWIND, MRS. EDWARD J. (HERMINIE TORREY) brought two monkeys with her to Newport and, fearing that they might be lonesome, purchased a pair of marmosets, paying a goodly sum for them as they have the fine manners found only in monkeys who have been at boarding school in Newport. *August 16, 1902*

BERWIND, JULIA, who could, and often did, execute an agile high kick even when she was in her eighties, died a few years ago, two shy of a hundred. For a time "The Elms," one of Newport's loveliest great cottages, was threatened with exploitation by a real estate entrepreneur, but fortunately it was saved at the eleventh hour by private capital and turned over to the able hands of the Newport Preservation Society. *July, 1963*

BEST, GENERAL CLERMONT LIVINGSTON was graduated with the highest honors at the age of nineteen from West Point. He served in the latter part of the Mexican War and was brevetted three times on the field of battle for bravery and gallantry. He was in arms throughout the Civil War; it was his guns that turned the tide of battle at Chancellorsville. *November 10, 1906*

BETTS, FREDERIC HENRY, who was an unusually efficient lawyer, was born at Newburgh, New York, in 1843. He was descended, on his father's side, from Thomas Betts, one of the founders of Guilford, Connecticut; from Josiah Rossiter, of Connecticut; and on the distaff side from John Eliot, apostle to the Indians; from Governors George Wyllys and Samuel Wyllys, of Connecticut; and from Colonel Andrew Ward. *November 18, 1905*

BIBBY, WILLIAM H. belonged to one of the oldest Knickerbocker families in New York. He was related to the Van Courtlandts, the Stuyvesants, the Schermerhorns, and the Astors. For years, he was Secretary of the Union Club. His great-grandfather was the famous Mr. van den Heuvel, whose country seat was a landmark on the Boulevard [Broadway] for many years. This old Colonial mansion, with its famous rooms and mantels and carving, was demolished six years ago, and a large apartment house stands on its site. *August 6, 1910*

BIDDLE, MRS. ALEXANDER WILLIAMS is a distinctively aristocratic figure. Mrs. Biddle is very apt at petit point, and during the after-luncheon coffee hour in the crystal room at the Homestead, Virginia Hot Springs, or on the Casino lawn during the concert hours, gave one an idea of how the Empress Matilda might have looked while working on her strip of Bayeux. *June 1, 1926*

BIDDLE, ALFRED The members of the Philadelphia Main Line horse set were known for brusqueness. One, Alfred Biddle, startled a dinner partner when she asked him what to do about the thistles in her fields. "Madame," was the terse answer, "I suggest that you get a camel." *September, 1992*

BIDDLE, ANTHONY J. DREXEL is making a most extraordinary collection of trophies of bloody fistic carnivals. He has now quite an extensive array of gloves worn in famous pugilistic contests, sponges used in cooling the fighters' brows, and autographed palm-leaf fans with which many a boxer's resuscitation has been aided. These are all carefully labeled, and no guest at Mr. Biddle's home departs without having the sanguinary relics tenderly shown him. *September 20, 1902*

BIDDLE, MR. AND MRS. ANTHONY J. DREXEL, JR. (MARY DUKE), were married at Duke's Farms, the estate of the bride's uncle at Somerville, New Jersey, a great property covering five square miles where Mr. Duke has erected hills and dug valleys, made lakes and waterfalls and about seventy very active fountains supplied by private water works. Each one is a copy of some famous fountain of the Old World. Mr. Duke's own railroad track runs into his estate, and special trains, one from New York and one from Philadelphia, brought guests to a station, whence motor buses carried them past the lakes and falls to the house. *July 1, 1915*

BIDDLE, MR. AND MRS. FRANCIS (KATHARINE GARRISON CHAPIN) The former United States Attorney General and his wife are among the many noted Washington art collectors who are represented in the current exhibition, "Privately Owned," at the Corcoran Gallery. Talk of art at the Francis Biddles' comes as naturally as discussions of books or politics. He has just written the widely praised analysis of McCarthyism in *The Fear of Freedom.* Mrs. Biddle is the author of three books of poetry. *February, 1952*

BIDDLE, MR. AND MRS. J. C. MERCER (ANNA THERESA BRENNAN) Philadelphia society was surprised by the announcement of the marriage of Mr. Biddle to Miss Brennan, a young woman in a different walk of life. It is said the bride's father was formerly a coachman. Mr. Biddle is a descendant of John Biddle, and is said to be the head of the Biddle family in this country. He was educated in Philadelphia and has been conspicuous in its fashionable set, being considered one of its most eligible bachelors. *August 30, 1902*

BIDDLE, MR. AND MRS. JAMES (LOUISA COPELAND) James Biddle, who heads the National Trust for Historic Preservation, believes that historic homes should vibrate with action rather than being served up to the public as museum pieces. Biddle keeps a dazzling array of projects going in the ten houses owned by the National Trust, of which he became President in 1967 (moving to the post from his former place as Curator of the Metropolitan Museum's American Wing). *September, 1970*

BIDDLE, MRS. (LENA GAINES) and her husband are at "Paradise," the old Gaines place on the outskirts of Warrenton, Virginia. The marriage of the Biddles was a most romantic one, for Mr. Biddle had spent nearly twenty years in a Trappist monastery, detained against his will much of the time, and effected his escape after many trials and tribulations. *August 1, 1922*

BIGELOW, MR. AND MRS. ALBERT S. left Burlington, Vermont, recently for a coaching trip in the Green Mountain State and western Massachusetts. Stops will be made at several towns. The coach left Cohasset several days before, so that the six horses were rested when Mr. Bigelow and his party started out. The trip will be made by easy stages, and there will be excursions on the lakes and mountain climbing and other diversion. *October 15, 1904*

BIGELOW, JOHN is one of the oldest members of the Thursday Evening Club. He was born in 1817 and graduated from Union College in 1835. Giving up his legal practice for journalism in 1849, he became the partner of William Cullen Bryant in the ownership of the *Evening Post.* From 1865 to 1867, he was Minister to France. Following this, he was Secretary of State for New York. *April 8, 1905*

BIGELOW, MRS. JOHN (JANE POULTNEY) It is said that Mrs. John Bigelow, wife of our late Minister to France, astonished the Parisian ladies by her wonderful pianoforte playing. She performs with a dashing disregard for the tenets of the art, her style being very fascinating and original. *August 21, 1867*

BIGELOW, POULTNEY, a son of John Bigelow, the venerable statesman, at one time in his life practised law. He has been a great traveler and has credit for being the first man to take a canoe through the Iron Gates of the Danube. *April 15, 1911*

BINGHAM, MRS. BARRY (MARY CLIFFORD CAPERTON), an erudite aristocrat, once the book page editor of the *Louisville Courier-Journal and Times,* the newspaper edited and published by her husband, is a crusading conservationist. Perched on its own hill, "Melcombe," her home, is a place of unparalleled splendor. An enormous southern Georgian Greek Revival mansion built in 1911, its spacious, courtly rooms are filled with magnificent French and English antiques. With ginger sarcasm, Mrs. Bingham muses about Kentucky hospitality as "living in The Compliment Belt." *April, 1970*

BINGHAM, MRS. HARRY PAYNE (MELISSA YUILLE) is one of three legendary, beautiful Yuille sisters. All married well, but Melissa married best. Husband was banker-philanthropist-sportsman. Old Guard. Was a confidant of the celebrated Consuelo Vanderbilt Balsan. Her estate, "Legerwood," in Southampton, is one of the best run, with a butler who serves in white gloves. *July, 1975*

BINGHAM, TIFFANY MITCHELL Binghams and branches of Binghams have been a staple at Groton for generations. Tiffany ticks off on her fingers: "Father, brother, sister, five uncles, cousins—well, I had some cousins who went to Westminster and Suffield Academy." Her ancestors were missionaries in Hawaii. *June, 1985*

BISHOP, CORTLANDT FIELD, who, with Mrs. Bishop (Amy Bend), has recently returned from a most remarkable automobile trip through Europe and Africa, is now at "Interlaken," his country place at Lenox. Mr. Bishop probably feels somewhat triumphant at seeing the signs, "Automobiles not allowed," taken down about Lenox, Massachusetts. Mr. Bishop's trip took him over a large part of Italy and northern Africa, including a long trip

BIDDLE

Brigadier General and Mrs. Nicholas Biddle and family.

According to legend, when Edward, Prince of Wales, visited Philadelphia during his American tour in 1860, he was introduced to so many people named Biddle that he finally asked in bewilderment, "What *is* a Biddle?" In 1981, on the 300th anniversary of William Biddle's arrival in America, *Town & Country* could only reply: "A family synonymous with the social, cultural, and financial life of Philadelphia."

William Biddle, Quaker and shoemaker in Oliver Cromwell's army, settled in West New Jersey in 1682. One hundred years later, numerous Biddles, despite their Quaker heritage, distinguished themselves as military and naval officers in the American Revolution. Clement Biddle organized "The Quaker Blues," a Pennsylvania volunteer regiment, and Nicholas Biddle, a sailor, made successful (and very profitable) raids on British shipping in the West Indies, until he was killed in action off Barbados in 1778.

Another Nicholas, the son of Charles Biddle, completed his course work at the University of Pennsylvania at the age of thirteen. When his degree was withheld because of his age, he moved on to Princeton. Diplomat, financier, writer, and editor, he acted as a vice-president of Pennsylvania under the constitution of 1776 and became president of the highly polit-

ical and controversial Bank of the United States in 1823. When it collapsed in 1841, he retired to his home, "Andalusia," sixteen miles from Philadelphia on the west bank of the Delaware River. A great admirer of classical Greece, Nicholas remodeled the house in the Greek Revival style and there entertained European visitors, American scholars, and statesmen.

The Biddle clan has produced its share of eccentrics: One of them, Anthony J. Drexel Biddle, Sr., had a passion for boxing, collected the gloves of famous fighters, and taught muscular Christianity in Sunday schools. His son, Anthony, Jr., married Mary Duke of the Duke tobacco fortune; Anthony, Jr.'s sister Cordelia married Anthony Duke, Mary's brother. The senior Biddle's life was the subject of a biography by Cordelia called *My Philadelphia Father,* later becoming the play *The Happiest Millionaire.*

The Biddle family has a deeply-felt respect for the past. Today, James Biddle, a former chairman of the National Trust for Historic Preservation, lives at Andalusia, and the house is protected as a National Historical Landmark. Nicholas Biddle Wainwright long served as director of The Historical Society of Pennsylvania, and Livingston Biddle is a former chairman of the National Endowment for the Arts.

What *is* a Biddle?
Clockwise from top left,
James Biddle; Laura Biddle in 1917;
Mr. and Mrs. George Drexel Biddle;
A. J. Drexel Biddle, Jr.; Major
General John Biddle in 1919; the Honorable
Francis and Mrs. Biddle (Katharine
Garrison Chapin), 1952; A. J. Drexel
Biddle, 1911; Craig Biddle, Jr.

into the great desert of the Sahara, where his big car frightened the camels into running away, but had little or no terrors for the natives. *October 1, 1904*

BISHOP, MR. AND MRS. HEBER A red domino party in a white and gold ballroom made a rather striking sight. It was evoked by Mr. and Mrs. Bishop's dance. Both men and women wore dominoes and, as a rule, half masks with a fall of lace. At the supper table, there were red flowers and red lamp shades, and in the favors for the cotillion afterward. The spirit of the occasion was duly reflected. The favors were elaborate trifles of silver, dolls drawn from a large scarlet boot, sachets, and fancy articles. *February 2, 1898*

BLABON, MRS. GEORGE W. (LILLY MAGNUS)—PREECE She was born to the Busch beer barony; married heir to linoleum fortune. At one of her famous parties, on her birthday, she received guests from inside a baby carriage, swaddled in pink blankets, sucking a pacifier, and sipping from a baby bottle filled with gin. *July, 1975*

BLACKWELL, BEATRIX is thirteen years old, of the ninth generation of Blackwells born on Long Island and of the clan who gave the name to the East River island. She is a descendant of Robert Blackwell, who settled in America in 1661. An expert horsewoman, she follows the Meadow Brook, Smithtown, and West Hills hounds. *October 1, 1922*

BLAIR, BOWEN The dynasty's central figure was William McCormick Blair (1884–1982), the distinguished investment banker who founded William Blair & Co., in 1935. But through both him and his wife, today's Blairs trace their Chicago roots all the way back to the city's very first settlers. His sons Edward and Bowen succeeded him at the firm; Bowen recently followed in his father's footsteps as head of the Art Institute, as well. Third son, William, Jr., is former U.S. Ambassador to Denmark and the Philippines. *September, 1990*

BLAIR, C. LEDYARD graduated from Princeton in 1890 and at once became a banker. Aside from his own firm, he is a director in several other banking institutions and in a number of railroads. He has a country home at Peapack, New Jersey, that has been the objective of many a run of the New York Coaching Club, of which Mr. Blair is an ardent supporter. He has been Commodore of the New York Yacht Club and has acted in high official capacity in a number of other clubs as well. *October 20, 1915*

BLAIR, DE WITT CLINTON was a graduate of Princeton, class of '56, and he gave Blair Hall to the Halstead Observatory at Princeton. His father, who was a noted railway man and one of the original directors of the Union Pacific Railroad, gave $70,000 to Princeton and $100,000 to the Blair Presbyterian Academy and built eighty churches in the West. *June 20, 1915*

BLAIR, JENNIE The big event was the long-heralded cotillion, the first in more than a decade, at which Miss Jennie Blair entertained. Mr. Edward M. Greenway, once czar of San Fran-

cisco society, and at whose famous balls Miss Blair was frequently his partner, led the cotillion. He had previously drilled six of the couples in the figures, many of which were revived from the old affairs. Miss Blair had selected the favors two years ago during the winter she spent in Paris, and they were all exquisite bits of finery or dainty articles of bric-a-brac. *February 1, 1922*

BLAIR, DR. AND MRS. MONTGOMERY Blair House in Washington, D.C., once belonged to Dr. Montgomery Blair's aunt and uncle, Major and Mrs. Gist Blair, and when they died he inherited it. Having two homes in Washington, Dr. Blair and his wife were most generous with the famous house, lending it to the White House for guest overflow. Now they have sold the house to the Government, with its original furniture, china, and silver, though the portraits are still on loan. *September, 1943*

BLAIR, MRS. WILLIAM (SARAH SEYMOUR) is the widow of William Blair, of Chicago. Mrs. Blair came to Chicago on her marriage in 1854 and for nearly seventy years was identified with the social, religious, and charitable life of the city. Her name was found on the list of every charity and was well known in foreign lands, where her church, the Presbyterian, had established work. *April 15, 1923*

BLAKE, BRIAN P. T. presides over the St. Nicholas Society. Founded by Washington Irving in 1835, the St. Nicholas is one of the oldest New York hereditary societies and draws male descendants of those who settled in the colony before 1785. *September, 1987*

BLAKELEY, MRS. GERALD W. (TENLEY ALBRIGHT) took up skating to strengthen her legs after being afflicted with polio. In costumes made by her grandmother, Miss Albright skated her way into national and international prominence. In 1952, she won a silver medal in the Olympics and, in 1956, the gold. Then, following the family tradition of her father and brother, she entered medical school and now is a surgeon at New England Baptist Hospital. *July, 1982*

BLANEY, MR. AND MRS. DWIGHT (EDITH W. HILL) of Boston are, as usual, at their summer home, "Blaney Castle," on Ironbound Island. Mr. Blaney, whose artistic work is familiar to all art lovers, is truly monarch of all he surveys in his island stronghold, with its perpendicular cliffs surmounted by its dense growth of trees. Ironbound is one of the most beautiful of the many islands which lend charm to the scenery about Bar Harbor, and Mr. Blaney is almost its sole possessor and inhabitant. *July 8, 1905*

BLEECKER, JAMES FORSYTH (of the Bleecker Street Bleeckers, the Jones Beach Joneses, and the Hudson Valley Verplancks) is a 27-year-old photographer and audio-visual producer specializing in historic preservation. He is now a member of the board that administers his own family's Hudson Valley homestead, "Mount Gulian," which von Steuben used as his headquarters and in which the Society of the Cincinnati was founded. A circa 1730 stone

Dutch Colonial built by Gulian Verplanck and restored by Mr. Bleecker's father, Bach Bleecker, it is on the National Register. *September, 1987*

BLEECKER, MRS. LYMAN C. (RUTH BLISS)—SCHWAB The New York Junior Assembly shows off one hundred girls, who automatically become the debs of the season. Nobody quite knows how they're selected. The Chairman of the Invitations Committee, Mrs. Lyman C. Bleecker, wife of an Episcopal clergyman in Cold Spring Harbor, comments, "Money simply does not count with us. As for the other debutante balls, they are much larger and they're benefits. But here at the Assemblies, we are not impressed with money." *June, 1966*

BLISS, CORNELIUS N. was Secretary of the Interior in President McKinley's administration and Treasurer of the Republican National Committee in four successive campaigns. Mr. Bliss began his business career in 1848 with James M. Beebe & Co., of Boston, and afterwards opened a branch dry goods house in New York. He was President of the Fourth National Bank and on the board of many financial institutions. *October 14, 1911*

BLISS, E. JARED, JR. "This house on Martha's Vineyard was in my family for five generations. It was built by my great-great-grandfather, Jared Fisher, Sr.," Bliss said. Commodore for many years of the Edgartown Yacht Club and a trustee of Mystic Seaport, Bliss, who served on the *America*'s Cup Race Committee, is revered for his sailing skills. *July, 1981*

BLISS, MRS. ROBERT WOODS (MILDRED BARNES) One of America's truly remarkable women, she lives in a house sprinkled with enormous collections of Lowestoft and Crown Derby, covered with miles of Gobelins tapestries. Outside, there are gardens, acres of greenhouses, and a Hollywood pool. The key to the personality of "Dumbarton Oaks" lies in the hands of industrious Mrs. Bliss, herself Washington's most distinguished institution. *December, 1938*

BLOODGOOD, ANTOINETTE Narragansett's "Black and White" ball was given at the Casino. The ballroom was a solid interior of black and white, one thousand yards of bunting being used to create a startling effect in an overhead roof and sides. The pillars of the ballroom had panels in large black-and-white-check cretonne, and the improvised boxes in the balcony were paneled in checks. The central piece of the decorative scheme was a big black bird cage suspended from the center of the ballroom, containing four white doves, the lower part being filled with white rose petals. At the psychological moment, Miss Antoinette Bloodgood of New York pulled a cord which released the rose petals and was supposed to release the doves. These, however, slept serenely on, seemingly unconscious of their surroundings. *August 10, 1915*

BOARDMAN, THOMAS DENNIS, one of Boston's best-known real estate men and prominent in yachting and club circles, died at his summer home "Chubbs," West Manchester, Massachusetts. He was the last of the original members of the Eastern Yacht Club, of which he was Commodore in 1878 and 1879. *October 1, 1919*

BOGGS, MRS. HALE (LINDY CLAIBORNE) is serving her seventh term as a U.S. Representative from Louisiana; her daughter Barbara Boggs Sigmund is the Mayor of Princeton, New Jersey. They represent the tenth and eleventh generations of the remarkable Claiborne family to serve the public. They number among their many political ancestors William C. C. Claiborne, whose vote in the contested 1800 presidential election denied the office to Aaron Burr and made Thomas Jefferson President. *October, 1986*

BONAPARTE, MRS. CHARLES JOSEPH (ELLEN CHANNING) is the widow of Mr. Charles Joseph Bonaparte of Baltimore, Secretary of the Navy under President Roosevelt and Attorney General of the United States from 1906 to 1909. At the age of eighteen, she first met her future husband, a grandson of Jerome Bonaparte, King of Westphalia, and Madame Betsy Patterson Bonaparte, of Baltimore, at a gymnasium ball at Harvard, where she was then a student. She had no children and was the last member of the Bonaparte family in Baltimore. *August 1, 1924*

BONAPARTE, JEROME NAPOLEON, a student at Harvard, sailed for Europe last week. He is the third Jerome Bonaparte in the American branch of the family. His father was the late Jerome Napoleon Bonaparte. His grandfather, Jerome Napoleon Bonaparte, who died in 1870, was the only child of Prince Jerome Bonaparte. Young Mr. Bonaparte is destined to become the head of the American branch of the Bonaparte family. He goes abroad to visit his sister, Countess von Moltke-Huitfeldt, formerly Louise E. Bonaparte. *July 6, 1898*

BONAPARTE, MADAME JEROME (ELIZABETH PATTERSON) It is nearly seventy five years since the beautiful and fascinating Miss Elizabeth Patterson won the heart of Jerome Bonaparte, then a captain in the French Navy. Married by Bishop Carroll, December 24, 1803, the honeymoon was scarcely over when the young couple were aroused by the anger of Napoleon, at what he called his brother's mésalliance. Jerome's cowardly desertion of his young wife, their divorce, and his subsequent marriage to the Princess of Württemberg, are matters of history. Her elder grandson, Colonel Jerome Napoleon Bonaparte, distinguished himself in the Franco-Prussian war and is a great favorite of the Empress Eugénie. In 1871, he married Mrs. Newbold Edgar, granddaughter of Daniel Webster. *June 19, 1878*

BONCOMPAGNI-LUDOVICI, PRINCE AND PRINCESS ANDREA (MARGARET PRESTON DRAPER) In the minds of scores of people quite beyond her ken, Miss Draper stands as a sort of American Princess Royal—with a great house, wealth unlimited, marvelous entertaining, social leadership in Washington and Newport, travel abroad, and her father's career as Ambassador to Italy. Prince Andrea Boncompagni-Ludovici comes of the old Roman aristocracy. The house has given two Popes to the church, Gregory XIII and Gregory XV, and several Cardinals have borne the same historic name. *October 20, 1916*

BOND, MR. AND MRS. ALFRED HEIDOKOPER (LOUISE DAVIES) The President of the Calumet Club in New York City looks personally after every detail, knows every member of his club, and has a kindly greeting alike for the newest recruit and the oldest member. Mrs. Bond is a descendant of Mr. and Mrs. van Beuren, who built on their property in Fourteenth Street the old-time mansion that is the one oasis in that center of trade. *October 22, 1904*

BONSAL, FRANK ADAIR The Harford County Hunt is situated in the town of Monkton, about twenty five miles or so outside Baltimore, and Monkton is in a lovely country, where foxes abound and where the galloping is always good. Mr. Frank A. Bonsal is the Master of the Harford County. His long experience, unrivaled knowledge of the country and the ways and wiles of foxes, are mainly responsible for the fine sport so long enjoyed in this part of Maryland. *February 1, 1924*

BORDEN, GENERAL HOWARD S. and his son, Mr. Arthur B. Borden, are both members of the Old Oaks polo team, which recently won the Southeastern Intra-Circuit tournament at Rumson. General Borden has been prominently connected with polo and sport in New Jersey for many years. He is one of the veterans of the game and apparently still playing as well as ever. His son is one of the coming players, and he distinguished himself in intercollegiate polo this spring as a member of the Princeton team. *September 1, 1927*

BORDEN, MR. AND MRS. JOHN (ELLEN W. WALLER) of Chicago have invited one hundred of their friends to a house party at their large place in Mississippi. The wonderful Borden farm in the South has, among its attractions, a large polo field, and the game will be played daily during the party. Bridge and, of course, mah jongg will while away hours indoors. A house party of such heroic proportions sounds quite regal and suggests prewar days in England or on the Continent, rather than America. *October 15, 1923*

BORDEN, M. D. C. was the largest cotton manufacturer and printer in the world. His father was Colonel Richard Borden, a pioneer manufacturer of Fall River, Massachusetts. After graduating at Yale, Mr. Borden became partner in the American Print Cloth Works at Fall River. He decided to manufacture his own cotton cloth, and he built three mills. He never acted in concert with others in business, and he saved the situation in a labor crisis by keeping his mills busy and raising wages. *June 8, 1912*

BORDEN, WILLIAM WHITING, an heir to one of the largest estates in Chicago, practically has renounced the world and will go to Kansu province in China as a missionary. Mr. Borden, who is worth some $5,000,000, is the son of the late William Borden, whose residence was one of the finest on the Lake Shore Drive and who left other immense property holdings in Chicago. W. W. Borden became imbued with the idea of becoming a missionary to China's darkest spot when he visited some missionaries on his world tour taken shortly after he became a Yale student. At Yale, he became known as a worker for the "down and outs" and established a mission in New Haven while a student. *October 5, 1912*

BOSTWICK, ALBERT C. returned last week from the Riviera, where he has been passing the winter with his family. Mr. Bostwick has been the victim of many paragraphs in American and foreign newspapers, because he chose to take over with him a retinue of servants rather than trust to what he could obtain on the Midi. For a time, Mr. Bostwick was a well known figure in open air sports, in coaching, and on the turf. He is the son of the late Jabez Bostwick, one of the Standard Oil millionaires. In the retinue (which excited so much comment) were only governesses and a tutor for his children, a banjo instructor for everyone, and personal servants. *May 6, 1911*

BOSTWICK, ALBERT C., JR. We think a good deal of the three young Mr. Bostwicks because they are so very active, and the public takes such a very keen interest in the sports in which they participate. Mr. Albert C. Bostwick, the oldest of the three brothers, is one of the youngest members of the Jockey Club. Mr. George H. ("Pete") Bostwick has made a brilliant record as an amateur steeplechase rider both here and abroad. And then he hies himself to his beloved Aiken, South Carolina, to play polo. Mr. Dunbar G. Bostwick, pursuing his way at Yale, is perhaps having the most strenuous time of the three, so far as his legs are concerned. When you happen to be one of the most brilliant members of the Yale varsity hockey team, you have to make the good old dogs work overtime. *April 15, 1931*

BOSTWICK, MR. AND MRS. GEORGE (LAURA ELIZABETH CURTIS) The wedding of Miss Laura Elizabeth Curtis to Mr. George "Pete" Bostwick, internationally-known young horseman, came to a thrilling climax when the couple galloped home from Trinity Church in a coach-and-four. The coach belongs to, and was driven by, the bridegroom's uncle, Mr. F. Ambrose Clark. *November 1, 1933*

BOURNE, FREDERICK GILBERT was a well-known yachtsman, member of many clubs, and financier. He began his career as a clerk at the Mercantile Library. While there, he was observed by Alfred Corning Clark, who had inherited from his father Edward Clark, $20,000,000. Young Bourne also sang in the choir of the church attended by Mr. Clark. By his voice and his personality, he won a place in the heart of the great financier, who gave him a chance in the business in which he had large interests. His advance was rapid. *April 1, 1919*

BOWDITCH, ALFRED was a member of the Suffolk Bar of Massachusetts, trustee for many large estates, and director in many Massachusetts enterprises. He was a representative member of a family that has stood for the best in New England traditions in law, business, and in medicine for many generations. *March 10, 1918*

BOWEN, MRS. EZRA (CATHERINE DRINKER) For all its understatement, the Philadelphia tradition has managed to produce some pretty remarkable individuals. Possibly no one in Philadelphia represents this better than the historian-biographer Catherine Drinker Bowen (*A Yankee from Olympus; Miracle at Philadelphia*). The Philadelphia Drinkers include Papa, who was President of Lehigh University; brother Henry, whose fame as a lawyer was almost equalled by his fame as a musician; Cecil, the world-famous physiologist who was also an alcoholic; Philip, inventor of the iron lung; and Aunt Cecilia Beaux, the portraitist. *October, 1970*

BOWEN, HENRY C. Woodstock, Connecticut, can hardly be mentioned without reference to the Bowen family. Henry C. Bowen, owner of *The Independent,* was a native of Woodstock and did much in his lifetime for the pretty town and its people. He gave them Roseland Park, and on every Fourth of July would invite famous men to make addresses before large audiences. Mr. Bowen's numerous descendants form a group of well-known men and women who still make their summer homes in Woodstock and carry on many of his benefactions. *August 7, 1909*

BOWEN, MR. AND MRS. JOHN DE KOVEN (ELIZABETH WINTHROP STEVENS) No church out of town could have been chosen for the wedding, for the bride would have thought it irreverent to be married before an altar other than St. Mark's, where Peter Stuyvesant in stained-glass window portraits and many other old Knickerbockers look down on the congregation. In the outer wall one may read: "In this vault lies buried Petrus Stuyvesant." Miss Stevens is eighth in descent from Peter Stuyvesant. *July 2, 1910*

BOWEN, MRS. JOSEPH (LOUISE DE KOVEN) once said crisply, "Debuts, since World War I, have no point. In my day, our parents invited old family friends and only men close to thirty who were established in law or banking. They were matrimonial timber." She made her debut in the 1870s, when guests supped on chicken salad and danced on white canvas floor covering. *November, 1958*

BOWES, MR. AND MRS. JOHN GARLAND (FRANCES FAY) When the San Francisco Museum of Modern Art celebrates the opening of its spectacular new $60 million building, the Boweses' sizable contribution will be acknowledged with the dedication to them of the museum's galleries for architecture and design, long-held interests of the couple. With his longtime business partner John Rosekrans, Bowes last June sold their Kransco Group, America's largest privately owned toy company, to Mattel for $260 million. That's a lot of Frisbees, the best-known item in the Kransco line. *December, 1994*

BOWLER, WALTER SCOTT comes of the old Metcalf Bowler family of Revolutionary days, whose town house in Newport is still in good repair and whose country place at Portsmouth has dwindled down to a few acres, the old house still standing almost without alter-

ation from that day to this. There Washington and Lafayette were royally entertained, and there Bathsheba Bowler was married to the Marquis de Lisle, aide-de-camp to Lafayette. *August 16, 1902*

BOWLES, SAMUEL, who was Editor and Publisher of the *Springfield Republican,* was the son of the late Samuel Bowles, who was also a distinguished publisher, and of Mary S. D. Schermerhorn, a daughter of the late Henry Van Rensselaer Schermerhorn. His grandfather established the *Springfield Republican* in 1824. *April 1, 1915*

BOYESEN, MR. AND MRS. ALGERNON (ADELAIDE BARCLAY) have taken an apartment at Thirty First Street and Fifth Avenue. Mrs. Boyesen's father, Mr. James Lent Barclay, is a descendant in the seventh generation of Colonel David Barclay, who defied Cromwell. His son, Robert Barclay, wrote the famous *Apology for the Quakers* praised by Voltaire. Young Mr. Boyesen is the son of the late Hjalmar H. Boyesen, the Norwegian scholar and author. *October 24, 1903*

BOYLAN, DR. AND MRS. GEORGE HALSTEAD (MARY KEY)—GILMOR Dr. Boylan graduated from the medical school at Yale and afterwards studied his profession in Leipzig and Paris. He was in the latter city when the Franco-Prussian War broke out and immediately offered his services to France. During the war, he was promoted to the rank of Assistant Surgeon Major of the Army of the Rhine. After his return to this country, he was for a number of years family physician to the late Samuel L. Clemens (Mark Twain) and also to the late James Gordon Bennett, whom he accompanied on many of his yachting trips around the world. His second wife was Mrs. Mary Key Gilmor, widow of William Lloyd Gilmor of Baltimore and granddaughter of Francis Scott Key, author of "The Star Spangled Banner." *February 10, 1919*

BRADISH, MRS. PHILIP gave one of her long-talked-of private theatricals. Her elegant residence is well adapted for theatrical performances, having a long drawing room with a dining room connected, where a stage with scenery, footlights, etc. had been erected for the occasion. The guests numbered about sixty and were all in evening dress. The programmes were printed on perfumed pink paper, in gilt letters. The charming domestic drama, entitled *Little Barefoot,* was most creditably performed by the lady and gentlemen amateurs. *April 24, 1867*

BRADLEY, COLONEL E. R., one of the great Kentucky breeders, is the owner of the "Idle Hour" Stock Farm that has sent to the races so many notable winners. At Colonel Bradley's farm, outside Lexington, stand the famous sires Black Toney, North Star, and others, and a select band of beautifully bred mares. *September 1, 1927*

BRADLEY, MR. AND MRS. EDSON (JULIA W. WILLIAMS) gave a ball entertaining sixty couples. Many novel features, in the nature of favors, were introduced. Very effective were the hand-painted butterflies, mounted on

gilded wands, which were illuminated by incandescent lights at the dancer's will. Chinese hats, hand-painted hat boxes, musical instruments, gold enameled salve-boxes, and gold pencils were the favors for the cotillion. *April 19, 1913*

BRADLEY, MR. AND MRS. HERBERT (MARY HASTINGS) sailed last month for England. From there, they embark for the west coast of Africa. Mr. Bradley will hunt specimens for the new zoo, while his author wife assembles story material. In their Chicago apartment, the Bradleys have a "jungle room" filled with trophies of former expeditions. Their African dinners are famous, where the guests are served only such food as the host and hostess can offer when they entertain in the heart of the Dark Continent. *January 15, 1931*

BRADY, JAMES COX The well-known horse show exhibitor, who is building up a racing stable, recently created a record at Saratoga by paying $50,500 for a yearling filly out of Man O' War. *September 15, 1925*

BRADY, MR. AND MRS. JAMES C., JR. (JOAN BABCOCK) The Bradys live in a 1760 farmhouse on the Lamington River on the enormous land parcel in Far Hills, New Jersey, bought by Joan's husband's grandfather in 1916. There are vestiges of a mill and, across the river, an old stagecoach stop that Joan converted into a studio. Joan says the kitchen is "the center of my life. I love to cook and I often paint there; it's a frequent subject of my work." *June, 1986*

BRADY, NICHOLAS F. was elected to the presidency of the New York Edison Company, succeeding his father, Mr. Anthony N. Brady. The new President is thirty four years old. Mr. Brady made welfare work among the employees of the company his especial study. It was largely due to his effort that a medal was awarded to the company by the American Museum of Safety for the protection of the life and limb of its employees. *April 19, 1913*

BRAINARD, NEWTON CASE Newt's ancestors were early leaders of the Aetna Life Insurance Company in Hartford. For generations, summers have taken Brainards to the Victorian family cottage at Fenwick, on Long Island Sound. Despite his Connecticut roots, Newt preferred small Groton over large Hotchkiss or Kent, in Connecticut, "because I felt I could make a difference here." *June, 1985*

BRANDT, MIRIAM was a member of a family prominent in the more exclusive element of Baltimore for several generations. The pioneer woman real estate operator in Maryland, she achieved success in this field, and the extent of her transactions steadily increased. Nearly all of the big transfers of property among the fashionable element of Baltimore and its vicinity during recent years were put through by her. She never, however, relinquished her place in society. *May 1, 1919*

BRANNAN, ELEANOR The late Charles A. Dana's granddaughters are particularly fine young women. Take the little militant, Eleanor Brannan: It was Eleanor whose genius for organization made the humorous suffrage play so great a success. Following her schooldays at Brearly, she spent a year with the militants in London. She headed the scheme leading to the extension of courtesies to the suffragists among the circus women while they were in Madison Square Garden. At a tea, the acrobats and "hoop-la" ladies drank tea with society. And much amazed was society to learn that these performers lead practically ascetic lives. Those elegant persons who do "the turkey trot" expected to learn something about circus-Bohemianism, and here were women leading strict lives, adhered to usually for the sake of dependent children or parents. *April 20, 1912*

BRAYTON, ALICE Newport's favorite spinster is not only a first cousin of the late lamented Lizzie Borden but also a lady of some eighty-two consecutive summers. "Newport will go on as long as nice people go on. When you are little, you are told by your Nannie that So-and-so and Such-and-such are 'nice people.' You don't question it. You believe it, at least until you meet them. In those days, anybody you didn't know was a 'nice person.' The trouble is that nowadays, even in Newport, everybody meets everybody else and that, naturally, makes a mess. But we'll come out of it. We've been here, you know, since 1636." *September, 1958*

BRECKINRIDGE, JOHN, Attorney General in the cabinet of Thomas Jefferson, brought his young wife and aged mother to this new country in 1793. He established in Kentucky a distinguished and delightful family, counting among its sons Joseph C. Breckinridge, Vice President of the United States; Breckinridge Long, former Ambassador to Italy; and Desha Breckinridge, beloved and charming publisher for many years of *The Lexington Herald.* Among its daughters were the peerless Mary Breckinridge, of the Frontier Nursing Service in the Kentucky mountains, and the late, scholarly Dr. Sophonisba Breckinridge, of the University of Chicago. *May, 1950*

BREESE, ELOISE gave a fancy dance, the guests being those favored few who under the title of "the Carbonites" are accustomed to assemble at this studio for similar affairs. Mrs. Cooper Hewitt gave her famous skirt dance; Miss Emily Hoffman was Carmen and danced a Spanish *cachuca.* Mr. James Barnes was a medieval sorcerer in black tights, with a black cap of the period, and performed feats of legerdemain. Mr. Stanford White had shaved his hair very close, and had his arms and legs and chest padded with huge stuffed sawdust muscles. He wore a suit of fleshings and trunks, and represented Sandow, the strong man. *March 22, 1899*

BREESE, JAMES L. A unique entertainment fore-shadowing the perfected combination of kinescope and phonograph was given at the studio of Mr. James L. Breese, an amateur photographer of great skill, at 5 West Sixteenth Street. The entertainment was called "a picture play" and consisted of the play, which was read by the author, Mr. Alexander Black, while photographs illustrating the text were thrown upon a screen. The photographs,

some three hundred in number, were taken by Mr. Breese, his friends and acquaintances sitting for him in his studio. *October 17, 1894*

BREESE, ROBERT POTTER, who is an expert auto driver, carried off new honors when, at the Motor Races at Riverhead, he broke the track record in his tiny "Peanut" automobile (really a Peugeot, Jr.), which made the mile in 1 minute 14 seconds. *August 1, 1920*

BREESE, SYDNEY All the members of the Breese family in New York are descendants of Sydney Breese, who was a wealthy merchant and a society man noted for his wit. He is buried in Trinity churchyard, and on the stone is the inscription: Sydney Breese, June 19, 1767. Made by himself. "Ha, Sydney, Sydney! Lyest thou Here? I here Lye 'Till Time is flown To its Eternity." *December 21, 1907*

BREESE, WALTER Golf was at first considered ridiculous, and when the Shinnecock Hills Golf Club opened in 1902, the country's first eighteen-hole golf course with a clubhouse, all Southampton paraded out to admire each player as he drove off from the first tee. Newspapers made fun of the "Shinnecock swells who think they have to wear a red coat to play the game." One Shinnecock player, Walter Breese, upon being told by his teacher that he should keep his eye on the ball, proceeded to take out his one glass eye and place it on top of the ball. *July, 1975*

BRINCKERHOFF, GENERAL ROELIFF B. had an international reputation as a prison reformer. He was brevetted a Brigadier General in the Civil War. He was born in Oswego, Cayuga County, New York, in 1828, of old Dutch stock. For three years, he was a tutor in the family of Andrew Jackson, Jr., adopted son of General Jackson, at "The Hermitage." He thus saw the old life in one of the slave states in its fullest development. *June 10, 1911*

BRISTED, CHARLES ASTOR is now at Baden-Baden, where he has bought a splendid villa and is astonishing the natives with his American trotters. He is a "fast" young man, but his brains keep pace with his other velocities. Were he poor, there would be few more brilliant authors. *October 10, 1857*

BROKAW, HOWARD AND IRVING Elberon, New Jersey, boasts the possession in the Brokaw brothers of the two best all-round athletes on the New Jersey coast. Mr. Howard Brokaw has been winning laurels by his fine polo playing at Narragansett Pier and Newport. Mr. Irving Brokaw has been very busy with golf at both the Deal Beach and Seabright links, and also figures in the Saturday polo matches at the latter resort, being the owner of one of the most beautiful polo ponies thereabouts. *August 31, 1901*

BROKAW, ISAAC VAIL was the guest-of-honor at a dinner given by his partners at Sherry's, in celebration of the fiftieth anniversary of the founding of the firm of Brokaw Brothers. The cloth of gold upon the table, the gold-decorated china and glassware, and the candelabra shades all betokened the golden anniversary. The favors were gold match boxes in the form of a miniature bolt of cloth. *February 10, 1906*

BROKAW, W. GOULD The *Amorita,* Mr. W. Gould Brokaw's yacht, will race this season. The *Amorita* always plays an important part in the social life of the resorts where she anchors during the season. Both Mr. Brokaw and his younger brother, Mr. Clifford V. Brokaw, have spent a number of summers at "Manhanset," Shelter Island. The *Evira,* Mr. Clifford V. Brokaw's yacht, was the scene of many little entertainments, and pretty girls at the hotel used often to go out in groups to have tea on the *Evira,* rather than in the palm room of the hotel. *May 3, 1902*

BROOKS, BLAIR MCKEAN is a member of that large and important family connection founded in Baltimore by the late prominent banker and one-time President of the Baltimore and Ohio Railroad, Mr. Chauncey Brooks; and popularly known as "the Brooks of Cloverdale." *June 10, 1920*

BROOKS, MRS. HENRY S. (MARGARET ARMSTRONG) was the widow of Henry S. Brooks, author and journalist. Her daughter, Miss Lilian Brooks, was married to Mr. Arthur Gouverneur Morris. Her husband, the late Mr. Brooks, was at one-time Editor of the *California Mountaineer* and Associate Editor of *The Pacific. August 13, 1910*

BROOKS, MRS. AND MRS. HORACE are well remembered by old New Yorkers, and their large house on Gramercy Park was long noted for the lavish hospitality of its owners. One of the delightful features of city life was their eleven o'clock breakfast, when all friends were welcome to drop in. He was a firm believer in the future of the Harlem River Railroad, one of the few large holders of that stock who stood by Commodore Vanderbilt when it sold down to seven, refusing to sell a share below par and lending valuable aid to Mr. Vanderbilt in winning his great fight. *March 22, 1893*

BROWER, GEORGE V., of Brooklyn, who, although he has been best known as Park Commissioner with a lively interest in his duties, held several other important public offices. His residence in Park Place, Brooklyn, was some fifteen or twenty years ago much like a country home, and here there were many garden parties and memorable treats for the schoolchildren. On Brandt Island, Massachusetts, Mr. Brower has a country residence in a colony made up of people who are old friends. He is well known in New York and is a member of the St. Nicholas Society. *January 1, 1910*

BROWN, ALEXANDER For many years, he was at the head of the banking firm of Alexander Brown and Sons, which is the oldest banking fund in the United States. The firm dates back to 1800 and was founded by Mr. Brown's great-grandfather. Mr. Brown has retired from business, but he has by no means retired from fox hunting. Today, beautifully mounted as always, he is a familiar figure with the Elkridge and Hartford hunt. *January 15, 1926*

BROWN, J. CARTER He knew from an early age that his life would be devoted to the arts. He recalls returning from boarding school in New England to Washington: "We drove past

BUSCH

At Grant's Farm: Trudy Valentine, daughter of August A.
Busch, Jr., and her husband John.

When Adolphus Busch, an emigrant from the Rhineland, arrived in St. Louis in 1857, the city of 200,000 already had forty breweries. Nevertheless, he began making beer himself and soon married Lilly Anheuser, daughter of another brewer. The firm was called Anheuser-Busch, but the Anheusers were reduced to minority shareholders. Adolphus and a stern-faced Lilly produced thirteen children.

Adolphus called his beer Budweiser. It was immediately popular, and he was immediately wealthy. Few millionaires have enjoyed their rewards more: in his private railroad car, Adolphus shuttled between St. Louis and his house in Pasadena, where thirty-five acres of gardens were maintained by fifty gardeners. When he and his wife celebrated their golden wedding anniversary, they gave a party for 13,000 guests at the St. Louis Coliseum. He chummed with presidents (he was especially close to William Howard Taft) and royalty; Adolphus visited Kaiser Wilhelm on his many trips to Germany.

The Busch family kept close ties to their fatherland. Adolphus died in 1913 at a castle he bought in the Rhineland. Some of his descendants married into the minor German nobility and spent World Wars I and II in Germany, creating serious problems with U.S. authorities when they attempted to return to the United States or transfer assets.

Adolphus was succeeded by his equally colorful son, August A. He bought "Grant's Farm," a property eleven miles

outside St. Louis where Ulysses S. Grant had once unsuccessfully tried to make a living as a farmer. In the early 1900s he added a Bauernhof, a German farm manor, behind the enormous main house filled with Louis C. Tiffany glass. Grant's Farm was—and still is—a private menagerie inhabited by elephants, deer, flamingos, and blue pigs. Each year when he went to his summer place near Cooperstown, New York, August took a trainload of animals, including an elephant, along with him.

August was president of Anheuser-Busch at the worst possible time for a brewery—Prohibition. The company survived thirteen years of American abstinence by selling yeast and a near beer with the unpromising name of Bevo. It never really caught on, but after Prohibition's repeal Anheuser-Busch emerged stronger than ever.

August A. ("Gussie") Busch, Jr., became president of the company, after family disputes, in 1946. He bought the St. Louis Cardinals baseball team, developed Busch Gardens theme parks, and christened Budweiser "The King of Beers." He had three wives and eleven children.

August Busch III, Gussie's son, succeeded him. In 1995, Budweiser accounted for 25 percent of the U.S. beer market, and family shares were estimated to be worth more than $1 billion. The company is still firmly controlled by the family. And they maintain the tradition that the first liquid a male Busch tastes is a sip of beer.

Spirits of St. Louis: *below,* brothers Adolphus and Andy Busch; *right,* Mrs. Adolphus Busch (Lilly Anheuser) in 1904; *bottom,* August A. ("Gussie") Busch, Jr.

this building," he says, referring to the National Gallery, "and I remember pointing to it and saying, 'That's the job I'd like to have some day.'" "Some day" arrived about two decades later. In 1969, Carter Brown, then just thirty-four, was appointed Director of the National Gallery. *September, 1975*

BROWN, JOHN NICHOLAS Founder of the Preservation Society, Mr. Brown is the scion of a Yankee family which, for two-and-a-half centuries, has made signal contributions to Providence. Among them is the mansion designed by Joseph Brown in 1786 for his brother John and donated by their descendant John Nicholas to the Historical Society. *July, 1979*

BRUCE, MRS. DAVID K. E. (AILSA MELLON) The late Andrew Mellon's tall, elegant daughter, said to be the richest woman in the country, has a fortune approaching a billion dollars. Every time Gulf Oil goes up a point, her net worth increases $3,000,000. When Ailsa married David K. E. Bruce (now United States Ambassador to Great Britain), Andrew Mellon reportedly gave the honeymooners $10,000,000 so they wouldn't have any trouble making it down life's highway together. *October, 1964*

BRUCE, MR. AND MRS. DAVID K. E. (EVANGELINE BELL) On a tree-lined driveway at the edge of the Palace Park, off the road leading from Versailles to Saint Cyr, lies the estate of "La Lanterne." This beautifully proportioned, late-eighteenth-century house is owned by the French government but is now occupied part of each year by former American Ambassador and Mrs. David K. E. Bruce. Perhaps no other historic house has exercised more influence on American architecture. Copies of it may be seen in Newport, Philadelphia, and Cincinnati, as well as in other cities. *July, 1955*

BRUCE-BROWN, DAVID LONEY The will of the wealthy young sportsman who drove a ninety horsepower Fiat to his death on the new Wauwatosa automobile course at Milwaukee on the eve of the eighth Vanderbilt Cup race bequeaths all his property to his mother. His estate is valued at more than $100,000. Some of his fortune was inherited, some was made at auto racing. *November 9, 1912*

BRUEN, MATTHIAS One of the Bruens who lived in the early part of the nineteenth century was Matthias Bruen, a scholarly clergyman, who once had charge of the American chapel of the oratory in Paris and who did work in New York that resulted in the establishing of the Bleecker Street congregation. *June 29, 1907*

BRUGUIÈRE, MRS. LOUIS (MARGARET L. POST)—VAN ALEN In 1958, *The New York Times* sadly noted that "In all Newport only Mrs. Louis Bruguière, Miss Julia Berwind, and Miss Edith Wetmore have liveried footmen to assist their butlers." *July, 1963*

BRULATOUR, MRS. JULES (HOPE HAMPTON) The indefatigable Hope, aglitter with her sequins and bugle beads, recently starred as a socialite in Paramount's *Hey, Let's Twist* movie filmed at the Peppermint Lounge. Hope's Twist is a determined leftover from the days of the

shimmy. Her succession of partners always falls by the wayside as she goes bravely on. Not averse to showing her legs—simply wild. *March, 1962*

BRYAN, JAMES PERRY, JR. New Englander Moses Austin, who won the contract from the Spanish governor to settle the first 300 colonists in Texas, never lived to see Houston founded. But through his daughter, Emily Austin Bryan Perry, his descendants are influential in the city today. Among them is James Perry Bryan, Jr., president of an oil and gas company and a former President of the Texas Historical Society. *September, 1991*

BRYCE, CARROLL was a brother of General Lloyd Stevens Bryce, Minister in the Netherlands, and of the late Mrs. Nicholas Fish. He was a familiar figure on Fifth Avenue for many years, always walking alone and dressed more according to the Paris than New York and London standards. He seldom spoke to anyone, and for the last three years has been almost a complete recluse at the Hotel Gotham. A member of the New York Bar, he never practised but kept in touch with all current events and was a man of wide reading and extensive knowledge. *December 16, 1911*

BRYCE, GENERAL AND MRS. LLOYD STEVENS (EDITH COOPER) Mrs. Bryce was the granddaughter of the late Peter Cooper. She was one of the beneficiaries under the will of the late Allan Thorndyke Rice and was left the *North American Review*. General Bryce, who is a littérateur and who has published many brilliant articles and some readable books, acted as editor of the *Review* for years. *February 14, 1901*

BUCHANAN, DIANA DOW ("DEDE") For Dede's debut, at the Pan American Union, Washington, D.C., on December 21, 1961, 600 guests entered "a pink palace with pink plumes and giant peppermint sticks" designed by Valerian Rybar. Wiley Buchanan, her father, gave a generous donation to Latin American charity in appreciation for the loan of the Union, but some diplomats bristled with indignation about the madcap frivolity in a setting where major Western Hemisphere issues are debated. Out of respect to the consternation, the flashing neon "Dede's Peppermint Lounge" was finally removed. "All these complainers are just jealous," Wiley Buchanan was moved to counter. "Some Communist sympathizer started all this." *June, 1965*

BUDD, SAMUEL was the founder of the men's furnishing store which has been located at Fifth Avenue and Twenty Fourth Street since 1861. Mr. Budd was a descendant of an old English family. The name was brought to America by the Rev. Thomas Budd, vicar of Montague, whose grandson founded Burlington, New Jersey. *July 27, 1912*

BULL, GEORGE HENRY Everybody in Saratoga knows Mr. Bull: As a founder and the President of the Saratoga Reading Rooms in the Grand Union Hotel; as an active Governor of the Saratoga Golf Club; and as the genial, energetic gentleman who is President of the Saratoga Association for the Improvement of the Breed of Horses. He left college after his

junior year to work for Rhoades & Co., brokers. In 1910, he became a member of the Stock Exchange, specializing in General Motors, but sold out in 1927 in order to devote his whole attention to racing. *August 1, 1934*

BULL, HENRY W., President of the Turf and Field Club, the delightful racing Club on the grounds of Belmont Park, is one of the best known sportsmen in the country. He finds time, in addition to his responsibilities as senior partner of the Stock Exchange firm of Harriman and Company, to be a very active steward of the National Steeplechase and Hunt Association and a Director of the Westchester Racing Association. *May 15, 1927*

BULL, MRS. OLE (SARA CHAPMAN) opened her studio on Brattle Street, Cambridge, for over a week to exhibit the painting of three of the artists of the Nippon Bijit Suin (Japanese Fine Arts Academy). The exhibition closed with a tea. Two or three typical Japanese dishes were served. Seaweed, prepared like salad (coleslaw), was one, and chopsticks took the place of forks. The tea was brewed three times and passed by Japanese maids. Some of the ladies present wore gorgeous Oriental apparel. *December 3, 1904*

BULL, MRS. WILLIAM TECUMSEH (MARY NEVINS)—BLAINE was the daughter of Colonel Richard Nevins, who owned the *Ohio Statesman*. Mrs. Bull was much interested in music and made an effort to help students in New York. Opera singers were often present when she gave musicales and suppers at her home in New York, and in her music room, always lighted by old-time unshaded candles, there were signed portraits and little gifts from distinguished people. *February 18, 1911*

BULLOCK, HUGH At Edgartown, Massachusetts, there's Commodore Hugh Bullock, chairman of the investment-counseling and mutual-fund firm Calvin Bullock Ltd, at the helm of his 41-footer, *Prettiemarie*. His wife, Marie, who founded and heads the Academy of American Poets, may well be thinking of new programs or preparing to entertain some of the member poets. *August, 1971*

BUNNER, H. C. gained the sympathy of his readers with a whimsical humor and with delicate sentiment. His books and stories were unique in style. For many years preceding his death, Mr. Bunner was the editor of *Puck*. He was a direct descendant of General Philip Schuyler and also a relative of the Tuckermans. *December 5, 1908*

BURDEN, ARTHUR SCOTT, member of one of New York's best known families and an ardent follower of amateur sport, particularly hunting and polo, died following an illness of seven years, which had its start with an accident from a horse in England. He was considered both a daring and expert horseman. In 1906, he married Miss Cynthia Roche, sister of Baron Fermoy. *July 1, 1921*

BURDEN, MRS. ARTHUR SCOTT (CYNTHIA BURKE ROCHE) became the bride of Mr. Guy Fairfax Cary at "Elm Court," the home of her mother, Mrs. Burke Roche, of Newport. Mr. Cary is a son of the late Clarence Cary, of

New York, and formerly of Virginia. His mother was Elisabeth Potter, daughter of the late Howard Potter, head of the international banking firm of Brown Brothers. *August 15, 1922*

BURDEN, CARTER, twenty-eight, was the youngest man ever elected to the New York City Council when he won as the Democratic-Liberal candidate in 1969. He served as Legislative Assistant to the late Senator Robert F. Kennedy for New York City and State Affairs and drafted position papers and speeches for the Senator on subjects such as environmental protection. *January, 1971*

BURDEN, GWENDOLYN Last week, in the Madison Avenue car, Miss Gwendolyn looked like a pretty schoolgirl. In a dark blue gown and a large black chiffon hat circled by a fascinating frill, her gray furs and a bunch of gardenias fastened in the fur stole, she seemed as much out of place as a fairy princess in the corner of the car. A whole row of tired, shabby but appreciative women shoppers seated opposite scrutinized even the lace ruffles on her cuffs. *April 9, 1904*

BURDEN, HENRY, who was born in Dumblane, Scotland, came to this country about 1820. He devoted himself to the manufacture of agricultural implements. His greatest invention was the machine for making horseshoes, devised in 1857. Henry Burden was also interested in navigation, and built a steamboat which from its shape was named "the cigarboat." *September 29, 1906*

BURDEN, ISAIAH TOWNSEND was for many years a leading figure in the social life of New York, London, and Newport. He was the son of Henry and Helen McOuet Burden, who came to this country from Scotland. By virtue of patents on iron working processes, which were used in the factory he had established in Troy, Henry Burden built up a great fortune. I. Townsend Burden entered his father's business as a partner. With his brother, James, Mr. Burden inherited the property upon the death of his father, in 1871. Mr. Burden and his wife, who was Miss Evelyn Byrd Moale, have been prominent socially. They originally lived at 5 East Twenty Sixth Street, where their entertainments gained for them much popularity. When trade began to make inroads in the once fashionable Madison Square section, Mr. Burden bought property from Andrew Carnegie at Fifth Avenue and Ninety Second Street, and there built the house in which he died. *May 3, 1913*

BURDEN, MR. AND MRS. JAMES A. (F. ADELE SLOANE) The prototype of their residence at Syosset may be found in the Whitehall house at Annapolis, although there have been many variations in the development of the details. Advantage has been taken of a characteristic of the site to introduce a corridor over a long arcaded basement somewhat in the manner of Robert Adam's famous Adelphi terrace. This corridor connects two of the wings, one given over to the service quarters, the other to the two-story wing occupied by the young sons of the family. *May 20, 1920*

THERE ARE MANY GIFTS

The will of Elias Boudinot, of New Jersey, has just been proved. It contains the following clause: "I give to the president and managers of the New Jersey Bible Society two hundred dollars, to be laid out in the purchase of spectacles, to be given by them to poor old people, it being in vain to give a Bible to those who cannot obtain the means of reading it." *February 6, 1864*

BURDEN, SHEILA The feminine eye at Meadow Brook, Long Island, noted, among other things equine and dashing, that the waist line, so long lost and well-nigh forgotten, has apparently returned. Some of the smartest costumes showed a decided drawn-in effect, notably a very lovely white crepe flounced frock worn by Miss Sheila Burden with a drooping white Milan hat. *September 1, 1924*

BURDEN, W. DOUGLAS is responsible for the great organization which journeyed to the Canadian woods, and there, after months of work, with incredible patience, made the pictures for the drama of Indian and forest life, *The Silent Enemy,* now showing at the Criterion Theatre. Because he knew the Canadian woods from years of sojourning there, Mr. Burden and his associates determined to record for the world a pictorial representation of the life of an Indian tribe, the Ojibway. *July 1, 1930*

BURDEN, WILLIAM A. M. Mr. Burden's interest in sport is primarily scientific. He accepts the luxury appointments of high-powered cars, airplanes, and dirigibles as symbols of progress. But romance for him is centered in the engines which represent their brain center. His research into aeronautics has carried him back to the early ascensions. Everything in Mr. Burden's balloon room at 10 Gracie Square records the famous balloon ascensions in the eighteenth century. *July, 1939*

BURDETT-COUTTS, WILLIAM LEHMAN ASHMEAD BARTLETT Fifty-five years ago, there was born in Massachusetts the second son of the late Professor Ellis Bartlett, of Princeton University. That boy is today Mr. Burdett-Coutts, a British member of Parliament and the husband of the richest woman in the world, who is also a peeress in her own right—namely, the Baroness Burdett-Coutts, proprietor of Coutts' Bank. Baroness Burdett-Coutts was thirty-seven years his senior, but the union has been exceedingly happy and felicitous. Husband and wife have each contributed in no small way to the welfare of the world. *February 3, 1906*

BURKE, MR. AND MRS. CARLETON FRANCIS (MYRTLE WOOD)—HOOKER Man of the month in the horse world is Carleton Francis Burke, guest of honor at the testimonial dinner of the Thoroughbred Club of America. Born in Arkansas fifty seven years ago, young Carty Burke was taken to California by his father, whose Los Angeles real estate is today the son's business interest. The Burkes have a house in Los Angeles but spend most of the

time at Greenfield Farm, their magnificent breeding establishment. Mr. Burke's maxims: "Wait and see" and "Better build more places to raise horses and fewer places to race them." *October, 1939*

BURKE, MRS. JACKSON (MARY L. GRIGGS) serves on the Asia Society's board of trustees. A native of Minnesota, her involvement with Japan did not begin until the 1950s, when she decided to build a country house in Oyster Bay, Long Island, and made a trip to Japan to study gardens there. In 1955, she married Jackson Burke, a typography designer and executive of the Mergenthaler Corporation, and started to build her collection, which now includes some 750 pieces. Mrs. Burke has acquired two extra apartments on her floor to house new acquisitions and to show them "in the proper ambience" created by the Japanese sculptor and designer Yasuhide Kobashi. *September, 1986*

BURKE ROCHE, CYNTHIA Mrs. Burke Roche will give a coming-out ball in Newport for her daughter, Miss Cynthia Roche, who, as a matter of fact, is not as fond of "society" as her mother. She enjoys automobiling, riding and driving, yachting, and tennis far better. At a recent Casino hop, she had partners for every dance and added to her already intense popularity by dancing a part of a dance with one and saving the rest for another swain. *August 23, 1902*

BURKE ROCHE, EDMUND MAURICE is one of the twin sons of the Hon. James Boothby Burke Roche, an Irish member of Parliament and brother and heir to Lord Fermoy. Mr. Burke Roche's mother is Mrs. Burke Roche of New York and Newport, and the daughter of the late Frank Work. Frank Work detested foreigners, and in his will he left a fortune of $2,700,000 to each of his twin grandsons on condition that they become American citizens, kept a legal residence in this country, and assume the name of Work. Also there is a codicil in which they are forbidden to travel in the Eastern Hemisphere or to marry a foreigner. Mr. Maurice Burke Roche and his brother did not change their names, but they both went to work in America. *April 26, 1913*

BURKE ROCHE, HON. MRS. JAMES BOOTHBY (FRANCES ELEANOR WORK) has an important place in the society of Newport; and the applause from the crowds, when she wins a blue ribbon at the Newport Horse Show, proves the esteem in which she is held by all classes. Her interest in horses is well known; her beautiful garden, in which every flower that blooms is blue, is a feature of her dainty Newport home and indicative of her personality. *September 9, 1905*

BURROWS, SENATOR AND MRS. JULIUS C. (FRANCES S. PECK) Mrs. Burrows, the wife of Senator Julius C. Burrows of Michigan, has found time to interest herself in youthful patriotism, believing that patriots are made from the cradle up. As President-general of the Children of the American Revolution, Mrs. Burrows has been enthusiastic. *April 4, 1908*

BURT, MR. AND MRS. HENRY C. (SARAH ROQUES) His father was a pioneer resident in the development of Cleveland; he was a descendant of Henry Burt, one of the earliest settlers of Springfield, Massachusetts, who, with Governor Pynchon, was a signer of the deed which purchased from the Indians the land which became the site of Northampton. His wife, Sarah Roques, descended from that little band that took trans-Atlantic passage on the *Mayflower*. *February 1, 1919*

BUSCH, MR. AND MRS. ADOLPHUS (ELISE ANHEUSER) One of the representative families of St. Louis is that of Mr. Adolphus Busch, one of its most prominent citizens. The entertainments given in his spacious South Side mansion savor of the magnificence of the *Arabian Nights*. Mr. and Mrs. Busch frequently receive their guests in what they call the "wine room." This apartment is hung with old tapestries, while overhead are trailing green vines, from which twinkle myriads of electric lights contained in bunches of blue and green grapes. The finest collection of steins in America ornament this unique banqueting hall. *December 26, 1903*

BUSCH, AUGUST ANHEUSER, JR. is President of the St. Louis Cardinals baseball team and honorary Chairman of the board of Anheuser-Busch, Inc. When he retired in 1974, the brewery had a capacity of 35 million barrels per year at nine plants across the country, and the company was far and away the world's largest brewer. Busch is 82 now, but he has lived life: He has had three wives and eleven children (the last fathered when he was 67). *October, 1980*

BUSCH, CARLOTA The big house on "Grant's Farm," the Busch family homestead outside St. Louis, was reopened this June for the wedding reception of the former Carlota Busch and her second cousin, John Flanigan, both great-grandchildren of Adolphus Busch, who came to this country from Germany in 1857. A historical landmark because of the two-room log cabin built by Gen. U. S. Grant (he farmed here in the 1850's with so little success that he dubbed the place "Hard Scrabble"), the farm has become under the Busches one of the show places of the nation. *September, 1948*

BUTLER, MRS. CLARENCE (SARAH TURNER) is the granddaughter of W. C. Bradley, Ernest Woodruff's partner in the purchase of Coca Cola. Bradley had only one child, a daughter, who married D. Abbott Turner, so that the Bradley fortune, estimated at some $300,000,000 to $400,000,000, is now the Turner fortune, and Mrs. Butler is the Turners' daughter. Bradley was an interesting entrepreneur in his own right. A cotton planter late in the nineteenth century, he owned steamboats to supply his plantation on the Chattahoochee from Columbus, Georgia. He didn't really see the need of buying groceries retail, so he started his own wholesale grocery in Columbus and, using the same logic, started a fertilizer company, a plow company, warehouses, mills and eventually owned most of Columbus. *May, 1969*

BUTLER, FRANK OSGOOD II, son of Paul Butler, Board Chairman, Butler Aviation, lives with his mother in Palm Beach. His diversions: collecting elephant figures—he now has a valuable collection in jade, copper, bronze, ivory, etc. Sports: His great sport is sky diving with parachute; also likes skin diving and shooting, right or left hand. *June, 1964*

BUTLER, GEORGE PRENTISS was a son of William Allen Butler, and a grandson of Benjamin F. Butler, who was Attorney General of the United States. William Allen Butler was also an author, his satirical poem "Nothing to Wear" being widely known. *April 15, 1911*

BUTLER, LAWRENCE SMITH The annual Smithtown Horse Show, which customarily initiates the fall sporting and society season on Long Island, will take place at "Fifty-Acre Field," the beautiful property of Lawrence Smith Butler, near the Smithtown Polo Field. *September 1, 1925*

BUTLER, NICHOLAS MURRAY President Butler's career as an educator began at Columbia in 1885, and he succeeded Mr. Seth Low as President of the University. He was the founder of the New York College for Training Teachers, and as a writer his reputation is, of course, international. That he is fond of golf (he is a member of the Ardsley Club) is of greater interest to society, for it indicates that he will be likely to take interest in the lighter pleasures of New York. *March 2, 1907*

BUTLER, PAUL This family traces its Chicago origins to a nineteenth-century paper company. Paul Butler ran Butler Paper Co. from 1930 to 1965 and founded Butler Aviation in 1945. But he's best known in Chicago for developing Oak Brook as the first prototype of the modern office village—"for people who worked with their heads and not their hands"—in 1956. He planned every aspect of the village, including seventeen fields for polo, his personal passion. *September, 1990*

BYERS, FRICK Ever since he took up ice hockey at Brooks School, Frick Byers' closets have been crammed with skates, tennis rackets, and other sporting gear that he admits he is "constantly updating." A budding photographer now studying at New York's Parsons School of Design, he says, "I don't think there has ever been a sportsman who didn't constantly hanker after more and better equipment." *December, 1992*

BYRD, MR. AND MRS. RICHARD (HELEN BRADSHAW) are the owners of "Rosemont," a Greek Revival mansion once the home of Richard's father, the late Senator Harry F. Byrd. "It's the love of the land that sets Clarke County, Virginia, apart from its neighbors," explains the Senator's son, a prominent local apple grower. "Land is an integral part of our life here, not some kind of status symbol." *October, 1985*

C

CABANNE, JULIA "At eleven o'clock antemeridian," read the invitations sent out by the Captain and officers of the battleship *Missouri* for the pretty ceremony at Fortress Monroe, Virginia. Miss Julia Cabanne was chosen to present on this date the great silver bell which hung in the *Missouri* building at the World's Fair to the battleship *Missouri*. It is because of a lineal descent from Pierre Lacleade Liguest, associated with the start of the city of St. Louis, that Miss Cabanne was selected. *June 10, 1905*

CABOT, MR. AND MRS. FRANCIS HIGGINSON (CURRIE DUKE)—MATHEWS "Quatre Vents," Mr. and Mrs. F. Higginson Cabot call their farm, because it is on high land and open to the four winds. It is part of the enormous family holdings at Murray Bay established by Mr. Cabot's grandfather, George Bonner of New York, who bought the *seigneurie* of "La Malbaie" more than fifty years ago. Mr. Bonner left the *seigneurie* and the responsibility of looking after the welfare of, and providing a living for, the *habitant* tenants to his daughter, Mrs. Francis H. Cabot, who still runs a very large farm, giving employment to several hundred French Canadians. *June, 1942*

CABOT, GODFREY LOWELL The most prolific and the most active of the great Boston families, the Cabots began their American line when George, John, and François emigrated from the Isle of Jersey in the early eighteenth century. John's sons became wealthy Salem merchants; grandsons John and Andrew founded the first cotton mill in America. The first Samuel Cabot married the daughter of Boston's largest shipper, Thomas Handasyd Perkins, and built another fortune on top of the existing one. Godfrey Lowell Cabot, a great philanthropist and longtime head of what is now the Cabot Corporation, was the wealthiest man in Boston and the protector of its morals, as patron saint of the infamous Watch and Ward Society. This institution, under the stern eye of Cabot, made "banned in Boston" a national joke by prohibiting works by, among others, Dos Passos, Sinclair Lewis, Hemingway, and Dreiser. *April, 1976*

CADWALADER, JOHN LAMBERT He was Assistant Secretary of State under Hamilton Fish during Grant's administration, and he was at one time the law partner of former Attorney General George W. Wickersham. He succeeded John Bigelow as the President of the New York Public Library. It was he who drew up the will of his friend Benjamin Altman, bequeathing his art collection to the city and making his business a trust to the Altman Foundation. Lambert Cadwalader, whose name he bore and who had a home in Trenton in the eighteenth century, represented New Jersey in the Continental Congress. *March 21, 1914*

CADWALADER, MR. AND MRS. RICHARD M. (EMILY M. ROEBLING) The yacht *Savarona* was 104 feet long. She was not an ocean-going yacht; she was a river-going houseboat. The Cadwaladers kept her for three years after her launching, but in 1928 decided they would graduate to something more practical. In '32 she became the property of the U.S. government and designated a Presidential yacht. Mr. C. died, and Mrs. C. decided to build the most luxurious yacht in the world, the 408-foot *Savarona III*. She succeeded, but the Depression forced her to charter her until 1938 and finally to sell her to the Turkish government as a training ship. *June, 1975*

CALDWELL, MRS. J. EMOTT (HANNAH LOCKE) is the great-granddaughter of Nathaniel Parker Willis, first "seeing-eye" of *Town & Country*. Although Mrs. Caldwell's soft Quaker "thee" and tiny waist might belong to the last century, she is no vaporous damsel; besides flying her own plane, she is a champion skater and skier, member of the American Women's Ski Team in 1937 and 1938. *December, 1946*

CALHOUN, JULIA At the third British court of the season, one of the young women presented was Miss Julia Calhoun, the daughter of General and Mrs. John C. Calhoun. Mrs. Calhoun is a niece of Richard M. Johnson, Vice President of the United States. General Calhoun is a grandson of Vice President John C. Calhoun, the great statesman and orator of South Carolina. He is an able financier. He is President of the Baltimore Coal Mining and Railway Company and holds high office in many corporations. *July 3, 1909*

CAMERON, MRS. GEORGE TOLAND (HELEN MARGARET DE YOUNG), a petite but very grand woman, is the eldest of the three surviving de Young sisters. Their father, the late Michael Henry de Young, established the *San Francisco Chronicle,* ducked a bullet aimed at him by the late Adolph B. Spreckels, and gave the city its de Young Memorial Museum. Mrs. Cameron's late husband was in what she calls "cement and oil." And when she is not at "Rose Court," the pink-stucco château she and her husband built in Burlingame in 1913, she is in Europe, palling around with the Duke and Duchess of Windsor. In the old days, before her husband got rid of it, Mrs. Cameron could be depended upon to play the saxophone. She also has had a go at the harp and the piano, but now prefers to watch and listen while others perform. *September, 1965*

CAMERON, SENATOR AND MRS. J. DONALD (ELIZABETH SHERMAN) Mrs. Cameron is the daughter of Judge Sherman of Ohio, whose brothers were the famous General William Tecumseh Sherman and John Sherman, Secretary of State and Senator from Ohio. Mr. Cameron was Secretary of War under President Grant till 1877, when he was chosen Senator to fill the vacancy caused by the resignation of his father, Simon Cameron, the great statesman who was, at one time, Minister to Russia and Secretary of War during Lincoln's administration. *March 27, 1909*

CAMMANN, HENRY LORILLARD The view of Queensborough Bridge in New York City seen through the arched windows of his dining room makes sufficient pictorial point of the scenic reward gained by the reclamation of one of New York's waterfronts. It was a little over a year ago that Sutton Place came into the news, but the little-known two-block thoroughfare already contains the homes of various well-known people in social, artistic, and professional circles. *February 15, 1922*

CAMOYS, LADY (MILDRED SHERMAN) Probably no debutante ever came out with more of a bang than Mildred Sherman, daughter of that super-socialite Mrs. W. Watts Sherman. In the midst of this ball, which took place at Sherry's just before World War I, a huge swan floated among the twelve hundred guests and exploded, shooting thousands of pink roses all over the place. *November, 1958*

FULL OF BEANS

Godfrey Lowell Cabot, present-day Cabot family patriarch, is a charming example of social independence. At gatherings where he is in attendance, conversation must be tailored to suit him. Though he was once active in Boston politics himself, politics under a Democratic administration would never be a fit subject for discussion. So bitterly was he opposed to the policies of Woodrow Wilson—a man, he once said, "who could not run a peanut stand"—that even his closest friends never cared to find out where he stood on Franklin D. Roosevelt. *July, 1947*

CAMPBELL, ANDREW COURTNEY, JR. was a representative of one of Chicago's oldest families. This first of Chicago's heroes left the halls of the University of Virginia, "to do for France," as he put it, "in my small way, what Lafayette and Rochambeau did in a big way for America." His six months in the Lafayette Escadrille was a series of triumphant exploits. His last act was one of chivalry. On October 1, 1917, near the town of Pargny, France, he deliberately drove his plane into one of four enemy planes in order to save the life of a French airman. He brought down the German plane, but himself fell, in a mass of wreckage. *March 1, 1919*

CAMPBELL, MRS. FREDERIC SCOTT, JR. (ELIZABETH CECIL CARY) is Southern as the Virginia reel. Tested for "Scarlett" during the casting of *Gone With the Wind,* she is the former Elizabeth Cecil Cary, whose F.F.V. dates from a Cary in the House of Burgesses in 1627. *October, 1943*

CANFIELD, AUGUSTUS CASS claimed descent from Lewis Cass, the statesman and scholar, at one time Minister to France and later the author of a book entitled *France, Its King, Court and Government.* His son, Lewis, was appointed Chargé d'Affaires to the Papal States. Every one with the name Cass, of course, since the time of the first Lewis Cass, has had affiliations with Detroit. *April 2, 1904*

CANFIELD, MRS. CASS (JANE SAGE) exhibits her sculpture under her maiden name. The figures she modeled for the entrance court of the new house at Upperville, Virginia, designed for Lieut. and Mrs. Paul Mellon are six animals. A fox on the alert and a hound baying at the moon represent Virginia's famous hunts. A rabbit, squirrel, beaver, and another lop-eared dog scratching in the sun are humorous in a perfectly natural way without resorting to caricature. *June, 1943*

CANNON, HARRY LE GRAND left three thousand dollars in his will to be used in establishing an art students' prize. Mr. Cannon was widely known as a prominent New York society and club man, but did not receive the credit he deserved for his unusually clever work as a sculptor. Had he been compelled to work at his art as a professional, rather than as a dilettante, he would probably have made his name famous. *July 17, 1895*

CANTACUZENE, PRINCE AND PRINCESS MICHAEL (JULIA DENT GRANT) were married at "Beaulieu," Newport, the residence of the bride's aunt, Mrs. Potter Palmer, on Monday by the picturesque ceremony of the Greek church and on Tuesday, at All Saints' Chapel, in accordance with the laws of Rhode Island. Mrs. U. S. Grant, the bride's grandmother, gave a magnificent necklace of pearls, with pendants of diamonds and emeralds, presented to her when she and General Grant visited Mexico in their trip around the world, nearly a quarter of a century ago. *September 27, 1899*

CANTACUZENE, PRINCE AND PRINCESS MICHAEL (CLARISSA CURTIS) In the quaint little church at Nahant, capable of holding less than three hundred people, and where generations of the Curtis family have worshipped and been given in marriage, Clarissa Curtis became a princess. The bridegroom is Prince Michael Cantacuzene, Count Speranski, of Russia, whose mother was Miss Julia Dent Grant, a granddaughter of General Ulysses S. Grant. The estates of the Cantacuzenes are in the Ukraine, and their magnificent old dwelling there has been destroyed and the lands confiscated. The family dates back to the Emperor Cantacuzene of Constantinople, who reigned in 1293. *July 20, 1921*

CAREY, MRS. GEORGE Up from North Carolina, she now lives at "Nonesuch," her house in Lutherville, Maryland. A champion party-giver, her place in the country is remarkable in that she is one of the few top hunting people who cares about music. In the last two years, Mrs. Carey has been concentrating on the violin in order to be able to play with the Woman's String Symphony. *June, 1939*

CARHART, AMORY SIBLEY was Commander of the Military Order of Foreign Wars of the United States, a member of the Society of Mayflower Descendants, and also Lieutenant Governor of the Society of Colonial Wars, State of New York. His collection of pictures and objets d'art was most complete, and he wrote on art subjects and kindred topics. *March 30, 1912*

CARMAN, RICHARD, the descendant of an old New York family, from whom a part of Harlem, where their country seat was situated, derives its name, is one of the prominent exhibitors of coaching horses at the New York Horse Show. He is considered by many to be the best whip in New York. His summer home is at Huntington, Long Island. *November 11, 1905*

CARNEGIE, ANDREW arrived in Pittsburgh during the Depression of 1848 and took his first job with the Blackstock Cotton Mills, at a salary of $1.20 a week. Later, he became a telegraph operator with the Pennsylvania Railroad. After the Civil War, Carnegie turned his attention to iron and steel and soon formed a company of his own that was to become a pattern for big business throughout America. In the year of 1900 alone, Carnegie Steel showed a profit of $50,000,000. It was one of Carnegie's precepts that it was a disgrace to die rich, and the later years of his life he devoted to giving away $350,000,000. *March, 1959*

CARNEGIE, MRS. THOMAS MORRISON, JR. (DOROTHY DUNCAN) The daughter of a very old family has changed her name. The bride is a granddaughter of the late Mr. and Mrs. Theodore Havemeyer, the latter prominent leaders in society thirty years ago. Mr. Carnegie is the third in line to bear the name of his grandfather. He is a great-nephew of the late Andrew Carnegie. *July 1, 1922*

CARNEGIE, MRS. THOMAS MORRISON, JR. (BLANCHE STREBEIGH)—SLOAN deserts New York early in the season to spend her winters on the Carnegie island off the coast of Georgia. Besides being a paradise for her two small sons, it gives Mrs. Carnegie the sandy beach and woods she loves and one of her favorite sports, trap shooting. In the summer, she is at Newport in her lovely house. She is a deft and delightful hostess, and her shrimp Newburgh, southern style, is excelled only by her Georgian wild turkey with wild rice. *February 1, 1934*

CARNEGIE, MRS. THOMAS W. (LUCY C. COLEMAN), of Pittsburgh, has been proposed for membership in the New York Yacht Club. Mrs. Carnegie is an enthusiastic yachtswoman and has owned the *Missoe,* steam yacht, for several years. During the winter Mrs. Carnegie goes to Jekyll Island, that exclusive sporting retreat off the coast of Georgia, part of which she owns. In applying for admission, Mrs. Carnegie has no other motive than the advantages to be gained from flying the club burgee in foreign waters. *January 10, 1894*

CAROLAN, MRS. FRANCIS (HARRIETT PULLMAN), daughter of the late George Pullman, of Chicago, is engaged to Colonel Arthur Frederic Schermerhorn, a member of a distinguished family, ninth in direct descent from Jacob J. Schermerhorn, who came to America from Holland in 1636. *May 15, 1925*

CARPENTER, MRS. JOHN ALDEN (RUE WINTERBOTHAM) The Equity Ball at the First Regiment Armory, Chicago, was a very gay affair. The scheme of decoration, planned by Mrs. John Alden Carpenter, was a winter scene, with the boxes converted to mimic sleighs. There were sleigh-bells jingling clear, snow icicles, fir trees gleaming with electric light, and snow-covered mountains. *February 15, 1924*

CARROLL, MR. AND MRS. CHARLES (SUZANNE BANCROFT) His election to the Jockey Club in Paris is quite an event, as very few, if any, Americans are members of that organization. Mr. Charles Carroll is a son of the former Governor of Maryland and a direct descendant of Charles Carroll, of Carrollton. Mr. and Mrs. Carroll have been living abroad for some years. They have been quite active in the hunting field at Pau and have also been residents of Biarritz. *January 17, 1901*

CARROLL, LAUREN, the son of General and Mrs. Howard Carroll, has come forward as one of the best amateurs in New York since he appeared as "John Perrybingle" in the performance of *The Cricket on the Hearth* given at the Plaza for the benefit of the Union Settlement. No one quite expected such good acting from an amateur, but the first few lines that "John" spoke made the audience settle in its seats. Only the cricket himself was at fault in his part, for his chirrup sounded more like the shake of a rattlesnake's tail. *December 21, 1912*

CARROLL, ROYAL PHELPS He has always been a sportsman, but he has recently devoted his energies to new fields. He will follow in the tracks of Theodore Roosevelt and go lion-hunting in the jungles of Africa. Royal Phelps Carroll is one of the sons of the late John Lee Carroll, who was State Senator in Maryland and Governor of that state from 1876 to 1880. His mother was a daughter of the New York banker Royal Phelps. He is a direct descendant of the famous Charles Carroll of Carrollton, one of the signers of the Declaration of Independence. *June 10, 1911*

CARTER, ALICE ATWATER, the daughter of the late Captain Fitzhugh Carter, of "Shirley," on James River, Virginia, will be wedded to Mr. Robert Valentine Reid, of Glasgow, Scotland. Shirley, the ancestral home of Miss Carter's fathers, has been identified with the family since the days when John Carter, Secretary of State in Virginia, lived there. The Carters come down from King Carter, the most elegant and the wealthiest Colonial gentleman of the Virginia Colony. *April 22, 1905*

CARTER, C. HILL, JR. Look at Shirley Plantation, Virginia. For nine generations, it has remained in the Carter family and now belongs to C. Hill Carter, Jr. The place is estimated at $1,500,000, but to convert the assets to spendable cash Carter would have to do the one thing he is committed not to do: sell Shirley. Instead, he nets barely $15,000 a year, renting his land and giving personal tours to the 23,000 visitors who pay $2 a head. *December, 1975*

CASE, WILLARD E. won recognition at home and abroad for the results of his research work in the field of electricity. He was descended from John Fitch, one of the first inventors of steam navigation. His grandfather, Erastus Case, was a prominent figure in science before the time of steam railroads. He was the owner of the Clark collection of Indian relics from the Cayuga and Onondaga tribes. *November 10, 1918*

CASSATT, ALEXANDER JOHNSTON, who seeks diversion from the multitudinous cares of looking after the details of a great railroad system in his extensive stock farm, "Chesterbrooke," at Berwyn, is about to extend his interest in horses. He now has a representative in Lexington, Kentucky, looking for a suitable farm. He purposes placing his celebrated Bard, who has won for his owner almost $100,000 on the turf, at the head of the stable. *September 13, 1902*

CASSATT, MARY, who is one of the celebrities in whom Philadelphia has pride, has been decorated with the cross of the Legion of Honor by the French government in recognition of her achievement as a painter. She is a sister of Mr. A. J. Cassatt, of railroad fame; and her niece, Mrs. W. Plunkett Stewart (Elsie Cassatt), won fame as a golf player. Mr. Cassatt has a home on Rittenhouse Square, but his artist sister lives abroad. She went to Europe in 1875. Her first exhibition at Durand-Ruel's in New York was during her visit to this country in 1898. *January 14, 1905*

CASSELL, GLADYS A great-grandniece of General Robert E. Lee, idol of the South, has come to San Francisco to continue her stage career, and she made her debut on the Alcazar Stage in *Civilian Clothes.* She is Miss Gladys Cassell of Virginia and so far has appeared in ingenue roles. She inherits the beauty of her grandmother, who was one of the Carters of Virginia. *September 1, 1922*

CASSINI, MARGUERITE, with her proverbial fondness for that variety which constitutes the spice of American life, has, as might have been expected, entered into the spirit of the era with the greatest enthusiasm. Her uncle, Count Cassini, the Ambassador from Russia, has an automobile, and Miss Cassini has spent so much time in this vehicle that she now holds undisputed, in so far as feminine automobilists are concerned, the record for both speed and skill in the manipulation of a machine. *November 1, 1900*

CASTELLANE, COUNT AND COUNTESS BONIFACE DE (ANNA GOULD) have left Deauville for Biarritz. The Countess is gaining in charm as she grows more matronly, and the independence which characterized her as Anna Gould has given place to a more docile manner, which makes her the kindliest of hostesses. *September 20, 1902*

CATHCART, MRS. REBECCA (MARSHALL), Minnesota's oldest settler in point of residence, died at the age of ninety five years. She was a sister of the late Governor William Marshall of Minnesota. *August 15, 1925*

CHAFFE, WILLIAM H., JR., of the fine old New Orleans French family of the same name, was, as usual, General Chairman for the Bal des Arts of the Baltimore Charcoal Club and exercised his usual discreet oversight of the invitation list, so consequently high society and high art were equally in evidence. *February 15, 1924*

CHALLONER, JOHN ARMSTRONG A great deal of discussion seems to be still going on in urban and suburban localities as to the desirability of keeping laborers on the farms. Thus far, Mr. John Armstrong Challoner of New York and "Merry Mills," Albemarle County, Virginia, seems to be the only one who has found a wholly successful answer to the problem. Mr.

Challoner has transformed one of his barns at Merry Mills into a very presentable movie theatre, where performances are given twice a week. The performances are free, and there is no limit to the audiences either in number or caste. *December 20, 1920*

CHAMBERS, MRS. ANNE (COX), former Ambassador to Belgium, heads a communication giant: Cox Enterprises, Inc., which has the *Atlanta Journal-Constitution* as the flagship of a chain of twelve newspapers and also owns eighteen radio and fifty-six cable TV companies. The daughter of James M. Cox, Jr., newspaper publisher, Congressman, Governor of Ohio, and Democratic candidate for the United States presidency—she inherited from him the basis of today's empire. *January, 1986*

CHANDLER, KENT, JR. Perhaps the real Lake Forest forte was best described by its Mayor, Kent Chandler, Jr. Chandler is a second-generation mayor, since he was preceded in the office by his father in 1938. Now, in 1971, Kent, Jr. says, "Lake Forest is the last unexploited space close to Chicago, and we want to keep it that way. We have pretty tight zoning here." *March, 1971*

CHANLER, MR. AND MRS. JOHN (AMELIE RIVES) Miss Rives resided in a pretty house high up on Franklin Street, in Richmond, Virginia. The *jeunesse dorée* of Richmond thronged her doors. They were frequently kept waiting until Miss Rives dashed off a poem, sub rosa. Then, as now, those who knew Miss Rives intimately were her ardent and sincere admirers. It is unfortunate that her novel *The Quick and the Dead* should place those chosen friends either in the position of condemning that book and some unrefined passages in her other stories, or else upholding the worst and most unhealthy tone that American literature has ever known. *September 26, 1888*

CHANLER, LEWIS STUYVESANT The present Lieutenant Governor of New York is an interesting type of the "gentleman in politics" and has been termed an "aristocrat turned proletarian." He is the great-great-grandson of the first John Jacob Astor. Mr. Chanler's democracy has never been questioned. During lengthy residence in Ireland, he advocated broad rights for the Irish, was associated with the Parnellite party, etc. As a lawyer in New York, he formerly made a practise of appearing in courts and pleading the cases of poor people, free of charge. *June 22, 1907*

CHANLER, MARGARET ASTOR Should it come to pass that Margaret Astor Chanler should die, there will be no hero of the war with Spain who will deserve a higher monument or a more flattering epitaph than she. As "Sister Margaret," she has nursed sick soldiers, braved yellow and typhoid fevers, and brought the sunshine of her beauty into hospital wards. Her fortune is very large. Her personal income is $30,000 a year. She is the great-great-granddaughter of the first John Jacob Astor. *September 28, 1898*

CHANLER, ROBERT W. The leonine mane, tortoise-shell spectacles, and robust presence of Chanler are an integral part of every comprehensive modern art show and ditto every

Bohemian gathering of the more exclusive sort. He has done Gothic panels for Mrs. Harry Payne Whitney and has decorated rooms for Mrs. William K. Vanderbilt, Mrs. Temple Emmet, Mrs. John W. Chapman, and Mr. Lloyd Warren. He has decorations in the Vanderbilt Hotel and in the new Colony Club. *April 20, 1916*

CHANLER, MRS. WILLIAM ASTOR (MINNIE ASHLEY) The Lafayette Memorial not only maintains as a shrine the birthplace and former home of the Marquis de Lafayette, it gives schooling and health conservation to three hundred French children annually. The Château at Chavaniac was bought in 1915 by the Lafayette Fund, which is headed by Mrs. William Astor Chanler. *January 1, 1926*

CHANLER, WILLIAM C., a movie-making explorer, is the lawyer-son of former Lieutenant Governor Lewis Stuyvesant Chanler and a nephew of the late Sheriff Bob Chanler, of Mrs. Richard Aldrich, wife of the music critic, and of Mrs. John Jay Chapman. The Chanlers spring from Dutchess County, where they are connected through the Astors with the Delano side of our new President's almost equally complicated family. *March 1, 1933*

CHAPIN, MR. AND MRS. ALFRED CLARK (GRACE STEBBINS) He was born in Massachusetts, and not so long ago gave $100,000 to Williams College, from which he was graduated in 1869. He was a member of the New York Assembly and Speaker of the House, when President Roosevelt was Governor. When he had been married only a few years, he was Mayor of Brooklyn. Mrs. Chapin is a great-granddaughter of Henry Hamilton Schieffelin. Much of her girlhood was spent in one of the beautiful old Schieffelin houses on Twenty Fifth Street that face Madison Square. *May 30, 1908*

CHAPIN, CORNELIA VAN AUKEN, who has recently been visiting her sister, the wife of Attorney General Francis Biddle, is a well-known sculptor and head of the sculpture division of Artists for Victory, Inc., a clearinghouse that brings together painters and sculptors with war organizations that need posters or want to arrange exhibitions. It even supplies models. *May, 1943*

CHAPMAN, MRS. HENRY CRAFTON (ELEANOR JAY) is one of the oldest remaining members of the Jay family in New York. Her father was John Jay, second of the name, who was United States Minister to Germany in the early years of the last century. John Jay, the first Chief Justice, was Mrs. Chapman's great-grandfather. Miss Beatrix Mary Jay Chapman, her daughter, married Sir George Head Barclay, who has had a distinguished career in the British diplomatic service. *July 1, 1921*

CHAPMAN, MRS. JOHN D. II (SALLY PUTNAM), granddaughter of Amelia Earhart Putnam, is a licensed pilot and used to fly her Piper Club everywhere. Now skiing's her sport, especially in Taos, New Mexico. *September, 1966*

CHARLES, MRS. ROBERT (MARION S. OATES)— LEITER Reminiscing recently at her magnificent house overlooking the ocean at Newport, Rhode Island, Mrs. Charles recalls past visits to Hot Springs, Virginia: "It was

one of the grand traditions. In the Forties, each spring we would bring the horses up from Aiken. We would stay for three weeks, leave the horses for the cool summers while we went north, and then return for an additional three weeks in the fall. Then we would take the horses back to Aiken. It was all so very civilized, and great fun." *December, 1983*

CHASE, KATE, who has dropped the name of Sprague since her divorce, is said to be still living quietly at Fontainebleau, where she is engaged in superintending the education of her three daughters. She used to be considered extremely ambitious; but after her father's failure to obtain the Democratic nomination for the Presidency in 1868, of which, as well as his election, both he and she were confident, she lost heart and hope. *January 20, 1886*

CHATFIELD-TAYLOR, HOBART was guest of honor at the dinner of the Society of Midland Authors, of which he was the first President. Guests at this dinner were asked to come in dress of the World's Fair period, this being the thirtieth anniversary of that notable event in Chicago's history. At the conclusion of the program, Mr. Chatfield-Taylor, who used to lead all the cotillions in those halcyon days, was asked to turn back the hands of the clock and repeat his early successes. It is a far cry from fox trots to the schottische, the polka, and the glide, but the Society of Midland Authors stood up gallantly to the test. *November 15, 1923*

CHATFIELD-TAYLOR, MRS. HOBART (ROSE FARWELL) has always been one of the leaders in the country life at Onwentsia, Lake Forest, Illinois, where she has made some enviable golfing records. She is the daughter of former Senator Charles B. Farwell, who with his brother, Mr. John Villiers Farwell, built the Texas State Capitol in 1887, receiving in payment 3,000,000 acres of land, now the site of the Farwell ranch. *September 16, 1905*

CHATHAM, THURMOND, of Winston-Salem, whose family for generations has worked and played in this enchanting country and whose mills at Winston-Salem make the most beautiful and softest wool blankets we have ever seen, is an enthusiastic sportsman, and his herd of Guernseys is one of the most notable in the state. *June 15, 1931*

CHEATHAM, MRS. OWEN ROBERTSON (CELESTE WICKLIFFE) "Men and women are equally enchanted by interesting jewels," explains Mrs. Cheatham. That is how the idea occurred to her to show Salvador Dalí's magical jewels around the world to benefit charitable organizations. There are forty pieces with religious themes, mythological or surrealistic, in the Owen Cheatham Foundation. They are worth approximately $5 million. *February, 1970*

CHEEVER, MRS. DAVID W. (ANNA NICHOLS) Mrs. Cheever's mother was Sarah Chamberlin, who was born in the house erected on the site of the Old Liberty Tree in Washington Street, Boston. She was a member of the Colonial Dames and the Fragment Society. Her town residence in Copley Square is today the last private residence in that once fashionable neighborhood. *October 20, 1917*

CHENEY, COLONEL FRANK WOODBRIDGE was at the head of the firm of Cheney Brothers, manufacturers of silk. About 1840, this great industry was founded in South Manchester by Ward and Charles Cheney and their brothers. The Cheney brothers made a scientific study of sewing-silks. On their estate at South Manchester, they established a model manufacturing village with cottages, a hall, and a theater. Mr. Frank Woodbridge Cheney traveled extensively in China and Japan to make a study of silk industries. *June 5, 1909*

CHENEY, JOHN S. was, as the oldest member of the firm of Cheney Brothers, one of the foremost manufacturers of the United States. His father, George Wells Cheney, was one of the original Cheney Brothers and a descendant, in the seventh generation, of John Cheney, who came to this country in 1635 and settled in Roxbury, Mass. *March 19, 1910*

CHENOWETH, MRS. ALEXANDER CRAWFORD (CATHERINE RICHARDSON WOOD) The Daughters of Holland Dames, descendants of the ancient and honorable families of New York, held their annual dinner. The descendants of the early Dutch colonists claim the highest distinction that an American can boast of, even to the chief executive of the United States. The society was created for the purpose of commemorating the events of the early Dutch period. The founder is Mrs. Alexander Crawford Chenoweth, a daughter of one of the Mayors of New York City, the late Hon. Fernando Wood. *February 11, 1905*

CHESTON, CHARLES S. is Master of the Whitemarsh Drag, which around Chestnut Hill furnishes such good sport to the sportsmen of Philadelphia. He hunts as assiduously as his brother, Mr. Radcliffe Cheston, Jr., and his cousin, Mr. Edward M. Cheston, and has been known for years as one of the finest gentleman riders in the country. Both Mr. Charles Cheston and his brother are connected with the old established Philadelphia banking house of E. B. Smith and Company. *February 1, 1928*

CHEWNING, MRS. EDMUND TAYLOR An authentic Cave Dweller, Mary is descended from Richard Wallach, the next-to-last Mayor of Washington, D. C., before it came under the jurisdiction of Congress in 1881, and from President Lincoln's Postmaster General, Montgomery Blair. Of the FDR years, she recalls: "I was only a child then, but I remember how divided my family was about these new people with only money moving in, and how upset some of them were when Aunt Rose Merriam, who had fallen upon hard times and became the first social secretary, began helping girls to be debutantes whose family nobody had ever heard of." *September, 1975*

CHEYLESMORE, LADY (ELIZABETH FRENCH) is a daughter of Mrs. Francis Ormond French and a sister of Mrs. Alfred Vanderbilt. Lady Cheylesmore met Colonel Herbert Eaton (now Lord Cheylesmore) in Bermuda, when he was an officer in the famous Grenadier Guards. His mother was a member of the Harmon family of New Orleans. Lady Cheylesmore, besides her favor with royalty, is noted also for the industry she started among working women—that of dressing dolls to represent celebrated people. *November 4, 1905*

CHILDS, GEORGE W. A report of the inauguration and ceremonies which marked the opening of the Philadelphia Centennial Exposition would necessarily be incomplete without a description of the social event of the evening. Mr. Childs, with the President, received. The foreign gentlemen, and the army and navy officers, were in full court dress and uniform. The Emperor of Brazil roamed through the brilliant apartments, speaking sometimes broken English. At eleven o'clock, McClurg's Liberty Cornet band appeared in front of Mr. Childs' residence and serenaded the President; shortly after which came to a conclusion the most brilliant social event which has ever occurred in the City of Brotherly Love. *May 17, 1876*

CHISHOLM, HUGH J. was born at Niagara-on-the-Lake, Canada. He began his business career in the railway news service of the Grand Trunk Railway and became a publisher and dealer in railway literature at Portland, Maine, and a manufacturer of paper and pulp. He was active in the formation of the International Paper Company. *July 20, 1912*

CHRIST, MR. AND MRS. DONALD (IRIS V. SMITH) — VAN INGEN — PAINE — RUSSELL like to combine formal black-tie dining and bridge. Iris has designed a room in the couple's Mill Neck, Long Island, home, "Wuff Woods," with optimum bridge-playing amenities, right down to the special lighting. Her dining room overlooks a surprisingly pastoral scene in any season: From its windows, guests have a view of Iris' private animal preserve, where her pairs of donkeys and llamas roam freely. Iris, who is the daughter of Consuelo Vanderbilt and Ambassador Earl E. T. Smith, inherited her love of animals from her mother. She is past President of the Animal Medical Center. *June, 1983*

CHRYSLER, MR. AND MRS. WALTER, JR. (PEGGY SYKES) There is Peggy Sykes, who, before she went off to the Continent a while ago as the bride of Walter Chrysler, Jr., planned every inch of her trousseau, her way of living, her city and country backgrounds. A music maniac who concentrated for years on Wagner in Munich, she has seen to it that her summer place on Long Island harbors two vast pianos. (The garden of this Chrysler house boasts the famous brooding *Story of Mankind* statue by Lachaise.) *June, 1938*

CHURCHILL, LADY RANDOLPH (JENNIE JEROME) Hers was one of the first Anglo-American marriages. In 1874, she wedded the Right Honorable Lord Randolph Henry Spencer Churchill, the third son of the seventh Duke of Marlborough. One of her two sons, Winston Leonard Spencer Churchill, has inherited much of his mother's energy and brilliance. In addition to becoming Vice President of the Ladies' Grand Council of the Primrose League, Lady Randolph is Editor of the sumptuous *Anglo-Saxon Review,* an entirely new departure in periodical literature. *July 26, 1900*

CHURCHILL, THOMAS J. comes from a prominent Southern family. His grandfather was the famous Confederate General Churchill, and his mother was Miss Hooper, daughter of Dr. T. O. Hooper, a surgeon in the Confederate army and in later years President of the American Medical Society. The Churchills have been residents of San Francisco for but a few years. They live in a charming home in Post Street and entertain in the true Southern hospitable way. *April 27, 1907*

CLAFLIN, JOHN The new President of the Chamber of Commerce is a representative New York merchant at the head of a house which has stood in the front rank of mercantile life in this city for over a half-century. Mr. Claflin is a great traveler, and he has made several trips to the East. He crossed the South American Continent from Pacific to Atlantic, at the Equator, in 1877, then quite a remarkable feat. *May 11, 1912*

CLAGETT, BRICE McADOO Typical of the first families who have lived with one foot in Washington and the other in Maryland—and probably the most prolific—are the Clagetts. Although the Clagetts have been actively involved in various causes (Brice's main interest is historic preservation), they haven't been great patrons of the arts: "Oh, I had a great aunt who died during the first act of *Lohengrin* at the Metropolitan Opera," says Brice. "She was Eliza Brice Clagett, and her husband was a man named Ethan Allen." About seven years ago, Brice was able to buy "Holly Hill," a 1663 house built by Richard Harrison, one of Brice's ancestors, in Friendship, Maryland. *September, 1975*

CLAGETT, MR. AND MRS. CHARLES THOMAS (NANCY LEITER) Among the direct descendants of Thomas Clagett, who came to America from London in 1670 to settle in Maryland, is Charles Thomas Clagett, whose wife is the former Nancy Leiter. Her grandfather came to Washington in 1880 from Chicago, where he was in business with Marshall Field. *September, 1975*

CLAIBORNE, MRS. HERBERT (KATE CABELL) On West Grace Street, Richmond, is the home of Mrs. Herbert Claiborne. This house breathes of the spirit of heirlooms, and the wall space is covered with old portraits. The ancient sideboard sparkles with old silver, and each piece of furniture tells a story of the Washingtons, to whom Mr. Claiborne is nearly allied. There is a community in Richmond representative of old families, who consider birth before money, and hospitality before splendor. *August 24, 1901*

CLARK, AGNES, a granddaughter of the picturesque Senator and a niece of Mr. Richard Tobin, one-time American minister at The Hague, was educated at a convent in Paris, studied music, and practiced hours abroad and last season in New York. The results of her work were wildly applauded when Miss Clark made her debut as a piano soloist with full symphony orchestra in the Woodland Theatre at San Mateo. *September 15, 1932*

CLARK, ALFRED CORNING The most pretentious private residence, perhaps, of Cooperstown, New York, is that of Alfred Corning Clark, who is travelling in Europe, where he spends most of his time. The house (at a cost of one hundred thousand dollars, it is said) was built by this gentleman's father, Edward Clark, who left an estate valued at all the way from twenty to thirty millions of dollars, all made out of the Singer sewing machine. *August 11, 1886*

CLARK, MR. AND MRS. EDWARD Last Monday, Mr. and Mrs. Edward Clark and family, of West Twenty Second Street, started for their summer residence at Cooperstown, Otsego County. They make the journey in a novel and leisurely way—that is, in their own carriage, and are accompanied by Signor Severini, the popular tenor. During the month of August, Mr. and Mrs. Clark are to receive as visitors several of the most distinguished amateur vocalists of New York. *June 17, 1868*

CLARK, EVELYN, daughter of Mr. and Mrs. J. Francis S. Clark, of Newport and New York, made her New York debut. Miss Clark is the granddaughter of Mr. Poultney Bigelow and a great-granddaughter of John Bigelow, Minister to France under Lincoln's administration. *April 15, 1928*

CLARK, F. AMBROSE has the good fortune to live in enchanting Georgian surroundings, and something of the atmosphere of that most delightful period of English history has crept into his bones. He is surrounded by sporting paintings by Ferneley and Ben Marshall, by lovely old Waterford glass and ancient books of a century ago, by an infinite number of reminders of the days when life was very pleasant and unhurried and tranquil. *July 15, 1927*

CLARK, FORRESTER A., SR. The Clarks of "Fox Hollow Farm," in Hamilton, Massachusetts, are building a dynasty. Related to such first family names as Winthrop, Thayer, and Burrage, there was a Clark ancestor on the *Mayflower*. "Tim" Clark, Sr. has really created the modern family and its fortune. He was virtually the last seven-letter man at Harvard, rowed on the U. S. Olympic crew in 1928, and is responsible for the installation of the current United States Equestrian Team on donated Clark property at Hamilton. The family controls H. C. Wainwright and Co., one of the most successful institutionally-oriented brokerage firms in America, and the largest Lincoln-Mercury dealership in New England. *April, 1976*

CLARK, JANE FORBES is the first woman President of the American Horse Shows Association. Known in Cooperstown as her family's "arbiter of taste," she is also President of the Clark Foundation, with assets of some $250 million (the fortune stems from a forebear who helped found the Singer sewing machine company). In addition, she's chairman of the company that manages the family's financial and philanthropic interests. Over the years, Clarks have enhanced their beloved Cooperstown with countless benefactions, including museums, a hospital, and an annual $2 million in regional college scholarships. *June, 1993*

CLARK, MRS. MARSHALL (VIRGINIA KEEP) is one of a group of clever young Chicago women who has not permitted the fact of their being members of the city's well-known families to keep them from advancing their talents. Mrs. Clark only recently returned from abroad—where, if memory serves rightly, she was a pupil of Sorolla. She has set up a studio in the building on Pearson Street where many of the interesting young artists hold forth. On Easter Monday, she gave a tea-exhibit which proved of sufficient interest to draw a most exclusive company, albeit the building is without elevators and Mrs. Clark's studio is perched on one of the upper floors. *April 20, 1912*

CLARK, W. A. The wealth of Senator W. A. Clark, of Montana and New York, is fabulous in the sense that it seems to pass the limits of credibility. It is not known, even approximately, how much over $100,000,000 he is worth; even he himself does not know, for his riches, barring some thousands of acres in coffee, rubber, and sugar in Mexico and California, are in his copper mine, which is known as the United Verde and is located in Jerome, Arizona. Its riches cannot well be estimated; so far, only the earth's surface has been scratched, as it were. *October 18, 1899*

CLARKE, JAMES KING and his younger brothers are interested in the automobile factory at Ardmore, Pennsylvania, and while independently wealthy they work from morning until late in the afternoon as busily as any mechanic employed in the factory. Their chief relaxation is a motor ride over the country roads round Philadelphia, and they are constantly having friendly discussions with the town authorities as to speed limits. *June 18, 1904*

CLARKE, RICHARD H., LL.D, a distinguished lawyer and author, gave a notable reception at his residence to his fellow members of the New York Society of the Sons of the American Revolution. The guests thus assembled represented the history of the nation—descendants of the Lees, the Warrens, the Gerrys, the Clarkes, the Hancocks, and other revolutionary fathers in the field and cabinet. He is a descendant of Hon. Robert Clarke, who was a colonist under the Baltimores in Maryland in 1634. *January 29, 1896*

CLARKE, THOMAS B. Members of the Motto Club were entertained by their chief, Thomas B. Clarke, at his house, 203 West Forty Fourth Street. The menus were each adorned with watercolor paintings of such animals as the frog, the stork, the owl, happily hitting off the special club distinction of the several members. After dinner, the guests visited Mr. Clarke's gallery of American art and examined several garnitures of antique Chinese porcelain. *December 22, 1880*

CLARKSON, GLADYS EVELYN On her mother's side, Miss Clarkson is a descendant of Bishop Samuel Provost, the first Episcopal bishop of New York, who read the prayers, standing at St. Paul's Church, when Washington was inaugurated. On the paternal side, Matthew Clarkson, made secretary to the Colony of New York by William and Mary, is one of the ancestors Miss Clarkson may claim. The Clarksons have intermarried with the Livingstons and de Peysters and the old families that still hold great estates along the Hudson at Tivoli. *April 15, 1911*

CLEMENS, SAMUEL L. (MARK TWAIN) went to Hamilton upon his arrival in Bermuda. He is forbidden by his medical men to attend dinners and receptions and has refused the invitations of the local clubs anxious to entertain him. This is the fourth visit of the great author to Bermuda, the climate of which he enjoys greatly, and where he is appropriately clad in his favorite suit of white flannel. *February 15, 1908*

CLEVELAND, ROSE ELIZABETH has become wealthy through her ownership of an island a few miles from Camden, Maine. Twenty years ago, she paid four thousand five hundred dollars for the island, and since then she has cleared two hundred thousand dollars from the sale of building lots. She is absolute queen of the island, and enforces her rules as rigidly as though it were situated in the South Seas. From March, 1885, until June, 1886, when her brother was married, Miss Cleveland was mistress at the White House. It was a short reign, but she certainly has very solid consolation now in a whole island. *November 4, 1905*

CLEWS, ELSIE WORTHINGTON was married at Newport to Mr. Herbert Parsons, of New York. Miss Clews is an authoress and has received degrees from several colleges, notably from Columbia, which made her a doctor of philosophy and honored her by making her work on philosophy one of its textbooks. *September 6, 1900*

CLEWS, HENRY, JR. It was always supposed that he would follow in the footsteps of his father and become a figure on Wall Street. From his early youth, however, he rather affected the startling and original; and as he showed all evidences of the artistic temperament, his parents wisely let him have his own way. He used to delight to shock the more staid element in Newport by some little oddity in dress and to keep these good people on the *qui vive*. After he reached his majority, he elected to take up the career of a painter and went to Paris to study. Young Clews has had a studio in Paris several years, and he has one now at Newport. *September 16, 1911*

CLEWS, JOHN HENRY was a member of the banking firm of Henry Clews & Co., of which Mr. Henry Clews, his uncle, was the organizer in 1877. The Clews family is one of the old families of Staffordshire, England, where Mr. Henry Clews was born. *April 20, 1907*

CLOTHIER, WILLIAM is inseparably associated with tennis. In 1906, he won the All-Comers Tournament. In 1909, Mr. Clothier again won the All-Comers. Since retiring from active participation in tennis, he has been very keen about foxhunting. He is Master of the Pickering Valley Hounds, which hunts the country around Phoenixville, Pennsylvania. *December 1, 1926*

CLOTHIER, MRS. WILLIAM I. The Philadelphia Pony Show was started by Mrs. William I. Clothier and her committee of ardent sportswomen in 1912, for the purpose of teaching youngsters to love, to care for, and to show their own horses and ponies in the true spirit of sportsmanship. Originally held near the Clothier estate in Wynnewood, The Pony Show has moved gradually away from town with the passing years and now takes place in the Radnor Hunt country of Malvern. *March, 1955*

CLOVER, EUDORA remains unmarried, and she has deserted Washington for California. The daughter of the late Rear Admiral Richardson Clover and a granddaughter of Senator Miller of California, a "forty-niner" who struck it rich, she has settled down on the family ranch in the Napa Valley and, after taking various agricultural courses, has developed into a successful farmer. *April 15, 1923*

CLUETT, MRS. WILLIAM GORHAM (HELEN STEDMAN) is the widow of one of the most respected civic leaders in Palm Beach history, William Gorham Cluett, of Cluett Peabody (Arrow shirts and Sanforizing). His name is synonymous with the top-drawer Everglades Club. Under Cluett's presidency, the club's impeccable standards were established. *March, 1979*

COBB, DARIUS, painter of portraits and landscapes, was a twin brother of the late Cyrus Cobb, painter and sculptor. The twins were born in Walden, Massachusetts, in one of the historic houses of New England. Their father was an eminent theologian. Their mother was the first President of the Ladies' Physiological Institute of Boston. Both the father and mother were descendants in a direct line from Elder Darius Cobb, who came over on the *Mayflower*. The twins helped each other in everything, though Cyrus turned his attention mostly to sculpture. The twin brothers served through the Civil War in the Forty-fourth Massachusetts Regiment. In 1866, on the same day, they married sisters. *May 20, 1919*

COBB, DR. W. MONTAGUE The Montague Cobbs trace their family history back to William H. Montague, who was born in Georgetown in 1820. He later emigrated to Springfield, Massachusetts, where he made a tidy fortune as a manufacturer of black hair preparations and cosmetics. His son had, by 1900, risen to the position of assistant tax assessor for the District of Columbia, an unusually high position for a black in those days. He married the daughter of a man named Cobb, and their son W. Montague Cobb today is a distinguished anatomist, professor of anatomy at Howard University, and editor of the *Journal of the American Medical Association*. *September, 1975*

COCHRAN, ALEXANDER SMITH is one of the latest converts to aeronautics. It has been recently announced that he has purchased a standard Wright biplane and will enter the field as an aviator. Mr. Cochran has suddenly come to fame as the wealthiest bachelor in society. He is the head of the carpet house of Alexander Smith & Sons Company at Yonkers. His mother was the sister of Alexander Smith, the founder of the fortunes of the family, and his father, the late William F. Cochran, was also a wealthy man. *May 13, 1911*

COCKE, GENERAL WILLIAM H., the resident owner of "Claremont Manor," Virginia, is of the family for whom the celebrated "Bremo" in Fluvanna County, Virginia, was built. Bremo was originally designed by Thomas Jefferson in 1815, and the first stone laid for the famous residence General John Hartwell Cocke was to dwell in was laid in 1818. General and Mrs. Cocke came into possession of the house in 1928. The manor is one of the very few examples in this country of the William and Mary and Queen Anne style. *June 1, 1934*

COCKS, WILLIAM WILLETS is a descendant on his mother's side of the great Quaker who founded Swarthmore College, where he was educated and of which he is now a manager. He is also a trustee of the Friends' Academy at Locust Valley. He remains loyal to the tenets of his ancestors, to whom charity is a synonym for peace, yet he had the fighting spirit to go into politics. In 1904, he was elected a member of Congress from the first New York district. *May 6, 1911*

CODMAN, COLONEL CHARLES RUSSEL was well known as a lawyer and was prominent in the affairs of the Republican party. His family has been identified with Boston since 1640. For several years, Colonel Codman was President of the Board of Overseers of Harvard College. He had served a term in the State Senate and took an active part in the local affairs of Brookline. *October 20, 1918*

CODMAN, OGDEN reversed the customary procedure of architects who, for centuries, have paid reverence to the architectural masterpieces of Italy and Florence and returned home to give a dash of European culture to their native buildings. Mr. Codman, on the contrary, built, for his own use, a foreign villa on foreign soil; a villa of noble proportions and authentic magnificence on a site overlooking the Mediterranean. The ambition was born when Mr. Codman, looking for a villa in 1929, was shown the Domaine de La Leopolda, created by Leopold II, King of the Belgians, from eighteen small parcels of land. Impressed with the beauty of the estate, Mr. Codman decided to buy the Domaine and build there a villa in the style of those along the Mediterranean dating from the eighteenth century. *September, 1947*

COE, WILLIAM ROBERTSON "Cherokee Plantation," near Yemassee, South Carolina, covers an area of over ten thousand acres. It is three miles from the outer to the inner gates, along a tree-bordered road. The land, once a part of the famous Blake plantation, created under a grant to Daniel Blake from the Crown in 1710, continued to belong to the family until Mr. Coe purchased it about two years ago. Stretching out on the south, along the Combahee River, the rice fields add further interest to the setting and provide an ideal feeding ground for ducks. *November 1, 1933*

COFFIN, TRISTRAM There is to be a great reunion of the Coffin family on the island of Nantucket to commemorate the anniversary of the death of Tristram Coffin, the first of the race who settled in this country in 1642 and to whom, with nine other companions, the island of Nantucket was deeded in 1659. The program will open on the first day, as is most proper, with a clambake, to come off near the site of Tristram's dwelling house. The third day will be ushered in with a breakfast given under a mammoth tent, at which such dainties as lobscouse, plum-duff, and chowder will grace the board. *August 3, 1881*

COFFIN, WILLIAM SLOANE is the newly elected—and very youthful—head of that infinitely august assemblage, the Board of the Metropolitan Museum. There was his ability as Treasurer, no less than his membership in W. & J. Sloane and in both the Sloane and Coffin families (for the duties of the board are not infrequently a matter of inheritance), that carried his name to the top of the ballot. *February 1, 1932*

COLBY, HOWARD A., of Llewellyn Park, Orange, New Jersey, is winning laurels for himself in a new field. Not content with being the champion of several New Jersey golf clubs, he has but recently become the champion squash tennis player of the Knickerbocker Athletic Club. *April 5, 1902*

COLEMAN, MRS. G. DAWSON (MARIANA W. GOWEN) is one of the Philadelphia society women whose work for the Devon Dog Show has actually made it one of the outstanding and ranking events of the country. Mrs. Coleman, who is Chairman of the Committee, is a fine woman to hounds and hunts regularly with the Radnor and Middleburg. Although keen as mustard on the king of beasts, she is far from impervious to the charms and merits of the friends of man. *May 15, 1928*

COLEMAN, BISHOP LEIGHTON From 1866 to 1869, he was rector of St. John's Church, Wilmington, Delaware. In 1877, with his wife, the daughter of Alexis du Pont of Delaware, he visited England. He was organizing secretary of the Church of England Temperance Society for three years and made Oxford his residence. In October, 1888, returning to America, he was ordained Bishop of Delaware and went to Wilmington to make it his home. *December 21, 1907*

COLEMAN, ROBERT S. ("COLEY") The Turf and Field Club is the oldest private club of racing in the United States. In 1895, when the club was founded, the Turf and Field was designed to be a horse fancier's recreational society, "a resort for polo, golf, and other sports and generally for the purpose of a country club." "The aim of the club is to give people a haven, if you will, of tranquility and camaraderie," says Robert S. ("Coley") Coleman, the current President. "We do try to improve things. We have had to adjust and roll with the punches, but our fundamentals remain the same as those of our founders." *July, 1982*

COLGATE, MRS. SAMUEL (CORA E. SMITH) has been repeatedly referred to as "the widow of the late soap millionaire." There are three distinct divisions of the Colgate clan in New York. One of these is engaged in the white lead business, one is in the banking business, and one is in the soap and perfume business. Samuel Colgate belonged to the branch which manufactures white lead, and was a very different man from Samuel Colgate, the soap maker, with whom he is so often confounded. *December 21, 1898*

COLLIER, PETER FENELON, who was one of the most successful publishers in this country, was born in Ireland. He was the founder and owner of *Collier's Weekly* and, for many years, had been at the head of the publishing firm of P. F. Collier and Son. Both he and his son, Robert J. Collier, have done much for the charities of the Catholic Church. In his box at the opera this spring, three priests were once seated, to illustrate how closely he kept in touch with the interests of the church. *May 1, 1909*

COLLIER, ROBERT JOSEPH provided some novel entertainment for the fifty weekend guests who attended a house-warming at "Rest Hill," Wickatunk, New Jersey, his country home. There was a ten-mile hunt from East Freehold to the polo grounds on the Colliers' estate, with two aeroplanes racing overhead. With T. O. M. Sopwith, the English aviator, in a Wright biplane, was James H. Hare, who took photographs of the hunt during the rest periods. The other aeroplane was driven by A. L. Welch, who carried Mr. Collier from Rest Hill to East Freehold, the starting point. Mr. Collier in his pink coat made a striking picture as the machine rose above the autumn landscape. At Freehold, he dismounted the aeroplane for one of his eighteen ponies and led the chase. *October 21, 1911*

COLLIER, MRS. ROBERT JOSEPH (SARA STEWART VAN ALEN), instead of giving a theater party which requires transportation of guests by auto or omnibus, brought the play to the house for the enjoyment of the people at her dinner party. After the dinner, *How He Lied to Her Husband* was given by George Bernard Shaw's company in the drawing room, which is a great square apartment at the corner of the house, once occupied by the Fish family and overlooking Gramercy Park. *January 14, 1905*

COLLIER, MR. AND MRS. WILLIAM MILLER (FRANCES BEARDSLEY ROSS) The present American Minister at Madrid and Mrs. Collier first distinguished themselves by a novel and most enchanting dinner, which created a sensation and no end of surprise and comment in the aristocratic circles of the Spanish capital. The table on this occasion was literally banked with deep red roses. The walls of the room were hung with purple velvet, and the ceiling was made to represent the canopy of the heavens at night. The guests entered the dining room in the gloom of semi-darkness, but as they took their places there suddenly burst forth from the petals of every flower on the table and from the "sky" above and from countless places on the purple-hung walls, thousands of twinkling, glittering, ever-changing stars, illuminating the room with intense brilliancy. The effect was startling and brought forth exclamations of admiration and surprise from the assembled guests. *October 31, 1908*

COLLINGWOOD, MR. AND MRS. FRANCIS (ELIZA W. BONNETT), of Elizabeth, New Jersey, have opened their summer home at Avon-by-the-Sea. Mr. Collingwood, who was associated with the Roeblings in the building of the Brooklyn Bridge, is devoted to the use of rod and line. After the bridge was finished, Mr. Collingwood was made a fellow of the Royal Geographical Society. He is a collateral descendant of the Admiral Collingwood who was second in command at Trafalgar. *July 2, 1904*

COLLINS, A. M. lives in the sporting town of Bryn Mawr, Pennsylvania, in his quieter moments. He has always played polo with the club there. But occasionally the urge for sport of another kind will be at him, and then he abandons the life of a peaceful country gentlemen with a vengeance. He is a noted big game hunter. He has made expeditions to Africa and South America and India and Alaska. He has brought back specimens so alarming and superb that his trophy room in his house at Bryn Mawr is recognized as containing one of the finest collections in the country. *March 1, 1927*

COLLOREDO-MANNSFELD, COUNT AND COUNTESS FERDINAND (NORA ISELIN) Surely this was not an international alliance of the sort in regard to which the public is always so vulgarly inquisitive, with its questions regarding the father's estimate of the bridegroom and paternal humility or obstinacy in regard to settlements. Though Miss Iselin's father, Mr. C. Oliver Iselin, is a Protestant, her grandfather, the late Adrian Iselin, was a Catholic whose generosity in building schools and churches in New Rochelle and in bequests to charity is surely a matter of record in Rome, where the bride will go with Count Ferdinand, as he is an attaché of the Austrian Embassy in "The Holy City." *May 15, 1909*

COLT, LE BARON The Colts are a very old family in Rhode Island and have maintained for many decades a social prestige in Providence which may be compared to that of royalty. Judge Colt is a brother of Colonel Samuel P. Colt, the president of the rubber trust and a multimillionaire, and is himself a man of means. *March 22, 1913*

COMBS, LESLIE II A potentate of brilliant commercial sense, Combs is unimpeachably the most successful seller of thoroughbreds alive today. For the second year in a row, he was America's number one money-winning breeder. For all those contemplating the horse game, Combs' suggestion: "You've got to be prepared to spend a million to begin with. Start with a four-year program. And come to get some good advice from good old Leslie Combs." *May, 1971*

CONGER, EDWIN HURD served in the Civil War; was State Treasurer of Iowa, 1882–1885; a member of Congress, Minister to Brazil and later to China, where in 1900 he had an active part in the quelling of the Boxer uprising. *May 25, 1907*

CONKLIN, MR. AND MRS. ROLAND R. (MARY MACFADDEN) have one of the most interesting estates on Long Island. They entertain in a novel way. For instance, on the night before Christmas, Mr. Conklin gave a dinner served as in the fashion of four hundred years ago in England. One enters the dwelling through a loggia with ivy on the walls and an Italian marble seat. The house is filled with curious lamps and tapestries and furniture taken from monasteries and convents abroad. The sixty servants employed on the place are sometimes invited into the theater on holidays, given remembrances, and entertained with music. *April 15, 1911*

CONNELLY, JOANNE was one of the Queen Debs of the year 1948. After reams of newspaper space, Joanne married golfer Bobby Sweeny. A subsequent wedding to tin heir Jaime Ortiz-Patiño was ill-fated, and, on the 49th day of their honeymoon in Capri, Joanne ran away. Patiño chased her. She became ill, and eventually Patiño divorced her to the tune of newspaper headlines. Joanne finally died of an overdose of sleeping pills. The last of the glamour girls had passed. *June, 1962*

CONOR, MR. AND MRS. DAVID MARION (OTELIA CARRINGTON CUNNINGHAM) A beautiful summer wedding interestingly reminiscent of the Old South occurred recently in Petersburg, Virginia. Through her mother (Otelia Carrington), the bride is descended from Judge Paul Carrington of Colonial days, for thirty years President of the Supreme

Council of the Old Dominion. On the paternal side, she is connected with the Alston, Kearney, and Somerville families of South Carolina. Mr. Conor is a son of the late Henry Groves Conor, formerly Judge of the Supreme Court of North Carolina. *September 1, 1925*

CONVERSE, FREDERICK S. must have been gratified by the attention given his new opera, *The Pipe of Desire,* which had its initial performance at Jordan Hall, Boston. The audiences were large and fashionable, and the list of patronesses included many of the smartest people. Mr. Converse is Assistant Professor of music at Harvard and, as he is a man of means, has time to perfect his musical ideas, and thus to insure their success. *February 10, 1906*

CONVERSE, HARRIET MAXWELL will leave town this week for a visit to the Cataraugus reservation to celebrate the anniversary of her adoption by the Seneca Indians. The Senecas are making great preparations for the occasion, designing to give the white daughter of the tribe a feast in the olden style. She is writing an account of the "Festivals and Legends of the Iroquois" in verse. *June 9, 1886*

CONVERSE, MRS. JAMES C. (LITA BERRY) Her beauty made her one of the most conspicuous brides of November, 1902. She is a niece of Mrs. John di Zerega (the di Zeregas tracing their origin back to the Danes) and a lineal descendant of Major John Berry, second Governor of New Jersey and proprietor of an extensive manor in Bergen County, granted him by the Duke of York. *March 26, 1904*

CONVERSE, JOHN W. plays polo during the summer at Bryn Mawr and Narragansett Pier, hunts with the Radnor and other Philadelphia packs during the autumn, and perhaps goes to England with Mrs. Converse, an excellent woman to hounds, for a season in the Shires. But whether in his home country or elsewhere, he does not let anything interfere with his civic duties and his responsibilities as Lieutenant-Colonel of the 103rd Cavalry of the Pennsylvania National Guard. *May 1, 1927*

COOK, CHARLES T. entered the service of Tiffany & Co. in 1847. He had been President since the death of Charles L. Tiffany in 1902 and was one of the oldest members of the Union League Club. In 1900, Mr. Cook was made an officer of the Legion of Honor of France, and in 1903 was decorated by the King of Italy as Knight Officer of the Royal Order of the Crown of Italy. *February 2, 1907*

COOK, MRS. NORMAN, who was not only born in Newport and lives there all the year round but who represents old Newport on her mother's side (Collins) and relatively new Newport on her father's (Norman), says, "I can never remember, not remembering Newport." She is convinced most people write off the resort too soon. "Even when we're alone here, in the winter, we don't just eat—we dine. In the old days, it was soup and fish, and now it's fish and chips, but we're still at it. We've still got what dear old Maude Howe Elliott used to call 'the pure silk thread through the tapestry of synthetics.'" *September, 1958*

POLITICS MAKES STRANGE DINNER-FELLOWS

John Vietor invited to dinner a contemporary of his at Yale, the young James Copley, heir to the Copley chain of newspapers and the powerful publisher of the chain's cantankerously Tory flagship, the *San Diego Union.* A polite Old Blue time was being had by all until Vietor happened to mention he was a Democrat. Copley was a man who took his politics passionately and seriously. "Jim turned a deep red," Vietor recalls. "He stood up and announced: 'I'm very sorry, but I cannot dine with a Democrat.' Then he walked out. That's the last I ever saw of him socially." *May, 1975*

COOKE, JAY One of the most picturesque hunting boxes owned by Philadelphians is that of Mr. Jay Cooke, at Larry's Creek, near Williamsport. It is called "Ogontz Lodge" and is commodious enough for the entertainment of quite a large party. *August 16, 1902*

COOKE, STARR A descendant of one of Hawaii's first missionary families, Starr Cooke is Executive Vice President of Carlton-Santee, a real estate and land-development company in Los Angeles. But he plans to return to Hawaii and to return with enough business experience to handle his family's vast holdings. "Too many of Hawaii's founding families stayed behind; outsiders had to be brought in to develop the islands and help them grow. I think we should learn how to handle things ourselves." *May, 1975*

COOLIDGE, T. JEFFERSON, JR. The beautiful art objects purchased by Mr. T. Jefferson Coolidge, Jr., at the Stanford White sale are installed in the home at Manchester, Massachusetts. This house, a feature of Coolidge Point, is one of the show-palaces of the shore. Originally, the point was owned by the grandfather of Mr. Coolidge, Jr., who was a direct descendant of President Thomas Jefferson, and much of the land on which the Essex Country Club stands was in the family. No one on the shore has done more for the town of Manchester than Mr. Coolidge and his father, who gave the town its magnificent public library. *May 25, 1907*

COOPER, MR. AND MRS. DOUGLAS (DIANE PITCAIRN) are a pair of Philadelphians to be reckoned with. Diane and Doug are such a many-sided duo—in Montego Bay, they have just bought an octagonal house with plans for hexagonal rooms. Doug is a jeweler and is active in the Smithsonian's efforts to establish America's equivalent to the crown jewels of Europe's monarchies. Diane is the daughter of the Reverend Theodore Pitcairn of the Swedenborgian community of Bryn Athyn outside Philadephia and a famous art collector. *October, 1966*

COOPER, EDWARD is and has been a notable figure in the civic and social history of New York. He was born in 1824, and is the son of the late Peter Cooper, the philanthropist. He is a profound scholar, a graduate of Colum-

bia University, and has been associated for years in the conducting of the iron industries which the Cooper family has instituted. At his home on Washington Square, one of the row of quaint, old-time brick residences on the north side of that historic park, Mr. Cooper has his library. One cannot fail to know the house, as a grateful city placed, years ago, a pair of gas lamps before the door, the tribute to mark the residence of a Mayor. *October 22, 1904*

COOPER, PETER The heirs of Peter Cooper have signed deeds whereby $550,000 will be added eventually to the endowment fund of Cooper Union. The sum is the principal of the trust fund left by Peter Cooper for the support of his family. Under the agreement between the heirs, his entire estate will thus have been devoted to the institution which he founded. *March 15, 1899*

COOPER, MRS. WYATT EMORY (GLORIA VANDERBILT)—DE CICCO—STOKOWSKI—LUMET, who paints and creates singingly joyous collages from bits of silver foil, gingham, and all sorts of *objets trouvés,* is considered by other Vanderbilts to have the most daring, personality-expressing style. An inveterate jewelry collector, she wears her chunky, weighty, marvelous embellishments like master craftsworks of some ancient civilization. *January, 1969*

COPLEY, MRS. JAMES S. (HELEN KINNEY), publisher of *The San Diego Union* and *The San Diego Tribune,* is also the Chairman and chief executive officer of The Copley Press, the parent corporation that publishes a variety of newspapers—eleven daily, thirty weekly, and one biweekly. Born in Cedar Rapids, Iowa, she attended Hunter College in New York, married James S. Copley, and, after his untimely death in 1973 at the age of 57, assumed his position as Publisher. *January, 1986*

CORBIN, AUSTIN "Blue Mountain Farm" is the estate of Mr. Austin Corbin, at Newport, New Hampshire. Shooting the wild boar is one of the chief pastimes on the farm, which comprises some twenty six thousand acres, all enclosed in a fence nine feet high, so that the immense herds of buffaloes, deer, and other game cannot escape. The boar hunters get out at half after three in the morning, lying in wait in the great apple orchards until the animals come out to feed. *October 1, 1904*

CORCORAN, GEORGE EUSTIS The change in name of Mr. George Peabody Eustis, by permission of the Supreme Court of the District of Columbia, was to that of George Eustis Corcoran. It is believed that he was moved by his desire to perpetuate the name of his late grandfather, William W. Corcoran, after whom the celebrated art gallery in Washington given by him was named. *March 1, 1921*

CORCORAN, W. W. The Washington philanthropist retired in 1854 from the banking house of Corcoran & Riggs and devoted his life to charitable deeds, which his financial and real estate speculations enabled him to execute on a grand scale. Among his most notable gifts to the public is the Corcoran

Art Gallery. The "Louise Home" is another one of his bequests to the public, on which he spent $400,000. The home is intended for refined ladies in reduced circumstances. *February 29, 1888*

CORCORAN, WILLIAM WARWICK, U.S. Vice Consul at Boulogne-sur-Mer, France, prominent in Washington society and particularly in the riding set at the Capital, has been elected first whip of the smart Le Touquet Hunt Club at Le Touquet, a fashionable resort on the north coast of France. *May 1, 1922*

CORLIES, MARGARET L. A notable acquisition to women's club life in Philadelphia is found in a fashionable motor club for women who drive their own cars. This is called "La Moviganta Klubo," and the club owes its existence to Miss Margaret L. Corlies, who founded it last May. It has been a great success from the start, and now has on the active members list twenty nine women who are their own chauffeurs. They are fortunate in having for their headquarters the beautiful and historic Benedict Arnold Mansion in Fairmount Park, built in 1761. *October 19, 1907*

CORNING, ERASTUS, of Albany, has two curious hobbies. Just at the present moment, he spends his spare moments in endeavoring to augment his rare collection of about twelve hundred orchids. About fifteen years ago, he busied himself for a long time getting together fifty thousand butterflies. His collection of butterflies is perhaps the second or third best in the United States. *February 3, 1886*

CORNWALLIS-WEST, MRS. GEORGE (JENNIE JEROME)—SPENCER-CHURCHILL It is to the credit of Mrs. George Cornwallis-West that the status of American society is upheld in the English metropolis. "The Americans have spent vast sums in entertaining and living on a scale of magnificence almost unknown before. This has led the English arbiters of fashion to adopt American lavish ways, until only a few of the wealthiest social leaders are able to keep up the American pace. As a result, many of them are unable to longer participate in the grander functions, and the effect on society as a whole is toward exclusiveness." *September 20, 1902*

CORRIGAN, MRS. JAMES (LAURA MAE WHITROCK)—MACMARTIN The most unusual party was given by her, a cabaret dinner and ball, with over a hundred guests seated at tables holding eight and ten. There was singing from soup to dessert. The decorations were elaborate and beautiful, real butterflies hovering over bowers of pink roses. Between each cabaret effort, individuals appeared bearing large cards, on which was written "silence." *July 1, 1923*

COTTENET, RAWLINS is a bachelor who is one of the most popular in New York society and who is especially interested in all sports connected with the turf as well as with music and the drama. He is quite a power at the Metropolitan Opera House and is one of the best riders to hounds and one of the oldest members of the Meadow Brook Club. Mr. Cottenet has written a number of songs, but he has never, as yet, come out in anything much more ambi-

tious. As he is a thorough musician with a remarkable faculty for melody, there is no reason why the musical world should not yet hear from him. *November 25, 1911*

COWDIN, JOHN E. is a well-known man in society whose knowledge about horses is authoritative. He is a polo player of renown and a whip; and he is one of the older members of the Turf and Riding Clubs. Mr. and Mrs. Cowdin live on Gramercy Park where, at their handsome residence, they entertain frequently during the winter, their summer home being at Far Rockaway. *November 10, 1906*

COWDIN, MRS. WINTHROP (RENA T. POTTER) was the daughter of the Right Rev. Henry C. Potter, D.D., Bishop of New York. Mrs. Cowdin, true to the principles of the Potter family, was zealous in humanitarian schemes and lost her health during the Spanish-American War, when she worked nobly to recruit a corps of nurses to go to Cuba. *October 27, 1906*

COWLES, MRS. THOMAS H. (BARBARA GRANGER) Onwentsia Club, Lake Forest, was the setting for one of the gayest of summer parties, an "inappropriate" dance. Mrs. Thomas H. Cowles had the inspiration for the affair. Mrs. Cowles belied her efficient manner by wearing a little girl dress of pink chambray and a pink bow on her unbobbed dark curls. Four debutantes of last season took the party quite by storm in their burlesque "rum sleuth" costumes, consisting of too-large policemen's outfits, tin stars, red noses and wigs, and Chaplin feet. *September 1, 1925*

COX, MRS. HOWARD ELLIS (ANN C. DELAFIELD FINCH) is descended from one of the oldest and most distinguished families in the United States. Among her ancestors are three signers of the Declaration of Independence. Her mother, Mary Livingston Delafield, made her debut in the family's townhouse in New York (opposite the Public Library, on 42nd Street) in 1898. In turn, Mrs. Cox made her debut in her family's townhouse, near the Metropolitan Museum, in 1936. Known professionally as Ann Cox, Mrs. Cox designed clothes for debutantes in her salon for over ten years. For the last four years she has been a fashion advisor at Bergdorf Goodman. *June, 1963*

COX, MARY ANN LIVINGSTON DELAFIELD The mere logistics of this girl's debut at the family's summer home in Westhampton, Long Island, are staggering. The party, first of the deb season in the New York area, will be preceded by a cocktail bash for 500. After that, comes a dinner party for 250 youngsters. Then comes the actual debutante party at the Cox house on Quantuck Bay. The Coxes will rent all the rooms in Westhampton's Inn for their guests, some coming from as far as Alaska for the event. They will also put up about thirty five boys and girls in their guest house. *June, 1963*

CRAM, MR. AND MRS. J. SERGEANT (CLARE BRYCE) He is another of the clubmen who has gone into politics and succeeded. There is no doubt but that he is an out and out Tammany man, and his first prominent position was that of President of the Dock Board. The family made a large fortune in the beginning of the

last century and have intermarried with several old and notable New York houses. In 1906, he married Miss Clare Bryce, a great-granddaughter of Peter Cooper. Both Mr. and Mrs. Cram are expert golfers, and each summer they go to Scotland to enjoy the ancient game in its best aspect. They are skillful whips, ride to hounds, and are much interested in sports of all kinds. *June 10, 1911*

CRAM, LILY, a daughter of Mrs. Henry A. Cram, is very enthusiastic about the birds in Lenox, Massachusetts. Almost every day at noon, she goes into the woods at "Highwood," sets a small table and feeds and studies the birds. Some are very tame and have learned to observe the feeding hour, flying about her closely. Recently, Miss Cram had an ornithologist give a lecture at Highwood with the birds that fly about her estate as a subject. She can imitate the songs of the Berkshire species. *July 18, 1908*

CRAMP, MRS. EDWIN S. (D. R. KEEFER), mother of the now Mrs. Theodore Roosevelt Pell, has been decorated by the Sultan of Turkey. The decoration was bestowed upon Mrs. Cramp for the christening of the Turkish man-of-war *Medjidie,* at the Cramp shipyard, when she acted as sponsor for the vessel. *December 12, 1903*

CRANE, CORNELIUS The sailing date has been set for a new expedition for the Field Museum. Cornelius Crane, son of Richard T. Crane, Jr., of Chicago, will be in charge of the venture and is to lend his yacht for the voyage. A twenty-five-thousand-mile cruise is planned, and the party hopes to bring back new specimens of sea monsters. *October 15, 1928*

CRANE, MR. AND MRS. JOHN OLIVER (CONTESSINA TERESA MARESCOTTI) were married in the private chapel of the Palazzo of Prince Allesandro Ruspoli, uncle of the bride. Mr. Crane was for four years secretary to President Masaryk of Czechoslovakia, and his father, Mr. Charles Richard Crane, was formerly American Minister to China. *December 1, 1929*

CRANE, WINTHROP MURRAY, JR., son of Senator Crane of Massachusetts, may be said to have entered upon his business career this week, when he assumed a partnership in the firm of Crane & Co., makers of Government money paper. His engagement to Miss Ethel Eaton of Pittsfield was recently announced, and their marriage will, in a way, unite the two largest paper-making industries of the Berkshires. *December 10, 1904*

CRANMER, GEORGE is one of Denver's first citizens. Long before the gold rush, his family were cattle tycoons, then switched to real estate in the 1880s. He is shown at Red Rocks Park, which he conceived as a great theater for music and drama festivals and later supervised during construction. Mr. Cranmer and his wife are distinguished art collectors, music patrons, world travelers, and civic leaders. *August, 1959*

CRARY, REV. ROBERT FULTON was a grandson of Robert Fulton, inventor of the steamboat. The Rev. Mr. Crary was founder of the parish of the Holy Cross, Warrensburg, New York. He was rector of the Church of the Comforter at Poughkeepsie for forty years. A composer of church music, he also exhibited paintings at the National Academy of Design. *December 12, 1914*

CRAVATH, PAUL D. The three days of celebration being over, residents of the North Shore of Long Island, with a sprinkling of those who have estates and homes to the southward, are calmly enjoying the many delights and luxuries and comforts of the new Piping Rock Club. It was only natural that, on the opening day, no man should have been more in evidence or the subject of more congratulations than Mr. Paul D. Cravath, to whose efforts and enterprise the club owes its existence. *June 15, 1912*

CRAWFORD, F. MARION The education of F. Marion Crawford, the author of *Mr. Isaacs* and *Doctor Claudius,* was commenced in Rome, continued at St. Paul's, Concord, and was completed at Cambridge, England, where he took high rank. He may not know as much Hebrew as his accomplished aunt, Mrs. Julia Ward Howe, but like her he is familiar with Latin, Greek, French, Italian, Spanish, etc. He inherits from his father, Thomas Crawford, the sculptor, a certain perceptive power, only he clothes his thoughts in words rather than in clay. *June 20, 1883*

CROCKER, MRS. BENNETT, daughter of the Auxiliary Bishop of Rhode Island, stepped into the Gotham picture frame a few years ago as a hostess of note and an industrious charity worker. When not busying herself with the poor, entertaining at the River Club, or adding up bridge scores, Mrs. Crocker does considerable trotting around. Last year, she had a schloss in Salzburg; this Christmas saw her at Saint Jovite; next month she appears in Palm Beach. She is often seen at night in well-cut black, exquisitely detailed, under a full-shouldered ermine coat. *February, 1939*

CROCKER, CHARLES FREDERICK, who went to California from Troy, New York, in 1849 and who was a member of the legislature in 1860, was one of the great men of California. He was associated with Leland Stanford, Mark Hopkins, and Collis P. Huntington. His enterprise and genius in promoting railroad enterprise made possible the building and extending of great railroad routes. He furnished means for much of the surveying that helped toward the progress of the Far West. *December 2, 1905*

CROCKER, CHARLES TEMPLETON While a student at Yale, he was a member of the Dramatic Club and gave evidence of considerable talent as an actor. Of late, he has shown a desire to do something besides motor and play polo. He is working to be a playwright. He does not care for comedy or society drama, but has plunged into the making of a gigantic allegorical spectacle, something fitted to the largest stage or to an open-air theater, with the noblest natural surroundings. He has taken for his theme the transformation of China. *July 20, 1915*

CROCKER, FRANK LONGFELLOW When a new luxury club opens its doors, Frank Longfellow Crocker is likely to be involved. An organizer of the Piping Rock, Creek, Links, and

Twenty-nine clubs, he is President of the Terrace Club, which will open any day now on a World's Fair lagoon. Successful before the Bar nearly forty years, he figured most recently in the press as counsel for Mrs. Harry Payne Whitney in the suit over little Gloria Vanderbilt. At Harvard, class of '98, he played football and rowed on the crew. Since that time, his horses have collected ribbons and his boats trophies. From his mother's family, relations of the poet Longfellow, he inherits typically New England enthusiasms for old prints of whalers and shipwrecks, for book collecting, and for service on the directorates of Latin American railroads. *June, 1938*

CROCKER, GEORGE, son of the late California millionaire, has just received $500,000 as a reward for five consecutive years of total abstinence from intoxicants. The father's will failed to bequeath a portion of his property to George, who was given to over-indulgence in intoxicants. He placed, however, four hundred and ninety bonds of the Southern Pacific Company in trust for George, with the proviso that if, within fifteen years after the death of the founder of the fund, George Crocker should remain sober for five consecutive years, the principal should be turned over to him. *November 4, 1896*

CROCKER, JENNIE ADELINE is one of the great heiresses of America. In 1905, she came into a fortune of over eight millions, which had been held in trust for her. Her father was the late Charles F. Crocker of San Francisco. Miss Crocker is well known in the world of sport, as she has, since coming into her inheritance, maintained kennels in San Francisco that are known all over the world. Boston terriers are a specialty in the Crocker kennels; when they died, they were given elaborate funerals. *April 20, 1912*

CROCKER, WILLIAM H. The rigor of the Lenten season was considerably lightened by Mr. William H. Crocker, Mrs. Charles Templeton Crocker, and Mr. Richard McCreery, who were hosts at a brilliant mi-careme ball. It was styled the Ball of the Roses and was held at the Hotel St. Francis in San Francisco. The guests were bidden to wear fancy dress and came in every color in which roses grow — pale pink, white, yellow, American Beauty, Gold of Ophir, the costumes made as much like roses as possible. Many of the men went as buds and leaves, and some of them as full-blown blossoms. *April 1, 1923*

CROMWELL, MR. AND MRS. OLIVER EATON (LUCRETIA ROBERTS) have a country place at Manursing Island, Portchester, New York, and they are among the most notable entertainers in the Westchester set. Mr. Cromwell is an enthusiastic yachtsman, one of the officials of the New York Yacht Club and a member of the Union, Century, and other New York clubs. For some winters, Mrs. Cromwell has made her home in Washington while her summers are spent at Manursing. *March 11, 1905*

CRONIN, JOHN W., JR. is one of America's Fifty Most Eligible Young Men. Son of John W. Cronin, of Shaker Heights, Denver, and Aspen; grandson of late William Boyer Robin-

son, founder in 1880 of Robinson Brick & Tile Co., still owned by his family. He has degrees from both Yale and Harvard. *June, 1964*

CRONLY, MRS. JOHN HILL (MARTHA VALENTINE) Richmond's gracious grande dame Mrs. John Hill Cronly takes a keen personal interest in the Valentine Museum founded by her grandfather, Mann S. Valentine II, in 1898. Sitting among paintings and sculpture in her turn-of-the-century townhouse, the daughter of the late author and historian Edward Pleasants Valentine speaks in snappy but elegant tones: "I never liked the War Between the States. Never was interested in it. The Civil War, the Civil War, the hell with it. It did nothing but divide family and country." *February, 1983*

CROSBY, ERNEST HOWARD was the son of the Rev. Dr. Howard Crosby, founder of the Society for the Prevention of Crime, who was actively interested in the welfare of the Indians and in the establishing of an international copyright law. William Bedlow Crosby, the philanthropist, who inherited a great part of the old Rutgers estate, was the grandfather. Colonel Ernest Howard, who was born in New York and resided here at 665 Fifth Avenue, was a social reformer, lecturer, and author. He was appointed a Judge of the International Court at Alexandria, Egypt, the first President of the Social Reform Club, Chairman of the New York committee of Friends of Russian Freedom, and also served at one time as President of the New York Vegetarian Society. *January 12, 1907*

CROSBY, COLONEL JOHN SCHUYLER on his father's side is a great-grandson of William Floyd, a signer of the Declaration of Independence from New York. On his mother's side, he is a lineal descendant of the Schuylers of Revolutionary fame. Colonel Crosby served in the Army of the Potomac under McClellan and was General Sheridan's personal aide-de-camp for five years. He was made Governor of Montana by President Arthur in 1881 and was one of the original organizers of polo in this country. *June 18, 1904*

CROSBY, KATHARINE VAN RENSSELAER Countless descendants of old New York journeyed to Madison Avenue Presbyterian Church for Katharine Van Rensselaer Crosby's and John Gregory's wedding. She married a promising young architect in John Gregory, winner one year of the Prix de Rome, and very well known in the best of the art group here in New York. Mrs. Gregory's colonial ancestry extends to the Delafields, Floyds, Kings, Schuylers, among well-known old families. *July 1, 1922*

CROSBY, KATHERINE SCHUYLER A marriage that will unite two families prominent in American annals is that of Miss Katherine Schuyler Crosby to Mr. Robert Burnet Choate. Miss Crosby is the only daughter of Mr. and Mrs. Stephen Van Rensselaer Crosby. Miss Crosby is a descendant of that General Philip Schuyler of revolutionary fame, who was one of the first four Major Generals in the U. S. Army. Two of her direct ancestors, Philip Livingston and William Floyd, were signers of the Declaration of Independence. *March 10, 1921*

CROSBY, MRS. ROBERT RALSTON (JANE MURRAY LIVINGSTON) was born in the old Livingston homestead in Linlithgow Place, Poughkeepsie. She was the granddaughter of the Rev. Dr. John Livingston, first President of Rutgers College and a minister of the Dutch Church of New York, and a great-granddaughter of Philip Livingston, one of the signers of the Declaration of Independence. *June 3, 1911*

CROWNINSHIELD, FREDERIC is the new Director of the American Academy in Rome. As an artist, he has made a specialty of wall paintings and stained glass windows. He is a poet as well as an artist. In this country, he has served as President of the Fine Arts Federation in New York, as acting President of the National Society of Mural Painters, and as Vice President of the Architectural League. *November 6, 1909*

CROWNINSHIELD, MRS. SCHUYLER (MARY BRADFORD) There is probably no woman better able to write a real blood-curdling piratical opera than Mrs. Schuyler Crowninshield, the brilliant wife of Admiral Crowninshield. Mrs. Crowninshield's first success from a literary viewpoint was *Where the Trade Winds Blow,* a series of stories of life in the Sea Islands of the South (a life very familiar to the author, for she has spent years there with her son, who owns a small island in this part of the world). At the time she visited her son, they were the only white people on the island. *March 25, 1905*

CRUGER, MRS. S. VAN RENSSELAER (JULIE STORROW), the woman of fashion and writer of clever society novels, pursues her course serenely. She is very happy in her fine old mansion, just on the border of that part of the capital city known as Georgetown. To keep up the colonial air, she has tabooed gas and electricity, and only candles light her home. When the mood for writing is upon her, Mrs. Cruger shuts herself away from everybody and works eight or nine hours a day. But when her book or story is finished, she becomes again the woman of fashion and grande dame. *April 11, 1903*

CRYDER, ETHEL One read this week, "Last of the Cryder Sisters Engaged." This to New Yorkers and to residents of Boston in no way suggested that the last member of a religious sect had decided to embrace matrimony. It meant that Miss Ethel Cryder, one of the triplet daughters of Mr. and Mrs. Duncan Cryder, is now among brides-to-be. Her sisters are Mrs. F. Lothrop Ames of Boston and Mrs. William Woodward of New York. Her fiancé is Mr. Cecil Higgins. Young Mr. Higgins's mother was Lady Hilda Higgins, a daughter of the eleventh Earl of Winchilsea. New York has always been proud of "The Cryder Triplets." Each is tall and exceedingly good-looking. When all were still unmarried, they dressed alike, and strangers were often bewildered—though not the men who came to woo. *September 19, 1908*

CUDAHY, JEAN made her debut in Omaha society this year and was honored by the local organization known as the Knights of Ak-Sar-Ben, being chosen fourteenth Queen of their civic order. The Omaha Ak-Sar-Ben corresponds to the secret societies that exist in New Orleans and St. Louis, for the purpose of giving parades and a carnival, and has fifteen hundred members. *June 19, 1909*

CULLEN, MR. AND MRS. HUGH ROY (LILLIE CRANZ) In 1947, they gave some hundred and fifty million dollars worth of producing oil properties to a Cullen Foundation, which made history as the largest single donation of its kind ever made by anyone. The principal beneficiary of Cullen money has been Mr. Cullen's pet project, the University of Houston. To date some twenty five million has been used from foundation funds to build buildings and launch a great institution of higher education. *March, 1954*

THE DANGER OF SPORT

Mrs. S. Van Rensselaer Cruger is confined to her home with injuries received from a bicycle mishap which occurred while she was taking an afternoon spin on her wheel last week in Central Park. It has been the custom of Mrs. Cruger, like many others in the fashionable world, to convey her wheel in her carriage to a secluded place in the park, and there pursue the exercise. Mrs. Cruger, who is not yet an expert in the art of wheeling, lost control of her machine and was flung violently to the ground. *May 29, 1895*

CULVER, MRS. EVERETT M. (MARY J. C. CLARK) For absolute cleverness and originality, no entertainment in New York has ever approached the St. Valentine's fancy dress dance at her apartment. It was a gathering of all nations. The guests, being assembled, were placed in various rooms, according to the country they represented. The procession of nations was then arranged and started, headed by a brass band, to be reviewed by Uncle Sam and Miss Columbia. The first surprise was an enormous papier-mâché head, the mouth of which made the entrance to the reception room and through which the procession passed. The eyes of this head were arranged with electric lights, with a real "goo-goo" wink, and they blinked as each couple passed through the open jaws. Mrs. Culver, the hostess, was a Chinese Empress, and she was brought into the room on a palanquin with bearers. One room was reserved as a cannibals' den, in which Dr. Culver, dressed as a Zulu chief and surrounded by charred bones and other evidences of a meal of roasted missionary, received the guests. *February 21, 1901*

CUNARD, LADY (MAUD BURKE) Born an American, Lady Cunard is still an emerald in the rough. Or perhaps, one should say, that she still exhibits the persistence suggested by her real name, Maud, more than that of the polished "Emerald," to which she answered in London. Her ladyship has been trying to get back to England. After achieving a reservation, Emerald Cunard has pursued the shipping agents to find out whether the boat has linen or cotton sheets, because if they are only cotton she will sleep between her own linen from here to Lisbon. A second complication arises in the presumed hour of sailing from Baltimore. Lady Cunard finds herself on the horns of a dilemma pointing either to a night on the boat at dock, because the Baltimore hotels are crowded, or, more horrible still, an 8 A.M. train from New York. Still a third problem is a guarantee that she will be able to take her sapphire clock through the Portuguese customs. *November, 1942*

CUNEO, MRS. JOAN NEWTON No woman has ever attracted such wide attention throughout the country as a driver of motor-cars. For several years, her remarkable driving in automobile races and endurance contests has caused unlimited comment. In the fifth annual reliability and endurance contest of the American Automobile Association for the Glidden trophy this year, Mrs. Cuneo was the only woman contestant to pilot a car over seventeen hundred miles of good, bad, and, for the most part, mountain roads and reach the finish line at Saratoga, New York, with a perfect score. *October 24, 1908*

CURRAN, MR. AND MRS. GUERNSEY (ELISE POSTLEY), of New York, are passing several weeks at The Greenbrier, White Sulphur Springs. They were hosts at a recent dinner in the Tudor grill, one of the novel features of which was an aeroplane made of ice, with a revolving propeller from which caviar was served. They entertained their guests afterward in their apartments at The Greenbrier with motion pictures taken by Mr. Curran at White Sulphur. *June 1, 1928*

CURTIS, MARGARET Important for the golfing circle was Miss Margaret Curtis's well-earned honors as champion of the United States Women's Golf Association, which she secured in a final match of the tournament at the Boston Country Club. Miss Curtis is still a schoolgirl, and will not make her debut for another year. She is a niece of Captain Nathan Appleton, of the Somerset Club. *June 22, 1901*

CURTIS, PAUL ALLAN, one of the founders of the New York Athletic Club, died at the age of seventy six. A group of twenty four athletes, chiefly oarsmen, formed the New York Athletic Club at a meeting at Mouquin's in 1865. Mr. Curtis had been "No. 1" on the books of the club since that time. His son, Paul Allan Curtis, Jr. is Editor of *Field and Stream.* *July 15, 1925*

CURTISS, EDWARD M. gave a superb dinner in honor of Miss Kathryn Kidder, who has made such a pronounced success in *Mme Sans Gêne.* The favors were purple and white satin Napoleonic hats filled with bon-bons. Throughout the dinner, the Napoleonic keynote was maintained. The soup had floating in it miniature signboards with "Mme Sans Gêne" upon them. The sweetbreads were decorated with empire wreaths cut from truffles. The Roman punch was served as suds in a wash tub, while the ices came on as French *vivandières.* *January 30, 1895*

CURZON, LADY (MARY LEITER) The "Decree of the Duchesses" is the name of the act accredited to their Graces of Portland and Marlborough in declining to curtsy to Lady Curzon of Kedleston while in India. Technically, in accordance with court etiquette, they are perfectly correct in their attitude, for the wife of a Viceroy, who is erroneously called a Vice-reine, has no official rank. For the Duchess of Portland or the Duchess of Marlborough, particularly the latter, to curtsy to her would be a recognition of the former Miss Leiter as a lady of royal rank. *January 17, 1903*

CUSHING, MRS. HARRY COOKE III (CATHLEEN VANDERBILT) Her wedding was attended by a gathering representative of the social walks of life in New York. She married the son of Mrs. J. Henry Lienau, by the latter's first marriage to Mr. Harry C. Cushing, of Boston. The bride is fifth in line of descent from Commodore Vanderbilt, founder of the family in New York. *July 15, 1923*

CUSHING, DR. HARVEY, eminent brain specialist, White House father-in-law (his daughter is Mrs. James Roosevelt), and a Pulitzer Prize winner for his biography of Sir William Osler, culled his book *From a Surgeon's Journal* from the more than a million words of his war diary. There is an occasional glimpse of ponderous inefficiency and military arrogance, but in general the book is singularly free of bitterness and disillusionment. At the end of the war, Dr. Cushing (he was an officer, of course) was still a patriot. *September, 1936*

CUSHING, MR. AND MRS. HOWARD GARDINER (ETHEL COCHRANE) There is to be erected on the grounds of the Art Association at Newport a fitting memorial to the late Howard Gardiner Cushing, the distinguished artist. Those who know the art of Mr. Cushing know Mrs. Cushing, too, for she was painted many times, her wealth of red hair that is like burnished copper in the sunlight making a striking note in some of his pictures. *April 10, 1919*

CUSHMAN, CHARLES VAN B. rides in many hunt races himself, plays polo, is as active in sport as it is possible to be, and, with his family, is the proprietor of the Eastland Farms Stable. The Cushman family are good stout New Englanders from Pomfret, and their racing colors are Harvard crimson with black sleeves and cap. *July 15, 1929*

CUSTER, MRS. GEORGE ARMSTRONG (ELIZABETH BACON), widow of the gallant and ill-fated General Custer, is a resident of New York, and to her social graces adds fine literary tastes and achievement. She lives in a pretty little flat on East Eighteenth Street. She is personally a sweet-faced woman of quiet, pleasing manners, her naturally bright disposition still shadowed and subdued by the great grief of her life. *March 3, 1886*

CUTLER, JOHN W. A New England which stamps its products quite as distinctively as Old England ever did is responsible for the family of Cutler. They came from Maine, settled in Brookline, and from that genial and sporting suburb of Boston there emerged the Cutler boys of Harvard, famed in song and story. John W., as the oldest brother, forsook rowing and, concentrating on the gentle pastime of football, developed into one of the outstanding players of his time and all time. After graduating, Mr. John W. Cutler went into the

banking business. He has been elected President of The Hangar, a new club which has been started in New York. Its members have a common interest in aviation. *April 1, 1930*

CUTTING, MRS. BROCKHOLST (MARION RAMSAY) and her son William Cutting, Jr., of New York, have founded a public charity in memory of Mrs. Cutting's son, the late Francis Brockholst Cutting. It is to be known as "St. Anthony's Bread." The fund is for the sick poor within the limits of St. Mary's parish, which is more than half of Newport; but it is to be dispensed without regard to creed, color, or nationality. *September 14, 1898*

CUTTING, JULIANA is again at Palm Beach. Miss Cutting was a leader in the gaiety at the Florida resort last winter. She is an unusually graceful dancer. Her ability in this direction extends to fancy dances, and last winter just after the cakewalk in the Cocoanut Grove, at which Mr. James Henry Smith and Mr. John Jacob Astor were judges, she and the latter essayed at a little impromptu dance in a private ballroom. *February 21, 1903*

CUTTING, MADELINE is "not like other girls." For benefit of charity, it is related, she goes hatless, and the money that other girls are now spending for fascinating pokes to go with their gowns she lays aside for the benefit of her protégés, the children at the new hospital in Pittsfield. *May 28, 1904*

CUTTING, ROBERT L., JR. The family of Robert L. Cutting, Jr. (who, it will be remembered, incurred the anger of his family several years ago by marrying actress Minnie Seligman) has become reconciled to the young man and his wife. Young Mr. Cutting, who was disinherited by his father, is again in the enjoyment of fortune. *June 10, 1896*

CUTTING, MR. AND MRS. WILLIAM BAYARD, JR. (LADY SYBIL CUFFE) He died in Assouan, Egypt. He was, at one time, secretary of Ambassador Choate, and in London he met Lady Sybil Cuffe (daughter of the Earl of Desart), who became his wife. For several years, he was Deputy United States Consul at Milan and was appointed Secretary of Embassy at Tangiers. *March 19, 1910*

CUYLER, CORNELIUS died as the result of injury in a motor-car accident in Biarritz, France. He was a nephew of Mrs. Morris K. Jesup and inherited from the late Mr. Jesup a legacy of $400,000. In the banking business, he was associated with Junius C. Morgan. Socially, he was much interested in the Princeton Club, of which he was at one time the President in New York City. *August 7, 1909*

CUYLER, REV. DR. THEODORE LEDYARD was the last survivor of the famous Brooklyn preachers known as "The Great Four." He was graduated from Princeton in 1841, and from Princeton Theological Seminary in 1846. He became the pastor of the Lafayette Avenue Presbyterian Church. He was one of the best-beloved of Brooklyn's clergymen, but one with a popularity that extended far beyond this part of the country, for he was the author of some four thousand articles in religious papers. *March 6, 1909*

D

DAHLGREN, MRS. JOHN ADOLPHUS BERNARD (MADELEINE VINTON) is the widow of Admiral Dahlgren and has long been acknowledged as a leader in the highest social circles of the capital, and as authority on etiquette in Washington. Six years ago, Mrs. Dahlgren purchased a site for a country seat on the apex of South Mountain, in Washington County, Maryland. The settlement of poor people upon the mountain is undoubtedly of gypsy origin, and the people are exceedingly superstitious. All manner of spooks, ghosts, and goblins are said to be seen by them. It is among this people, whose straggling village adjoins her estate, that Mrs. Dahlgren has gathered the material for her book. *South Mountain Magic* is proof of the present existence, in the very borderline between two rich and thickly populated valleys, of the superstitions of the Middle Ages, still pure and undiluted by education or civilization. *August 10, 1882*

DAHLGREN, MR. AND MRS. JOHN VINTON (ELIZABETH DREXEL) were married in quaint but sensible fashion at "Dahlen," the Maryland mountain home of Mrs. Madeleine Vinton Dahlgren, the bridegroom's mother. The young couple remained quietly in this beautiful retreat until Saturday, when the bridal reception began which will continue a week. The big old-fashioned barn has been converted into a ballroom, but on two evenings the barn will be turned into a theatre and private theatricals given. *July 10, 1889*

DALRYMPLE, OLIVER was the first of the bonanza wheat farmers of the Northwest, and his farm of 75,000 acres was world famous. He was born in Pennsylvania and came to Minnesota in 1855. Ten years later, he gave up the practice of law and took up farming, beginning the experiments that made him an authority on wheat culture. Mr. Dalrymple and his family made their home on Summit Avenue, St. Paul, but spent a large part of every summer on the big wheat farm, where many distinguished people were entertained. *September 26, 1908*

DANA, CHARLES A. In the retirement of Charles A. Dana, Esq., from the *Tribune,* the editorial fraternity of all parties will miss the productions of one who is universally esteemed, not only by his literary friends but by his political opponents. *April 19, 1862*

DANA, DAVID T. As soon as he was graduated from Princeton's class of 1901, he started for the Far West to gain his riding experience from the cowboys, the best riders in the world. A strenuous athlete himself, living among cowboys, working for wages as they do, the fact that he was a gentleman in no way detracted from his popularity. After four years of this rugged life, he returned to Lenox, Massachusetts, in the spring of 1905. Little wonder that he was chosen from among his fellows for the position of M. F. H. of the Berkshire Hunt, the youngest man in America to hold such a position. *January 11, 1908*

DANA, JANET P. was introduced by her mother, Mrs. Paul Dana. As a daughter of a distinguished editor (and a grandfather, Charles A. Dana, still more eminent in the history of journalism), and on the maternal side a grandchild of Mr. and Mrs. W. Butler Duncan, Miss Janet has very enviable distinctions as to family. The two houses occupied, respectively, by the Danas and Duncans are the first residences at the very beginning of Fifth Avenue, the fine, old-fashioned blocks opening into Washington Square. *December 10, 1904*

DANA, NAPOLEON JACKSON TECUMSEH had an eventful career as a soldier in the Civil War, this being preceded by several years' residence in St. Paul, where as early as 1855 he was prominent as a banker. He was a nephew of Dr. Samuel Luther Dana, who had international fame as a chemist and who founded a great American industry in Waltham, Massachusetts. *February 11, 1911*

DANA, MRS. RICHARD HENRY, JR. (SARAH WESTON) was the widow of Richard Henry Dana, Jr., the author, who died at Rome, Italy, in 1882, and whose *Two Years Before the Mast* was the result of his voyage as a seaman from Boston round Cape Horn to the western coast of North America. Mrs. Dana is survived by her son, Richard Henry Dana, who, in 1898, was married to Miss Edith Longfellow, the second daughter of Henry Wadsworth Longfellow, the poet. *December 7, 1907*

DANFORTH, MR. AND MRS. WILLIAM (ELIZABETH ANNE GRAY) A member of Missouri's illustrious Danforth family, Bill, a cardiologist, is chancellor of St. Louis's Washington University. As head of the distinguished institution, he and his wife Elizabeth probably do more entertaining than anyone else in town. Headquarters for all this festivity is the Chancellor's House, built in 1913. *March, 1989*

DARLING, COLONEL AND MRS. JOHN AUGUSTUS (CLARA HASTINGS)—CATHERWOOD Mrs. Darling was famous for her hospitality and for the originality of her entertainments when she was foremost in San Francisco society, first as Miss Hastings, daughter of Governor Hastings of California, and afterwards as Mrs. Catherwood. Colonel Darling has published charming compositions under the name of August Mignon, a pretty play of words upon his own name. *June 18, 1904*

DAVIDGE, JOHN WASHINGTON is a lawyer, a clubman, and a student of genealogy who can make the subject more fascinating than any contemporary cocktail chitchat. Mr. Davidge owes his membership in the Society of the Cincinnati—direct descendants of Washington's officers—to the first President's brother, John. Mr. Davidge's grandfather was Dr. John Beale Davidge, who was instrumental in founding the University of Maryland. Still another ancestor is Dr. Bailey Washington, a handsome naval hero of the War of 1812. *February, 1952*

DAVIDSON, MARY LOUISE The Davidsons are one of Charlotte, North Carolina's early families and founders of the town and college of Davidson, seventeen miles north of the city.

Mary Louise Davidson, a Colonial Dame, Daughter of the American Revolution, and charter member of the Mecklenburg Historical Association, lives today in the family manse, "Rosedale," built between 1790 and 1800 and listed in the National Register of Historic Homes. Taking out a silver warming dish from 1811 and showing the house's original wallpaper from 1790, Miss Davidson remarks, "We still live in the 18th century in a great many respects." *January, 1979*

THE CONFEDERACY PASSES

Mrs. Jefferson Davis died at the Majestic Hotel, in New York. Mrs. Davis, the widow of the President of the Confederacy, was born in 1826 at Natchez, Mississippi. Her grandfather was the Governor of New Jersey, and her father was connected with the United States Bank. Until Jefferson Davis died in New Orleans, in 1889, his wife was with him, in peace and war. As devoted to the Confederate cause as her husband himself, she could hardly be persuaded to leave Richmond when Grant began to close in around it in 1865. *October 27, 1906*

DAVIS, ARTHUR VINING, Chairman of the Board of the Aluminum Company of America, has built a winter home at Rock Sound, on Eleuthera Island, Bahamas, where he is developing a multimillion-dollar resort. *February, 1955*

DAVIS, BRITTON is one of the most prominent men connected with the progress in Texas. Born and brought up in Texas, his grandfather and father were as much interested in statehood as doughty Sam Houston. The family has been identified with Texan history ever since the days of the Alamo. Mr. Davis's father was the first Republican Governor of the state. *June 11, 1904*

DAVIS, DWIGHT F. is the champion tennis player of the world, founder of the international tennis cup tournament, and, this year, chairman of the state championship tournament that meets at Magnolia, Massachusetts. *July 16, 1904*

DAVIS, MR. AND MRS. L. CLARKE (REBECCA HARDING) Mr. Davis, up to the time of his death, was the Editor of the *Public Ledger* in Philadelphia. His wife was the author of many charming tales under the *nom de plume* of Rebecca Harding Davis. The literary talent of this distinguished family descended to the two sons, Mr. Charles Belmont Davis and his brother, Mr. Richard Harding Davis, who began his literary career on the *Philadelphia Press*. *April 15, 1911*

DAVIS, MR. AND MRS. THEODORE M. are again spending the winter in a leisurely way along the Nile in their dahabiyeh, *The Bedouin*. Mr. Davis is devoting his life, and a large part of his fortune, to collecting relics and curios of early Egypt, China, and Japan. Although many Americans hire the curious dahabiyehs, the picturesque boats of the Nile, Mr. Davis is one of the very few Americans who own them for their own pleasure. *February 11, 1905*

DAY, MR. AND MRS. HENRY E. (SOPHIE NORTON SCHUYLER) She is a member of one of the oldest of New York's notable families. The Rev. Dr. Montgomery Schuyler, her father, was dean of Christ Church Cathedral in St. Louis. One of the bride's brothers was the late Louis Sandford Schuyler, a member of the brotherhood of St. John the Evangelist, who went to Memphis, Tennessee, during the yellow fever epidemic. He died a victim of the disease. Another brother of the bride, the Rev. Philip Schuyler of Bennington, Vermont, performed the ceremony, and Mr. Montgomery Roosevelt Schuyler, also a brother, gave her away. *September 14, 1907*

DAYTON, MARK The department store heir became active in alternative philanthropy in 1977, after attending a California conference for socially responsible inheritors. Mark subsequently helped found Rebuilt America, a national bipartisan economic think tank. The causes he supports include the American Refugee Committee, the St. Paul Food Bank, and Esalen Institute's Soviet-American exchanges. *December, 1989*

DAYTON, ROBERT J. is a retailing entrepreneur whose great-grandfather founded Dayton's, Minneapolis's largest department store. In due course, Dayton's was run by Bob's grandfather and then by five Dayton brothers, including Bob's father. (Today, it is part of the Dayton Hudson Corporation, the nation's seventh-largest retailing conglomerate.) *December, 1987*

DEACON, MRS. PARKER (FLORENCE BALDWIN) The "Mrs. Deacon" whose name appears as a new American beauty, and to whom the Prince of Wales requested an introduction, is a daughter of Commodore Baldwin, of the United States Navy. Miss Florence Baldwin was married about a year and a half ago, while she was still in her teens, and is beautiful enough to justify the admiration of His Royal Highness. Mrs. Parker Deacon is too young and too artless to be enrolled among the professional beauties of the Prince of Wales' set, and we trust that she may be spared the unenviable distinction. *September 1, 1880*

DE ACOSTA, MERCEDES Her first full-length novel, *Until the Day Break,* has been published by Longmans-Green. Aside from being socially prominent as the wife of Abram Poole, the portrait painter, Miss de Acosta already has achieved considerable fame in the field of poetic literature and in dramaturgy. *June 1, 1928*

DE BORCHGRAVE D'ALTENA, COUNTESS CAMILLE (RUTH SNYDER REILLY) is the daughter of Mr. Thomas Alexander Reilly, of Philadelphia, and a niece of Ambassador Charlemagne Tower. The Countess was a bride last week. She has had the distinction of being presented at the courts of Belgium, England, Germany, and St. Petersburg. The bridegroom belongs to a distinguished Belgium family and is gentleman-in-waiting to King Leopold. *October 1, 1904*

DE BRAGANCA, PRINCE MIGUEL, son and heir of Dom Miguel, Duke of Braganca and pretender to the throne of Portugal, husband of the former Anita Stewart, died in the home of the latter's father, Mr. William Rhinelander Stewart. The home of Prince and Princess de Braganca was at Tuxedo Park, New York. *March 15, 1923*

DE CHAMBRUN, COUNTESS CHARLES (CLARA LONGWORTH) is the sister of Representative Nicholas Longworth. Her husband, Count Charles de Chambrun, a Colonel in the French army, is a great-great-grandson of Lafayette and is now stationed in Morocco. The Countess is an author and holds a doctor's degree from the Sorbonne. *September 15, 1923*

DE CHARETTE, MARQUIS AND MARQUISE (SUSANNE HENNING) In the Lady Chapel of St. Patrick's Cathedral on Fifth Avenue, New York, Miss Susanne Henning was married to the Marquis de Charette. The bride's parents, Mr. and Mrs. James Williamson Henning, have lived of late years in either New York or Tuxedo Park. They were, however, originally residents of Louisville, and at the horse show while the Marquis was visiting his mother's people, he met the young woman now his bride. The Marquis is a son of Baron de Charette and Baroness de Charette, who is a daughter of the late Colonel Andrew J. Polk of Kentucky and a granddaughter of Leonidas Polk, who was a general in the Confederate Army and a bishop in the Episcopal Church. With Bishop Stephen Elliott as his helper, he succeeded in the plans that resulted in the opening of the University of the South at Sewanee, Tennessee. *November 20, 1909*

DE CHAULNES, DUC AND DUCHESSE (THEODORA SHONTS) Mr. and Mrs. Theodore P. Shonts have hearts almost too big for their house. Consequently, there was a crush at the marriage of their daughter, Miss Theodora Shonts, to the Duc de Chaulnes at 123 East Thirty Fifth Street, New York. After the ceremony, guests entered the drawing room to present themselves to the bride and the receiving party. Waiters with trays holding glasses of the wit-inspiring beverage came out into the hallway in search of any timid guest. In the breakfast room, the candle light shone through white shades on which the crest of the Duc de Chaulnes was worked out in blue, and even the bonbons had this crest. *February 22, 1908*

DE CHOISEUL-PRASLIN, COUNT AND COUNTESS GILBERT (CLARA SUTRO)—ENGLISH She is the youngest daughter of the late Adolph Sutro, who was Mayor of San Francisco. She has lived in Paris for fifteen years. Adolph Sutro was a millionaire with imagination. He built the Sutro tunnel in Nevada, and he was a collector of books and objects of art. When the war broke out, Mrs. English was the first American woman to enroll as a nurse. She was one of the stirring spirits in getting the American Ambulance started, and she endowed a number of beds. *July 20, 1915*

DE COURCEY, DR. WILLIAM HENRY resided on the ancestral estate of the family, "Cheston on the Wye," in Queen Anne County. For years, his stables were noted for fine horses. Mr. de Courcey was the oldest member of the Maryland Club. *April 15, 1911*

DEEDS, COLONEL EDWARD A. His home in Dayton has his own flying field and an aeroplane anchorage in front of his house, which fliers from all over the world have used for experimental purposes. Colonel Deeds is a devoted enthusiast of aviation and owns a three-motor all-metal Ford plane, in which he does most of his traveling. *February 1, 1929*

DEERING, CHARLES was as well known in Europe as a patron of art as he was in his native Chicago. Perhaps his most romantic ventures in the art field were centered in Spain. In one village, he restored a whole street of ancient houses and stocked them with priceless treasures. He also purchased the ruined castle of Tamarit, with its feudal site on a high cliff overlooking the Mediterranean, its history dating back to early Roman days. At one time, this American benefactor thought of endowing one of his castles as an art school, but this proved impractical; and his priceless collections of Spanish art were moved to America. *September 15, 1930*

DEERING, WILLIAM was born in 1826 in moderate circumstances in Maine. He became head of Deering, Milliken & Co., wholesale and commission merchants of Portland, Maine. In 1870, he acquired the Marsh harvester business in Plano, Illinois. He renamed this business the Deering Harvester Company in 1880 and moved to Chicago. When the Deering and McCormick interests were amalgamated into the International Harvester Company in 1902, he retired, leaving his son, Charles, as Chairman of the Board of Directors. *January 1, 1918*

DE FOREST, LOCKWOOD, now so prominent in the art world of New York, owes his knowledge of the achievements of the Orientals to his travels in the Far East. With Mr. Louis C. Tiffany, in 1879, he was associated in his decorative work, and in the years directly following he visited India. At the Lahore Exhibition in 1882, he exhibited India woodcarving made under his direction, and both at the Colonial Exhibition in London and at the World's Fair in Chicago received medals for this sort of work. *November 11, 1905*

DE FOREST, MR. AND MRS. ROBERT W. (EMILY JOHNSTON) are representative of everything that is most admirable in the society of New York. They have a home in Washington Square. It is simple and dignified in its furnishings, and here cultivated people come together to listen, perhaps, to music. Mrs. de Forest was one of the first hostesses who had the Dolmetsches play on their old-time instruments for a musicale in a private house. Mr. de Forest's work for the betterment of the poor is well known in New York. He was the first tenement house commissioner in the city; was the founder of the Provident Loan Society; and was made President of the Charity Organization Society in 1888. *September 14, 1907*

DE FORESTA, COUNTESS ALBERT (CHARLOTTE C. SKINNER) The marriage of Miss Skinner to Count de Foresta was a fashionable event, taking place in St. Patrick's Cathedral, April 30, 1891. Count de Foresta was Italian minister to the Bavarian Court, where the Count and Countess have resided until this year,

when the former was appointed minister plenipotentiary from Italy to Sweden. *June 25, 1904*

DE FRISE, ALEXANDER POWYS, the great-great-grandson of Levi Leiter, co-founder of Marshall Field's, is also the grandnephew of Lady Curzon, former Vicereine of India. Alex, who is currently in industrial sales, has an interest in politics. The family apartment was designed in 1928 by David Adler, Chicago's "great houses" architect. Adler spared no expense in workmanship or materials: Marble pilasters are topped with pewter capitals, and the ebony floor is striped with stainless steel. *December, 1988*

DE FRISE, MRS. ALISON (CAMPBELL)—CLARK The Leiter family's Chicago presence is maintained today by Levi Leiter's aristocratic California-raised great-granddaughter, Alison Campbell de Frise, a fundraiser for countless civic and charitable boards. Her sister, interior designer Juliet Campbell Folger, makes her home in Washington, D. C., as does another Levi Leiter great-granddaughter, Juliette Clagett McLennan, who is a U.S. delegate to the United Nations. *September, 1990*

DE GUIGNE, CHRISTIAN I Soon after gold-rush days, Christian de Guigne I married Mary Parrott, daughter of John Parrott, an early California land developer who had several beautiful daughters—one of whom, Regina May, married Christian's cousin, Auguste de la Lande. Auguste and Regina's daughter, named Regine, married Count Louis de Tristan, and cousins Marc de Tristan and Christian de Guigne III married, respectively, the Christenson sisters, Jane and Eleanor, daughters of a shipping and lumber magnate, thus becoming twice cousins (through their grandparents) and double brothers-in-law. *December, 1980*

DE GUIGNE, CHRISTIAN IV is one of America's Fifty Most Eligible Young Men. Son of a chemical corporation executive, with a family prominent in San Francisco and Peninsula, Chris works in Wall Street, plans to join his father's chemical firm. His four cars: two Ferraris, a '35 Ford, and a VW. *June, 1964*

DE GUIGNE, MRS. MARIE LOUISE (ELKINS), of San Mateo, became the bride of Mr. Paul Thayer Iaccaci of New York, the marriage having been solemnized in that city, where the bride and her mother, Mrs. William Delaware Nielson, have been sojourning. The young matron is one of the prettiest and most popular young women in California society. She is the granddaughter of the late Senator Charles Felton of Menlo Park, one of the early day millionaires of the state. *February 15, 1922*

DE KERGOLAY, COUNT JEAN died at "Dagnoles d'Orme," the family estate in France. He was widely distinguished as a scientist, explorer, and author. His wife was formerly Mary Louise Carroll, eldest daughter of the late ex-Governor John Lee Carroll, of "Doughoregan Manor," Howard County, Maryland. *September 15, 1923*

DE KOVEN, MR. AND MRS. REGINALD (ANNA FARWELL) She is a woman of talents, in addition to the usual social accomplishments. Her translation of Pierre Loti's *An Iceland Fisher-*

man is recalled, and she has contributed much prose and poetry to the magazines. Mr. de Koven's accomplishments as a composer are well known. *January 21, 1911*

DELAFIELD, CORNELIA VAN RENSSELAER On Tuesday, the fair sex was greatly in prominence by virtue of the fencing contest. What good results in fencing may be attained after one season's instructions was proved. In the senior class, the championship medal and foils were won by Miss Cornelia V. R. Delafield, daughter of Dr. Francis Delafield. Several of the contestants wore accordion-pleated skirts of silk and alpaca, with thin silk or nainsook shirt waists, but Miss Bettie Collamore and Miss Enid Locke, with their faultlessly-fitting velvet skirts and plain white jackets of white duck, were perhaps the most appropriately prepared for this rather strenuous sport, which if it mercilessly reveals all awkwardness also shows a graceful woman to the best advantage. *May 9, 1903*

DELAFIELD, EMILY and Dr. Rolfe Floyd were married at the residence of the bride's mother, Mrs. Lewis Livingston Delafield, at Fieldstone-on-Hudson. He is of old Revolutionary stock, a great-grandfather being one of the famous generals of that period. Mrs. Delafield was a Miss Prime, and she is representative of the old Knickerbocker aristocracy of New York. The young couple will live at "Mastic," the country seat of the Floyds for generations, on Long Island. *June 29, 1901*

DELAFIELD, RICHARD To incorporate a family is perhaps a novel proceeding, but it has been done this past week at Albany. The Delafield Family Association is the new corporation with principal offices in New York City. There are few New York families of older or more distinguished lineage. The Delafields are French in origin, and they antedate the year 1000. The Delafields of America are descended from John Delafield, a Count of the Holy Roman Empire, who came to this country from England during the last century. Richard Delafield is one of the incorporators. In financial affairs he is prominent, being President of the National Park Bank of New York. *May 11, 1912*

DE LA GUERRA, JOSEFA The marriage of Miss Josefa de la Guerra of Santa Barbara and Alejandro Savin of Los Angeles was celebrated in the Paulist Church of San Francisco. Mrs. Savin is a member of the famous old de la Guerra family of Santa Barbara, who received their grant from the Spanish king long before the gringos were known to the West. Some portion of the old estate is still in the family, among that two of the few adobe houses still standing in Santa Barbara. *May 10, 1920*

DE MENIL, MRS. JOHN (DOMINIQUE SCHLUMBERGER) She's the heiress-daughter of Conrad Schlumberger, co-founder of Schlumberger Ltd., the huge oil equipment company. Although French-born, she has lived since 1941 in Houston, where she and her late husband, John, were leading patrons of the arts. In 1971, they underwrote the Rothko Chapel in Houston, to house the last dark paintings of Mark Rothko; she bequeathed both the building and paintings to the city. *December, 1983*

DEMING, GEORGE, of Cleveland, has purchased seventeen islands off the coast of North Carolina, with an area of nearly three thousand acres. His summer home is located on Davis Island. He is now in his eightieth year, but it is said that four o'clock every morning finds him up and digging in his beautiful gardens when at home in Cleveland. *October 28, 1905*

DE MONSTIERS MERINVILLE, MARQUISE (MARY CALDWELL), sometimes singled out as an illustration of the misfortune that comes from marriage with a foreign nobleman, has, nevertheless, been more shrewd than most frail women, and her property in Kentucky remains intact. The Marquise and her sister, Baroness von Zeidlitz, are the heaviest taxpayers in Louisville. Although so much of her life has been spent abroad, she is true to her country, and founded the Catholic University in Washington. *June 18, 1904*

DEMOREST, MR. AND MRS. WILLIAM CURTIS (ALICE ESTELLE GILBERT) gave one of the most original of the fortnight's entertainments in the Adirondacks. About two hundred guests were invited to a water carnival given in the bay which their camp, "Hukeween Lodge," on Coon Lake, overlooks. The carnival was followed by an Indian play with interpretation of Indian songs and dances, arranged by Mr. Ernest Thompson Seton. *September 18, 1909*

DENMAN, MR. AND MRS. WILLIAM (LESLIE VAN NESS) William Denman is Chairman of the Federal Shipping Board, which has already begun the construction of an emergency wooden cargo fleet to aid the Allies. Mr. Denman married Miss Leslie Van Ness, whose forebears had interesting connections with the Capital in post-Revolutionary days. John Peter Van Ness, one-time Representative from New York and later Mayor of Washington, was her great-uncle. Judge Van Ness, as he was called, was the son of General Peter Van Ness, of Revolutionary fame, and his brother, William P. Van Ness, was Burr's second in his duel with Alexander Hamilton. Afterward, he secreted Burr at the family home, in Kinderhook, where later Washington Irving lived and wrote, and which still later became the residence of Martin Van Buren. *May 10, 1917*

DENNY, JAMES O'HARA III, whose family on both sides goes back into Pittsburgh history to 1751, stands in front of the Block House of Old Fort Pitt, site of the O'Hara homestead. Mr. Denny is a professor of industrial engineering at West Virginia University. *February, 1975*

DE PEYSTER, CAROLA represents the very best "blue blood" of American society, and is associated with the old stronghold of aristocracy situated along the Hudson River, the chain of great estates situated just north of the little village of Tivoli. The de Peysters have one of the most beautiful of these homes along the "Woods Road," and among their relatives and neighbors are the Livingstons, Clarksons, Beekmans, and Van Rensselaers. The de Peyster family came originally from Normandy, driven to Holland from Brabant. Mr. Garrett Bergh Kip, Miss de Peyster's future husband, is a member of a family originally of France, and later also driven to Holland by virtue of religious persecution. *January 24, 1903*

DE PEYSTER, CATHERINE AUGUSTA was the last of the de Peysters, a family famous since Colonial days. The New-York Historical Society will get the bulk of the estate, including many articles of furniture and bric-a-brac of historical value. All family portraits, Miss de Peyster directed, shall never be copied in any form of art, nor the old Chelsea figures which were buried under the greenhouse, the first ever built on Manhattan Island, during the Revolutionary War. *February 18, 1911*

DE PEYSTER, MRS. FREDERICK J. (AUGUSTA MORRIS) Of the sewing classes, that of which Mrs. Frederick J. de Peyster is considered the leader is the one credited with the most serious work, and just plain sewing, rather than afternoon tea and gossip, are the watchwords. The Infant Orphan Asylum, one of the oldest institutions in New York, where the babies enjoy the personal acquaintance of the society people who protect them, will profit by the work of this class. *February 27, 1904*

DE PEYSTER, MAJOR GENERAL JOHN WATTS At a brilliant commemorative party, the dinner was prepared by the General's own cooks and was pronounced "unsurpassable." Some of the wines consumed were nearly a century old and were inherited by General de Peyster from his maternal great-grandfather, the Hon. John Watts, the last royal recorder of New York. A noteworthy feature of the occasion was the speeches, each officer recounting some gallant deed in war in which he had participated or been an eyewitness. *March 16, 1881*

DE POLIGNAC, PRINCESSE EDMOND (WINNARETTA SINGER), that famous and formidable daughter of the Singer who so fortuitously sold us sewing machines, passed through New York from her visit to Florida, where she has been surveying the fantastic and magic real estate activities of her brother, Paris Singer. She is one of the few Americans to have accomplished the rare feat of establishing a salon. Much of the new music we have heard in the public concert halls of New York has had its premiere in the private music room of her Paris home. Many artists are grateful for the eager impulse her patronage has afforded them. *April 1, 1926*

DERBY, DR. RICHARD is a direct descendant of Richard Derby, the Salem merchant whose ships and brigantines crossed the ocean during the French Revolution. His father was Dr. Richard H. Derby, who was noted in New York as an opthamologist. The most famous man in the family was Elias Hasket Derby the first, who built ships during the Revolution and who has always been called "The Father of American Commerce." *February 22, 1913*

DE RENNE, WYMBERLEY JONES "Wormsloe," the country place of Mr. de Renne, about ten miles from Savannah on the Isle of Hope, is interesting, not only because of the picturesque country surrounding it and the treasures of art and literature which it holds but because it is the only one of the old plantations still possessed by the family to which it was originally granted. *March 22, 1902*

DE TRISTAN, MARC, JR. is one of America's Fifty Most Eligible Young Men. The eldest son of Count and Countess de Tristan (the Countess is the former Jane Christenson), he is a third generation Californian and Harvard grad. *June, 1964*

DE WINDT, E. MANDELL, Chairman and chief executive officer of Eaton Corp., is head of the Cleveland Commission on Health and Social Services. "It isn't hard to find things to do in any community," says de Windt, a direct descendant of President John Adams. "The main thing is to keep a balance between civic and community interests and your family and business." *October, 1971*

DE WOLFE, ELSIE When the ship of the New York bachelor girl comes in, she gets herself a home like that of Miss Elsie de Wolfe and Miss Elizabeth Marbury, at 122 East Seventeenth Street. One of the most distinctively individual homes of its sort in New York, the house is rich in beautiful old things picked up in France, particularly in Versailles, where Miss de Wolfe lives in summer. In the bay window is a marble baptismal font of the sixteenth century, which Miss de Wolfe brought from Venice and which she uses for gold fish. The two clever women who have made this home for themselves are among the most successful professional women in New York. *March 28, 1903*

DI BASSANO, PRINCESS (MARGUERITE CHAPIN) was a member of Springfield's first family. In the modern penthouse atop her Renaissance palace, her exhibits include the work of her daughter, Lelia Caetani. In Paris, with Mrs. John W. Garrett, she opened a gallery for famous painters; in Rome, a lottery for struggling artists. Her husband composed the opera *Hypatia,* sung in Basel this winter. *April, 1937*

DI CARPEGNA, COUNTESS ALFREDO (KINTA DES MARE)—MERRILL—DE RHAM A New Orleans beauty who buried three husbands: "Charlie" Merrill, founder of Merrill Lynch brokerage firm; Whitney de Rham; and a Roman Count, who gave her a title. Her fortune comes from Merrill, who divorced her because he "couldn't afford her." *July, 1975*

DICK, MRS. C. MATHEWS (C. GARNETT CROSSAN), whose husband strode into Washington from Chicago about a dozen years ago, took to entertaining in the capital via Newport. Mrs. Dick has special European crystal and china made for her table, special bodies for her Rolls, and makes a special effort to keep secret the name of her hatmaker (Nicole de Paris). At home, Mrs. Dick shines behind the tea table in beige velvet stenciled in gold. *January, 1939*

DICK, MR. AND MRS. EVANS ROGERS (ELIZABETH TATHAM) are former Philadelphians who now have a residence in New York City and who spend their summers at Garrison-on-the-Hudson, New York. At present, Mr.

and Mrs. Dick are living in a picturesque bungalow, awaiting the completion of a large house that is truly like a castle situated on an eminence near old Storm King, overlooking Constitution Island and just across the river from the Military Academy at West Point. This castle-like house is being built according to plans made by Mrs. Dick. *August 27, 1910*

DICK, MRS. FRANKLIN A. (MYRA ALEXANDER), the oldest member of a prominent Philadelphia family, died in Paris, where she had lived most of her later life with her daughter, the Marquise de Breviaire d'Alaincourt. Five grandsons were in active service in the war, all having commissions. She leaves a large fortune, a trust fund left by her late husband. *January 20, 1919*

DICKINSON, JOHN S., the son of the former Commodore of the New York Yacht Club, is a tall, handsome fellow and one of the best amateur swimmers ever seen at Palm Beach. When a boy, he spent his summers at Shelter Island and even then astonished his comrades by his daring. *March 25, 1905*

DIETRICH, MR. AND MRS. H. RICHARD, JR. (CORDELIA BIDDLE) At thirty two, he has inherited the presidency of three companies: Dietrich Corporation Investments, Dietrich Foundation, and Ludens Cough Drops. "My family left me and my brothers a certain amount of wealth. It gives us great opportunities but also great responsibilities. You can't think of yourself only," says Dietrich. "We've both seen so much waste in our own families, by people who live for only their own generation," adds Cordelia. "Consequently, we try to do everything for a long term, thinking ahead," Richard says. *February, 1971*

DIETZ, MRS. HOWARD (TANIS GUINNESS)—MONTAGUE spends considerable time in her townhouse on 11th Street, a little less time in California, and several weeks of the year hopping up and down the Eastern seaboard when one of her husband's shows opens on the road. In her clothes, there is generally a significant intimation of what tomorrow's fashions may be. America has seen crownless turbans since last year, but no one except Mrs. Dietz had appeared at lunch with two small bunches of silver fox held smack on the top of her pate with a narrow piece of black velvet ribbon. *December, 1937*

DILLINGHAM, MR. AND MRS. WALTER F. (LOUISE OLGA GAYLORD) The gaunt dead crater of Diamond Head crouches like a headless sphinx with its paws in the sea guarding the city of Honolulu. Well up on its slopes lies "La Pietra" (the Jewel), the Italian villa of Mr. and Mrs. Walter F. Dillingham. From this coral-tinted Italian villa, the wide and varied view includes the Island of Oahu, a survey of the Manoa Valley, the interesting pattern of the city, with the deep blue of the Pacific breaking into the white surf to the south. *February 1, 1926*

DILLON, C. DOUGLAS The former Treasury Secretary and Ambassador to France is the son of Clarence Dillon, the late founder of Wall Street's Dillon, Read & Co. The Dillon Fund, a foundation established jointly by father and son, has given away more than $2 million

in some years. Douglas is Chairman of the Metropolitan Museum of Art in New York. *December, 1983*

DINSMORE, CLARENCE GRAY Mr. Dinsmore's interest in automobiling, and his efforts to promote the sport and the development of the Mercedes machines, were unfailing. He once loaned a seventy horse-power Mercedes to the German Emperor. He received many favors from the Kaiser. He was present at both races for the Vanderbilt Cup, and was often seen standing in his box and closely keeping score. *November 18, 1905*

DINSMORE, MR. AND MRS. WILLIAM B., JR. (MARION DE PEYSTER CAREY) He won first prize at the recent lawn tennis tournament in Tuxedo and is a son of Mr. William B. Dinsmore, one of our best-known country gentlemen, sharing with his brother, Mr. Clarence Gray Dinsmore, the ownership of the large estate at Staatsburg, New York. Young Mr. Dinsmore, together with his wife, is identified with the life of Tuxedo. *July 2, 1904*

DISSTON, MR. AND MRS. WILLIAM (ELIZABETH DUNLOP) After a meet of the White Marsh Valley Hounds, Mr. and Mrs. William Disston, of Philadelphia, gave a breakfast at their stock farm above Chestnut Hill. The huntsmen and huntswomen were told that their host had very kindly given the use of his farm residence as a clubhouse for the hunt club. Mr. Disston's farm is situated at the foot of Militia Hill, overlooking the broad acres of the White Marsh Valley, and on the spot where the militia of General Washington's army was encamped previous to the battle of Germantown and only about a mile from the historic Fort Washington. *January 7, 1905*

DIX, REV. DR. MORGAN belonged to New York. He was not one of the clergymen called from other parts of the country. He was born in this city, and his father, John Adams Dix, was Governor of the state, and his mother was Catherine Morgan, the daughter of Congressman John J. Morgan. Before he was Governor, General Dix was appointed Minister to France and during the forties was a United States Senator. The Rev. Dr. Dix began his work for the Episcopal Church as assistant minister in Trinity Parish in 1855. He became rector in 1862. *April 16, 1910*

DIXON, FITZ EUGENE, JR., principal heir to the nineteenth-century Elkins and Widener streetcar fortunes, gives away about $1 million a year, mostly in the Philadelphia area. Widener College changed its name from Pennsylvania Military College after Dixon and his mother rescued it from financial ruin in 1972. *December, 1986*

DIXON, GEORGE DALLAS, JR. is a great-grandson of George Mifflin Dallas, the statesman who was appointed Minister to Russia by President Van Buren, elected Vice President on the ticket with Polk, and later made the United States Minister at the Court of St. James. Mr. Dixon's mother was Miss Mary Quincy Allen, a daughter of the late William H. Allen, who was President of Girard College and of the American Bible Society, and a granddaughter of Samuel Quincy of Boston, who was one of a long line of scholarly men. *March 28, 1908*

DOANE, BISHOP WILLIAM is representative in his family of a long line of men noted as scholars and dignitaries of the Church. Bishop Doane organized the Cathedral of All Saints in Albany and founded both St. Agnes's School and the Child's Hospital in Albany. His father was Bishop George Washington Doane of New Jersey, who was so active in founding St. Luke's Hospital. His brother, Monsignor Doane, left the Episcopal Church and was educated for the priesthood in France. *March 19, 1910*

DODGE, BAYARD, grandson of the late William Earl Dodge, the philanthropist, will go shortly to Syria as a missionary. Under the auspices of the Foreign Department of the International Y.M.C.A., he will go to Beirut, Syria, and he will serve as Y.M.C.A. secretary among the students in the Syrian Protestant College. Mr. Dodge is one of the richest young men in New York, and there is no one in the foreign field propagating the gospel who represents greater wealth. *April 26, 1913*

DODGE, MR. AND MRS. MARCELLUS HARTLEY (GERALDINE ROCKEFELLER) The initial show of the recently formed Morris and Essex Kennel Club, held on the private polo field at "Giralda Farms," the magnificent estate of Mr. and Mrs. M. Hartley Dodge, at Madison, New Jersey, was marked by the most elaborate arrangements, open hospitality, and sincere social and sporting spirit. Colloquially termed "Mrs. Dodge's Show" (it was this foremost fancier of shepherd dogs who conceived the organization of the club and the materialization of the event to a signal success), it will long be remembered as an ideal dog show. *July 15, 1927*

DONAHUE, MRS. JAMES P. (JESSIE WOOLWORTH) Because her sons James and Woolworth like to shoot ducks, Mrs. Donahue bought a tiny house at Manorville, near Riverhead, Long Island. Because Woolworth went to Africa and shot enough elephants, lions, leopards, zebras, rhinoceros, and smaller fauna to start a private museum, she had a hunting lodge built with a sixty-foot lounge to house the collection and eight bedrooms to take care of the family and guests. The original little house still exists as a bachelor wing. *July, 1939*

DONNELLEY, MR. AND MRS. GAYLORD (DOROTHY RANNEY) R. R. Donnelley & Sons has grown in four generations from a small print shop into the nation's largest commercial printer. Founder Richard R. Donnelley opened his Chicago print shop in 1864. His son, Reuben H. Donnelley, married Laura Thorne, daughter of the co-founder of Montgomery Ward, and became a major Ward's shareholder. Gaylord Donnelley is one of Chicago's most accomplished citizens. He was Chairman of the University of Chicago trustees and President of the Community Fund. *September, 1990*

D'OREMIEULX, MR. AND MRS. MARIE THEOPHILE (LAURA WOLCOTT GIBBS) She was the daughter of George Gibbs and, on the maternal side, a granddaughter of Oliver Wolcott, Secretary of the Treasury in Washington. She

married the son of Count Henri d'Oremieulx de Belleville in 1835. Her husband became a naturalized American citizen and served for eighteen years as an officer in the United States Army and instructor in French at West Point. During the Civil War, Mrs. d'Oremieulx was a member of the New York branch of the United States Sanitary Commission and was an active worker in the big fair held in New York in 1864 for the commission. *December 5, 1908*

DOREMUS, MRS. CHARLES AVERY (ELIZABETH WARD), a clever woman playwright, was born in Kentucky. Her mother was the grandniece of President Zachary Taylor, and the blood of three presidents—Thomas Jefferson, John Quincy Adams, and Zachary Taylor—flows in her veins. Mrs. Doremus's latest success is *The Four-in-Hand,* which was performed in Washington a few weeks ago. In this play, Miss Elsie de Wolfe made a decided hit. *February 28, 1894*

DORRANCE, MR. AND MRS. JOHN (ETHEL MALLINCKRODT) The Quaker City has not had a wildly hilarious season, and but a few red letter days (or nights) can be vividly remembered. Prominent among these, however, is the wonderful ball which Mr. and Mrs. John Dorrance gave to open the New Year and, incidentally, to present to society their daughter, Miss Elinor Dorrance. It has been many years since such a lavish display has been seen in Philadelphia; the entire ballroom floor of the Bellevue-Stratford had been transformed into a scene of tropical splendor. Huge palm trees outlined the walls, with hanging moss and feathery ferns forming a background to a grove of orange trees, from which the guests could pick at will. In a cleverly arranged enclosure were live tropical birds and monkeys. *February 1, 1926*

DOUGLAS, MR. AND MRS. JAMES, JR. (GRACE McGANN) President Hoover's appointment of James Douglas, Jr., as Assistant Secretary of the Treasury removes a brilliant young Chicagoan from social and business circles here. His wife inherits the stately beauty of her mother and her two aunts, daughters of the late Senator Farwell. *April 15, 1932*

DOUGLAS, MR. AND MRS. LEWIS W. (PEGGY ZINSSER) The new Director of the Budget is often called "the eleventh member of the Cabinet." His grandfather was an Arizona prospector who discovered the famous copper mine, "Bisbee Queen." Douglas, Arizona, was named for him. Lew's father, "Rawhide Jim," prospecting on his own account, discovered the equally famous "U.V.X." As a boy, Lew Douglas rode and shot as boys do in that glorious West before he went East to school and to Amherst and to Massachusetts Tech, where he studied metallurgy. Meanwhile, there had come his marriage to Peggy, daughter of F. G. Zinsser, the chemist, and niece of another scientist, Hans Zinsser. *April 1, 1933*

DOUGLAS, MARION is a direct descendant of Richard Douglas, one of the Pilgrims who came from Scotland to Plymouth in 1649, who subsequently removed to New London, Connecticut, and whose great-great-grand-

son was Captain Richard Douglas of the Continental Army. Through her great-grandmother on her father's side, Miss Douglas is a descendant of Sir Robert Hempstead, who founded Hempstead, Long Island, in 1640. *September 5, 1908*

DOUGLAS, WILLIAM PROCTOR was an old lover and supporter of yachting and polo. He was a member of the first American polo team, and one of his yachts played its part in helping to keep the *America*'s Cup. *July 1, 1910*

DOUNE, LADY (BARBARA MURRAY) An outstanding international event in Paris was the wedding in St. George's Church of Miss Barbara Murray of New York to Lord Doune. His father, the Earl of Moray, came from a family in the old Celtic line of the Earls of Moray, of whom the most famous was Macbeth. *August 1, 1924*

DOWNING, THOMAS DANIEL The Downing family, although lifelong friends of the Heckschers and many of the representative Catholic families of Manhattan, are best known socially in Brooklyn, where they have lived for over a score of years. They are of Quaker origin, but the branch represented at St. Ignatius Loyola have been Catholic for three generations. The Downing homestead, the family estate midway between Rye and Port Chester, is one of the ancient landmarks in that portion of Westchester County. *January 20, 1906*

DOWNS, MRS. GEORGE F. (SALLIE WARD)—LAWRENCE—HUNT When America's social Pantheon shall be erected, the fitting representative for Kentucky's proud old Commonwealth will easily be found in Sallie Ward. She was the first woman in Louisville to introduce the custom of "at home" days, giving weekly receptions and balls which have never been eclipsed. Her first marriage was to an immensely wealthy young Bostonian, Bigelow Lawrence. It did not prove a lasting one, for the senior Mrs. Lawrence immediately sought to change the petted, willful Southern girl into a demure, straitlaced New England matron of her own type. At the next session of the Kentucky Legislature, a special enactment was passed, divorcing the couple. Her second husband, Dr. Robert W. Hunt of New Orleans, was a courtly gentleman of the old school. The match was violently opposed by the Hunt family, but the gallant doctor sent word to his relatives that he would far rather go to Hell with Sallie Ward than to Heaven without her. In 1882, her last marriage was celebrated, to Major George F. Downs, who had been a beau at her mother's receptions forty years before. *August 16, 1900*

DOWS, MR. AND MRS. DAVID (GWENDOLYN BURDEN) He is an ardent foxhunter, plays polo at Aiken or Meadowbrook, shoots and fishes and sails. His wife hunts likewise, so it is hardly surprising that their daughter, Miss Evelyn Byrd Dows, has taken to it zealously. Miss Dows takes her name from the famous Evelyn Byrd of history, a daughter of all the famous Byrds of Virginia. Mrs. Dows is connected through her mother with this family, who have recently been acquiring new fame.

DUKE

Doris Duke at El Morocco in 1942 with Chilean Emilio Tagle.

James Buchanan Duke was the son of a Confederate veteran who, as his family told it, returned to North Carolina from the Civil War with half a dollar and two blind mules. James (called "Buck") and his brother Benjamin planted a small quantity of leaf tobacco, which they processed and sold under the name Pro Bono Publico. With the invention of cigarette-making machines, the Duke boys were able to increase their relatively modest sales of chewing and pipe tobacco to millions, and eventually billions, of cigarettes.

Buck Duke had a genius for merging companies, and by 1890 he had organized the American Tobacco Company (called by antimonopolists "The Tobacco Trust"), with more than 150 factories and a capitalization of a half-billion dollars. At one time, the American Tobacco Company controlled an estimated 90 percent of America's cigarette business. Buck made even more money with his Duke Power and Light, one of the world's largest utility companies.

Buck Duke was a notorious diamond in the rough, but he was also philanthropic: he gave $40 million to Trinity College, a small Methodist school in North Carolina that changed its name, in 1924, to Duke University. The Duke Endowment, which aided mainly North Carolina charities, received $40 million the same year.

Totally indifferent to society, J. B. built a showplace in Somerville, New Jersey, but entertained only his old North Carolina cronies there. Over fifty when he married his second wife, Nanaline (really "Nannie Lee") Holt, he became a father at age fifty-six. His only child was named Doris.

Nanaline had all the social ambition her husband lacked, and for many years entertained the Newport set at "Rough Point," the spectacular Duke house originally built by Frederick Vanderbilt at the end of the island. She insisted on boarding school, a New York debut, and presentation at Buckingham Palace for her daughter.

Doris, her father's adored child, inherited most of his $70 million estate on his death in 1925. She was then thirteen. Reclusive by nature, she restlessly divided her time through the years between the Moorish palace, called "Shangri-La," that she built in Hawaii, Rough Point in Newport, Somerville (where there were 400 in help), and Hollywood, where she owned "Falcon's Lair," the house built by Rudolph Valentino. She collected art and artifacts (she once bought an entire Thai village and had it sent to Hawaii, where it was never unpacked) and restored many colonial houses in Newport.

Married first to James H. R. ("Jimmie") Cromwell, son of the famous Palm Beach hostess Mrs. E. T. Stotesbury, she also was briefly wed to international playboy Porfirio Rubirosa. Rubirosa later married Barbara Hutton, Doris's competitor for the title of "richest girl in the world" (Doris, in fact, was much richer). Doris Duke died at Falcon's Lair in 1994, leaving a highly publicized, problem-riddled estate estimated at around $1 billion, most of it eventually destined for a Doris Duke Foundation.

Doris's cousins, children of Buck's brother Benjamin, have led generally happier and more public lives. Angier Biddle ("Angie") Duke served as U.S. ambassador to many countries and chief of protocol during the John F. Kennedy presidency. It was he who arranged the assassinated president's state funeral. Angie had his share of Duke exuberance; he was killed by a car while roller-blading near his Southampton home at the age of seventy-nine. His brother, Anthony Drexel ("Tony") Duke, has been much honored as the founder of Boys Harbor, Inc., a philanthropic organization for educating New York inner-city children.

The peerless Dukes: *left,*
Mrs. Angier B. Duke in 1917,
with a Belmont jockey;
below, at Boys Harbor
in 1959, *left to right—*
Mrs. Angier Biddle Duke,
John Duke with his father
Anthony, December,
Mrs. Anthony, Cordelia Drexel
Biddle Robertson, Angier.
Josephine in center.

One of them is the present Governor of the State of Virginia, and another is Richard Evelyn Byrd, intrepid explorer of the North Pole. *April 15, 1927*

Dows, Mrs. Tracy (Alice Olin), whose second volume of verse, *Illusions,* has just been published, is something of a phenomenon for Washington. Entirely without "official position," with no "political influence" whatever, she nevertheless is frequently the center of interesting political discussion. Her house is all pale colors, pointed curiously by the flash of the red on her own fingernails. Above the jars of delicately yellow roses there is a picture of her great-grandfather Robert Livingston; one of her father, Stephen H. Olin; and one of her grandfather, the famous Methodist preacher, President Olin of Wesleyan College. *January 1, 1932*

Drake, Francis Marion, who ten years ago was Governor of Iowa, was one of the pioneer railway builders of the West. He was President of the board of trustees of Drake University, which he endowed very liberally. Drakeville, in Iowa, was founded by his family. In 1852, at the head of a company of sixteen men, he crossed the plains with ox-teams, and on this journey had a severe encounter with the Pawnee Indians. During the Civil War, he was a Brigadier General of volunteers in the Union Army. *February 8, 1908*

Draper, Carlton The Drapers (Alexander Draper came over from Bolton, England, in 1640) made their fortune in Delaware. Milton, Delaware, a few miles west of Rehoboth, is headquarters for Draper-King Cole, Inc., one of the largest canneries in the country. The force behind the company's success was the now-retired Carlton Draper, who has homes in Lucarno, Switzerland, Boca Raton, Florida, and Rehoboth. *July, 1981*

Draper, Mrs. Henry F. (Anna Palmer) While hundreds of New Yorkers were in Madison Square Garden or at the opera, she was entertaining the members of the Academy of Science at her residence, 271 Madison Avenue. Mrs. Draper is the widow of Dr. Henry Draper, and connected with her house by a passageway there is a laboratory that she built as a memorial to her husband. From year to year, Mrs. Draper invites her friends to an important lecture, followed by a reception, given in the laboratory. In 1903, at a lecture given there, society had its first opportunity to see radium. *November 23, 1907*

Draper, Ruth is a granddaughter of the late Charles A. Dana and a niece of Mr. Paul Dana. Her father, the late Dr. Draper, was a New Englander. He was President of the New York Academy of Medicine and had a chair in the College of Physicians and Surgeons. Miss Ruth Draper, his fourth daughter, writes monologues without number and delivers them in a way that has made a great stir in society. At the Colony Club this spring, her monologues received vigorous applause. As the German governess, the debutante in the conservatory, or the Scotch lassie she was truly wonderful. *May 16, 1908*

Drexel, George Washington Childs succeeded his namesake George Childs as proprietor of the *Philadelphia Public Ledger* in 1894. But just eight years later, he sold the paper. The remaining forty two years of his life were devoted to yachts and motor cars: He became an expert mechanic and was instrumental in shaping Philadelphia's early automotive speed laws. *November, 1991*

Drexel, Mr. and Mrs. George Washington Childs (Mary S. Irick) have purchased one hundred and sixty acres of land at Ryders Cove, Ilesboro, in Penobscot Bay, and will build a cottage that will be the largest on the island. When asked why they did not build on the fashionable side of the island, Mr. Drexel replied that "The coal strike was responsible for it all." Last summer, while cruising about in their steam yacht, they were obliged to use soft coal. A south wind carried the smoke ashore, much to the annoyance of the New Yorkers whose houses were near the water's edge. They sent word to Mr. Drexel, asking him to anchor a bit further on. This he did, going to Ryders Cove. And at the latter spot, he found just the place desired for his house. *January 10, 1903*

Drexel, Mrs. John R. (Alice G. Troth) wore, without doubt, one of the most exquisite gowns seen in Newport for a long time. It was of cloth of silver; the strands of genuine silver, which were woven in the fabric, glimmered and glistened under the many lights. Her jewels were a dog collar and tiara of diamonds and turquoise, also a long double chain of the same gems, festooned from shoulder to shoulder. This, by the way, is an exclusive fad with Mrs. Drexel: Her long chains are always worn in this manner. *September 12, 1903*

Drexel, Mr. and Mrs. John R. III (Hon. Noreen Stonor) Although Mrs. Drexel was the daughter of Baron Camoys of England, on her mother's side she traces her ancestry to Roger Williams, who founded the state of Rhode Island and established its capital at Providence in 1644 as a haven for those seeking religious freedom. Her descent from Williams is through the Browns of Providence, one of America's foremost families, famed in financial, educational, cultural, and philanthropic activities for over two centuries. Among their distinctions was the endowing of Brown University. The Browns have been visiting Newport since its earliest days. The Drexels are the great Philadelphia banking family who appeared on the Newport scene in the '80s. *September, 1958*

Drexel, John R. IV "Somebody in the family decided to be passive—to teach their children that one shouldn't be commercially aggressive," he says. "I'm the first in my family in four generations to work. Why did they decide to drop out and become professional socialites? Nobody got the message that you have to have money to have the wherewithal to be philanthropic." *November, 1991*

Drexel, Louise Bouvier, daughter of the late A. F. Drexel, was married to Edward DeV. Morrell. This wedding has attracted much attention on account of the great wealth of the bride, who is the youngest of three sisters, each possessing an annual income of three hundred thousand dollars. The bride as well as her sisters is noted for her great interest in charitable and industrial institutions and in Christianizing the Indians. One novel feature at the church was the presence of fifty servants belonging to the two households, and seated in pews by themselves. *January 23, 1889*

Driscoll, Clara, daughter of Mr. Robert Driscoll of Texas, spent her childhood on her father's ranches in the shade of the tragic Alamo. Therefore, when she was grown to womanhood, and there came a sad possibility that this sacred Alamo would be sold for public purposes, it was Miss Driscoll who advanced the necessary $75,000. The Texas legislature refunded this money just last year, but Texas remembers that it was Miss Driscoll who stepped forward at the crisis. *February 3, 1906*

Drummond, Bettina, a granddaughter of Marshall Field, is an expert in Haute Ecole, an exacting poetry of movement made famous by the Spanish Riding School. "When people say, 'What do you do?' and you say 'The art of dressage,' they look at you as if you are absolutely loony," laughs Bettina, one of the very few Americans to have experienced the airs above the ground. *August, 1983*

Drummond, Mrs. Harrison I. (Mary W. Prickett), who is one of the prominent matrons of St. Louis, is likewise known to society in the East. Until quite recently, with Mr. Drummond she occupied a residence at Dobb's Ferry, New York. *November 28, 1903*

Dryden, John F., President of the Prudential Insurance Company of America and former United States Senator from New Jersey, amassed a very large fortune in his business life, personal friends estimating it as high as $50,000,000. Mr. Dryden devoted his talents to study of insurance questions. He founded the Prudential Insurance Co. in Newark in 1873, was also one of the founders of the Fidelity Trust Company of Newark, and was interested besides in several traction companies in New Jersey. *December 2, 1911*

du Bois, Guy Pène Although born in Brooklyn, the son of Henri du Bois, a critic of art, literature, and music, the artist descends from a family that landed in New Orleans fifty years before the Revolution. Besides building a painter's reputation, Guy Pène du Bois followed his father's footsteps into art criticism, which he published in three of New York's leading dailies. *June 15, 1931*

Dudley, Mr. and Mrs. Guilford (Jane G. Anderson) U.S. Ambassador to Denmark and Mrs. Guilford Dudley are the most popular and admired couple in Nashville. The Ambassador formerly was President of Life & Casualty Insurance Co. of Tennessee, of which his father was a founder. Mrs. Dudley was the first chairman of the world-renowned Swan Ball. "Guilford Dudley is the most integrated personality I've ever met," says the scion of one of Nashville's oldest and most prominent families. *June, 1971*

DUER, HARRIET ROBINSON was a daughter of the late John Duer, Justice of the Supreme Court, and a great-granddaughter on her maternal side of Lord Stirling of Revolutionary times. She was born in New York and spent the greater part of her life in this city and at Newport. Miss Duer was buried in the Alexander family vault in Trinity churchyard, which has been in the family for more than two centuries. *May 21, 1910*

DUER, KATHARINE ALEXANDER represents the fourth generation in descent from Colonel William Duer, and for more than a century and a half the Alexander name has been associated with the Duer family. The family ramifications are wide, and the years, supplemented by dignified lives, have added prestige to the names. *May 15, 1923*

DUER, WILLIAM ALEXANDER was a grandson of William Alexander Duer, Judge of the Supreme Court and President of Columbia College from 1829 to 1842. The first William Duer died in New York in 1799. His wife was Catherine Alexander, second daughter of General William Alexander, claimant of the Scottish Earldom of Stirling. In this generation, the Duers had a brilliant part in New York society, were the first family to have liveried servants, and the number of wines served at table was a matter of comment. *November 4, 1905*

DUKE, MR. AND MRS. ANGIER BIDDLE (ROBIN C. TIPPETT)—LYNN are rapidly creating a new ambassadorial style in Madrid. The incorrigibly social Angier is entertaining at a great rate and getting a lot of mileage out of his comparatively small embassy. Robin has vastly impressed the Spanish by exhibiting a great many American painters, mainly abstract. "Our Spanish friends rightly love their Zurbaráns and Goyas, but I think the newer American painting stimulates even when it baffles them." *January, 1966*

DUKE, DORIS One well-known restoration-minded member of Newport's glittering summer colony is Doris Duke. She became increasingly interested in those eighteenth-century structures on the rambling streets of the Point and Historic Hill. Miss Duke quietly began buying up houses for a few thousand dollars each and drawing together a staff of architects and researchers and craftsmen who would execute her very personal vision of what this part of old Newport could be. In 1968, this increasingly reclusive woman issued a statement establishing the Newport Restoration Foundation, endowing it, over the years, with an estimated $10 million. *December, 1984*

DUKE, JAMES BUCHANAN The country estate of Mr. James B. Duke, in Central New Jersey, about half-way between Orange and Princeton, comprises over two thousand acres of fertile farm lands. This vast area has been transformed under engineers, landscape architects, and roadmakers. Farm houses and fences have disappeared, public roads have been widened, miles of new macadam drives sweep among rolling hills and dales. The whole panorama of woodland, rolling valley, and winding river now form a landscape scheme that for original design and decorative treatment may find few counterparts. *March 21, 1903*

DUKE, MARY, the daughter of Mr. and Mrs. Benjamin N. Duke, was to be presented at the Court of St. James. The gown she selected was of white soft satin with a trellis of shaded gold roses in a graceful design. The long empire train of chiffon was draped in rose buds. Miss Duke is an amateur musician of much ability. She was educated at Trinity College, Durham, North Carolina, which was built and endowed by her grandfather, Washington Duke, the founder of the company of which his youngest son, Mr. James B. Duke, is now the President. *May 23, 1908*

AT THE DUKE BOX

After World War II, Angier Biddle Duke gave his bachelor friends a stable at Southampton with a "stall" for each "stud," which became known as The Duke Box. The Duke Boxers always had beautiful women around, kept a retainer to cook their meals, gave one big bash a year with 700 invited guests, and made a point of not dressing in black tie. *July, 1975*

DUKES, SIR PAUL AND LADY Their visit to Chicago was made the occasion for many dinners before the very interesting talk the former gave of "hairbreadth escapes in the imminent deadly breach" in Red Russia. Lady Dukes is the daughter of Mrs. W. K. Vanderbilt and was the wife of Ogden Mills, before her divorce. *March 1, 1923*

DULANY, HELEN HUGHES, who designed the first wide gold bracelets to decorate chic American arms, is now concentrating on industrial designs and murals. She lives in a penthouse on Lake Shore Drive in Chicago, beneath the rays of the Lindbergh Light: Here, on a terrace wall, Tony Sarg drew mad marine scenes one day, which was further complicated when Walt Disney sketched in Mickey Mouse, grinning here and there behind the seaweed. *November, 1936*

DUNCAN, WILLIAM BUTLER was a power in the business life of this city. He was educated at Edinburgh and in Brown University. At the latter, he received the degree of Bachelor of Arts in 1850. In Mr. Butler's home on Fifth Avenue, King Edward, the then Prince of Wales, was entertained when he visited this country. From 1874 to 1888, Mr. Duncan was President of the Mobile & Ohio Railroad Co. Mr. Duncan had the distinction of being the only American member of London's exclusive club, the Travelers. *June 29, 1912*

DUNCAN, MRS. WILLIAM BUTLER (JANE PERCY) died at her home, 1 Fifth Avenue. Mrs. Duncan, before her marriage in New Orleans in 1853, was Miss Jane Percy, a granddaughter of Winthrop Sargent, the first Governor of Mississippi, who was also an ancestor of John Singer Sargent, the artist. Mrs. Duncan was one of the patronesses of the famous dancing class held at Delmonico's. Mr. and Mrs. Duncan had one of the proscenium boxes at the Academy of Music in the days of Italian opera on Fourteenth Street. *December 23, 1905*

DUNN, MRS. JAMES CLEMENT (MARY A. ARMOUR) Born a Kansas City Armour, she has a house in Washington, but she takes her autumns in New York, suns herself in Palm Beach, and sails off for holidays in Honolulu. When the sun is high, she likes to sally forth in a trim, slim *tailleur* and a pert little sailor tilted over her brow. But she turns to Vionnet for the right gown to set off her sapphires and diamonds. The wife of an authority on protocol, she is continually amazing Washington by mixing all sorts of people together and making them love it, and one of the successes of the summer was her out-of-doors beer party. *January, 1939*

DU PONT, MRS. ALFRED IRÉNÉE is the daughter of Judge Edward G. Bradford and, on the maternal side, the granddaughter of the late Alexis Irénée du Pont and a niece of Admiral S. F. du Pont. Mr. and Mrs. du Pont own a large estate in Wilmington, Delaware, where the family with which they both have kinship has been prominent for many generations. *April 17, 1909*

DU PONT, AMY Santa Barbara is most fortunate to have in the adjoining acres of Hope Ranch a locale in which the far-sightedness of its creators and developers visioned a corner of English park lands for every form of equestrianism, forever free from the dangers of the highway and the open road. The club is equipped for all kinds of equestrian sport and was organized by Miss Amy du Pont, of Wilmington and Montecito, who is its first President. *March 15, 1931*

DU PONT, ETHEL is Wilmington's number one debutante. The du Pont name, with its connotations of greatness, is becomingly worn by this young representative of the famous house. She is the daughter of Mr. and Mrs. Eugene du Pont of "Owl's Nest," Greenville, Delaware, and Northeast Harbor, Maine, and her hobby is riding and hunting. She is considered the most interesting debutante of the Philadelphia-Delaware season. *January 15, 1938*

DU PONT, MR. AND MRS. EUGENE ELEUTHÈRE (KATEDULWE MOXHAM) In the du Pont family, there are many old French names, for its members are all descendants of Pierre Samuel du Pont de Nemours, the French economist and statesman, who lived and died in Wilmington, Delaware (where all the du Ponts make their home); of Victor Marie du Pont, who was the French Consul General of New York; and of Eleuthère Irénée du Pont, who founded the famous powder mills of Wilmington. *February 1, 1908*

DU PONT, HENRY B. Nowhere will one find a more sustained enthusiasm for aviation than that which centers around the perfectly planned private airport of Henry B. du Pont, near Wilmington. Mr. du Pont was the first of his family to take up flying. It was no fad with him, but an undertaking in which he became absorbed and which he carried through with characteristic thoroughness. He built his fly-

du PONT

Flying enthusiast Henry du Pont, 1932.

Even before coming to the United States, the du Ponts were a distinguished family. Pierre Samuel du Pont de Nemours ("of Nemours," to distinguish him from the many du Ponts from other towns in France) was a well-known economist, diplomat, and correspondent with Thomas Jefferson. Liberal but disgusted by the excesses of the French Revolution, he came to this country hoping to establish an agrarian colony in Virginia, bringing with him his sons, Victor and Eleuthère Irénée, and their wives and children. They landed at Newport, Rhode Island, on New Year's Day, 1800.

The du Ponts decided against distant Virginia and settled on the Brandywine River in Delaware, instead. Soon they were producing gunpowder, an item in great demand in the new republic. The idea was Eleuthère Irénée's, and he gave his name to the enterprise: E. I. du Pont de Nemours.

Eleuthère Irénée fathered three sons: Alfred Victor, Henry, and Alexis. Among them, they produced twenty-four grandchildren. Henry du Pont headed the firm from 1850 to 1889. Like many early du Ponts, he was a dedicated worker, writing 6,000 business letters a year in his own hand. A pattern was

set in which a family member was always president of the company: three sons of Lammot du Pont, for example, headed the firm in turn. And there was never a lack of heirs in this prolific family: in 1950, when the du Ponts celebrated the 150th anniversary of their arrival in the United States, 1,800 members of the family attended.

Nylon, Teflon, synthetic rubber, and cellophane: all have, through the years, served to bankroll various du Pont family estates throughout Delaware. Among the family's philanthropies in the state are the Eleutherian Mills, located on the original site of the gunpowder factory, the Brandywine River Museum, the Delaware Natural History Museum, Longwood Gardens, and the Henry Francis du Pont Winterthur Museum of American decorative arts.

Antimonopoly investigations, which lasted for years and generated much unwanted publicity, eventually resulted in the forced sale of the du Ponts' one-third holding in the General Motors Corporation, and many du Ponts, today, lead lives that are guardedly private. However understated, total du Pont wealth is still estimated to be in the billions.

D̲elaware's own family, du Pont de Nemours: *clockwise from top left,* Ethel du Pont Roosevelt; Mrs. A. Felix du Pont; Mr. and Mrs. William du Pont; Mrs. Alfred Irénée du Pont in 1909; the 1933 Alexis du Pont Memorial Shoot; former Governor and Mrs. Pierre S. du Pont IV.

ing field partly for the use of his family and friends and partly because there were no airports in Delaware at the time where he could keep his plane. *May 1, 1932*

DU PONT, MR. AND MRS. HENRY F. (RUTH WALES) kept four footmen in livery at Southampton, imported snapdragons from their Winterthur estate just to match the color of their ruby-red glasses, and stored bins of china, plate, and candlesticks in the cellar, so none of their parties would ever repeat a theme. *July, 1975*

DU PONT, PIERRE SAMUEL III was the great-great-grandson of the original Pierre Samuel du Pont de Nemours. From 1915 to 1940, he headed du Pont, and he also served for a time as both President and CEO of General Motors; but his most enduring legacy is probably Longwood, a magnificent display garden just over the Pennsylvania border in Kennett Square. When he died in 1954, he left his beloved gardens "… for the sole use of the public for purposes of exhibition, instruction, education and enjoyment." *August, 1990*

DU PONT, MRS. RICHARD C. Now the center of the Maryland thoroughbred country, the fertile land on the banks of the Bohemia River was first pioneered as breeding grounds for fine-blooded, good-boned animals by Mrs. du Pont. She is known around the world as the owner of Kelso, history's most admired horse. Kelso was five times Horse of the Year, won 39 races, a world record of $1,977,890. He once received so much fan mail that it warranted a special mailbox in Mrs. du Pont's gray-and-yellow colors. The mailbox is a Woodstock landmark. Mrs. du Pont now fox hunts Kelso and rides him around her vast land, in the company of her three yellow Labradors. *May, 1971*

DU PONT, T. COLEMAN In addition to running the Equitable Building and controlling the Equitable Assurance Society, he is actively and actually engaged in the hotel business, the coal business, the traction business, several trust companies, and a surety company. He is very fond of yachting, and his hydroplane racer, *Tech, Jr.,* holds the mile record in her class. He is a moving spirit in the National Highways Association, one of the foremost factors in the good roads movement in this country. *June 20, 1916*

DU PONT, WILLIAM III Following in the illustrious tradition and adroit equine footsteps of a renowned sporting family, William du Pont III is an outstanding young horseman and everybody is watching him. He is the last son of "Old Willie" du Pont, of the far-famed "Foxcatcher Farm" in Delaware. Energetic Bill doesn't miss a daylight hour working at his huge 2,000-acre-plus Pillar Stud in Lexington, Kentucky, where he stands nine internationally pedigreed stallions and keeps mares, foals, and sales yearlings on two separate farms, which lie in 635 choice Bluegrass acres. *July, 1983*

DU TEMPLE DE ROUGEMONT, COUNT AND COUNTESS RENÉ (EDITH DEVEREUX CLAPP) Remarkably good looking, in view of all the disappointments among representatives of

French nobility who have found their way here, is Count René du Temple de Rougemont. He looks very honest and manly and quite as tall as his tall American ushers. *December 10, 1904*

DWIGHT, HELEN was the only daughter of Timothy Dwight, formerly president of Yale University. In New Haven, Miss Dwight was active in charitable work and, as a member of the Connecticut Society of Colonial Dames, did much toward preserving the historical landmarks of the city. *October 23, 1909*

DYER, ELISHA Providence, Rhode Island, takes the liveliest interest in politics just now, for former Governor Elisha Dyer is slated for Mayor on the Republican ticket. That Governor Dyer will be elected to any office for which he is nominated is a foregone conclusion, since he is quite as popular with the voters in the lower walks of life in the state where his father and grandfather were Governors as with "the aristocracy," for Providence still claims an aristocracy. *October 28, 1905*

DYER, MRS. ELISHA, JR. (SIDNEY TURNER)—SWAN always gives the first formal dinner of the season at Newport, and for several years has succeeded in giving the last one, as well. "Wayside" is a popular "dinner house," the library and smoking room please the older set, while the younger people are equally charmed with the perfect floor of the ballroom or the cool darkness of the north porch. *September 24, 1904*

E

EARLE, VICTOR DE LA MONTAGNE, son of General and Mrs. Ferdinand P. Earle of "Earle Cliff," Washington Heights, gave a birthday party. Master Victor is a lineal descendant of General Johannes de la Montagne, chief military commander of Manhattan Island, 1640–1645, and a member of Governor Stuyvesant's council. *May 29, 1895*

EASTMAN, GEORGE In announcing his benefaction, which disposed of the last large block of his personal holdings in his Kodak company, Mr. Eastman said that he wanted to see his money work for him while he was alive to watch it. Most of his latest gift will go to the University of Rochester. Mr. Eastman's total benefactions now total $58,602,900. *January 15, 1925*

EDGAR, CONSTANCE, stepdaughter of Colonel Jerome Bonaparte and great-granddaughter of Daniel Webster, took the black veil at the Convent of the Visitation, Baltimore. The ceremony was performed in the convent chapel by Archbishop Gibbons, in the presence of the dark-robed nuns and a few of the relatives and friends of the family. Miss Edgar is about twenty years old and was much admired in the social circles of Baltimore, Washington, New York, and Boston. *May 12, 1886*

EDGAR, MR. AND MRS. NEWBOLD (AGNES STRACHAN) He was one of the pioneer summer residents of Southampton. He went there first as a boy and, for thirty years, had been

there every year, often remaining with Mrs. Edgar into the winter. Throughout their residence there, he and Mrs. Edgar took an active interest in social and club affairs. He had much to do with the development of the club life and in bringing that phase of summer life to its present high standard. *September 10, 1918*

EDGAR, MRS. NEWBOLD LEROY (MARIE J. MANICE) has lost none of her enthusiasm for all aerial sports, but prefers ballooning. She attended the international aviation meets at Rheims and Brescia; she describes aeroplaning as marvelously interesting, but a nervous sport. The motor makes a discomforting noise, and one can never feel very secure. Mrs. Edgar has never gone up in an aeroplane, but has made several balloon ascensions. The costume she advises for air travel is a simple tailored gown and a small hat, covered with a thick veil, as the sun's rays are very hot in the summer, and as one goes with the wind, there is a considerable breeze. *December 25, 1909*

EDGAR, MR. AND MRS. SELWYN own a shooting lodge in Louisiana, where, with their invited guests, they repair about once in six weeks, exchanging the conventional atmosphere of the city for the pleasures of this rural abode. Mrs. Edgar is acknowledged as one of the famous women shots of America, and it is no uncommon thing for her to return from a hunting expedition with a big bag of game. *December 26, 1903*

EDIE, CLEMENTINE ELIZABETH is engaged to Mr. Joseph Catherwood. The marriage will unite two of the old California families. The future bride is a great-granddaughter of the late Bishop William Kip, who was one of the first Episcopal bishops of San Francisco. Mr. Catherwood is also a member of an old and notable San Francisco family. His great-grandfather was the late Judge S. C. Hastings, Chief Justice of California and founder of the Hastings Law College. He is a nephew of Marquise Joaquín de la Pereyra of Paris. Countess Lewenhaupf of Falkenstein is among his cousins. *June 15, 1923*

EDWARDS, GORDON W. was recently selected as one of the one hundred and ten San Francisco bachelors who are to act as dragoons escorting Miss Virgila Bogue, the Queen of the Portola Festival, which will be one of the most brilliant pageants ever given in the city of the Golden Gate. To meet the requirements demanded of a member of Miss Bogue's Dragoon escort, the bachelor must be five feet, ten inches in height and of the guardsman type of masculine attractiveness. *August 14, 1909*

ELIOT, MRS. SAMUEL (EMILY MARSHALL OTIS) was a direct descendant of the patriot James Otis, and her mother was the famous beauty Emily Marshall, who, a hundred years ago, when Boston was a village in comparison with its present size, was "the toast of the town." Mrs. Eliot stood for all that was typical of the Boston woman of the old school, and was one of the last survivors of that class. *March 17, 1906*

ELIOT, THOMAS H. Washington University in St. Louis has made great strides under Chancellor Eliot, and the American Council on Education places it among the top twenty five universities. Thomas Eliot's grandfather, the late Charles W. Eliot of Harvard, was a cousin of the founder of Washington University, the Rev. William Greenleaf Eliot. *March, 1970*

ELKINS, KATHARINE The appearance of Miss Katharine Elkins in the ring at the National Capital Horse Show, wearing the red and green of the Keswick Hunt Club, was the first intimation many persons had of the change in Miss Elkins's happy hunting ground. Her resignation from the Orange County Hunt, with its headquarters at "the Plains" in Loudoun County, took place more than a year ago, when she surrendered all claim to this most exclusive and high priced hunt club in the United States, to which she paid an initiation fee of $10,000 when she and the former Miss Mary Harriman enjoyed the distinction of being its only girl members. *May 18, 1912*

ELKINS, STEPHEN BENTON was admitted to the Bar in Missouri in 1863, was Secretary of War from 1891 to 1893, and United States Senator from West Virginia, from 1895 to 1906. His wife is a daughter of Senator Henry G. Davis. Senator Elkins has large coal mining and railroad interests in West Virginia. *January 14, 1911*

ELLETT, THOMAS HARLAN The architect of the new Cosmopolitan Club is the designer of a number of the most charming country houses in the East. His work, like his life, is essentially agreeable. Recognition has come from the Architectural League in the Silver Medal and from the American Battle Monuments Commission. *February 15, 1933*

ELLIOTT, MR. AND MRS. JOHN (MAUD HOWE) are in Newport with Mrs. Elliott's mother, the venerable Mrs. Julia Ward Howe. Mr. Elliott, who is well known as an artist, has painted some notable landscapes of Newport. Mrs. Elliott, like her mother, has had success as an author, and has many of her mother's social graces. Every year, there is entertaining at Mrs. Howe's cottage, and her receptions, at which new pictures are often shown, are altogether different from the gay events with which *Newport* is supposedly surfeited. *July 25, 1908*

ELLIOTT, MR. AND MRS. JOHN D., JR. (ELEANOR THOMAS) Eleanor Elliott's roster of jobs would make a hardened business executive quake: Chairman of the board of trustees of Barnard College, Chairman of the $30 million Foundation for Child Development, Governor of New York Hospital, and first woman director of the giant Celanese Corporation. Her husband, known as Jock, is board chairman of Ogilvy & Mather, the worldwide advertising agency. *November, 1975*

ELLIOTT, MR. AND MRS. JOHN G. (ALINE DICKERSON) On the death of his father, Mr. Elliott succeeded as head of the firm of James Elliott & Co., one of the leading linen houses in this country. He was married in 1895 to Miss Aline Dickerson, daughter of the late John S. Dickerson, a well known yachtsman and the owner of the *Madeleine,* the last schooner to defend the *America*'s Cup. *March 12, 1910*

PEYTON PLACE NORTH

"They wanted to shoot that movie, *Peyton Place,* in Woodstock, Vermont," recalls Betty Emmons, a former New Yorker whose Dana family ancestors date back to the 1700s here. "And a lot of people were for it, for the income. Well, the alarm buttons really went off; friends even called us in St. Croix! They were horrified that all that business about small-town scandals would be connected with Woodstock. So they kicked out the movie people, who went to Camden, Maine—which made millions off it." *October, 1992*

ELLIS, RALPH N., master of the Meadowbrook hounds, one of the best-known packs in America, and the only one hunted regularly on Long Island, is an accomplished exponent of two sports. Mr. Ellis, though one of the best horsemen and cross-country riders in the American hunting field, is even better known as a yachtsman and as the owner of the famous schooner *Iroquois*. He is a clever helmsman who figured prominently in yachting long before he became prominent as a huntsman. *October 25, 1900*

ELLIS, WILLIAM D., JR. An Atlantan, 28, from one of that city's oldest families. Doug's great-grandfather was Judge W. D. Ellis, his father is Board Chairman of Southern Mills, of which Doug is V.P. and General Manager. He also teaches Sunday school. *June, 1964*

ELLSWORTH, LINCOLN In 1926, Lincoln Ellsworth flew in a dirigible over the North Pole. In 1926, he also inherited the castle of Lenzburg, in Switzerland, from his father, Mr. James W. Ellsworth. As Mr. Ellsworth bequeathed an age-hewn castle in Switzerland to his son, so his daughter, Mrs. Bernon S. Prentice, inherited from her father the Villa Palmieri, located near Florence in the Fiesole Hills. About this villa, Giovanni Boccaccio was pleased to write in hyperbolic terms. *June 1, 1928*

ELY, MR. AND MRS. GEIST live in the farthest reaches of the Main Line in a smallish house on a vast family compound (180 acres, including riding stables). If you ask Geist—who lived fifteen years in New York after graduating from Princeton—why he came home, he says, "Look, one of the reasons I left Philadelphia was the restrictiveness. I wouldn't know what it's like to be on the outside. If you're on the inside, Philadelphia is very warm and welcoming; but fifteen years ago, you just didn't see anybody you weren't brought up with, which isn't exactly mind-expanding." *October, 1970*

ELY, MRS. ROBERT ERSKINE (RUDOLPHINE SCHEFFER) is a young woman of much intellectual charm and has many friends among men of letters. The week before her marriage, she presided at a luncheon given for Mr. Henry James, the novelist, following his lecture on "Balzac, the Teacher." Mr. Ely has given very interesting little dinners at the City Club, and has members of the 400 to meet men of letters and other lions. *July 1, 1905*

EMERSON, CHARLES CHASE, a well-known Boston artist, died at his home in Allston. He was mostly engaged in the work of illustrating books and magazines. He was a lineal descendant of that Parson Emerson, of Concord, credited with firing the shot "heard around the world" in the Revolutionary War. *May 10, 1921*

EMERY, JOHN J. comes closer than anyone else in the city to meriting the title "Mr. Cincinnati." He is President of Thomas Emery's Sons, founded by his grandfather 125 years ago, an organization with large holdings in core property, including the Carew Tower, the city's tallest building. He is also Chairman of the Board of Emery Industries, a large and flourishing chemical company. *September, 1963*

EMMET, ROBERT R. M. TEMPLE is a direct descendant of Thomas Addis Emmet, brother of the great Robert Emmet, the Irish patriot. Among the Temples and the Emmets, there have been many brilliant men and women. Henry James, in his reminiscences, speaks of the intermarriage of Emmets and Temples: "The Temples and Emmets being so much addicted to alliance that a still later generation was to bristle for us with a delightful Emmetry." *October 24, 1914*

ENDICOTT, MR. AND MRS. WILLIAM C., JR. (LOUISE THORON) will return to "Old Farm," their summer home at Danvers. This estate is one of the noted New England homes and was purchased by the great-grandfather of Mr. Endicott, Captain Joseph Peabody, at the time of the War of 1812, as a place of refuge for his family and his cargoes in case of invasion by the British. One of the original barns, where the cargoes were stored, is still standing. *July 4, 1908*

EUSTIS, MRS. JAMES B., one of the most charming of the younger gentlewomen in New York, has a clever scheme that delights all the harrassed "captains of industry," who have found a wonderful cure for insomnia in the puzzle-pictures—the cut-up conundrums in wood that have become one of the most infectious fads that ever took the fancy of New Yorkers. These puzzles, however, no matter how fascinating, are quickly put together and are of no further use. So Mrs. Eustis has established a puzzle exchange. Puzzles, like books in a circulating library, are sold, purchased, and exchanged. Mrs. Eustis, in her simple, clinging black gown as she presides over the puzzles, makes a picture even more attractive than when at the opera in evening costume. *October 24, 1908*

EVANS, AUGUSTA BINNEY Her marriage to Mr. Algernon Brooke Roberts was celebrated at the Bryn Mawr Church. It was an event of unusual interest, in that it recalled a period of Philadelphia's fashionable life which is rapidly passing away. The bride is a member of one of the oldest and most distinguished families of the Quaker City, while the groom is the son of the late George B. Roberts, former President of the Pennsylvania Railroad. Both families are proud of their Welsh ancestry, and evidences of this are found in the sweet-sounding names they have bestowed upon their country seats: "Pencoyd," being the name of the Roberts estate, and, "Penchyn-y-coed," that of the Evans place. *June 21, 1902*

EVANS, BETH, a favorite in society, recently became the wife of David Dearborn, Jr., of New York. He was one of New York's "confirmed bachelors," of New England derivation. His sister is Mrs. Lewis H. Lapham (Antoinette Dearborn), of New York and New Canaan. *September 1, 1925*

EVANS, JOHN is the grandson of the first Territorial Governor of Colorado, appointed by Abraham Lincoln in 1862. By his marriage to the former Gladys Cheeseman, two of the most important families in the state were merged, and there is scarcely a single institution that does not bear some sign of their cultural, industrial, or philanthropic contributions. *August, 1959*

EVANS, MRS. ROBERT DAWSON (MARIA ANTOINETTE HUNT) She was one of the richest women in New England, and her name and that of her husband will go down to posterity as the giver of the Robert Dawson Evans wing of the Boston Art Museum as well as in countless lesser gifts of church organs, valuable pictures, and other works of art. *November 1, 1917*

EVANS, WILLIAM T., formerly President of Mills & Gibbs, was well known for his interest in struggling artists, among those he helped being Ralph Blakelock and Henry W. Ranger. He was a friend to Innes, Wyant, and Martin, the work of whom passed by him to the National Gallery. It is stated that, within the last fifteen years, he gave to public use paintings estimated now at $1,000,000. *December 10, 1918*

EWING, MRS. RUMSEY (ROSALIE MCREE) In 1940, she carried both the bouquet of three hundred and fifty orchids grown from seed in the Missouri Botanical Gardens especially for the queen of the Veiled Prophet Ball in St. Louis and the gold and jeweled scepter that had been added to the royal panoply. *September, 1952*

EWING, MRS. THOMAS, JR. (LUCIA CHASE) Yale men from Hong Kong to Moscow agree that Lucia Chase was the outstanding prom girl of all time. Living in Waterbury, only thirty miles north of New Haven, she enjoyed such a whirl at Yale that she never had time to wander further afield. In the years of Yale's greatest triumphs, no party was ever a party without Lucia Chase. Sons of Yale still sigh over their memories of her: her dark, curly hair, blue-green eyes, feather-footed dancing, even her leopard coat and cap. Now the widow of Thomas Ewing, Jr., she has returned seriously to her dancing, appearing this season as an important new American ballerina. *December, 1936*

EXMOUTH, PROFESSOR CHARLES EDWARD PELLEW, VISCOUNT The father of Professor Pellew was the sixth Viscount Exmouth and died in Washington, leaving his son to inherit the title. Lord Exmouth is a grandson of Judge William Jay of New York and a great-grandson of John Jay, our first United States Chief Justice. He graduated from Columbia in

1884, joined the faculty as chemistry professor, and has been with the University ever since. He will renounce his American citizenship now, become a British subject, and take the seat in the House of Lords to which he is entitled. *June 1, 1923*

F

FAHNESTOCK, MR. AND MRS. HARRIS (MABEL METCALF) will open "Eastover," their, new and attractive Lenox, Massachusetts, country estate. Eastover crowns a hill that has a wonderful outlook. It is a brick structure decorated by London artists. Abundance of hand carving abounds, especially in the dining room and library. Mrs. Fahnestock's own room is in rose. A feature of her boudoir is concealed doors, which open by hidden springs giving entrance into spacious closets. There is an enormous system of gardens, terraces, and fountains underway at Eastover, which will be a year in building. *June 10, 1911*

FAIRCHILD, MR. AND MRS. DAVID G. (MARIAN HUBBARD GRAHAM BELL) "Twin Oaks," Mrs. Gardiner Hubbard's country house, was the place of the marriage of her granddaughter, Miss Marian Hubbard Graham Bell, daughter of Professor and Mrs. Alexander Graham Bell, to Mr. David G. Fairchild. It seemed most fitting that this daughter of a famous inventor should marry a scientist, for Mr. Fairchild is an explorer for the Agricultural Department. *April 29, 1905*

FAIRCHILD, FRANCES The midnight performance in the ballroom of the Ritz-Carlton, at the Egyptian Pageant and Ball, culminated in a really beautiful scene. Miss Frances Fairchild was asked to take the part of Tut-ankh-Amen in the Pageant and appeared in all the colors found upon the figures in the tomb. The idea of the dramatic skit was to show, through pantomine, what transpired when Cleo made the acquaintance of Tut. *May 15, 1923*

FAIRFAX, MRS. HAMILTON R. (ELEANOR VAN RENSSELAER), decorated by Queen Mary for her services at home and abroad during the World War, was for seven years President of the Colonial Dames of New York State. She also founded the Churchwoman's League for Patriotic Service, a strong unit in the Episcopal Church. When the drive commenced to raise the building fund for the Cathedral of St. John the Divine, she was made the Chairman of the women's division and made a marvelous showing with the cooperation of teams that worked gallantly under her leadership. *February 1, 1926*

FAIRFAX, COLONEL JOHN WALTER was a veteran of the Civil War. He fought as ranking officer on the staff of General Longstreet, and is referred to in history as "Longstreet's fighting aide." In 1850, he acquired the historic country seat of President James Monroe near Aldie, Virginia. "Leesylvania," the old home of the Lee family where he died, was the birthplace of the Revolutionary hero "Light Horse Harry" Lee. *March 28, 1908*

FAIRFIELD, RICHARD CUTTS Into the hands of Mrs. James C. Barr, of Boston, will soon be placed one of the highest decorations Italy has to offer. It is the *Medaglia d'argento al valore militare,* won by her son, the late Richard Cutts Fairfield, for conspicuous bravery in collecting wounded under fire on the night of January 26, 1918, during an aerial bombardment at Mestre, Italy. Young Richard Fairfield was named for his ancestor, Richard Cutts, who graduated from Harvard in 1790 and married the sister of Dolley Madison, the wife of a President of the United States. *June 1, 1918*

FANSHAWE, MRS. WILLIAM S. (JESSIE JEROME) was the daughter of Leonard and Fanny Jerome. With his brother, Lawrence R. Jerome, Leonard Jerome was associated with William R. Travers and the late August Belmont in creating Jerome Park and founding the American Jockey Club. Mrs. Fanshawe's sister, Jennie Jerome, married first Lord Randolph Churchill, the English statesman, and secondly Mr. Cornwallis-West. *December 19, 1908*

FARGO, JAMES CONGDEL was the brother of the late William S. Fargo, who in 1844 organized the first express company running west from Buffalo. In 1871, he organized the Merchants' Despatch Transportation Company, of which he became President. Until six months before his death, he was president of the American Express Company. He established the money order system and the system of travelers' checks. *March 1, 1915*

FARISH, WILLIAM, grandson of one of the founders of Humble Oil & Refining Company (now Exxon Company, U.S.A.), wields considerable clout in both thoroughbred and polo circles. The current Vice Chairman of the Jockey Club and a member of the Breeders' Cup Executive Committee has such an impeccable reputation as a breeder that equine expert Queen Elizabeth has twice been his guest at "Lane's End Farm" near Versailles, Kentucky, where he has such top-notch stallions as Spend-a-Buck at stud. *January, 1988*

FARWELL, MR. AND MRS. JOHN VILLIERS III (MARGARET WILLING) In 1845, more than two centuries after his ancestors settled in Concord, Massachusetts, twenty-year-old John Villiers Farwell arrived in Chicago on a load of wheat. Within five years, he was partner in the dry goods firm that eventually became J. V. Farwell Company. John and his brother Charles, a United States Senator, were partners in both the dry goods firm and in real estate ventures. Their most dramatic acquisition occurred in the mid-1880s when, in exchange for funding construction of the Texas state capitol building in Austin, their company received the XIT Ranch, the largest ranch of the Old West, more than 3,000,000 panhandle acres that stretched over and into ten counties. The grandchildren of John V. include 95-year-old John V. Farwell III, who, with his 83-year-old wife Margaret, gives some of the most engaging dinner parties on Astor Street. The sheer dash that prompted

John, in the 1920s, to fly an airplane under five bridges in New York City is still in evidence. *September, 1990*

FELLOWES, CORNELIUS In New York, he and his ancestors and his family are among the "old set." He has taken a deep interest in the Horse Show since its very first exhibition. As Mr. Fellowes represents the more conservative element in New York society, so does he the same class in the Horse Show Association. And this conservative element is one of its strongest features. The show is alike popular with the quiet old families and the more fashionable ones. Mr. Fellowes is largely interested in racing, and he is a familiar figure at Belmont Park and Gravesend and Sheepshead Bay. *November 11, 1905*

FENTRESS, MR. AND MRS. CALVIN (FRANCES E. WOOD) The Chicago Fentresses are great-grandchildren of James Fentress, who was brought in as Solicitor General of the Illinois Central Railroad after the Civil War. In 1931, his grandson, Calvin, Jr., married a daughter of General Robert E. Wood, the innovative President of Sears Roebuck. The following year, Calvin became President of Sears' newly formed insurance company, Allstate, which he led until 1966. *September, 1990*

FENWICK, MR. AND MRS. CHARLES C., JR. (ANNE D. STEWART) An investment banker, Mr. Fenwick and his wife are ardent steeplechasers. "It's a matter of getting up early in the morning and riding before work" is Charlie's simplistic explanation of how he managed to combine the winning of three Maryland Hunt Cups and the 1980 Grand National with success in the business world. Both Charlie and Anne come from a long line of dedicated foxhunters and steeplechasers. Both Anne's granduncle and grandfather, Plunket and Redmond Stewart, rode their own horses to win the Maryland Hunt Cup at the turn of the century. *March, 1981*

FENWICK, MRS. HAMMOND (MILLICENT VERNON HAMMOND) is the daughter of the late Ogden Hammond, wealthy New Jersey banker and onetime Ambassador to Spain. He survived the sinking of the *Lusitania;* his wife did not. On her mother's side, Mrs. Fenwick is descended from John Stevens, who purchased quite a bit of land around Hoboken, New Jersey. The ancestral Stevens family home is the spot where the Stevens Institute of Technology now stands. Millicent Fenwick, a Republican, who is 65, says, "I think I'm probably the oldest freshman Congressperson there's ever been." *September, 1975*

FERGUSON, CHESTER The inescapable and benign totem of the Tampa-ocracy is Lykes family patriarch Chester Ferguson. He is a Lykes by marriage to Louise, a granddaughter of progenitor Dr. Howell Lykes, who founded the first of the family holdings: cattle and steamshipping. Today, the family-held enterprises, estimated at over a billion dollars' worth, include shipping, steel, cattle ranching, meat packing, citrus processing, electronics, banking, insurance, law, and real estate. *January, 1980*

FERGUSON, MRS. WALTON (JULIANNA WHITE) In Huntington, Long Island, there is a place unique even in these days of homes arranged in original and luxurious ways. It is the house of Mrs. Julianna Ferguson, the niece of Philip Armour. It is copied after an Italian monastery with upper and lower gardens, inner and outer courts with playing fountains, grotesque gargoyles, numerous corridors, and many fireplaces. Looking from the water, the lines of the exterior are softened by distance, and it has the appearance of an ancient castle set in the wooded hills of Long Island. Mr. Louis Comfort Tiffany, master of many arts, is directing the work. *August 20, 1910*

FIELD, CYRUS W., long known as an extensive dealer in paper in the city of New York, has lately rendered his name familiar to the world by his prominent connection with the ocean telegraph. *September 5, 1857*

FIELD, FREDERICK W. is the great-great-grandson of Chicago merchant prince Marshall Field. After he and his half-brother Marshall Field V dismantled their Field Enterprises media empire in 1983, Ted established Interscope Corporation in Westwood, a moderately successful film production company. Of late, he and his wife have been donating increasingly to environmental causes and projects in Chicago. Although he lived in Chicago only briefly, "he feels an obligation to begin giving money back to the city," says a spokesman. *December, 1989*

FIELD, GWENDOLYN, the daughter of the late Marshall Field of Chicago, was married to Mr. Charles Edmonstone at St. Martin's-in-the-Fields. The bride was given away by her uncle, Admiral of the Fleet Earl Beatty. Earl and Countess Beatty held a reception after the ceremony at their residence, "Mall House," which forms part of the Admiralty Arch. Among the wedding gifts was a little token such as a Scottish castle from Mr. Edmonstone's parents. *May 15, 1923*

FIELD, MRS. HENRY (NANCY PERKINS) The greatest interest is felt in Chicago in the announcement of the marriage of young Mrs. Henry Field to Arthur Ronald Lambert Field Tree. Mrs. Field is, of course, well known in New York society, her mother having been one of the famous "Langhorne sisters." Lady Astor, recently elected to the British Parliament, is one of these sisters, as is also Mrs. Charles Dana Gibson. Nancy Perkins made her debut in Richmond, Virginia, in 1915. She married Henry Field, son of Marshall Field II, in February 1916, and he died in July of that year. Mr. Tree is a first cousin of Mrs. Field's first husband, being also a grandson of Marshall Field I. By the terms of his father's will, Arthur Ronald Tree must live in America. *May 20, 1920*

FIELD, HICKSON W. has recently purchased in Rome a portion of ground, including the ruins of the Baths of Titus, and is erecting a palace that will be in size and splendor the marvel of its time. The grounds are already converted into a Garden of Eden, and the views commanded from different portions of them include many of the finest ruins of Rome, the Coliseum being almost within their gates. The only child of Mr. and Mrs. Field has married Prince Brancaccio. Though Mrs. Field has resided seventeen years abroad, she retains the most vivid remembrances of her friends in America, and is always ready to give them a hearty welcome in her Italian home. In this respect, she presents a pleasing contrast to many of our country people, whose heads and hearts have been strangely displaced by association with titles, and are only the ridicule of the society, for they all but ignore associates of their earlier years. *March 9, 1881*

FIELD, MARSHALL I Chicago people were greatly affected by the death of Mr. Marshall Field. The great stores which bear his name were closed from the time of his death until the day after his burial, and for an hour all of the large retail stores, together with innumerable other concerns, were closed. The Board of Trade, of which he was a member, suspended all business. Mr. Field was born at Conway, Massachusetts, in 1835. In 1856, he traveled westward to Chicago. He was first the junior partner and then senior partner in the house which became, in 1865, Field, Palmer & Leiter. In 1881, Mr. Field became the head of Marshall Field & Co., having the largest wholesale and dry goods business in the world. *January 27, 1906*

FIELD, MARSHALL III, who was educated at Eton, and early in life, while living on his parents' estate near Leamington, England, learned all the fine points of horsemanship, has been practising polo almost daily at Meadow Brook. Recently, his nineteen polo ponies were turned loose in the stretches of forest land encircling his vast country estate, now in the process of development at Lloyd's Neck on Long Island. *September 1, 1914*

FIELD, MRS. MARSHALL III (EVELYN MARSHALL) The Dramatic Committee of the Arts Club presented George Bernard Shaw's *How He Lied to Her Husband.* Interest centered in the appearance of Mrs. Marshall Field III as the wife. Mrs. Field scored a real success. She was not only letter-perfect in her part—an achievement rather rare in amateur theatricals—but she did some actual acting, and her enunciation was clear. Her beauty helped, to be sure, but it was not all. *March 10, 1920*

FIELD, MARSHALL V He's been civically active in Chicago since he arrived there in the mid-sixties to succeed his late father. Today, he devotes half his workday to his role as President of the board of The Art Institute of Chicago. In 1979, Field and Chicago's Crown family jointly funded the Crown-Field Education Center at Chicago's Lincoln Park Zoo—where, in gratitude for Marshall's generosity, a rhinoceros has been named for him. *December, 1989*

FIELD, MARY STUART Stockbridge, in the Berkshires, will have its eyes wide open to see all that it can of the wedding of Miss Mary Stuart Field and Mr. Edmund Clarke. As a granddaughter of Jonathan Edwards Field, the

FIELD

Mr. Marshall Field and Marshall Field, Jr., 1923.

In 1905, a year before his death, Marshall Field, America's merchant prince, was also the United States' largest individual taxpayer. The secret of his success: "Give the lady what she wants," he decreed, at the largest and one of the most innovative stores in the world.

As a boy, Marshall Field worked as an apprentice at a dry-goods store in Massachusetts. When he moved to Chicago in 1856, he became junior partner in a department store with Levi Leiter and Potter Palmer, whom he eventually bought out. Courtly but frosty in manner, Marshall Field lived modestly. His wife, with whom he was on distant terms, stayed mostly in the countryside in England, as did their two children and most of their grandchildren.

Two months after his only son died from a gunshot wound that may have been self-inflicted, Marshall Field died himself. The 22,000-word will he left was a masterpiece of lawyerly caution, tying up funds for his two grandsons, Marshall III and Henry, then age twelve and eight, for the next thirty-nine years. The estate was valued between $100 and $150 million. Field had donated the land for the new University of Chicago and left $8 million to build the Field Museum of Natural History along Lake Michigan.

Marshall Field III, hailed by newspapers as "the richest boy

in the world," returned to the United States, but not to Chicago, in 1914, at age twenty-one. He and his first wife, Evelyn Marshall, settled down on nearly 2,000 acres in the sporting country of Long Island.

In middle age, Marshall III suddenly gave up business interests to devote himself to social causes and the establishing of liberal newspapers, first *PM* in New York and then, on his return to Chicago, the *Sun*, which he started in 1941 and later merged with the *Chicago Times*.

Criticized during the 1930s for supporting liberal causes while enjoying vast inherited wealth, he once angrily said, "I happen to have a great deal of money; I don't know what is going to happen to it, and I don't give a damn." Asked for a comment, the usually reticent John D. Rockefeller, Jr., replied, "I don't care what happens to Marshall Field's money, but I do care what happens to mine."

Marshall Field V, great-great-grandson of the family founder and past president of the Art Institute of Chicago, is the last male Field in Chicago. He and his half brother, Frederick W. ("Ted") Field, disbanded the family's publishing business in 1983. Ted, who lives in California, established Interscope Corporation, a film production company, and contributes to environmental causes.

Merchandise and manners: *far left*, Mrs. Marshall Field, Jr., and Marshall III in 1918; *left*, Mrs. Marshall Field III, 1933; *below, from left*, Jamee, Stephanie, Abby Field and their parents, Mr. and Mrs. Marshall Field V, in 1990.

bride is likewise a descendant of the Calvinist Jonathan Edwards, who wrote his *Freedom of the Will* in the Berkshires. All the famous Fields spent part of their life in Stockbridge. *June 18, 1904*

FIELD, WILLIAM BRADHURST OSGOOD Cricket and baseball still survive in Lenox, Massachusetts, and seldom a game of either is played that does not bring Mr. W. B. Osgood Field into action, just as golf and tennis do. At baseball, he has become renowned as the captain of the "Elm Court" team, composed of employees of Mr. William Douglas Sloane's great estate. When it comes to cricket, Elm Court is just the place for games of this sort, and Mr. Sloane is one of the few country gentlemen who would give up a large portion of very beautiful lawn for such purposes. *October 1, 1904*

FINDLAY, JOHN VAN LEAR His oratorical powers, well displayed in Congress, date, perhaps, from "Maryland Day," at the Centennial Exhibition in 1876, when he was the official orator for his state. His uncle was John King Findlay, the jurist, while William Findlay, Governor of Pennsylvania, was also his relative. *October 27, 1906*

FINLEY, MR. AND MRS. DAVID (MARGARET MORTON EUSTIS) "Oatlands," another National Trust property in Leesburg, Virginia, was the donation of the David Finleys. He was the first director of the National Gallery of Art and founder of the National Trust for Historic Preservation; she is the former Margaret Morton Eustis, an heiress of Washington's first philanthropist, William Wilson Corcoran, who gave Washington the Corcoran Gallery of Art. *September, 1975*

FIRESTONE, A. BROOKS Although there were a few small, respected vineyards in the Santa Ynez Valley, not until Firestone dropped out of the family business and turned his hand to growing grapes on 300 acres above Los Olivos did the local wines gain national attention. The Firestone Vineyard has the gold medals and the sales, both here and abroad, to prove that the valley is productive. *June, 1984*

FISH, HAMILTON For eleven years he was a member of the New York Assembly and Speaker thereof in 1895–96. Always an ardent Republican, he went to Congress from the Twenty-first New York District in 1909–1911. The Fish family is one of the most distinguished and notable in New York. Its country headquarters is at Garrison's, where generation after generation have held a position similar to that of an English county family. Around the little Episcopal Church there are monuments to the many members who have been known to fame in the past century. The founder of the fortunes was named Preserved Fish, because he, as a small child, was cast up by the sea. The great shipping house of Fish & Grinnell, and afterwards Grinnell & Minturn, was a power in the first half of the nineteenth century in New York. *May 11, 1912*

FISH, HAMILTON III There is something singularly pathetic in the death of Hamilton Fish, third, the young man who was killed by Spanish bullets in the Spanish-American War.

He was of athletic build, and this, with his youth, tempted him into various predicaments, sometimes involving physical force for their solution but usually ending favorably to Fish. Hitherto, he has been heard of not perhaps so much in polite society as in the college athletic field, and as a boyish culprit in the local police courts. But, in enlisting and in meeting death, he has written his name in United States history, and has added lustre to the ancestry of the famous family whence he springs. *June 29, 1898*

ON LAND, ON SEA

The only hostess who gave a dinner with a spectacular table arrangement this summer at Newport was Mrs. Stuyvesant Fish. The center of the table was arranged so that a tank and a miniature lake could be placed there, and among the ferns and the aquatic plants there were gold-fish swimming and little yachts sailing, which bore the names of the contesting boats in the recent trials to choose the *America*'s Cup defender. *August 8, 1903*

FISH, HAMILTON IV Col. Nicholas Fish, an officer in the Continental Army, fought at Saratoga and Yorktown and became New York's first Adjutant General. Nicholas' son, Hamilton Fish I, became a New York Representative and Governor as well as U.S. Senator and Secretary of State. His son, Hamilton Fish II, was speaker of the New York Assembly before becoming a Representative, and his son, Hamilton Fish, held the same House seat as his forefathers for twenty five years. Congressman Fish remains committed to the family's five-generation tradition of public service. "I have been a banker, a lawyer, and a foreign service officer, but nothing is as fulfilling as being in Congress." *October, 1986*

FISH, MRS. NICHOLAS (CLEMENCE SMITH BRYCE) was the widow of the diplomat and banker, who died in New York in September, 1902, and the mother of Hamilton Fish, who lost his life in Cuba during the Spanish-American War. She married Nicholas Fish at Newport, Rhode Island, about the time that he was appointed Second Secretary to the United States Legation at Berlin. He was Chargé d'Affaires to the Swiss Confederation (1877–81) and United States Minister to Belgium in 1882–86. In 1887, Mr. and Mrs. Fish returned to New York and took a cottage at Tuxedo. *December 19, 1908*

FISH, STUYVESANT "The chief reason for forming the Knickerbocker Greys was to keep Satan from finding mischief for our idle hands," wrote Stuyvesant Fish, one of the original company. The Knickerbocker Greys was founded on the rather hopeful premise that a son's dream of glory on the battlefield could perpetuate a mother's dream of drawing room civility. *May, 1981*

FISH, MRS. STUYVESANT (MARION ANTHON) has been quoted as desiring to dispose of "The Crossways," a beautiful Newport property only recently built and already the scene of many delightful entertainments. Mrs. Fish

says, "I have determined that in order to entertain properly and to have just the degree of exclusiveness one desires, it is the proper thing to have a big estate. I have plenty of ground here, but that is not what I want. And, besides, I think that Newport is becoming too contracted for the society of the future. It is becoming too much a place for people to come who want to break into society." *August 1, 1903*

FISHER, ALFRED JOSEPH III Scion of the Fisher Body family, he is an enthusiastic polo player and member of the Georgetown Polo Team. Fisher loves good food (he's a member of The Fussers, a select Washington gourmet group), hunts and has shot bear in the wilds of Canada. *June, 1968*

FISHER, DR. JOHN RUSH STREETT won the Maryland Hunt Cup twice; his grandfather rode in 1924; his uncle William B. Streett finished second or third five times; and another uncle and cousin, Janon Fisher, Jr. and Janon Fisher III, almost retired the Hunt Cup with Mountain Dew. His wife Dolly's grandfather won three times with his horse Garry Owen at the beginning of the century, and her father owned an entry. Her uncle rode in the race five times and owned a winner. *May, 1979*

FISHER, MRS. WILLIAM (JUSTINE VAN DEN HEUVEL) Her grandfather was Gouverneur Bibby, who married a daughter of John C. Van den Heuvel, the site of whose country home, the last of the old-time mansions on Broadway, was that on which the new Astor apartment house was erected. John C. Van den Heuvel was at one time Governor of British Guiana. *September 26, 1908*

FISHER, MRS. WILLIAM A. (CHARLOTTE C. BAYLOR) The Baylors have a name interwoven with that of Virginia. It was George Baylor of Virginia who, as aide-de-camp to Washington, participated in the surprise of the Hessians at Trenton and carried the news to Congress. *October 27, 1906*

FITCH, JUDGE JOHN, a member of the Society of Cincinnati and various New York clubs, died in his seventieth year. He was a descendant of Governor Fitch of Connecticut and the Livingstons of this state, a picturesque figure in New York society whose uncouth ways and gruff speech disguised many sterling qualities. A man of the old school, he, in the broad daylight of our city streets, still wore the dress-coat of "ye olden times." *September 4, 1889*

FLAGLER, HENRY M. began life in Republic, Ohio, where he worked in a grocery. After several reverses, he was backed by money put up by a relative and went into the oil business with the Rockefellers. This was the basis of his enormous fortune. He was Vice President of the Standard Oil Company until 1908, when he retired. For a quarter of a century, he has been devoted to Florida, and he has spent over fifty millions there. He created Palm Beach. He invested twelve millions in hotels, eighteen into oil railroads, and a million in steamships. *May 31, 1913*

FLAGLER, MRS. HENRY M. (MARY LILY KENAN) Standard Oilman Henry Flagler, builder of Palm Beach, built "Whitehall" for his third wife. Even Mrs. Flagler's closet was a house in itself. She had several hundred dresses and several hundred hats, not one of which, she liked to boast, she ever wore twice. She also boasted she could have fifty guests for dinner each night in the week and never use a single item of service twice. *February, 1962*

FLEISCHMAN, JULIUS, millionaire sportsman and well-known businessman, died at Miami, Florida, at the age of fifty three, while playing polo. For years, the Fleischman Bakery maintained the Fleischman bread line at Broadway and Eleventh Street, where homeless men were fed. Mr. Fleischman had an extensive place at Sands Point, Long Island, which was the polo-playing rendezvous of the British contenders for the International Polo Cup and where the Prince of Wales was frequently a visitor. *March 1, 1925*

FLEISCHMANN, COLONEL AND MRS. MAX, of Cincinnati, since their return from their wedding journey to the Arctic regions, have related thrilling experiences with ice packs and a leaky boat. They had great luck with big game and brought home many trophies, two live bear cubs being among them. The Fleischmanns are now planning a season in South Africa in pursuit of big game. *October 20, 1906*

FLETCHER, HENRY P. is the recently-appointed Ambassador to Mexico. Mr. Fletcher's last diplomatic appointment was to Chile, as Minister and later as Ambassador. Fletcher sprang into prominence overnight over the matter of the famous Hu-Kwang loan. He was the first American diplomat to realize that the United States had something to do with the business and future of China. *May 20, 1916*

FLINT, ANNIE, the daughter of Dr. Austin Flint, Sr., is one of those young women of fine mind who do so much to refute the once popular notion that girls born to good social position have thought only for the lighter pleasures of life. Miss Flint, through her mother, is a relative of the old Smith family of Ballston Spa, New York, and a cousin of the Countess of Strafford. Since the appearance this spring of her successful book, *A Girl of Ideas,* she has written a charming little volume of children's stories. *November 28, 1903*

FLOOD, JAMES C. He is descended from James Flood, 1870's Bonanza king. His grandmother is listed in the phone book as simply and imperiously, "Mrs. Flood." Stanford '61, and currently working at Wells Fargo Bank, Jim is Treasurer of The Bachelors of San Francisco. *June, 1964*

FLOYD-JONES, MR. AND MRS. EDWARD HENRY (EDITH CARPENDER) She is related to the Lispenards, who descend from Leonard Lispenard, the Huguenot. Several streets in New York were named after the early representatives of this family: Leonard, Anthony (now Worth), and Thomas Streets were named after three of the brothers. The bridegroom is a descendant of Richard Floyd, whose family was famous in Suffolk County. One of the later Floyds married a daughter of Judge David Jones, and, for reasons of inheritance, the name of the wife took precedence over that of her husband. By the inversion of the name, the great estate at Fort Neck, Long Island, came into the Floyd family. *December 2, 1905*

FOLGER, HENRY C. accumulated his fortune in Standard Oil of New Jersey and of New York. In his youth at Amherst College, he had become ardently devoted to Shakespeare. So that it was not primarily as a collector but as a Shakespeare lover that he began the accumulation of the greatest Shakespeare treasure in the world. His buying went on through his long life. As quietly as he had made his collection, Mr. Folger during the past few years had bought various "parcels" of land on Capitol Hill, where he intended to house it. *November 15, 1930*

FOLSOM, ETHEL Those who predicted that Miss Ethel Folsom, daughter of Mr. and Mrs. George Folsom of New York, would tire after a season or so of her philanthropic project, a sanitarium for women convalescents from New York hospitals that she established near Lenox, apparently little understood how absolutely wrapped up in this project was its promoter. Last month, Miss Folsom opened the sanitarium for its fourth season, and there, forsaking the allurements of the brilliant social life among the hills, she will devote the entire season in caring for the comfort of those sent out to regain health amid delightful surroundings. *July 1, 1905*

FORBES, MALCOLM, Chairman of the Board and Editor-in-chief of *Forbes* magazine, is an obsessive collector. His eight major collection areas are housed in three museums which are open to the public, and they could not be grander or more personal. The Château de Balleroy in Normandy is both the family's French residence and a museum of ballooning; the Palais Mendoub in Tangier, Morocco, is an Arabian Nights palace staffed with Forbes' standing army of 70,000 toy soldiers; while Battersea House in London, the Forbes' London home, is a repository of Victorian art. Forbes set six ballooning records and won the Harmon trophy as Aeronaut of the Year in 1975, before his life insurance company put a stop to his exploits. Now his trips are limited to an occasional joy ride at his New Jersey home and to the ballooning festival at Château de Balleroy every June. *March, 1982*

FORBES, MURRAY, a member of Boston's prestigious Forbes family, is the oldest son in eight generations of oldest sons. Forbes is founder of the Navigator Foundation, an organization that presents exhibitions of Eastern European art, music, and film. "I began my odyssey to Eastern Europe in 1972," he says. "I then won a painting fellowship in Cracow, and while there became involved in creating an awareness of the culture." *February, 1987*

FORBES, WILLIAM CAMERON This stern, amazingly fit bachelor of nearly seventy, former Governor of the Philippines, grandson of Ralph Waldo Emerson, is now Chief of the Long-Tail Forbeses. (The Forbes clan almost split up fifty years ago over the question of docking their horses' tails.) Naushon, Massachusetts, an island of hills and forest seven miles long and one and a half miles wide, became Forbes property when Cameron's great-uncle Swain took title to the island in 1843 with John Murray Forbes, Cameron's other grandfather. Now, there are sixteen family houses on the island, all filled with Forbes sons and daughters and their children. The "Mansion House" is the feudal hub of the island. The Governor, a rigid martinet as well as a patriarch, runs Naushon almost as if it were the Philippines. *October, 1939*

FORD, ANNE AND CHARLOTTE The most highly publicized coming-out parties in recent years were the two lavish parties Henry Ford II gave for his daughters, Anne and Charlotte. Charlotte's Grosse Pointe debut in December 1959 was characterized by the press as "The Party of the Century." It cost about $250,000. Paris decorator Jacques Frank worked months to turn The Country Club of Detroit into a fairyland, with precious French tapestries on the walls, crimson carpets, and duplicates of a marbled Grecian room, the garden of Versailles, and a medieval castle. In January 1961, the Fords repeated with another for daughter Anne. There were 50,000 roses in tiny glass tubes. (The flowers had been planted a year before on Long Island, and it required 270 man-hours to place the roses alone.) *June, 1962*

FORD, HENRY II A more conspicuous show place is Henry Ford's 227-acre estate in Water Mill, Long Island, recently sold for close on $2 million. This figure, neighbors say, was a bargain, considering the artificial lake Ford built to insure privacy, the two-story entrance hall, the library paneled in eighteenth-century *boiserie,* a wildlife preserve, and a mammoth thirty-by-sixty-foot pool with pool house, patio, and four levels of gardens spilling down to the ocean. "We used to spend all day," said one of Ford's sisters-in-law, "sitting around in wet bathing suits." *July, 1975*

FORD, PAUL LEICESTER A social event of general interest was the marriage of Miss Grace Kidder to the popular novelist Mr. Paul Leicester Ford. Mr. and Mrs. Ford will occupy their new home in the "court end of town"—37 East Seventy Seventh Street—as soon as it is completed. It is a wide house with light on all sides. A unique feature is a room for the storage of automobiles on the street floor. *September 27, 1900*

FORD, STELLA DUNBAR is known as Detroit's "Lady Bountiful." Her large fortune was left to her by her father, the late E. Leyden Ford, Sr., son of the man who made the Ford millions in the glass industry in Pittsburgh and Toledo. Miss Ford has been noted for her judicious donations of huge sums to charitable and civic movements. She has given much to the anti-tuberculosis campaign and presented the civic government with twenty five specially constructed drinking fountains for horses and dogs. *May 2, 1914*

FISH

In 1928: Mrs. Sydney W. Fish, one of the famous Wiborg sisters.

In the Gilded Age of the nineteenth century, two tireless and inventive hostesses, Mrs. William B. Astor and Mrs. Stuyvesant Fish, ruled Society in New York. Born Marion Anthon, of a distinguished New York family of professors and lawyers, "Mamie" Fish remained on visiting but distant terms with her rival; Caroline Astor regarded Mamie as a decidedly disintegrating social force. Unabashed and unretiring, Mamie Fish inspired fear among her less entertaining dinner guests with her cutting remarks. Aided by Harry Lehr, a champagne salesman who was the professional jester of her set, she shook up New York and Newport society by reducing the length of dinners from the customary three hours to exactly fifty minutes. She varied the usual cotillions with circus, vaudeville, and farmyard galas, and once dressed Western Union telegraph boys as cupids for a "heavenly party."

According to one of the most widely trafficked anecdotes of the time, Mamie Fish once gave a dinner for an Italian "Prince del Drago," who turned out to be a formally dressed monkey. (The editors of *Town & Country,* with whom Mrs. Stuyvesant Fish was a great favorite, stoutly denied that the dinner ever took place.)

Mr. Stuyvesant Fish abstained from Society, insofar as his wife would let him. *Town & Country* noted in 1910 that he had "little part in society, so far as it means cotillion-leading or trying to win loving-cups or blue ribbons at sports." He did like,

though, to build bonfires on holidays for the enjoyment of guests.

Stuyvesant Fish also abstained from the politics that engaged most of his relations; instead, he was president of the Illinois Central Railroad, a position usually held by gentlemen of impeccable social credentials. Politics, both before and after Stuyvesant Fish, has been the family's primary business. Descended both from New York's Dutch Governor Peter Stuyvesant and from Robert Livingston, first Lord of Livingston Manor, their record of public service has been characterized by a startling longevity. Nicholas Fish, a soldier in the American Revolution, was the first adjutant general of the state of New York. In direct line, Hamilton Fish I served as governor of New York (in 1849), U.S. senator and secretary of state; he also acted as president-general of the Society of the Cincinnati, an aristocratic group limited to male descendants of French and American officers in the American Revolution. He lived to be eighty-five. Hamilton II was also a congressman from New York; he lived to age eighty-seven. Hamilton III, also a congressman, survived to be 103. In 1986, *Town & Country* noted that he introduced himself as "a man who talked to a man who talked to Lafayette." His son Hamilton, the fifth generation in public service, as a member of Congress served in the 1974 Nixon impeachment hearings. At present, there is no Hamilton Fish in the House of Representatives. Members of the family continue to reside in upstate New York.

Party-givers and public servants:
clockwise from top left,
the redoubtable Mrs. Stuyvesant Fish in 1914;
Hamilton Fish, Sr., and Jr., 1986;
Mr. and Mrs. Stuyvesant Fish, Jr.
and their 1910 bridal attendants;
a young Janet Fish in 1905.

FRELINGHUYSEN

Horse show goer Theodore Frelinghuysen in 1911.

The Frelinghuysens came to New Jersey to convert and remained to represent. The Reverend Theodorus Jacobus Frelinghuysen, a pastor of the Dutch Reformed Church who was called "the Apostle of the Raritan," settled in 1720 in Somerville, New Jersey—an area represented in Congress in this century by Peter H. B. Frelinghuysen, Theodorus Jacobus's great-great-great-great-great-grandson, and, today, his son, Rodney P. Frelinghuysen. Half a dozen members of the family have been U.S. senators, mayors of New Jersey cities, and state attorneys-general.

Theodorus Jacobus was a combative evangelist who alienated members of his congregation by dwelling at loving length on their sins. He painted his sleigh with the slogan "No man's tongue and no one's pen / Can make me other than I am." His five sons and two sons-in-law became ministers of the Dutch Reformed Church as well. One daughter, Maria Frelinghuysen Cornell, was an early temperance advocate and founder of the Sober Society in Allentown, Pennsylvania.

Theodorus Jacobus's grandson, Frederick, was the first Frelinghuysen to put politics before God. Regarded as the leading Dutch-American at a time when the Dutch comprised about one-sixth of the American population, he became a member of the Continental Congress and a U.S. senator from New Jersey in 1793. Since then, there has always been a New Jersey Frelinghuysen on the political horizon.

The second Frelinghuysen U.S. senator was Theodore, Frederick's son, who also ran for vice-president of the United States as the running mate of Henry Clay. Their slogan: "Hurrah! Hurrah! The country's risin' / For Henry Clay and Frelinghuysen." Senator Theodore was true to the religious traditions of his family: he kept a Bible by his razor so he could meditate on a text while he shaved, and his main legislative program in Congress, where he was known as the "Christian statesman," was trying (unsuccessfully) to prevent the delivery of mail on Sunday. He eventually became chancellor of New York University.

Through the generations, Frelinghuysens have successfully forged family alliances with other political and financial dynasties. Theodore's daughter, Sarah Helen Frelinghuysen, married John Davis, grandson of a Massachusetts senator; their daughter, Matilda Davis, wed the son of Massachusetts Senator Henry Cabot Lodge. George Griswold Frelinghuysen's marriage to Sarah Ballantine tied the family to the brewing dynasty; their son, Peter H. B. Frelinghuysen's wedding to Adaline Havemeyer brought "Sugar Trust" funding. Of cousin Suzy Frelinghuysen Morris, an operatic soprano, her husband once explained: "She is descended from a long line of bluenosed Dutch clergymen who would jointly turn in their graves at the spectacle of their scion portraying ladies of such dubious reputation as Salome, Tosca, and Santuzza."

Frelinghuysens, past and present:
clockwise from top left,
Los Angeles' George Frelinghuysen, 1974;
Mrs. Frederick T. Frelinghuysen
in 1917; in 1986, Peter H. B.
Frelinghuysen and his son, Rodney.

FORRESTAL, JAMES V The Secretary of the Navy, a broker and banker who in his Princeton days was an amateur boxer, once said that his hobby was "obscurity." He is brilliant, serious, and one of the hardest-working men in the Capital. He disapproves of frivolity in wartime and hates dressing up at any time. *August, 1944*

FOSTER, JOHN W., known as the "Dean of the American Diplomatic Corps," was the first professional diplomatist produced by the Foreign Service of the United States. He began practising law in Evansville, Indiana, in 1856. His first diplomatic service was rendered in 1873, when General Grant appointed him Minister to Mexico. He became Secretary of State in 1892. *December 1, 1917*

FOX, JOSEPH M. is a descendant of James Logan, the eminent statesman of Scotch-Irish parentage. In 1699, James Logan came to America with William Penn, as his secretary. After an active life and a term as a Mayor of Philadelphia, he spent his last years at his country seat, "Stenton," now a part of Philadelphia. Botanists named plants in his honor, and scientists all regarded him with great reverence. *October 29, 1904*

FRANCIS, CHARLES S. was proprietor of the *Troy Times* and late Ambassador to Austria-Hungary. His diplomatic career began as secretary to his father, who was United States Minister to Greece. From 1900 to 1902, he was Envoy Extraordinary and Minister Plenipotentiary to Greece, Rumania, and Serbia. *December 9, 1911*

FRANCKLYN, DORIS was the center of an adoring bevy of debutantes when she made her first appearance as an author. Her little operetta, "Flora-Florizel," is a clever story of the Queen of the Fairies, who, through love, becomes a mortal woman and forsakes her throne for a man. The imagery is certainly quaint and beautiful. After the performance, there was a storm of applause from the audience. There were repeated cries for the author, led by Miss Gladys Vanderbilt, who was also the first to pelt Miss Doris with her violets when the young girl stepped out on the stage. *April 1, 1905*

FRASER, MRS. HUGH, who is the originator of the Japanese entertainment to be given at the Belasco Theater, is not only the sister of a well-known novlist—Marion Crawford—but the daughter of the late Thomas Crawford, the noted sculptor. So Mrs. Fraser, who is the widow of the late British envoy to Japan, has knowledge of the truly beautiful and talent inherited from a sculptor. The entertainment promises to be so poetic and beautiful that people whose principles forbid their endorsing charity for the Japanese may quiet their consciences by going for a purely selfish purpose. *May 6, 1905*

FRAZER, MR. AND MRS. PERSIFOR II planned an intimate debut for their daughter, Elizabeth (Bettina), at "Oakwood," their Newport estate, on July 26, 1941, but the guest list mushroomed to 600 people. Meyer Davis played toe-tapping melodies, there was a gypsy string orchestra, and a piano player in an Uncle Sam outfit played boogie-woogie on a Tom Thumb piano that floated on an improvised island in the swimming pool. *July, 1965*

FRAZIER, BRENDA, the most important Glamour Girl of 1938 and of all time, hit a high-water mark of debutante bedazzlement that hasn't been equaled since. Brenda came into $4,000,000 at the age of twenty-one. She was not the richest, most pedigreed, or most beautiful of the 1938 debs. But she was a nice combination of the three and had, besides a dead-white complexion and slashing dark-red lips, a very photogenic way with cameramen. Brenda became a national institution, turned down a possible screen career, and enjoyed highly publicized romances with artist Peter Arno and Italian playboy Piero Mele. She went on to marry John Simms "Shipwreck" Kelly, former football player, and, later, Thomas Chatfield-Taylor. *June, 1962*

FOR THE LOVE OF SPORT

Childs Frick, the only son of Mr. Henry C. Frick of Pittsburgh and Pride's Crossing and New York, has recently sailed from London at the head of an expedition to Abyssinia for the purpose of making natural history collections for the Smithsonian Institution. The work will occupy about seven months. The explorers will go through a country said to be infested with hostile tribes and rampant with disease. Mr. Childs Frick is a noted polo player and is as adept in many outdoor sports. *January 13, 1912*

FREEMAN, JOHN The engagement is announced of Mlle. Beatrice de Béarn, daughter of Prince Henri Gallard de Béarn, to Mr. Freeman, the son of the late Mr. William Freeman. He is an American, but through his mother, who was Princess Marie de Bourbon Braganza, he has a most romantic history. Moreover, Mlle. de Béarn is half-American, her mother having been the beautiful Beatrice Winans, daughter of the late Mr. Ross Winans, of Baltimore. *February 15, 1926*

FREER, CHARLES L., the art collector of Detroit, was born at Kingston, New York. He made his money in railroads and manufacturing in Detroit, retiring from active business in 1900. From that time on, his interest lay in the search and discovery of art objects. He travelled to the Far East, to Egypt and to the most remote places. In 1915, he made the announcement that he had sold his entire collection to the Smithsonian Institute at Washington, for the sum of one dollar. At the same time, he announced he would provide a million dollar art gallery to house the collection. It is said to include 5,000 objects in all. *October 20, 1919*

FRELINGHUYSEN, MRS. FREDERICK (ESTELLE B. KINNEY) The marriage was celebrated at "Woodside Hall," the country seat of the bride's mother, Mrs. Thomas Talmadge Kinney. Mr. Frelinghuysen owns a large estate at "Oakhurst," near Elberon, New Jersey, and his retinue of servants as well as those belonging to the Kinney ménage were served with a hearty repast in the barn. *August 2, 1902*

FRELINGHUYSEN, MRS. FREDERICK (MAI D. WATSON) It is nothing unusual to have breakfast in Newport and hop, as they say, down to New York for lunch. The airline is proving a great success, and Mrs. Freddie Frelinghuysen, who is always among those to do things first, was one of the first women passengers. *August 1, 1923*

FRELINGHUYSEN, MR. AND MRS. HENRY O. H. (MARIAN C. KINGSLAND)—SEHERR—THOSS In 1720, the Dutch Reformed Church sent an evangelist, Reverend Theodorus Frelinghuysen, to New Jersey, and he, in turn, founded one of America's great political dynasties. Marian, married to the twin brother of former Congressman Peter, has decorated an 1800 farmhouse on Rattlesnake Bridge Road, Far Hills. She also owns a chalet in Gstaad. *June, 1986*

FREMONT, REAR ADMIRAL JOHN C., U.S.N. was a son of the late John C. Fremont, famous as a soldier and explorer. Rear Admiral Fremont commanded the *Porter* during the war with Spain, and was one of the most distinguished flag officers in the Navy. His mother, Jessie Benton Fremont, who was a daughter of Senator Thomas H. Benton, was well known as an author. *March 18, 1911*

FRENCH, MRS. SETH BARTON, at a Colonial Ball in Newport, wore a white satin petticoat draped in old lace and pink roses, with a train and bodice of pompadour brocade. She also wore, among other ornaments, a locket, on one side containing hair of George Washington and on the other that of Richard Henry Lee, an ancestor of Mrs. French; also a miniature of General Lee, both of which were family relics. *August 30, 1902*

FRENCH, MRS. STUYVESANT LEROY (MAUD COSTER)—SALM—HOPE "We don't live in any kind of grandeur here. We don't want to," remarks Mrs. Stuyvesant French, ninety-year-old grande dame of Tuxedo. "Tuxedo is a very unpretentious place. There are some people who move here and try to be pretentious, but they don't last." *May, 1984*

FRICK, HELEN CLAY Helen's father, Henry Clay Frick, dominated Pittsburgh's coke industry during the Carnegie era; when he died in 1919, she inherited $38 million, which she subsequently expanded through canny business dealings. She established the Frick Collection in New York in memory of her father, whom she worshipped. *December, 1983*

FRICK, HENRY CLAY was an art collector and one of the country's greatest financiers, who is said to have spent over $10,000,000 in the collection of paintings and art objects. He was born in West Overton, Westmoreland County, Pennsylvania, in 1849. He started his career as a dry goods clerk and later became a bookkeeper in his grandfather's distillery at Broad Ford. His real start was marked from the time he began acquiring small tracts of land and to try coke making. In 1871, he organized the firm of Frick and Company. *December 20, 1919*

FROTHINGHAM, REV. PAUL is one of the shining exceptions to the rule that there are few brilliant preachers among the younger generation of ministers. A member of a distinguished Boston family, this namesake and descendant of the man whom Longfellow has immortalized in "Paul Revere's Ride" weekly fills the spacious Arlington Street Church with an attentive audience such as few of Boston's large churches can boast. *July 8, 1905*

FULLER, MRS. HENRY BROWN (LUCIA FAIRCHILD) Her little portraits on ivory have been getting a good share of popular approval from the throngs who have been visiting Knoedler's during the annual exhibition of The American Society of Miniature Painters. Mrs. Fuller, now the wife of the landscape painter, was a prominent society girl of Boston who preferred art and an artist to the conventional pleasures of society and the more conventional society husband. *February 6, 1904*

FULLER, MELVILLE WESTON, eighth Chief Justice of the Supreme Court of the United States, was a grandson of Judge Henry Wild Fuller, a friend and associate of Daniel Webster, and, on the maternal side, of Nathan Weston, Associate Justice of the Supreme Court of Maine. While still a young man, he went to Chicago. In 1862, he was a member of the convention to revise the Illinois constitution. His defense of Bishop Charles Edward Cheney against the charge of Canonical disobedience brought him much fame. Chief Justice Fuller was twice married and was the father of eight daughters. *July 9, 1910*

FURNESS, DR. HORACE HOWARD was a lawyer and considered one of the first Shakespearian authorities in the country. His father, the Rev. William Henry Furness, was pastor of the First Unitarian Church of Philadelphia. Dr. Furness was admitted to the Bar in 1859 and immediately devoted himself to the study of Shakespeare. In 1871, he brought out the first volume of a new variorum edition designed to summarize the conclusions of the best authorities in all languages. He also served on the Seybert commission for investigating modern spiritualism. *September 7, 1912*

G

GALE, MR. AND MRS. THOMAS BRUTON are from the South, but have long been identified with New York's "Southern colony." Mr. Gale comes from Mobile, Alabama, and Mrs. Gale from Montgomery. She is a great-granddaughter of Andrew Dexter, the founder of Montgomery. *February 20, 1904*

GALLATIN, CORNELIA LANSDALE, a great-granddaughter of Albert Gallatin, Secretary of the Treasury under Presidents Jefferson and Madison and afterwards Minister to France and to England, married Mr. Alfred Fitz Roy Anderson, a direct descendant of King Edward I and the early Princes of Wales; in Grace Church, New York City. *May 15, 1924*

GALLAUDET, REV. HERBERT DRAPER is a member of a famous family. His grandfather was the late Thomas Hopkins Gallaudet, who made the education of deaf mutes his life work and who established his first school in Hartford, Connecticut. Sophia Fowler, later his wife, was one of his pupils. Dr. Edward Miner Gallaudet, his son, established The Columbian Institution in Washington for the deaf, dumb, and blind. An uncle, the Rev. Thomas Gallaudet, founded St. Ann's Church for deaf-mutes in New York. *August 28, 1909*

GAMBRILL, RICHARD is a wealthy young man who is just beginning to go in society. His father was from Baltimore, and he died while the boy was a small child. His mother was a Miss Van Nest. Her fortune is derived from street railroad stocks, the family having had large holdings in the old Sixth Avenue horse car line. Mrs. Gambrill has kept her son away from Newport as much as possible, but he is studious and ambitious and has not as yet cared for society. *August 19, 1911*

GARDINER, DOANE At North East Harbor, Maine, beautiful tableaux were given at the Parish House for the benefit of the athletic field. Mr. Doane Gardiner, as Merlin, the magician of King Arthur's court, invoked each passion, such as "Despair," "Jealousy," "Hate," "Love," and "Charity," represented by different young ladies, who recited appropriate lines. *September 2, 1905*

GARDINER, MRS. J. LYON (ELIZABETH C. JONES) —LIVINGSTON will spend a great part of the summer at "The Manor," Gardiner's Island. The Gardiner homestead is associated with much of historic interest, and in the house there are many relics and heirlooms. A cloth of gold, presented by Captain Kidd to the mistress of the manor, has been divided into pieces, each representative of the family owning a part. The house is very lonely in its situation, almost hidden by tall trees, and there is no social life there excepting when Mrs. Gardiner entertains. *April 19, 1902*

GARDINER, ROBERT DAVID LION, present Lord of the Manor of Gardiner's Island, differs from many of the old families' descendants in that he happily displays his wealth. It is not unusual for Mr. Gardiner to accost total strangers on a Long Island Sound ferry and pull out a twenty-carat diamond from his pocket or brag about how much IBM he owns. He is a member of fourteen clubs, owns five big houses, speaks six languages, knows everything about eighteenth-century art. Has a smashing young wife and $27,000,000 of IBM stock. *September, 1973*

GARDINER, MR. AND MRS. WINTHROP (ISABEL T. LEMMON) Under the auspices of the Committee of the Historical Round Table, a pageant setting forth the Colonial Days in Old New York was beautifully presented. Captain Kidd brought two direct descendants of the Gardiner family into the cast for that episode—Mr. and Mrs. Winthrop Gardiner and Isabel Gardiner. The programme contained an insert of historical interest, in an itemized list of the contents of Captain

William Kidd's famous treasure chests, which list is in the possession of Mr. Winthrop Gardiner, descendant of the Gardiners, who originally occupied Gardiner's Island at the time Captain Kidd arrived there, seeking a place to hide his plunder. *April 15, 1925*

GARDNER, AUGUSTUS PEABODY By virtue of his election to the House of Representatives from the sixth district of Massachusetts, he has compelled that body of legislators to listen to some unpalatable truths. By birth, and again by marriage, Gardner is a member of the Brahmin caste of New England. His father-in-law is Henry Cabot Lodge. He has the most inaccessible office in the United States Capitol, located down amid the boilers and coalbins of the sub-cellars, somewhere under the landings which form the western approach to that building. *February 10, 1916*

GARDNER, CATHERINE, a grandniece of Mrs. Jack Gardner, manipulates her big motor car with much dexterity and is giving pleasure to her family and friends by taking them for long daily spins to the suburbs. Miss Gardner is wearing the most up-to-date auto costume in town, a gown and jacket of brown leather with jaunty hat to match. She has much of the individuality and independence of her much discussed aunt, the chatelaine of "Fenway Court." *April 29, 1905*

GARDNER, DR. CHARLES HUNTINGTON was the Principal of the Gardner School, which he founded in 1858. He was born at Worthington, Massachusetts, was graduated from Williams College in 1847, and shortly after engaged in missionary work among the Choctaw Indians, establishing a new mission in the Choctaw Agency. Returning to the East, Dr. Gardner devoted himself to educational interests, serving as President of the Rutgers Female Institute. Many prominent women in this and other states are graduates of the Gardner School. *April 27, 1907*

GARDNER, MRS. JOHN LOWELL (ISABELLA STEWART) Mrs. John Gardner's Venetian palace, "Fenway Court," Boston, was opened on New Year's night by a concert, given in the beautiful music room, said to be the largest room in a private residence in this country. It is all white, with the exception of orange-colored silk draperies at the windows. A conservatory, much like a garden in the tropics, adjoins this room, and from the balcony, where the hostess received her guests, there is a vista including several rooms hung with rich tapestries. *January 10, 1903*

GARNETT, MRS. EDWARD MALCOLM (EMILY HAYWARD) was a descendant of Thomas Savage, the first white settler on what was to be the most aristocratic Colonial portion of Maryland, the Eastern Shore. Her early schooldays were spent in Tallahassee. One of Mrs. Garnett's brothers, Dr. William Randolph Hayward, was Mayor of Tallahassee and Treasurer of Florida. In 1851, she was married to Colonel Garnett, a descendant of the earliest Cavalier settlers of Virginia, who was at that time living on his plantation at Tallahassee. *March 1, 1921*

GARRETT, MRS. JOHN W. (ALICE WARDER) She is a great lover and patron of all the arts. In the Garrett family house, "Evergreen" in Baltimore, she built a lovely little theatre which Bakst decorated. There she occasionally would do a classic Spanish dance in one of the great collection of Spanish costumes she owns, or sing an old French ballad for intimate friends. At Evergreen, she has been wont to gather all sorts of people from the ranks of the littérateurs, the painters, the musicians of New York to listen to a series of concerts by string quartets or do charades or simply to dine most exquisitely. *September 15, 1929*

GARVAN, MR. AND MRS. FRANCIS P. (MABEL BRADY) In the Cathedral of the Immaculate Conception in Albany, for the marriage of Miss Mabel Brady and Mr. Francis P. Garvan, "There were three hundred palms, six hundred yards of laurel roping, three hundred ropes of asparagus, two thousand white lilies and an equal number of white peonies." Miss Brady's father, Mr. Anthony N. Brady, is one of the best known capitalists of Albany. He first controlled the street car lines of Albany, Troy, and Chicago. He planned the consolidation of the New York surface lines, and in other cities also he has controlled similar combinations. *June 18, 1910*

GATELY, MRS. CHARLES LINCOLN Mrs. Gately is a sister of the late Justice Lamar, one of a long line of distinguished men descending from Lucius Quintus Cincinnatus Lamar, the first great legal light of the family Lamar. The name "Cincinnatus" in no way implies affiliations with Cincinnati. An eccentric uncle was given the privilege of naming his sister's children and chose his favorite historical authors when burdening the helpless infants at their baptism. The first Lucius Quintus Cincinnatus very happily, however, became a great lawyer instead of a cotillion leader, and the weighty name was well carried. *November 12, 1904*

GATES, MERRILL EDWARDS is a son of the late Merrill Edwards Gates of Washington, D. C., who was President of Rutgers College and later of Amherst College. As the result of his work for the Government among the Indians, he wrote several books recommending better methods in their education. His brother, Lewis Edwards Gates, has a professorship at Harvard and was at one time in Congress. The grandfather, Seth Merrill Gates, also had considerable fame in his time. He was ardent in his hostility to slavery, and in history it is recorded that a Southern planter of much wealth offered a large reward for "his delivery in Savannah, dead or alive." *April 11, 1908*

GAYNOR, MR. AND MRS. NORMAN J. (BETSY PAGE) She is a daughter of the Rev. Mr. Frank Page and a niece of Ambassador Thomas Nelson Page, the most noted, perhaps, of all the writers about Virginia. She is a great-great-granddaughter of John Page, the Governor of Virginia, who was Thomas Jefferson's friend. Both the bride's father and her illustrious uncle, whose wife was formerly Mrs. Henry Field of Chicago, were brought up on the family plantation, which was part of the original grant to an ancestor among the colonists. *April 25, 1914*

GAZZAM, MRS. JOSEPH M. (NELLY MAY ANDREWS) is a great-granddaughter of Baron Frederic Eugene François de Beelen Bertholff, Austria's first resident minister to this country. She is the daughter of Mr. and Mrs. Benjamin Andrews, of New Orleans. Her father was one of the pioneer cotton-seed oil men of the South. Mrs. Gazzam has accomplished some clever literary work, including a book of recognized authority on bridge whist, and is, too, a musician of more than ordinary ability. Today, Mrs. Gazzam acknowledges the possession of three fads—music, pearls, and old laces. *August 6, 1904*

GERARD, JUDGE AND MRS. JAMES W. (MARY DALY) He comes from distinguished old New York stock. His father was the late James Watson Gerard, who was a lawyer of much note and State Senator in 1876, and his grandfather—also James Watson Gerard—was likewise a lawyer and a philanthropist who procured the incorporation of the House of Refuge for Juvenile Delinquents and who was the first person in this country to advocate a uniformed police. Judge Gerard was admitted to the bar in 1892 and was Chairman of the Democratic campaign committee in New York County for four years. He is one of the silk stocking Tammany members, but he has been one of the hardest workers for his party. He married Miss Mary Daly, daughter of the late Marcus Daly, the wealthy Western mine owner. *September 14, 1912*

GERRY, MR. AND MRS. EDWARD (MARTHA B. FARISH) Like most other top horsewomen, she was born to serious money. Bloodstock inherited from her father, oilman William S. Farish, put Martha and her mother in the horse business. "We decided to breed as well as race. The fillies were very good. We got off to a good start." *July, 1984*

GERRY, MR. AND MRS. ELBRIDGE T. (LOUISA MATILDA LIVINGSTON) were poison to social climbers. At their mansion on 61st Street, where the Pierre now stands, they gave the most exclusive annual balls in New York history. Their complete set of solid silver, including plates and cups for 600 people, became famous. Elbridge, twice Commodore of the New York Yacht Club, was familiar to the public for the black astrakhan hat he wore sleighing. *April, 1939*

GERRY, PETER GOELET Believers in the British theory that young men of good family should go in seriously for politics are pointing with pride to the recent election of Peter Goelet Gerry to be United States Senator from Rhode Island. Grandson, maternally, of Peter P. Goelet, and great-grandson of Elbridge Gerry, Vice President of the United States under Madison and signer of the Declaration of Independence, he is a member of the inner circle of Revolutionary aristocracy. More than that, his life has been lived in accordance with the tenets of his position. He has been a polo player, a whip, and an all-around sportsman. *December 1, 1916*

GERRY, ROBERT is an excellent whip, an expert master of hounds, and he has established a large horse farm near Tuxedo. His equipages are as near perfection as can be, and his stables in town are models. He has established the coach running between Belmont Park and the Holland House during the racing season and is one of the most energetic members of the Coaching Club. *November 11, 1905*

GERRY, MR. AND MRS. ROBERT LIVINGSTON (CORNELIA HARRIMAN) His out-of-door interests are almost wholly concerned with horses. He married Miss Cornelia Harriman, and the interest in horses of the sons and daughters of the late Mr. E. H. Harriman has been as widespread as that of any family in existence. Mr. Gerry for some years was Master of the Orange County Hunt, which hunts the country around The Plains, in Virginia. It was one of the great sights of the Bryn Mawr Horse Show to see the Orange County horses in that team class, when all horses were ridden by ladies, and Orange County sent out their magnificent performers, ridden by the three sisters, Mrs. Gerry, Mrs. C. C. Rumsey, and Mrs. R. Penn Smith. *October 1, 1926*

GIANNINI, MR. AND MRS. GABRIEL (OLGA HARRINGTON) Dr. Giannini is a physicist and technical consultant for industry and has based his Giannini Institute near his ranch in La Quinta, 45 minutes east of Palm Springs. Mrs. Giannini is the daughter of George P. Harrington, a former General Motors Vice President, and Princess Olga Bagration-Moukhransky, whose ancestors once ruled the republic of Georgia in Russia. *May, 1975*

GIBBS, GEORGE was a noted mineralogist who lived for many years at Newport, Rhode Island, but who, with his wife, Laura Wolcott, went to Sunswick, now Astoria, Long Island, to make his home. His son, George Gibbs, was a noted student of Indian dialects; another son, Oliver Wolcott Gibbs, was a very great man, indeed; and a third son, Major General Alfred Gibbs, was a gallant soldier. Oliver Wolcott Gibbs was a professor at Harvard. During the Civil War, he was one of the chief workers for the United States Sanitary Commission, and out of this commission the Union League was formed in New York City with the idea that it should be devoted to "the social organization of sentiments of loyalty to the Union." *May 21, 1910*

GIBBS, PROFESSOR WOLCOTT was the son of George Gibbs, the mineralogist, and his wife, Laura Wolcott, the daughter of Oliver Wolcott, Secretary of the Treasury under Washington. Professor Wolcott Gibbs held the chair of physics and chemistry in the College of the City of New York, and following this was elected to the Rumford professorship in Harvard. *December 29, 1908*

GIBSON, CHARLES DANA In 1925, the inventive Gibson built his family a unique folly-by-the-sea on Seven Hundred Acre Isle, Penobscot Bay, Maine: a medieval-looking stone structure with a square Norman-style tower affording a grand lookout. Over the years, the little fortress has not only astonished passing sailors, it's been the site of Gibson family christenings, weddings, and memorial services. *July, 1994*

GIBSON, HARVEY DOW Switzerland, that suburb of the world, was the country chosen for Mr. Gibson's wedding to Mrs. Helen Whitney Bourne. His spectacular successes as banker, Red Cross Commissioner for France, and, later, member of the War Council and War Finance Committee, have made him one of the important figures amongst the younger men in the New York area. *April 1, 1926*

GIBSON, MRS. HARVEY DOW (HELEN C. WHITNEY)—BOURNE gave a supper after the opening of the new Gilbert Miller play, which was for her lovely debutante daughter, who, nearly everybody admits, is the hit of the season. She had to do something about her hankering for the stage and made her debut in *Firebird*, getting a great deal out of even her tiny maid's part. *January 1, 1933*

GIBSON, PRESTON is a young man of many talents. Baseball and negro minstrels were among his early delights. Mr. Gibson is the youngest son of the late Senator Randall Lee Gibson of Louisiana. Mr. Gibson maintains a dramatic office on Broadway and is said to own considerable stock in a sporting newspaper. Several playlets and one comedy have been written and produced by him with success, and he was also the inspiration of the Playhouse in Washington, where the turkey trot was first danced. *August 17, 1912*

GILBERT, MR. AND MRS. FITCH were married on June fifteenth, but not until they left for Mr. Gilbert's home in Gilbertsville was their marriage announced. Gilbertsville, which is named after Abijah Gilbert, Mr. Gilbert's ancestor, is in Otsego County not far from Cooperstown. Abijah Gilbert settled in Otsego County in 1787. His grandson, another Abijah, was a United States Senator. *July 11, 1914*

GILBERT, MRS. SEYMOUR PARKER (LOUISE ROSS TODD) has slipped with astonishing ease into a very special niche in Berlin's official and diplomatic life. Prior to her marriage to the brilliant financial genius, now Agent-General under the Dawes Plan, she was well known in Washington society, where she distinguished herself by her extremely clever work in amateur theatricals. She recently had an opportunity of displaying her gifts in this direction as the star member of the *Berlin Midnight Frolics* cast, given in the Kaiser Hall of the Hotel Adlon. *May 15, 1925*

GILDER, RICHARD WATSON He became Editor for the Scribner firm monthly called *Hours at Home* in 1869. From 1870 until his death, he was on the editorial staff of what was first *Scribner's Magazine* and later the *Century Magazine*. He was one of the founders of the Society of American Artists and the American Copyright League and President of the New York Association for the Blind. He also was the founder and first secretary of the New Jersey Society for the Prevention of Cruelty to Animals. *November 27, 1909*

A PENNY SAVED...

Over the years, there has been a lot of comment about Mr. J. Paul Getty's ostensible "meanness," as they put it in England. When Mr. Getty installed a pay phone at Sutton Place, it made more headlines than the end of the Korean War. Almost everyone believes that it's still there. Mr. Getty says, "Oh, yes. There were dozens of men working here for a long time. I had the phone booth installed for the workmen to use from time to time." *January, 1974*

GILDER, MRS. RICHARD WATSON (HELENA DE KAY) The Gilder residence was at 103 East Fifteenth Street, where Mrs. Gilder had a studio. It is marked today by two medallions of the Saint-Gaudens brothers, who were among the eminent men who often came together there. Mrs. Gilder was studying art with John La Farge at the time of her marriage in 1874. Later, the family moved to "The House of the Vine" on Eighth Street. "You must never forget this of the Gilders," said Walt Whitman, "that at a time when most everybody else in their set was throwing me down, they were nobly and unhesitatingly hospitable." *May 6, 1911*

GILL, WILLIAM FEARING, who has bought the Poe cottage at Fordham, near the old Kingsbridge Road, announces that he intends to keep it as a memorial of the poet. It was here that Poe wrote some of the poems that have rendered his name immortal, here his wife Virginia died, and here he passed through some of his severest struggles with poverty and mental cares. The land about the cottage includes four and a half city lots, and the price paid was $3,487.50. *April 14, 1889*

GILLET, MR. AND MRS. F. WARRINGTON, JR. (ELESABETH R. INGALLS)—BOYKIN As Palm Beach grows and grows up—the winter population now swells to 40,000—its society becomes more and more fragmented. F. Warrington Gillet, Jr., whose new wife Eles is a Birmingham Ingalls steel heiress, sees them this way: "The WASP Establishment, the Jewish Establishment," and "a group busy getting their pictures taken." *March, 1983*

GILMAN, PROFESSOR DANIEL COIT was at one time President of the University of California, and in 1875 was called to the Presidency of Johns Hopkins University in Baltimore. He was also President of the Carnegie Institute in Washington. During his career in Baltimore, Dr. Gilman took an active part in the affairs of the city and of the state. For many years he was President of the Baltimore Charity Organization Society and also of the Municipal Art Society of Baltimore. *October 24, 1908*

GIMBEL, MRS. ADAM (SOPHIE HAAS)—ROSSBACH, who married not so long ago into one of Philadelphia's great merchant families, is now identified with New York and Elberon, New Jersey. Mrs. Gimbel merges in her own person artistic talent with business dexterity. She not only runs the Salon Moderne but turns her hand at designing with a *je ne sais quoi* touch that nearly out-Parises the French. *October 1, 1932*

GIMBEL, JACOB, senior member of the merchandise house of Gimbel Brothers, died at Atlantic City. From one little store in Vincennes, Indiana, in 1851, the industry of the Gimbel Brothers has led to a chain of great department stores in New York, Philadelphia, Milwaukee, and Paris. *December 1, 1922*

GIZYCKA, COUNTESS FELICIA The wedding of Countess Felicia and Mr. Drew Pearson, which took place in San Diego, California, brought to light the fact that this tall, slim child with the honey-colored hair, had run away from home. Possessed with the idea of earning her own living, she had ridden thirty miles from the Gizycka ranch in the Jackson Hole Country, had sold her horse for money to pursue her journey, and had been working as a waitress in a railway restaurant. *May 1, 1925*

GLENN, IDA URQUHART Her marriage to Captain S. J. Bayard Schindel will take place in early November. Miss Glenn is a Southern woman of a long line of people distinguished in history: the Cobbs, Lamars, Guerrards, and Garterays. She is a cousin of the late artist Whistler, and just before his death it was decided that she should visit Paris to be both his model and pupil. Miss Glenn has glorious hair of reddish-gold. *October 3, 1903*

GODDARD, MOSES BROWN IVES was a member of the old firm of Brown & Ives, President of the Providence and Worcester Railroad. His father, William Giles Goddard, once had the chair of moral philosophy and metaphysics at Brown University. His grandfather, William Goddard, established the first printing press in Providence and was widely known as a publisher. *May 25, 1907*

GODDARD, ROBERT H. IVES, JR. is related to several of the most notable families in Rhode Island. His sister, Miss Madeleine Ives Goddard, was married in January of 1907 to the Marquis René d'Andigné, of the "Château Monet" in Anjou. *July 18, 1908*

GOELET, MAY Mrs. Ogden Goelet announced the engagement of her daughter, May, to Henry John Innes Ker, eighth Duke of Roxburghe. Miss Goelet is, perhaps, the richest heiress in America and belongs to an old and distinguished family. The American branch was founded by Francis Goelet, of the French

Huguenot family, who settled in America in 1676, and his descendants engaged in business in New York and wisely invested their savings in Manhattan real estate. The enormous increase in realty values in New York had made the late Ogden Goelet and his brother, Robert, millionaires from birth. The father of the future Duchess, Ogden, was an enthusiastic yachtsman. During the latter part of his life he became prominent in English society. He leased "Wimborne House" in London, where he entertained lavishly and where he gave a dinner to the then Prince of Wales at the Queen's jubilee. He had built at Newport the superb villa, "Ochre Court." His town house was at 606 Fifth Avenue. *September 12, 1903*

GOELET, PETER AND ROBERT The Goelet millionaires had an ancestor, who, following the honorable craft of ironmongery, learned in it how to turn iron to gold, and then into city lots. The story goes that, upon a time, they found themselves cramped for pasture for their cow, and, to accommodate her, they bought a pasture lot of some forty or fifty acres, for a trifle. That pasture now is covered with brick and stone along Fifth, Lexington, and Fourth Avenues, and the Goelets still own it. *May 6, 1868*

GOELET, MRS. ROBERT (HARRIET WARREN) No American woman has been more honored abroad by royalty than was Mrs. Goelet. Every summer, she visited Kiel in her splendid yacht, the *Nahma,* and was entertained by the Kaiser and Prince Henry of Prussia. She was their hostess on a number of occasions. During the winter, the *Nahma* cruised in the Mediterranean and at Cannes and Nice. Mrs. Goelet received visits from the different European sovereigns. The *Nahma,* which was a large ship built on the lines of a cruiser, was detained some years ago by the Turkish officials for forty-eight hours in the Dardanelles, being mistaken for a foreign warship. When the mistake was discovered, the Turkish government was all apologies, and Abdul Hamed II, Sultan of Turkey, conferred on Mrs. Goelet the cordon of the Chefakat, a most notable decoration. *December 14, 1912*

GOELET, MR. AND MRS. ROBERT G. (ALEXANDRA CREEL)—TUFO Ownership of Gardiner's Island at the end of Long Island, said to be worth $50 million, recently passed to Alexandra and her brother Robert Creel, after their uncle Robert Gardiner refused to pay taxes on the 3,380-acre island, which has been owned by the Gardiner family since 1639. Her husband is heir to an old New York landowning family and serves as President of the American Museum of Natural History. *September, 1988*

GOELET, ROBERT WALTON The houseboat has suddenly glided into fashionable favor, and now no large household is complete without one. It is as necessary as the motor and the yacht and the special train and the half-dozen estates in different parts of the country. One of the largest is the *Aunt Polly,* which belongs to Robert Walton Goelet. The boat is a complete summer residence afloat. There are two stories and a wide staircase and high ceilinged suites of rooms, with private baths. A pecu-

liarity of this craft is that the interior work is all of notched pine. There are over four thousand notches in ceilings and stair rails and in some of the rustic seats, no two are alike. This rough wood gives one the impression of being a species of floating camp in the Adirondacks. *July 4, 1903*

GOLDSBOROUGH, ELEANOR WINDER The ceremonies held in connection with the centennial celebration of the laying of the cornerstone of the Washington Monument in Baltimore also served in a manner as a time of resurrection of the old order of Maryland aristocracy. Little Miss Eleanor Winder Goldsborough appeared in the program as the bearer of the identical golden trowel used by her ancestor, Governor Winder, at the laying of the cornerstone, July 4, 1815; while Master John Ridgely, 3d, of Hampton, represented both his great-great-grandfathers General John Eager Howard and General Charles Ridgely, when he raised the historic flag for which both forebears so valiantly fought and conquered during the wars of the Revolution and of 1812. *July 10, 1915*

WOMEN AT WORK

Mrs. Douglas Gill has for several months been a member of the working fraternity, the hostess in a famous New York gown establishment. The story is told of the type of reporter in whom tact is not nurtured. Loth to recognize Mrs. Gill's right to her own reservations as to why she was at work, the reporter voiced the following conclusion: "I suppose you're ashamed of it!" "On the contrary," replied the imperturbable Sallie, "working is one of the few things in my life of which I have really been proud!" *July 15, 1925*

GOODHUE, BERTRAM GROSVENOR was a Fellow of the American Institute of Architects, a member of the National Institute of Arts and Letters, and one of the chief exponents of the Gothic design in architecture in the United States. He was the architect who was discovered to have woven into the design of a part of St. Thomas's Church, Fifth Avenue, New York, different emblems indicative of the life and types that passed its doors. The dollar sign, hidden in a maze of carving over the Bride's Door, created considerable of an uproar at the time it was discovered. *May 15, 1924*

GOODRICH, MR. AND MRS. CHARLES C. (MARY A. GELLATLY) The little theater on their estate at Llewellyn Park, Orange, New Jersey, while small, is unique in many respects and may be said to set a new standard for the private theater in this country. The building was originally used as a stable and carriage house. The theater was formally opened by a dedicatory performance written and produced by the architect, Mr. Howard Greenley, *Star Dust,* a masque in two parts. *April 20, 1917*

GOODSELL, BISHOP DANIEL AYRES completed his fiftieth year of ministry in the service of the Methodist Episcopal Church in March, 1909. He was resident Bishop of Boston for many

years prior to his appointment, in May, 1908, to be Bishop in New York. He caused a discussion when in his Episcopal address he advocated a more liberal construction on the plan of amusement of the young people of the Methodist Church, permitting theatergoing and even card-playing within reasonable limits and under wise supervision. *December 11, 1909*

GORDON, JOHN B. "Sutherland," a noted Georgia home standing on historic ground a few miles out of Atlanta, is a stately-looking mansion of colonial design. To the stranger, it is pointed out as the home of General John B. Gordon. The house itself, though of recent construction, is almost an exact facsimile of the ancestral home of Mrs. Gordon. On the beautiful lawn in front, under the magnolia trees and oaks, General Gordon has written not a little of his book, *Reminiscences of the Civil War. February 28, 1903*

GOUDY, HELEN comes from one of Chicago's oldest families. Her maternal grandfather was the late Mr. Samuel J. Walker, noted among the businessmen of Chicago in the days before the fire. He was an early real estate dealer and not only amassed a big fortune but was possessed of the civic pride which caused him to do much for Chicago in general. It was Mr. Walker who secured the 1865 commission which gave to the city Lincoln Park. On the other side, Miss Goudy's paternal grandfather was the late William C. Goudy, widely known as an early Illinois lawyer. *October 25, 1913*

GOULD, ANNA, daughter of the late Jay Gould, has announced her engagement to Comte Boniface de Castellane of Paris. Miss Gould has just passed her twenty-first birthday. Under her father's will, she inherited about $12,000,000 and, according to report, $2,000,000 will be settled upon her husband, agreeably to foreign custom. The Comte de Castellane is a scion of one of the oldest families in France, the title dating back to the year 1000. His especial accomplishments are horsemanship and drawing. *February 13, 1895*

GOULD, FRANK JAY In speaking of the court tennis tournament, I said that in all probability Mr. Jay Gould again would be champion. But he is not, because illness prevented his getting in shape to defend his title. The retiring champion first earned his honors in 1906, and he has held them ever since. Mr. Gould is a master technician, and his absolute mastery of every phase of the game gave him an unexcelled technique. He it was who developed the railroad service which was so largely responsible for his supremacy. *May 15, 1926*

GOULD, GEORGE J. Those who are interested in such matters may like to know that it has been estimated that Mr. George Gould's expenses for himself and family during his recent foreign trip have been $600,000, or at the rate of $4,615.38 a day. They were wide open to their newly-made titled acquaintances, and money was spent as only a Gould could spend it. Upon his personal merits, Mr. Gould has gained a recognized social position in England that cannot be cavilled at and has proven himself, in the language of the day, a "dead game sport." *October 24, 1894*

GOULD, HELEN Her home, "Lyndhurst," on the Hudson, is a gray and blue marble structure, so solid, so sombre, that it verges upon the monastic. Since her father's death, Miss Gould has changed nothing within the castle or without. All the old-fashioned furniture, each and every jug, vase, and picture, remains as Jay Gould left it. The castle contains forty six rooms, separated into suites by wide and lofty halls. The style of the furniture and decorations within, like the style of architecture without, is Gothic. All the simplicities and severities of this style are relentlessly adhered to. *July 5, 1899*

GOULD, MR. AND MRS. HOWARD (VIOLA KATHARINE CLEMMONS) The son of the late Jay Gould was married to Miss Viola Katharine Clemmons, who was formerly an actress, having, however, but limited experience on the stage. The Gould family seem to have been opposed to the match, and, by the terms of Mr. Jay Gould's will, any of his children marrying without consent of his executors and trustees was to forego one-half the bequest allotted to him, in this case representing the pretty penny of $5,000,000. At all events, married they were. *October 19, 1898*

GOULD, JAY The value of the estate left by the late Jay Gould has just been appraised at $80,934,580.79. For about twelve years prior to Mr. Gould's death, there existed between him and his son George J. Gould an arrangement to the effect that the latter should devote himself entirely to his father's business affairs, making no other business engagements or connections. The compensation to be paid him was agreed upon some months before the testator's death, at $500,000 per year. *January 9, 1895*

GOULD, MR. AND MRS. JAY (ANNE D. GRAHAM) The duplex home of Mr. and Mrs. Jay Gould at 444 East 57th Street is the first smart apartment to go modern from the beginning to the end, from the foyer to the littlest dressing room. The living room has what all twentieth-century rooms should have; that is, solidarity; not that concrete and metal solidarity the Teutons love but a reasonable and restful mass effect; a simplification of line and form which repudiates Parisian fussiness as well as German absoluteness, which eliminates curves and exploits angles. *April 1, 1929*

GRACE, JOSEPH PETER, JR. has just succeeded his father as President of W. R. Grace & Co., the international trading and shipping company founded by his grandfather, William R. Grace, who came from Ireland and became Mayor of New York. Educated at St. Paul's School and Yale ('36), "Pete" Grace entered the family business as a clerk after graduation and by last year had been advanced to Vice President. *July, 1946*

GRACE, MRS. WILLIAM R. (LILLIAS GILCHREST), widow of the founder of W. R. Grace & Co., died at "Gracefield," Great Neck, Long Island. The late Mr. Grace was the eighty-fifth and eighty-seventh Mayor of New York. She was the daughter of George W. Gilchrest, a noted shipbuilder and shipowner of Maine. *November 15, 1922*

GRAHAM, MRS. WILLIAM MILLER, whose presentation at the Court of St. James this month was of much interest in California, will give a ball at her home, "Besselguardos," Santa Barbara, in honor of Admiral Evans and his staff during the squadron's three days' stay in the channel. Everyone is expecting much from the Grahams, for they never entertain in a commonplace way, and their home is spacious. It is a white marble Italian villa that stands on the bluff overlooking the city of Santa Barbara and the channel. *March 21, 1908*

GRANARD, BERNARD ARTHUR FORBES, 8TH EARL AND COUNTESS OF (BEATRICE MILLS) The days of their honeymoon were passed at the beautiful country home of Mr. and Mrs. Ogden Mills, the bride's parents, at Staatsburg, New York. The bride, one of the twin daughters of Mr. and Mrs. Ogden Mills, the granddaughter of Mr. D. O. Mills, the millionaire philanthropist, and the niece of Mrs. Whitelaw Reid, the wife of our Ambassador to the Court of St. James, has had, as a young girl, a brilliant social career. On her mother's side, she is the granddaughter of the late Maturin Livingston and a descendant of Governor Lewis, one of the historic figures of the Revolution. The Earl of Granard is Master of the Horse, Lord-in-Waiting to King Edward VII, and Deputy Lieutenant for the County Longford, Ireland. *January 23, 1909*

GRANT, FREDERICK DENT Along with the bodyguard of General Grant rides his son, Fred, a stout lad of some twelve summers. He endures all the marching, follows his father under fire with all the coolness of an old soldier, and is, in short, a chip off the old block. *September 19, 1863*

GRANT, GEORGE DE FOREST is one of the oldest of the young bachelors in town. He is very wealthy and is frequently pointed out as the uncle of the Countess of Essex and the Countess Gaston de Breteuil. He has always had a penchant for keeping bachelor house in a very delightful manner. For years, he and his brother, R. Suydam Grant, lived in a house near Gramercy Park. One seldom passes the Union Club without seeing Mr. George de Forest Grant in the window. *July 30, 1904*

GRANT, NELLIE WANSHALL The President's daughter was married at the White House to Mr. Algernon Sartoris, a young Englishman of wealth and honorable connections. The bride's presents amounted to $60,000 and were displayed in the library. Among the most costly gifts was a complete dinner service by A. J. Drexel, of Philadelphia, worth probably $4,500; by A. T. Stewart, of New York, a lace pocket handkerchief of the largest size, $500. The President gave the bride $10,000 and two handsome sets of lace made to order in Brussels. *May 27, 1874*

GRANT, ULYSSES S. III Another member of the famous Grant family has come to San Francisco to reside. The newcomer is Major Ulysses S. Grant III, who, with Mrs. Grant, has come west to live for the next few years. Major Grant is attached to the Engineer Corps of the army. His mother was a sister of the late Mrs. Potter Palmer of Chicago. Mrs. Grant is a daughter of Elihu Root, and her marriage to Major Grant took place in the national capital, where her father was Secretary of State under President Theodore Roosevelt. *December 1, 1920*

GRAVES, HENRY, JR. A short distance from the Gould camp on Upper Saranac Lake in the Adirondacks is Eagle Island, for which Mr. Henry Graves, Jr., of New York, not long ago paid the Hon. Levi P. Morton close to $1,000,000. Mr. Graves, who is now in camp with his family, is a lover of motor boating, and recently purchased a new speed boat, larger than any other in use on Adirondack waters. This he christened *The Eagle*. *August 20, 1910*

GRAY, FRANCIS CALLEY It is reported that the late Francis C. Gray has bequeathed his large and munificent collection of engravings to the Boston Athenaeum. Mr. Gray has been for many years collecting the engravings and has expended, it is thought, upwards of twenty five thousand dollars for the purpose. *January 10, 1857*

GRAY, MRS. GEORGE GRISWOLD On New Year's in New York, Mrs. George Griswold Gray received at the residence of her father, Mr. Richard Irvin. She was attired in her wedding dress and wore magnificent jewels. Representatives of old New York—that class of genuine Knickerbockers fast dying away—were numerous at Mrs. Gray's reception, which was among the most aristocratic of the day. *January 8, 1873*

GREEN, ANDREW HASWELL was a descendant, through his grandmother, from John Tilley, who was a passenger on the *Mayflower* in 1620. Mr. Green was the founder of the New York Zoological Society and was also the originator of the plan which resulted in the founding of the American Museum of Natural History. *November 21, 1903*

GREEN, MRS. EDWARD HOWLAND (HETTIE ROBINSON) The richest woman in America is Mrs. E. H. Green, the wife of the Vice President of the Louisville and Nashville Road. She was a Miss Robinson, and her father was a whaling master at New Bedford. He owned a fleet of ships known as the blue line of whalers, and from his profession was known as "Blubber Robinson." He died when his daughter was a mere girl and left her a fortune of about eight millions. As her tastes were simple and her wants few, she was able to transfer her enormous income almost every year to the body of the fortune itself, and it has now accumulated to more than $27,000,000. Her husband, Mr. Green, was a very rich man when she married him and has been successful since. It is said that the income of this couple is $2,500,000 a year. *May 26, 1880*

GREEN, ELEANOR, daughter of Dr. James O. Green, of New York, and great-granddaughter of Peter Cooper, is engaged to Prince Viggo of Denmark, son of His Royal Highness Prince Valdemar and a cousin of the Kings of Denmark and of England. *March 1, 1924*

GREEN, DR. JAMES O. was a descendant of Robert Green, who settled in Virginia in the early part of the eighteenth century. His wife was Amy Hewitt, daughter of Abram S. Hewitt, one-time Mayor of New York. He was

GOULD

Mr. and Mrs. Frank Jay Gould, in 1913.

"The most hated man in America" is how Jay Gould described himself. It may well have been true. Gould's stock manipulation, shady associates, and persistent untrustworthiness horrified nineteenth-century America. As a poor boy in upstate New York, the young Jay invented a mousetrap, clerked in a store, wrote a history of his home county of Delaware (which he printed and hawked himself), and saved enough to invest in railroad stocks. When he died of tuberculosis at the early age of fifty-seven, in 1892, the owner of the Western Union Telegraph Company, the Missouri Pacific, Texas Pacific, and other railroads left his wife and six children an estate of about $80 million.

Their legacies enabled the Gould children to set examples of extravagance that astounded even the Gilded Age, as they slowly made their way into the New York Society that had never accepted their father. Son Frank Jay Gould belonged to twenty-seven private clubs at one time, played polo and court tennis, and sailed the world in his oversized yacht. When *Town & Country* chronicled his saga in 1956, the story was called "He Had Fun With His Money: The Long, Happy Spree of Frank Jay Gould." But Frank also inherited his father's gift for replenishing the family coffers. An expatriate in France who did not visit the United States for thirty years, he foresaw the possibilities of developing the French Riviera as a summer resort. He bought land, built casinos and hotels, and when he died in 1956 left an estate of more than $100 million. On the death of his wife Florence La Caze, the inheritance was passed on to French and American charities.

His brother George was not as lucky. At one point, the younger five siblings sued George, the eldest son, for $50 million for mismanaging their father's estate. They won, and seem to have been justified: by 1918, under George's direction, all the Gould railroads had slipped from the family's control.

But George lived well. At his estate, "Georgian Court," in Lakewood, New Jersey, an eighty-foot-long mural decorated the entrance hall; for entertainment, there was a lagoon for boating, three polo fields, and a shooting range. With his wife, actress Edith Kingdon, George fathered five children. He also had three children out of wedlock with another actress. Eventually, George's style of life swept away his inheritance. When he died at his French villa in 1923, he left an estate of only $5 million.

Other Gould marital sagas were equally sensational. Brothers Frank Jay and Howard also married actresses; Howard later sued his wife for divorce on the grounds of her adultery with "Buffalo Bill" Cody. Frank's wife had him in court thirteen times between 1918 and 1929. One sister, Anna, married Comte Boniface ("Boni") de Castellane in one of the most publicized international marriages of the 1890s, then divorced him after he had spent $5 million of her money on parties and a reproduction of the Petit Trianon. She next married the Comte's cousin, the Duc de Talleyrand-Périgord. The other sister, Helen Miller Gould, wed Finley J. Shepard, a YMCA worker, when she was middle-aged and adopted four children she found abandoned on the steps of St. Patrick's Cathedral. "Lyndhurst," the Gothic house on the Hudson River where the Gould children grew up, is now a property of the National Trust for Historic Preservation.

The style of the times, as the Goulds saw it: *clockwise from top left,* Silvia, Edith, and Kingdon Gould, Jr., 1929; debutante Marjorie Gould, 1908; Edwin Gould; the children of George Jay Gould with the family chauffeur. Each had his or her own specially built car to play in.

devoted to sport pertaining to horses, and did much to help establish polo at Jerome Park and Meadow Brook in the early days of the game in this country. *April 1, 1924*

GREEN, COLONEL WHARTON was the only son of General Thomas J. Green, the author of the act fixing the Texas-Mexico boundary. He was twice married, his second wife being Mrs. Addie Burr Davis, widow of Vice President Davis. In 1882, he was elected to Congress from the Fayetteville, North Carolina, district and served two terms. *August 13, 1910*

GREENE, GENERAL FRANCIS VINTON is well known as an author, and his books are the result of his experiences as a soldier. He was, for instance, a military attaché of the United States Legation at St. Petersburg; was with the Russian Army in Turkey in 1877 and 1878, and was present at the battle of Plevna. Following this, he received decorations and a campaign medal from the Emperor of Russia *June 8, 1907*

GREENOUGH, ELLEN The wedding of the daughter of Dr. Robert Greenough and Mrs. Greenough to Mr. Hardwick Stires, of New York, is still another Gotham-Boston alliance linking two notable family lines. Mrs. Greenough is the niece of Dr. Charles W. Eliot, President Emeritus of Harvard University, and Mr. Stires is a son of the Reverend Ernest M. Stires, rector of St. Thomas's Episcopal Church in New York. *February 1, 1924*

GREER, RIGHT REVEREND DAVID HUMMELL was the Protestant Episcopal Bishop of New York. At the time of his death, he was surrounded by a mass of work and interests—namely, the union of Christian Churches, the development of closer relations between the Protestant Episcopal and the Greek Catholic Churches, and the completion of the Cathedral of St. John the Divine, which consummation was very dear to his heart. *June 10, 1919*

GREW, EDWARD WIGGLESWORTH The engagement of Miss Ruth Dexter and Mr. Grew has aroused more interest in Boston than any similar event for a long time. Mr. Grew, who is a member of the Somerset and other clubs, has three sisters who married brilliantly— Mrs. J. Pierpont Morgan, Jr., of London, Mrs. Boylston Beal, and Mrs. Van Rensselaer Crosby. *January 10, 1901*

GRIFF, MR. AND MRS. GARY JOHN (M. LAURIE MACDONALD) He is a fifth-generation Californian, and, although she was born in Connecticut, Laurie Griff is a member of the Carson-Domínguez family, who received one of California's original Spanish land grants. "Our roots are here, but I still see California as a pilot state. That's probably why I love it." *May, 1975*

GRIFFITH, MRS. (SUSAN BINNEY MONTGOMERY) (a combination of names that thrills the heart of the high-born Philadelphian) is engaged to Mr. Parker Ross Freeman. The prospective bride is a representative of distinguished families. She is a grand-daughter of the celebrated Horace Binney, and her father, Mr. Richard Montgomery, was descended from a French family of nobility. His sister married the

Count de La Rochefoucauld. Mr. Freeman is a descendant of George Ross, one of the Declaration's signers. *July 19, 1902*

GRINNELL, ADMIRAL HENRY WALTON comes from an old New Bedford family, and it was his grandfather who organized the expedition that went to the Arctic to relieve Sir John Franklin. When the Japanese applied to the United States naval board for an officer to help them organize their navy, Admiral Grinnell received the appointment, was given the rank of Rear Admiral by the Japanese Government, and was for several years Inspector General of Japan's navy. He inherited a fortune from his father and has a large estate in Florida and a summer home in Westport, Rhode Island. *July 30, 1910*

BEASTLY TO TRUMAN

Truman Capote told me Mrs. Winston Guest came to see his Long Island place and said all it lacked was a lion. Truman isn't much for lions, so when he uncrated the one C-Z sent him he found all those fangs a bit hard to live with. After a while, though, he became quite attached to the lion—until Winston called him to say C-Z had no right to give away that lion. "My mother and I shot that lion," said Winston, "and I have to have it back. Come on over and take anything in the house you want." Now lionless but happy, Truman is making out with the zebra he chose. *February, 1966*

GRISCOM, LLOYD CARPENTER, son of Clement A. Griscom, President of the American line, who has been appointed Secretary of the United States Legation at Constantinople, was on the staff of General Wade in Cuba during the war with Spain and was previously secretary to Ambassador Bayard in London, distinguishing himself in both capacities. *October 11, 1899*

GRISWOLD, F. GRAY The first fox hunt of the season took place at Bryer's farm, three miles from the city of Newport. At five o'clock, the master of the hounds, Mr. F. Gray Griswold, appeared. As the amateur riders went north in full view of several hundred spectators, they presented the appearance of the tail of a comet, the redcoats being a long distance in advance. The ladies rode straight as an arrow, Miss Coats following closely the huntsmen. The first in at the death was the master of the hounds. The brush was awarded to Miss Coats, whose riding was superb. *August 11, 1880*

GRISWOLD, JACK SYMINGTON Son of Mr. and Mrs. B. H. Griswold III, of "Fancy Hill," Monkton, Jay's father is a senior partner in Alexander Brown and Sons, the oldest investment banking firm in the nation, also a trustee of Johns Hopkins and Director of Sun Publishing. Jay is a top rider, often entered in Hunt Cup and Grand National races. *June, 1964*

GROSVENOR, GILBERT M. The Grosvenors are an old Washington family who, for generations, have dedicated their efforts to a project of national importance. Gilbert M. Grosvenor, great-grandson of Alexander Graham Bell, is the fifth generation of his family to serve as President of the National Geographic Society,

founded in 1888 by his great-great-grandfather Gardiner Greene Hubbard and thirty two other men. *February, 1988*

GUEST, MR. AND MRS. WINSTON FREDERICK CHURCHILL (HELENA McCANN) After the service in the garden of "Sunken Orchard" at Oyster Bay, the Winston Frederick Churchill Guests received in an indoor tennis court filled with palms from the McCann place in Florida and painted to resemble the Royal Poinciana and Whitehall hotels. The bride is a daughter of Mr. and Mrs. Charles E. F. McCann and granddaughter of the late Frank W. Woolworth. Mr. Guest's maternal grandfather was also a celebrated figure in American business, the late Henry Phipps, Carnegie's partner. As the son of Captain the Hon. Frederick E. Guest, he is descended from the first Duke of Marlborough. Bagpipers were one of the many musical units involved. After a trip to the South Seas, the young couple will return for participation in the East-West polo. *July 1, 1934*

GUEST, MRS. WINSTON FREDERICK CHURCHILL (LUCY DOUGLAS "C-Z" COCHRANE) The famous C-Z, one of Mainbocher's star clients, is one of New York's most interesting hostesses. She doesn't limit herself to just one group. Her "crowd" may just as well be the Long Island horsey set—C-Z being a first-class horsewoman—the Palm Beach money set, or the international set. Today, she is famous for topping the list of best-dressed women. Before she married the handsome Winston Guest, she had a fling at Hollywood, played in the line of the *Ziegfeld Follies*—all this, even though she is a member of a very proper Bostonian family. *December, 1959*

GUGGENHEIM, MRS. HARRY (ALICIA PATTERSON) She began her newspaper career in 1927 at her father's paper, the *New York Daily News,* was successively a reporter, staff writer, and—for eleven years—the newspaper's literary critic. In 1939, she married financier-sportsman Harry Guggenheim; the following year, they began *Newsday,* a suburban Long Island paper that soon became successful. *January, 1986*

GUGGENHEIM, MR. AND MRS. SIMON (OLGA HIRSH) Mr. Guggenheim, who is a Philadelphian by birth, went to Pueblo, Colorado, in 1889 to engage in the smelting and refining business with his brother. He soon became a factor in political affairs of that state. He was elected to Congress during the Sixtieth Congress now in session. When Mrs. Guggenheim had been only a few weeks in the capital city, her dinners and entertainments came into general favor. She cares little for society as such, however, and is more interested in her philanthropies, to which she devotes much time. *April 4, 1908*

GUGGENHEIMER, RANDOLPH He was noted for all that he accomplished in behalf of the public schools of New York. When he was nominated for the office of President of the Municipal Council, he was elected by a large majority. He was one of the pioneers in introducing large office buildings on Broadway. *September 21, 1907*

GUILD, CURTIS, JR. The appointment of former Governor Curtis Guild, Jr., of Massachusetts to be Ambassador at St. Petersburg seems to have given general satisfaction. The new Ambassador comes of an old Massachusetts family, has a recognized social position in Boston, is a Harvard graduate, and has a number of degrees from universities in this country and Europe. He was Lieutenant Governor of Massachusetts for three years and followed it with three terms as Governor. *April 29, 1911*

GUNTHER, FRANKLIN MOTT His great-grandfather was Dr. Valentine Mott, called "the father of American surgery" and founder of the New York College of Physicians and Surgeons. The Motts first settled at Hempstead, Long Island. He occupied the position of private secretary to Thomas J. O'Brien, Ambassador to Japan, from 1908 to 1909. He was detailed to the American Embassy in London in 1914. *April 10, 1918*

GURNEE, WALTER A most wonderful monkey was one of the first to arrive at the Noah's Ark party given by Mr. and Mrs. Andrew McKinley. The animals came in two by two, numbering about seventy in all. The monkey proved to be Mr. Walter Gurnee, attired in soft brown wool, forming a complete and close-fitting covering. He carried the character still further by emitting strange and awful squeaks. Miss Brittin dawned on the room as a white French poodle. Above her arms and ankles were bands of sheep's wool, which made her look like a high-bred animal. On a white wool tail, she wore a huge bow of ribbon, which was much admired when the appendage was in motion. *March 21, 1903*

H

HACKETT, MR. AND MRS. JAMES KETELTAS (MARY MANNERING) At a remarkable dinner given recently by Mr. and Mrs. James K. Hackett, the table decorations were certainly a surprise to many of the guests. Instead of the regulation polished mahogany, covered with finest damask, the table top was of plate glass and the cloth was of sheerest, most beautiful Japanese grass linen. No ordinary candle lights were on this unique board, but all the lighting was done from underneath the table by an arrangement of electric wires that made the upper surface ethereally luminous. So far as is known, nothing of the kind has ever been attempted in this country or at a private dinner, and the sensation it created may well be imagined. *February 7, 1903*

HADDEN, ALEXANDER, who is prominently identified with the social labor of leading cotillions, is an amateur missionary and worker among the city's poor and unfortunate. His example in this particular is an excellent one for bachelors of means and leisure. It is an excellent sign of the times when wealthy young men appreciate and act upon the opportunities for doing good that the great metropolis presents. *February 15, 1893*

THE SENATE ABHORS THE HOUSE

It is said that Senator Eugene Hale's superb home in Washington, D.C., came very near costing him his seat in the Senate. When he married the heiress Miss Chandler, he was a poor man, having but little over his salary as a Senator. Hardly had the magnificent residence neared completion when a wily political enemy of the Senator had a negative taken of the house and several hundred photographs printed from it. These were distributed in Maine and aroused a flood of unpopular feeling. The members of the State Legislature, in whose hands Hale's re-election lay, contrasted the palatial home with their own modest dwellings. It took much tact and political skill to overcome their prejudices. *February 22, 1902*

HAGGARD, MR. AND MRS. WILLIAM D. III (HOLLISTER D. HOUGHTON) Among the many appealing couples in Aiken, South Carolina, are Hollister and Billy Haggard. They live in a white-and-yellow, slim-columned Victorian house with a modern interior. Hollister is the daughter of Arthur Houghton of the Metropolitan Museum. She hunted at Fairfield in Far Hills, New Jersey. Billy hails from Nashville, was on the U.S. Three-Day Olympic Equestrian Team. *March, 1977*

HAGGIN, JAMES BEN ALI is the last of the Forty-Niners, the famous band of pioneer miners and bankers who went to California in the golden days. During the season, at the Metropolitan Opera, he is in his parterre each Monday evening. It cannot be said that he thoroughly enjoys the opera, but he takes his ease, sitting in a large chair, bringing the evening newspapers to read and occasionally having forty winks. *June 10, 1911*

HAINES, MRS. JOHN P. (MARY MERRITT) was a woman of broad charities; and at the time her husband was President of the Society for Prevention of Cruelty to Animals, she assisted him ably in his work. The Haines residence, "Cranmore Farm," at Tom's River, is one of the show places in that part of New Jersey. Here also is the famous dog cemetery, where the canine pets of the household are buried in a fenced-in plot of ground, with headstones to mark their resting places. *March 25, 1911*

HAINES, MRS. WILLIAM A. (EMILY S. STAGG) She was a member of one of the oldest Knickerbocker families of New York. Her great-uncle on the paternal side was George Washington's secretary during the Revolutionary War, and the first secretary of the Society of the Cincinnati. *September 21, 1907*

HALE, REV. DR. EDWARD EVERETT was the last of that brilliant group of men who were known as the New England school in American literature. He was licensed to preach as a Unitarian, and his first regular pastorate was in Worcester, Massachusetts. He became pastor of the South Congregational Church in Boston in 1856 and remained in that post until shortly before he was appointed Chap-

lain of the Senate in 1903. As an author, his greatest work was *The Man Without a Country*. He is survived by his wife, who is a niece of Henry Ward Beecher. *June 19, 1909*

HALE, NATHAN II With Henry D. Sedgwick, Nathan Hale, 2d, edited the *Boston Weekly Messenger,* the first weekly periodical in the United States devoted to literature and politics. He was also the first President of the Boston and Worcester Railroad, the first company in New England to use steam power. He was a nephew of Nathan Hale, the patriot who died a martyr to his country. *June 19, 1909*

HALE, SUSAN is to spend the winter on the Mediterranean. Though Miss Hale allows *Who's Who* to give the year of her birth as 1833, one can readily believe that this bright sister of the author of *The Man Without a Country* could write a most entertaining book about the winter she will enjoy on the Riviera. With her brother, it will be remembered, she wrote the *Family Flight* series of travels. *October 22, 1904*

HALL, DR. G. STANLEY was the first President of Clark University, distinguished psychologist, and descendant of William Brewster, John Alden, and five other *Mayflower* Pilgrims. *May 15, 1924*

HALL, MRS. W. ALEXANDER REMBERT (GERTRUDE LUQUEER LANE) Her wedding was celebrated in the house in which she was born (a very noteworthy item in unstable New York), and the ceremony was performed by the clergyman who baptized her. She is a direct descendant of Nacassius de Pille, Vice Governor of New York, with Peter Stuyvesant, in 1638. *October 22, 1904*

HALL, MRS. WALKER PIERCE (LAVINIA BAKER) is one of the young matrons well known in the society of Cincinnati. She is a niece of Mr. and Mrs. Louis C. Nelson, with whom she lived at their beautiful country home, "Nelsonia." Mrs. Hall's grandfather six times removed was Governor William Bradford, of the *Mayflower* party. Mr. Hall, who is a prominent young broker of Cincinnati, is the son of the late Joseph L. Hall, the manufacturer of safes. *September 23, 1905*

HALL, WILLIAM CLAIBORNE His family is one that is well known in the South. His great-great-grandfather was William Claiborne, the early Governor of Louisiana, who figures so prominently in history. His great-grandmother married Jean Baptiste de Marigny, son of le Marquis de Marigny. Mr. Hall also has family connections in Baltimore. His grandfather was the first President of the B. & O. Railway. *April 24, 1909*

HALSEY, MRS. FREDERIC R. (EMMA G. KEEP) was a niece of former Governor Roswell P. Flower. She was much interested in the charitable work of St. Thomas's Church in New York and built the Halsey Day Nursery. She was also interested in the Flower Hospital, of which Governor Flower was the founder. *October 24, 1908*

HALSTEAD, MURAT was for many years Editor of the *Cincinnati Commercial-Gazette,* at a time when it ranked as one of the most brilliant newspapers in the country. He was a war-correspondent in the Franco-Prussian war of 1870. Mr. Halstead on March second, 1857, was married to Miss Mary Victoria Banks, and there was much romance in the wedding. The bridegroom, who was booked to report the inauguration of President Buchanan, was in quarantine with varioloid until within a few hours of the ceremony. In order to make railway connections, which were decidedly primitive in those days, the ceremony was delayed until four o'clock in the morning but conducted with all the formality of a wedding at a more customary hour. *March 9, 1907*

HAMMERSLEY, LOUIS GORDON The Court of Appeals has handed down a decision in the famous Hammersley will case, a civil *cause célèbre*. M. Louis Gordon Hammersley, the son of the late J. Hooker Hammersley, under this ruling profits by the estate. He was born years after the will was made, and he was long known as "the infant" and still is under the law, although he is a student at Harvard University. The Hammersleys were a very rich and influential New York family, and their progenitor made a fortune in hardware over a century ago. They were the first New Yorkers to mount liveries, and there was an art gallery at the home of the founder of the house, who lived in a great mansion on Greenwich Street. *June 14, 1913*

HAMILTON, ALEXANDER was his party's nominee for the State Senate in 1930 and a delegate to this year's National Republican Convention. The descendant of our first Secretary of the Treasury and the grandson of J. P. Morgan actually means little enough to the body of voters a few blocks north of Sutton Place. To them, a graduate of St. Paul's and Harvard is better presented as a governor of the Manhattan Council of Boy Scouts and an active member of the increasingly active Ivy Club, oldest Republican Club in New York City. *November 1, 1932*

HAMILTON, HELEN M. Her father, Mr. W. Gaston Hamilton, is a direct descendant of Alexander Hamilton. Her brother, who was popular at Yale and noted for his work with the crew, married a daughter of Mr. J. Pierpont Morgan. Miss Hamilton, who is known best as "Miss Daisy" Hamilton, has a pretty accomplishment in the singing of ballads. During the seasons she spent at Newport, she was prominent in all the entertaining given at Mrs. Schuyler Hamilton's house. *March 18, 1905*

HAMILTON, WILLIAM GASTON is a direct descendant of Alexander Hamilton, and, when younger, his daughters had little enthusiasm for Princeton—perhaps because Aaron Burr's father was once President of the university. *February 20, 1904*

HAMILTON, MR. AND MRS. WILLIAM PIERSON (JULIET MORGAN) have closed their town house to open their home at Tuxedo. Mrs. Hamilton is a wise mother, who believes in developing the individual personalities of her children. J. Pierpont Morgan Hamilton already shows many traits of his grandfather, which are considered by the family irresistibly funny in so small a boy, but which may mean a great deal to the young man later in life. *May 3, 1902*

HAMLIN, MR. AND MRS. HARRY They are always prominent attendants at the New York Horse Show, for the Hamlin stables in Buffalo have for half a century had world-wide fame. "Village Farm," famous as the breeding place of some of the finest horses in the world, was founded half a century ago by the Hamlins and has been conducted by them ever since, Mr. C. J. Hamlin and his son, Mr. Harry Hamlin, being the active owners. *July 29, 1905*

HAMMOND, EMILY SLOANE Her engagement to Mr. John Merryman Franklin, elder son of Mr. and Mrs. P. A. S. Franklin, the former the head of the Mercantile Marine, is announced. Miss Hammond is a great-granddaughter of the late William H. Vanderbilt and therefore fifth in line from Commodore Cornelius Vanderbilt, founder of the Vanderbilt family. General John Henry Hammond, U.S.A., was her paternal grandfather. Mr. Franklin's mother's family belongs to the haute monde of Baltimore's most exclusive circle. Mrs. Franklin was Miss Laura Merryman, of "Hayfields," Cockeysville, Maryland. As head of the International Mercantile Marine, Mr. Franklin is one of our great captains of industry. *May 1, 1922*

HAMMOND, GOVERNOR JAMES H. Governor Hammond has one of the largest landed estates of the South—his "farm" comprising over eleven thousand acres—and may be set down, with propriety, as a representative man of South Carolina. *December 12, 1857*

HAMMOND, NATALIE HAYS "A museum devoted to the human spirit" is how she describes the lively cultural center she created on a pastoral hilltop in northern Westchester County, New York. The annual Blessing of the Land and the Animals brings together priests, rabbis, and monks, children bearing cats and pet insects, housewives bearing houseplants, and, once, a city policeman with his police horse. The monks chant, the frogs in the pond chant, and spring happens as Natalie Hays Hammond believes it should happen. *March, 1982*

HAMPTON, AMBROSE Wade Hampton, a cavalry hero during the Revolution, conquered the wilderness, too. He became one of the South's largest planters, with cotton and sugar lands ranging all the way to Louisiana. Wade's son, Wade II, was famous for his one-horse marathon ride from New Orleans to Washington bearing the glad tidings of Andrew Jackson's victory. Wade III equipped and commanded his own crack legion during the Civil War. Today, in Columbia, South Carolina, the Hamptons are still kings of the upcountry. Ambrose and Harry Rutledge Hampton own Columbia's morning and evening newspapers. Their brother Frank is a gentleman dairy farmer and thoroughbred raiser. *November, 1977*

HANCOCK, ARTHUR BOYD III Scion of a family which for a century has been in the business of breeding distinguished race horses, he grew up at "Claiborne Farm," the world's most important thoroughbred breeding establishment. In January of 1973, Arthur withdrew from Claiborne (subsequently receiving $3.5 million for his share) and devoted all his attention to his own "Stone Farm." From 100 acres and five mares, Stone Farm grew to 2,500 acres, 210 broodmares, and nine stallions. *July, 1983*

HANCOCK, JEAN BARCLAY PENN-GASKELL is a lineal descendant of two Colonial governors who had large grants from the Crown: William Penn, proprietary Governor of Pennsylvania, and Sir Robert Barclay, proprietary Governor of East New Jersey. She was introduced in the old family home at 906 Spruce Street, Philadelphia, which is in the notable group of aristocratic houses in the block called Portico Row, formerly owned by such families as the Wistars, Brocks, Sculls, and Halls. *January 10, 1914*

HANCOCK, CAPTAIN R. J. owns "Ellerslie," a great estate in Charlottesville, Virginia, covering 18,000 acres along the eastern slope of Carter's Mountain. Ellerslie is one of the famous stock farms of the country. The horses bred there "in the purple" furnish a chapter in the history of the American turf. It is an estate also famous for its elms, and this bears out the belief of English horsemen that where elm trees flourish, thoroughbred horses will thrive. *September 21, 1907*

HANCOCK, SETH, master of Kentucky's "Claiborne Farm," syndicator of champions, youngest member of the Jockey Club and still in his early thirties, has already demonstrated his classic potential. Given command of the world's most highly revered thoroughbred breeding farm in 1973 after the sudden death of his father, mythic horseman A. B. "Bull" Hancock, Jr., he immediately showed the will to leap to the front. Less than one month later, he syndicated Secretariat in four days for the then impossible figure of $6,080,000. Last year, the farm established another world record with the $36.4 million syndication of Conquistador Cielo. *July, 1983*

HANES, JOHN W. Of the famous families of the Winston-Salem area and one of the oldest is the Hanes clan, whose founding father, Marcus Hoens, came to Salem in 1774. His descendants were farmers who prospered in the growing and later manufacturing of tobacco. John W. Hanes, the 88-year-old head of the family, is a noted New York financier who retains his ties with North Carolina and, indeed, during the Depression, helped bail the state out of financial distress. Of his late brothers, banker Robert Hanes built the Wachovia Bank and Trust Company into one of the nation's foremost banks; and James G. Hanes developed the great Hanes Hosiery Company and left the bulk of his estate to encourage the arts in Winston-Salem. *March, 1981*

HANNA, MARK A. [in the nineteenth century] kept a big place in Lenox, Massachusetts. The house was always full of an assortment of ladies, the stable full of an assortment of horses. His special carriages were pulled by a team hitched in tandem, and the road in front was kept clear by outriders equipped with trumpets to herald his arrival. *August, 1949*

HANNA, RUTH Mark A. Hanna's daughter, who is a fine horsewoman, refuses to wear skirts on horseback and rides astride, dressed in a suit of clothes that might have been made for a man. One of the suits she wears is of fawn-colored stuff. The breeches are of the regulation riding style, loose and full at the hips, gradually narrowing down to a close fit at the knees. Below them she wears gaiters of the same color. Her jacket is a sort of semi-cutaway of the same color and, opening at the neck, reveals a stiff shirt and collar and a jauntily-tied necktie. *September 9, 1896*

HANNUM, MRS. JOHN B. (NANCY PENN SMITH) is the Master and huntsman of Mr. Stewart's Cheshire Foxhounds, a private pack of English hounds which, for the last sixty years, has made Unionville, Pennsylvania, a mecca for fox hunters. Born with a silver hunting horn in her mouth, Nancy lists six Masters of Foxhounds in her immediate family. E. H. Harriman, her maternal grandfather, founded the Orange County Hounds in New York, and her paternal grandfather, R. Penn Smith, was M.F.H. of the Chester Valley Hounds in Pennsylvania. The overwhelming majority of the 130 hunts in the United States are clubs or subscription packs, supported by members or subscribers. The Cheshire is a private hunt; Nancy Hannum owns the hounds and horses, pays the staff, and bears all expenses. Friends and neighbors hunt by invitation only. The costs are staggering. *January, 1975*

HARE, HORACE V. is M.F.H. of the Radnor Hounds. The hunt was started in 1880 by Mr. James Rawle. The present master, since accepting the mastership in 1909 and carrying the horn himself, has fully kept up the reputation for good sport which has always been the heritage and pride of this old Philadelphia hunt. A keen horseman and a really close observer of hounds in their work, he has labored conscientiously to improve his country and his hounds. *January 3, 1914*

HARE, MONTGOMERY is a grandson of the late Rev. George Emlen Hare, who was famous for his Biblical learning, and great-grandson of Bishop John Henry Hobart, who was active in founding the General Theological Seminary which occupies Chelsea Square in New York City and where Hobart Hall contains a famous library of twenty three thousand volumes. *March 14, 1908*

HARGRAVE, WILLIAM A. A sixth-generation Chicagoan, Billy Hargrave is the grandson of actress Colleen Moore, who later became a partner of his grandfather's firm, Merrill Lynch. Hargrave's mother was a Pirie of Carson Pirie Scott. Retail stores are a recurring theme in old Chicago families. Hargrave is in the brokerage business. *December, 1988*

HARKNESS, HARRY S. was President of the Sheepshead Bay Corporation, owner of the Sheepshead Bay Speedway, President of the Harkness Estates, and one of the largest stockholders in the Standard Oil Company. With two sisters, he shared the $150,000,000 estate left by their father. Mr. Harkness owned

the U.S.S. Yacht *Wakvia II,* sunk in May, 1918. It was claimed for the yacht that she had sunk three German submarines. *February 10, 1919*

HARKNESS, WILLIAM L. left an estate of over $53,439,437. No part of the fortune goes to charity, although he made a gift of $400,000 to Yale for a recitation building shortly before his death. His will gave his widow one half of the residuary estate, $26,366,794. The remainder of the estate went to his daughter, Louise H. Harkness, and son, William H. Harkness. *May 1, 1921*

HARPER, MRS. FLETCHER (JANE FREELOVE LYON), the wife of the well-known publisher of the house of Harper & Brothers, has set on foot an admirable charity. At her instigation, Mr. Fletcher Harper has purchased the Seashore Cottage at Atlanticville, New Jersey, and is about to have it fitted up as a hotel, to be devoted exclusively to the entertainment of working girls during the summer months. *March 27, 1878*

HARRIMAN, E. ROLAND is Wall Street's air commuter from Arden, New York. Head of the Grand Circuit, founder of the Trotting Horse Club of America, and owner of Goshen's Historic Track, he has just been made honorary President of the new U. S. Trotting Association, a merger of racing organizations he has been trying to bring about since 1926. *March, 1939*

HARRIMAN, EDWARD HENRY Some years ago, Mr. E. H. Harriman made a journey to Alaska. His first reason for making the venture was a desire to shoot a Kodiak bear. But eventually, it became a scientific expedition, with twenty five men of science and three artists, all at the expense of Mr. Harriman. But though handicapped by men who were poking around with microscopes and other implements of scholarly inquiry, Mr. Harriman did bring down his bear, the first of the species ever to be measured or photographed. *June 26, 1909*

HARRIMAN, MRS. J. BORDEN (FLORENCE JAFFRAY HURST) The Colony Club formally opened this week. Society women who, perhaps, had not been so "chummy" since their schoolgirl days were brought together by their interest in the club. Miss Elsie de Wolfe made good her promise to create "the club beautiful" so far as interiors go. Mrs. J. Borden Harriman, a typical "out-door matron," makes a good President of a club which will include in its membership not only the strictly society element but women who are bread-winners. *March 16, 1907*

HARRIMAN, W. AVERELL occupies today in the world of shipping a position certainly comparable with that held by his father in the railroad industry twenty years ago. In his college days, Mr. Harriman was not robust enough to make the crew or football team. But he did achieve the distinction of becoming head coach for both the freshman and varsity eights. Now he is the driving force in a half dozen shipping organizations and a leader in the movement to establish a permanent merchant marine. In April of 1915, he rescued Miss Kitty Lanier Lawrence when she was thrown from a runaway horse. The following September, they were married. *November 15, 1922*

HARRINGTON, MRS. DONALD D. (SYBIL BUCKINGHAM) was born and reared in Amarillo, Texas, the granddaughter of some of the town's first settlers. Grand opera is Sybil Harrington's grand passion. Since 1978, this vivacious widow of a pioneer Texas oilman has personally bankrolled eleven new productions at the Metropolitan Opera. Mrs. Harrington has given more to the company than any other individual in its history. She has given, through the Don and Sybil Harrington Foundation, many times more to eighty nine little-known charities in and around her hometown. *December, 1988*

HARRINGTON, GEORGE The assistant to the Secretary of the Treasury at Washington, sailed for England on a three-months' leave of absence for his health. This distinguished state officer takes abroad with him, fortunately, one whom it will be a great pleasure to present to the brilliant circles of London diplomatic society—Mrs. Harrington, a lady holding a position, both before and since her marriage, as the most brilliant conversationalist our country ever produced. *October 3, 1863*

HARRIS, JOEL CHANDLER "Uncle Remus" dined at the White House the other day, and you may be sure that when President Theodore Roosevelt and Joel Chandler Harris got to telling stories, the bison and the elks on the walls of the great state dining room heard yarns that reminded them of "the times that was." *November 30, 1907*

HARRISON, MRS. BURTON N. (CONSTANCE CARY) Born in Fairfax County, Virginia, she is connected through both her parents with some of the foremost families in this country. Her father, Archibald Cary, was nearly related to Thomas Jefferson, and her mother was a descendant of Lord Fairfax. She was married to Mr. Burton Harrison, who had been private secretary to Jefferson Davis. Mrs. Harrison's summers are spent for the most part at Bar Harbor, Maine, where her villa, "Sea Urchins," is a center of the social life of that watering place. Indeed, Mrs. Harrison is so much a part of society that her novels pertaining to that phase of life may be quoted as a true picture of the ways and manners of society folk. *August 9, 1900*

HARRISON, MR. AND MRS. CHARLES LEARNER III There have been Harrisons in Cincinnati for at least five generations. Charles Learner Harrison III is a partner in the stockbrockerage firm of Harrison & Company, and he and his pretty wife, who is also Cincinnati born, live in a large, sprawling house in countrified Indian Hill. "We never traveled much," Molly Harrison recalls with a smile. "The feeling was that Cincinnati is such a pleasant place, so why should anyone go anywhere else?" *October, 1975*

HARRISON, FRANCIS BURTON The official announcement of his appointment as Governor General of the Philippines was made in Washington. He was for ten years the Representative in Congress from the New York district. He has always been a staunch supporter of the Democratic party. It will be remembered that Mr. Harrison's father, an able and brilliant lawyer, was secretary to Jefferson Davis at Richmond when the latter was President of the Confederate States. *October 11, 1913*

HARTFORD, HUNTINGTON Hunt has more pies than he has fingers. These include the A&P heir's new resort heaven, Paradise Island, in the Bahamas; that new slick magazine of the arts, *Show;* the Oil Shale Corporation; a Handwriting Institute for psychological research in New York; the Huntington Hartford Theatre in Hollywood; an automatic-parking operation called Speed-Park, Inc., in New York; a new Gallery of Modern Art being built on Columbus Circle in New York; and a standing offer to build a sidewalk cafe for the people of Manhattan in Central Park. *August, 1962*

HARTRIDGE, MR. AND MRS. WALTER Mrs. Hartridge is directly descended from both Charles Augustus Lafayette Lamar and Henry Jackson. (Charles Lamar bought the yacht *Wanderer* from the New York Yacht Club and imported slaves in it in 1858, fifty years after their importation was outlawed; Henry Jackson prosecuted Lamar in a famous trial on nearby St. Simon's Island.) Mrs. Hartridge's husband is descended from James Wayne, a justice of the United States Supreme Court who presided at the trial. *May, 1969*

HASBROUCK, CHARLES "My father, genealogist Kenneth Hasbrouck, has been referred to as 'Mr. History,'" Hasbrouck says, "and I was raised in New Paltz, which was settled by a dozen Huguenot families, including the Hasbroucks, in 1677. I grew up in a stone farmhouse that was built in 1798. When I went to college, I was determined *not* to be a historian. But," he grins, "here I am." Today, Mr. Hasbrouck's speciality is restoration. *September, 1987*

HASTINGS, MRS. THOMAS (HELEN BENEDICT), who is the elder daughter of Mr. E. C. Benedict, is always much in the "Public Eye" during the week of the National Horse Show, as she usually drives for friends. Often she is spoken of as the best four-in-hand driver in this country. At the outdoor horse shows she has driven this fall for Mr. Clarence Mackay, winning blue ribbons for his "four." Mrs. Hastings is the wife of Mr. Thomas Hastings, one of the greatest of American architects. *November 10, 1906*

HAUPT, MRS. IRA (ENID ANNENBERG) The retired editor-publisher of *Seventeen* magazine (from 1953 to 1970) is the sister of Walter Annenberg and the widow of financier Ira Haupt. Her main avocation is horticulture, for which she has won many citations and trophies; it's also her main philanthropic interest. Since 1978, she has given more than $10 million to the New York Botanical Garden; she's also planted hundreds of cherry trees on Park Avenue in New York. *December, 1983*

HAVEMEYER, HENRY OSBORNE One of our representatives was present at the marriage of Mr. Henry Osborne Havemeyer and Miss Mary Louise, daughter of George Elder, at the South Reformed Church, Fifth Avenue. The four ushers created several blunders and considerable confusion by their want of tact and composure. Ladies were hurried up the aisle in the most unceremonious manner, gentlemen were rudely addressed, and, altogether, the inefficiency of the ushers marred the enjoyment of the occasion. Nor did the organist give satisfaction. He performed the most doleful and inappropriate selection of music it has ever been our duty to listen to. *March 9, 1870*

HAVEMEYER, HORACE has formed the new sugar company to be known as Welch, Havemeyer & Fairchild. Mr. Havemeyer has been recently engaged in a long legal contest with the American Sugar Refining Company over an allotment of $10,000,000 of the stock of the National Sugar Refining Company made to his father. The old Sugar Trust so called, which began in a humble way nearly a century ago in Williamsburg, New York, has been more or less a family affair. His father, the late Henry O. Havemeyer, married twice, both of his wives being members of the Elder family who were also in the sugar business. The separation of business interests which have lasted so many years, in a little set of people all related to each other, means quite a wrench, and a drifting away from old associations. *August 10, 1912*

HAVEMEYER, THEODORE A. The New York Farmers is a society of very rich men who come together for a dinner in the Metropolitan Club. Each member is a specialist in some line of farming. A conspicuous member of the society is Theodore A. Havemeyer of the American Sugar Refining Company. He follows dairy farming with such force and common sense that from three thousand enfeebled New Jersey acres, he gets a yearly dividend of from seven to ten per cent. *March 10, 1897*

HAVEN, GEORGE GRISWOLD, who was born in 1837, was graduated from Columbia University in 1857. He was the President and Managing Director of the Metropolitan Opera and Real Estate Company. He was one of the first members of the Coaching Club of New York and, for many years, was a member of the New York Yacht Club. He had been a member of the Stock Exchange and had large financial and railway interests. *March 28, 1908*

HAVEN, LEILA is granddaughter of the late George Griswold Haven of New York and a great-granddaughter of John Arnot, the first citizen of Elmira, New York, to take a place among the great magnates in this country. It was the three sons of John Arnot who founded the Chemung Canal Bank. Mr. Matthias Arnot, who invented an aeroplane, is a son of John Arnot, 2d. *December 11, 1909*

HAWKES, McDOUGALL is a direct descendant of General Alexander McDougall, who was the first President of the Bank of New York and of the New York Society of the Cincinnati. His father, the late W. Wright Hawkes, was well known as an orator and for some time had the chair of English literature at Trinity College. As a lawyer, Mr. Hawkes was commissioner of docks and is an authority on engineering and real estate matters concerning the waterfront and the port of New York. *May 30, 1908*

HAWKINS, RALPH CLYMER The Order of the Founders and Patriots of America is not a large organization, but it is organized in a score of states. To be a member, one must not only be lineally descended from a "Founder" (an ancestor who settled in the Colonies prior to May 13, 1657) but also descended in the same line from a "Patriot" (an ancestor who, in the Revolutionary period, either served in the Armed Forces or by some overt act definitely attached himself to the American cause). Ralph Clymer Hawkins has been a member of Founders and Patriots for forty years. "The real thing about this organization," he said feelingly, "is the uniqueness. It's that double badge of honor— both a Founder and a Patriot *in the same line,* remember." *July, 1962*

HAWLEY, EDWIN, the bachelor railroad man, who left an estate worth about $25,000,000, died intestate, according to a statement issued by John B. Stanchfield, as attorney on behalf of his heirs. The fact that Mr. Hawley left no will came as a windfall to none of these so much as to Frederick Crandell, a nephew, who had been cast off by his uncle in a quarrel many years ago, and who had been making a precarious living ever since, lately as a bookkeeper for a firm of stevedores. *February 17, 1912*

HAXALL, MR. AND MRS. BOLLING (ELIZABETH DODGE) live on Club Island off the town of Clayton, further up-river toward the St. Lawrence's source, Lake Ontario. Their grandchildren, summering on the wooded ten-acre island with them, comprise the sixth generation of Mrs. Haxall's family in the Thousand Islands. Relatives are still around them in their island group, with cousins on the points of nearby Grindstone Island and Mrs. Haxall's father on a neighboring Canadian island. *August, 1978*

HAY, HELEN The wedding of the daughter of Secretary and Mrs. John Hay to Mr. Payne Whitney, the son of Mr. William C. Whitney, was a matter of more than local social interest. The parentage of both the bride and groom made the wedding one of national importance, and Miss Hay's achievements in the literary field, moreover, have made friends for her among thousands who may never have seen her. The President and Mrs. Roosevelt were the only guests other than relatives who attended the wedding breakfast. *February 13, 1902*

HAY, JOHN, President Lincoln's private secretary and co-author of his life, has been selected by President-elect McKinley for the post of Ambassador to Great Britain. Colonel Hay has served as Secretary of legation at Paris, Vienna, and Madrid. *January 6, 1897*

HAYES, MR. AND MRS. AUGUSTUS, JR., 112 East Twenty Fifth Street, gave a reception in compliment to Oscar Wilde, the poet. Mr. Wilde wore a Prince Albert coat, tightly buttoned, and held in his hand a pair of light gloves. His manner exhibited the unconsciousness of a gentleman. The lines of his face are essentially feminine, but these are on so large a scale that their soft curves indicate none of the weaknesses which might hastily attach to the adjective.

Otherwise his broad, sturdy physique is as English as if trained in athletics instead of aesthetics. *January 11, 1882*

HAYES, MRS. FRANCIS B. (NINO K. HUNT) Another new house in Aiken, South Carolina, just brought to completion is that of Mrs. N. K. Hayes. Mrs. Hayes is well remembered as the champion horsewoman who rides at Meadowbrook and owns Chappie, the champion jumper of the world. *March 1, 1902*

HAYES, MRS. JOEL ADDISON (MARGARET HOWELL DAVIS) Mr. William Beverly Rogers, who is to marry Miss Lucy White Hayes, a granddaughter of Jefferson Davis, is at the El Paso Club in Colorado Springs. Mrs. Joel Addison Hayes, the mother of the young bride-to-be, is the recognized leader of society at Colorado Springs; and in bringing out a handsome bulletin to illustrate the progress and prosperity in Colorado Springs, a portrait of Mrs. Hayes was used to aid in representing the social conditions of life in this health-restoring place. *February 18, 1905*

HAYWARD, HARRIET TAFT, daughter of Mr. and Mrs. Harry Taft Hayward, of Franklin, Massachusetts, has just opened a hat shop at Wellesley for the exclusive clientele of the Wellesley College girls, calling herself The Mad Hatter. *March 1, 1929*

HAYWARD, MR. AND MRS. LELAND (PAMELA DIGBY)—CHURCHILL Pamela is a big-city girl who has always moved in geopolitical society. She was formerly married to Randolph Churchill, and her son is Winston Churchill. With the flair of a cosmopolite, she manages to make the right scene always, but always, at the right time. During the war, she made the No. 10 Downing Street scene. The late '40s and '50s found her in Paris, where the action was. And now she is where it's all happening, in Manhattan. *September, 1967*

HAZARD, CAROLINE, President of Wellesley College since 1889, is a descendant of Thomas H. Hazard, founder of Newport, Rhode Island. She is the author of much interesting literature about the "Narragansett Country" and the Quakers, who once inhabited Newport and the neighboring region. *November 14, 1903*

HEADLEY, MR. AND MRS. GEORGE (BARBARA WHITNEY) start the ball rolling at Keeneland, Kentucky, with their Saturday evening Winter Wonderland Ball, a beautiful heat-of-July refresher, properly chilled by ice-colored and silver-sparkled decorations. Two tents are pitched around the famous Headley bibelot museums, shell grottos, and porcelain collections to accommodate the more than 500 very international and very horsey guests who drink champagne ice, wander around the museums, and dance to two Palm Beach orchestras. *July, 1977*

HEARN, GEORGE A., 46 East Sixty Ninth Street, New York, gave a brilliant reception in honor of the St. George's Society, an organization composed of residents of the United States, English-born or of English ancestry. Gentlemen only were present, and the guests, having received a specially-bound catalogue on their entrance, bent their attention to the rare treasures of art that line the walls of the

reception room and library, and which are hung in every part of the spacious house. It is a matter of common knowledge among connoisseurs that Mr. Hearn owns one of the largest and finest individual collections of paintings in this country. *May 4, 1898*

HEARST, MRS. GEORGE A. (PHOEBE APPERSON) has been appointed a regent of California State University. This is the first time a lady has ever been appointed on the board. Her appointment was asked for by the women graduates of the university. *August 25, 1897*

WITH THE WISDOM Of SOLOMON

While making his fortune as an engineer in South Africa, John Hays Hammond became the associate of Cecil Rhodes, played a part in his dream of empire. Trekking to the northward, he casually built his fire on the edge of some pits. Daylight aroused his curiosity. He had rediscovered King Solomon's mines. Fortune made, he became in Washington the consultant not only of ephemeral Presidents but steady Western politicians—not a king-maker so much as a maker of king-makers. *December 1, 1931*

HEARST, WILLIAM RANDOLPH Mr. Hearst's ranch high above San Simeon combines wild California mountain country and palace splendor. Mr. Hearst inherited the ranch from his father. He has enlarged it until it now extends over almost three hundred thousand acres. To get a feasible site for the "Casa Grande" and its suite of guest houses, swimming pool, plaza, and gardens, a top was sliced off the mountain. Superb gardens were developed on different levels, approached by sweeping flights of stairs. Whole facades of celebrated palaces have contributed to the building up of "La Cuesta Encantada." The large menagerie in a huge enclosure near the house becomes a legitimate part of the fantasy, a link with the wild trails Mr. Hearst likes to ride, trails which often provide the merest footholds for the horses. *November 15, 1931*

HECKSCHER, MR. AND MRS. AUGUST (ANNA P. ATKINS) will be at Huntington, Long Island, in the late spring. Mr. Heckscher takes great interest in his estate, and in the development of the gardens from the very beginning of the season. The grounds of the Heckscher estate are particularly beautiful because they are so natural. The fine strip of woodland has been carefully preserved, and the road leading through it has been left open to the public, so that it is possible for anyone to take the drive through the woods, coming out where there is a view of Huntington Harbor. *March 11, 1911*

HECKSCHER, JOHN GERARD was the son of the late General Charles A. Heckscher and Georgiana Coster Heckscher. He was born in New York in 1837 and was the namesake of his maternal grandfather, John Gerard Coster, who came to New York about 1790 and was for many years one of the best known mer-

chants in New York and President of the Bank of the Manhattan Company. Mr. Heckscher was one of the founders of the Coney Island Jockey Club and one of the organizers of the National Horse Show Association. *July 11, 1908*

HECKSCHER, MAURICE, of New York, is at present the hero of Burlingame. Mr. Heckscher is making his large investments in California, and recently he bought the "Hope Ranch" at Santa Barbara. When he heard that the San Mateo Polo Club's polo field was to be divided and sold for residential lots, he bought the polo field for $100,000 rather than see the polo field the home of hundreds of unknown Smiths and Joneses, who never heard of the game of polo. *November 10, 1918*

HEFFELFINGER, MR. AND MRS. FRANK TOTTON (LUCIA LOUISE PEAVEY) The most novel holiday event in The Twin Cities was the mask ball given by Mr. and Mrs. Frank T. Heffelfinger at Minnetonka. A special train was arranged to carry the two hundred guests to the lake, but the night was so beautiful and warm that many of them preferred to travel by motor and preserve their disguises. The road to the station, a mile away, was hung with colored lights. Mrs. Heffelfinger was Brunhilde, and Mr. Heffelfinger a very effective Mephistopheles with an evil eye whose light was brightened by an electric attachment tucked in his belt. *January 12, 1907*

HEINE, MARGUERITE ALICE The maiden name of the Duchesse de Richelieu, who is to marry the Prince of Monaco, was Heine, her father being M. Michel Heine, an American banker. Her father was a cousin of the poet Heinrich Heine, and, after being a banker at New Orleans, he has settled in Paris. The bride will be the first Jewess by birth legitimately married to a reigning Catholic prince. *November 13, 1889*

HEINZ, MR. AND MRS. HENRY J. II (DRUE M. ENGLISH)—ROBERTSON—MACKENZIE—MAHER Drue Heinz will tell you that she's just another housewife. Says she. Well, she's got the houses. There's the mansion of the Heinz dynasty in Pittsburgh named "Sweet Water." There's a villa on the French Riviera. There's a house in Paris. There's a little mews house in London's Berkeley Square. There is the place in Greenwich, Connecticut. Throw in an apartment of three floors overlooking the East River, right here in Manhattan. And there's an island in the Bahamas with a fishing lodge. *September, 1967*

HEINZ, HOWARD, Vice President of the H. J. Heinz Company of Pittsburgh, is a Yale man, was one of the most popular men in his class, and has spent much time abroad. He is as much interested in college settlement work as he is in the great industry that bears his name. He founded and maintained "Covode House" in Alleghany, where the greatest amount of intelligent, well-directed, only settlement work is carried on. The time a young society man usually spends at his club, Mr. Heinz devotes to philanthropy. *February 3, 1906*

HENDERSON, MR. AND MRS. FRANK, of New York, who are spending the season at "Whitehall," Palm Beach, gave a very novel beefsteak dinner in February. The guests motored to

HEARST

Joanne Hearst with Hearst cousins, 1959.

George Hearst, a Missouri farm boy fascinated with mining, went to California in 1850. After nine lean years of prospecting, he hit pay dirt in three separate metals; soon he was a major investor in the Nevada Comstock (silver) Lode, the Homestake Mine in South Dakota (gold), and the Anaconda copper mine in Montana. Among other properties, he developed a million-acre ranch in Mexico. Active in Democratic party politics, he eventually served as senator from California. In 1880, he acquired the *San Francisco Examiner*, for the price of its debts. His wife, Phoebe Apperson, became a major benefactor of the fledgling University of California at Berkeley and a founder of the National Cathedral School for Girls in Washington, D.C. She played an active role in the women's rights movement and in the American Red Cross.

When the Hearsts' only child, William Randolph, left Harvard, he asked to manage the *Examiner.* Full of new ideas, he immediately began to expand the newspaper, adding more colorful news coverage. In 1895, William Randolph came to New York and bought the ailing *Morning Journal*—he cut the paper's price to a penny, introduced biting cartoons, and aggressively investigated municipal scandals. Going head-to-head with Joseph Pulitzer's *World,* he instigated circulation wars at the turn of the century, finally trouncing the *World* with his coverage of the Spanish-American War. He printed the first newspaper front page in color in 1897 and pioneered movie newsreels when his photographers recorded the inauguration of President Woodrow Wilson in 1913. Hearst added *Town &*

Country to his successful stable of popular magazines in 1925.

Despite his New York publishing and political ties (he was congressman from New York in 1903–07), Hearst never forgot his California origins. His favorite home of several was "San Simeon," which he began building along the Pacific coast in 1919. During the 1920s and 1930s, statesmen, royalty, writers, and movie stars arrived on a special train from Los Angeles on Friday evening and found themselves the next morning surrounded by grazing zebras and wildebeests from W. R.'s private zoo. In 1981, *Town & Country* itemized San Simeon's many riches: 123 acres of gardens, terraces, two swimming pools, three guesthouses, and a castle known as La Casa Grande, with 38 bedrooms, 31 bathrooms, 14 sitting rooms, a movie theater, caves of wine, a library with over five thousand books, and underground vaults to store an endless assemblage of treasures.

In 1903, W. R. married Millicent Wilson, who was for many years head of the Milk Fund; they were the parents of five sons, all of whom worked in the Hearst empire. Today, The Hearst Corporation is one of the largest diversified communications companies in the world and has operations in magazine, newspaper, and book publishing, radio and television stations, cable networks and programming, television production, newspaper syndication, and new media services. The company is owned by the Hearst Family Trust, which is operated for the benefit of William Randolph Hearst's descendants.

Empire builders: *clockwise from top left,* Mrs. William Randolph Hearst, in 1934; Phoebe Hearst, 1947; William Randolph Hearst; Mr. and Mrs. Randolph Hearst, 1989; in 1942, brothers John, William R., and David Hearst.

Boca Raton, where dinner was served on the beach opposite the Ritz-Carlton Cloister, the steaks being cooked over an open fire by a chef from the Green Room Club, of New York. A band of fifteen played for dancing. There were special entertainers, also a treasure hunt and many other surprises for the guests. *March 15, 1926*

HENDERSON, MRS. JOHN B. Remarkable indeed was the dinner given by Mrs. John B. Henderson, wife of ex-Senator Henderson, at her picturesque home, "Boundary Castle," in Washington, D. C., in honor of twenty four delegates to the National Society for the Study and Prevention of Tuberculosis. Mrs. Henderson is a stern vegetarian, so she and Dr. Kellogg, of Battle Creek, Michigan, connived to invite the most rabid meat advocates to partake of a strictly vegetarian menu, which started off with fruit soup, followed by mock-salmon, with sauce Hollandaise and cucumbers. The menu also had a supplementary card, showing just how many "food units" were supplied by each dish. *May 27, 1905*

HENRY, J. NORMAN III Though by profession an investment counselor, he also collects paintings and antique cars, owns an art gallery, and publishes limited-edition fine art books. It's only natural; his great-great-grandfather, Henry C. Gibson, was a major donor to the Pennsylvania Academy of Fine Arts, and his great-great-aunt was Mary Cassatt. *November, 1984*

HENRY, SALLY DREXEL Probably no Philadelphia debutante is having a more brilliant season planned in her honor than Miss Sally Drexel Henry, the daughter by a former marriage of Mrs. Gouverneur Cadwalader. Named for her grandmother, Mrs. Alexander Van Rensselaer, who was Miss Sally Drexel, she is the first debutante for many years in the many branches of this family, and an almost endless chain of entertaining is being planned in her honor. *October 1, 1923*

HENRY, MR. AND MRS. W. BARKLIE (ALICE BELKNAP) closed their country home at Radnor. Mrs. Henry is well known to New York people and was in this city last spring at the Coaching Parade. She is a daughter of William Worth Belknap, the soldier who came into prominence during Sherman's march to the sea, and who was Secretary of War during Grant's administration. William Goldsmith Belknap, Mrs. Henry's grandfather, made his name for gallantry with General Taylor's Rio Grande campaign. *January 14, 1905*

HERRICK, EDWIN W. was one of the prominent pioneers of Minneapolis, having come from Ohio in 1867. He was active in all movements that tended to develop the musical and artistic interests of the city. His ancestors settled in Virginia in 1653, and he was intimately connected with the Herricks who, for three hundred years, have held the estate "Beau Manor Park" in Leicester, England. *May 20, 1911*

HERTER, MRS. CHRISTIAN (MARY MILES), the mother of two distinguished New Yorkers, is establishing a salon in Santa Barbara, California. A short time ago, for example, she induced Rear Admiral McCalla, U.S.N.

(retired) to read parts of his lectures to a group of her friends. These lectures were of the series delivered by the Admiral at the War College after he had led Seymour's column to the relief of the legations during the Boxer uprising in China in 1900. One of Mrs. Herter's sons is Dr. Christian A. Herter, an authority on neurology, and the other, Mr. Albert Herter, the artist. *April 6, 1907*

HEWITT, MRS. ABRAM S. (SARAH AMELIA COOPER) was the widow of Mr. Abram S. Hewitt, who was Mayor of New York City in 1887 and 1888, and for many years a Representative in Congress. Mrs. Hewitt was the only daughter of Mr. Peter Cooper, founder of Cooper Union. Mrs. Hewitt, who was very wealthy and owned much valuable real estate in the city, also had the distinction of having been the wife of a Mayor of New York City and a sister of another Mayor, Mr. Edward Cooper, who was in office in 1879 and 1880. *August 24, 1912*

HEWITT, ELEANOR GURNEE, daughter of the late Abram S. Hewitt, Mayor of New York, and one of the dignified representatives of the social regime of old New York, died at her country home, "The Forges," at Ringwood Manor, New Jersey. She founded the Cooper Union Art and Decorating Museum, as her grandfather, Peter Cooper, had founded Cooper Union. *December 15, 1924*

HEWITT, FREDERICK COOPER of Oswego, New York, left an estate estimated to be worth over $5,000,000. The principal bequests are $2,000,000 to the New York Hospital, $1,500,000 to the Metropolitan Museum of Art, which society is also made his residuary legatee, and $500,000 to Yale University. The will stipulates that should any of his heirs attempt to break the will he shall forfeit his inheritance, which shall then go to the Metropolitan Museum of Art. *September 19, 1908*

HEWITT, PETER COOPER, the American inventor, was a son of Mr. Abram S. Hewitt, Mayor of New York, and a grandson of Peter Cooper, the philanthropist. The incandescent light which bears his name is about eight times stronger than the ordinary incandescent light produced by the same amount of power. *October 1, 1921*

HEWLETT, RICHARD, whose engagement to Miss Althea Livingston Schoonmaker is announced, is one of the Long Island Hewletts, whose ancestor, Richard Hewlett, was a famous Loyalist during the Revolution. At Southold and Setauket, he was staunch in his support of the King. Later, he was made Mayor of St. Johns, New Brunswick, and grantee of the town. His son was prominent on Long Island later. Marius Schoonmaker, Miss Althea's ancestor, is identified with the locale of Kingston and was the author of its history. *May 6, 1905*

HEYE, MR. AND MRS. GEORGE (BLANCHE A. WILLIAMS) have closed their country home at Woodmere, Long Island, and are at their city home, 667 Madison Avenue. While at Woodmere, Mrs. Heye gave several of the clever dinners for which she has acquired a name. For one of the dinners, the walls were covered with fish nets, in which imitation fish,

lobsters, and crabs were entangled. In one corner of the room, a life-sized figure of a fisherman stood. The table was a reproduction of a bridge and a pond. Souvenirs in clams, all sorts of droll features, enlivened the dinner. *October 19, 1907*

HICKS, JOHN D. was born in Westbury, Long Island, where his ancestors settled over two hundred years ago. One of his forefathers was Elias Hicks, the famous Quaker minister, who was born in Hempstead in 1748. Mr. Hicks was prominent in the financial world and was greatly interested in the welfare of Swarthmore College, founded by Samuel Willets, the Quaker philanthropist. Mr. Hicks is survived by his wife, who is a member of the Haviland family of France. *December 28, 1907*

HIGBIE, MR. AND MRS. HUGO S. The Higbies do so much entertaining that the Grosse Pointers have nicknamed their house with its formal backyard garden "The Embassy." Says Mrs. Higbie, "We always try to have congenial people. I do a lot of careful planning, having good service, lots to drink, and good old-fashioned Lester Lanin type music. Never any of that rock-n'-roll." *May, 1972*

HIGGINSON, A. H. is one of the best-known sportsmen in America, a steward of the National Steeplechase Association, President for many years of the Masters of Foxhounds Association, and master of many packs, first of his own pack in South Lincoln in Massachusetts and now Joint Master of the Cattistock in that romantic southwest county of England. *July 15, 1931*

HIGGINSON, MAJOR HENRY LEE Since the death of J. P. Morgan, he had been regarded as the dean of American financiers. He was the head of the firm of Lee Higginson Co., one of the leading banking houses of the world, and the founder of the Boston Symphony Orchestra. *December 10, 1919*

HIGGINSON, JAMES JACKSON was one of the original members of the New York Stock Exchange and President of the Harvard Club. He was a great-grandson of Stephen Higginson, of Salem, and a brother of Major Henry Lee Higginson (who did much in the interests of music in Boston in his work to organize the symphony orchestra). *January 14, 1911*

HIGGINSON, COLONEL THOMAS WENTWORTH Stephen Higginson, his father, was steward of Harvard University from 1818 to 1834. The first Stephen Higginson, grandfather of Colonel Higginson, was a delegate to the Continental Congress. Colonel Higginson graduated from the divinity school in 1847, and in the same year was ordained pastor of the first Congregational Church in Newburyport, Massachusetts. He left this church on account of his anti-slavery principles and preaching. He was an earnest advocate of women's suffrage and of the higher education of both sexes. *May 20, 1911*

HILL, MRS. CHARLES E., of Baltimore, was a descendant of John Clayton, Attorney General of Virginia and Judge of the Admiralty Court, who was frequently a member of the Virginia House of Burgesses. John Clayton was a son of Sir John Clayton, of Hawkshurst, Kent County, England. Mrs. Hill was also descended from the Ridgely, Stockett, Page, and Pendleton families of Maryland and Virginia. *April 20, 1907*

HILL, J. JEROME has been winning laurels as an artist. The young man is the second son of Mr. and Mrs. Louis Hill and the grandson of the late J. J. Hill. His talent for, and interest in, canvases has been recognized since his young boyhood, and he has delved into the subject seriously. *November 1, 1924*

HILL, LOUIS W. succeeded his father, Mr. James J. Hill, as Chairman of the Board of Directors of the Great Northern Road. In the development of the great territory through which the Great Northern passes, he has been continually active. In the current biographies, he is called the "Prince of Press Agents—the Discoverer and Inventor of the Northwest" that after his father had built his empire, the son came along and put it in the show window. *September 14, 1912*

HILLMAN, MR. AND MRS. HENRY LEA (ELSIE MEAD HILLIARD) stand in front of the $12 million Hillman Library, completed in 1969, at the University of Pittsburgh. Hillman is head of Pittsburgh's Coke & Chemical and, through the Hillman Co., the family investment holding company, controls and influences vast corporate and banking interests. Elsie Mead Hillman is the very visible member of the family through her work for the local Republican group. *February, 1975*

HINES, EDWARD Edward Hines Lumber Company, founded in 1892 by the philanthropist of the same name, provided the wood that helped build the Chicago Stockyards, the Great Lakes Naval Base, major Loop office buildings, and Chicago's Century of Progress Exhibition in 1933. His grandson Edward sold off the lumber mills and other assets in 1983 and bought out the retail operations, converting the company into a new Edward Hines Lumber Co., technically preserving the company's identity as one of only three major Chicago concerns founded in the nineteenth century which are still run by their founding families. *September, 1990*

HINKLE, ANTHONY HOWARD was for years one of Cincinnati's most prominent and philanthropic citizens, and an active promoter of opera. Mr. Hinkle entered the publishing house of W. B. Smith & Co., from which issued the McGuffey school books in 1862. He was constantly promoted while with the firm, and between 1865 and 1890 he filled every position from shipping clerk to proprietor. *June 3, 1911*

HITCHCOCK, ANNE made her debut at St. Petersburg when her father, Ethan Allen Hitchcock, was stationed there as our Minister to Russia. It is very remarkable that Mrs. Hitchcock and her two daughters have returned in person every call made upon them since their sojourn in Washington, in spite of the fact that expediency long ago decided that it was impossible for the family of a cabinet officer to make a thousand calls in one season, and even the

practice of sending a card by a footman has been abandoned. However, Mrs. Hitchcock has been heard to say: "If people do me the honor of calling on me, I certainly should return the compliment. And," she added, "I frequently have the pleasantest visits in the humblest houses." *September 16, 1905*

HITCHCOCK, CENTER He was educated at Oxford, and besides his interest in outdoor sports he was a patron of art and of music. He was the President of the Brook Club, of which he was one of the founders, and was a member of the majority of the important clubs of New York. *January 2, 1909*

HOME, HOME ON THE RANGE

A buffalo hunt is a novel sport these days, when there are in existence only a few herd. Mr. James J. Hill of St. Paul has a herd at his farm at North Oaks, not far from St. Paul; and as it had grown to twenty animals, it was considered too large by its owner. Accordingly, he gave his son, Mr. Walter Hill, permission to have a buffalo hunt. Mr. Hill took the first shot. He failed, however, to drop a big bull who started for the hunters and, according to authoritative tales, they were forced to climb a tree to escape from the angry beast. They were treed for some time; but at last the buffalo roamed away and the hunters descended. *January 22, 1910*

HITCHCOCK, ETHAN ALLEN was in China when a young man as a member of the firm of Olyphant & Co. Later, he was engaged as the president of mining and railroad companies, was United States Minister to Russia from 1897 to 1898, and in the latter year was made Ambassador. From 1899 to 1907, he was Secretary of the Interior. *April 17, 1909*

HITCHCOCK, FRANK is the son of Mr. and Mrs. Thomas Hitchcock, and a brother of Mr. Thomas Hitchcock, Jr. As might be expected, young Mr. Hitchcock is an enthusiatic polo player, and this year is captain of the Princeton team. *June 1, 1928*

HITCHCOCK, THOMAS His refusal to give up his box at the Metropolitan Opera House on the occasion of the gala performance in honor of Prince Henry of Prussia has been magnified by the daily papers. It may be doubted that he ever referred to Prince Henry as a "snip" of royalty. A fellow club member of Mr. Hitchcock's pronounced him a nervous, excitable man, quick to resent a fancied insult, and consequently a target for many practical jokes. *February 8, 1902*

HITCHCOCK, MRS. THOMAS (MARY LOUISE CENTER) belongs to the old school. There really is a Newport of the formal sort, so the looker-on concludes when Mrs. Hitchcock's coupe drives up to a florist's shop. Via the maid seated beside her, and then via the footman, the attendant in the flower-shop is informed that Mrs. Hitchcock would be pleased to speak to him. And then, after consultation, he carries out a big bouquet of

American Beauties and tearoses from which to choose. After respectful assistance from the florist, the selection is made. *August 10, 1912*

HITCHCOCK, THOMAS, JR. Thomas Hitchcock, Sr. and his son Tommy were the only father and son in the history of American polo to earn ten goal ratings, the highest and best you can rank. The elder Hitchcock, who enjoyed a reputation of being the greatest developer and trainer of steeplechase horses in the U.S. or England, got his ten goals in 1891 at Meadowbrook. Tommy, a pilot who was killed in World War II, got his ten goals in 1920 at Sands Point. *March, 1977*

HITCHCOCK, MRS. THOMAS, JR. (LOUISE M. EUSTIS) Horse is king at Hempstead and emperor at Aiken, South Carolina. One of the cottage colony at Hempstead owns nine autos, but when he goes South, he is careful to leave all of them. The puffing of one of them on the Aiken roads would snuff him out socially. There is not an auto in all Aiken. The leader of the Aiken set is the wife of Thomas Hitchcock, Jr. She was a Miss Eustis, a niece of Miss Celestine Eustis, who is reckoned as the discoverer of Aiken. From a delicate girl, the young woman who is now Mrs. Thomas Hitchcock, Jr. has developed into one of the finest horsewomen and best all around sportswomen in the country. *February 7, 1903*

HOCKADAY, IRVING O., JR., a keen athlete with a wry, philosophical bent, graduated from Princeton and, as his father before him, set out to explore the world, which included climbing the Matterhorn. Irv props his lean, ascetic face on his fingertips and ponders the city he loves, "You have to look at a city not as a fixed entity but as something that's continually evolving." Hockaday, civic leader of the upcoming generation, is channeling exploratory energies into rebuilding downtown Kansas City. *October, 1983*

HOE, ROBERT III He was the third man of this name identified with the development of printing presses. His grandfather, Robert Hoe, founded a press manufactory in this country in 1803. Mr. Robert Hoe, 3d succeeded to the management of the firm in 1884 and made by his inventions many improvements in printing presses. He owned one of the finest private libraries in this country, was one of the founders of the Metropolitan Museum of Art and of the Grolier Club, of which he was the first President. *October 2, 1909*

HOFFMAN, CHARLES F. He occupied himself chiefly with the properties of the Hoffman family. The estate included the old Hoffman House facing Madison Square and other property around or near Bryant Park. He was the President of the Union Club. *September 20, 1919*

HOFFMAN, MURRAY "Dere ———: Won't U Kame To My Little Bolshevik Baby Party. Put On Your Best Bib & Tucker. A Turble Punishment Will Befal Those That Dress As Grown-Ups. After Supper The Famous Jazz Piece, 'Boozleless Blues' Will Be Rendered" This appealing notice was served on a number of the friends in the younger set of Murray Hoffman, who originated one of the most amusing parties given in New York this winter. When the majority of the guests had arrived, a servant appeared with a large tray of milk bottles and lollypops. The milk bottles contained milk punch. Later on, a futurist "Bolsheviki drama" said to be "a play without scenery, costumes or words," was given in total darkness. *March 20, 1919*

HOGUET, HENRI ANTHONY LOUIS is the only living grandson of the late Anthony Hoguet, the first of the family to come from France doing a fur-trading business. Later, he became a gold broker and afterwards was the founder of the firm of Wilmerding, Hoguet & Co., the great wholesale auctioneers. At Lake Mahopac, New York, is situated the country estate of the Anthony Hoguets. It was for years composed of a French colony. *July 1, 1905*

HOGUET, ROBERT LOUIS belongs to one of the oldest of the Catholic families in America. On the maternal side, he is related to the Noels, each member of which has a given name betokening French ancestry. The Hoguets are descendants of Henry Louis Hoguet, through whose efforts the New York Catholic Protectory was founded, and who received the title of Knight of St. Gregory the Great from Pope Pius IX. The old Hoguet place on West One Hundred and Forty First Street is in a bit of green country, though not far north of Grant's Tomb. *June 15, 1907*

HOLLINS, HERRY B., JR. His marriage to Miss Lilias Livingston, daughter of Mr. and Mrs. Harry B. Livingston, will take place at Islip, Long Island. The bride's father is a well-known banker and a cousin of Mrs. Ogden Mills. Mrs. Livingston is a member of the old Redmond family of New York. Mr. Hollins is well known as a golf player. In 1896, when only fourteen years of age, he won an open handicap at Meadow Brook and in the same year captured the gold medal at the Westbrook open tournament. *June 18, 1904*

HOLMES, FIELDING A chief ornament of young social St. Louis, he hit his peak at the "Veiled Prophet" Ball 1965, as escort of the Veiled Prophet Queen. All-round chap: Athletic, intellectual, sports minded, he races his own Maserati, Porsche, and Cobra. Likes to paint, especially still lifes. *June, 1967*

HOLT, WINIFRED, who is a sculptor (her works have been exhibited at the Architectural League and by the National Sculpture Society in New York and also in Italy and Germany) is famous, also, for the work she does for the blind. She is the daughter of Henry Holt, the publisher. In dainty pale blue evening attire, and as gay as any butterfly debutante, she was seen at the Charity Ball. Then the following week, in large black letters on the bulletin-board of the Charity Organization Building, one saw her name among those of the dignitaries who had part in a meeting of the New York Association for the Blind. *February 23, 1907*

HOMANS, MRS. ROBERT (ABIGAIL ADAMS), the great-great-granddaughter of John and Abigail Adams, lives in a Beacon Hill apartment. "There's a great deal to look forward to in

Boston," she says. "We've got a lot of colleges. There's an aroma of intellect here, although it's been salted up a lot. Boston used to be a center of intellect, and I like to think of it as that again." *March, 1968*

HONE, HESTER GOUVERNEUR She has an interesting pedigree that includes relationship with notable families in both New York and in Philadelphia. One of her ancestors was the courtly Philip Hone, one of the founders of the Hone Club that gave many famous dinners for Daniel Webster. At "The Crinoline Ball," which was given in April, 1906, at the old Astor House, Miss Hone wore a white tarlatan and pale blue satin gown that was a copy of an old daguerreotype-portrait of Hester Gouverneur, her grandmother. *December 7, 1907*

HONE, PHILIP He is New York's most honored gentleman, in the best sense of the word, and he is so used to the large influence given him by his sound mind, fine person, noble manners, and benevolent heart, that he is universally approved and loved, and eligible to any office by which this feeling can fairly express itself. *April 28, 1849*

HOOKER, MRS. JOHN (ISABELLA BEECHER), in a recent lecture before the Constitution Club, advocated the appointment of a woman as superintendent of the city's police force, and an appointment of an equal number of men and women to the ranks. As to the ability of women to command such a semi-military force, Mrs. Hooker referred to Zenobia of Palmyra, Catherine of Russia, and Maria Teresa of Austria, as women who successfully commanded troops in the field. *April 13, 1887*

HOOPER, ROBERT CHAMBLET is often referred to by old-fashioned followers of the turf as one of nature's noblemen. However, he had other endowments and privileges, for he belonged to an old Back Bay Boston family. He became the moving spirit of the Brookline Country Club and owned the best of steeplechase horses. He was noted for his strict integrity. He never ran a shady race or started a horse when he was not fit. *July 20, 1912*

HOOVER, ALLAN Like father, like son! In catching a thirty-eight pound game fish during his Hawaiian vacation, Allan Hoover displayed an aptitude for the sport to match President Hoover's flair for fishing. Young Hoover landed his catch off the Kona coast of Hawaii. In Honolulu, Hoover was honored with numerous functions in which government officials and members of the younger social set were hosts. One of the highlights of his trip, he said, was the outrigger canoe ride at Waikiki Beach. *October 15, 1931*

HOPKINS, LYDIA Society throughout the West received a shock when it discovered that Miss Lydia Hopkins, daughter of Mr. and Mrs. Timothy J. Hopkins, of San Francisco and Mayfield, had entered the workaday world to sell hats in one of San Francisco's larger department stores. Furthermore, the heiress to millions announces that she is earning her living as a necessity and that she means to continue in her position and advance as far as she is able. *February 15, 1923*

HOPKINS, MRS. MARK (MARY FRANCES SHERWOOD) inherited from her husband, who was one of the five men who built the Central Pacific Railroad, a fortune of about thirty millions. She is described as a woman of great strength of character; in appearance and in mental characteristics strongly masculine; thoroughly acquainted with the ways of business, and, like her husband, passionately fond of horses. During her visits to Great Barrington, Massachusetts, Mrs. Hopkins may be seen on the afternoon of every fair day driving out behind a pair of fine trotters, she herself holding the reins. *January 28, 1885*

HOPPIN, BAYARD is the youngest son of Mr. and Mrs. William Warner Hoppin of New York and a descendant of William Warner Hoppin, who was Governor of Rhode Island, the state with which the Hoppin family has been identified for generations. In all books of American biography, one finds men of this name. With few exceptions, they were born in Providence and were either statesmen, artists, or scholars interested in art or archaeology. On his mother's side, Mr. Hoppin is a relative of the Beekmans, one of New York's notable families. *March 26, 1910*

HORNBLOWER, LEWIS WOODRUFF is a son of Mr. William Butler Hornblower, the lawyer; a grandson of the late Rev. William H. Hornblower of Allegheny, Pennsylvania; a nephew of Mr. Joseph C. Hornblower, one of the architects of the United States National Museum; and a great-grandson of Joseph C. Hornblower, who was Chief Justice of New Jersey, one of the original members of the American Bible Society, and President of the New Jersey Historical Society from its foundation in 1845 until his death in 1864. *November 14, 1908*

HORNER, DOUGLASS DUBOSE Handsome, outdoorsy, son of one of St. Louis' oldest and most distinguished families, he plays soccer, football, and baseball. Drives a Mustang. *June, 1968*

HORSFORD, CORNELIA The most interesting home on Shelter Island is that now presided over by Miss Cornelia Horsford. In the books which give bits of her biography, one sees in apposition the awe-inspiring word "archaeologist." As a daughter of the late Eben R. Horsford, Miss Cornelia continued his archaeological researches after his death in 1893; and in 1895 sent out archaeological expeditions to Iceland to examine the ruins of the Saga time. She is the author of several very deep books, including one entitled *Graves of the Northmen*. *July 9, 1904*

HORWITZ, DR. ORVILLE was a son of the late P. J. Horwitz, who was Surgeon General and medical director of the Union Navy during the Civil War. His mother was Miss Caroline Norris, a direct descendant of Mr. Isaac Norris, one of the Provincial Councillors of Pennsylvania, and of Mr. Thomas Lloyd, the first Governor of that state. Dr. Horwitz was one of Philadelphia's most noted surgeons. *February 8, 1913*

HOUGH, MRS. AND MRS. DAVID LEAVITT (HELOISE BEEKMAN) To New Yorkers who know their social history, Miss Beekman was a very interesting bride, as she is a descendant of the first William Beekman who sailed to New Netherlands with Peter Stuyvesant. Mr. Hough has an equally interesting ancestry, as before him there was a long line of soldiers and men who have been prominent in educational progress. As an able engineer himself, he is an excellent example of an American aristocracy that retains its best qualities. John Hough, one of his forefathers, was an engineer who served his country during King Philip's war. *December 5, 1903*

HOUGHTON, ARTHUR A., JR. For the Chairman of the board of the Steuben Glass Company, cattle breeding is a business—a very serious one. He owns "Wye Plantation" in Queenstown, on the Eastern Shore of Maryland. His rolling 1,400-acre spread, bordered on three sides by the brackish Wye River, is a pastoral masterwork. In 1937, Houghton founded Wye to breed Black Angus. Today, he is considered one of the most famous of modern Black Angus breeders. *February, 1978*

HOVING, WALTER Born in Stockholm in 1897, the son of a Swedish grand-opera singer and a Finnish doctor, he is out to raise $10,765,000 for 360 Army recreational clubs. His organizing ability is already attested by executive jobs at Macy's and Montgomery Ward and the current Presidency of the Fifth Avenue Association and Lord & Taylor. *August, 1941*

HOWARD, MR. AND MRS. POLK STEELE When they entertain for dinner, they prepare an irresistible Eastern Shore feast including hardshell, softshell, and Imperial crabs and Maryland beaten biscuits. Howard is the tenth lineal descendant of Augustine Herrman, who held the original Bohemia Manor grant of 20,000 acres from Lord Baltimore. *May, 1977*

HOWE, MARK A. DE WOLFE The best known of living Howes is the Pulitzer Prize biographer Mark A. De Wolfe Howe, whose elder son, Quincy Howe, has brought *The Living Age* back from Lazarus' estate. His other son, Mark, is Secretary to Mr. Justice Holmes, and a brother, Wallis Howe, is probably the best architect in Providence, with his son, George, as associate. *February 15, 1934*

HOWE, MRS. SAMUEL GRIDLEY (JULIA WARD), whose ninetieth birthday had national recognition last week, has long been identified with "The City by the Sea." But she represents a Newport quite different from that pictured by the press: It is a Newport that has old-fashioned scruples and quiet pleasures; books and talks with people who wrote them, and pictures, with chat over afternoon tea with perhaps the very artist who painted them. *June 5, 1909*

HOWELL, MRS. GEORGE, of Philadelphia, describes the visit of the Prince of Wales, who afterwards became the brilliant English ruler Edward VII, to her early home in Allegheny. He was tendered a reception by an ancestor of Mrs. Howell, General William O'Harra Robinson. He showed great interest in the young daughter of the house, when she made

her presentation curtsy to him. Mrs. Howell, pleased to recall this feature, relates how the Prince stooped to kiss her and exclaimed at the same time: "Well, you are a very nice little girl." Mrs. Howell adds, in telling the story: "I've saved all the souvenirs of this visit that I can. I am sorry to say that I never put any especial mark upon the place where the Prince of Wales kissed me." *June 25, 1910*

HOWELL, REV. DR. RICHARD LEWIS died at his home in the Hotel Aberdeen in New York City, which he owned. Dr. Howell was assistant rector of the old Church of the Epiphany in Philadelphia and rector of St. Margaret's Church in Washington. He owned a large island-estate at Newport, Rhode Island. He is survived by his wife, who is a daughter of Mr. and Mrs. Thomas Delano Whistler of Baltimore and a greatniece of Whistler, the artist. *February 12, 1910*

HOWELLS, MR. AND MRS. JOHN MEAD (ABBY WHITE) The bridegroom, like his uncle, Mr. William Rutherford Mead, is an architect, and he made the plans for St. Paul's Chapel at Columbia University, where the wedding service was read. The bride's father, Mr. Horace White, was at one time Editor of the *Chicago Tribune,* but for many years has been associated with the *New York Evening Post,* of which he is Editor-in-chief. Both Mr. White and Mr. William Dean Howells, the bridegroom's father, our "representative man of letters," attended the ceremony. *December 28, 1907*

HOWLAND, GARDINER was a man who lived in the exercise of large influence. As one of the wealthiest of our citizens, he had the power which the world at present most recognizes, and he had qualities of character which made his varied exercise of this power a blessing to his fellow men. *November 22, 1851*

HOWLAND, HENRY E. A novelty in entertainment was provided for the Thursday Evening Club of New York—the entertainment being a mock trial, with Mr. Howland as judge. Mock trial used to be a very popular entertainment, especially on shipboard twenty years ago. It offers exceptional scope for the display of wit and mental ingenuity. *March 21, 1894*

HOWLAND, MR. AND MRS. LLEWELLYN III (JESSIE WILLIAMS) One cannot talk of Boston history without mentioning the whaling industry, and no name is more associated with the days of the New Bedford fleet than Howland. The first of the family, Henry Howland, came to America on the *Speedwell,* directly after the *Mayflower.* Several years later, he owned more than a million acres on Cape Cod. Llewellyn Howland III, a senior editor at Little, Brown & Co., is one of publishing's most productive talents and a notable collector of marine paintings. He is married to Jessie Williams, granddaughter of Ben Ames Williams, the novelist, and daughter of Ben Ames Williams, Jr., current chief of the Old Colony Trust and President of The Country Club. *April, 1976*

HOYT, BEATRIX In golf, women have found at last an athletic game at which they can command masculine respect unmixed with condescension. Since the ladies' championship of Amer-

ica was instituted in 1895, the improvement in American women's play has been remarkable. Since Miss Beatrix Hoyt, of the Shinnecock Hills club, flashed upon the scene as a mere schoolgirl in 1896, neither she nor anyone else has very obviously advanced the work she then set up. For three years, Miss Hoyt romped through the field. She constituted a class by herself. *June 8, 1901*

HOYT, CONSTANCE is the daughter of the Solicitor General, Mr. Henry M. Hoyt. Her mother was, before her marriage, Miss Anne McMichael, a daughter of Mr. Morton McMichael of Philadelphia, well known as a publisher, and a sister of Mr. Clayton McMichael, who was at one time the Editor and the proprietor of *The North American. December 28, 1907*

HOYT, JOHN WESLEY was graduated from the Ohio Wesleyan University in 1849, later studied law, and finally received the degree of M.D. from the Ohio Medical College. Mr. Hoyt was sent by the United States as commissioner to expositions in London, Paris, and Vienna. He was appointed Governor of Wyoming 1878–1883, making peace with the Indians. Mr. Hoyt was the founder and first President of the Wyoming Academy of Arts, Letters, and Sciences. *June 1, 1912*

HUBBARD, GENERAL THOMAS HAMLIN He is prominent as a lawyer, but in 1865, for service in the Civil War, was brevetted Brigadier General. He has been the president of railroads, including several in Guatemala and Mexico, but is attached to things soldierly and is the Commander of the Military Order of the Loyal Legion, New York. *July 27, 1907*

HUBBARD, WILBUR ROSS His family has lived ten generations on the Eastern Shore of Maryland. Mr. Hubbard grew up in his Georgian town house, "Widehall," where the door handles and hardware are made of sterling silver, and the lawns roll down to the Chester River as if in a scene from 18th-century England. A Yale graduate, a bachelor, a Lieutenant in World War I, he keeps one of the few remaining private packs of foxhounds in the country. *May, 1977*

HUGHES, CAROLYN CONDE, daughter of Mr. and Mrs. Felix T. Hughes, is a cousin of Rupert Hughes, author, and a great-great-granddaughter of the Thomas Conde who came here with Lafayette and fought in the Revolution. As for her own achievements, Miss Hughes was graduated from Spence with her class's vote for pulchritude. *October 15, 1929*

HUMPHREY, MRS. GILBERT (LOUISE IRELAND) She is a member of the U. S. Equestrian Team and master of the hunt at Chagrin Valley Hunt Club. At her sprawling estate, "Humphrey Hill," the Humphreys hire grooms, deliberately, who can't ride so they can be sure the horses will respond perfectly to their own riding habits. She digressed momentarily into the complexities of the relationships between the Hanna, Ireland, Bolton, and Humphrey families. And she explained that the famous private preserve in Georgia to which her father-in-law, George Humphrey, former Secretary of the Treasury, used to take President

Eisenhower, had first been brought to the family's attention because Mark Hanna and William McKinley went there in the belief that the climate was beneficial to the treatment of arthritis. *September, 1966*

HUMPHREY, REV. AND MRS. WILLIAM BREWSTER (MARY E. IVES) have several times during Lent given an entertainment which they call "An Hour with the North American Indians." At their home, 118 Waverly Place in New York City, the Indian folklore music was discussed by the Rev. Mr. Humphrey, and to illustrate his talk he sang some of the Indian songs. "The Sunrise Call," which has been sung by the Indian priests for hundreds of years, was of especial interest. Mrs. Humphrey, as usual at these entertainments, explained the legends and the symbolism of Indian baskets and their makers. *March 28, 1908*

HUMPHREYS, DR. FREDERIC H. was President of the Humphreys Homeopathic Medicine Company. One of his ancestors, John Humphreys, was one of the settlers of the Massachusetts Bay Colony. His ancestors included Colonel David Humphreys, who was General Washington's aide, and Joshua Humphreys, who designed and built the frigate *Constitution*. *February 1, 1919*

HUNDLEY, MRS. MARY (GIBSON), an honors graduate of Radcliffe, who for years taught languages at Washington's prestigious Dunbar High School, speaks with a broad-A Boston accent and is a woman of promptly revealed opinions. "I am not black," she says, "and I do not like to be called black. I like the expression the French use as a designation. I am an *Américaine de couleur*. At Radcliffe, I was just another one of the girls. I was invited to parties in Boston houses where they wouldn't even receive the Irish!" *September, 1975*

HUNNEWELL, FRANCIS WELLES was one of Boston's leading businessmen and philanthropists. He was especially prominent in all the works and charities of the Episcopal Church. For many years, Mr. Hunnewell was one of the directors of Calumet and Hecla and of the C.B. & Q. Railway, and at the time of his death was President of the State Street Exchange. *October 20, 1917*

HUNTINGTON, COLLIS P. said of his new son-in-law, Prince Francis Edmund Hatzfeldt-Wildenburg: "The Prince, like other men in his position, has had an inordinate capacity for spending money and getting into debt and difficulty. I wish he had a cleaner record, but he is a bright man, of many and varied talents, and will doubtless make my daughter happy. The sum which the Princess receives as her dower is no more and no less than what she would have taken if she had married a Connecticut farmer." *September 13, 1889*

HUNTINGTON, BISHOP F. D. describes fashionable society "as a something too formal for an institution, too irregular for an organization, too vital for a machine, too heartless for a fraternity, too lawless for a school, too decent for a masquerade, with too much lying for a bureau, and too many passions for a pageant." *October 16, 1889*

HUNTINGTON, DR. AND MRS. FRANCIS C. (PATRICIA SKINNER) Like so many of his ancestors in the past 300 years, Frank Huntington chose the ministry as his career after Exeter, Harvard, and degrees in theology from Princeton Seminary and General Seminary. Still an active clergyman, he is now Deputy Director of the Seaman's Church Institute in New York. One year after graduating from Smith, Patricia received her M.A. in African history from the University of California at Los Angeles. *January, 1979*

HUNTINGTON, HENRY EDWARDS is one of the wealthiest men on the Pacific Coast. He is a nephew of the late Collis P. Huntington, the railroad magnate, and he is actively engaged in the same interests. Mr. Huntington's residence on Nob Hill, San Francisco, was destroyed by the earthquake, but his library and wonderful collection of art treasures are at one of his three estates in Southern California. *May 6, 1911*

HUNTINGTON, MRS. HENRY EDWARDS (ARABELLA DUVALL YARRINGTON)—WARSHAM—HUNTINGTON was the wife of the late Henry E. Huntington and of Collis P. Huntington. Her first husband was A. D. Warsham, of Alabama. She married Mr. Collis P. Huntington, the noted railroad man, in 1884. He died in 1900, and in 1913, she married her second husband's nephew in Paris. *October 15, 1924*

HUNTINGTON, LAWRENCE D. was for sixty years an associate of Mr. E. C. Benedict in the brokerage business. He was the second oldest member of the New York Stock Exchange. Mr. Huntington was an enthusiastic yachtsman, a naturalist, and a fisherman. He was an intimate friend of Grover Cleveland, and often went fishing with the ex-President in Buzzard's Bay. *April 10, 1909*

HUNTINGTON, MARIAN believes in "seeing America first." Recently, she started for New York from California, driving her own machine. Miss Huntington is an expert chauffeuse, and she is expert in everything she undertakes. She is like the Huntington family in that she seldom undertakes anything that most other young persons, heiresses to millions, are attracted by. She is the daughter of Henry E. Huntington of Los Angeles by his first marriage. H. E. Huntington inherited nearly forty millions from his childless uncle. *May 20, 1917*

HUTCHINS, STILSON, whose career has included the duties of an editor, publisher, and newspaper proprietor, is a New Englander by birth, but he founded the *Times* in St. Louis and

served in the Missouri as well as in the New Hampshire Legislature. As an art collector, he has been well known, and one finds in issues of the old *Home Journal* long columns devoted to "appreciations" of the pictures in his famous gallery in Washington. *March 27, 1909*

HUTTON, MR. AND MRS. EDWARD F. (MARJORIE MERRIWEATHER POST)—CLOSE Their new Florida residence has a very special location, on a stretch of land running between Lake Worth and the Atlantic Ocean. It is appropriately called "Mar-a-Lago," for the lake and the sea, and extends generously over a property a thousand feet deep. Strictly speaking, Mr. Hutton's residence is not one house but several houses, united by ambulatories and terraces. There are the main house, the owner's house, the guest house, and the baby's house, which has nothing in it but the apartments pertaining to the baby and its comfort. *May 1, 1928*

HUTTON, MRS. GAUN M. (CELESTE MARGUERITE WINANS), widow of the former American Vice Consul to Russia, died at her residence, "Alexandroffsky," Baltimore. She was a daughter of the late Mr. Thomas De Kay Winans, who built the first railroads in Russia during the reign of the Czar Alexander II, for whom he named the picturesquely imposing mansion erected as his permanent home in Baltimore in 1845. Her grandfather, the late Mr. Ross Winans, founder of the Baltimore branch of the family, was the inventor of the "camel-back" locomotive and the eight-wheel car, and established some of the largest machine shops in this country. *April 1, 1925*

HYDE, MR. AND MRS. JAMES HAZEN (MARTHA LEISHMAN)—DE GONTAUT-BIRON Mr. James Hazen Hyde is an international figure. He is the son of the late Henry Baldwin Hyde, founder of the Equitable Life Assurance Society. He was graduated from Harvard in 1898 and in the same year was elected second Vice President of the Equitable Society. His disposing of his stock to Mr. Thomas F. Ryan and his taking up his permanent residence in Paris are facts known to everyone. She was Miss Martha Leishman, elder daughter of Mr. John G. A. Leishman, formerly American Ambassador to Germany. It was while Mr. Leishman was Minister to Turkey that she was married to the Comte Louis de Gontaut-Biron. One of the wedding gifts was the Grand Cordon of the Nichan Shefekat order in diamonds. This is the only order which the Sultan confers upon women. *November 22, 1913*

HYDE, LADY (MARGUERITE LEITER) The Leiter trial, which is the dispute between Lady Marguerite Hyde, the former Daisy Leiter, and her brother, Joseph Leiter, over a question of the alleged mismanagement of the late Levi Z. Leiter's fifty-million dollar estate, is attracting much attention. With Mr. Leiter are Mrs. Leiter and his sister, Mrs. Colin Campbell, the former Nancy Leiter. In the courtroom, Mrs. Leiter and Mrs. Campbell work each day on their petit point, while the trial, which promises to last three months, goes on. *April 15, 1926*

I

IGLEHART, D. STEWART He was a most highly esteemed member of the Great Neck team and for many years afterwards was a most enthusiastic participant in polo games all over the world. In South America, as resident manager of the great interests of W. R. Grace and Co., he was a familiar and tremendously popular player on fields in Peru and Chile and the Argentine. *August 1, 1931*

IGLEHART, PHILIP had a seven-goal polo rating when he was 23 and 24, then went to work with General Foods and Grace Steamship Lines. During this period, he was also Ambassador to Chile. Philip came back at the age of 46 and regained his seven-goal form, quite an athletic accomplishment. It was at this time that polo was slipping in Florida; so in 1964, with seven stockholders, they moved the Gulfstream activity to Lake Worth. *March, 1980*

ILYINSKY, PAUL Noted Cincinnati businessman and Palm Beach Councilman Paul Ilyinsky, grandnephew of Czar Alexander III, who is running for reelection unopposed, says, "Palm Beach is really an American town. A town for Americans who've made it to the top. These people don't go to night clubs. They come down here and put on black tie to visit with their friends." *March, 1983*

INGALLS, MR. AND MRS. FAY (RACHEL C. HOLMES) have called their new breeding farm on a lower Warm Springs, Virginia, mountain, "Hobby Horse Farm." Here is a very charming "hobby" indeed—a perfectly arranged breeding farm with track and stables and cottages for the keepers and attendants. And in a dear little ravine is a rustic camp on the side of a tiny river. *October 1, 1927*

INGERSOLL, RALPH II The Ingersoll Publication Company, his daily and weekly newspaper chain, now numbers close to 200 papers. He's a leading supporter of "Prep for Prep," which tutors disadvantaged children so they can attend prep schools. And he's paying off a $500,000 pledge toward a new building for a School of American Ballet in New York. *December, 1989*

IRVING, LOUIS DU PONT is a son of Mr. Alexander Duer Irving, who is now the owner of "Sunnyside," the home of his illustrious great uncle, Washington Irving, the author. Sunnyside is today one of the most fascinating of the historic homes of this country. Its walls, for example, are partly covered by ivy grown from cuttings from Melrose Abbey and given to Washington Irving by Sir Walter Scott. *October 19, 1907*

ISELIN, MR. AND MRS. C. OLIVER (HOPE GODDARD), who will manage for the fourth time the defender of the *America*'s Cup, has been a yachting enthusiast since he was a small boy. Mrs. Iselin shares her husband's fondness for the sport, and during the international series of races in 1899 she sailed with him on the *Columbia,* making her headquarters on a houseboat moored in the harbor off Atlantic Highlands. There was more than the usual number of "flukes" that year, and two of the daily newspapers attempted to connect Mrs.

Iselin's presence on the defender with the difficulty in winning a race. Mr. Iselin's confidence never abated, and there was a joyous greeting between Mr. J. Pierpont Morgan and Mr. and Mrs. Iselin when the financier was taken on board the houseboat after the determining race. *December 27, 1902*

ISELIN, ERNEST is the son of Mr. and Mrs. Adrian Iselin, Jr. His grandfather, Mr. Adrian Iselin, has a wide fame as a banker and philanthropist, the Iselins as a family having spent nearly one million dollars for the building of Catholic schools and churches in New Rochelle. The last church as a gift from Mr. Iselin to the town was planned for the benefit of the Italian colony. *November 7, 1903*

ISHAM, LIEUTENANT COLONEL RALPH is a financier, big game shooter, late officer in His Majesty's army, and book collector. Small fry leaves him absolutely cold, and as if to demonstrate this he has brought back to America the long-missing James Boswell manuscripts, which are, without doubt, the literary discovery of the century. *November 15, 1927*

ISHAM, ROBERT T., JR. Dr. Ralph Isham, a surgeon, traveled west for his health in 1855 and married the daughter of George Snow, one of the dozen pioneers who had incorporated Chicago as a town in 1833. In 1873, Edward Swift Isham and Robert Todd Lincoln, son of the President, formed the firm that was to become Isham, Lincoln & Beale, which was, until it dissolved in 1988, one of the city's most influential law firms. Robert T. Isham, Jr., now in his mid-thirties, is a lawyer who delighted the family by joining Isham, Lincoln & Beale and practicing with the firm established by his great-great-granduncle. *September, 1990*

IVES, BRAYTON has been conspicuous in financial and railroad circles for over a generation. Mr. Ives has been identified with many stirring episodes in Wall Street. A former President of the Northern Pacific, as senior member of an influential Stock Exchange banking and brokerage house, he has shown always vigor. Mr. Ives is distinguished by a refined taste as a collector of rare books and is the possessor of a famous collection of antiquities. *December 26, 1903*

IVES, MRS. ELIZABETH (STEVENSON) Her great-great-great-grandfather, William Stevenson, arrived in the Colonies in 1748. Mrs. Ives' grandfather, Adlai Ewing Stevenson, served two terms in the House of Representatives and was elected Vice President under Grover Cleveland in 1893. Stevenson's wife, Letitia Green, served four terms as President General of the Daughters of the American Revolution. Their grandson, Adlai E. Stevenson, was Governor of Illinois, Ambassador to the U.N. in the Sixties, and a three-time Presidential candidate. *March, 1988*

IVINS, WILLIAM M. is the lawyer of stern integrity who was Republican candidate when there was such an exciting political battle between McClellan and Hearst for Mayor of New York. Only last week Mr. Ivins had a great deal to say on the question of recounting the votes. During the Eighties, he was Judge Advocate General of the State of New York. *July 20, 1907*

IZARD, JOSEPHINE, daughter of Colonel and Mrs. Adam Cadwallader Izard of South Carolina, is the great-grand-daughter of Ralph Izard, who married Alice De Lancey, daughter of Peter De Lancey, Lieutenant Governor of the Province of New York. Ralph Izard, although Minister to the court of the Grand Duke of Tuscany, refused to be presented at court because he would have to bow the knee, which he said he "would never do to mortal man." *June 13, 1894*

J

JACKSON, JOHN B., former Minister to Persia, will arrive in Havana early in 1910. Mr. Jackson will succeed Mr. Edwin V. Morgan of New York as Minister to Cuba. In the diplomatic corps, Mr. Jackson is said to have served more years continuously than any man in the service. He was first Secretary to the legation in Berlin, Minister to Chile in 1897, and later appointed Minister to Greece. Mr. Jackson is a member of one of New Jersey's oldest colonial families. He is an able linguist, speaking fluently seven languages. *January 1, 1910*

JACKSON, GENERAL JOSEPH COOKE graduated with honors at Yale University in the class of 1857. General Jackson had a brilliant military career, participating in twenty one engagements. During the Civil War, nine state and eight federal appointment commissions were tendered him. He was brevetted Brigadier General in the field. General Jackson's father was the Hon. John P. Jackson of Newark, New Jersey, a descendant of the Brinckerhoff, Schuyler, Van Voorhis, and other well-known Dutch and English families. *June 7, 1913*

JACKSON, M. ROY The Rose Tree Hunt, of which Mr. Jackson accepted the mastership in 1914, is fairly entitled to be known as the oldest fox-hunting club in the United States. Mr. Jackson had had a long experience with his own private pack and with a natural genius for venery added to experience and determination in crossing a country, he became a notable figure among the fox-hunting men in the United States. From Rose Tree, Mr. Jackson went in 1918 to the neighborhood of Rye to help in the building up of the Fairfield and Westchester Hunt. He has accepted the mastership of the famous old Radnor, one of the best known packs in the country, the nearest to Philadelphia of all those many packs surrounding the city. *March 15, 1930*

JACOBS, MRS. HENRY BARTON (MARY FRICK)— GARRETT is "the Mrs. Astor" of Baltimore. Mrs. Jacobs' return to her city home is still of much moment to the social world, for, although she entertains just a degree more quietly than she did as Mrs. Robert Garrett, her influence and favor are of the same importance. Mrs. Jacobs' attitude toward social life is decidedly conservative. At her house last winter, one met the same families seen there twenty years ago, perhaps, in some cases, represented by a younger generation. Mrs. Jacobs has done much to preserve the dignity of Baltimore society, and also its characteristic simplicity and informality. *October 31, 1903*

JAMES, DANIEL WILLIS died at the Mount Washington Hotel, Bretton Woods, New Hampshire. He was one of the most noted merchants of New York, and he was well known as a philanthropist. He was at one time President of the Children's Aid Society and was a trustee of Amherst College, and through his generosity, the university was enabled to carry on its special astronomical work in observations of eclipses of the sun. *September 21, 1907*

JAMES, MRS. ELLERY SEDGEWICK The lioness of LVIS — Ladies Village Improvement Society — is East Hampton's Mrs. Ellery Sedgewick James, a white-haired dynamo of both the summer set and the year-round residents. Her husband was a direct descendant of East Hampton's first minister, Thomas James (1602–1636). "He's buried in that graveyard there," Mrs. James pointed out, "with his feet toward his congregation." For half a century, Mrs. James has fought East Hampton's good fight against billboards, neon lights, and even against sale signs in windows of chain grocery stores. *September, 1962*

JAMES, HENRY During his recent visit to Boston, Mr. James offended several people by not acknowledging their dinner invitations. In straightening the matter out, Mr. James explained that he had received sixty dinner cards for the same night, all of which his besieged secretary had answered in as personal a manner as possible. Unfortunately, a few were overlooked. *August 12, 1905*

JAMES, WILLIAM was an active member of the faculty at Harvard University from 1872 to 1907, when he retired to devote his time to psychological studies and writings. He was a son of Henry James. Professor James is survived by a brother, Mr. Henry James, the eminent novelist. *September 3, 1910*

JANVRIN, DR. JOSEPH E., who is one of the noted physicians in New York, was born in Exeter, New Hampshire, where he still owns the old home that was built two hundred years ago, the second house erected in the historic town. Besides the famous John Alden, who was led to speak for himself, Dr. Janvrin is a descendant of Governors Bradstreet, Dudley, and Winthrop and of the Adams family of Quincy, Massachusetts. *December 26, 1908*

JARVIS, GRACE is a debutante representative of one of Michigan's old families. She is a granddaughter of the late Senator James McMillan. She is the niece of Lady Harrington, the wife of Sir John Lane Harrington. The grandfather of this debutante, the late Senator McMillan, was one of Michigan's great "captains of industry." In 1864, with Mr. John S. Newberry, he organized the Michigan Car Company. He was also one of the organizers and later the President of the Detroit, Mackinaw and Marquette Railroad Company. *December 28, 1907*

JAY, CORNELIA was the daughter of the late John Clarkson Jay, one of the seven founders of the New York Yacht Club. His home was the beautiful old Jay place at Rye, New York, about which Fenimore Cooper wrote his novel *The Spy*. It was John Clarkson Jay who made a specialty of conchology. His collection of shells and his library on this branch of science were purchased by Catherine Lorillard Wolfe and presented to the American Museum of Natural History. *October 26, 1907*

JAY, ELEANOR She had the center of the social stage as a young woman just affianced. She is piquant and girlish, and ever so attractive. Her engagement was announced to Mr. Arthur Iselin. As the daughter of Colonel William Jay, doyen among gentleman whips, she is a descendant of the first John Jay, of Huguenot descent, and prominent in the history of his country. *September 24, 1904*

SERVED UP ON A SHELL

A house-warming requires only music for dancing, wine, and good things in plenty for the dinner. The dedication of a garden is a more delicate matter. The entertainment held last week on Commodore and Mrs. Arthur Curtiss James's estate at Newport had, however, close connection with their house built on a rock close to the sea. The garden was lighted only softly, an orchestra played dreamy music, trumpeters in costume gave a musical warning, *Parsifal*-like, that the pageant would begin. A stately lady was seen advancing. "Why, it's Mrs. James!" In a rich voice that carried well, she expressed her hopes for her garden in poetic prophecy and welcomed her guests. The final scene surpassed anything that even Newport had ever seen. *Aphrodite* was carried in, enthroned in a gigantic white shell. *Aphrodite* leaped from her throne, dived into the pool in front of her, and danced with reckless grace, water splashing around her. Suddenly, the whole garden bloomed with small electric lights of blue and white. Led by the trumpeters, the guests passed under the blue canopy to the house. The dance on the marble floor began even before a fanfare announced the bringing in of the boar's head for supper. *August 23, 1913*

JAY, JOHN His death removes if not the last, certainly the most active, survivor of the grand generation which carried the slavery conflict to its final triumph. There was every temptation in life to a young man in 1836, gifted as he was with fortune, good connections, illustrious ancestry, and honorable ambition, to eschew the anti-slavery cause on leaving college. But he did not. He threw himself into the thick of the fight, and for the thirty years following he labored for the emancipation of the negro. *May 16, 1894*

JAY, JOHN Born in New York City in 1745, Jay served the fledgling nation in an extraordinary number of high offices, as President of the Continental Congress, first Chief Justice of the United States, Governor and Chief Justice of New York State, and author of the Jay Treaty. His retirement home is situated near Katonah, in New York's northern Westchester County. Five generations of Jay's direct descendants lived in the homestead. The last resident, great-great-granddaughter Eleanor Jay Iselin, added the elegant west wing, displaying portraits by Stuart, Trumbull, and Sargent, to the simple clapboard, shingle, and stone farmhouse constructed in 1787. *October, 1981*

JAY, PETER AUGUSTUS had been in and out of Washington a half dozen times prior to starting off for his new post in the Argentine. Oil looms large on the horizon in Argentina, and the arrival of Mr. Jay, who is said to have done wonders in straightening out the tangled situation in Rumania, in which oil figured so momentously, is waited somewhat impatiently by the Argentinians. *August 15, 1925*

JAY, COLONEL WILLIAM The formal organization of the Coaching Club was made about two years since, and on the suggestion of Mr. Jay, now President of the club, a formal effort was undertaken to make coaching popular in New York. A year ago, the first public parade was made. The club now numbers sixty members and has seventeen drags; and if crowded streets and repeated cheers are any criteria, the enterprise has the public goodwill. *May 30, 1877*

JEANES, ANNA T. By the will of Miss Anna T. Jeanes, which was admitted to probate October first, $1,000,000 is bequeathed for the benefit of the Negro Race. This has already been paid over to Messrs. Booker T. Washington and Hollis B. Frissell. The will bequeaths to Swarthmore College all the testator's coal and mineral lands on condition that the management abandons all participation in intercollegiate sports and games. The sum of $250,000 is bequeathed to the trustees of the Philadelphia Yearly Meeting. Nine relatives are given $5,000 each. *October 19, 1907*

JEFFORDS, MR. AND MRS. WALTER M. (KATHLEEN McLAUGHLIN) During the race meet at Saratoga, the indefatigable Jeffordses give six-course, six-wine lunches for twenty, and legend has it that they've never missed a day. The Jeffordses' Victorian house is decorated in green and white, their racing colors since 1915. Mr. Jeffords, whose great-uncle owned Man O' War, is a Vice President of the Saratoga Reading Room and the National Museum of Racing. *August, 1985*

JENKINS, MICHAEL was one of the most widely known financiers and philanthropists in this country. From 1896 until his resignation in 1907, Mr. Jenkins was President of the Merchants and Miners Transportation Company. He was one of the founders of the Catholic University at Washington, and for his splendid work for the Catholic University and his numerous other services in behalf of Catholicism in the United States Pope Pius X ennobled Mr. Jenkins and his wife as Duke and Duchess of Llewellyn of the Holy Roman Empire. The recipients of these titles, however, never made any use of them, although the honor of their bestowal was highly appreciated. *October 1, 1915*

JEROME, LEONARD W. Fifth Avenue and Central Park, on last Saturday afternoon, presented a very lively and gay appearance. The drives were thronged with stylish equipages, the rides with equestrians, and the promenades with thousands of well-dressed ladies and gentlemen. While riding up the avenue, about four o'clock, we passed Mr. Leonard W. Jerome, driving his handsome four-in-hand coach, with a delegation from the Union Club seated on top. *May 13, 1868*

JESUP, MORRIS KETCHUM Take any board of directors of any of the many New York institutions, and the names of the same millionaires will be found, who think little of subscribing $100,000 a year to maintain expeditions, the arts, sciences, charities, literature, and philanthropies. Morris K. Jesup, the banker, may well stand near the head of the list, as his purse is freely opened to all institutions. His donations to the American Museum of Natural History are rapidly approaching the million dollar mark. In the Botanical Garden, the Zoological Garden, and the Y.M.C.A., his trail is marked by gifts of thousands of dollars. *April 18, 1903*

JEWELL, MR. AND MRS. CHARLES (SARAH ANNE RIDLEY) "Bethel Place," in Columbia, Tennessee, is one of three ante-bellum manor houses built for the Pillow brothers in the late 1840s and '50s of wood, brick, and stone, all found on the family's 5,000-acre holding. For the past twenty years, Bethel Place has been the home of Mr. and Mrs. Charles Jewell. A former Kentuckian, Charlie Jewell came to Tennessee to raise tobacco in the early 1940s and purchased Bethel Place for his bride, a Pillow descendant. *November, 1977*

JOHNSON, MR. AND MRS. AYMAR (MARIAN K. HOFFMAN) The wedding of the only daughter of Mrs. Charles Frederick Hoffman, of New York and "Blickling Hall," Norfolk, England, was performed at the Cathedral of St. John the Divine. Mr. Johnson is a grandson of Bradish Johnson, whose house at Fifth Avenue and Twenty First Street was a social landmark in New York. *December 1, 1924*

JOHNSON, MRS. DEANE F. (ANNE McDONNELL)—FORD was born in New York, one of fourteen children. She was brought up on a silk cushion, since the Irish clans of Murray (her mother's family) and McDonnell were two of America's greatest, richest, and most influential families. Twenty nine-room apartments in New York, fifty-room houses in Southampton—with separate kitchens for the children's quarters—and access to the Pope. When Anne married Henry Ford in June 1940, it was ecstatically rhapsodized by the press and everyone else as "The Wedding of the Century." Henry Ford took on 116 new in-laws just by giving Anne McDonnell his name. *May, 1975*

JOHNSON, MRS. F. KIRK (ELIZABETH McGHEE) From Fort Worth, very sports-minded, the Johnsons spend every weekend at their Possum Kingdom Lake ranch, where they "pass the time" practicing at their two shooting ranges, swimming in the pool, and playing shuffleboard. They also raise cattle. Business or competition shoots take them to various cities in Europe and around the States. They have also been on safari in Africa, where Ellen shot antelope, elephant, lion, buffalo, and rhinoceros. *January, 1966*

JOHNSON, JANE ALVA What the Assemblies are to Philadelphia and Boston, the Cotillions to Baltimore, and the St. Cecilia to Charleston, this and more is the Veiled Prophet Ball to the good people of St. Louis. This year, the queen of the ball, the fifty-fourth in its history, was Miss Jane Alva Johnson, the daughter of Mr. and Mrs. Andrew Johnson. Miss Johnson acts as a whip when hunting at Aiken or with the Bridlespur hounds around St. Louis. *December 15, 1933*

CHEERIO, AS THEY SAY

When Mr. William Waldorf Astor became convinced that there were many things about these United States that he did not like, he said he would not be an American any more, and went over to London and assumed British citizenship. Another eminent American who does not like the way we have been doing things lately has announced that he likewise will no longer play in our backyard. He declares that he will swear allegiance to King George. However, it is so long since Mr. Henry James has actually played in our backyard, that we shall perhaps not miss him very much. *August 1, 1915*

JOHNSON, JOHN H. Walt Whitman, the poet, was entertained at a reception given by Mr. John H. Johnson, No. 113 East 10th Street. A number of the friends of the venerable poet embraced the opportunity to renew their acquaintance with him. *March 7, 1877*

JOHNSON, OWEN, son of Robert Underwood Johnson, sometime Editor of *The Century* and Ambassador to Italy, is famous as the author of *The Varmint, Stover at Yale,* and *The Salamander,* which was one of the first novels to expose how Ladies Lived in the Big City. *August, 1949*

JOHNSON, PHILIP To isolate a water faucet, mount it on a pedestal like a Greek statue, and display it under specially-constructed muslin ceilings through which the light diffuses evenly over functional curves is one of the ideas that Philip Johnson has put over at the Museum of Modern Art. His apartment is designed around furniture bought in Berlin from Mies van der Rohe, one of Germany's most progressive figures. Besides his own surroundings, Philip Johnson has designed everything from watches to tea gowns. At Harvard, he spent most of his time in the Fogg Museum between long trips to Potsdam. *April 1, 1934*

JOHNSON, ROBERT UNDERWOOD gives up his office as Editor-in-chief of the *Century* magazine after forty years of splendid service. Mr. Johnson was decorated in 1891 with the ribbon of the Legion of Honor, for the conspicuous part he took in the attainment of international copyright. He has published several volumes of verse and was the originator of the Keats-Shelley Memorial in Rome. He planned and forwarded the creation of Yosemite National Park and has for many years been a prominent figure in conservation conferences. *June 7, 1913*

JOHNSON, MRS. WARREN (M. CONSTANCE WOODWORTH)—WARBURG Her ex-es include dashing Warren Johnson and Paul F. ("Piggy") Warburg, of the financial clan. A journalist with a career on newspapers and magazines, she writes a column for *The Palm Beacher*. *July, 1975*

JOHNSON, DR. WOOLSEY was the greatgrandson of Dr. Samuel Johnson, the first president of Columbia College, whose son, William Samuel Johnson, was one of the ratifiers of the Constitution of the United States. The family is remarkable for the number of distinguished college presidents closely related to it, there being nine. *July 13, 1887*

JOHNSTON, MARTHA is the fiancée of Mr. W. De Lancey Kountze. She is a daughter of Colonel and Mrs. J. Marshall Johnston, of Macon, Georgia, who live in a great spreading mansion of the old time. On her mother's side, Miss Johnston is related to the Huguenins, of Macon, who have the very bluest of old Huguenot blood. *November 14, 1903*

JONES, ALICE One of the most brilliant weddings of the week was that of Miss Alice Jones, daughter of Mrs. Mary Mason Jones, to Mr. Adrian Iselin, son of Adrian Iselin, the Wall Street banker. The gifts of the bride included a flower-built schooner, the hull of which was formed of violets. This beautiful ship floated upon a sea of white and red roses, an emblem, we trust, of the happy destiny upon which the happy pair have embarked. *April 11, 1877*

JONES, BEATRIX CADWALADER, who studied with Professor Sargent of Harvard, took a course in the Arnold Arboretum, and her travels abroad were largely for the purpose of studying famous gardens in England and on the Continent. Her landscape gardening is so far from being an ephemeral fad that she hangs out her "shingle," inviting competition with all the "mere men" who are classed as landscape architects. *July 16, 1904*

JONES, MR. AND MRS. E. PEMBROKE (SADIE W. GREEN) gave a large and most charming entertainment at "Friedheim," in Bellevue Avenue, Newport. The cotillion was composed of figures of different nations. The Italian figure demonstrated the art of glassmaking. For the Swiss figure, there were pretty alpine staffs. The last figure was an American figure, wherein the feature was a large illuminated, electric-lighted ball to represent the globe, surmounted by an American eagle, with letters of gold encircling the globe, "We Want the Earth." *August 23, 1902*

JONES, E. PEMBROKE was actively interested in railway affairs and prominent socially in New York and in the South. His country home was "Airlee-on-the Sound," Wilmington, Delaware. A Christmas custom with him was to ask all the children of the first families of

Wilmington to his home for a Christmas tree party, sending them away laden with gifts. In June, 1917, he placed his New York house at the disposal of the Italian mission visiting New York, and the invitation was accepted. *February 10, 1919*

JONES, ELLEN ROOSEVELT The wedding of Miss Jones, daughter of Mr. De Witt Clinton Jones, and Mr. Frederick G. Payne, Assistant Paymaster in the Navy, took place in Elizabeth, New Jersey. The bride is a great-granddaughter of Governor De Witt Clinton of New York, and the bridegroom is a descendant of Alexander Hamilton and Major General Philip Schuyler. *September 28, 1901*

JONES, FERNANDO The sale of the old Fernando Jones property down on Prairie Avenue carries an interest and a reminiscence outside of Chicago's limits. The Jones residence was the first dwelling to be erected in Prairie Avenue after the great fire. The family always held a high place in the Chicago annals of society and business, and so their big home became the center not only of the society life of the growing city but a gathering place of the great who came as visitors. It was there that the famous reception to Mme. Sarah Bernhardt was held a dozen years ago. *May 31, 1913*

JONES, G. NOBLE A Savannah engagement of considerable interest to Southern society is that of Miss Frances Meldrim to Mr. G. Noble Jones. Mr. Jones is on the board of managers of the Cotillion Club, a member of the Georgia Society of the Cincinnati and the Georgia Society of the Sons of the Revolution. He is a collateral descendant of G. Noble Jones, who came from England in 1733 with Oglethorpe, and to whom an original grant of land was made by George II, the property known as "Wormsloe," and now owned by Mr. Wymberley Jones De Renne. *March 12, 1904*

JONES, MRS. ISAAC (MARY MASON) The site of the house now occupied by Mrs. Mason Jones has been in possession of the family since 1804, when it was bought, together with forty acres of adjacent land. The family occupied the old homestead as a country seat, removing from the part of the city now known as Wall Street. The marble buildings were erected in 1867, Mrs. Jones moving in 1869 to the present residence. Sixty four years ago, Mrs. Jones presided at the first ball of her wedded life, and though now eighty years of age, conducts personally her household affairs and manages the estate. *February 16, 1881*

JONES, MRS. OLIVER LIVINGSTON, for her reception to the Society of Holland Dames, chose the day that celebrates the organizing of the municipal government of New York. On February second, 1653, Governor Peter Stuyvesant appointed the first burgomaster and schepens, officers corresponding to those of the Mayor and Aldermen of today. Had the Governor been present on Saturday, he would have heard in the greetings the names of many of his schepens and patroons and would have seen how the achievements of his day are remembered. *February 9, 1907*

JORDAN, EBEN D. was a citizen who left his mark on Boston. He founded the great department store Jordan Marsh and built the imposing mansion, 46 Beacon Street, which has housed since 1924 the Women's Republican Club. He built the Boston Opera House in 1909 and met its deficits until it was disbanded in 1914. *June, 1950*

JOY, MRS. HENRY BOURNE (HELEN HALL NEWBERRY), who is one of the most prominent matrons in Detroit, is a sister of Assistant Secretary of War Truman H. Newberry and is a great-niece of Oliver Newberry, known as "The Steamboat King." Mr. Joy is a son of the late James Frederic Joy, President of the Michigan Central and the organizer and builder of several railroads in the West. For generations, both the Joy and the Newberry families have been identified with the progress of Detroit. Mr. and Mrs. Joy are well-known in the East, for they have spent many summers at Watch Hill, Rhode Island. *July 20, 1907*

K

KAHN, MR. AND MRS. OTTO (ADDIE WOLF), who are at "Villa Arcadie" in Bar Harbor, will leave this country late in August, to take possession of "Cassiobury," Lord Essex's estate at Watford. Though there is rumor that Mr. and Mrs. Kahn may go to England to make it their permanent home, they have one of the finest residences in Morristown, New Jersey. Every afternoon at five, when tea is served, there is the children's hour, and the eldest daughter, Maud Emily Kahn, who is herself still a schoolgirl and not yet out in society, brings the family in a merry little troop to the table which is presided over by Mrs. Kahn. *July 20, 1912*

THE ENTERTAINMENT WAS FLAWLESS

Did millionaire Otto Kahn really hire 1,000 "flunkies" in Louis XVI costumes and powdered wigs to line the Ritz-Carlton ballroom for his daughter Maud's debut? Only 75 flunkies in phlox-pink breeches bowed and scraped on tiptoe to serve Maud Kahn's elegant guests. However, the entertainment in honor of Miss Maud was matchless for the 'twenties. Enrico Caruso sang during dinner (two songs for $10,000), *chanteuse* Yvette Guilbert vocalized between dances, and the Ballet Russe starring Nijinsky performed at three o'clock in the morning. *June, 1965*

KANE, DE LANCEY ASTOR will establish a line of English coaches to run from this city to New Rochelle on the Sound. The undertaking will necessitate an outlay of about twenty five thousand dollars. Mr. Kane will hold "the ribbons" himself. Other lines, to be driven by gentlemen coachmen, are to be projected, one of which is to extend along the North [Hudson] River. This is a London fashion which deserves to be appreciated in

New York. The drives are beautiful, and the people will be glad of the novel opportunity presented. The best horses will be provided. *February 16, 1876*

KANE, MR. AND MRS. JOHN INNES (ANNIE C. SCHERMERHORN) Their reception, given in their new home at the corner of Fifth Avenue and West Forty Ninth Street, marked a new era, perhaps, in social history. With all due reverence, many of the guests spoke of it as "a resurrection party," for so many people were seen who have been lost to society, overwhelmed by the tidal wave of wealth and loath to accept invitations because unable to return courtesies in the prodigal style of the day. *January 9, 1909*

KANE, WOODBURY Besides being a descendant of John Jacob Astor, Captain Kane was a collateral relative of Elisha Kent Kane, the famous Arctic explorer, and also of Chancellor James Kent, one of the most eminent jurists of the eighteenth century. He was the author of a legal work considered the first judicial classic of the United States. John Kintzing Kane, the jurist, was President of the American Philosophical Society. His son, Elisha Kent Kane, the Arctic explorer, added to geography the most Northern lands known in his day. *December 16, 1905*

KAVANAUGH, MRS. GEORGE WASHINGTON (MARIE M. MILLER) stepped out on her own this year and hit all the newspapers by buying champagne for the reporters on the opening night of the Opera. It seems she asked these gentlemen to pull her hair to satisfy themselves that it was her very own. Either of those exploits would have made her celebrated— both have assured her a niche in New York's Hall of Fame. *March, 1938*

KAWANANAKOA, PRINCESS ABIGAIL KEKAULIKE is a direct descendant of Hawaiian royalty and cousin of Edward Keliiahonui Kawananakoa, the man who would be king had the monarchy not been abolished in 1893. The handsome imperial Princess is President of Friends of Iolani Palace, an organization that has spearheaded the restoration of the only royal palace in the United States. Princess Abigail is an accomplished equestrienne and rancher/breeder. *January, 1981*

KEAN, THOMAS H. Seven generations after his ancestor William Livingston became New Jersey's first governor, Thomas Kean is immensely proud of his work in the same office—a feeling shared by his fellow citizens, who re-elected him by the largest majority in the state's history. In facing such challenges as creating a new image for the state, he keeps his family's tradition in mind. "My father," he says, "a Congressman for twenty years, taught me that public service is a very noble profession." *October, 1986*

KEENE, FOXHALL His father, James R. Keene, a Wall Street megatherium, had a standing offer of $100,000 to back Foxhall against any one man in the world at ten sports of his own choosing. Foxhall Keene was one of the greatest flat-racers, steeplechasers, and fox hunters of his time. He was a superb golfer and motor racer. He was a crack at lawn tennis, court tennis, and racquets. He was a ten-goal poloist for thirty years. He also boxed and played football. *December, 1936*

KEENE, JAMES R. passed his boyhood on a Virginia farm near Lynchburg. In 1852, he went to the Pacific Coast, and at the age of twenty five was a curb broker in San Francisco. For fifteen years, Mr. Keene had ups and downs; and when the Bank of California failed in a memorable panic, he was on the right side of the market and walked off with $4,000,000. He then came to New York, where for years on Wall Street he was the boldest plunger. *January 18, 1913*

KELLOGG, MR. AND MRS. FRANCIS (FERNANDA W. MUNN) Mrs. Francis Kellogg, a wild-game buff and highly experienced safarier, is just back from another long stay in Stanley-and-Livingston country. As President of the Louwana Fund (named for her mother, the former Mary Louise Wanamaker), she's been dedicating most of her time since 1963 to raising funds for planes and Land Rovers and other anti-poaching aids needed in Kenya's big-game preserves. A safari that Mrs. Kellogg took one year was devoted to collecting specimens of small mammals and birds for the National Museum. This took her to some parts of Kenya where white women had never before been seen. *September, 1970*

KELLOGG, PETER, a New York financier, tossed a toga party in Bay Head, New Jersey, that featured invitations in Latin, a whole roasted pig, and "chariot races" in which male guests pulled female-piloted boat trailers through a street conveniently closed to traffic by local police. *June, 1981*

KEMBLE, MR. AND MRS. WILLIAM (MIMI MADDOCK) Included in this 30-to-40-year-old group of young couples in Palm Beach are former Bostonian Bill Kemble, who is with Shearson, and his wife Mimi, who works as a decorator. Mimi's father, Paul Maddock, a key figure in saving some of the town's oldest buildings on the picturesque Lake Trail, owns the charming, gabled "Duck's Nest," the oldest house on the island. *March, 1983*

KEMPER, WILLIAM T. The seldom-disputed leaders of Kansas City's financial, social, and cultural life now are the Kempers, descendants of William T. Kemper, who arrived in the city in 1893. His family now owns the first- and third-largest banks in Kansas City and controls or has large interests in 21 smaller banks in Missouri, Kansas, Colorado, and Oklahoma. They own some seven blocks of downtown real estate and, through directorships or investments, influence many of the city's major businesses and such national firms as Owens-Corning Fiberglass and the Missouri Pacific Railroad. *May, 1968*

KENDALL, MRS. WILLIAM SERGEANT (CHRISTINE HERTER) gave an exhibition of her new paintings at "Garth Newel," her home on Warm Springs Mountain, Virginia Hot Springs. Here, Mr. and Mrs. Kendall have separate studios, and they give as much attention to their paintings as they do to their romantic Arabians, which drew so many blue ribbons at the recent horse show. *October 1, 1928*

KENDRICK, MRS. RODNEY (EDITH HUNTINGTON)—SPRECKELS—WAKEFIELD San Francisco society was surprised by her marriage to Mr. Rodney Kendrick, of Sausalito, which took place in Truckee, California. Mrs. Kendrick is the daughter of the late Mr. and Mrs. Willard V. Huntington, of San Francisco, and a niece of Mr. Henry Huntington of Pasadena and the late Mr. Collis P. Huntington. *August 15, 1925*

CAMELOT BY THE CLOCK

With the arrival of the John F. Kennedys in the White House, the social climate of Washington has changed. What was once occasional socializing in a serious vein is now constant, gaily spirited, and dynamic. "It used to be so quiet around here after 11 o'clock, you could shoot ducks," says Charles, the faithful White House steward for years. "Things certainly have changed." *December, 1963*

KENNEDY, JOHN STEWART The second appraisal of the estate of John Stewart Kennedy gives the gross value of $67,137,735. Some $30,000,000 of the estate goes to charitable and philanthropic institutions, about $17,000,000 goes to the widow, Mrs. Emma B. Kennedy, and $15,000,000 more goes to relatives. Mr. Kennedy left no children, but divided his estate among seventy two individuals and sixty institutions. *November 4, 1911*

KENNEDY, MR. AND MRS. JOSEPH P. (ROSE FITZGERALD) The strapping, red-headed Irishman, as Chairman of the Securities and Exchange Commission, was Wall Street's only darling in the Rooseveltian cabal. The son of a contractor who was also a politician, he played ball at Boston Latin. It was through his father that he met his wife, a daughter of Mayor John F. ("Honey Fitz") Fitzgerald. Politically, Mr. Kennedy belongs in the category of "Roosevelt before Chicago." He contributed $40,000 to the party fund, accompanied the Democratic nominee on his campaign tour, and then, after the election, returned to his own affairs. *October, 1935*

KENNEDY, MR. AND MRS. MOOREHEAD C. (LOUISA LIVINGSTON) He is one of the few diplomats who successfully completed the School for Arabic Studies in Lebanon, after Princeton and Harvard Law School. They have been stationed in Yemen, Athens, Beirut, and now live in Washington, D.C., where he is director of the Office of Investment Affairs for the State Department. *September, 1973*

KENT, MR. AND MRS. JAMES (MARY BRINCKERHOFF VERPLANCK) One of last Saturday's nuptial ceremonies recalled all the early history of New Amsterdam and brought together a representation of the old Dutch families descendant from the Protestants of Holland. The bride numbers among her distinguished ancestors Daniel Crommelin Verplanck, member of Congress. The Verplanck estate at Fishkill, New York, where Mr. and Mrs. Robert N. Verplanck, the bride's parents, still own the homestead, was the property of the family as early as 1682. In the little old house, Baron Steuben had his headquarters. The groom likewise has a pedigree to be envied, for he is a relative of the Van Cortlandts, and through his mother, Mrs. James Kent, is also a connection of the Morrises. *October 31, 1903*

KERNOCHAN, FREDERIC has been Chief Justice of the Court of Special Sessions since 1916. In support of his present candidacy on both the Fusion and Republican tickets for Judge of General Sessions, William Travers Jerome, heretofore a fellow Democrat, has emerged to break a long silence. During the great reform days of District Attorney Jerome, Frederic Kernochan was one of the young crusaders on his staff. *November 1, 1933*

KERNOCHAN, MRS. JAMES LORILLARD (ELOISE STEVENSON) was chosen President of the Ladies' Kennel Association of America, a society formed on the plan of the English one to further the breeding of dogs among women. Her kennels, well known as the Meadows Kennels, are perfection, built with every luxury for dogs. Passing through the library, one enters an enclosed piazza, around the sides of which, under a curtain, are comfortable dog-boxes. Here, in cold weather, they can have the luxury of steam heat, besides the odor of rare, sweet flowers and the songs of numbers of birds. *August 31, 1901*

KERNOCHAN, MRS. JAMES P. (CATHERINE LORILLARD) has been given the credit of saying that, at Newport, the old conservative element must be asked to the largest functions of the millionaires, because their presence gives an air and a tone to the entertainments, just as antique furniture and bric-a-brac and family portraits and heirlooms would to a drawing room. *August 5, 1905*

KERNOCHAN, MARSHALL R. is one of the most versatile young men in New York society. He plays an excellent game of tennis, drives an automobile like a professional racer, is a near scratch man at the golf club handicap, is one of the best dancers among young men in the Lenox colony, and is known as a composer of merit by singers of male songs. *September 16, 1911*

KETELTAS, ALICE The Keteltas mansion at Eighth Street and Fifth Avenue is perhaps the last large private house in that part of town. The house is the home of a charming gentlewoman, Miss Keteltas. The Keteltas house was the scene of many entertainments a generation ago, and Miss Keteltas elected to reside in her ancestral residence long after the neighborhood had been deserted by her friends. To the people living in that section, the sight of liveried servants was a mystery, and the owner was obliged to have a sign placed near the main entrance stating that the house was not an institution and forbidding people from annoying its inmates by ringing the bell. Now it is covered with large advertising placards. With the two Rutherfurd residences, it remains now about the last to tell of the glory of the former court end of New York in the Forties and Fifties. *June 29, 1912*

KEYES, MRS. HENRY WILDER (FRANCES PARKINSON), being the wife of a Senator and a thoroughly nice woman, has painted extensive pictures of the Washington she knows for a very wide audience. Her readers retained the traditional picture of a glittering and romantic Victorian capital, in which everyone is happy and in which the only problem is the love life of a rural Senator. *January 1, 1933*

KEYSER, MATHILDE One of the most important engagements announced in Baltimore for several years is that of Miss Keyser and Mr. William Maurice Manly. She is a descendant of one of Maryland's oldest and purely Maryland families. The old family home was opposite "Mount Vernon." Mr. Manly belongs to an old Colonial family of North Carolina, and in every way represents all that is best in a gentleman of the old regime. To his energy, the Baltimore Horse Show Association owes its success. *March 8, 1902*

KING, DOROTHY Very interesting to New Yorkers, because of the bride's wide connections, has been the wedding of Dorothy King to Mr. Alexander Nelidow. The Nelidow family has been traceably established in Russia for hundreds of years. Mrs. Nelidow is a granddaughter of the late Edward King of Newport and a great-great-granddaughter of Colonel Nicholas Fish. She is also a descendant of Peter Stuyvesant and of John Winthrop, the former the last Dutch Governor of New York and the latter the first Colonial Governor of Massachusetts. *January 15, 1926*

KING, EDWARD was at one time President of the New York Stock Exchange, a governor of the New York Hospital, and President of the St. Nicholas Society. His father, James Gore King, represented this country during a financial crisis of his time, when he convinced the governors of the Bank of England that they might with safety assist American merchants. James Gore King was the son of Rufus King, the statesman, who in 1825 went on a mission to England at the urgent request of John Quincy Adams and whose life history was part of the history of this country. *November 28, 1908*

KING, GENERAL HORATIO C. was soldier, lawyer, writer, orator, publicist, musician, businessman, and wit. He joined the National Rifles, the crack military company of Washington, D.C., and demonstrated his efficiency as a sharpshooter from the house tops on Pennsylvania Avenue, at Lincoln's first inauguration! He served till the end of the war, receiving credible promotions, and then became Associate Editor of the *New York Star* and later, Publisher of the *Christian Union*. His interests grew wider in scope until, to those who knew him, the handling of them became little short of a marvel. *December 1, 1918*

KING, NICHOLAS LEROY, a direct descendant of Peter Stuyvesant, says that he has "a village feeling about New York, based not only on coming from a tradition-minded family but on sense of location. I live within four blocks of where my parents, grandparents, and one great-grandparent lived." Mr. King (whose family tree also includes Edith Wharton and various Livingstons, Fishes, Bayards, and Rhinelanders) adds, however, that he wouldn't dream of "talking about who one's ancestors are, except maybe to other cousins." *September, 1987*

KING, MR. AND MRS. THOMAS W. (CORNELIA PEABODY) At their house at Cedarhurst, Mr. and Mrs. King are very much interested in dogs. They have some very good Griffons. In fact, the best Griffon in this country is Mrs. King's dog named "Piggy," which won at the Ladies' Toy Dog Show at the Waldorf-Astoria and again at the Westminster show. *March 18, 1905*

KIP, MR. AND MRS. HENRY SPIES (FRANCES C. JONES) have taken the cottage "Caselo," on Kay Street, in Newport. Mr. Kip, as a descendant of the Kip's Bay Kips, has the privilege of taking up his residence, when he so chooses, at "Ankony," the old estate at Rhinebeck, where the Kip cows are in adjacent pastures to those of Mr. John Jacob Astor. Mrs. Kip was independent and original while still very young and had a "studio" where artists and clever people in general were well pleased to drop in for a chat and music. *July 23, 1904*

KIP, IRA J. is the originator of the delightful plan for the enjoyment of the society people of South Orange, New Jersey. Mr. Kip has purchased a fine four-in-hand coach and horses, and trips will be made three times a week from the clubhouse of the Essex County Country Club to the Baltusrol clubhouse and return. The coach is the "Olden Time," which took the first prize at the World's Fair at Chicago. Matched leaders and wheelers of fine action and style have been purchased, and the entire outfit is complete in every detail. *May 25, 1901*

KIP, ISAAC L. was a retired physician and a member of one of New York's old families. Dr. Kip married, in 1858, Cornelia Brady, a daughter of the late William V. Brady, a former Mayor of New York, and in 1873 began to manage the Brady estate. Dr. Kip was also one of the claimants to the Kip Bay estate in First Avenue, to which his ancestors had obtained a grant about two hundred years ago. *October 14, 1911*

KIP, WILLIAM RULOFF is named after Roeloff de Kype, his ancestor. Coming closer to the present day, he is a descendant of the Knickerbocker who built the Kip mansion taken down in 1854 to make way for the cutting through of East Thirty Second Street. Since his graduation from Yale, Mr. Kip has given much time to art. *January 31, 1914*

KISSEL, GUSTAV EDWARD was the senior member of the firm of Kissel, Kinnicutt & Co. He was interested in charities and was President of the People's Symphony Concert Society. His wife is a daughter of William K. Thorn and Emily Vanderbilt. *April 22, 1911*

KLEBERG, ROBERT The "King Ranch," that incredible barony of close to a million acres of land in Texas alone, is only part of a stultifying 11,500,000 acres in the world over, spread throughout such diverse domains as Australia, Venezuela, Spain, and Morocco. The ranch is headed up by 78-year-old Bob Kleberg. The present "family" is a conglomerate of Klebergs, Armstrongs, Clements, Larkins, Sheltons, Johnsons, Sugdens, and Meyers in the older generations alone. *November, 1974*

KNIGHT, MR. AND MRS. EDWARD COLLINGS (ANNA MAGILL) The dinner dance they gave their debutante daughter, Clara Waterman Knight, was held at the Bellevue-Stratford in Philadelphia. Nothing like the magnificence of the Knight affair had ever been seen here. A citizen of the world, Mr. Knight drew upon his continental experiences for ideas. Those ideas cost him roughly $35,000, but the result was to put the $20,000 ball of James W. Paul, which has heretofore marked the limit of costly functions in Philadelphia, in the shade. There were rose trees from which the women plucked the blossoms and cast them at the men until the floor was a fragrant carpet. It took three cars to bring up from the South the trees and blooms that went with the roses. *February 3, 1906*

KNIGHT, MR. AND MRS. LOUIS ASHTON (CAROLINE RIDGWAY BREWSTER) He is an artist like his father, Mr. Daniel Ridgway Knight, and when he arrived from abroad he received due mention and there was reference to his achievements as a painter. Few readers of the papers realized, however, that it was this artist who, shortly after his arrival, was married to Miss Caroline Ridgway Brewster. The bride, on her father's side, descends from the Brewsters of colonial times. Her maternal grandmother, before her marriage, was a Miss Ridgway, and her ancestors in Philadelphia were also the ancestors of Mr. Knight. *October 26, 1907*

KNOX, DOROTHY HENESS Pittsburgh is giving much attention to the success of Miss Dorothy Heness Knox. Miss Knox has published a book, *The Heart of Washington,* and according to the critics it has much merit. Her grandfather was the late W. W. Knox, a writer of distinction in his day; her great-grandfather was the Rev. Jeremiah Knox, and her great-great-grandfather, the Rev. William Knox, a clergyman of the Presbyterian faith who lived in Pittsburgh in 1800. Secretary Knox claims the same family tree, the Knoxes of Knoxville and Brownsville being as well known as Pittsburgh itself. *September 4, 1909*

KOCH, DAVID H. He's one of the four sons of the late Fred Koch, co-founder of Koch Industries of Wichita, Kansas. He's also an eclectic philanthropist with particular interests in science, libertarian politics, education, and performing arts. A devotee and generous supporter of ballet, he's among the financiers of a current Yale archaeological excavation project in Egypt, which seeks to learn how common people lived in ancient times. *September, 1989*

KOONTZ, MR. AND MRS. HENRY CLAY gave a series of five parties to celebrate the centennial of their "HK Ranch." Located outside of Victoria, Texas, the HK Ranch was carved out of the Keeran ranch founded by Koontz's great-great-grandfather, John N. Keeran. The final wing-ding centered around a quail hunt.

The birds that were bagged that day provided that night's banquet. The night before, there had been a gala get-together at the Koontz "ranch house"—an old church they bought for $4,000 and moved some thirty miles out to the HK Ranch. *September, 1979*

L

LA FARGE, FRANCES AIMEE, youngest daughter of Mr. John La Farge, the artist, and Mr. Edward Herrick Childs were married at Newport. Mrs. Childs is a direct descendant of Commodore Oliver Hazard Perry. She was selected by the Secretary of the Navy to christen the gunboat *Newport* when it was launched four years ago. *June 21, 1900*

LA FARGE, MR. AND MRS. GRANT (FLORENCE B. LOCKWOOD), who were with the President and Mrs. Roosevelt at the Jamestown Exposition, are old friends of the Chief Executive and his gentle wife. Mr. La Farge is an architect, a son of John La Farge, one of the greatest of our artists and art-writers, his picture of *The Ascension* being considered the finest example of mural painting in this country. Mr. and Mrs. La Farge have a modest home on East Twenty Second Street and a summer home at Saunderstown, Rhode Island. *June 15, 1907*

LA FARGE, MARIE ANGELE was a sister of John La Farge, the famous American artist. Miss La Farge's life was typical of the aristocratic old French element represented by her family. It was a beautiful life in which her duties consisted of ministering to the unfortunate and in which her chief recreation, her interest in her flowers at her beautiful home, seemed typical of her gentleness. *February 2, 1907*

LA FARGE, OLIVER is now in Washington as special consultant to the Army Air Transport command. His duties include flying air transport routes, visiting bases, and writing up his experiences for the Command. Mr. La Farge has been on numerous archaeological and ethnological expeditions and has done research at Tulane and the Pennsylvania Museum. He won the Pulitzer Prize with his Navajo novel, *Laughing Boy*. *March, 1943*

LA MONTAGNE, MRS. AUGUSTE A. (ANNIE DAVIS) is survived by her daughters, Mrs. Nicholas Murray Butler, wife of the President of Columbia University, and Mrs. Francis K. Pendleton, wife of the former Supreme Court Justice. Her husband was a brother of the late Edward La Montagne, a member of the Racquet and Tennis Club. *March 1, 1924*

LA MONTAGNE, RENE is the goaler of the Rockaway Hunt Club hard riders, but he makes their thraldom pleasant, and shows them such good sport, that his popularity knows no bounds. His hunting education was excellent, and consisted of a very thorough apprenticeship in England and two rattling good seasons at Pau. The country around Pau is stiff, and his experience there got him in good condition for the Long Island rail fences. *October 23, 1889*

LADENBURG, MRS. ADOLPH (EMILY STEVENS) Society is electrified by the news that Mrs. Adolph Ladenburg, who is one of the most graceful and accomplished horsewomen in the country, is to open a sales and exchange stable conducted on business lines at her new place on the Hempstead Plains, Long Island, opposite the Meadowbrook clubhouse. A recent very clever sale of horses by Mrs. Ladenburg gave her the idea of trading in horses as a practical venture. *September 5, 1903*

LADEW, HARVEY When Harvey Ladew decided to settle in the hunting country of Maryland, he found an old farm in Harford County with a simple farmhouse that had been standing about a hundred years. Today, it stands transformed both outwardly by beautiful gardens and inwardly by distinguished decoration. The owner is a man of many interests, but his greatest love is fox hunting, and he has spent years amassing collections which have to do with this sport. For over twenty seasons, he hunted in England. *October, 1951*

LAIDLAW, CHARLES E. was a brother of Mr. Henry B. Laidlaw, with whom, in 1875, he founded the banking firm of Laidlaw & Company. For twelve years, he was one of the governors of the Stock Exchange. *February 13, 1909*

LAMONT, CORLISS is the second son of Thomas W. Lamont of the J. P. Morgan firm. Young Corliss Lamont showed signs of becoming a firebrand as early as 1922 when, as a Harvard undergraduate, he became head of the Progressive Club of the Harvard Union and invited Eugene Debs to speak there. He campaigned for Norman Thomas, Socialist candidate for President in 1929. Mr. Lamont has become an important figure in all radical movements. He has been arrested for picketing. He has lectured at such places as meetings of Friends of the Soviet Union. *December, 1940*

LAMONT, ROBERT P., JR. is the son of President Hoover's Secretary of Commerce. He is the young man who upset Washington's politicians three years ago by going to Russia and advising the Soviet Government how to improve its livestock industry. The owner of 7000 acres (Perry Park Ranch in Colorado), 300 head of registered Herefords and 750 Hampshire Down sheep, he has served as President of the National Western Stock Show. Mrs. Lamont does her best work at the ranch. Sculptor of the War Memorial in New Canaan, Connecticut, her portrait busts and animal figures have been exhibited across the country. *May 1, 1935*

LAMPTON, DINWIDDIE, JR. is a gentleman farmer who works as hard as he plays. As much businessman as he is father, as much farmer as he is patron of the arts, Dinwiddie Lampton, Jr. is the supreme country gentleman. He is President of The American Life and Acccident Insurance Company of Kentucky, a privately held family corporation. In the land of bourbon and blue-blooded horses, on the fourth Saturday of May, Kentucky's first families and their special guests gather at Dinwiddie Lampton, Jr.'s "Hard Scuffle Farm" for one of America's premiere steeplechase events: Hard Scuffle Race Weekend. *May, 1983*

LANAHAN, MRS. WILLIAM WALLACE (ELEANOR ADDISON WILLIAMS) confines her remarkable energies to playing the role of top Baltimore hostess. The Lanahan luncheon before the Maryland Cup had to be abandoned because it became too popular: Last time six hundred guests came. *June, 1939*

LANE, MRS. FRANKLIN KNIGHT (ANNE WINTERMUTE), widow of Franklin K. Lane, who was Secretary of the Interior under President Wilson and was recognized as one of the strong men of the Administration, has returned to California to make her home. Mrs. Lane is a believer in spiritism, and she and Mrs. Harriet Blaine Beale, daughter of James G. Blaine, together published a small volume containing a series of "lessons" which they were convinced came to them from a spirit in the other world by means of automatic writing. *September 1, 1923*

LANGFORD, NATHANIEL PITT came to St. Paul in 1854. In 1862, he aided in opening an overland wagon road to Walla Walla, Washington. He accompanied General Henry D. Washburn, Surveyor General of Montana, to the Yellowstone country, and in recognition of services then rendered, Mr. Langford was appointed the first superintendent of Yellowstone Park. He was twice married, both times to sisters of Dr. Charles A. Wheaton of St. Paul. *November 4, 1911*

LANSING, ROBERT The country now has an able man as Secretary of State, a man possessed of many interesting and admirable qualifications. He has represented the United States in more international arbitrations than any living American. He is an author, a poet, and an editor. He makes a good diplomat because he is a keen golfer and a patient angler. He has an ingratiating smile, and is considered one of the best dressed men in public life in Washington. *July 1, 1915*

LARSEN, JONATHAN Z. One of America's Fifty Most Eligible Young Men. Son of the Roy Larsens, his father is Chairman of the Board, Time, Inc. Jon attended Hotchkiss, has an A. B. Harvard '61. At 21, he came into a small fortune. Hobby: photography (which he probably inherits from mother's brother, Jerome Zerbe). Serious about writing, he leans toward essay rather than fiction. *June, 1964*

LASKER, MRS. ALBERT (MARY WOODARD) The soft-spoken widow of Chicago advertising pioneer Albert Lasker has given millions to medical research, mostly through the foundation she and her husband set up in 1942. Her efforts to beautify New York by donating hundreds of thousands of flowers to the city earned her the sobriquet, "Primavera in an asphalt desert," but medical research is her top priority. *December, 1983*

LAUGHLIN, MADELAINE E. She is a member of a family associated with the great steel interests of Pittsburgh. She is a granddaughter of the late Benjamin Franklin Jones, who established the American Iron Works, the firm name being Jones & Laughlin. In 1884, he was made President of the American Iron and Steel Association and was later a candidate for

United States Senator. She is a fearless horse-woman, and her riding last fall was a feature of the Sewickley Horse Show. *January 20, 1906*

LAW, GEORGE, SR. was a man whose name will always have a place in the annals of his country's progress. He was foremost in the project of erecting High Bridge in New York City, and his name, cut in stone, may still be seen. In 1849, he carried the first passengers to the Isthmus of Panama by steamship, and he was the owner of a great ferryboat system on New York's East River. *June 18, 1904*

LAW, WALTER W. It is to the credit of Mr. Walter W. Law and his magnificent estate at "Briarcliff Farms" in the Westchester Hills that the invention of the name Briarcliff leaves such a refreshing impression. The instinct which prompted Mr. Law to develop Briarcliff Farms on business principles has also led him to take an active interest in the formation of a School for Practical Agriculture and Horticulture. *March 15, 1902*

LAWRANCE, CHARLES LANIER was designer of the motor which was installed in the *Spirit of St. Louis,* which, with a modern Icarus for pilot, made history. It is quite possible that finance lost a distinguished pupil when Mr. Lawrance, on graduating from Yale in 1905, rebelled against entering the banking house of Lanier & Winslow, of which his grandfather, the late Mr. Charles Lanier, was senior partner. But it is very certain that science benefited. His great triumph began when his friend, Captain Lindbergh, hopped off from Roosevelt Field on that historic Friday morning of May the twentieth for Le Bourget. *June 15, 1927*

LAWRANCE, FRANCIS C. was at one time a notable figure in New York club and social life. For the past quarter of a century, he has been living a great part of the year at his villa at Pau. He was a man of independent means. He married the wealthy Miss Garner, a sister of the late Commodore Garner, who, with his wife, drowned in his yacht off Stapleton, S. I. Mr. and Mrs. Lawrance had charge of the three orphan daughters of the Garners. These young women are now the Marquise de Breteuil, Mrs. Gordon-Cumming, and the Countess Leon von Moltke. *August 26, 1911*

LAWRENCE, AMORY APPLETON was at the head of important cotton industries in Ipswich and was made President of the Boston Merchants' Association. He was the brother of Bishop William Lawrence of Massachusetts and active, therefore, in behalf of the Episcopal charities of his state. *July 20, 1912*

LAWRENCE, EFFINGHAM is a namesake of the first Effingham Lawrence, whose name was given to him in compliment to the Howards of Effingham, later the Earls of Effingham. Joseph Lawrence, so the story goes, married a daughter of Sir Richard Townley, a relative of the Howards of Effingham. There was another Effingham Lawrence who founded the famous Tontine Coffee House Association of New York. Then a third Effingham Lawrence was the first judge of Queens County and was a brave officer in the Navy. *April 20, 1907*

LAWRENCE, FRANK R. was President of the Lotos Club for thirty years, and eminent among corporation lawyers of the city. Mr. Lawrence was noted for his gift as a toastmaster and is remembered as presiding at the now famous Lotos Club dinner when Colonel Harvey arose and unofficially proposed Woodrow Wilson, the guest of honor, as a candidate for the Presidency of the United States. *November 10, 1918*

LAWRENCE, RT. REV. FREDERIC C. Bishop Lawrence's father was William Lawrence, Bishop of Massachusetts. His brother, William Appleton Lawrence, was bishop of Western Massachusetts. The bishop who followed his father, Charles L. Slattery, was his brother-in-law. His grandfather Parker was elected bishop but died before his investiture. Great-grandfather Amos Lawrence built the family fortune as a Boston merchant between 1790 and 1840. Amos was one of Boston's great philanthropists and gave away two-thirds of his income. *March, 1968*

LAWRENCE, MRS. JAMES There have been established in different parts of devastated France, by the American Committee for Devastated France, tea rooms where one may obtain typically American cool drinks, ice cream sodas, sundaes, college ices, and various other delectable refreshments unknown to the European palate. These tea rooms are found at Coucy-le-Château, Couy, and Laon, that at the latter place being in charge of Mrs. James Lawrence, of Boston. *August 20, 1920*

LAWRENCE, JAMES, JR., who has just been chosen Chief Marshal for Harvard Class Day, the highest honor in the gift of the University, has been receiving many congratulations. In spite of his aristocratic affiliations and all that goes with the name, which has always been one to conjure with socially in Boston, young Lawrence is as democratic in the true sense as any man in college. He is a splendid-looking fellow, tall, with well-knit frame, and has a distinguished manner. *December 27, 1900*

LAWRENCE, JOHN S. is one of the most noted amateur yachtsmen of the country, head of the syndicate which built the *Yankee,* one of the four sloops built for the defense of the *America*'s Cup. The Lawrences for generations have been associated with Massachusetts, and in particular with that part of Massachusetts which is the hub of the state and, for that matter, the hub of the Universe. *July 15, 1930*

LAWRENCE, PRESCOTT If the fashionable audience at the National Horse Show felt that it would have been correct to applaud, the appearance of Prescott Lawrence would certainly have been the signal for such a performance. Prescott Lawrence has always been regarded as a mascot. He is thoroughly English in his garb and appearance, and at the same time an enthusiastic American. His clothes were a study for the man who wished to know what was the latest thing in London worn by gentlemen. Mr. Lawrence never goes to extremes in his attire, but he always makes the dress fit the occasion. *November 22, 1900*

LAWRENCE, RIGHT REV. WILLIAM, Bishop of Massachusetts, is a member of the historic Lawrence family of Boston and his mother was a Miss Appleton. His father was the late Amos Adams Lawrence, the builder of Lawrence Hall, the Episcopal theological school at Cambridge, Treasurer for some years of Harvard College, and an overseer thereof. The town of Lawrence, Kansas, and the Lawrence University at Appleton, Wisconsin, were named in his honor. In fact, there is a long line of notable Lawrences, the head of the family being Amos Lawrence, son of Samuel of Revolutionary days, and the benefactor of the famous academy at Groton. *October 18, 1913*

LAWSON, THOMAS W. Is it not strange that a successful man should choose for the name of his country home "Dreamwold," which literally translated means "a place to dream in." Yet that is what Mr. Thomas W. Lawson, of Boston, has done in giving title to his spendid establishment at Egypt, Massachusetts, on Cape Cod. One of the most notable features here is a racetrack enclosure containing two speeding courses and a polo field. Stretching away in the distance is the blue Atlantic, and in the foreground stands the lighthouse on Minot's Ledge. Along this rise of ground and in the valleys are the farm buildings, stables, cow barns, poultry houses, kennels, a dove cote, a beehive, a fire department house, the great Dutch windmill, a blacksmith shop, and an animal hospital. *February 14, 1903*

LAWSON-JOHNSTON, JOHN ROBERT has leased from the Duke of Argyll the historic castle of Inverary, with its extensive deer forests, grouse moors, and salmon rivers. It is the first time that the castle has been let. The rent is $15,000 a year. Inverary is a stately, but gloomy-looking house. *July 19, 1900*

LAZARUS, EMMA Her translations from Heine were first published in *Scribner's Magazine,* and her miscellaneous poems, *Songs of a Semite,* were widely read when published in 1882, during the winter that thousands of Russian Jews came to this country to escape persecution. As a result of their arrival, and the need for devising employment for them, Miss Lazarus wrote a series of articles indicating a system of technical education to solve the difficulty. Many of her translations from medieval Hebrew are now incorporated with the ritual of many American synagogues. *June 3, 1905*

LE BOUTILLIER, JOHN A. was a descendant of the firm of Le Boutillier Brothers, a famous dry goods house once situated in West Twenty Third Street, and a member of a silk thread manufacturing house. *May 15, 1924*

LEARY, BETH was the last American woman to be made a Countess by Pope Leo XIII. She was invested with her title through Archbishop Corrigan in May, 1902. *July 25, 1903*

LEAS, MR. AND MRS. DONALD S., JR. (FERNANDA WANAMAKER) A night in Bombay was the theme of the lavish costume ball given by the Donald S. Leas, Jr. in Southampton. Mrs. Leas confesses to a weakness for anything

"Oriental and mysterious," and this time she let herself go with one of the most spectacular parties Southampton has ever seen. An enormous tent was erected over a sunken garden at "Westerly," the Leas estate. Centered on the dance floor over a fountain was a splendid onion-domed "Taj Mahal." Three artificial palm trees supported the tent, which was swathed in hundreds of yards of pink and fuchsia China silk. *August, 1966*

LEATHERMAN, MR. AND MRS. RICHARD, JR. (CARROLL SEABROOK) Both husband and wife come from distinguished politico-military-cotton stock. Mr. Leatherman is a Polk. As in President James Knox Polk. And as in Leonidas Polk, a man for all seasons: Founder of the University of the South at Sewanee, Tennessee; Episcopal Bishop of Louisiana; great planter and gallant general; the "fighting bishop" of the Confederacy. Richard Leatherman's grandfather, Samuel Richard Leatherman, was a cotton king. Carroll Leatherman is a direct descendant of William Carroll, six times Governor of Tennessee and a military leader who helped his friend Andrew Jackson win the Battle of New Orleans. In addition to Governor Carroll, Mrs. Leatherman's lineage includes a Governor of Kentucky, a Minister to Spain, and a ferocious Civil War general. *November, 1977*

LEE, ANNE CARTER, granddaughter of the heroic General Robert E. Lee, married Lieutenant Edward Hanson Ely. In addition to her famous Lee ancestry, the bride is also a direct descendant of Parke Custis, son of Madame Washington and adopted son of General Washington. Through her mother (Miss Anne Willing Carter), she further counts among her ancestors that magnificent Colonial magnate and land owner of the Old Dominion, "King" Carter. A reception followed at "Nordley Regis," the ancestral home of the Carters, near Upperville. Instead of cutting the great wedding cake with the bridegroom's sword, the bride used the historic sword of her grandfather, General Lee, which was temporarily released for the purpose from its place of safe deposit in the Confederate Museum in Richmond, Virginia. *September 20, 1921*

LEE, ELIZABETH was the daughter born to Mr. and Mrs. Brooke Lee, the first girl child to open her eyes in historic Silver Spring, Maryland, the home of former Senator Blair Lee. Old Francis P. Blair of Andrew Jackson's day and "Kitchen Cabinet" fame, was among her forebears, and so was Montgomery Blair, who was in Lincoln's cabinet. *July 15, 1923*

LEE, ELLEN BRUCE, only daughter of Mr. and Mrs. Arthur Lee, of Elkins, West Virginia, and Washington, D.C., became the bride recently of Mr. Stoddard Pintard Johnston, of New York, in the Presbyterian Church, at Elkins, the church a memorial to the great-grandparents of the bride and built by her grandfather, the late Henry Gassaway Davis. *August 15, 1923*

LEE, GIDEON was a Mayor who had a part in the history of New York City, for he was courageous and energetic in quelling the riots in 1833. A daughter of Gideon Lee married Mr.

Charles M. Leupp, who was well known as a patron of art in the days when comparatively few New Yorkers had time or mind for painting and music. *January 22, 1910*

LEE, MARY CUSTIS was the eldest daughter of the late General Robert E. Lee and Mrs. Mary Custis Lee. Miss Lee was born at Arlington, then the residence of her maternal grandparents, Colonel and Mrs. George Washington Parke Custis, the former of whom was a step-grandson of General Washington. Nearly her entire life was spent at Arlington. A woman of commanding presence, brilliant intellect, and great cultivation, Miss Lee was eminently a *grande dame* of the old aristocracy of the South, and was everywhere received and deferred to as such. *December 10, 1918*

LEE, MR. AND MRS. WILLIAM HENRY FITZHUGH (MARY TABB BOLLING) A social event which attracted more attention in the state of Virginia than anything of the kind that has occurred there for many years—the marriage of young General W.H.F. Lee to Miss Tabby Bolling—occurred on Thursday last in Richmond. General Robert E. Lee was present. On the whole, it was the grandest and most aristocratic social event that has been celebrated in Richmond since the breaking out of the war. *December 4, 1867*

LEEDS, MR. AND MRS. WARNER M. (LOUISE T. HARTSHORNE)—MOORE The ball at "Greenway Court," Bar Harbor, had to do with the sea and with costumes of the sea. "Au Fond de la Mer" it was called, and each newcomer stepped down three granite steps into the under-ocean court of Poseidon. Brilliant fish of the Orient were everywhere strung on invisible thread. A ship's keel appeared through the water overhead and swayed there, heavy with barnacles. Into this scene floated a full three hundred and fifty guests, costumed as mermaid or sea foam, pearl or anemone, eel, frog, or goldfish. A trumpet sounded, and green fire flashed from the deck of the Leeds's yacht, the *Duchess*. Through green fire marched a group of men singing the chorus from *The Flying Dutchman* and halted there before closed gates. Slightly in advance of the others stood Mr. Leeds as the god of the sea and Mrs. Leeds as his consort. *August 22, 1914*

LEEDS, MR. AND MRS. WILLIAM BATEMAN (NONNIE STEWART) are regular summer residents of Newport. Last fall, Mr. Leeds purchased "Rough Point," which had been in the market for a long time. With its location at the lower turn of the cliff walk, with the grounds bounded by the ocean and Bellevue Avenue, the estate has long been one of the showplaces of Newport. The rough stone house, with its brown walls, seems part of the rocks above which it is built. The rocks extend out into the water many feet, and at the change of the tide or during a storm, the surf is magnificent. *August 24, 1907*

LEEDS, MR. AND MRS. WILLIAM B., JR. (PRINCESS XENIA OF RUSSIA) Their recent marriage in Paris was an event of international interest. The Princess Xenia is the youngest daughter of the late Grand Duke George

Michaelovitch of Russia and a niece of the King of Greece. Mr. Leeds is the son of Princess Anastasia of Greece, who was formerly Mrs. William B. Leeds of New York. *November 20, 1921*

LEFFERTS, GERTRUDE, daughter of John Lefferts, of Flatbush, Long Island, was married to Henry L. Brevoort. The Lefferts homestead, in which the ceremony was solemnized, has been occupied by the family since 1661. It was partially burned during Revolutionary times, but was rebuilt on the same timbers. On the library walls hangs a deed of property signed by Governor Stuyvesant. *November 15, 1882*

LEFFERTS, COLONEL MARSHALL was one of the great civil engineers of his time. He was the consulting engineer of the Atlantic Cable Company and was the inventor of much that improved electric cables. The Seventh Regiment under his command left New York during the Civil War, and after the war he died while on the train with the Seventh Regiment on the way to the Fourth of July celebration in Philadelphia. *April 24, 1909*

LEGARÉ, MRS. KENT The superbly groomed woman who gives great care and thought to her appearance stands out in Washington. Mrs. Kent Legaré is definitely one of those. She likes black, in lines running like a Vertés sketch, pointed up with staccato notes of color. She likes star sapphires and has a superb collection of them, likes minks and martens and has a pile of them. Mrs. Legaré takes her chic, her exquisite hands, her well-coiffed head over her own little circuit every year: from Washington to her summer house in Connecticut to her plantation in South Carolina—with considerable trotting across the Atlantic thrown in. *January, 1939*

LEGGETT, FRANCIS H. To a tiny village in New York State belongs the honor of being perhaps the first to own a church decorated throughout in the old spirit by one artist. St. Peter's Episcopal church at Stone Ridge, Ulster County, has been decorated and restored entirely as a memorial to Francis H. Leggett, the great merchant of New York, whose beautiful country seat, "Ridgely Manor," is one of the features of the district. Mr. Stephen Haweis, the well-known English artist, was commissioned to paint a series of pictures of Bible subjects, and he has recently completed the work quite in the old spirit of a French or Italian church. *June 1, 1920*

LEGGETT, SARAH HULL A commendable example in extending the field for the practical activities of ladies is offered by Miss Sarah Hull Leggett, who has just opened a bookstore at 1184 Broadway. Miss Leggett is a young lady of culture and refinement, a member of one of our oldest and most respected families. Her personal attractiveness indicates that it is no necessity that has led to this step, but a worthy desire for independence and a congenial employment for her talents. *November 3, 1875*

LEHMAN, MR. AND MRS. ROBERT (RUTH OWEN MEEKER) Robert Lehman is the polo-playing banker and nephew of New York's Governor. Mr. Lehman is the only son of Philip Lehman, who, in one of the few remaining private houses in the West Fifties (it is diagonally across from the Rockefellers) has one of America's finest collections of Old Masters. *October 1, 1934*

LEHR, HARRY has loyal friends in great numbers, and both he and his adherents are not only weary of but making strong protests against the constant ringing the changes on Mr. Lehr's fun-loving propensities. Some of the supposed escapades, so much written up, are of course fabrications, and the reader who believes all the tales has but a superficial knowledge of Newport society. Even the stuffed coon, brought in as a joke at dinner as a reminiscence of an amusing hunt at the Pembroke Jones estate in the South, was made to figure as a monkey; and the populace still believes in the "monkey who dined with the '400'." *August 15, 1903*

LEITER, JOSEPH is one of the few young men, sons of millionaires, who have shown the inherited ability to continue the financial successes of the father. From 1891 to 1898, he was his father's assistant agent, and it was in the beginning of the latter year that he became the largest individual holder of wheat in the history of the grain trade. The famous Leiter Chicago wheat corner is historic. *March 29, 1913*

LENOX, JAMES has never made money, and has never attempted to do so. Indeed, he is the one, and the only one, of our rich men who, it is claimed, makes it a matter of conscience not to add house to house and lay field to field. It is asserted that every year he dispenses his vast income in his own ways, but that he scrupulously avoids reinvesting it. And yet, in spite of himself, he grows richer and richer thus: Years ago, his father was obliged to take a piece of property, far beyond civilization, to satisfy a mortgage of eleven or thirteen thousand dollars. He held on, and James Lenox has held on. Now it is on the east side of the Central Park about Seventieth street—six blocks of the most desirable property in the city, and of which Mr. Lenox has sold to the amount of three-quarters of a million, and has enough left to make a million. *May 6, 1868*

LESER, MR. AND MRS. CHARLES CARROLL FULTON (PAULINE POTTER) Miss Potter, the great-granddaughter of one of the Bishops Potter, great-grandniece of the other, descendant of Thomas Jefferson, and former news reporter, was married to Charles Carroll Fulton Leser, the eminent picture restorer. Mr. Leser has spent many a happy hour rubbing the years away from the ladies of the Frick and Morgan Collections. In the course of his career with the Fogg Museum, he has already uncovered a Titian and a Tintoretto. *December 1, 1930*

LEVY, MRS. FANNY (MITCHELL) had for many years presided over Monticello, Virginia, the home of her eldest son, Jefferson M. Levy, which had been the family homestead since the death of Thomas Jefferson. Last fall, she received the Daughters of the American Revolution and presided at the grand colonial ball given to them at Monticello, at which the minuet was danced by the descendants of the original signers of the Declaration of Independence. *January 18, 1893*

SOCIAL ARBITER AND ARTISTE

Harry Lehr, with Mrs. Lehr, who is a daughter of Mrs. Joseph Drexel of Philadelphia, has been in Europe for some time. But he has been much in the public eye abroad, and Americans have read with interest of his being received by King Edward. He is a son of Mrs. Robert Lehr of Baltimore, where he was one of the founders of the Paint and Powder Club. At the first performance of this organization, he bounded into favor in the part of a ballet-girl wearing long yellow curls and a short fluffy skirt. As a cotillion leader, his talents are considered equal to those of Mr. Elisha Dyer. To use his own words, when once complimented upon this accomplishment he said, "Ah, yes! But I shine at the wrong end, you know." *September 19, 1908*

LEWIS, ELEANOR PARKE CUSTIS has an array of names that indicate a very desirable pedigree. Her mother was a daughter of Edwin A. Stevens, son of John Stevens, who created the estate "Castle Point," at Hoboken, New Jersey. In the Stevens family, there has been a line of eminent engineers. Edwin A. Stevens, grandfather of Miss Lewis, founded Stevens Institute, where engineers, who have won fame and wealth in their profession, invariably send their sons. *June 25, 1904*

LEWIS, MR. AND MRS. OWEN BATCHELDER (FRANCES JACQUELINE WASHINGTON) If the United States had come into being as a constitutional monarchy instead of a republic, and if George Washington had been made its king, then the tale might have been different. For the new Mrs. Lewis's father is the nearest living kinsman of the first President, a direct descendant of his brother, Bushrod Washington, and was the last Washington born at "Mount Vernon." *May 10, 1917*

LIDGERWOOD, MR. AND MRS. JOHN H. Unlike many of the Morristown, New Jersey, residents, they never go to New York for the winter season, leaving "Speedwell" only for their summer home at Shelter Island. Speedwell is one of the historic places of Morristown—Morse having sent the first telegraphic message from a building on the estate—and has been occupied by eight generations of Mrs. Lidgerwood's family. *April 5, 1902*

LIHME, ANITA, daughter of Mr. and Mrs. C. Bai Lihme, of Chicago and Watch Hill, is engaged to Prince Edward Joseph Lobkowicz. Miss Lihme and Prince Lobkowicz met at the Everglades Club, at Palm Beach. He is twenty-six years old and is a descendant of one of the oldest families in Europe, dating back a thousand years. His ancestors were made princes in 1624 under the Holy Roman Empire. He came to America a year ago, and owing to his extensive knowledge of Old Master and antique furniture, is connected with the Gainsborough Studios, of New York City. *August 1, 1925*

LIMBERG-STIRUM, COUNT AND COUNTESS (MARY JOY NEWLAND) Detroit is represented at the court at Berlin by a bride of the year, Countess Limberg-Stirum, daughter of the late Henry A. Newland and of Mrs. Newland, who was the daughter of the Hon. James F. Joy. The Countess is a typical American beauty and of retiring, quiet manner. Count Limberg-Stirum is of the Royal Guards in Emperor William's Court, and has ancestral estates in Berlin. *September 25, 1909*

LINCOLN, MRS. ABRAHAM (MARY TODD) Mrs. Lincoln made several purchases of books at Appleton's store last week. Our lady readers may like to know how she was attired. In a few words it can be told—so neat, plain, and simple was her costume. The dress consisted of a black and white small pattern checkered silk, worn long and trimmed with flounces. A shawl of the same material fell gracefully from the lady's shoulders. The bonnet, of white Tuscan, was trimmed with the same colored silk as the dress and shawl—the tout ensemble forming a most lady-like dress, which was quite becoming to the wearer. *July 9, 1864*

LINCOLN, ROBERT TODD At Manchester-in-the-Mountains, one of the notable summer homes is owned by Mr. Robert T. Lincoln of Chicago, who was formerly Secretary of War and also Minister to Great Britain. With him at his mountain residence is his daughter, Mrs. Beckwith, while his son-in-law and daughter, Mr. and Mrs. Charles Isham, with their son, young Lincoln Isham, occupy a fine old New England home at Manchester-in-the-Mountains. *September 4, 1909*

LIPPINCOTT, MR. AND MRS. J. DUNDAS (ISABEL ARMSTRONG) Philadelphia is looking forward to meeting the new mistress of the Lippincott "Yellow Mansion," as the family residence at Broad and Walnut Streets has been known to three generations. The marriage of Mr. J. Dundas Lippincott to Miss Isabel Armstrong took place last Saturday. The bride is a Southern woman, and is descended on both sides from leading Tennessee families. Her mother is a grand-niece of President Polk, and with her parents, Mr. and Mrs. Knox Walker, lived in the White House during the Polk administration. *November 28, 1903*

LIPPINCOTT, MRS. JOSHUA The old families of Revolutionary times are many of them still prominent in Philadelphia. One of their leaders is Mrs. Joshua Lippincott, who lives in the old Lippincott mansion at the northeast corner of Broad and Walnut, one of the most valuable properties in the city. Her charming old-fashioned garden is unfortunately walled in from the public gaze, but her wonderful elm tree has been celebrated for many years, and in the summer is one of the sights of Walnut Street. Mrs. Lippincott entertains not very largely but with great magnificence, and to be received by her is a mark of social security. *July 6, 1901*

LIPPINCOTT, MRS. WALTER (BESSIE T. HORSTMANN) Her suburban home, "Alscot," is one of the show places of Bryn Mawr, Pennsylvania. Last week she had as guests, at a garden fete, about three hundred members of the country set. The number of men present gave occasion for remark, many of them being those whose names are invariably associated with tickers and long-distance telephones leading to New York headquarters—men who are supposed to have never a moment's time for such a frivolity as a garden party. A scattering of fashionable Episcopal rectors, making dark somber spots on the lawn, gave a truly British aspect to the gathering. *June 28, 1902*

LITCHFIELD, BAYARD SANDS was graduated from Harvard in 1903. He is the son of the Honorable Edward Hubbard Litchfield of New York, and a grandson of the late Edwin C. Litchfield, who did much towards giving Prospect Park, Brooklyn, its reputation for beauty. There his home, "Litchfield Mansion," the picturesque building on the hill, was built. On the distaff side, young Mr. Litchfield is a descendant of Joshua Sands and of Anne Ayscough Sands, in memory of whose good works St. Ann's Church in Brooklyn received its name. *August 22, 1908*

LITCHFIELD, EDWARD ("DIMI") In 1913, Edward H. Litchfield, Dimi's grandfather, saw the completion of his country home in the Adirondacks, which is still the summer gathering place for the family. Bears and tigers, zebras, moose, and elk found their way into the Great Hall, along with nearly 190 other animal trophies, all dated and bearing Litchfield initials. Dimi eventually took charge of the family's financial investments and holdings, which include farmland in the Midwest, a small chemical company, and timber interests in the Adirondacks. Having taken on the stewardship of the 14,000-acre Litchfield Adirondack home in 1949, he has worked diligently ever since to maintain his grandfather's legacy. *August, 1983*

LITTLE, MR. AND MRS. WILLIAM C. (MAY SIMON) One of the newest homes in St. Louis, yet one of the most pretentious as regards size and appointments, is "Alden Hall," built last season by Mr. and Mrs. William C. Little and named after the historic ancestor of the Little family, John Alden. On the walls of the spacious living room hangs that familiar picture of "Priscilla," who was wooed by the family's progenitor. The Little family, as seen in the society annals of St. Louis, is one of the best established. *July 9, 1904*

LITTLETON, MR. AND MRS. MARTIN (MAUD WILSON) made a visit to "Innocence at Home," the new residence of Mark Twain at Redding, Connecticut. Mr. Littleton, whose geniality even softened some of the aspects of the Thaw trial, and who over his usual glass of buttermilk at luncheon had good jokes for the benefit of even the most down-trodden reporter, is a good match for our most famous humorist, so all sorts of cynical and amiable remarks were tossed about prodigally. *July 11, 1908*

LIVINGSTON, MR. AND MRS. GERALD MONCRIEFFE (ELEANOR HOFFMAN RODEWALD) He was a former Governor of the New York Stock Exchange and a nationally-known breeder and exhibitor of sports dogs. Gerald was

descended from the Livingston Manor Livingstons, but he was born in St. Paul. He reinstated the family fortune by making a huge sum in milling in the Middle West and was shrewd enough to sell short in 1929. His widow has a large limestone town house in Manhattan's East Sixties, a rambling estate touching Huntington Harbor on the North Shore of Long Island, a *pied-à-terre* for the winter months in Palm Beach, an impressive stone castle near Litchfield, Connecticut, plus the enormous "Dixie Plantation" in Quitman, Georgia. *September, 1973*

LIVINGSTON, HENRY H. is unique among Livingstons in that he is the last one to own a piece of the original Livingston land. His 200 acres overlooking the Hudson in the southern half of Columbia County are part of the original 160,000 acres acquired by the First Lord of the Manor, Robert Livingston. "It's been a real struggle to keep it up. But we're determined to have it stay in the family. It means a great deal to all of us," explains Henry H. Livingston. *September, 1973*

LIVINGSTON, JOHN has never mingled much in public life. He was formerly a prominent and successful merchant in New York City, and was distinguished for the munificence with which he dispensed the hospitality of his princely residence in Broadway, now the site of the Broadway House. *October 11, 1851*

LIVINGSTON, JOHNSTON has been the President of the Knickerbocker Club for several years. It is a very exclusive organization, and it is the most difficult club into which to gain admission in New York. Johnston Livingston comes in a direct line from the Livingstons of Livingston Manor. It was his daughter who was chosen to dance in the *quadrille d'honneur* at the famous Columbian Centennial ball at the Metropolitan Opera House. She has since married the Marquis Laugier Villars. *October 22, 1904*

LIVINGSTON, LORNA, direct descendant of Chancellor Robert R. Livingston, whose Beekman Place coming-out party and Junior Assembly debut was prominently noted by *The New York Times* back in the 'fifties, is now the Managing Editor of *Manhattan East*, an upper East Side weekly newspaper, where she juggles features about politics and police, diplomats and decorators. *September, 1973*

LIVINGSTON, PETER W. By his death at Morristown, New Jersey, the direct male line of the Livingston family, famous in the annals of New York State, was ended. The only representatives of the manor Livingstons now left are among the male descendants of the late Moncreiffe Livingston, of Columbia County, New York. After them comes Henry Walter Livingston. The family is of Scotch origin, and since its settlement in this country two centuries ago has always been prominent in society, while it has furnished many noted men to public life. *June 23, 1886*

LLOYD, ELIZABETH KEY is a member of one of the most distinguished old family connections of Maryland including, on the paternal side, the Keys, Howards, and Leighs, while through

her mother she is a granddaughter of the late Mr. and Mrs. William Donnell of Baltimore. In addition to "Wye House," on the Wye River, the ancestral home of the Lloyds and one of the finest existing specimens of genuine Colonial architecture, the Lloyds have another handsome home in Baltimore familiarly known as the old Donnell house, which for several generations has been the scene of a continuous succession of brilliant entertainments. *October, 1917*

LODGE, SENATOR HENRY CABOT He was known familiarly as the "senior" Senator from Massachusetts in the United States Senate, where he served continuously for thirty one years, leaving a marked impression on the nation's history. He was, as well as a statesman, an historian of note, a publicist, a lawyer, a man of leisure and independent means. Mrs. Lodge, who died in 1915, was Anna Cabot Mills Davis, daughter of Admiral Charles Henry Davis, U.S.N. *December 1, 1924*

LODGE, HENRY S. has been prominent in supporting the arts and in managing the affairs of the Metropolitan Boston Transit Authority. He is also probably the most stylish dresser in the city. "No one has the taste of Harry Lodge," a friend told me. "And he wouldn't be caught dead in Gucci loafers." *April, 1976*

LODGE, MR. AND MRS. JOHN DAVIS (FRANCESCA BRAGGIOTTI) Scion of a family which has been prominent in state affairs since the Revolutionary War, Governor Lodge of Connecticut is a graduate of Harvard, an ex-lawyer, a sometime Hollywood and Broadway actor, a Second World War naval officer, and a former United States Congressman. Mrs. Lodge, whose family is as noted in the arts as her husband's is in politics, made her dancing debut in the Milan Opera House. *March, 1953*

LOEB, JOHN L., member of a New York "Our Crowd" family, ran Loeb Rhoades & Company before its 1979 merger with Shearson Hayden Stone; through another merger, he's honorary Chairman of Shearson American Express. Most notable gift: $8.5 million to Harvard, alma mater of son, John, Jr. *December, 1983*

LOEW, WILLIAM GOADBY With Mrs. Loew, he has hunted in England and Ireland and with any number of packs in this country; and just at present, he is more interested in hunting than ever, because Mrs. Loew is the Lady Master of the Harford Hounds just outside Baltimore. Every year, she and Mr. Loew take their big stable of hunters to that charming and sporting country and stay there all autumn and into the winter. *August 1, 1927*

LOEW, MRS. WILLIAM GOADBY (FLORENCE BAKER) was considered the best-dressed American in London this season, and has returned with a trunkful of wonderful Paris frocks. At a recent concert, she wore a magnificent Paquin creation in dull ash gray, hand embroidered, crepe mignon. She has a pretty fad of never wearing more than a single color at a time, so gloves, shoes, and hat were of the same dull grey. *August 30, 1902*

LONGWORTH, NICHOLAS was one of the leading men of Cincinnati for years—the wealthiest, we believe, and among the first introducers of the wine culture upon the banks of the Ohio

LIVINGSTON

At the dog show: sisters Mary and Eleanor Livingston, 1927.

The first tally of the socially select in the new United States was the "Dinner and Supper List for 1787 and 1788" drawn up by Mrs. John Jay, wife of the first American secretary of state. She was born Sarah Van Brugh Livingston, of the Hudson River landed aristocracy. A century later, Ward McAllister enshrined more Livingstons than any other family in his Four Hundred. In the 1990s, the *Social Register* cites thirty-five individual Livingstons, with as many more entries including "Livingston" as part of their name.

Public service as much as social credentials accounts for Livingston prominence through the years. Between 1716 and 1961, innumerable Livingstons and their in-laws held the offices of U. S. senator, governor, justice of the Supreme Court, cabinet member and ambassador. During the American Revolution, Livingstons supported the patriot cause body and soul: eight Livingstons fought in the battle of Saratoga in 1777; a Livingston foiled Benedict Arnold's plot. Philip Livingston signed the Declaration of Independence.

And, always, there was land. Robert, the first Livingston in America, was descended from the Lords of Callendar, a noble Scottish family. But as the eighth son and fourteenth child of a Presbyterian minister, he had his own way to make in the world and arrived in colonial New York in 1673. By a fortunate marriage to heiress Alida Van Rensselaer of the Dutch colonial aristocracy and a royal grant from King Charles II, he managed to secure a staggering 157,640 acres extending for miles along the Hudson River. His grandson, curiously named Robert Robert Livingston, added another 240,000 acres through his marriage to Margaret Beekman. On the Hudson between New York City and Albany, numerous Livingstons (the three Lords of the Manor before the American Revolution begat a total of thirty-two children) built houses on the original manorial grant, many of them surviving to this day. "Montgomery Place" and "Clermont," burned by the British but later rebuilt, are both now open to the public. A few estates still remain in the hands of Livingston descendants; one tract is Bard College.

While most of the Livingstons have been New Yorkers, Edward Livingston, great-grandson of the first Lord of the Manor, had the distinction of representing first New York, then Louisiana in the U.S. House of Representatives. He was mayor of New York City, a senator from Louisiana, U.S. secretary of state, and finally U.S. minister to France. Livingston descendants have made careers in politics up to the present: among them, former Congressman Hamilton Fish, Jr., of New York, former Governor Thomas Kean of New Jersey, and Congressman Robert Linlithgow Livingston, Jr., who today represents Louisiana as Edward Livingston did in 1823.

A Hudson River heritage: *left,*
at Clermont, their ancestral home, the family of Mr. and Mrs.
Henry H. Livingston in 1973; *right,* World War I Lieutenant Goodhue Livingston, Jr.

River. He foresaw, at an early period, the future importance of Cincinnati, removed there, and early invested his surplus means in real estate, which in time made him a millionaire. *February 21, 1863*

LONGWORTH, MRS. NICHOLAS (ALICE ROOSEVELT) The "Princess Alice," now the wife of Congressman Nicholas Longworth of Ohio, is about to emerge from the quietude which she has insisted upon since her marriage and is to campaign actively in the Middle West for Messrs. Harding and Coolidge. Recently she made her maiden political speech in Ohio and held the attention of her audience from start to finish. *October 10, 1920*

LOOMIS, MRS. HENRY P. (JULIA J. STIMSON) The Society of the Colonial Dames of America is to be congratulated upon its selection of a new President, Mrs. Henry P. Loomis of New York and Tuxedo. Mrs. Loomis is without question one of the few very strong women in New York, in position and influence. One of the records connected with the war was her raising of an approximate $2,000,000 for the education of the orphans of the French officers of the army and navy. *June 1, 1923*

LOOMIS, HORATIO was for many years professor of mineralogy in the University of Vermont and was well known as an analytical chemist. He is survived by his wife, who is the only daughter of the late Edward J. Phelps, Minister to England during Cleveland's first administration. *February 13, 1909*

LORD, MRS. FREDERICK R. (EDITH TIFFANY) is a daughter of Mr. and Mrs. Henry Dyer Tiffany, of "Foxhurst," the quaint old homestead on Westchester Avenue, New York. The Fox family belonged to the old Quaker aristocracy and intermarried with the Leggetts. Mrs. Lord is a representative of the tenth generation to live at Foxhurst, a grant to her ancestors in 1651. *September 16, 1905*

LORILLARD, LOUIS L. has taken possession, with his family, of the magnificent villa at Newport bequeathed to him by Miss Catherine Lorillard Wolfe. During his two years' absence in Europe, she instructed her agent, who was buying the treasures for the adornment of the house, to consult his tastes in all matters. Every day, he finds stored away in the commodious closets of the villa surprises in the shape of costly embroideries or bric-a-brac, of whose existence nobody seems to have been aware. *May 25, 1887*

LORILLARD, MR. AND MRS. LOUIS LIVINGSTON are the youngest members of one of Newport's oldest and most respected families. Louis, a slender, handsome, aristocratic-mannered man, is an heir to the tobacco fortune. His wife, the attractive Elaine, is the mother of two and a jazz enthusiast. Vitally interested in the cultural life of Newport, the Lorillards have made a labor of love out of the bringing of fine musicians to the beautiful island-resort community. At the beginning of 1954, Elaine decided that Newport could lead the way in immortalizing what is America's basic musical contribution to the world—jazz. *July, 1957*

LORILLARD, PETER It has been said that "There never was a poor Lorillard." Appearances seem to indicate that there never will be one. Wealth, like poverty, if not a disease, seems to be contagious. This immense estate is now some seventy years old; for as far away as 1810, P. & G. Lorillard were very rich and never gave a note. When George died, his estate was estimated at over $2,000,000. Tobacco did the work. *May 6, 1868*

LORILLARD, PIERRE A large force of men is employed upon the grounds of the new game preserve of the Tuxedo Park Association, organized by Mr. Lorillard. Mr. Lorillard's tract originally embraced about five thousand acres, but he secured for this park one thousand acres more from the Sterling Mountain Company. Near the station at Lorillard's, the grounds are being graded and several buildings are in the process of erection, one of which is to be an English inn for the accommodation of visitors. Mr. P. Lorillard will have a residence for himself on one side of the lake, and directly opposite a house will be built for his son, P. Lorillard, Jr. The park will be freely opened to visitors, though, of course, the sporting privileges of the place are restricted to members of the association. *December 23, 1885*

LORIMER, MRS. GEORGE HORACE (ALMA V. ENNIS) has inaugurated in Philadelphia a novelty in the way of amusement. Known as Six Actors Afternoons, society at large has been invited to subscribe to six large informal afternoon receptions in the foyer of the Academy of Music, when the guest, or guests of honor, are literary or dramatic celebrities. *November 20, 1921*

LORING, DANIEL, JR., who has been traveling for the past five months and has visited Cape Nome, Alaska, and some other out-of-the-way places, returned to New York. Mr. Loring's father, a multi-millionaire, owns mines in the Far West, and the young man has been investigating their value—investigating with a pick and shovel, working as a day laborer and the hours of a laborer. He comes back strong and muscular, in all the better health for his mining experience. *November 1, 1900*

LOTHROP, MARGARET MULFORD At "The Wayside," the former home of Nathaniel Hawthorne at Concord, Massachusetts, Mrs. Daniel Lothrop (whose pen name is "Margaret Sidney") introduced her debutante daughter, Miss Margaret Mulford Lothrop. This "bud" is of general interest far beyond the confines of society, for "Margaret Sidney" wrote all those books about the *Five Little Peppers*. Her father, Daniel Lothrop, founded, moreover, the publishing house of D. Lothrop & Co. *November 2, 1906*

LOUBAT, JOSEPH FLORIMOND has endowed Columbia University library with $1,000,000 in property. He is a New Yorker by birth. A scholar and a diplomat, he has received many orders and dignities at the hands of various sovereigns. He is known in Europe as the Duc de Loubat, the title having been conferred upon him by the Pope. *March 9, 1898*

LOUNSBERY, RICHARD P. belonged to one of the oldest Westchester families and died on an estate which has been in their possession for over 150 years. Mr. Lounsbery was born in 1841 and was a member of the brokerage firm of Lounsbery & Haggin. *October 28, 1911*

LOVETT, H. MALCOLM, JR. Over eighty years ago, his grandfather became the founding President of Rice University. A professor of astronomy and mathematics at 36, Lovett was a brilliant scholar with seven degrees from American and European universities. After graduation from Rice, son Malcolm Lovett earned his law degree at Harvard and became a partner in the firm of Baker & Botts. H. Malcolm Lovett, Jr. graduated from Rice and Harvard and headed the Bayou Club board. *September, 1991*

LOW, ABBOT AUGUSTUS lived at No. 3 Montague Terrace in the Low Homestead, overlooking New York Harbor, which was built in the early forties by his father, Mr. Abiel Abbot Low. Mr. Low was born in Brooklyn and entered the lumber business when a young man. His operations in that field were confined largely to tracts of wooded land in the Adirondacks. He was at one time President of the Brooklyn Association for Improving the Condition of the Poor. *October 5, 1912*

LOW, MARY ANGELINE The Lows are among the very pillars of Heights society in Brooklyn. To be even an "S.R.L."—some relation to the Lows—is considered a mark of social distinction. Miss Mary Angeline Low, whose engagement to the Rev. Roger S. Forbes was announced, is a granddaughter of the late Josiah O. Low, who left a fortune running up into the millions. Josiah O. Low was a son of the original Seth Low of Salem, Massachusetts, and came to Brooklyn with his father, and also his brother, the late Abiel Abbot Low, with whom he engaged in the China tea trade. *May 18, 1907*

LOW, SETH, the candidate for Mayor of New York, sometimes called Greater New York, is a well-born, wealthy descendant of an old Brooklyn family and the President of Columbia University. His grandfather, after whom he was named, was the first Mayor of Brooklyn. His father was Abiel Abbot Low, a famous merchant who advocated the consolidation of New York and Brooklyn when Seth was a little boy. *September 8, 1897*

LOWDEN, FRANCES, whose engagement to Mr. John B. Drake, Jr. is of the deepest interest to Chicagoans, is the youngest of the three daughters of ex-Governor and Mrs. Frank O. Lowden of Illinois, and granddaughter of George M. Pullman. The first John B. Drake, grandfather of Miss Lowden's fiancé, began the great hotel business which has been carried on successfully by his sons. *September 15, 1924*

LOWELL, ABBOTT LAWRENCE is the President of Harvard University. Outside of New England, President Lowell may be known for his relatives. To some, he is the brother of the late Percival Lowell, the astronomer. To others, he is the brother of Amy Lowell, the poet. He is a descendant of the Percival Lowell who came

LODGE

In 1902: Massachusetts Senator Henry Cabot Lodge.

In comparison with the colonial Adams, Cabot, or Saltonstall families of Boston, the Lodges were relative latecomers. Giles Lodge arrived in Massachusetts after the American Revolution, in 1791, and became a successful merchant. His son, John Ellerton Lodge, linked the Lodges to old Boston when he wed Anna Cabot, granddaughter of the U.S. senator. The Cabots were also rich merchants who owned cotton mills and shipping lines. Later marriages allied the Lodges with other political families. When George Cabot Lodge, great-great-great-grandson of Giles, ran for the Senate from Massachusetts in 1962, he counted eight forebears who were past members of Congress.

Republican Senator Henry Cabot Lodge, son of John Ellerton Lodge, represented his state in Congress for a total of thirty-seven years (1887–1924). A dyed-in-the-wool conservative (H. L. Mencken said, "He was as cool as an undertaker at a hanging"), he could be surprisingly liberal on some issues. A bitter foe of Woodrow Wilson, he led the successful fight against America's entrance into the League of Nations, and he opposed women's suffrage. Yet he was an author of the

Sherman Antitrust Act and the pure food and drug laws. His wife, Anna Cabot Mills Davis (called "Nannie"), daughter and sister of admirals, was noted for her beauty and enthusiastic hospitality. She called the formidable Senator Lodge "Pinky."

Henry Cabot Lodge's sons did not enter politics, but his daughter Constance married Augustus ("Gussie") Peabody Gardner, a congressman. Grandsons Henry Cabot Lodge, Jr., and John Davis Lodge both enjoyed active careers in politics. Henry, who married the Boston Brahmin Emily Sears, became a senator from Massachusetts and ambasssador to South Vietnam and to the United Nations. In 1960, he ran for vice president on the Republican ticket headed by Richard Nixon.

His brother, John Davis Lodge, reached politics by a more circuitous route. He began as a movie actor, spending three years in Hollywood and then at British film studios, where he appeared in B-grade movies such as *Bulldog Drummond at Bay*. Following World War II, John Davis Lodge was elected a member of the House of Representatives from Connecticut. After serving as Connecticut's governor, he was named U.S. ambassador to Spain.

to Massachusetts in 1637, and of the John Lowell who enlivened the Revolution with his letters of "A Boston Rebel." James Russell Lowell, the poet and an earlier professor of Harvard, was his grandfather's cousin. This grandfather founded the Lowell Institute. His mother was Miss Katherine Bigelow Lawrence, probably the most learned lady of her generation in Boston society, speaking five languages, singing, and playing three instruments. *November 20, 1917*

LOWELL, AMY The magic of Miss Amy Lowell's name always sends a thrill through the intermingled circles of Boston's society and literati. The occasion of a farewell dinner to the distinguished authoress was signal for an outpouring, both smart and important, at the Hotel Somerset, where the state ballroom was gorgeously beflowered in her honor. Miss Lowell, with a fat, two volume, red-bound *Keats* as her latest contribution to literature, was to have sailed away soon after for British centers of learning and culture, and also a number of lectures. *May 1, 1925*

LOWELL, MRS. CHARLES RUSSELL (JOSEPHINE SHAW), whose name is prominently before the public just now because she accepted the leadership of the anti-Tammany league of women, has been long and favorably known for her good deeds. Through her efforts, police matrons were appointed in New York, working girls' clubs formed, and the Consumers' League inaugurated. One good work of the latter has been better provision, including seats behind the counter for shop girls. *November 7, 1894*

LOWELL, GUY designed the new Piping Rock clubhouse at Locust Valley, which is one of the finest buildings of its kind in the country, and he is also the architect of the new Boston Museum of Fine Arts. His father, the late Edward J. Lowell of Boston, was a first cousin of James Russell Lowell, and a cousin of A. Lawrence Lowell, President of Harvard, where Mr. Lowell was graduated in 1892. *April 26, 1913*

LOWELL, RALPH Away back in 1837, John Lowell, Jr., decided he wanted to give half his money to establish free public lectures for the people of Boston. It amounted to $250,000 at his death; it's worth $4,000,000 now. Every trustee must forever be a male descendant of Lowell, and Ralph Lowell is only the fourth generation from merchant John to carry on the trusteeship. The trustee, with the President of the Boston Athenaeum, posts a letter with the name of the next trustee, and when he dies, a representative goes to the Athenaeum and asks: "Have you got a letter for the Lowell Institute?" The Athenaeum has yet to answer "No." *March, 1968*

LUNGER, MRS. HARRY W. (MARY JANE DU PONT) is the younger daughter of du Pont heir Philip Francis du Pont (1878–1928), but his favorite: He left her all but $2 million of his $58 million fortune. She owns Christiana Stables in Delaware; husband Harry W. Lunger is a stockbroker; son Brett was an occasional Grand Prix racer. *September, 1988*

LYMAN, MR. AND MRS. RONALD THEODORE (ELIZABETH VAN CORTLANDT PARKER) She is a granddaughter of Mr. Cortlandt Parker, the lawyer who has had a conspicuous part in the history of New Jersey. His father, James Parker, who was graduated from Columbia in 1791, gave to Rutgers College the land on which its buildings now stand. Mr. Lyman belongs to a family in which there have been several Theodores of much distinction. In 1835, Theodore Lyman, the philanthropist, rescued William Lloyd Garrison from a mob at risk to his own life. *October 29, 1904*

LYNE, CARRIE MONCURE, who, as the descendant of Anne Ball, sister of Mary Washington, and great-great-great-granddaughter of Colonel William Byrd, founder of Richmond, leaves New York this week for her home, "Frascati," one of the most famous and elegant colonial houses in the Richmond section of Virginia, the birthplace also of Princess Troubetzkoy (Amelie Rives) and Mrs. Charles Dana Gibson. *May 25, 1898*

M

MABON, MR. AND MRS. JAMES B., JR. (MARY FROST) She is known as the original hat designer at Hawes, Inc., who studied stage design in Vienna. The wife of James B. Mabon, Jr., a piano-playing broker, is as cosmopolitan as she is versatile. Her family, including uncle Frederick Sterling, Minister to the Irish Free State, comes originally from St. Louis. But the three daughters flowered on a California cattle ranch and in a Florentine villa. *February 1, 1933*

MACARTHUR, GENERAL AND MRS. DOUGLAS (JEAN FAIRCLOTH) Apartment 37A in New York City's Waldorf Towers, now occupied by General and Mrs. Douglas MacArthur, has the unique distinction of being the official quarters for the first meeting of the Big Four, and here the first postwar treaties were signed. A plaque in the apartment's entrance hall commemorates this historical event. In the entrance hall, a framed fingernail tapestry—a copy of a ninth-century painting in the Shosoin—and a Japanese screen are two of Mrs. MacArthur's finest treasures. *October, 1951*

MACARTHUR, WILLIAM T., a small farmer and wandering evangelist in Pennsylvania's coal region, produced four remarkable sons who wound up in Chicago. The wealthiest,

John D. (1898–1978), became a billionaire by pioneering the concept of direct-mail health insurance sales. The $3 billion MacArthur Foundation, created from his estate, is the largest in Chicago. His older brother Alfred (1885–1967) also became a centomillionaire as President of Central Standard Life Insurance Co. of Illinois. Brother Telfer (1891–1960) founded the Pioneer Press chain of Chicago suburban newspapers. And perhaps the best-known MacArthur brother, journalist Charles (1895–1956), wrote *The Front Page* and married actress Helen Hayes. *September, 1990*

MACDONALD, MRS. BYRNES (ALLETA MORRIS) has summered at Newport since the age of one, growing up at "Malbone," the historic house of her father, Lewis Gouverneur Morris. After her marriage to Princetonian Byrnes MacDonald, they embarked on a wedding trip around the world. Mr. MacDonald became secretary to the fiery Mayor La Guardia in the stormy 1934–1941 period. He was also one of the founders of the Police Athletic League. Mrs. MacDonald is noted as an expert duck and pheasant shot and can slug through rugged terrain for hours as doggedly as most men. At one time, she raised Irish wolfhounds. *September, 1958*

MACDONALD, CHARLES BLAIR, who, with his family, formerly lived in Chicago, is one of the most famous of the amateur golf players in this country. He was the winner in the first United States Golf Association championship held at Newport in 1895. He also won international golf honors in Canada, and was in the public eye as the projector of the plan in regard to "The Ideal Golf-Course." *August 1, 1908*

MACKAY, CLARENCE H. The effort exerted by him in entertaining the Prince of Wales at a dinner and dance at "Harbor Hill," Roslyn, Long Island, resulted in what will undoubtedly go down in social history as one of the most remarkable affairs ever tendered to royalty in America. The genius of electrical experts turned the estate of hundreds of acres into fairyland. The approach was hung with Meadow Brook blue lanterns, and bay trees and orange trees were lit with little clusters of electric lights. Flood lights stationed at different points, one on Bar Beach, another thrown on part of Glen Cove, another on the harbor, lit up the vessels. *October 1, 1924*

MACKAY, MRS. CLARENCE H. (KATHERINE A. DUER) was the sensation of the evening at the James Hazen Hyde ball. Mrs. Mackay, clever, poetic, and quick to be in sympathy with Mr. Hyde's idea, was magnificently arrayed. At first glance, people whispered, "Surely the Queen of Sheba!" but, instead, she was Adrienne Lecouvreur, as she appeared in *Phedre.* Her beautiful black hair in thick masses at the temple and her great dark eyes make her look medieval even sometimes at the opera, and with her robe studded with turquoises, a crown on her head thrown back, with pages to carry her train, she had just the imperious carriage for the part. *February 4, 1905*

MACKAY, DONALD was a former President of the New York Stock Exchange and a resident for many years of Englewood, New Jersey, of which city he had been Mayor three times. He was a member of the Wall Street firm of Mackay & Co. and the President of the Englewood Bank. At Englewood, he gave a hospital, a library, and a park. *March 9, 1912*

MACKAY, EVA The marriage of Eva Mackay, step-daughter of John W. Mackay, of California, to Don Ferdinand Julien Colonna, Prince of Galatro, is wholly dissociated from selfish motives. Miss Mackay's prospective millions had nought to do with it. It was a genuine love affair—love at first sight. His uncle, the old Prince of Galatro, wrote a letter to Mrs. Mackay in Paris, asking the hand of her daughter for his nephew. Mrs. Mackay replied that she had forwarded the substance of the letter for her husband's consideration and took pains to add that "She, her husband, and her daughter were all true Americans, who loved their country, its institutions, and, especially, its matrimonial customs, and that therefore it would be quite out of the question to think of arranging a 'dot' or any other sort of wedding portion in advance." *February 18, 1885*

MACKAY, MRS. JOHN W. (MARIE LOUISE HUNGERFORD)—BRYANT, wife of the "bonanza king" of California, now possesses the magnificent robe manufactured for the Empress Eugénie and presented by the municipality of Paris to her Majesty! The robe is of lace, entirely covered with flowers *en point a l'aiguille.* It took fourteen years to complete by the five first hands of the *fabrique* at Chantilly, and one hundred thousand francs ($20,000) was paid for it by the city. Mrs. Mackay is now having her portrait painted by Bonnat, with the imperial robe hanging from her shoulders and brought in light transparent folds over her bosom. *February 1, 1882*

MACMILLAN, EMERSON is one of the most interesting figures in the modern financial world. The architect of his own fortunes, he has also given his time to esthetic pleasures. Mr. MacMillan, who as a businessman is first of all a banker, was the founder of the American Light and Traction Company. He has a camp on the Rangeley Lakes, Maine, but it had long been his intention to own an estate and now he has an ideal home at Darlington, New York. *July 23, 1910*

MACVEAGH, LINCOLN is the son of a former Ambassador to Japan. Though not himself a career man, Lincoln MacVeagh succeeds two State Department Ministers to Greece with a more than brilliant preparation. A scholar, and one-time proprietor of The Dial Press, he is the grandson of two celebrated attorneys, Wayne MacVeagh, who was Garfield's Attorney General, and Sherman S. Rogers, of Buffalo. Among Lincoln MacVeagh's literary connections one might list his uncle, Robert Cameron Rogers, who wrote *The Rosary,* and first cousin Cameron Rogers, biographer of Walt Whitman. Ellery Sedgwick, Editor of *The Atlantic,* and the novelist John Marquand are both in-laws. *January 15, 1935*

MACY, V. EVERIT The first Josiah Macy who came to this country arrived on his good ship, the *Prudence,* bringing the first news of the declaration of war between the United States and Great Britain. With his son, William H. Macy, he established his business in New York in 1828. This son was a distinguished New Yorker; he became President of the Seaman's Bank for Savings in 1848. Mr. V. Everit Macy, one of the most interesting members of the present generation of the family, has given much of his time to civic betterment. *April 4, 1914*

MAGRUDER, JULIA was the daughter of the late Allan Bowie Magruder, of Charlottesville, and a niece of John Bankhead Magruder of the United States and Confederate Armies. In her *Realized Ideal,* the story assumes the three-fold division of man into body, soul, and spirit, the two former making the mortal personality and the latter the immortal individuality. *June 15, 1907*

MAHONY, WALTER BUTLER has one of those much-prized New England pedigrees that go back to some sturdy Puritan who arrived on the *Mayflower.* He is a grandson of Carey Allen of the Vermont family which Ethan Allen made famous; a lineal descendant of William White, one of the *Mayflower* voyagers, and a great-grandson of Justin Morgan, owner of the famous horse that bore his name. *February 27, 1909*

MALLORY, HENRY ROGERS was the former President of the Mallory Steamship Company. Mr. Mallory's father was Charles H. Mallory, and he was the grandson of the founder of the Mallory lines. In 1908, with four others, he formed the holding company known as the Atlantic Gulf and West Indies Steamship Company. *March 20, 1919*

MANCHESTER, DUKE AND DUCHESS OF (HELENA ZIMMERMAN) "Kylemore Castle" is the Connaught home of the Duke and Duchess of Manchester, a present from the latter's father, Mr. Zimmerman, of Cincinnati. He paid something over 60,000 pounds for it. Kylemore Castle is the private property of the Duchess, for it was settled upon her by her father. She has proved herself a first-class farmer; her prize breeds of cows bring high prices, and the animals are being sold all over the kingdom. *August 31, 1907*

MANICE, MRS. WILLIAM (SARAH REMSEN) is a daughter of the late William Remsen, of the old Dutch family which has intermarried with the de Peysters and Livingstons. Mr. William Manice is a son of the late William de Forest Manice, the owner of the old homestead, now the Turf Club. *May 13, 1905*

MANIGAULT, PETER The family name was synonymous with the most genteel wealth. Their graceful town house, a monument to Charleston's gilded rice age, still stands on Meeting Street. The current Peter Manigault is maintaining his family's preeminence, not by the traditional power of the purse but by power of the press. He followed his father into the newspaper business, becoming president of the company that publishes the *Charleston Evening Post* and the morning *News and Courier.* His typically Charlestonian pride in the past has rendered Manigault an indefatigable worker for the National Trust for Historic Preservation. *November, 1977*

MANVILLE, THOMAS, JR. No one has matched that well-known "leading man" Thomas Manville, Jr. for cast changes. At least seven of Tommy's ten wives were courted in El Morocco, and there have been times when as many as three of them, in the role of ex-wives, have found themselves seated close enough to be able to watch Manville's attentions to their latest successor. *January, 1960*

MARIÉ, PETER Easter Monday, 1875, was the date of one of the smartest functions of the season in New York society, a calico and chintz costume ball at Delmonico's. Peter Marié, a prominent bachelor noted for his art collection, hospitality, and light verse, had photographs made of a number of the charming ladies present, from which miniatures were made, after which the subjects were invited to a private view of the collection. *March 1, 1921*

MARLBOROUGH, DUCHESS OF (CONSUELO VANDERBILT), bent upon knowledge and experience that will help her in her sociological work, spent much time in New York with Mrs. Clarence Mackay, who believes that wealth and leisure bring with it great responsibility. But though the Duchess, like Mrs. Mackay, has no time or taste for a vigorous pursuit of society as popularly understood—just the aim to have pleasure and prestige—she did much to illuminate New York socially during Lent. The most noteworthy entertainment in New York was the dinner that her mother, Mrs. O.H.P. Belmont, gave for her at the Plaza Hotel. Following the dinner there was a lecture on "The Modern Issue"; and those people who deny the existence of a serious-minded social world should have seen how tractably, even cheerfully, all the well known bachelors submitted to this mental nourishment. *April 4, 1908*

MARLBOROUGH, DUCHESS OF (LILY WARREN PRICE)—HAMERSLEY Her marriage to Lord William Beresford took place in St. George's Church, Hanover Square. She was originally Miss Lily Warren Price, daughter of Commodore Price of the United States Navy. In 1881, she married Mr. Louis C. Hamersley, who was possessed of enormous wealth. All his money, amounting to about $7,000,000, was left to his widow for life. On her death, it was to go to such local charities as she might designate unless Mr. J. Hooker Hamersley should have a male child. In the spring of 1891, Mrs. Hooker Hamersley presented her husband with a son, and this child is consequently heir to the whole seven millions. After four years of mourning for her husband, Mrs. Hamersley became, in 1888, the wife of the eighth Duke of Marlborough. *May 8, 1895*

MARQUAND, HENRY G. has a life history with which the majority of Americans are familiar. In his management of his brother Mr. Frederick Marquand's real estate, he became interested in the architecture of New York; and as a result of his efforts to improve "The

Chocolate City," he was made the first honorary member of the American Institute of Architects. His art collection given to the Metropolitan Museum of Art, the chapel given to Princeton University, the gymnasium that he gave to the same college, and the pavilion to Bellevue Hospital to which his brother also contributed are some of the gifts with which the name of Marquand is associated. *January 9, 1909*

MARQUAND, MR. AND MRS. JOHN PHILLIPS (ADELAIDE FERRY HOOKER) Ever since Harvard ('15) and an active war career begun on the Mexican border, Mr. Marquand has devoted himself exclusively to work. In his family strain are Anne Hutchinson, whose dissenting beliefs caused her to leave the Massachusetts Bay Colony for New Rochelle, and an aunt who is a successful novelist, Margaret Fuller. Matching these, his fiancée Adelaide Ferry Hooker offers Thomas Hooker, founder of the Connecticut colony, and the Irish veteran Ernie O'Malley, a sudden best-seller, who married her sister Helen, the sculptor. Another Hooker sister, in marrying John D. Rockefeller, 3rd, united two of the driest families east of Topeka. *April, 1937*

MARSHALL, CHARLES HENRY was a son of Charles H. Marshall, the great shipping merchant who died in New York City in 1865, who became proprietor and master in the Old Line of packets between New York and Liverpool. Charles H. Marshall, first, was the third President of the Union League Club. Charles H. Marshall, 2d., who was born in 1838, became manager of the Black Ball line of packets from 1865 to 1881. On account of his interest in civic affairs, he was appointed Commissioner to the World's Fair in 1876. In 1888, he married Josephine Banks, niece of James Lenox, the philanthropist. *July 13, 1912*

MARTIN, MR. AND MRS. BRADLEY (CORNELIA SHERMAN) have given evidence of their intention to make their permanent home in England. Bradley Martin, who is related to the Van Rensselaers, Lansings, and Townsends, came to this city from Albany. Mrs. Martin was a daughter of Isaac H. Sherman, who bought and exported barrel staves. When he died, he left a fortune of about $10,000,000. Mrs. Martin has always been a lavish entertainer, but all her former entertainments were eclipsed on February 10, 1897, when she gave the famous Louis XV costume ball at the Waldorf, which cost $30,000 of itself, $150,000 on the part of the guests for the costumes and so forth. *May 4, 1898*

MARTIN, ESMOND BRADLEY, SR. A grandson of steel magnate Henry Phipps and an ace at chess, he is also a connoisseur of stamps, minerals, fine eighteenth-century English antiques, and gold pocket watches made by Abraham Louis Breguet, the famous Parisian watchmaker active between 1795 and 1820. He's knowledgeable as well about the great salmon streams of the world, many of which he has fished. Over the past several years, he has devoted himself to lawsuits (thus far unsuccessful) against the Bessemer Trust Company, which controls his multimillion-dollar trust fund. *June, 1985*

MARTIN, FREDERICK TOWNSEND The arrival of Mr. Frederick Townsend Martin in Palm Beach means an added impetus to the devotion to bridge whist. Mr. Martin proved himself during his stay here last season to be not only a skillful but an indefatigable player of "bridge," and this year he is not belying his reputation. Bridge whist has great vogue at Palm Beach. Every afternoon in the hotel rotundas and on the verandas are little gatherings of devotees of the game, and there are frequent "bridge" parties at the various cottages. *March 7, 1903*

MARTIN, JUDGE AND MRS. J. WILLIS will give a ball on New Year's Eve, at the Bellevue-Stratford in Philadelphia, in compliment to the First Troop Philadelphia City Cavalry, the oldest military organization in the United States. Judge Martin served for fifteen years on the active roll of the troop. The First Troop was organized November 17, 1774, by a number of young gentlemen of birth and fortune who were mounted, armed, and equipped at their own expense. The date chosen is appropriate, for the battle of Trenton was fought just before the close of 1776 and that of Princeton at the very beginning of the new year 1777, and the troop had a part in each battle. *December 28, 1907*

MARTIN, MRS. JAMES E. was the hostess at the "exotic" birthday-feast given at "Martin Hall," Great Neck, last week, the first Lucullan feast New Yorkers have read of this fall. The table was laid beneath a bower of trailing wisteria, and had as its center an ideal lily-pond, many of the lilies furnishing an excuse for lighted tapers that cast an opalescent glow on the tiny goldfish swimming in the waters. Each woman present represented a flower, and all had powdered hair and wore patches. *November 10, 1906*

MARTIN, MR. AND MRS. PETER D. (LILY OELRICHS) Their new French motor car is one of the most gorgeous in Newport, and is one of the few of its kind in America. They do all their traveling and shopping by means of the automobile. Its body is of white, with enclosed carriage top with linings of red, which can be removed and the machine used for speeding. Automobiling will be more popular than ever among the cottagers next summer, as the sales of different styles of horseless vehicles have been numerous. *April 25, 1903*

MASON, MRS. FREDERICK THURSTON It is almost time that the invitations to subscribe to her Monday Night Dancing Class were out in Philadelphia. Mrs. Mason never indicates who are the sheep and who are the goats until the very, very last moment. It seems almost like the refinement of cruelty to keep so many on the anxious bench, although it is done out of a spirit of pure, though mistaken, kindness. There are so many climbers nowadays and some are such "awfully nice," likable people, too. It will cast a shadow over many a Christmas, will that list, because the first class meets positively on December eighteenth. *December 2, 1905*

MASON, GERTRUDE FRANCHOT belongs to one of the most important family connections in this country. She is a direct descendant of George Mason of "Gunston Hall," signer and framer of the first American Bill of Rights, and also of John Stevens Mason, former Minister to France. A younger John Stevens Mason, her great-uncle, was first Governor of Michigan and United States Senator from the same state. *January 20, 1916*

MASTERSON, MR. AND MRS. HARRIS III (ISLA C. STERLING)—COWAN—WINSTON Though the Masterson family came to Texas from Tennessee in the 1820s, James Roane Masterson and his brother Archibald first came to Houston in the 1860s. Both were lawyers. They and all their brothers became judges. Today, the clan has branched out into journalism, the Episcopal priesthood, real estate development, and the theatre. The most prominent, Harris Masterson III and his wife, a daughter of a founder of the Humble Oil Company, are leading philanthropists. *September, 1991*

MATHER, CHARLES E. For a long period, he assumed with success the mastership of the Radnor Hounds, one of the oldest packs in America. A few years ago, Mr. Mather gave up the Radnor and, with his private pack of English-bred hounds, moved to that lovely and historic country around West Chester bordering on the Brandywine. The Brandywine is a private pack, the personal property of the Master. They have no fixed days of meeting but go out when the Master is so inclined. All the horses seen in the field come from the Master's stable, and as at times he has to mount some fifteen to twenty people, it can readily be seen that a big stud has to be kept up. *October 24, 1914*

MATHER, CHARLES E. IV enjoys life in a Philadelphia Gothic villa. The young banker is interested in travel and art, particularly the works of American Luminists, and loves the William Merritt Chase portrait of his great-great-grandfather in the hall. His late grandfather, who was President of the National Museum of Racing in Saratoga, inherited "Avonwood Farm," one of America's oldest thoroughbred stables, from his grandfather, the first Charles Mather. *November, 1984*

MATTHEWS, GEORGE G. is President and trustee of the Henry Morrison Flagler Museum, housed in "Whitehall," the Palm Beach landmark built by his great-grandfather Henry Morrison Flagler, the visionary "founder of Palm Beach." George Matthews was on the Palm Beach town council for sixteen years, including seven terms as President. *March, 1988*

MAXWELL, ELSA The amazing thing about Elsa is that she has run a large section of cosmopolitan society for a great many years and that she has made a lot of friends but no money doing it. Arriving on the scene from nowhere in particular and being endowed with neither money nor great physical advantages, she has nevertheless had a marvelously good time ever since the war and has given all sorts of people a good time, too. She has a great vitality, a considerable musical gift, and a wild desire to give the best parties in Europe or America. Not being rich enough to provide the parties, she has not hesitated to elect willing millionaires to the office of party giver. *November 15, 1932*

MAXWELL, MR. AND MRS. LAWRENCE, JR., who entertained a great deal for Sir Edward Elgar and Lady Elgar when they were in Cincinnati, gave a musicale at "Maxwellton," the splendid Gothic room where one of the finest organs in this country is installed. The mirrored walls, the cathedral windows representing the depths of the forest: These are details of the wonderful room that Cincinnati considers one of its seven wonders. Mr. Maxwell, though a former United States Solicitor General, is never so busy that he neglects his music. *January 12, 1907*

MAY, MRS. CORDELIA (SCAIFE) A Mellon heiress with liberal leanings, she's estranged from her right-wing brother Richard Mellon Scaife. Her Laurel Foundation, set up in 1951, concentrates on environmental and population causes, especially in western Pennsylvania. *December, 1983*

MAYHOFF, MRS. CARL VON, is one of the board of lady managers of the Louisiana Purchase Exposition and represents the State of Virginia. She is a daughter of the late Captain J. P. Levy, who was a descendant from the distinguished Knickerbocker family who settled in New York about 1665. Hon. Jefferson M. Levy, her brother, is the well-known owner of "Monticello," and she acts as his hostess both at the famous Jefferson home and at their home in New York. *May 2, 1903*

MAYHOFF, MUNROE Some of the most gallant of the soldierly Knickerbocker Grays came together for a jolly little theater party. They were the guests of Master Munroe Mayhoff, who though just eight years old on Saturday of last week, waited to celebrate his birthday on the holiday established in tribute to Lincoln. The little Knickerbockers were taken to see the matinee performance of *Buster Brown,* and Buster never had more sympathetic spectators. *February 18, 1905*

McALLISTER, WARD The Patriarchs' Ball at Delmonico's in New York was the first of the twenty-second season of the organization. Mr. McAllister, who founded the organization, says: "There was a necessity for the Patriarchs in 1870, and that necessity seemed to be dying out. Recently, however, a new one has arisen. London society may be too large for public balls, and there the necessity does not exist. Every one has a fixed position, but in New York they have not. The present is an era of multi-millionaires, who aim at keeping out as many of their own kind as possible from the inner circle which they have formed." *December 12, 1894*

McCLELLAN, GEORGE B. represents society in New York in a high degree. His wife was Miss Heckscher, the sister of Mrs. Egerton L. Winthrop, Jr., and the daughter of Mr. John Heckscher, and the first cousin of Mr. Philip Lydig, Mrs. Lorillard Spencer, Miss Wilmerding, and Mrs. Casimir de Rham, and the niece of Mrs. Stephen Van Rensselaer. The McClellans have always held a very excellent position in New York, and the late General and Mrs. McClellan entertained delightfully in the old Alsop mansion on Washington Square. *September 26, 1903*

IT'S A BIRD, IT'S A PLANE, IT'S A McCORMICK

Aero teas and aeroyachting made a leap into Chicago society with the debut of Harold Fowler McCormick's airboat, Edith. For the first time, friends of Mr. McCormick were taken up in the Edith, previous to an aero tea on the lakefront of his Lake Forest villa. Mr. McCormick found the airyacht so successful that he has decided to discard his swift motorboat in his trips between Lake Forest and Chicago and rely on the Edith. The thirty miles between his Lake Forest home and Grant Park took him twenty-eight minutes. He has planned to keep a lookout on top of the Harvester building to signal the approach of the Edith. The signal will send a chauffeur with an automobile to the landing place, so that Mr. McCormick can be rushed through Grant Park to his office on Michigan Avenue. *August 16, 1913*

McCONIHE, MRS. D. MORAN (MARGUERITE C. HAGNER) Peter Hagner, "Margot" McConihe's first forebear to settle in Washington, arrived in Georgetown in 1778. He had been sent from Philadelphia by the federal government to help move the capital to the banks of the Potomac. Another descendant, Isabel Hagner, was the first White House social secretary; she worked for Mrs. William Howard Taft. The McConihes live on "Piney Spring Farm," in Potomac, Maryland, where Margot owned and operated a country newspaper, *Potomac Almanac,* for fifteen years. Her husband, F. Moran McConihe, was in the Eisenhower administration, at GSA, and later founded the Potomac National Bank. He owned the Potomac Hunt, and, according to Margot, he is "on the board or head of eighty per cent of the things in Washington." *September, 1975*

McCORMICK, BROOKS, JR. A son of the International Harvester family, he is an avid art enthusiast whose collection includes works by Picasso, Matisse, Calder, Buffet, Giacometti, etc. He writes short stories and is on the board of trustees of *Poetry* magazine. *June, 1968*

McCORMICK, MR. AND MRS. CYRUS III (DOROTHY LINN) Chicago's most important society event preceding the coming of Lent was their marriage. The ceremony took place in the new Fourth Presbyterian Church, known in Chicago as the "McCormick Church." During the seating of the guests, the choir chanted a chorus composed by Mr. Cyrus McCormick, the bridegroom's father, who long has been one of Chicago's music patrons. The noted McCormick marriage pillow was used. This pillow, upon which all of the McCormick bridal couples for many years past have knelt, is of gold satin with the monogram of each of the couples embroidered upon it. *March 10, 1915*

McCORMICK, HAROLD FOWLER, JR., of Chicago, left for Africa, where he will be a member of an expedition headed by Dr. Carl G. Jung, the Swiss psychologist. Mr. McCormick accom-

---

panied Dr. Jung on a trip through the southern sections of the United States last winter, just prior to going into the International Harvester Company plant at Milwaukee, where he worked for some time as a day laborer, in order to learn the business of his paternal forefathers. The young explorer is intensely interested in research work connected with psychology, which he began with Dr. Jung last winter. *September 1, 1925*

McCORMICK, J. MEDILL, since his election as junior Senator from Illinois, may be considered to have succeeded in the process of emerging from the shadow of the grandfather's and his father's name. Grandson of William Sanderson McCormick, a member of the great reaper firm, and son of Robert Sanderson McCormick, formerly American Ambassador to France, he inherited great wealth and greater business interests in his home town, Chicago. *January 20, 1921*

McCORMICK, MURIEL, eldest child of Mrs. Rockefeller McCormick, was married to Mr. Elisha Dyer Hubbard of Middletown, Connecticut. He was a wealthy bachelor prior to his marriage to John D. Rockefeller's granddaughter, living the life of a gentleman farmer on his country estate, "Lone Tree Farm." The former Miss McCormick has always been interested in music and the stage and was associated with the Palm Beach Play House both as director and a member of the company. *October 15, 1931*

McCORMICK, ROBERT S. was the son of William S. McCormick and a nephew of Cyrus H. McCormick. He married Miss Katherine Medill, a daughter of the late Joseph Medill. In 1889, Mr. McCormick was appointed First Secretary of the United States Legation in London, thus beginning what was to be a long and useful career in the diplomatic service. The year 1901 saw him named as Minister to Austria. In 1903, he was transferred to Russia. He became Ambassador to France in 1905. *May 10, 1919*

McCUTCHEON, MRS. JOHN BARR (CLARA GLICK) The McCutcheon family is very well known, not only in Chicago but far and wide, for the three sons of Mrs. John Barr McCutcheon have won fame by their clever pens. The eldest, Mr. George Barr McCutcheon, is the author of those popular novels *Graustark* and *Brewster's Millions.* The second brother, Mr. John T. McCutcheon, applied his pen differently and has won a worldwide reputation for his cartoons. A third and younger brother, Mr. Ben F. McCutcheon, has written several books of value and has won considerable fame by his little half-column sketches illustrating weather conditions or market quotations. Altogether, the family is one which stands out prominently in the ranks of society. *September 21, 1907*

McDONALD, JAMES was a brother of the late Alexander McDonald of Cincinnati, and the great-uncle of the Princess Murat and the Princess Rospigliosi. He was one of the organizers of the Standard Oil Company and its representative abroad. He had a home in Cadogan Square, and his wife has been one of the most popular American hostesses in London. *February 1, 1915*

McCORMICK

Mr. and Mrs. William W. McCormick and daughter, in 1919.

Cyrus Hall McCormick was the second generation of his family to try to make a machine to reap the wheat fields of America. His father, blacksmith and part-time inventor Robert McCormick, experimented for twenty years, to little avail. In 1834, Cyrus finally succeeded in patenting a reaper that revolutionized farming—first in Midwest America, then throughout the world. It made him immensely rich. When his son, Cyrus, Jr., merged the McCormick firm in 1902 with William Deering's, it became the giant International Harvester.

The McCormick brothers, Cyrus and William S., descended from Thomas McCormick, a weaver who emigrated from Northern Ireland to Pennsylvania in 1734. William's great-grandson Brooks McCormick, who retired in 1980, was the last McCormick to head International Harvester.

Both brothers' children became prominent in Chicago's social world. Harold Fowler McCormick, son of Cyrus, married Edith, a daughter of John D. Rockefeller. For thirty years, she was one of the most eccentric members of Chicago Society. Famous for her $2 million pearl necklace and gold dinner service originally made for Napoleon's sister, she was convinced that she was the reincarnation of Tutankhamen's child bride. Chilly in demeanor (only two of her many servants were permitted to speak to her), Edith was a great supporter of the Chicago Opera and Lincoln Park Zoo. After her death in 1932, one of the Chicago newspapers elected another member of the family, Mrs. Chauncey McCormick (born Deering), "queen of Chicago society."

William S.'s son, Robert Sanderson McCormick, ambassador to Austria-Hungary and to Russia, married Katherine Medill, daughter of the editor of the *Chicago Tribune* and founder of the great Medill-Patterson newspaper dynasty. Their son, Medill McCormick, sometime senator from Illinois, wed Ruth Hanna, later a U.S. congresswoman. Son Robert R. McCormick, editor and publisher of the *Tribune,* was famous for his isolationism, hatred of unions, and virulent Anglo-phobia (despite his own upper-class English accent acquired at school in England). A noted polo player in the 1920s at the Onwentsia Club at Lake Forest, where many McCormicks had houses, and at Aiken, South Carolina, and Miami Beach, he flew between polo grounds in his own plane at a time when private planes were rare.

McCormicks and their philanthropic foundations today continue in their support of Chicago institutions, among them Northwestern University, the Illinois Institute of Technology, and the Art Institute of Chicago.

McCormicks, reaping the benefits: *clockwise from top left,* Colonel Robert R. McCormick, 1930; in 1913, Mrs. Harold Fowler McCormick and children Fowler, Muriel, and Mathilde; Senator Medill McCormick, his farm superintendent, and prize bull in 1923.

McDonnell, Mrs. James F. (Anna Murray) She is the matriarch of the McDonnell clan who led the "Irish invasion" of Southampton during the twenties. Her husband's brokerage firm went bankrupt in '69—after he fulfilled a promise to make $1 million for each of their thirteen children. She goes to Mass every morning, often twice on Sunday. Conservative, straitlaced. *July, 1975*

McIlhenny, Edward has donated a large island tract in Vermilion Bay, Louisiana, as for the purpose of a refuge for game birds which flock to this locality in the winter. The income of the McIlhenny family was enhanced by the sale to a stock company of the recipe for a famous pepper sauce, which was one of the many delicious accompaniments to the serving of fish and game at their hospitable board. It is made from small peppers, very hot, which grow in abundance on the island, and it is world famous, having the name "Tabasco." *October 19, 1912*

McIlhenny, Henry P. Satisfied, in summer, by the thirty thousand acres of wild moors, mountains, lakes, and rivers of his "Glenveagh Castle" in County Donegal, Eire, Henry P. McIlhenny relishes the happy contrast of city life during the rest of the year, in his newly renovated house on Rittenhouse Square in Philadelphia. Since he is the curator of Decorative Arts at the Philadelphia Museum of Art, Chairman of the Philadelphia Metropolitan Opera Committee, and Chairman of the Philadelphia Orchestra's student concerts, Mr. McIlhenny's new town house is the vital center of the artistic and musical social life of the city. *May, 1952*

McIlhenny, Mr. and Mrs. Irvin Avery (Anita Stauffer) The marriage was solemnized in St. Louis Cathedral, New Orleans. The bride, on the maternal side, is a granddaughter of General Richard Taylor, only son of Zachary Taylor, twelfth President of the United States. Sarah Taylor, who became the wife of Jefferson Davis, was a sister of General Richard Taylor, who owned a great sugar estate in St. Charles Parish about twenty miles above New Orleans. The bridegroom, during the Spanish-American War, was one of the Rough Riders. He is a grandson of General Dudley Avery, part owner of Avery Island, which lies above Vermilion Bay in Louisiana. *December 7, 1907*

McIlhenny, Walter A grassy knoll rising out of the marsh, 192 feet high, is one of five salt domes in southern Louisiana—Avery Island: a feudal enclave in the 20th century, some 2,500 acres of hillsides surrounded by another 10,000 acres of marsh. It has been in the family since 1818, one piece of land, ruled by one family. Three industries sustain the bayou-rimmed island: the salt mines, which run deep underground, the red-pepper fields that produce the chief ingredient for the world-famous Tabasco sauce, and 150 oil wells. Mister Walter and his family are of English descent. Their major problem is certainly not one of sustenance but how to preserve their private Xanadu against the press of their own

people, the sixty or seventy blood descendants, each having an equal claim on a finite piece of property. The island is owned as a corporation, founded in 1903 by the descendants of Judge Dudley Daniel Avery, from whom all the stockholders descend. *January, 1976*

McKean, John is descended from Thomas McKean, a signer of the Declaration of Independence, and a great-great-nephew of Colonel Robert Gould Shaw, who during the Civil War led a famous march of black soldiers against the South. He is a lawyer, secretary of the Myopia Hunt Club, and interested in flat racing as well as the management of a 2,000-acre family estate in North Carolina. *February, 1987*

McKelway, Dr. St. Clair His election as Chancellor of the Regents of the University of the State of New York gives universal satisfaction. The Editor of the *Brooklyn Eagle* is one of the ablest newspapermen in this country. Nearly all his life, he has been in newspaper work, although a member of the New York Bar. *March 1, 1913*

McKim, Charles Follen In 1872, he began to practise his profession as an architect. In 1877, he became a partner of Mr. William R. Mead, and in 1879 the late Stanford White became a member of the firm. He was one of the founders of the American Academy in Rome. The Public Library and the Algonquin Club in Boston are among the examples of architecture deemed monuments to his ability. Early in his career, he married Julia Appleton of Boston. *September 25, 1909*

McKinney, Price has made a great fortune in Michigan copper mines. He is very fond of out-of-door sports, and drives the swiftest thing in motor-cars. His motorboat, the *Standard,* carried off the prize in the races on the Hudson River last summer. *October 20, 1906*

McKnight, Turney is joint Master of Fox hounds for the Elkridge-Harford Hunt in Green Spring Valley, Maryland. McKnight is also one of the foremost amateur steeplechase jockeys in the country. In 1975 Mister (the prefix given to amateur riders) McKnight won the Blue Grass Cup of the Hardscuffle in Kentucky. He had a hardscuffle of his own when the architect for his over-a-quarter-million-dollar house refused to let interior designer Baby Jane Holzer paint the outside of the house black. (Mr. McKnight not only has a way of spellbinding race crowds but also of raising local eyebrows.) *March, 1977*

McLane, Fanny King doesn't bother so much about permanents in the hunting field as she does about the behavior of the beginners. Having taught her two nieces, Mrs. R. Curzon Hoffman and Mrs. Edwin Warfield, how to rank as the first two women riders in the Maryland countryside, she is well qualified, even at seventy five, to take the field and correct anybody's manners (she always insists upon a child's hunting in a derby). "Uncle Fanny," as she is affectionately known, broke her wrist at seventy but continued to hunt five days a week. She races her own horses at Pimlico. *June, 1939*

McLaughlin, Helen Malcolm, daughter of Mr. and Mrs. Frank McLaughlin, is a descendant of Hugh Roberts, the first Mayor of Philadelphia, and of the Howards of Virginia, whose estate joined that of President Madison. The great-grandfather of this debutante was Howard Malcolm, who was a clergyman and man of letters. He was at one time President of the Georgetown College in Louisville, resigning when he took a brave stand as an abolitionist. He was the first man in Kentucky to free his slaves. Mrs. McLaughlin's father was at one time President and Publisher of the *Philadelphia Times,* his inheritance from his father. *November 28, 1908*

McLean, Mrs. Donald (Emily N. Ritchie) is the regent of the New York City Chapter of the Daughters of the American Revolution. Mrs. McLean is the daughter of the late Judge Ritchie, of Frederick, Maryland, and inherits her patriotism and judicial bent of mind from a long line of soldiers and statesmen. She is a splendid parliamentarian, with commanding personality and a voice of carrying power that can be distinctly heard all over a large auditorium. *April 22, 1905*

McLean, Edward ("Ned"), only child of Mr. John R. McLean, is described as a blond giant. He is the grandson on the maternal side of General Edward Fitzgerald Beale, for whom he is named. He will inherit the bulk of the Washington McLean estate, beside the colossal fortune of his father and a goodly amount from the Beale estate. *June 18, 1904*

McLean, John R. has bought, for the rumored price of $600,000, half or a little more than half interest in the Washington *Post* Company, thereby securing control of Washington's only morning daily. Mr. McLean is a Democrat, and everybody is much interested to see what effect this purchase will have upon the policy of the *Post,* which has hitherto been an independent paper. Mr. McLean is the owner of the *Cincinnati Enquirer.* Mrs. McLean was Miss Emily Beale, daughter of General Beale, of Washington. *October 28, 1905*

McLean, Mr. and Mrs. Robert (Clare Randolph Goode) The bride belongs to a particularly large and distinguished family connection. On the paternal side, she is a granddaughter of the late Judge John Goode of Bedford County, Virginia, widely known as the "Virginia Gladstone," and—more familiarly—as "The Grand Old Man of Virginia" or the "Bronze Lion of Bedford." Her maternal grandfather was the late Colonel W. Stewart Symington, a gallant officer of the Confederacy. *May 1, 1919*

McManus, Charles J., Jr. stays in exquisite isolation at "Mercers Creek," Antigua, one of the only two remaining sugar estates on the island that have been turned into private homes. His unique cut-stone house, parts of which were built in the 1690s, is the lordly idiom of the plantation aristocracy. *December, 1976*

McMillan, Senator James was one of Michigan's great "captains of industry." In 1864, with Mr. John S. Newberry, he organized the Michigan Car Company. He was one of the organizers and later the President of the Detroit, Mackinaw and Marquette Railroad Company. In 1886, with Mr. Newberry, he contributed a large sum of money toward the establishing and maintenance of a large hospital in Detroit. *October 19, 1907*

McNALLY, MR. AND MRS. ANDREW III (MARGARET MACMILLAN) They met at the old Thousand Islands Yacht Club. Today they summer on *La Duchesse*, George Boldt's 100-foot houseboat, tied off Wellesley Island. There are four generations of McNallys in residence in the island compound to which the boat is moored. Mr. McNally's father was commodore of the Yacht Club, bringing the staff up from the Ritz. Andrew III was also involved in social duties. "I'll never forget interviewing orchestras on Broadway one season to get a group up here for the Club," he says. *August, 1978*

McVICKAR, MRS. HARRY WHITNEY (MAUD ROBBINS) is Chairman of the dog show committee of the Southampton Kennel Club. Mrs. McVickar is an authority on well-bred dogs, and at an impromptu bench show given a few seasons ago on the grounds of one of the Main Street cottages, she exhibited several blue ribbon winners who wore the badge of their honor with face and aplomb. *August 2, 1913*

MEAD, GEORGE H. of Dayton is one of the leading poloists of the country, whose interests are varied and many; in the Midwest, at Aiken, South Carolina, during the winter, and fox-hunting in Maryland and Virginia. *August 1, 1928*

MEADE, RICHARD WORSHAM Since the time of George Meade of pre-Revolutionary days, there have been three or four, perhaps five, Richard Worsham Meades who have been distinguished in history. George Meade was the founder of St. Mary's Church, in Fourth Street, Philadelphia, the oldest Catholic Church save one in this country. The first Richard Worsham Meade went to Spain, was a ship-owner in Cádiz, and one may read of the part he had in the Peninsula War. *December 16, 1905*

MECKLENBERG-SCHWERIN, DUCHESS OF (LILY OELRICHS)—MARTIN and her son, Mr. Charles Martin, were in San Francisco for several weeks. The young man, who is interested in agriculture, has entered the School for Agriculture connected with the University of California at Davis. The Duchess, who was Mrs. Peter Martin before her marriage, enjoyed a quiet time. After a visit on the Atlantic Coast with Mr. and Mrs. Charles Oelrichs, she will return to the south of France, where she has an attractive villa. *November 1, 1922*

MEDILL, JOSEPH, Editor of the *Chicago Tribune,* is traveling with Mrs. Medill in Europe. In a recent letter to his paper, he describes London in the fashionable season. Speaking of the moral aspects of the British capital, he says that in the male ranks of all classes of the English people agnosticism is becoming frightfully prevalent. The great problem in church-circles is how to arrest its spread and finally extirpate it. *August 2, 1882*

MEEKER, ARTHUR, JR. There has been considerable comment here over a series of satirical articles in the *Chicago Herald Examiner* by Arthur Meeker, Jr., who writes on the follies and foibles of the present generation in society. The articles were in the form of letters of advice to the feminine parvenue desirous of breaking into Chicago society, with the possibility of larger fields ahead after the Middle West has been conquered. *December 15, 1928*

MELLON, ANDREW The North Shore has ever been a happy hunting ground for Official Washington. A newcomer is Mr. Andrew Mellon, Secretary of the Treasury, who has taken the Ayer place, "Avalon," at Pride's Crossing. While he himself will only flit back and forth, his daughter, Miss Ailsa Mellon, is installed and has a houseful of guests constantly. The house, which is of the Italian villa type, with red tiled roof, nestles close by the water against a background of dark pines. *September 1, 1922*

MELLON, PAUL has devoted most of his life to disbursing money to worthy causes. Recipients of his largess have included universities, mental health programs, and especially the National Gallery of Art in Washington, which his father established in 1937 and which Paul has headed since 1963. He attended Choate, Yale, and Cambridge, maintains elegant homes in Virginia, Washington, Cape Cod, and Antigua, owns one of the world's finest private art collections, and his famous Rokeby Stables have produced champion thoroughbreds at the Belmont Stakes and Epsom Downs. *May, 1978*

MELLON, RICHARD KING Since 1937, when he assumed management of the great industrial empire left by his uncle, Andrew Mellon, Dick Mellon has been one of the nation's most conscientious and influential financiers and, in 1948, was acclaimed through a nationwide poll as one of "America's Fifty Foremost Business Leaders." To thousands of sports enthusiasts in other parts of the globe, from Melton Mowbray to the Yukon, he is admired principally because he is an exceptionally fine horseman, crack shot, and all-round sportsman. *June, 1951*

MELLON, MR. AND MRS. WILLIAM LARIMER, JR. (GWEN GRANT) A grandnephew of Andrew W. Mellon, at the age of twenty five he read of the work of Albert Schweitzer. So impressed with Dr. Schweitzer's work, he entered Tulane University at age 41 as a pre-medical student, while his wife prepared herself to be a laboratory technician. In vacations during his seven years of study, Mr. and Mrs. Mellon traveled about the world searching for the location where they thought their services would be most needed. They found just such a place in the Artibonite Valley of Haiti. Here Dr. Mellon and his wife invested some two million dollars in their very own Albert Schweitzer-model hospital. For the past twenty years, the Mellons have faithfully continued their project. *January, 1976*

MENDES, REV. DR. HENRY PEREIRA of New York has been appointed Grand Chaplain of the grand lodge of Masons of the State of New York. Dr. Mendes is the first rabbi selected for this office since the existence of the grand lodge, which is over one hundred years old. *July 8, 1896*

MENDL, LADY (ELSIE DE WOLFE) After a successful decade as an actress, she turned to interior decorating and was, in a sense, a pioneer of that subsequently abused occupation. She became the most successful dean of decorators in this country. As her business increased, she spent much of her time in Europe and established a second home for herself at Versailles. Her distinguished activities during the war added lustre to her already brilliant achievements and now, at the age of sixty one, she has married an Englishman. *April 1, 1926*

MENKEN, MRS. S. STANWOOD belongs to the monotony school. She has made her reputation by getting dressed up yearly in some elaborate fancy-dress costume for the Beaux-Arts. When the Beaux-Arts folded right under her, so to speak, she didn't surrender—she just moved on to another parade ground and dazzled the photographers with her red sequins at the Firemen's Ball. *March, 1938*

MERLE-SMITH, VAN SANTVOORD, commanding Company L of the old 69th Regiment, has received the American Distinguished Service Cross for heroic conduct and coolness under fire. He is the son of the Rev. Dr. Wilton Merle-Smith, pastor of the Central Presbyterian Church in New York City, and grandson of the late Commodore Van Santvoord, the founder of the Hudson River Day Line. *October 1, 1918*

MERRILL, MRS. CHARLES (EVANGELINE JOHNSON)—STOKOWSKI—ZALSTEM-ZALESSKY is Palm Beach's most irrepressible patroness of the arts, who's been collecting abstract painting for sixty years. Now, at eighty one, the heiress to the Johnson & Johnson fortune is co-chairing the Palm Beach Festival. Formerly married to Leopold Stokowski and Prince Zalstem-Zalessky, she recently married artist-sculptor Charles Merrill, forty three. *March, 1979*

MERRIMAN, REV. DR. AND MRS. DANIEL (HELEN BIGELOW) have just built and endowed a hospital near North Conway, New Hampshire, in memory of the latter's father and mother, Mr. and Mrs. Erastus B. Bigelow (Eliza Means). Mr. Bigelow was the inventor of the carpet loom. Dr. Merriman was at one time the pastor of the Central Church in Worcester and President of the board of directors of the Worcester Art Museum. *June 3, 1911*

MESEROLE, GENERAL JEREMIAH VANDERBILT was a descendant of Jean Meserole, a French Huguenot who founded the Meserole family of Williamsburg and Greenpoint, Long Island. His activity in military affairs began in 1855, when he enlisted in the Seventh Regiment. At the outbreak of the Civil War, he went to the front. After Lee's surrender, General Meserole returned to his old work as surveyor until elected President of the Williamsburg Savings Bank in 1891. *August 22, 1908*

MELLON

Secretary of the Treasury Andrew W. Mellon, 1921.

In 1994, *Town & Country* presented its Generous American Award to Paul Mellon. "The fact is," the magazine concluded, "no one alive today, not even the bountiful Walter Annenberg, can challenge Paul Mellon as America's preeminent philanthropist in the arts." His gifts, at that time, totaled more than $670 million. Among them: more than one thousand paintings given to Washington, D.C.'s, National Gallery of Art and the creation of the Yale University Center for British Art, the largest single collection of English paintings in this country.

Born in 1907, Paul Mellon came naturally to both giving and the arts. His father, Andrew W. Mellon, was one of the greatest collectors of all time. His Raphaels, Rembrandts, and Vermeers today fill the walls of the National Gallery, which Mellon, Sr. also endowed. The Mellon Foundation, which Andrew established to continue his history of giving, registered assets of over $2 billion in 1995.

Andrew Mellon's most famous role, though, was as America's longest-serving secretary of the treasury, from 1921 to 1931. Throughout the booming Twenties, he succeeded in reducing the national debt, gained a reputation for aloofness (with an "ice-water smile," contemporaries said), and took a stance that was eminently pro-business. For many years in the United States, "Mellon" and "banking" were practically synonymous. His wife, born Nora McMullen, was a granddaughter of Patrick Guinness, founder of the Dublin brewing dynasty.

Andrew's father, Thomas Mellon, was born in 1837 in a Pennsylvania town named Poverty Point. That was the last association of the Mellon name with lack of funds. Himself the son of an Ulsterman who arrived in this country in 1818, Thomas went to Pittsburgh to study law and became a banker and judge. Soon, he was in the enviable position of lending money to Andrew Carnegie and other founders of U.S. Steel. When the judge retired in 1886, the family banking business descended to his sons Andrew and Richard B. Under their aegis, their Union Trust Company of Pittsburgh became one of the major financial institutions in the United States. They expanded into Gulf Oil, the Carborundum Company, Koppers, and the giant Aluminum Company (Alcoa), which Andrew organized.

Today, the other main branch of the Mellon family descends from Richard's son, Richard King Mellon, who merged the various family banks and is credited with the modern-day renewal of Pittsburgh. In a reticent family, the exuberant "R. K." often served as spokesman. Richard King Mellon died in 1970, but Paul Mellon continues to maintain houses in Cape Cod, Antigua, Washington, Paris, and New York, and a horse-breeding farm, "Oak Spring," in Upperville, Virginia. His airplane, a Gulfstream II, is hung with canvases by Georges Braque, Paul Klee, and Ben Nicholson. Younger descendants in the Mellon and Scaife family branches today own banks and newspapers and fund innumerable philanthropies, including many devoted to conservation.

M ellons of many talents: *clockwise from top left,* Mrs. Richard K. Mellon, 1937; Andrew Mellon's children, Paul and Ailsa, in 1924; in 1932, Richard King Mellon takes the silver cup.

MESSINGER, MRS. WILLIAM (ALIDA ROCKE-FELLER)—DAYTON, daughter of philanthropist John D. Rockefeller III, has emerged as one of the nation's largest givers to progressive (as well as traditional) causes on an annual basis. She says she seeks to fund "social change at the grass-roots level." One example: She supports radio station KILI, owned and operated by Oglala Indians on the Pine Ridge Reservation in South Dakota. *December, 1989*

METCALF, MR. AND MRS. LAWRENCE (CATHERINE J. ROLPH) On the west shore lies Rubicon Beach, the gold coast of Lake Tahoe. Brothers Larry and John Metcalf, descendants of railway pioneer Collis Huntington, live side by side with their wives, Sue and K. J. (Catherine), and a constant flow of visitors. "We entertain very simply," says K. J. Metcalf. "We have two different cooks—a peanut-butter-and-jelly cook when the children and grandchildren are here, and our own. It's all outdoors, under the trees, or at our gazebo on the beach." *August, 1985*

MEYER, BARON ADOLPHE DE is quite a social personage in London. He is a banker, belonging to many of the fashionable clubs. The Baron de Meyer is very artistic, and he has made wonderful successes in photography. He has had sittings from nearly all the great beauties of the very fashionable set, and a number of his proofs have been published. He is coming for the *America*'s Cup races, and he will be the guest of Mr. and Mrs. Widener and Mr. and Mrs. John R. Drexel at Newport. *July 11, 1903*

MEYER, MR. AND MRS. GEORGE VON LENGERKE (ALICE APPLETON) He was of the Harvard Class of 1879, and made a record while in college as a class oarsman. His political career began in the Boston Common Council in 1879, and from that he went steadily higher until he reached the highest honors both in this country and abroad. He had been Ambassador to Italy and Roosevelt's Ambassador to Russia, after serving as Postmaster General. He was President Taft's choice for Secretary of the Navy, and in every office he achieved unqualified success. *April 1, 1918*

MILBANK, JEREMIAH II The members of the Amateur Comedy Club, if any of them were present, probably honored the boys of the Cutler Comedy Club by being just a little jealous. *Caprice,* a little play, was presented by six clever young boys of the Cutler School. Music was furnished by the Cutler Mandolin Club, led by Mr. Jeremiah Milbank, 2d. *February 18, 1905*

MILBANK, JOSEPH was one of the builders of the Chicago, Milwaukee and St. Paul Railroad. He built the People's Palace in Jersey City in memory of his parents and was active in many philanthropies. He was the brother of Mrs. A. A. Anderson, who built public baths in New York and who gave Milbank Hall to Columbia University. *September 26, 1914*

MILBURN, DEVEREUX One of the speeches at the sportsmen's dinner at the Waldorf-Astoria in New York City was that of Mr. Devereux Milburn on "International Polo." He pointed

out that this was not a contest between nations but a contest of type of game, and that England had built up a restrained offensive code, as against the open, aggressive, fast galloping code of the United States. He admitted that the success of the future lay in "new blood," and that the new blood depended upon American polo development. He said that polo should be fostered in Army circles among civilians, the tyro encouraged, and every chance given him to play. *March 1, 1912*

PALACE INTRIGUES

Scarcely had society begun to speculate upon the outcome of Mrs. Cornelius Vanderbilt's brilliant coup in securing Prince Henry of Prussia for dinner, when Mrs. Ogden Mills sent out invitations to meet the Prince at luncheon on the day preceding, thus wresting from Mrs. Vanderbilt the distinction of being the first New York woman to privately entertain His Royal Highness. Those who had hailed Mrs. Vanderbilt as Mrs. Astor's successor are beginning to realize that Mrs. Mills, who has long considered herself the arbiter of the circle within the circle, has no intention of abating one jot of her power. *March 15, 1902*

MILES, MRS. NELSON A. (MARY HOYT SHERMAN), wife of the former commanding general of the army, died at West Point. She was the daughter of Judge Charles Sherman and a niece of the late Senator John Sherman of Ohio and General William T. Sherman, so by inheritance had the qualities valuable to a woman who is the wife of a prominent man. *August 13, 1904*

MILLER, MRS. ANDREW J. (CHARLOTTE P. TAYLOR) "We do not seek publicity, we do not wear costumes, and we do not march in parades," says Colonial Dames of America National President Mrs. Andrew J. Miller. "We do not think that's comely for ladies." *October, 1981*

MILLER, MRS. GILBERT (KATHERINE "KITTY" BACHE) She says she is not a real hostess, that she prefers spur-of-the-moment entertaining; in fact, she confesses, "I prefer being a guest." Nonetheless, Kitty Miller ranks high among New York's outstanding hostesses. The Millers have houses in Majorca and London and an apartment in New York in which Goya's masterpiece, *Don Manuel Osorio,* hangs six months of the year (the other six months it hangs in the Metropolitan Museum of Art). *May, 1965*

MILLER, MRS. HENRY WISE (ALICE DUER), who has been mentioned as one of the women whom popularity and probability point to as the Dean of Barnard College, is a daughter of Mrs. Elizabeth Duer, the author; a sister of Miss Caroline Duer, whose short stories one always selects to read first when one notes them in cutting the leaves of a new magazine; and a cousin of Mrs. Clarence Mackay. Mrs. Duer's father was James Gore King Duer. *April 4, 1908*

MILLER, RICHARD K. is quintessential Old Guard, springing from Old Family and Old Money. He is the son of the late Robert Watt Miller, Chairman of the board of the Pacific Lighting Corporation. As President of the San Francisco Opera Association, Dick Miller's father was instrumental in building the Opera into one of the best in the country. He is the son-in-law of Donald J. Russell, Chairman of the board of the Southern Pacific Railroad. His mother is the former Elizabeth Folger, who founded the Folger coffee empire. His grandfather, C.O.G. Miller, was one of the founders of the Pacific Lighting Corporation. *February, 1973*

MILLER, MRS. W. GRAHAM At her Italian villa in Santa Barbara, Mrs. Miller has given some wonderful entertainments. She has treasures in her home such as Mr. Morgan finds in his travels. In the great entrance-hall burns a lamp from the altar of an Italian church, and there are tapestries, each with a history. The Italian terrace, where guests may chat and walk after dinner, overlooks the Pacific Ocean. Often for Christmas dinners, the choirboys of St. Anthony's at Santa Barbara sing with one of the priests playing the accompaniment. *June 8, 1907*

MILLER, MR. AND MRS. W. STARR will soon take possession of their new villa near Bailey's Beach, Newport. The house has especial interest, as it was designed by Mrs. Miller's brother, Mr. Whitney Warren. *July 12, 1902*

MILLS, DARIUS OGDEN The will of the late Darius Ogden Mills was filed for probate. With the exception of six bequests to public institutions, the estate, which is estimated at between $50,000,000 and $60,000,000, is divided between two children, Mr. Ogden Mills, Jr., and Mrs. Elizabeth Mills Reid, wife of Ambassador Whitelaw Reid. *January 22, 1910*

MILLS, MRS. OGDEN (RUTH LIVINGSTON) A very handsome ballroom will be added to the Ogden Mills residence in town. This was much needed, as Mrs. Mills has not been able to give very large entertainments, owing to lack of space. In fact, for the fashionable woman, a ballroom has become an absolute necessity. Private houses are, more and more, becoming like small hotels, with the exception that the first three floors are built solely with the view of entertaining. *June 29, 1901*

MILLS, MRS. PAUL (ELLEN DREXEL PAUL) is a sister of Anthony J. Drexel Paul, and of Mrs. Charles A. Munn, who was Miss Mary Astor Paul. She is closely related to the clans of the Drexels, Biddles, and Astors and is a cousin of Lady Maidstone. "Woodcrest Lodge," the home of the late James Paul, is one of the most imposing English mansions along the Main Line. *November 15, 1923*

MINER, MRS. RANDOLPH HUNTINGTON Her father was a New Englander, her mother Spanish, and she was born in California. She has lived all over the world, owns a villa on the cliffs above the Mediterranean near Santa Margherita, and now calls Washington "home." Mrs. Randolph Huntington Miner is one of the wittiest people alive, numbers her friends by the thousands because, as she says, "I love people of all ages—from the cradle to the brink of the grave." *June, 1945*

MINOT, MRS. GARDNER (CONSTANCE GARDNER) has been much missed in Washington of late. Her position here has been rather extraordinary, for although she had no official position one met all the political big-wigs at her house. During the arms conference, she served as a sort of unofficial hostess for her grandfather, Senator Henry Cabot Lodge. Mrs. Minot's father was the late Augustus Peabody Gardner, like the Lodges of the Brahmin caste of Boston. *March 15, 1924*

MINOT, MRS. JOSEPH GRAFTON (HONORA E.T. WINTHROP) Boston was more or less given over last week to the entertaining of the General Society of Colonial Wars by the Massachusetts Society. The most notable occasion was the reception given at the Hotel Somerset, this having great social significance from the fact that Mrs. J. Grafton Minot and Mrs. Francis I. Amory, who are prominent in the most exclusive set, received the guests, together with Mrs. Frederic J. de Peyster of New York, whose husband is Governor of the General Society. The governors and lieutenant governors of both societies wore broad red ribbons of the order over their evening dress. *May 31, 1902*

MINOT, LAWRENCE has been one of the most prominent financiers and trustees of property in Boston. He carried on a business that was begun by an ancestor in the eighteenth century. Mr. Minot's country place at Wareham, Massachusetts, is widely known as one of the most beautiful in the country. It is called "Saffron Walden," after the estate of his ancestors in England. *July 1, 1921*

MINOT, WILLIAM VI The first Minot, Stephen, came to America on the *William and Mary* and soon acquired the entire town of Dorchester, Massachusetts, which he purchased for short-term profit. Minots served in the Revolution. One ancestor, George Richards Minot, whose portrait was painted by John Singleton Copley, was the aide-de-camp of George Washington. William Minot VI is in constant motion all over the world, helping to run the institutional operations of Advest, Inc., stockbrokers. *April, 1976*

MITCHELL, DONALD GRANT is widely known as "Ik Marvel," genial veteran of the world of letters. It has long been an honored custom among Yale undergraduates to make literary pilgrimages to his home in New Haven to gaze with affection upon the author of those classic works *Reveries of a Bachelor* and *Dream Life*. In 1867, Mr. Mitchell published a volume of *Rural Studies*. The first paper in this volume, "An Old-Style Farm," contains an accurate and realistic description of the farm at Salem, Connecticut, on which Mr. Mitchell spent the earlier years of his life. After his marriage to Miss Mary Pringle of Charleston, South Carolina, Mr. Mitchell disposed of his farm at Salem and went abroad as Consul at Venice, a position given him by President Pierce at the suggestion of his lifelong friend, Nathaniel Hawthorne. *April 6, 1907*

AND THEN CAME BIKINIS

On these beautiful August mornings, Spouting Rock Beach in Newport, from ten until one, is the scene of animated gatherings, when society meets for its morning dip. Very novel suits are being worn this year, and besides those made of silk there are a great many of satin. Miss Gladys Mills and Miss Beatrice Mills, the beautiful daughters of Mr. and Mrs. Ogden Mills, have the prettiest gowns seen on the sand. They are of dark silk, elaborately trimmed, but not at all startling, for, as one of the men in charge of the beach naively expressed it, "They look more as though they were going to church than in bathing." *August 2, 1902*

MITCHELL, JOHN J. The idea for the internationally known trail-riding club Los Rancheros Visitadores (The Visiting Ranchers) was conceived one summer evening at the 1928 encampment at Bohemian Grove. Chicago oilman John J. Mitchell—romanticist, outdoor man, and lover of horses—began to muse upon how great it would be if everything that was transpiring at the Grove could be "done on horseback." Mitchell was soon to purchase a 10,000-acre ranch in Santa Barbara County, to breed palomino horses. At the time married to Lolita Armour (of the meat-packing Armours), he named the ranch "Juan y Lolita," and it was to play a prominent part in the beginning of Los Rancheros Visitadores in April 1930. *May, 1975*

MITCHELL, S. WEIR One of the most celebrated members of the Bar Harbor colony is the Philadelphia scientist and psychological novelist, who has a charming residence, although not an imposing one, on West Street. Mr. and Mrs. Mitchell are on the very top strata of social circles but go out very little. Dr. Mitchell is an ardent bicyclist, and, clad in gray knickerbockers, can be seen almost any day out for a spin. *July 18, 1903*

MITCHELL, WILLIAM HAMILTON was Vice President of the Illinois Trust and Savings Bank, had lived in Chicago since 1873, and had been connected with many of its interests. From connection with the Alton packet back in 1852, he had come to build what is now the Chicago and Alton Railroad, and he was a man of much wealth, although in 1849 he had walked from Missouri to California beside his ox-team. *March 19, 1910*

MIXTER, MRS. JAMES More than anything, it is probably Cincinnati's atmosphere of continuity that attracts people to the city and keeps them there. Mr. and Mrs. James Mixter live in the turreted Gothic mansion that Mrs. Mixter's great-great-great-grandfather, John Mixter, built in 1852. "How many New Yorkers or even Bostonians or Philadelphians know who their great-great-great-grandfathers were?" Mrs. Mixter wonders. "Well, there he is," she says, pointing to the marble bust that stands in one of the twin front parlors. *October, 1975*

MIZNER, ADDISON Having thoroughly Latinized Palm Beach, Mr. Mizner is now extending activities to Boca Raton. He would probably describe himself something like this: six feet one, weight nobody's business, more or less blond, and somewhat of a placid nature. His first love of Spanish architecture was born at the age of thirteen, when the family moved to Central America, where his father had a special embassy to straighten out the Nicaragua Canal difficulties. *September 15, 1925*

MIZNER, LANSING No dinner in San Francisco is thought complete without one of the Mizners. It was Lansing Mizner who made the remark that if a man should drop dead in the library of the Pacific Union Club his body would not be found for a week. *April 10, 1915*

MONROE, GERTRUDE Next to Mobile's Strikers Ball comes the Twelfth-Night Revelers' Ball in New Orleans. These balls are the appetizers for the Carnival table d'hôte which is served until the Ash Wednesday demi-tasse closes the feast. To be the queen or a maid at Twelfth Night, chosen as they are by what is the "premeditated lucky chance" of finding the gold bean or silver bean in a cake of wedding-like dimensions, is one of the greatest of the debutante's honors. This year, the golden bean fell to Miss Gertrude Monroe, who is the third sovereign the family of Judge and Mrs. F. A. Monroe has produced, her two elder sisters having reigned at Carnival balls in the recent past. *January 26, 1907*

MONSON, ALONZO was the founder of the Knickerbocker Club, and he had a romantic history; his father was a Portuguese and owner of ships that plied in the beginning of the last century in the Spanish Main. Judge Monson went to California in 1850. On the Pacific Coast, he was wrecked and landed in Mexico and afterwards practiced law in California and was Judge of the Supreme Court there. Making a large fortune in real estate, he returned to New York and was prominent in society and club life. He was a governor of the Union, and, with Alexander Hamilton, Jr., and the late John Jacob Astor, he established the Knickerbocker. *July 1, 1911*

MONTGOMERY, HELEN HOPE To the almost endless chain of entertaining that has been planned in honor of the debutante daughter of Mr. and Mrs. Robert Leaming Montgomery, of Villanova, Pennsylvania, is added a new and novel link—invitations have now been sent out for a race meet. The meet will be held at "Ardrossan," the beautiful country home of Mr. and Mrs. Montgomery at Villanova, and it is safe to predict that the Quaker City's best will attend. *October 1, 1922*

MONTGOMERY, WILLIAM W. The Merion Cricket Club owes its introduction into the cricket world primarily to Mr. William W. Montgomery and Mr. Maskell Ewing, who, while on a pedestrian tour through the Blue Ridge Mountains in Berks County, Pennsylvania, in the fall of 1865, conceived the idea of organizing a cricket club in the neighborhood of Lower Merion. *November 22, 1902*

MORGAN

J. Pierpont Morgan in 1902; his children, *left and right,* J. P. Morgan, Jr., and Anne.

No other American has been described as "princely" more often than John Pierpont Morgan. His financial operations, his style of living, his art collecting were all on a scale seldom seen in America. Awed by his power and personality, contemporaries called him "the magnifico."

J. P. was a financier to his fingertips. Born to banking and to wealth (his grandfather was successful in the fire insurance business, and his father, Junius Spencer Morgan, invested British funds as a banker in the United States), Morgan was involved in most of the great money transactions of his time. Aiming to bring order to chaotic industries, he began with the railroads—consolidating dozens of lines into giant, nation-wide, more efficient systems. Dozens of iron and steel companies were merged into U.S. Steel: J. P. Morgan made millionaires right and left and almost single-handedly halted the Wall Street panic of 1907.

Famous for his taciturnity and dislike of the press, he rarely concerned himself with public opinion. He never chatted with associates, made speeches, gave interviews, or attended public meetings. Instead, he thought out his financial operations while playing solitaire in the study of his Madison Avenue house, surrounded by his Old Master paintings and first editions. People knew J. P. Morgan liked them if he invited them to sail on his yacht, the *Corsair,* which had a crew of eighty-five but usually not more than four guests, or gave them a collie from his famous kennels at Highland Falls, New York.

He seldom went to parties. A prominent Episcopal church-man, he had a special fondness for attending church conferences, arriving on a private train loaded with clergymen.

Well educated (he attended the University of Göttingen in Germany) and sophisticated, Morgan was one of the greatest collectors of all time, concentrating on Chinese porcelains, Old Master paintings, and, above all, books and manuscripts. He spent lavishly. When he died in 1913, he left $68 million, bringing forth John D. Rockefeller, Sr.'s surprised remark, "Why, he wasn't even a rich man."

Morgan's son, J. P., Jr. (who died in 1943), acted as American agent for the Allied countries in World War I, and after the war floated securities of foreign governments. As much an Anglophile as his father, he entertained the Archbishop of Canterbury on his yacht and invited King George VI shooting on his Scottish moors. Like his father, J. P., Jr. always maintained an English residence. His unmarried sister Anne was a Francophile, kept a home at Versailles, and was decorated by the French government for her help in World War I. An ardent promoter of women's rights, she was president of the American Woman's Association.

J. P., Jr.'s wife, Jane Grew, descended from a distinguished Boston family of bankers, and his son, Henry Sturgis Morgan, married Catherine Adams, also from Boston and the great-great-granddaughter of President John Quincy Adams. Descendants today are still connected with banking.

MOORE, ALEXANDER P. The lion's share of the credit for persuading King Alfonso and Queen Victoria of Spain to visit the United States goes admittedly to Mr. Alexander P. Moore, sometime Ambassador to Spain, who held a unique position at court in Madrid. Breath-taking tales were told of Mr. Moore's slapping the King on the back and sending candy to the Princesses quite as if they were American girls. But the facts remain that Mr. Moore is exceptionally popular in Spain, that he is persona grata with the *grandeza,* and that he enjoys the warm friendship of the King and Queen. *April 1, 1926*

MOORE, MRS. BLOOMFIELD H. Notable among Newport festivities this season is the children's fancy dress party given by Mrs. Bloomfield Moore, of Philadelphia, on the lawn of her villa at Newport. A large black shoe with red heel and huge tin buckle, a triumph of upholstered *chaussure,* was filled with children in various costumes. Miss Mary Paul and the Misses Agnes and Anna Lazarus were detailed to pick the strange fruit that hung from a symmetrical miniature pine tree, boxes of sweetmeats, tiny Japanese parasols and fans, and Italian straw bugles. The Misses Havemeyer looked very handsome in their Austrian peasant dress. Master B. La Farge was a French cook, his baton of office a large iron spoon. *October 3, 1877*

MOORE, CASIMIR DE RHAM, a retired lawyer, was a grandson of Clement Clarke Moore, author of *The Night Before Christmas,* and a great-grandson of Benjamin Moore, the second Bishop of the Diocese of New York. *June 1, 1925*

MOORE, CHARLES A., JR. He has allied himself with his father's business interests, and with such success that he is now Vice President of the big corporation, the Maxwell, Manning and Moore Company of which his father is President. But as a traveler, young Mr. Moore is of greatest interest. Only four years ago, he was graduated from Yale, but since then he has accompanied Lieutenant Peary on a summer excursion into the Arctic regions; and his recent trip to Turkey and Arabia was even more exciting. In Turkey, he became greatly interested in the natives, and believing them often maligned by the Christians is ready with arguments in their defense. *January 19, 1907*

MOORE, MRS. CLEMENT CLARKE (LAURA M. WILLIAMS) is considered one of the most popular matrons in New York society. She was a Miss Williams, and married the grandson of the author of *The Night Before Christmas.* Mr. and Mrs. Moore travel in the winter, generally in Europe, and a part of last winter they were in Egypt. This spring, Mrs. Moore took great interest in automobiling and was one of the first American women in Paris who had her own automobile. *October 11, 1900*

MOORE, JAMES HOBART, of Chicago, has been at Virginia Hot Springs but is expected to leave so that he will arrive in New York for the opening of the Horse Show, as he will, of course, have a great many entries. He is traveling in a private car and has an orchestra with him for the entertainment of his guests. He also has a car for his horses, and one for his traps and coaches. *November 15, 1902*

MORES, MLLE. DE Announcement has been made in Paris of the engagement of Mlle. de Mores, daughter of the widowed Marquise de Mores and granddaughter of Mr. Louis von Hoffman, of the Union Club, to Baron Pichon of France. The Marquis de Mores, who spent a number of years in New York and on cattle ranches in the West, was murdered in 1896 by his Arab guides while making his way from the southern borders of Tunis to Khartoum to join the Mahdi and his Dervishes in their fight against England. His son, M. Louis de Mores, who is now at Harvard, inherited from his paternal grandfather the title of Duke of Vallombrosa. He is Harvard's only duke. The Marquise de Mores has been engaged for a number of years in litigation with former French government officials of Tunis, whom she has publicly accused of having instigated the assassination of her husband. *September 30, 1905*

LEAVES OF CLASS

The finest cigars in the United States are said to be those smoked by J. Pierpont Morgan. The cheapest cigar that he uses costs him not less than one dollar and twenty five cents. They are made in Havana. Mr. Morgan sends a tobacco expert every year to the plantations in western Cuba to purchase the best tobacco before it matures. This agent remains on the spot directing the cutting of the plant and its forwarding to Havana, where another expert, a cigarmaker, takes charge. *October 6, 1897*

MORGAN, ALEXANDER PERRY When the Princeton estate of Junius S. Morgan, nephew of the great J. P., was subdivided into a development of sixty townhouses and condominium apartments, the splendor of the grounds and of the original Jacobean country house were successfully preserved in part because the architect on the project, Alexander Perry Morgan, was himself a great-great-nephew of J. P. Morgan and lived on the grounds. Today, he lives in one of the apartments in the carriage house he helped to restore. *October, 1984*

MORGAN, ANNE is the daughter of the late John Pierpont Morgan. She has gargantuan energy. She founded the Colony Club, of which she was Governor and Treasurer; she became Chairman of the Women's Department of the National Civic Federation; she organized the American Committee for Devastated France. Her work in the war is almost a matter of history. Certain decorations such as the Legion d'Honneur and the Croix de Guerre serve to remind her of its efficacy. *November 15, 1926*

MORGAN, EDWIN D., JR. He is a member of ten of the Harvard clubs and societies, has rowed on the varsity four-oared crew for two years, and is on the varsity eight. Mr. Morgan is already well known in the metropolitan world of amateur sport as a fearless rider, and he has taken part in some of the racing events at Meadow Brook. *June 28, 1913*

MORGAN, MRS. EDWIN D., JR. (ELIZABETH MORAN) Wheatley Hills, Long Island, is a stronghold of the Morgan family. Mrs. Morgan's father-in-law was the first to discover the manifold attractions of that now very exclusive and charming sporting centre. Mrs. Morgan is amongst the most interesting of the younger New York matrons, and her exhibition of drawings and pastels at the Ferargil Galleries last winter gained a great deal of favorable notice. *November 1, 1927*

MORGAN, GEORGE DENISON was the son of the late John Hale Morgan and Sarah Spencer Morgan, a sister of the late J. Pierpont Morgan. He was a collector of Japanese art, was interested in the work of the English church in Japan, and had a residence in Yokohama. *July 20, 1915*

MORGAN, REV. JOHN D. was rector of the American Church of the Holy Trinity in Paris, France. He was a cousin of Mr. J. Pierpont Morgan, and he married a sister of that financier, who was Miss Juliet Morgan. He was at one time assistant rector of St. Thomas's Church in New York but since 1872 was rector of the Protestant Episcopal Church of the Holy Trinity in Paris and was known to hundreds of Americans who were his parishioners. *January 27, 1912*

MORGAN, JOHN PIERPONT Of all the summer establishments at Newport, probably the most unique, least known, and most unostentatious is the red frame structure by the sea locally known as the "Graves End Fishing Club." Here it is that the great financier, Mr. J. Pierpont Morgan, makes his home for at least three or four days during the summer months for the sole purpose of enjoying the fresh lobsters, which are especially trapped for him off the ocean shores nearby. Mr. Morgan employs an expert lobsterman and fisherman all the year round, and the traps are placed in parts of the sea not frequented by the commercial lobster catchers. The largest and choicest of these toothsome creatures are lured into the traps by certain tempting bait provided by Mr. Morgan's deep sea caterer. *July 3, 1909*

MORGAN, MRS. JOHN PIERPONT, JR., and Miss Muriel White were presented to the Queen by Mrs. Henry White, wife of United States Chargé d'Affaires, at the first drawingroom held at Buckingham Palace. Mrs. Morgan wore a beautiful gown, with a train of white satin lined with pale blue velvet and outlined with trails of pink roses; her corsage and petticoat were of white satin. Miss White: white satin, covered with white chiffon; train of satin trimmed with chiffon and lilies-of-the-valley. *March 2, 1898*

MORGAN, MRS. W. FORBES, JR. (EDITH L. HALL) is a daughter of Mrs. Valentine G. Hall and a sister of Mrs. Stanley Mortimer, Mrs. Lawrence Waterbury, and the late Mrs. Elliot Roosevelt. Mr. Valentine Hall, a brother of Mrs. Morgan, was at one time noted for his talent shown in amateur theatricals. Mrs. Morgan is a daring equestrienne, a good swimmer, and an expert shot with the rifle. *July 30, 1904*

MORISON, SAMUEL ELIOT "Harvard is the central thing to Boston and it explains its character," insists Admiral Samuel Eliot Morison, the historian and Harvard professor. "It's the one city I've known where professors are fashionable. It's chic to be a professor here. I remember going to the wedding party of a relative in Philadelphia once where I was asked not to mention that I was a professor in order not to embarrass the bride's family." *March, 1968*

MORRIS, MR. AND MRS. A. GOUVERNEUR (LILIAN BROOKS) have just returned to their Monterey, California, home after several months on their plantation in Tahiti called "Hoe Taeme" (Once Upon a Time). This popular and well-known author is turning his attention to the raising of copra on his plantation. *December 1, 1928*

MORRIS, BENJAMIN WISTAR is architect of the Cunard Building, the Annex to the Morgan Library, and the Morgan Memorial at Hartford. From the first immigrant, Anthony Morris of "Oldgravelaine," London, who moved to Philadelphia in 1682 to join William Penn, to Mr. Morris's father, the Bishop of Oregon, and Mr. Morris himself, the family does not seem to have been noted for sitting down complacently. A cousin, Roland S. Morris, was Ambassador to Japan during the World War. Farther back was Captain Samuel Morris, who founded the City Troop of Philadelphia and during the Revolutionary War was its commander. *July 1, 1927*

MORRIS, CAMILLA ROSALIE was a member of a distinguished colonial family that received from King Charles Second a grant of the entire tract of land now included in the Bronx. The manor was named "Morrisania" by the original owner. Among her direct ancestors were Lewis Morris, first Colonial Governor of New York, and Gouverneur Morris, one of the framers of the Declaration of Independence and American Minister to France. Miss Morris was also connected with the Manigaults and other historic lines of South Carolina and with many of the leading colonial families of Maryland. *October 20, 1919*

MORRIS, DAVE HENNEN was recently elected President of the Automobile Club of America. He graduated from Harvard in 1896. In his junior year, he was married to Miss Alice Vanderbilt Shepard, daughter of Colonel Elliott F. Shepard, the owner of the *Mail and Express*. His personal hobbies are politics; horse racing; real estate, of which he is a large holder in New Orleans and Texas, as well as New York; yachting, shooting, and automobiling. *December 24, 1904*

MORRIS, MR. AND MRS. GEORGE L. K. (SUZY FRELINGHUYSEN) Although the George L. K. Morris' house did not actually create seismic disturbances in conservative Lenox and Stockbridge, Massachusetts, mild temblors are rumored to have resulted from the first shock of its uncompromisingly modern architecture. Whatever the Berkshireites think of it, it is the right kind of place for the owners. George and Suzy Frelinghuysen Morris are both artists. She recently exhibited with the American Abstract Artists show at the Riverside Museum. His polished and chased bronze sculpture was in the Artists for Victory exhibition at the Metropolitan Museum. *September, 1943*

MORRIS, GRACE ELLIOTT Dr. and Mrs. Robert Morris have announced the engagement of their daughter, Miss Grace Elliott Morris, to Mr. Philip Livingston Poe of Baltimore. Miss Morris is a great-great-granddaughter of Robert Morris, the great financier of the Revolution, and also a descendant of Chief Justice Marshall of Virginia. Mr. Poe is a member of the well-known Baltimore family, the Poe brothers being the famous football players of Princeton. He is the son of Mr. Nelson Poe and is a grandnephew of Edgar Allan Poe. *May 13, 1905*

A ROSE IS A ROSE

Mrs. George L. K. Morris listed a "Miss Rose" as her daughter in the New York *Social Register*. Rose, it turned out later, was a Pekingese. Mrs. Morris explained that when she was filling out her annual form young Rose nudged her ankle. "All right, Rose, I'll put you in, too," promised Mrs. Morris, and she did. The *Register* deadpanned, "Where family matters are concerned, we have to take the word of our subscribers." *August, 1966*

MORRIS, HELEN VAN CORTLANDT is a descendant of Helen Van Cortlandt, who married James Lewis Morris, a Captain in the Revolution and fourth son of Lewis Morris, the signer of the Declaration of Independence. She is a relative of Mrs. Robert Hall McCormick, Jr. (Eleanor R. Morris), whose marriage brought out the Morris history. There are so many people in Philadelphia who claim descent from the signers that New York is pleased, occasionally, to display a similar pedigree. *April 16, 1904*

MORRIS, DR. LEWIS RUTHERFURD There is no young man in New York society in whose veins flows as genuinely good and aristocratic blood as it does in Dr. Morris's. He is a direct descendant of one of the signers of the Declaration of Independence, Lewis Morris. The old family place, called "Butternuts," at Morris, New York, has been in his family in direct line since the time of Queen Anne. He is closely connected with the family of Senator John Kean, the Stuyvesant and Hamilton Fish families, Hamiltons, Gouverneurs, and all whom they have married. *June 14, 1900*

MORRIS, MRS. LEWIS S. (EMILY PELL COSTER) Her house on Wolver Hollow Road, Brookville, originally stood near Dijon. The late Ashbel Barney discovered it, fell in love with it, bought it in December 1926, and had it dismantled and brought over, piece by piece, stone by stone. In due course, Mr. Barney had it re-erected on its present site. The manor, known in France as the Château des Thons, was built in the seventeenth century. *January, 1948*

MORRIS, STUYVESANT FISH, JR. was a great-grandson of President Van Buren. He graduated from Columbia in 1898 and became a member of the Stock Exchange. His father was Dr. Stuyvesant Fish Morris, his mother Ellen J. Van Buren. *May 1, 1925*

MORRISON, CLINTON was the son of Mr. Dorilus Morrison, a pioneer of Minnesota. He was brought to Minneapolis by his father, and before he was twenty one he was engaged in the lumber industry. Since then, he has been associated with most of the large enterprises of the city and amassed a large fortune. A year ago, he presented to Minneapolis property valued at $250,000 for the site of the new Minneapolis Art Museum. *March 29, 1913*

MORSE, SAMUEL F. B. was the grandnephew of the American primitive painter and inventor of the telegraph, Samuel Morse. S.F.B. discouraged a strong association between the two men, for he maintained an un-executive disdain for hard work and perseverance. He once said, "Men do not get along in the world by hard work and perseverance; they keep you from meeting the right people." *June, 1977*

MORTIMER, RICHARD has been building his big house at Tuxedo Park, New York, for some ten years; and to the casual observer, it seems still far from completion. The owner's English origin is plainly discernible throughout the house and grounds, the posts of the two gateways being surmounted by the English lion. The house itself is very large, and reminds one of an old English manor house. At one side of the driveway there is a stone wall, a portion of which, near the house, is decorated with the busts of the Roman emperors. *October 11, 1900*

MORTON, JANE Her departure into business indicates the ambition and initiative of that young woman. She is the daughter of the Mark Mortons of Lake Forest and a sister of Mrs. William E. Swift. She has taken unto herself the Stutz motor car agency in Lake Forest, and having had dashing business cards inscribed and circulated, is now doing a rushing business. She attracted attention from the local barber's union some time ago with her non-union activities as a bobber of heads. Her friends liked her cut so well that they thrust their business upon her. *August 15, 1926*

MORTON, JOY One of the keenest encouragements to planting in Illinois is the Morton arboretum at Lisle founded by Mr. Joy Morton, brother of the late Paul Morton, Secretary of the Navy under President Roosevelt. The Morton family have always specialized in trees, as the family crest of an oak tree indicates. J. Sterling Morton, Secretary of Agriculture under Cleveland and founder of the family fortunes, emigrated to Nebraska as a young man. His famous Nebraska estate, "Arbor Lodge," went to his sons at his death. A few years ago, the family presented the place to the State of Nebraska, and it is being preserved as a horticultural museum and park. *May 15, 1932*

MORTON, LEVI P. The beautiful homes along the Hudson River approach more closely than elsewhere in these United States the character and dignity of great English estates. Noteworthy among these is "Ellerslie," the country residence of the Hon. Levi P. Morton. Ellerslie, situated fifteen miles above Poughkeepsie, at Rhinecliff, covers a thousand acres. The house originally was colonial in architecture, but Mr. Morton has expended one hundred and fifty thousand dollars on the present structure, which is Swiss in design. The largest of the farm buildings is the cow barn and, with its aristocratic occupants, it is far-famed, for Mr. Morton owns four hundred of the choicest Guernsey cows. *August 17, 1901*

MORTON, PAUL was the son of J. Sterling Morton, Secretary of Agriculture during Cleveland's administration. Mr. Morton was Secretary of the Navy during President Roosevelt's administration. He was made President of the Equitable Life Assurance Society of the United States in 1905. *January 28, 1911*

MOULTON, MRS. ARTHUR J. (CATHERINE T. LEWIS) The merry Christmas time had ideal celebration at the home of Mrs. Arthur J. Moulton, 413 Fifth Avenue, who gave a masquerade ball. The musicians placed in the small gallery overlooking the court played many of the melodies of *The Wizard of Oz,* and among the young people in character three of the most amusing were bright Miss Bessie Moulton, as "Dorothy," and Mr. George Kobbe, as the loose-jointed scarecrow, and Mr. Harry Ashmore, as the tin woodsman. These three young people sang a trio, and the scarecrow and the tin woodsman throughout the evening cleverly acted their parts. *January 7, 1905*

MOULTON, BESSIE R., who is the youngest daughter of Mrs. Arthur J. Moulton, and a great-granddaughter of the late Moses Taylor, will be married to Mr. Lloyd Aspinwall, a great-grandson of the late William H. Aspinwall, after whom Aspinwall, the Eastern terminus of the railroad crossing the Isthmus of Panama was named. *December 16, 1905*

MUNN, CHARLES "Mr. Palm Beach." His mother was a Breakers Row cottager, and you can't get any more Palm Beach than that. Charlie's famous definition of a gentleman: "A man who for three generations has pronounced 'to-may-to' 'to-mah-to.'" *January, 1968*

MUNN, ORSON D., of New York, nephew of the late Charles A. Munn, is to succeed his uncle as Editor and Publisher of *The Scientific American.* *May 1, 1924*

MUNROE, MRS. FREDERICK MITCHELL (ELIZABETH LEE BOWLES) was a daughter of the late Samuel Bowles, founder of the *Springfield Republican,* and the wife of Mr. Frederick Mitchell Munroe, formerly Editor of *Brooklyn Life* and at one time of *Town & Country.* *May 6, 1911*

MURPHY, EDGAR GIBBS, as well known as a sharp wit as a good pigeon shot, is about to start for Palm Beach, Florida, to prepare for the inaugural shoot there, under the auspices of the Florida Gun Club. The opening event of the club this winter will be the shooting for a trophy presented by Mr. August Belmont. *January 12, 1907*

MURRAY, THOMAS At one point, there were so many Murrays in Southampton that the resort was known, spitefully, as Murray Bay. Inventor Thomas Murray's estate included a chapel, stables, tennis court, and two swimming pools—one for adults, one for children. The neighbors were fascinated with his pools—his didn't have sand, as theirs did. Murray had invented a way to filter out the sand when salt water is piped in from the ocean. *July, 1975*

MURRAY, MRS. THOMAS Queen of the Murray dynasty of Southampton, she has eleven children. Her husband received three Papal decorations (the world record) and sat on the Atomic Energy Commission. Winters at Windham Mountain, and at her family Catskills ski compounds. *July, 1975*

MURRAY, MR. AND MRS. WILLIAM SPENCER (ELLA DAY RUSH) The bride and bridegroom both belong to families well known in American history. An interesting feature of the wedding is the fact that it is the second union of the two families. On August twenty ninth, 1809, the great-grandfather of the bride, the Hon. Richard Rush, of Philadelphia, distinguished as a statesman and diplomat, married Miss Catherine Eliza Murray, of Annapolis, a great-aunt of the bridegroom. *September 30, 1905*

N

NATHAN, EDGAR J. is President of Congregation Shearith Israel, the congregation founded by the original Sephardic settlers in New York City. The synagogue continues to use the Sephardic rituals derived from Spanish and Portuguese traditions. "The service is as it was," according to Mr. Nathan, "and it's said that if someone from the year 1654 magically appeared here to worship, he would feel completely comfortable." *September, 1987*

NEMOURS, DUCHESSE DE (MARGUERITE WATSON), of an ancient and honorable F. F. V. (First Families of Virginia), annexed a title of the F. F. of France. But as it is, she is only recognized by the cream of endorsement society. The Nemours preserve their ancient seat in the Haute-Savoie, where the Duchess, carefully turned out by Worth, Cartier, and Pond's two creams, was photographed recently with a lamb of a dachshund for the great international endorsement adventure. *May 15, 1931*

NEUHAUS, MR. AND MRS. JOSEPH RICE (MARGARET L. ELDER) The Neuhaus family was established in Texas in the 1840s by the German-born Ludwig Elder Neuhaus. Grandson Hugo—known as the Baron—married the beautiful Kate Rice, the great-niece of Rice University founder William Marsh Rice. The Baron established Houston's first investment banking firm and became President of the Houston Country Club. Joe Neuhaus is an officer of the family-founded investment firm. *September, 1991*

NEWBERRY, TRUMAN H., who went to Washington to be Assistant Secretary of the Navy, is but forty four. He served on the *U.S.S. Yosemite* throughout the Spanish-American War. This warship was manned by the most aristocratic young men from Detroit, who became enthused with patriotism as the result of Mr. Newberry's enthusiasm and rallied round him when he called for volunteers. His father, John Stoughton Newberry, as Provost General of Michigan, did work of the same patriotic sort during the sixties. His grandfather, Oliver Newberry, was a famous steamboat builder, known in the West as "The Commodore of the Lakes." *November 21, 1908*

NEWBOROUGH, LADY (GRACE CARR) is the daughter of the late Colonel Carr, of Kentucky. She married in 1900. She is very fond of her adopted country and of the English people, and is acknowledged to be one of the best dressed women in London. Both Lord and Lady Newborough are devoted to yachting, and they have enjoyed many interesting voyages in their pretty yacht, *Fedora.* *April 15, 1905*

NICHOLS, ALEXANDER R. THOMPSON was the youngest son of the millionaire clergyman Dr. Samuel Nichols and Susan Nexen Warner. Colonel Nichols was a lateral descendant of Sir Richard Nichols, the first English Governor of New York, and the ground on which Trinity Church and graveyard stand was known as "Governor Nichols's Garden." Colonel Nichols's maternal uncle, Effingham Howard Warner, donated the principal amount of money toward building the oldest St. Bartholomew's Church, whose facade was embellished with his coat-of-arms; and the Warner estate, early in the century, owned the ground on which the Grand Central Depot stands. *June 21, 1900*

NICHOLS, MR. AND MRS. CHARLES W. (DR. MARGUERITE SYKES)—CHRYSLER Charles is a director of Allied Singla Inc.—his grandfather co-founded its predecessor, Allied Chemical Company. Peggy, a consulting doctor of chemotherapy at Memorial Sloan-Kettering Hospital and an avid conservationist, is co-founder with Brooke Astor and Mimi Thorne of the women's committee of the Zoological Society. *July, 1986*

NICKEL, MRS. J. LEROY The richest woman in California is Mrs. J. Leroy Nickel, whose father, Henry Miller, the great land owner, just died and left her his entire fortune. No one knows precisely the value of the Miller fortune, but some people estimate it as high as a hundred million. Henry Miller came to this country from Germany as a small boy. He was the greatest land grabber of his time, and he owned several of the large Spanish estates. He could go from Oregon to the extreme southern part of California and always sleep on his own property. *November 20, 1916*

NICOLL, COURTLANDT There was considerable activity and unconfined merriment at Morristown, New Jersey, when the Whippany River Club gave its fall gymkhana on the club polo grounds. Then came the "Dead Man's Race." Prior to the start, there was a grand funeral march to dirge music, each competitor carrying his stuffed "dead man" past the grandstand. Then the contestants mounted ponies and, after circling the track, dismounted, picked up the dead one and rode around once more to the finish line. The glory of this great sport went to Mr. Courtlandt Nicoll and mannequin. *October 26, 1907*

NIVEN, MR. AND MRS. MICHAEL are both native Californians. In fact, he—a descendant of the Dohenys (an old California family that has made many outstanding contributions to the state)—would never want to live anywhere else. "It's all here. In California, you can be anything you want to be, do anything you want to do." *May, 1975*

NOBLE, DAVIDE YULEE is a debutante of the Washington, D.C. set who yet has affiliations with the official world, since her grandfather was the late Senator Yulee, who was at one time President of the Atlantic and Gulf Railroad and established his plantation in 1823. During the Civil War, he served as a member of the Confederate Congress. He served as a United States Senator from Florida from 1845 to 1861. *December 28, 1907*

NORRIE, CHRISTOPHER Good looking, cosmopolitan, socially top drawer, he's studying journalism at New York University, having prepped at St. Marks and Le Rosey. Considering the world of film as a career, Chris is already a very talented young photographer. He shoots in England and at his father's farm in Virginia. *June, 1968*

NORTON, DR. CHARLES ELIOT was a son of Andrews Norton, the scholar and theologian. He was graduated from Harvard in 1846. In 1862, he was married to Miss Susan Sedgwick of the famous Stockbridge family. In 1855, when in Switzerland, he met John Ruskin, who became one of his closest friends. During the sixties, he was associated with James Russell Lowell in editing *The North American Review.* He was professor of history at Harvard from 1847 until 1898. Mr. Richard Norton, the Director of the American School in Rome, and Mr. Eliot Norton, who is a lawyer, are his sons. *October 31, 1908*

NORWEB, MRS. R. HENRY (ELIZABETH GARDNER) lives in the one beautiful lakefront district of Cleveland, Bratenahl. She is President of the Garden Center, Vice President of the Art Institute, and a trustee of the Museums of Art and Natural History. She also raises prize poodles and is an expert on coins. *February, 1960*

NOYES, CROSBY STUART Editor of the *Washington Evening Star,* he made his reputation as a journalist during the Civil War. In his younger days, he traveled in Europe on foot, and later in his career journeyed to all parts of the world. He is survived by three sons, Mr. Theodore W. Noyes, President of the *Evening Star* Newspaper Company; Mr. Frank B. Noyes, Editor and Publisher of the *Chicago Record-Herald* and president of the Associated Press; and Mr. Thomas C. Noyes, news-manager of the *Star. February 29, 1908*

SOON, A HORSELESS CARRIAGE

Lester Norris, member of the executive committee and director of Texaco from 1933 to 1973, and his wife Dellora, a Texaco heiress and its largest stockholder, came from St. Charles, Illinois, to find Naples, Florida, by accident. But they liked it so much, they bought "Keewaydin," five miles of island five miles away. "That was almost thirty years ago, but we've kept it pretty much the same," said Mr. Norris, now a Naples conservationist and philanthropist. "Not too long ago, we added electricity and phone service, but that's as far as I'll go." *February, 1975*

O

OBER, ROBERT was killed in action in France. Lieutenant Ober was one of four brothers overseas with the American Expeditionary Force. Lieutenant Robert Ober graduated from Princeton and afterwards went to Winnipeg, Manitoba, to engage in wheat brokerage. When war was declared, he returned to Baltimore, where with his brothers and five cousins—also all now in France—he was largely instrumental in the formation of Battery A. *November 10, 1918*

OBOLENSKY, PRINCE SERGE, better known by his title of Colonel, earned as a parachutist in the U.S. Army during World War II, was one of the city's most dashing social figures for decades. Serge was married to Alice Astor, and although they were later divorced, he remained a close friend of her brother Vincent. Vincent put Serge in charge of public relations for one of his properties, the St. Regis Hotel. The Colonel made the hotel the hottest place in town, and later did the same for the Sherry-Netherland Hotel, with its famous Russian nightclub downstairs. The parties the Colonel gave and the international crowd he entertained became part of New York social legend. *March, 1984*

O'DUNNE, MRS. EUGENE (ELISE MANNING REARDON), whose home is in Baltimore, is the daughter of the late George Evett Reardon, a great-grandniece of John Quincy Adams, and a great-granddaughter of Joshua Johnson, Consul General to England. She was married (by Cardinal Gibbons) about five years ago, to Mr. Eugene O'Dunne, the present Deputy State's Attorney of Baltimore, the son of the late Edmond F. O'Dunne, the one-time Chief Justice of Arizona, who was knighted by Pius IX and created a count by Leo XIII. *August 1, 1908*

OELRICHS, BLANCHE ("MICHAEL STRANGE") took her first serious step on a New York stage in the Strindberg play produced by The Stagers. Her somewhat unsuccessful attempts at a career, which her husband, Mr. John Barrymore, so signally adorns, were begun last summer, when she appeared sporadically in Salem, Massachusetts. This is her only experience as an actress. But she is an undaunted and charming egoist. *April 1, 1926*

OELRICHS, MRS. HERMAN (THERESA "TESSIE" FAIR) Her fete will go down in history as the event par excellence of the season. "Rose Cliff," Mrs. Oelrichs' exquisite summer home, never looked more beautiful. The house is a replica of La Petite Trianon, only on a much larger scale. The cotillion was led by Mr. Harry Lehr and Mr. Elisha Dyer, Jr. An unusual idea was the "butterfly conflict." Tissue paper butterflies with iridescent bodies, to which were attached burrs, were thrown at the dancers in great numbers, immediately sticking to the pretty frocks and making quite a sensation. This throwing of butterflies should become as popular here as confetti throwing is in Rome. It is much more effective. *September 12, 1903*

OELRICHS, HILDEGARDE is renowned for her skill and pluck in the hunting field. When in Scotland at "Balmacaan," Mr. Bradley Martin's place, she brought down a large stag with her rifle, and last winter won golden opinions among the mighty hunters of the wild West by shooting a grizzly bear in the Rocky Mountains. *October 5, 1887*

OGDEN, HERBERT GOUVERNEUR is a son of Herbert Gouverneur Ogden, known throughout the country as an expert in topography; in 1870, he was with the first naval exploring expedition to the Isthmus of Darien, and in 1893 was in charge of the party that determined the international boundary between British Columbia and Alaska. The Ogdens "date back" to John Ogden, first Governor of New Jersey, so the family history is long. *April 13, 1907*

OGDEN, ROBERT C. was philanthropist, educator, author, and soldier. From 1885 until 1907, he was a partner of Mr. John Wanamaker. Mr. Ogden was also widely known as a foremost worker in the field of education in the South, for his interest in the uplifting of the Negro and his advocacy and support of the Hampton Institute in Virginia. For a long period, he was President of the Southern Educational Board and a trustee of Tuskegee. *August 16, 1913*

OLCOTT, GLADYS solemnized her marriage to Jean de Pendrill Waddington, C.G.M.O. of the French Cuirassiers. Though English originally, the Waddingtons have been for two centuries citizens of France. Mr. Waddington is a grand-nephew of the late William H. Waddington, for ten years French Ambassador to the Court of St. James, and a grandson of the late Richard Waddington, a one-time Premier of France. His widow, now living in France, was Miss Mary Alsop King of New York. Mr. and Mrs. Charles Waddington, of France, are the bridegroom's parents. Mrs. Waddington, was a Miss Harjes, her father the late John Harjes, founder of Morgan & Harjes. *November 1, 1922*

OLIN, STEPHEN HENRY was one of the veterans of the New York Bar, served for a time as acting President of Wesleyan University, and was a member of many genealogical societies, having descended from French Huguenot stock. His first wife, previously Alice Barlow, died in 1882. In 1903, he married Emeline Harriman Dodge, daughter of Oliver Harriman. *September 1, 1925*

OLYPHANT, ROBERT MORRISON Up to the time of his retirement in 1903, he had been President of the Delaware and Hudson for twenty years. The oldest alumnus of Columbia University, Mr. Olyphant was the grandson of Dr. David Olyphant, who came to Charleston, South Carolina, soon after the battle of Culloden and who, in 1776, was appointed Director General of Hospitals. *May 20, 1918*

ONASSIS, MRS. ARISTOTLE (JACQUELINE LEE BOUVIER)—KENNEDY came out as a young girl at an afternoon tea followed by dancing at Hammersmith Farm in Newport. Her brother Jamie was born several months before, and he shared the honors. Invitations read, "To meet Miss Jacqueline Lee Bouvier and Master James Lee Auchincloss." *June, 1969*

ORSINI, PRINCE AND PRINCESS DOMINICO (LAURA SCHWARTZ)—ROWAN are coming West to spend a part of the winter at the home of the princess in Pasadena. It will be the first visit to the United States of the prince, who belongs to an old and famous family in Rome. The daughter of Princess Orsini, Mrs. Robert H. McAdoo, and Mr. McAdoo will come West, too. Mrs. McAdoo was Miss Lorraine Rowan and was married a few weeks before her mother's marriage to Prince Orsini. *November 1, 1924*

ORTHWEIN, ADOLPHUS BUSCH, JR., a lawyer and developer, is the President of the Atlanta Polo Club. He founded the organization, now one of the leading young clubs in the country. Three years ago, the 2-goaler also completed a private field at his Polo Place housing development, where residents and local club members play in a 100-acre wooded setting overlooking the Chattahoochee River. *January, 1987*

ORTHWEIN, MRS. JAMES (ROMAINE "TOODY" DAHLGREN PIERCE)—SIMPSON—MILFORD-HAVEN Although her great-great-grandfather was first Governor of Missouri, it was marriage to the prominent businessman-sportsman that brought Toody Orthwein to St. Louis. Now she lives with as much panache in Huntley Village as she did in New York and in London (when she was the Marchioness of Milford Haven). *March, 1970*

ORTHWEIN, PETER B. serves as President of the Greenwich Polo Club. He is the family's most prominent high-goaler—"as good as a lot of pros," says Dolph Orthwein, Jr. Peter's Airstream team, named for the classic trailers produced by his company, $135-million-a-year Thor Industries, competes at Palm Beach in the winter and Saratoga and at Greenwich in summer. *January, 1987*

OSBORN, HENRY FAIRFIELD is one of the most outstanding figures in the whole field of American education. He is descended from a prominent family of Revolutionary stock and with means and position (Dr. Osborn is almost unique among Columbia professors in being listed in that sociological index, the *Social Register*). Early associated with the American Museum of Natural History, he is one of the men to whom its remarkable growth is largely due. He was also one of the group actively identified with the foundation of the New York Zoological Park in the Bronx. *October 20, 1921*

OSBORN, MRS. HENRY FAIRFIELD (LUCRETIA T. PERRY) Mrs. Osborn and Mrs. Ralph Sanger, her daughter, are doing faithful and arduous work for the historical tableaux that will be given on December twenty ninth in New York. There are to be twelve tableaux, each showing a living portrait of some celebrated American. Mrs. Clarence Mackay will appear as her ancestress, Lady Kitty Duer, and it is hoped that in the character of Commodore Matthew Calbraith Perry, one of his descendants will pose. His grandchildren, who are of the Belmont, Hone, Rodgers, and Tiffany families, will be seen as middies. Mrs. Arthur Iselin, Eleanor Jay, will represent an ancestress at the French court. *December 18, 1909*

OTIS, MRS. HARRISON GRAY (ELIZA A. WETHERBY) is one of Boston's very "best citizens," besides having been all her life a leader of its best society. Mrs. Otis, in her report of what the Relief Committee have done for the volunteers in the field, states that they have made, collected, and distributed some sixty thousand articles for the soldiers' comfort. *November 23, 1861*

OTIS, MR. AND MRS. WILLIAM are among those who bring the "surprises" of Colorado Springs most strikingly to the visiting stranger. Mrs. Otis is the niece of Senator Goddard, granddaughter of the Governor of Maine, and, it sometimes seems, is related to most of well-known New England. The doorway of the Otis townhouse is copied from the old residence in Portland, from panel to fan-light, where Mrs. Otis' family lived neighbor to Longfellow. Before a fireplace lies the mounted skin of a mountain lion they shot on their place in Pine Valley, where they love to spend weeks at a time in the charming little cabin or picnic in the open camp. *March 15, 1932*

OWEN, MR. AND MRS. KENNETH DALE (JANE BLAFFER) Houstonian Jane Blaffer Owen is the wife of Kenneth Dale Owen, geologist, oilman, cattle and horse-breeder, and a direct descendant of Robert Dale Owen, a Scots social reformer and leader of the second New Harmony, Indiana, utopian experiment. Mrs. Owen was among the first to recognize the town's future potential as a cultural center. Today, with its Harmonist structures, restored hostelries, rustic restaurants, and riveting contemporary buildings and sculptures by such modern masters as Philip Johnson, Richard Meier, and Jacques Lipchitz, New Harmony is decidedly a one-of-a-kind town. *December, 1981*

P

PACKER, HARRIET P. It is to her family that Brooklyn's famous school for girls, the Packer Collegiate Institute, owes its permanent establishment. When the Brooklyn Female Academy that had been opened seven years earlier was destroyed by fire in 1853, Miss Packer's mother gave $65,000 to rebuild the school as a memorial to her husband. At the time, this was the largest gift ever made for the advancement of the higher education of women. *December 4, 1909*

PAGET, SIR ARTHUR HENRY AND LADY (MARY FISKE "MINNIE" STEVENS) Minnie, Lady Paget, was one of the most prominent social figures of two continents in the past decade. She was born in Boston, and her father accumulated his means in the mercantile and hotel business. Lady Paget's career was based on an extraordinary amount of personal charm and an unusually bright mind. She was immediately popular with almost all who met her and became a social figure in New York and London. Lady Paget was active during the World War and, during the time Sir Arthur was British Minister in Belgrade, she made herself beloved for her services in the organization of hospital work in the first and second Balkan wars. *June 10, 1919*

PAINE, MRS. C. HAMILTON has, during her comparatively short residence in Paris, acquired a position as a leader of society which has hardly ever been attained by any American woman. The most distinguished people crowd her salons on her reception days, and it is a notable fact that some of the best French families are constant visitors at her charming home on the Avenue du Bois de Boulogne. *April 24, 1909*

PAINE, GEORGINA Her young friends were invited to a dance given at Copley Hall by her father, General Charles Jackson Paine, who owned the three defenders of the *America*'s Cup—the *Puritan, Mayflower,* and *Volunteer.* He is a great-grandson of Robert Treat Paine, one of the signers of the Declaration of Independence. *December 28, 1907*

PALMER, COURTLANDT At the second popular concert at the Arts Building in Bar Harbor, Maine, Mr. Courtlandt Palmer won the hearts of his audience. No artist at the new building has received a warmer welcome. Mr. Palmer, who is Mrs. Robert Abbe's son and who has studied both in Rome and in New York, played with much feeling and expression. It was a popular concert given outside the regular course, so that the townspeople might have a chance to see the new building; but the audience was most satisfactorily aristocratic, as Mrs. Abbe is one of the very pillars of Bar Harbor society. *August 17, 1907*

PALMER, MRS. JOHN S. (DAISY DYER) is the wife of television's popular sportscaster, Bud Palmer. She is the daughter of the Walter Gurnee Dyers, of "Farmlands," Newport. The Dyers are year-round residents of the beautiful old city, and both their families have been prominent there for several generations. Mrs. Dyer was Betty Tailer, daughter of the late T. Suffern Tailer, who built the country's most spectacular private golf course on his Newport estate early in the century. *September, 1958*

PALMER, POTTER of Chicago has a stud of six horses at Long Branch, New Jersey—five blacks and a bay. He drives a four-in-hand that excites the envy and admiration of all. *August 21, 1867*

PALMER, MRS. POTTER (BERTHA HONORÉ) She was the acknowledged leader of Chicago society most of her life and a prominent figure in the life of the big social centers she crossed—New York, Newport, London, and Paris. She married Mr. Potter Palmer in 1871, then regarded as the wealthiest resident of Chicago. In 1891, she was elected President of the Board of Lady Managers to the World's Columbian Exposition. Her success, resulting from her tact and executive ability, resulted in her appointment as the only woman member of the National Commission for the Paris Exposition of 1900, and thus she became an international figure. *May 20, 1918*

PALMER, MR. AND MRS. POTTER II (PAULINE KOHLSAAT) live a quiet, dignified life in an Astor Street, Chicago, apartment filled with priceless jade. Mrs. Palmer is more interested in art than in society (the Palmers have given many paintings to the Art Institute) and is active in the Needlework Guild and the Antiquarian Society. *April, 1939*

PALMER, THOMAS WITHERELL was a diplomatist and financier and at one time United States Senator. Among his many public gifts was a tract of one hundred and forty acres a short distance north of Chicago, now known as Palmer Park. Mr. Palmer could have had a Cabinet position under President Harrison but preferred to accept the position of Envoy Extraordinary and Minister Plenipotentiary to Spain, in which capacity he served from 1889 to 1892, and upon his return to the United States was made President of the World's Fair at Chicago. *June 7, 1913*

PALMER, COLONEL WILLIAM JACKSON He was the founder of Colorado Springs and the chief benefactor of Colorado College. When the Civil War broke out, he recruited a company of the Fifteenth Pennsylvania Cavalry, of which he was made Captain. In 1871, he and his associates laid out Colorado Springs as a residence city for health seekers. His home for many years was "Glen Eyrie," near the

Garden of the Gods, at Colorado Springs. He built a mansion on the model of Blenheim Palace. Wishing to see the members of his old regiment once more, he invited them to visit him in 1907, and 264 attended the reunion at his expense, which amounted to about $40,000. *March 20, 1909*

PARK, MR. AND MRS. DARRAGH, JR. (SALLIE MELLON) Another 1938 individualist who took her matrimonial project into her own graceful hands was Mr. and Mrs. Charles Henry Mellon's daughter Sallie, who came out last year and this May married Darragh Park, Jr. A tulle type and knowing it, she wisely took to a cloudbank of the fabulous stuff in her wedding gown and topped it off with yards of family rose point. She's one of the few brides of the season who decided to collect her bridesmaids for a spinster dinner when the groom called out his ushers to celebrate. Sallie Mellon Park herself decided on a linen trousseau of white, the simplest flat silver in the house of Gorham, and cupboard after cupboard of Steuben glass. *June, 1938*

IN CHICAGO, THEY OPEN MUSEUMS INSTEAD

Mrs. Walter Paepcke is the nearest thing Chicago has to a *grande dame*. "I love Chicago, but I hate the suburbs. The amusing people all live in town. Lake Forest is death in the afternoon. Everyone has a marble entry hall, everybody goes to Hobe Sound or Palm Beach, they all play bridge, swim at the country club, and they're all equally rich. The Lake Forest people have pots of money, but they just sit on it. We hear about it only when they die—then we find out they've been collecting Picassos under their beds." *February, 1972*

PARKER, MRS. JAMES HENRY, President of the New York Chapter of the United Daughters of the Confederacy, has just returned from the Charleston Exposition, where she was the recipient of many honors. On the trip North, the party were received at the White House by President Roosevelt. It is especially appropriate that Mrs. Parker should receive this tribute, as she is a representative Southerner and one of the leaders in New York where Southern interests are concerned. *May 3, 1902*

PARKER, JAMES V. is beloved by the lassies of all ages! Dignified grandmammas tell their debutante granddaughters that they did not consider themselves properly introduced unless asked by Mr. Parker as a partner. His stately gallantry is most charming in the present day. Mr. Parker's cottage on Merton Road, in Newport, is famous for its red rambler roses. Last summer, an electric landaulet was added to Mr. Parker's equipages, and this superseded his beautiful victoria and horses, which have been so much admired. *August 10, 1907*

PARKER, STEPHEN HILLS, the artist, is Mrs. Jules de Neufville's brother. He now has a studio in Florence, but New Yorkers remember him, when his sister was a very young girl famed

for beauty, as a bachelor equally famed for a fascinating personality. He was a frequent visitor to Stockbridge and Lenox, Massachusetts, then, as now, the "literary center" and meeting place of clever people. Mr. Parker is best known in this country perhaps for his painting of St. Sebastian in New York's Cathedral of St. John the Divine. *October 17, 1903*

PARROTT, EMILIE married Mr. Wilberforce Williams at "Baywood," the old family home in San Mateo of the bride's grandmother, the late Mrs. Abby M. Parrott. It was from this house that all the Parrott daughters of the last generation—Lady Archibald Douglas-Dick, Mrs. Robert Young Hayne, Mrs. Joseph A. Donohoe, the late Comtesse de la Lande, the late Comtesse Christien de Guigne, and the late Mrs. Albert E. Payson—were claimed as brides. *April 15, 1924*

PARROTT, MADELEINE belongs to an interesting family. She is a descendant of Robert Parker Parrott, who invented and perfected the Parrott system of rifled guns and projectiles first used in the Battle of Bull Run. "Arden," which Mr. E. H. Harriman purchased at Tuxedo, was the old Parrott estate, a part of which, including the homestead, has been retained by the family. *April 27, 1907*

PARSONS, JOHN E. was one of the most eminent lawyers in the state of New York. His most important work was in connection with the organization and building of the American Sugar Refining Company. For several years, he was President of the Board of Trustees of the Brick Presbyterian Church. He was on the committee called to revise the Presbyterian creed. *February 10, 1915*

PARSONS, SCHUYLER LIVINGSTON had a number of delightful parties by way of introducing to his friends "the sweet little, neat little" green house recently erected on Pleasure Island near Islip, Long Island, which looks as though it had been transplanted bodily from a forest where it might have grown, green from cellar to roof tree. Someone has described his little house as a place in which old globes, old books, old chintzes, old furniture, and new magazines, fresh flowers, and open fires abound. *July 1, 1924*

PATTERSON, ELINOR The opening of *The Miracle* in Chicago almost revivified the dying winter season. It was Elinor Patterson's night, with her father and mother, Mr. and Mrs. Joseph Medill Patterson, entertaining four boxes of guests in the back of the horseshoe. Elinor Patterson, who, two short years ago in her debut season, sat many a time with a gay group of debutantes and beaux on the other side of the footlights in the Auditorium, came into her own in her own home town. *March 1, 1926*

PATTERSON, GEORGE STUART is a son of Mr. C. Stuart Patterson, of "Gracehill," Chestnut Hill. In 1897, he captained the Philadelphia cricket team in England, and for many years he has been considered one of the best players of the game in America. *October 31, 1903*

PATTERSON, LAURA, who, for the past two generations, has been a prominent figure in Newport and Baltimore society, was the last of her branch of the distinguished Maryland family of the name. The late Madame Bonaparte (Betsy Patterson), who married Jerome Bonaparte, youngest brother of the great Napoleon, was her aunt. Miss Patterson's immediate relatives were at one time the principal property owners in Baltimore. Her paternal grandfather, William Patterson, was reckoned by his intimate friend General George Washington as the richest man in the United States. *May 10, 1918*

PATTERSON, ROBERT W. He began his journalistic career on the *Chicago Times* and later became an editor on the *Chicago Tribune.* From the position of Telegraph Editor, Mr. Patterson was promoted to that of Managing Editor. While he held the latter position, Mr. Patterson married Miss Eleanor Medill, daughter of Joseph Medill, after whose death he became Editor-in-chief of the *Chicago Tribune. April 9, 1910*

PATTON, MR. AND MRS. GEORGE S., JR. (BEATRICE BANNING AYER) Even the most ardent advocate of peace must confess that a military wedding is a little more picturesque than any other kind. Such was the opinion when Miss Beatrice Banning Ayer was married to Lieutenant George S. Patton, Jr., Fifteenth U.S. Cavalry, at St. John's Church, Beverly Farms, for the bridegroom and the ushers wore the dress uniform of their rank. Many of the men guests were also from the Army or Navy, and after the benediction the ushers drew their sabres, raised them above their heads, and formed an arch of steel over the pathway of the newly wedded pair as they left the chancel. *June 4, 1910*

PAYNE, COLONEL OLIVER H. will start for a European cruise on his new steam yacht *Aphrodite.* This handsome vessel is three hundred and three feet, over all. She carries three masts and is square-rigged on the two forward sticks; her far-reaching spars will spread no less than seventeen thousand square feet of canvas; and, while forced draught may push her to seventeen knots an hour, her ordinary cruising speed will be fifteen knots. *February 8, 1899*

PAYSON, MRS. CHARLES SHIPMAN (JOAN WHITNEY), spectator sportswoman extraordinary, shifts from baseball diamond to paddock and track without missing an inning or skipping a race—keeping score of both simultaneously with the aid of a transistor. New York baseball fans find her worthy of the Hall of Fame, for she has given them back a club of their own, the Mets. Obviously, she is a native New Yorker. *September, 1967*

PAYSON, MRS. CHARLES SHIPMAN (VIRGINIA KRAFT) Celebrated international sportswoman, big-game hunter, and current owner of more than one hundred thoroughbreds, Virginia Payson divides her time among Sands Point, Long Island, Hobe Sound, Saratoga, and Maine; that is, when she's not visiting her broodmares in Florida or watching her thoroughbreds in Lexington, Kentucky. *August, 1985*

PEABODY, ELIZABETH Of the three daughters of the celebrated Dr. Peabody of Salem, only one survives, Elizabeth, who is one of the most intellectual women of the century. Her sister Mary married Horace Mann, and her sister Sophia became the wife of Nathaniel Hawthorne. A mere family reunion would have brought her into contact with some of the finest minds in the country. *August 31, 1867*

PEABODY, ENDICOTT ("CHUB"), Harvard '42, was that college's last legitimate All-American football player until the 1974 squad. Called "the baby-faced assassin" in college, Chub Peabody became Democratic Governor of Massachusetts at the same time that his mother, Mary Parkman Peabody, was going on civil rights marches and his sister, Marietta Tree, was in official capacities at the United Nations. *April, 1976*

THE COOK WEARS EMERALDS

Mrs. Potter Palmer's livery is the swellest in Newport. The doorman presents himself with knickerbockers and patent leather slippers with gilt buckles, and his fine black silk hose are relieved with a wide gilt garter just below the knee. But this is not all that a guest observes at the door of the summer home of the Palmers, for, if he will glance beyond to the end of the spacious hall, he will very likely see the large and stately butler strutting about, if possible very much more gorgeously attired than this subordinate who has allowed one to enter. *August 26, 1896*

PEABODY, FRANCIS STUYVESANT, of Hinsdale, Illinois, died of a stroke of apoplexy while taking part in the opening hunt of the New Mayslake Hunt Club, recently organized near a clubhouse near the Peabody estate at Hinsdale. He was found dead, with his favorite horse, Dunbar, standing over his body, waiting for help to come. His Hinsdale estate, "Mayslake," was one of the finest in the country, while his collection of original manuscripts of Robert Louis Stevenson was well known among collectors. *October 1, 1922*

ENOUGH IS ENOUGH

Mrs. Henry Parish gave the wedding which united Eleanor and Franklin D. Roosevelt. Summering among the sixty families of Newport, she has continued to play hostess and sympathetic friend. But this winter, as the last disinterested supporters of the New Deal began to wane, Mrs. Parish's butler went solemnly to the telephone with a long list of her acquaintances. As each house answered, the person at the receiver heard this simple statement: "Mrs. Parish wants you to know that she is no longer in sympathy with the New Deal." *March, 1938*

PEABODY, GEORGE LEE was a graduate of Harvard, class of '86 and well known as a polo player. One of his brothers is the Rev. S. Endicott Peabody, and he was a member of a Boston family noted for many generations for intellectual achievements. *February 25, 1911*

PEABODY, JOSEPH Among the late arrivals at Hot Springs, Virginia, from Boston are Mr. and Mrs. S. Endicott Peabody. That genial bon vivant and raconteur, Mr. Joseph Peabody, a brother of Mr. Endicott Peabody, is with them. He just waited in New York long enough to see his friends of many years, the de Reszke brothers, off for Europe. Mr. Peabody speaks French like a native and leads the gaiety in the little colony of Dinard in France each summer. He is a Boston product of which that city is justly proud. *May 11, 1901*

PEABODY, LAWRENCE CARLETON II For him and his family, living old-world style in a grand Victorian gingerbread palace in Port-au-Prince, Haiti, is all very real and has been since 1960. Peabody's ancestors had been coming to Haiti since the 18th century, when they started the Plymouth Rope Company there. The Peabodys fell in love with the great house the first time they saw it and bought it immediately. Larry says, "It works so beautifully for the jungle we live in and as a backdrop for our collection of Haitian art and antiques from around the world." *January, 1976*

PEABODY, POLLY At 22, Polly Peabody is the first American woman to make a war reputation. At five, her governess took her to Paris to join her mother and stepfather, Henry Grew Crosby, exotic poet, nephew of Mrs. J. P. Morgan. At seventeen, she spent a New York winter with her mother at Delmonico's, made a formal debut among Whitneys and Harrimans. Last summer Polly worked at a talent agency. Over weekends, she became a crack shot under tutelage of Baron Bror von Blixen. With a group of Yale surgeons, Polly and the Swedish baron later organized a field hospital unit for Finland. *June, 1940*

PECK, THOMAS BLOODGOOD was a direct descendant of William Peck, who came to this country from London in the year 1627 and subsequently became one of the founders of the New Haven Colony. During his business days, Mr. Peck was interested in fire insurance. He was President of the Port Chester Savings and a trustee of the House of Mercy. *May 25, 1912*

PECKHAM, WILLIAM GIBBS, well-known lawyer and founder of *The Harvard Advocate,* died at his home in Valley View, Westfield, New Jersey. In 1914, he married Miss Marian Wheelock, a descendant of the Wheelock who founded Dartmouth College. *May 15, 1924*

PEIRCE, HERBERT H. D., third Assistant Secretary of State, who has been aptly dubbed "the Chesterfield of the administration," has been delegated the nation's official host at Portsmouth, where the world-talked-about Russo-Japanese peace conference begins its sittings. Mr. Peirce was for seven years secretary of our legation at St. Petersburg and is, therefore, well acquainted with the intricacies of Russian court etiquette. He is a Harvard man, a linguist, and was in France appointed a commander of the French Legion of Honor. *August 5, 1905*

PELL, REV. ALFRED DUANE, descendant of one of New York's oldest families, was ordained a priest of the Protestant Episcopal Church in the Cathedral of St. John the Divine and was shortly afterward appointed to be rector of the Church of the Resurrection. He was well known as a collector of old silver and rare china. *April 1, 1924*

PELL, CARRIE CHEEVER, who was married last week, had, among other things in her trousseau, twenty four pairs of different colored shoes to match the same number of dresses. *March 6, 1867*

PELL, SENATOR AND MRS. CLAIBORNE (NUALA O'DONNELL) The first American Pells settled at Pelham Manor, New York, in 1672; William Claiborne, the Senator's other namesake and the father of generations of Southern leaders, settled in Virginia in 1621. The Senator's wife, Nuala, has among her ancestors the Carrolls of Maryland, the Chews of Pennsylvania, and the Lees of Virginia. A portrait in their Washington home shows young Pell with his father, Herbert Claiborne Pell, a Congressman and foreign minister. *October, 1986*

PELL, CLARENCE C. This year, for the tenth time, Mr. Clarence C. Pell won the Amateur Racquets Championship of the United States, defeating in the final match his ancient rival, Mr. Stanley G. Mortimer, in three straight games at the Racquet Club in New York. In addition to his extraordinary record in the singles, Mr. Pell, playing with Mr. Mortimer, has won the doubles championship nine times. *April 1, 1931*

PELL, ELEANOR LIVINGSTON married Mr. Charles Harris Phelps in St. Thomas church in New York. The bride is the only child of John Augustus Pell, a direct descendant from Lord Pell, to whom was granted the manor of Pelham in the county of Westchester. The groom is the direct lineal descendant of the old Puritan William Phelps, one of the earliest settlers of the Massachusetts colony. *February 13, 1878*

PELL, ISABEL TOWNSEND, one of New York's younger set, has relinquished the byways of pure social amusement for a serious and successful career in the real estate world. This is not surprising, since Miss Pell's forebears have been engaged in buying and selling Manhattan since its early days. *September 15, 1928*

PELL, JOHN H. G. The most faithfully restored fort in America, Ticonderoga, is a beloved colonial treasure in spit-and-polish order. Were it not, however, for the bulldog determination of four generations of the Pell family, not a stone of Ticonderoga would be in place today. William Pell, importer of mahogany and marble, loved and bought the property in 1820. Today, John H. G. Pell is President of the Fort Ticonderoga Association, and in his tenure has added many acres of surrounding lands which once served as peripheral defenses. Some twenty six Pells are now members of that association, equaling almost a regiment. *March, 1982*

PELL, SAMUEL OSGOOD, whose recent expedition to the Arctic searched for treasure on an island in Baffin's Bay, is the well-known real estate man. The voyage of the *Neptune* was most successful, although gold was not found; but a valuable cargo of furs and walrus ivory was secured, and the captain and the crew of

the *Algerine,* which had been caught in the ice near Bylot Island, were rescued. Mr. Pell comes of a family of brothers interested in outdoor sports and adventures of all kinds. There is Mr. Theodore Roosevelt Pell, who has just distinguished himself in tennis and in athletics, and Mr. S.H.P. Pell, who is a great traveler. These brothers are the sons of the late John Howland Pell. They have all been identified with the different amateur sporting events on Long Island, where they have their summer home. *October 12, 1912*

MISS PAUL'S HEART WAS NOT A-FLUTTER

At Mary Astor Paul's debut in Philadelphia in 1906, her father, James Paul, had imported some ten thousand exotic butterflies from Brazil that were let loose on the guests at a given signal. The hoped-for effect was somewhat dimmed by the fact that many of the creatures had died in the excessive heat, and the deluge of dead insects falling into food and drink was hardly romantic. *November, 1958*

PELL, MRS. WALDEN (ORLEANA REDWOOD ELLERY) was for twenty years a prominent member of the American colony in Paris and a steadfast friend of young women seeking an artistic education in the French capital. She belonged to the well-known Ellery family, of Rhode Island. She was married in 1836 to Walden Pell, a member of the historic Pell family, and took an active part in New York society. *December 27, 1899*

PENFIELD, MR. AND MRS. FREDERICK COURTLAND (ANNE WEIGHTMAN WALKER) President Wilson sent to the Senate the nomination of Mr. Penfield to be Ambassador to Austria-Hungary. He was formerly a newspaper man, but he has served the government as Vice-consul in London and as Consul General and diplomatic agent in Egypt. Both Mr. Penfield and his wife are Catholics, and he has been decorated by the Pope with the Grand Cross of St. Gregory the Great in acknowledgment of generous support of Catholic educational and charitable work. Besides his Papal honors, Mr. Penfield has been decorated by the Sultan of Turkey, the Khedive of Egypt, and with the Cross of the Legion of Honor by the French Government. *July 19, 1913*

PENNOYER, PAUL GEDDES is the son of a wealthy department store owner. He first entered the University of California, and later went to Harvard, graduating there in 1914. He had a short diplomatic career during his sophomore year at Harvard, when he was granted leave of absence to serve as secretary to Mr. John W. Garrett, then Minister to Argentina. His eldest brother, Richard Pennoyer, is now second secretary of the American Embassy at London. His younger brother, Sheldon Pennoyer, is a painter, who received his training at the Ecole des Beaux Arts in Paris. *May 10, 1916*

PENNOYER, PETER Great-grandson of J. P. Morgan, he is an architect with Moore, Pennoyer & Turino and summers in Mishaum Point. Extensive European travels help to inspire his architectural talents. *September, 1987*

PENROSE, SPENCER Brother of the famous Senator Boies Penrose from Pennsylvania, Spencer Penrose would be a significant figure in any environment. Dark, magnificently built, and in splendid condition, he has a touch of the Orient in the drawing of his eyes and more than a little of the eastern potentate about his manner. Penrose is one of the makers of Colorado Springs. He it was who laid out Broadmoor, a fashionable residence neighborhood, built the new Broadmoor Hotel, added a lovely building to the group which makes up Fountain Valley School, and founded the Cooking Club. *March 15, 1932*

PEPPER, DR. WILLIAM, son of the late Dr. William Pepper, who was Provost of the University of Pennsylvania and one of Philadelphia's most eminent physicians, is dean of the faculty of medicine and assistant professor of clinical pathology in the University of Pennsylvania. Dr. Pepper's mother, Mrs. Frances Sergeant Pepper, was a granddaughter of Commodore Oliver Hazard Perry, hero of the battle of Lake Erie in the War of 1812. *October 20, 1918*

PERKINS, ALICE, daughter of the late Mr. and Mrs. Moncure Perkins, granddaughter of the late Colonel Langhorne, of Virginia, niece of our Mrs. Charles Dana Gibson, of Lady Astor, Mrs. Paul Phipps, and Mrs. Robert Brand, has become the bride of the Honorable Reginald Winn of London at St. James's Church, Piccadilly. *April 15, 1924*

PERKINS, ISABEL The richest little girl in the world is the seven year-old daughter of Captain George H. Perkins of the Navy. She is worth seven million dollars in her own name, the amount having been left her recently by her grandfather, William F. Weld, of Boston. Mr. Weld was the father of the little girl's mother, and when he died, four heirs, including the child, came into possession of the bulk of his fortune, twenty eight million dollars. Twenty thousand dollars annually is to be used in caring for the little millionaire heiress until she reaches the legal age and claims her millions. *June 18, 1884*

PERRY, JOHN MOORE is a son of Mr. Oliver Hazard Perry, who is well known as an artist and a member of the family that is kin to the two great Commodores. The senior Mr. Perry was born in Newport, Rhode Island. His relatives include Mrs. John La Farge, wife of the distinguished artist; Mr. Grant La Farge, the architect; and Thomas Sergeant Perry, at one time the Editor of *The North American Review.* Like the majority of the Perrys, he, too, was born in Newport, Rhode Island. *May 28, 1910*

PETER, ARMISTEAD III Washington blue bloods adore Georgetown. It is, for some, the only place to live. This probably stems from the fact that so many of the descendants of the original Georgetowners have roots there—families such as the Peters, whose ancestral home, "Tudor Place," was built in 1815 and has been in the Peter family ever since. The original occupants were Thomas Peter, a tobacco broker, and his wife, Martha Parke Custis, granddaughter of Martha Washington. Armistead Peter III, the present owner of Tudor Place, lives a quiet and private life. *September, 1975*

PETERS, ELEANOR HARTSHORN is a granddaughter of Mrs. Richard Peters of Atlanta, where the Peters family has always stood for what is best and highest in furthering the public good. The late Richard Peters, the grandfather of Miss Peters, went to Atlanta in 1837. He is numbered among the pioneer citizens who did much towards giving Atlanta its start toward great wealth. *December 11, 1909*

PETERS, HARRY T. The Master of the Meadow Brook is a sportsman and bibliophile, whose successes have been many with horses and hounds and who is the owner of one of the outstanding collections of sporting items existing today. *January 15, 1928*

PEW, J. HOWARD, the older of two brothers, and an elder of the Presbyterian Church, was best known socially for his dinner dances, at which no alcohol was served and at which many a guest spent the evening outside, fetching drinks from the car trunk. Joseph N., his brother, played some golf, but most of his time was spent disposing of his enormous assets, of which the lion's share ultimately went to the Pew Memorial Trust, one of the Pew Charitable Trusts, collectively the second-largest charitable trust in the U.S. *September, 1992*

PEW, JOSEPH, SR. was the youngest of ten children of a Western Pennsylvania farm family that occasionally assisted runaway slaves before the Civil War. In the 1870s, Joseph headed for the nearby oil fields. But while other fortune hunters scouted for oil, Joseph latched onto the natural gas escaping from the oil wells. He designed a pump capable of driving the natural gas hundreds of miles through pipelines, built a network of pipelines, and made a fortune. His children were also technical geniuses whose rare ability to work together often enabled their Sun Oil Company to move faster than its competition. *May, 1978*

PHELPS, MR. AND MRS. HARRIS The present home of Mr. and Mrs. Harris Phelps was once the residence in Paris of the King and Queen of Hanover. It is one of the most magnificent as well as one of the most artistic in the city. During many years, Mr. Harris Phelps has been a collector of tapestries, bronzes, pictures, porcelain, and art treasures of different kinds. His library is a notable example of order and care, where one finds everything card indexed in much the same fashion as at the British Museum in London. *April 24, 1909*

PHELPS, CAPTAIN JOHN J. will start with his wife on a three-month's trip on a four-horse tally-ho. He will drive a thousand miles up hill and down dale, from Hackensack, New Jersey, to Montreal. In 1896, he established the present record by driving eight hundred miles without a mishap. *May 24, 1900*

PHILLIPS, MR. AND MRS. LAUGHLIN (JENNIFER STATS)—CAFRITZ "Our house was built in the late 1800s," says Jennifer Phillips, "so we tried to decorate it as it was decorated then." Husband Laughlin Phillips is Director of The Phillips Collection, founded by his father in 1919 as the first museum collection in America devoted to modern art and now one of the world's best small museums. *February, 1988*

PHILLIPS, WILLIAM, recently U.S. Minister to the Netherlands and now Under Secretary of State, is with his family at his estate, "Highover," overlooking Wenham Lake. Mr. and Mrs. Phillips (Caroline Drayton) are very much in evidence socially. *August 15, 1922*

PHIPPS, HENRY The Phipps family owns extensive but unknown amounts of land along the entire eastern part of the country, and are reported to be the biggest single eastern landholders. The originator of the family fortune was Henry Phipps, onetime accountant for Andrew Carnegie, who himself became a multi-millionaire. *June, 1983*

PHIPPS, MRS. HENRY (ANNIE C. SHAFFER) is the wife of a great steel magnate, a partner of the late Mr. Andrew Carnegie and the late Mr. H. C. Frick. She is the mother of sportsmen and the grandmother of Yale heroes. Not to be outdone by the younger generations, she goes up to the Cascapedia Club and in a record season kills one of the biggest salmon of the year. The Cascapedia Salmon Club is one of the most noted clubs in Canada. It is some fifty miles northeast of the Restigouche River in Canada, and sport there has been famous for generations. *August 15, 1926*

PHIPPS, JOHN S. Very influential in the affairs and development of Palm Beach are Mr. J. S. Phipps and his brothers, Mr. H. C. Phipps and Mr. Howard Phipps. All three brothers are most enthusiastic polo players and for a long time have been playing regularly at Westbury at the Meadow Brook Club and other grounds. Mr. J. S. Phipps himself has on his place one of the finest fields in the country. *March 15, 1926*

PHIPPS, LAWRENCE CLINTON III The son of Lawrence C. Phipps, Jr., of the highly social Denver branch of the great Pittsburgh family, "Lawrie" is a grandson of the late Senator Lawrence C. Phipps and is President in his own right of General Optics Co. *June, 1964*

PHOENIX, LLOYD One of the most interesting yachts enrolled in the New York Yacht Club is the auxiliary steamer *Intrepid,* owned by Mr. Lloyd Phoenix, one of the earliest life members and one of the most thorough and popular yachtsmen in America. The *Intrepid* has done a great deal of cruising in West Indian waters, and she is frequently seen under sail alone. *September 28, 1901*

PICKERING, JOHN is the ninth John Pickering to occupy the Pickering House, built in Salem in 1651. Timothy was Adjutant General, Quartermaster General, Postmaster General, and Secretary of War and State under George Washington. The house is the oldest home in the country to be continuously occupied by the same family. *June, 1974*

PICKMAN, MRS. DUDLEY L. of Beacon Street is another Boston woman who, when on pleasure bent, takes thought for those less fortunate than herself. This summer, she is at her seashore home at Beverly Cove. On the estate is a smaller house, and this is kept open for the entertainment of working women who have seen better days and can appreciate refined surroundings, and who need a quiet vacation. Mrs. Pickman, who has a fortune in her own right, was a Miss Motley before her marriage. *July 30, 1910*

PIERCE, CHARLES ELIOT, JR. "The Morgan Library is something of a hybrid—part research library, part museum," notes its new Director, Charles Eliot Pierce, Jr. (pronounced "Purse," as in S.S. Pierce, the Boston firm of luxury comestibles founded by his great-great-grandfather). Mr. Pierce, another of whose great-great-grandfathers was President of Harvard, was plucked by the Morgan's search committee from Vassar College, where he headed the English department. He had taught there for seventeen years. *December, 1987*

PIERREPONT, HENRY EVELYN was the first President of the Brooklyn Academy of Music and did much toward laying out the streets of "The City of Churches." In his travels abroad, he made a study of the topography of all the large cities and in 1835, about two years after Brooklyn was incorporated as a city, prepared plans that were adopted by the Legislature. Henry Evelyn Pierrepont was a son of Hezekiah Beers Pierrepont. On the site of the farm owned by Hezekiah Pierrepont, the City Hall, the Brooklyn library, five churches, and other buildings were erected. *June 5, 1909*

PIERSON, MARGUERITE ("DAISY") has had a part in everything social that enlivens Tuxedo Park, New York. She is a daughter of General and Mrs. J. Frederic Pierson. Her father is seventh in descent from Abraham Pierson, first President of Yale College, who was a pastor of a church in Southampton, Long Island, in the seventeenth century, one of the ten clergymen elected to "found, form and govern" a college in Connecticut in 1700. *April 23, 1910*

PHIPPS

In 1913: Mrs. Henry Carnegie Phipps and son Ogden.

In the 1930s, the polo fields of America were dominated by a single family: the three sons of John S. Phipps, their cousins, Winston and Raymond Guest, and Townsend and Esmond Martin. Edward, Prince of Wales, was one of the chosen few to play on the private field at John Phipps's hundred-acre estate at Old Westbury, Long Island. Today open to the public, the Stuart-style house of cherry red brick, with its Chippendale furniture and portraits by Gainsborough and Reynolds, was initially completed in 1905. According to reports published at the time, Phipps financial holdings were then estimated at $35 million.

But polo was not the only Phipps family sport. Through the years, as both players and patrons, Phippses of Pittsburgh, New York City, and Palm Beach have enthusiastically ridden to hounds and played competition-level golf and tennis. Mrs. Henry Carnegie Phipps was one of the first women to own a major American racing stable. The present Ogden Mills ("Dinny") Phipps is chairman of both the New York Racing Association and the Jockey Club of America.

All has been possible because family founder Henry Phipps, born in Philadelphia to English immigrant parents, was a farsighted bookkeeper who bought an interest in a small western Pennsylvania iron forging company in 1861. Through mergers, the company became part of the Carnegie Steel Corporation and eventually U.S. Steel. Bessemer Securities Corporation, the family holding company, has diversified its interests through the years, especially into land. Phippses, for example, have been major developers of both the south and north shores of Long Island. Famed for its secrecy, Bessemer was reported in 1995 to manage about $3 billion for the 200 or so members of the Phipps family.

Today's main branches of the family descend directly from Henry Phipps's three sons (Howard Phipps; Henry Carnegie, who married a Mills of the California gold-mining fortune; and John, who wed an heiress of the Grace shipping family) and two daughters (Helen, married to Bradley Martin, an oil heir, and Amy, wife of the Honorable Frederick Guest). John S. Phipps and his father-in-law, Michael Grace, were among the prime early developers of Palm Beach; beginning in 1914, they bought up and began to build on most of the available acreage on the island. Phippses today remain among the first families of Palm Beach. "We never came here for business purposes," explained Ogden Phipps, in 1962. "We just kept trying to get away....Palm Beach just kept catching up with us."

Great sports: *clockwise from top left*, Sonia Phipps on the tennis court in 1933; H. C. Phipps, riding with hounds in 1913; tennis player John S. Phipps; Michael Phipps dressed for polo.

PIGNATELLI DI MONTECALVO, PRINCESS (CONSTANCE WILCOX) Her spring gesture is a delightful story called *Such Ways Are Dangerous,* which follows on the heels of her several successful books of plays. Princess Pignatelli lives in Sutton Place, primarily because she likes the flow of river life beneath her and the lines of the Queensborough Bridge darkening against the May sky. Deploring the segregation of ages in New York social life, she likes to entertain in the Continental manner with people of all ages coming in for tea or dinner. *May, 1939*

PILLSBURY, GEORGE, JR. On his 21st birthday, this heir to the Pillsbury baking flour fortune gave most of a $400,000 inheritance away to organizations aimed at changing the status quo. Since then, he has emerged as the most consistent patriarch of the "alternative philanthropy movement." Pillsbury launched the Haymarket People's Fund in Cambridge in 1973 and was an early financial supporter of food co-ops, *Ramparts* magazine, and documentary films on social issues. He also conducts conferences and counseling for wealthy inheritors, steering them toward "socially responsible" philanthropy and investing. *December, 1989*

PILLSBURY, JOHN SARGENT It was his father, the late Mr. Charles A. Pillsbury, who established the flour mills, famous as the largest in the world, in Minneapolis; and his grandfather, the late Mr. John S. Pillsbury, was Governor of Minnesota and a man much loved and respected in the Northwest. *September 9, 1911*

PILLSBURY, MRS. JOHN S. (MAHALA FISKE) After her marriage in 1856 in Warner, New Hampshire, she went to Minnesota with her husband. She took an active part in the pioneer life, and during the Sioux massacre of 1862 was a ministering angel to the refugees. Mr. Pillsbury's prominence in politics and business brought her much before the public, but she always found time for her philanthropic work. *July 9, 1910*

PINCHOT, AMOS R. ENO, after winning honors in the first tennis tournament at Kebo, is directing his attention toward awakening an interest in baseball. He is forming a nine, and the Bar Harborites will play games with other teams in the vicinity, including Northeast Harbor. This is all thoroughly American in its enthusiasm over our "national" game, but it seems even more strenuous than tennis. *August 6, 1904*

PINCHOT, ROSAMUND is the nineteen-year-old novice whose portrayal of the nun is one of the features of Max Reinhardt's spectacle, *The Miracle.* Stepping straight from a finishing school to the stage of the Century Theater, and, incidentally, abandoning rather elaborate plans for a social debut in doing so, Miss Pinchot gave some of the other members of the cast some mild surprises by the enthusiasm with which she undertook her role. *July 1, 1924*

PIRIE, JOHN T. was born at Erol, Ireland. In 1854, he came to this country with Samuel Carson. They went West and founded what is now one of the largest department store concerns in Chicago, Carson, Pirie, Scott & Co. His summers were passed at Sea Cliff, Long Island, where he owned a large part of the waterfront. *May 10, 1913*

PLANT, HENRY B. controls twelve different railway corporations, is President of the Southern and Texas Express Companies, President of steamship lines covering the coasts of the Gulf, founder of the most palatial winter resort in America, the Tampa Bay Hotel, Florida, and owner of four other beautiful resorts within the state. To Mr. Plant may be accredited the development, if not the real discovery, of the grand West, or Gulf, Coast of Florida. *March 4, 1896*

PLATT, THOMAS COLLIER entered mercantile life as a young man. Later, he was President of the Tioga National Bank and a member of Congress from 1873 to 1877. He was President of the Southern Central Railroad and of the Addison and Pennsylvania Railroad, and became a United States Senator in 1897, his term expiring in 1909. *March 12, 1910*

PLIMPTON, GEORGE A. is one of the well-known Republicans interested in political science and good government. His library of educational books, beginning with the date of printing, is the largest in the world. *November 3, 1906*

POE, ARTHUR is a son of Mr. and Mrs. John P. Poe, of Baltimore, and is a grandnephew of the poet Edgar Allan Poe. Young Mr. Poe, like all the male line of his family, is a graduate of Princeton and a famous football player. *June 11, 1904*

POLK, FRANK LYON is a grandson of Leonidas Polk, who was both a bishop and a general, and a great-great-grandson of Thomas Polk, the patriot, who made his home in Mecklenburg County, North Carolina. Leonidas Polk, who was killed with a cannon-shot while commanding the Army of the Mississippi during the Civil War, was bishop of the diocese of Louisiana during the Civil War. Dr. Polk, the father of young Mr. Polk, is now dean of Cornell University's Medical College. *September 21, 1907*

POMEROY, MR. AND MRS. EUGENE (ELIZABETH EAGAN) Early in the beginning of the development of Convent, New Jersey, a branch of Mr. Pomeroy's Ohio family was settled there, making it among the earliest residents in the history of the now fashionable little community. While Mr. Pomeroy was in the trenches in Europe, Mrs. Pomeroy bought an old farm at Convent. She succeeded in realizing a charming country home out of the fragments of a dream and some substantial timbers. *August 1, 1922*

POOL, DR. AND MRS. EUGENE HILLHOUSE (ESTHER HOPPIN) She is a descendant of a long line of distinguished Hoppins, beginning with William Jones Hoppin, the diplomatist. Later there were Thomas F. Hoppin, the artist; Augustus Hoppin, the author; and William Warner Hoppin, Governor of Rhode Island. The groom, Dr. Eugene Hillhouse Pool, can point to a worthy ancestor in James Hillhouse, who was spoken of by Cotton Mather as the "worthy hopeful young minister lately arrived in America." *May 7, 1904*

POOR, CHARLES LANE One of the first cottages opened at Manhanset Manor, Shelter Island, was the colonial residence close to the water that belongs to Professor Charles Lane Poor of Columbia University. His home is near the New York Yacht Club station, and while at Shelter Island he is the commodore rather than the professor and his interests are nautical rather than astronomical. Professor Poor was formerly one of the faculty at Johns Hopkins and since 1904 has been professor of astronomy at Columbia University. *June 12, 1909*

POPE, MR. AND MRS. JOHN RUSSELL (SADIE G. JONES) He is the young architect whose influence has been a factor in freeing New York from opprobrium as "The Chocolate City." She is the daughter of Mr. and Mrs. E. Pembroke Jones, who have a plantation-estate at Wilmington, North Carolina, and a residence at Newport, Rhode Island. Mr. Pope has unique distinction as an architect whose ideals have hearty, professional support. He was the architect of the residence of former Ambassador Henry White in Washington and of Mrs. Robert R. Hitt's residence in the same city, considered the two finest houses in America. *July 11, 1914*

PORTER, MRS. ALEXANDER S. (FRANCES WENTWORTH CUSHING) was a lineal descendant of James Otis, the patriot, and of General Benjamin Lincoln, of Revolutionary fame, and of Charles Chauncy, second President of Harvard College. *November 1, 1924*

PORTER, BENJAMIN C. A newcomer to Tuxedo Park, New York, is Mr. Benjamin C. Porter, the portrait painter, who has just bought a plot of ground here but who has not yet begun to erect his cottage. Mr. Porter has had among his sitters many of the beautiful women who live in Tuxedo. *October 11, 1900*

PORTER, COLE While contemporaries like Irving Berlin, Noel Coward, and the Gershwins were struggling for crusts, Porter was sharing the flamboyant benefits of a $7,000,000 inheritance, a social marriage, and a reckless extravagance. In Paris, for example, where Porter lived during the roaring '20s, he furnished his house from garret to wine cellar with zebra rugs, platinum wallpaper, and red lacquered chairs covered with white kid; and in Venice, he gave his "Red and Gold Balls," which make recent grade A coming-out parties seem shabby by comparison. One gorgeous Porter affair had fifty brawny gondoliers standing around dressed as statuesque footmen and an acrobat who ate his dinner swaying gently above the canal on a tightrope. *April, 1940*

PORTER, ELSIE The interest in the wedding of Miss Elsie Porter testified not only to her father's popularity but to her own success as a youthful hostess. The groom, Dr. Edwin Mende, is the son of a distinguished physician in Switzerland. Ambassador Horace Porter, the father of the bride, is a descendant of soldiers and lawyers. Andrew Porter opened a school in Philadelphia in 1767. Later, he was Captain of the Marines. The son of Andrew Porter was David Rittenhouse Porter, Governor of Pennsylvania. *March 11, 1905*

PORTER, KATHERINE WYMAN is engaged to Mr. George Hunt Pendleton. Miss Porter is a granddaughter of General Rodney Corning Ward. Mr. Pendleton is a grandson of Senator George Hunt Pendleton, at one time Minister to Germany and a great-grandson of Francis Scott Key. *May 15, 1924*

POST, MRS. EDWIN MAIN (EMILY PRICE) There is today a more real need for an intelligent, sensibly conceived book on social usage than there has been in this country since the crude days following the War of 1812. One can have nothing but commendation for the manner in which Mrs. Price Post has tactfully accomplished this task in her new book *Etiquette In Society, In Business, In Politics and At Home*. As a sample of what we mean about Mrs. Post, a sample both of her common sense and her sense of humor, we quote her remarks about eating corn on the cob: "If you insist on eating it at home or in a restaurant, to attack it with as little ferocity as possible is perhaps the only direction to be given." *September 1, 1922*

POST, MRS. MARJORIE MERRIWEATHER is a philanthropist, financier, horticulturist, and advocate of square dancing; Palm Beach's radiant, statuesque grande dame. The Post pad, "Mar-a-Lago," has a five-story tower, a million-dollar inlaid marble table in the dining room, 36,000 Portuguese and Spanish tiles in the patio and hall, a boudoir that looks like Versailles, a 9-hole golf course, and an underground tunnel that leads to a private cabana and pool. *January, 1968*

POST, MRS. WILLIAM Newport society had a "baby party" lately, the hostess being Mrs. William Post. The guests were asked to wear baby garments at dinner and at the dance following. Miss Edith Gray was the last to arrive, and her entrance was triumphal. She wore a long, white christening robe, that extended to the floor, and a lace cap encircled her chubby face. The "infant" was reclining in an improvised baby carriage, which was pushed by Robert L. Gerry, attired in plaid kilts and a black velvet blouse. *November 1, 1899*

POSTLEY, CLARENCE ASHLEY was the son of General Brooke Postley. He was formerly commodore of the New York Yacht Club. At his residence on Fifth Avenue, he had a large collection of silver cups won by yachts. *June 6, 1908*

POTTER, ALONZO, aside from the fact that he is the son of a well-beloved bishop, is a representative of one of New York's famous families. The Right Rev. Henry Codman Potter, Bishop of New York, who is so liberal and charitable in his views, is a descendant of Robert Potter, the evangelist, who was so stern and unmerciful in his ideas of justice. He was a settler in Massachusetts Plantations in 1634. There have been three bishops in the family since his time. *October 24, 1903*

POTTER, BISHOP HENRY CODMAN The cornerstone of the Cathedral Church of St. John the Divine was laid by the Rt. Rev. Henry C. Potter, Bishop of New York. The bishop smoothed the mortar with his silver trowel and made the sign of the cross in it with the point of the trowel. Several of the trustees passed through the congregation taking up the offering. Cornelius Vanderbilt and J. Roosevelt Roosevelt returned with their plates heaped up with greenbacks. *January 4, 1892*

POTTER, MRS. HENRY CODMAN (ELIZABETH SCRIVEN)—CLARK She built model tenements at Amsterdam and West End Avenues; she erected in memory of her first husband the Alfred Corning Clark Neighborhood House at Rivington and Cannon Streets, and supported the Young Men's Christian Association at Cooperstown, New York, where she owned a large country estate, and purchased the Fenimore Cooper grounds there for a public park. *March 13, 1909*

PRINCESS ELIZABETH OF CALIFORNIA

It is not an entirely remote possibility in the general rearrangements of maps and governments in Europe at the close of the war that an American woman may find a seat on one of the thrones. Miss Elizabeth Sperry, of Stockton, California, married Prince André Poniatowski. The Poniatowskis claim direct descent from Stanislaus II, of the house of Poniatowski, the last King of Poland. Therefore, if Poland is restored as an independent kingdom, Prince André seems to have the worthiest title to the crown. *May 10, 1915*

POTTER, MRS. JAMES BROWN (CORA URQUHART) To Mrs. Potter the feminine world is indebted for the invention of a dancing shoe that is warranted to unlace six times every half hour. As soon as the muscles of the instep are exerted the ribbons give way, then untie, and the next moment trail upon the floor. This, of course, necessitates a kneeling knight at Beauty's feet. *October 27, 1886*

POULTNEY, WALTER DE CURZON Baltimore is his one home, and the delightful old house, the home of successive generations of his race in that city, is his dearest hobby. In the hall hangs a portrait of William Poultney, Earl of Bath, who was Prime Minister of England, while in the dining room hang portraits of Mr. Poultney's earliest American ancestors, Mr. and Mrs. John Moale, the latter widely known in history as Ellin North, the first white child born in Baltimore. *October 1, 1915*

POWEL, SAMUEL is a namesake of his ancestor, who was Mayor of Philadelphia in the eighteenth century and who married Elizabeth Willing. She adopted her nephew, John Powel Hare, and he took the name of Powel by act of legislature. John Hare Powel died in Newport in 1786. He was secretary of the United States Legation in London under William Pinckney, was one of the founders of the Pennsylvania Agricultural Society, and was well known even abroad for books giving advice to husbandmen and agriculturists. *April 24, 1909*

PRATT, CONSTANCE is the second daughter of Mr. and Mrs. Dallas Bache Pratt of New York; a sister of Mrs. Lycurgus Winchester, formerly of Baltimore; and a niece of Mr. Francis H. Landon, who recently resigned from his post at the American embassy in Vienna. Mr. and Mrs. Pratt have a box at the Metropolitan Opera House on Wednesday nights, and their daughters, Miss Constance and Miss Beatrice Pratt, who dress alike with the exception of some detail of coiffure arrangement, are always much observed on account of their good looks and their striking costumes. *December 14, 1907*

PRATT, MRS. FRANCIS C. By now most people of the so-called *monde* have heard of Yeamans Hall Club, north of Charleston. A clubhouse, designed by James Gamble Rogers, stands on the site of the old Hall, and the immediately adjacent land has been mapped out into building sites. Mrs. Francis C. Pratt's house is one of the more successful. It was built in 1928 and is called "Goose Creek House," being the first of the club cottages to be built on the banks of that river. *March 1, 1931*

PRATT, JOHN T. The handsome new country house that he is building at Glen Cove will complete what is undoubtedly the largest group of summer homes belonging to one family in this country, if not in the world. It is the seventh new house to be built on the great Dosoris estate of some two thousand acres since the late Charles Pratt acquired it more than twenty years ago, the remaining five sons of the founder of Pratt Institute and the family of his elder daughter, the late Mrs. Frank L. Babbott, each having a summer home there, with an apportionment of acreage. *January 1, 1910*

PRATT, SHERMAN Of all the enterprising Pratts descended from the philanthropic Standard Oil magnate of Brooklyn, Sherman is the leading movie producer, the most democratic, the only member of the third generation to have followed the second to Amherst, and certainly the family's sole devotee of modern architecture, deep-sea expeditions, and the gentle art of bumming. Picking cotton and lumberjacking, he once worked his way to the Coast, and now as President of the Open Road organizes student tours into Soviet Russia or any other part of the world. *June 1, 1932*

PRENTICE, JOHN H. was a native of New Hampshire, but since 1839 the family has been identified continuously with Brooklyn. Mr. Prentice was one of the foremost citizens of his day. To his energy and public spirit, the Packer Institute and the Polytechnic Institute owe much, while he helped materially to make Greenwood Cemetery the beautiful place that it is today. He was among the first to foresee what bridging the East River would mean to Brooklyn. *June 22, 1907*

PRENTICE, MR. AND MRS. SPELMAN (LOLA PIERCE NOYES) now divide their year among New York, Southampton, where they have recently acquired an estate, and Palm Beach. Mr. Prentice is a grandson of the late John D. Rockefeller. When this popular young couple decided to make their winter home in Palm Beach, they soon felt the need for a club-type resort. An exceptional site at Manalapan seemed to fill the bill exactly. In this ideal setting, Mr. Prentice constructed "La Coquille" (The Seashell). *January, 1955*

PULITZER

Brothers Michael and Joseph Pulitzer, Jr., in 1980.

An emigrant from Hungary, Joseph Pulitzer arrived in the United States in 1864, when he was seventeen. Almost at once, he went to work at the *Westliche Post,* a German-language newspaper in St. Louis. By 1878, Pulitzer was owner, as his descendants still are, of the *St. Louis Post-Dispatch.* For more than a century, the Pulitzer name has been celebrated in American journalism.

Ready for the New York market, Joseph Pulitzer bought the *World* from Jay Gould in 1883 for $350,000. He immediately made the paper's policy liberal and pro-labor; it would oppose "the aristocracy of money," he wrote, with "America's true aristocracy—the aristocracy of labor." As a voice of the Democratic party, the *World* for years was one of the most flamboyant and influential newspapers in America.

After 1890, Joseph Pulitzer was virtually blind. He developed an extraordinary sensitivity to noise: his houses in New York and Bar Harbor, Maine, were soundproofed, and he finally escaped the din of civilization by cruising the world in his yacht, directing his newspapers by cable. At his death in 1911, he left funds to establish the Columbia University School of Journal-

ism and the famed annual awards called the Pulitzer Prizes.

The Pulitzer clan became a part of America's social elite when Joseph married Kate Davis, a cousin of Confederate President Jefferson Davis. Their son, Ralph, went on to marry Frederica Webb, a great-granddaughter of Cornelius Vanderbilt. Social connections did not prevent Ralph, though, from publishing an astringent little book in 1910 entitled *New York Society on Parade,* in which he penned various unkind comments about New York City hostesses, comparing their "indelible smiles" to those of "coiffeurs' models and Christian martyrs."

Ralph acted as publisher of the *World* until he and his brother, Joseph II, sold it to Scripps-Howard in 1931. The *St. Louis Post-Dispatch* continued to flourish under Joseph II and his son, noted art collector Joseph III (who died in 1993). Herbert Pulitzer, Jr., known as "Peter," another grandson of Joseph I, invested in Florida orange groves and hotels. His first wife, Lilly Lee McKim, a dress designer, developed a successful line of sportswear under the name Lilly Pulitzer, Inc. Today, Pulitzer Publishing, a publicly traded corporation, owns newspapers, radio stations, and a satellite network.

PRESTON, MRS. THOMAS (ANN BROCKEN-BROUGH) Generals in both Southern and Northern Armies branch from the family tree of Mrs. Thomas Preston. Her grandfather, General John R. Cooke, fought with the Virginians in the Civil War; his father, General Philip St. George Cooke, with the Union Army. *October, 1943*

PRESTON, ZELIA KRUMBHAAR The country wedding is quite in vogue this winter. There could hardly have been a prettier scene than that when Miss Preston was married to Mr. Charles Frederick Hoffman, at St. Mary's, in Tuxedo. The bride comes from distinguished lineage. Her mother was a Miss Krumbhaar, and she is related not only to the Philadelphia family of that name but to the Butlers of South Carolina, into which house married Fanny Kemble, the actress. She is a cousin of the late Ward McAllister. The bridegroom is one of the Hoffman family connected so long with the history of the Protestant Episcopal Church. *January 3, 1912*

PRINCE, MR. AND MRS. CHARLES (HELEN PRATT) have come to Boston to make an appeal for funds for Devastated France. The Prince villa is at Noir Moutier, on an island off the coast of La Vendée. When war broke out, Mrs. Prince threw herself into the work of alleviating the lot of the peasants about their place and with such success that word of her labors reached headquarters and she was "commanded" to Paris, where she has worked in close cooperation with the French authorities. *April 10, 1919*

PRINCE, FREDERICK H., SR., lived up to his classification in *Time* as "testy," "box-jawed," and "priest of all financial oldsters," when, at the age of seventy, in a pickup polo game at the Myopia Hunt, he first warned an opposing player that if he didn't get out of the way he would kill him. Then, when the man did not, he split his head open with his mallet. Five years later, Prince was forced to pay $15,000 in damages. *July, 1947*

PRINCE, MR. AND MRS. WILLIAM WOOD (ELEANOR EDWARDS)—DE RICOU The colorful Boston capitalist Frederick Henry Prince amassed among his various holdings a huge slice of Chicago manufacturing, real estate, and a controlling interest in Armour & Co. He groomed as successor his cousin's son, William Wood of Tuxedo, New York, on one condition: Young Wood must become Prince's adopted son and add "Prince" to his surname. The re-named William Wood Prince subsequently became chief executive of Armour from 1957 until its sale in 1969. Elegant Billy, now 76, and his Cincinnati-born wife Eleanor ("Queen of Newport"), have set Chicago's social tone for the past quarter-century. *September, 1990*

PROCTOR, COLONEL FLETCHER DUTTON, formerly Governor of Vermont, was one of the most prominent men of the state, being interested in various industrial enterprises and in politics. Upon his graduation from Amherst College, he became connected with the marble quarrying business carried on by his father; and when the late Senator entered President Harrison's cabinet in 1889, Colonel Proctor succeeded to the presidency of the marble company. In 1906, Colonel Proctor was elected Governor. In his term of office, 1906–1908, many progressive movements that are now part of state policy, such as forestry, improved highways, and skilled supervision, had their beginning in Vermont. *October 7, 1911*

WAIT 'TIL THEY SEE THE MALL

Gordon C. Prince, one of Myopia Hunt Club's oldest living members and former master of foxhounds, says: "The North Shore has developed, and it's no longer practical to hunt foxes. With foxes on the loose, they'd be running into grocery stores and all over the shopping centers, and you can't have that." Mr. Prince is a grandson of Frederick Octavius Prince, Mayor of Boston in the 1880s. *June, 1974*

PRONTAUT, MRS. JOHN HENRY (EMMA BIGNON) was a member of an old aristocratic French family. The first Catholic mass celebrated in Augusta, Georgia, was for her great-grandfather, in 1790. She was noted in the South for her philanthropies. Her residence at "The Pines" is one of the notable places of Augusta. *October 10, 1914*

PRYOR, MRS. ROGER ATKINSON (SARA AGNES RICE), wife of ex-Justice Roger A. Pryor, a Brigadier General in the Confederate Army, was the leader of a Southern literary group in New York. She was founder and first Regent of the National Society of the Daughters of the American Revolution and, for nineteen years, the honorary Vice President General of the organization. *February 24, 1912*

PULITZER, MR. AND MRS. HERBERT (LILLY McKIM) are the golden couple of Palm Beach. He's Tarzan, she's Jane, and they're both usually barefoot. It's all right, he's very big in oranges and grapefruits (Pulitzer Groves), and his grandfather was the newspaper publisher; and she's the Lilly behind all those Lillys the ladies wear. In Palm Beach, if you're Very Rich, Very Old Family, Very Social, and Very Successful, you can go barefoot any time you please. It's that kind of place. *January, 1968*

PULITZER, JOSEPH The summer home at Bar Harbor of Mr. Joseph Pulitzer, of the *New York World*, attracts a great deal of attention. A notable feature of the establishment is the baths in the basement of the stone tower. When the tide flows in, it fills a huge swimming tank, and the sea water is then warmed by steam. Beside the swimming tank, there are Turkish, Russian, and indeed every known kind of baths. *August 21, 1895*

PULITZER, MR. AND MRS. JOSEPH (EMILY S. RAUH) As Chairman of the Pulitzer Publishing Company, Joe Pulitzer presides over a media empire that includes TV, radio, and print. At home, he and his wife Emily (a former curator at the St. Louis Art Museum) live happily amid their extraordinary art collection. Other pieces are in the permanent collections of the Harvard University Art Museums. *March, 1989*

PULITZER, RALPH One of the most fruitful topics of conversation throughout the spring season has been furnished by Mr. Ralph Pulitzer's brilliant criticism of certain aspects of modern New York society in his *New York Society on Parade,* a keen, intelligent, and discursive account of the smart world from its more or less humorous, but never its scandalous, side. European society consists of a deep mill pond of assured position with a froth of probationary parvenus; New York society consists of a whirlpool of tentative novices with a sediment of permanent members. *September 3, 1910*

PULLMAN, FLORENCE is one of the most richly-paid women in the country for her labors. She is the daughter of George M. Pullman, and is said to draw a salary of $10,000 a year from the Pullman company for naming cars. Miss Pullman evidences a preference for euphonious names. There is a fine discrimination displayed in the naming of cars for special service. For example, dining cars are in most instances named after such celebrated cooks as Savarin, and the cooks of famous men and women. *February 19, 1896*

PURDY, AUGUST BELMONT He is said to have imported the first pack of fox hounds to this country, from Ireland, in 1880, which were hunted under the name of the Meadow Brook Hunt. The next year, the club was incorporated with Mr. Purdy the first M.F.H. He was M.F.H. at Pau, France, many years ago, and was among the leading supporters of polo in this country. He was identified equally prominently with amateur racing, being known as one of the best gentlemen jockeys over here during the heyday of his activities in sport. *June 20, 1919*

PUTNAM, GEORGE PALMER is Treasurer of G. P. Putnam's Sons and a grandson and namesake of the founder of the famous old publishing house. In his younger days, he spent several years in the West. He went in for newspaper work and became Editor and Publisher of the *Bulletin* in Bend, Oregon. Before he was thirty, he had served two terms as mayor of the town. His western training still crops out in his love of nature, his liking for long hikes, and his friendship for explorers, tramps, and out-of-door people generally. *September 1, 1925*

PUTNAM, MRS. GEORGE, SR. (KATHARINE HARTE), founder of the famous Puttencove Kennels, may not be the most active breeder of top-drawer poodles, but she has nevertheless been a breeder of poodles *longer* than anyone else in the United States, thus securing for herself the well-earned title of "Mrs. Poodle." "You see, the ideal poodle should be a very lovely person; a very nice, generous, steady, gay, intelligent person. And some of them are—*really.* No, I wouldn't say all of them. No, not for a minute, but then I haven't met many people as good as all that either," she concludes. *February, 1977*

PUTNAM, MRS. JOHN B., widow of one of the organizers of Union Commerce, one of Cleveland's five big banks, lives alone in Bratenahl, an enclave of some 1,400. The home has a Victorian exterior but is hung inside with her Picassos, a Matisse, and Modigliani. "Pictures," she says, "are my companions. They get a personality of their own." She expresses something of the feeling of the city's other old and moneyed families when she says, "If you have privileges and fail to take responsibilities, you're surrendering your privileges." *September, 1966*

PYNCHON, SARAH was a sister of the late Thomas Ruggles Pynchon, President of Trinity College from 1874 to 1883. She was a direct descendant of William Pynchon, founder of Roxbury and Springfield, Massachusetts. By her death, another tract of land in the new Vanderbilt Square of the Sheffield Scientific School is released to the university. The historic Pynchon residence will be torn down soon. *October 28, 1911*

Q

QUINCY, JOSIAH was a former Mayor of Boston and at one time Assistant Secretary of State. Mr. Quincy was the sixth in direct descent to bear this illustrious name, the first having been a prominent citizen of Boston in its infancy, the next a patriot of the Revolution, and three others Mayors of Boston in their generation. He was graduated from Harvard in the class of 1880, and he went to Washington as counsel for the Argentine Republic in the dispute with Brazil over boundaries. He was twice elected Mayor of Boston. *October 1, 1919*

QUINLAN, MR. AND MRS. ROBERT, JR. (KATHARINE LEA "KAYLEA" MURDOCK) Her great-great-grandfather, Jefferson Gilbert James, claim-staked 175,000 acres of land near what is now Fresno, California, in the 1860s. "My great-grandmother Maude James used to wear all her jewelry when she went to the opera," says Kaylea. "She'd have one armored car in front of her and one behind. She was known as the 'Cattle Baroness of the West Coast' and hated anything to do with cattle. But as the only child of Jeff James, she inherited it all when he died." Bob's background is admittedly more staid than his wife's. He traces it back to Captain John Quinlan, one of the city's first sea captains. His father owns what was once the first coffee, tea, and spice export-import house in San Francisco. *February, 1973*

R

RAMSAY, BARONESS CONSTANTIN (FRANCES WHITEHOUSE) is a granddaughter of the late Bishop Whitehouse of Chicago. Although she rarely appears in society, she is one of the richest Americans who visit London. Fine porcelain is her hobby; she paid $5,000 for a dessert service of Sèvres at the Paris factory last Easter. *October 20, 1906*

RAND, WILLIAM BLANCHARD has been in large measure responsible for all that has been accomplished in Old Chatham, New York. Cubbing three times a week in the late summer and hunting in the fall and winter, he has seen to the training of the hounds and the panelling of the country. Yet contrary to the common opinion that a good M. F. H. finds time for nothing else in life, he manages to supervise the administration of his farm, dairy, and riding school at Salisbury, Connecticut, as well as to be an active member of the State Legislature at Hartford. *November 15, 1932*

RANDALL, BURTON H. Randall is a great-grandson of President Thomas Jefferson and a grand-nephew of President Zachary Taylor. He achieved quite a bit of patriotic distinction for himself during his service of twenty months in France, as an artillery officer of the famous Rainbow Division. For the last six months, he has acted as town mayor over a zone including Mehun and twelve additional communes. *September 1, 1919*

RANDOLPH, DR. ARCHIBALD CARY Virginia is where the Randolphs have always lived and that is where the Randolphs have always hunted. From the beginning, they have been associated with the political and social and sporting life of their home state, and no history of the state could be complete without mention of their distinguished services. *June 1, 1929*

RANDOLPH, MRS. ARCHIBALD CARY (THEODORA AYER)—WINTHROP Just outside of Middleburg, Virginia, near Upperville, is the entrance to "Oakley," the 250-acre estate of Theodora Ayer Randolph. Around Middleburg and Upperville, they call her "The Kingfish." Some refer to her as "Empress of the Piedmont." To her next-door neighbor, Paul Mellon, she is unequivocally "The *grande dame* of the Virginia world of the horse." She has been President of The Upperville Colt and Horse Show for so long that many consider it "her" show. The same applies to the very prestigious Piedmont Foxhounds, for which "Theo" Randolph has served as M.F.H. since 1954. *June, 1984*

RANDOLPH, FRANCIS MERIWETHER died at "Clover Fields," his ancestral estate in Albemarle County, Virginia, held in unbroken succession by his family under the original deed dated 1634, and formerly embracing all of Albemarle and Greene counties. Mr. Randolph married his cousin, Miss Charlotte Macon, of "Clover Hill," Albemarle County. *October 15, 1922*

RANDOLPH, MARY occupies a unique position on the Washington, D.C., stage. The daughter of the late Brigadier General Wallace Fitz Randolph, who was the first Chief of Artillery since George Washington, she grew up in the regular Army and perforce acquired a sense of protocol as soon as her eyes were open. During the Coolidge administration, she was social secretary to Mrs. Coolidge and ran White House functions, including the local end of the difficult visit of Queen Marie of Rumania and entourage. *October, 1943*

RANDOLPH, MARY ETTA of St. Louis is engaged to Mr. Garneau Weld of Baltimore. Through his mother, Mr. Weld is a member of the old French family of Garneau, of St. Louis. On the paternal side, he is related to the Welds of Boston and the Carroll and MacTavish families of Maryland. *March 1, 1924*

RANDOLPH, OSCAR DEWOLF Until recently rector of Christ Episcopal Church in Lexington, Virginia, Captain Randolph may be primarily considered "a born fighter." As a descendant of the famous John Randolph of Roanoke, he comes of the distinguished old Virginia family which also numbers the Indian Princess Pocahontas and her father, King Powhatan, among its progenitors. Before entering upon his study for the ministry, Captain Randolph was a noted athlete and while at the University of Virginia was considered foremost among the many football stars that have carried the blue and orange to victory on the gridiron. *September 20, 1917*

RANDOLPH, PHILIP P. S. gave a ball in honor of Miss Dorothy Randolph at the Bellevue-Stratford Hotel in Philadelphia. Because a few goldfish swam in the basin of a small fountain, a silly story was telegraphed to New York stating that the guests angled for Japanese fantails with hook and line, and then threw them into the water again. None of the Philadelphia papers published fish-stories about Miss Randolph's ball. All the tales were reserved for New Yorkers whom the imaginative journalist doubtless considers more gullible than the descendants of William Penn. *January 18, 1908*

RANGHIERI, COUNT AND COUNTESS GIULIO The bride is an American, the daughter of W. Morgan Shuster, President of the *Century Magazine* Company of New York. The bridegroom is the last lineal descendant of an ancient Roman family that owns vast landed estates near Florence, Italy. *September 1, 1925*

RAVENEL, CHARLES A Huguenot pillar of Charleston is the Ravenel family. Coming directly to South Carolina after the Revocation of the Edict of Nantes, the family produced in addition to its lordly rice planters a complement of very distinguished scientists and physicians. Like most of the rest of the ruling elite, the Ravenels were victims of the economic malaise that gripped the city for so long after the Civil War. When present generation scion Charles "Pug" Ravenel went to Exeter and Harvard, he went not as a function of old family privilege but on a scholarship for being the city's best paper boy. *November, 1977*

RAWLE, HENRY is the son of Mr. Francis Rawle, of Philadelphia, well known as a lawyer, and a nephew of Henry Rawle, who was the great iron-master at the head of the works in Erie, Pennsylvania. The first Francis Rawle in this country founded the settlement known as "The Plymouth Friends." He was said to be the first person in the British colonies to write on the subject of political economy and its relations to the conditions in the new country. *April 20, 1907*

REA, SAMUEL It was to be expected that Samuel Rea would be re-elected to succeed himself as President of the Pennsylvania Railroad System. For nearly a generation, he has been associated with the Pennsylvania system. Samuel Rea is a descendant of an Irish Samuel Rea, who left the north of Ireland for these shores in 1754. His grandfather was in the War of the Revolution and the late unpleasantness in 1812 and was in the United States Congress from 1803 to 1815. *May 20, 1919*

REDMOND, MR. AND MRS. HENRY S. (JULIE R. PARSONS) The "cotton dinner" given at their residence, 11 East Fifty Fifth Street, New York, to celebrate the first anniversary of their marriage, was the most novel of this week's entertainments. Branches of cotton, just as it grows in the South, and scarlet poinsettia with electric light twinkling here and there, decorated the table, and miniature bales of cotton were the souvenirs. Southern melodies were played by an orchestra, and plantation songs were sung. *January 10, 1903*

REED, MRS. JOSEPH VERNER (PERMELIA PRYOR) The Hobe Sound mover and shaker is Permelia Reed. She is President and Secretary of the Hobe Sound Company, a very sound outfit which bought up most of the real estate on the island years ago and today owns virtually all Hobe Sound except the private houses. Her company owns the Jupiter Island Club, the nerve center of it all — and everything else from the Beach Club to the barber shop and beauty parlor. If you don't get into the Jupiter Island Club, alas and alack, not only can you not play golf — you can't even have your hair done. *April, 1974*

REED, MRS. SAMUEL PRYOR (ANNE F. ENGELHARD) An enthusiastic hostess, she considers her party a success when there is "spontaneity in the conversation and giggling in the air." The worst thing a hostess can do, she says, is to have a party where "everyone knows everyone. A good hostess must love being a hostess and look happy to see her guests, who should include lots of pretty, non-pregnant girls." *May, 1965*

REED, MRS. WILLIAM (EMILIE MCKIM) was a granddaughter of Mr. John McKim, Jr., who came in 1780 from Londonderry, Ireland, to Baltimore, where he became a founder of the Baltimore and Ohio Railroad and President and director in several of its early financial corporations. She was founder and incorporator of the National Society of the Colonial Dames of America. In 1895, she founded and incorporated the Maryland Society of the Daughters of the Confederacy. *June 1, 1924*

REEVE, J. STANLEY The Radnor Hounds met at the home of Mr. J. Stanley Reeve, who is the Secretary of the Bryn Mawr Hound Show and one of the most ardent supporters of the Bryn Mawr Horse Show. He will also be remembered as the author of *Radnor Reminiscences,* published a year or two ago. *December 1, 1923*

REEVES, NANNIE, daughter of Charles Reeves, of Baltimore, known also in New York and Philadelphia social circles, has applied for admission to the training school for nurses at Johns Hopkins Hospital. Her motive for entering this uninviting field of work is purely charitable. She will become a district nurse and care for the poor and sick in the lowest parts of the city. *February 8, 1899*

REID, MRS. OGDEN (MARY LOUISE STEWART), wife of Ogden Reid of the New York *Herald Tribune* family, former Ambassador to Israel and Congressman from New York, is a partner in Update, Inc., a marketing firm with emphasis on community relations. A summa cum laude graduate of Barnard College, with an M. A. from Columbia, she became the youngest trustee in the history of Barnard. Recently, she became the first woman trustee of the still all-male prep school, Deerfield Academy. *January, 1978*

REID, MR. AND MRS. OGDEN MILLS (HELEN MILES ROGERS) share the responsibilities of the proprietorship of the *Tribune* between themselves in a manner which, so far as our own knowledge runs, is unique. Mr. Reid inherited the *Tribune* from his father, Whitelaw Reid, and went to work in the *Tribune* at the traditional bottom of the ladder. In 1911, he married a Miss Helen Miles Rogers, of Racine, Wisconsin. Since their marriage, Mrs. Reid has continued to exercise a very active and important part in the control of her husband's newspaper. *July 15, 1922*

REID, WHITELAW In 1857, at the age of twenty, he purchased the Xenia, Ohio *News*. In 1868, he joined the staff of the New York *Tribune*. In 1869, he was its Managing Editor, and in 1872 he borrowed sufficient money to purchase a controlling interest in the paper. In 1881, Mr. Reid married the daughter of Mr. D. Ogden Mills, the millionaire and philanthropist. Mr. Whitelaw Reid was Minister to France in 1889. In 1905, he was made the American Ambassador to Great Britain. *December 28, 1912*

REIDL DE REIDENAU, BARON AND BARONESS are at present living in Madrid, after a sojourn in San Sebastian, where the Baroness received many social attentions. In Pittsburgh, the Baroness' old home, word was received this week that Baron Reidl is appointed Minister to Rio. The Baroness is the third daughter of Mrs. James Neale of Pittsburgh. Her grandfather, the late J. J. Gillespie, founded the well-known firm of art dealers in Pittsburgh. *September 28, 1907*

REISINGER, MR. AND MRS. HUGO (EDMEE BUSCH) As a collector of modern paintings, Mr. Reisinger was considered one of the best in the United States. He made the arrangements for the German government's exhibition of art in the Metropolitan Museum of Art and also organized an American art exhibition at the Royal Academy of Berlin and the Royal Art Society of Munich, paying all expenses. He is survived by his wife, who is a daughter of the late Adolphus Busch. *September 10, 1914*

REISINGER, MR. AND MRS. KURT H. (MARY LODGE MCKEE) She is the granddaughter of Benjamin Harrison, a President of the United States. When in the White House, the bride was known as "Baby McKee" and was as popular in the daily papers as Archie Roosevelt. He is a son of Mr. Hugo Reisinger, art collector and importer. *September 22, 1913*

REVEDIN, COUNT AND COUNTESS GIOVANNI (MARGARET TRIMBLE) When, with distinction, vitality, and poise, Margaret Trimble starts across the Atlantic with her new husband, she will step into another world as the wife of Italy's Under-secretary at Budapest. She will take with her from America an eagerness to cope with all European life, some disarming clothes, *and* the small brisk touches of her own that make for true chic. She has had Fira Benenson of Bonwit Teller's Salon de Couture make up her silkiest pieces—the timeless Chanel black lace spattered with nonchalant bows, the Alix black-on-white with the tied-on fluid skirt, the discreet blue Molyneux suit with the masterful pleats. *June, 1938*

REYNAL, MR. AND MRS. EUGENE SUGNY (ADELE FITZGERALD) have been among the most hospitable of the residents of White Plains, New York. When the cornerstone of their new home was laid on the outskirts of White Plains, there was a jolly "function." Photographs of the family, a bottle of whisky twenty-one years old, and all sorts of curious documents were buried in the stone. Following this, there was a cake-walk under the apple trees to the music of the band. *July 27, 1912*

REYNOLDS, NANCY SUSAN The youngest and only surviving child of tobacco magnate R. J. Reynolds, she gave $30 million in 1938 to establish, with her siblings, the Z. Smith Reynolds Foundation, which supports projects in North Carolina only. Her later gift of $11 million established the ARCA Foundation. Twice divorced, she has assumed her maiden name, gives anonymously, and prefers to shun the limelight. *December, 1983*

REYNOLDS, PATRICK is a grandson of the founder of R. J. Reynolds Tobacco Company; not coincidentally, he's also emerged as one of the nation's leading anti-tobacco crusaders. He says he's put $1.2 million into his Patrick Reynolds Foundation for a Smokefree America. His full-time efforts against tobacco include testimony in Congress and state legislatures in support of anti-cigarette ordinances. *December, 1989*

RHETT, EDWARD LOWNDES His mother, Mrs. Julia Brisbane Rhett, now of Brooklyn, is a descendant of Rawlins Lowndes. His father, the late Major Roland Rhett, was a descendant of Colonel William Rhett, who settled in Carolina in 1694, and in this way he can trace his ancestry to the aristocracy of the United Kingdom. *October 31, 1903*

RHINELANDER, ADELAIDE, daughter of Mr. Philip Rhinelander, is a post-debutante, having come out last year, and is one of the most aristocratic-looking girls in New York's younger set. Her father's New Year's Eve parties to "the old New Yorkers," friends whose families have lived in New York for at least a hundred years, have taken their place in the social history of the city. *January 20, 1921*

RHINELANDER, DR. PHILIP MERCER In the election of the Rev. Dr. Philip Mercer Rhinelander to the bishopric of Pennsylvania, an old New York family which has been lavish in its donations to the Episcopal Church has had its first member elected to the purple. The new bishop is quite a young man and was graduated from Harvard in 1891. *May 27, 1911*

RHINELANDER, SERENA has given to St. James's parish, New York, a large plot of land and a group of ecclesiastical buildings. The property is part of the original seventy-acre farm that was the summer home of Miss Rhinelander's grandfather, William Rhinelander, who purchased it in 1798. The land and the buildings will be worth half a million dollars. *April 14, 1897*

RHINELANDER, MR. AND MRS. T. J. OAKLEY (TATIANA HOLMSEN)—BRAINARD—KELLEY Oakley Rhinelander, whose family has been in the real estate business since 1744 in New York and, before that, in shipbuilding on the Hudson River since 1694, has always been a Newport summer resident. Two years ago, the Rhinelanders submitted to a yearning for the country and made Newport their year-round residence. Back in 1938, Oakley obtained a solo-flying permit at Roosevelt Field. He later was awarded the Distinguished Flying Cross by the Air Force during World War II. He is very enthusiastic about safariing. "I found East Africa one of the few things better than advertised." He managed to get two entries in Rowland Ward's *Record Book of Big Game* in 1967. "But," he says, "I doubt that I would shoot animals if I went back now." *January, 1972*

RHINELANDER, WILLIAM was the only son of the late William C. Rhinelander and a direct descendant of Philip Jacob Rhinelander, who came to this country in 1686, following the Revocation of the Edict of Nantes, and who made his home in New Rochelle. *January 11, 1908*

RHINELANDER, MRS. WILLIAM (MATILDA OAKLEY) At a recent dinner given by her, electricity was employed as an auxiliary in decorative effects. A storage battery, having been placed in the house, enabled the hostess to place in the foliage of a large azalea in the centre of the table a number of tiny little lights. When these were turned on, the effect was indescribably beautiful. *February 1, 1888*

RHINELANDER, WILLIAM C. He inherited the beginnings of his fortune; for the Rhinelander père was so lucky, or so wise, as to own a farm along the East River on Manhattan Island. Having the supreme faculty, also, of holding on, it came to his children, of whom our millionaire is the most distinguished representative. He, too, has had his struggles to keep, and to get more; and he has succeeded so that he owns "lots innumerable, from Thirtieth Street to One Hundred and Thirty First Street," and vast properties in Broadway, Park Row, Barclay Street, etc., etc. *May 6, 1865*

RHODES, MR. AND MRS. JAMES FORD (ANN CARD) are occupying their summer home, "Ravens Cleft," at Seal Harbor. Mr. Rhodes, who has but a few rivals among our leading American historians, has realized in his career a successful combination of business activity with literary genius. When he entered the University of New York in 1865 as a special student, it was to make history his main work. Further studies at the Universities of Chicago, Paris, and Berlin and the inspection of mines and mining in Germany and the British Isles completed his equipment for both business and literature. *July 1, 1905*

RICE, MRS. ALEXANDER HAMILTON (ELEANOR BLANCHE ELKINS)—WIDENER The most exciting pearls in this country belonged to Mrs. A. Hamilton Rice. Bought from the Gary estate, they consisted of three colossal, perfectly matched strands, which Mrs. Rice always wore with earrings of pear-shaped pearls set between two large diamonds. *November, 1937*

RICE, MR. AND MRS. CALE YOUNG (ALICE HEGAN) That well-beloved creator of Mrs. Wiggs, Alice Hegan Rice, with her poet husband Cale Young Rice, author of *Nirvana Days,* returned to her home in Louisville after six months wandering in the Orient. A devotee of Japanese legendary art, this Southern writer has brought from Nippon rare treasure to enrich her curio collection. Mrs. Rice is a niece of Fannie Caldwell Macauley, whose letters from Japan to her Louisville mate originated *The Lady of the Decoration. January 1, 1910*

RICE, MRS. CHRISTINE (WETHERILL) has shown much ability as an amateur actress and carried off a great part of the honors in the recent symbolic play, *Sister Beatrice,* in which she had the title-part. She belongs, as do all worthy and aristocratic Wetherills, to the family whose founder in this country was Christopher Wetherill, the famous Quaker, who gave to his fellow-believers the land in Burlington, New Jersey, on which they built their first meeting-house. He founded the society which received the name of "The Fighting Quakers." The Wetherills of later days have made world-famous discoveries as the result of their experiment with zinc ores. *April 4, 1908*

RICE, MRS. HENRY M. (MATHILDE WHITALL) was the widow of Henry M. Rice, and her name will always be associated with the early history of Minnesota and the Northwest. In 1849, she accompanied her husband to Minnesota. In the decade preceding the Civil War, she lived in Washington, where Mr. Rice represented his state in Congress, and their home was a rendezvous for distinguished men of the period. *November 3, 1906*

RICE, ISAAC L., SR. was a chess shark—the "Rice Gambit" immortalizes his fame. There is a special sound-proof vault in the basement of the Rice house on Riverside Drive, New York, all staged for international chess matches, and several have been played there. Mrs. Rice is leader of the anti-noise crusade which has converted the Hudson from a cross between a boiler-factory and a steam-calliope grounds to a relatively quiet thoroughfare. *July 20, 1916*

RICHARDSON, MRS. TOBIAS GIBSON (IDA ANN SLOCUM) not only inherited money from her husband but was an heiress, and is now the richest woman in the state of Louisiana. She has traveled extensively all over the world, and even her greenhouses contain treasures representing her journeys. Her collection of orchids from South America is famous. Through Mrs. Richardson's influence, the old calaboose on Congo Square in the French Quarter of New Orleans was abandoned and replaced by an ornate city prison above Canal Street. Built when Spain was in possession, the old Spanish jail was full of dungeons, horribly infected, and Mrs. Richardson's work was greatly appreciated. *July 10, 1909*

RICHELIEU, DUC AND DUCHESSE DE (ELINOR DOUGLAS WISE) Matrimony is in the air in Baltimore, for the past fortnight has witnessed several very prominent weddings and many engagements have been made. Quite the most important is that of Miss Elinor Douglas Wise, who returned to Baltimore from Europe, where she has been studying several years for grand opera. Miss Wise astonished her friends with the news of her engagement to the Duc de Richelieu, who belongs to one of the oldest families in France. The engagement ring that the Duke has given to Miss Wise belonged to the famous collection of his mother, the Princess of Monaco, and is a marquise of twenty five diamonds. *February 1, 1913*

RIDDLE, MR. AND MRS. JOHN WALLACE (THEODATE POPE) Miss Pope, even as Mrs. Riddle, intended to keep on with her architectural work, which has already won her favorable recognition in local circles. She is a member of the Colony Club, and a survivor of the *Lusitania* sinking. Mr. Riddle was Ambassador to Russia from 1906 to 1909. *March 20, 1916*

RIDGELY, JOHN lately inherited at his mother's death the old family home, "Hampton." This beautiful mansion, with acres of well-laid-out grounds, comes from Colonial ancestors and has passed for five or six generations from father to son. It is one of the few really old places in Maryland which are still owned by the original family. *October 1, 1904*

RIGGS, ELISHA FRANCIS, who was a resident of Washington, was the head of the Riggs National Bank. He was a son of George Washington Riggs, who in 1830 formed the banking house of Corcoran & Riggs, which took up the entire loan called for by the government in the Mexican War. *July 16, 1910*

RIGGS, WILLIAM P., member of the old aristocratic element of Baltimore society, was secretary of the Maryland Jockey Club. Mr. Riggs first became interested in racing in 1898 and was the leading spirit in the movement that took the Pimlico racetrack out of the slough into which it had long fallen. He was further responsible for the renewal of the Preakness and was the instigator of the big increases in the stakes of the feature races. *March 15, 1926*

RINEHART, ALLAN GILLESPIE is engaged to Miss Gratia Buell Houghton. The announcement was made in due form by her parents, Mr. and Mrs. Arthur Amory Houghton. Miss Houghton was introduced to society in Berlin a year ago, when her uncle, Mr. Alanson B. Houghton, was American Ambassador to Great Britain, and was presented at the Court of St. James's. Mr. Rinehart would follow in the footsteps of his famous mother, Mary Roberts Rinehart! He has chosen a literary career and has a lot of magazine articles to his credit in addition to his connection with a New York publishing house. *June 1, 1925*

RIPLEY, ANNAH is a debutante of great interest as the granddaughter of Mrs. Henry B. Hyde, a niece of Mr. James H. Hyde, and a daughter of Mr. and Mrs. Sidney Dillon Ripley. Sherry's, including even the rooms for private entertaining, was for that night reserved for the ball; and it was one great mansion with Mr. and Mrs. Ripley in complete possession. Mr. and Mrs. Ripley went back to the good old ways by allowing the reporters to use the word "ball," now so strictly avoided; and the entire occupation of Sherry's surely made impossible the term "a small dance." *December 24, 1904*

RIPLEY, HENRY To present his daughter Leslie on August 13, 1938, Henry Ripley, of Newport, built a ballroom onto his home at the cost of $50,000 (it was demolished the day after the party). Ripley's antipathy to publicity created a climate of intriguing secrecy, and so the party attracted round-the-clock attention from the press. One newspaper sent a helicopter with aerial photographers to snap the Ripleys at play, and Papa Ripley threatened to shoot down all other helicopters that intruded on the privacy of his guests. *June, 1965*

RIPLEY, SIDNEY DILLON is one of the most enthusiastic of Hempstead's gentlemen farmers. He has greatly improved his place on the edge of the plains, and it is now one of the most attractive of the many fine estates near the Meadow Brook Club. He is more interested in cattle than in horses. He has imported a great many lately and has a new breed of cows—brown Swiss, ungainly-looking animals but as valuable as they are ugly. *November 8, 1902*

RIPLEY, MR. AND MRS. SIDNEY DILLON II (MARY MONCRIEFFE LIVINGSTON) He is the eighth Secretary—as the Smithsonian chief administrator has traditionally been called—to rule the institution since its founding by an Act of Congress in 1846. Mr. Ripley, as this Harvard Ph.D. prefers to be called, is an erudite zoologist and articulate ornithologist. *February, 1980*

RIVES, G. BARCLAY, son of the present Corporation Counsel of New York City George L. Rives, has been appointed by President Roosevelt to be the third secretary of our Embassy at Berlin. Mr. Rives belongs to one of the most distinguished families in New York. In 1900, he married Miss Elizabeth Emlen Hare, and her death but a few months after their marriage caused his complete withdrawal from society. His manners are most courtly, and will serve to impress the German court as regards the culture and breeding of well-born Americans. *March 15, 1902*

RIVES, MR. AND MRS. GEORGE LOCKHART (SARAH WHITING) are having happy times at "Swanhurst" in Newport. Mrs. Rives, who is unusually democratic, is often spoken of as the "champion whistler of Newport." She has a sweet disposition, and at six o'clock every morning she can be found in her rose garden singing and whistling, while she culls from three to five hundred of the flowers she loves so well, delighting to arrange them herself. *June 4, 1904*

THE THREE B'S

Grande dame Mrs. T. Markoe Robertson married into the Duke tobacco fortune and co-authored *My Philadelphia Father,* about growing up as a Biddle. She's good-hearted, girlish, and scatter-brained. "I live on Ben-Gay, booze, and Bufferin," Mrs. Robertson explains. *July, 1975*

RIVES, HALLIE ERMINIE has recently returned to New York, and is now living in her studio-home, watching with interest the remarkable sale of her new novel, *A Furnace of Earth.* Her father was one of the old Rives family of Virginia; her mother was the daughter of William Edward Ragsdale, the noted tobacconist, who owned a thousand slaves. Her new novel has been likened to that of her cousin, Amelie Rives's *The Quick and the Dead,* yet to the discerning reader it is really of a different type. *The Furnace of Earth* is the story of a girl who renounces the love of a man because she imagines it to be lacking in spiritual qualities and who, after much agonized self-searching and the influences of certain dramatic occurrences, realizes her mistake. *October 18, 1900*

RIVES, REGINALD W. is Secretary Treasurer of the National Horse Show, a great whip still, and the present head of the Coaching Club. Reggie Rives saw the rise and fall of the fine harness horse, the great days of public coaching, and probably every show held by the National. *October 15, 1933*

ROBB, J. HAMPDEN was the son of James Robb of New Orleans, who built the first gas works in Havana in 1846 and who also built the first railroad connecting New Orleans with the North. J. Hampden Robb graduated from Harvard in 1866, and then studied in Switzerland. Returning to this country, he engaged in the cotton and banking business. He was a member of the Legislature of New York, Commissioner of the Parks of New York City, and Secretary of the American Museum of Natural History. In 1868, he was married to Cornelia Van Rensselaer Thayer of Boston. *January 28, 1911*

ROBBINS, REV. FRANCIS LE BARON founded a church in Kensington, Philadelphia, in the center of a great manufacturing district, and he also established the Beacon Presbyterian Church in Philadelphia, where he labored among one hundred thousand working people. His wife was the daughter of a clergyman and the niece of the Honorable Levi P. Morton, Vice President of the United States, who, in turn, is the son of a clergyman. *June 25, 1910*

ROBBINS, MR. AND MRS. WARREN DELANO (IRENE DE BRUYN) Berlin is in the midst of quite an unexpected little post-Easter social flurry. The American Embassy staff has taken the initiative in these gaieties, one of the outstanding events being a dance given at the Embassy itself. Mr. and Mrs. Robbins had engaged the services of "Buddy," whose prowess with the drumsticks has made a sensation even in sophisticated Paris, supported by "Mrs. Buddy" (named "Mattie"), equally famed for her pianistic proficiency. A distinguished company danced to Buddy's jazz and joined him in singing plantation melodies and the entire repertoire of American popular songs—including Mr. S. Parker Gilbert, Miss Ailsa Mellon of Washington, Mr. Sinclair Lewis, who for the first time this week walked down Berlin's "Main Street," Mr. William Coffin, and Baroness von Schoen (née Kathleen Burney, of Washington). *June 1, 1925*

ROBERTS, DR. CHARLES HENRY On the maternal side, he was a descendant of Van Braam, Holland's first minister to China, and a great-nephew of Owen Roberts, who owned a large estate on the island of Java. Dr. Roberts was at one time President of the Carolina Central Railway. He had a country home, "Cedarglen," in Ulster County, New York. *February 20, 1909*

ROBERTS, MARSHALL OWEN has been naturalized in England. He was educated at English schools, and is a graduate of Cambridge. The great fortune of Marshall O. Roberts, his father, had its foundation in a contract to supply the United States Navy with oil in 1837. He afterward became interested in navigation, was one of the early advocates of the Erie Railroad and one of the projectors of the Delaware, Lackawanna, and Western Railroad. *July 12, 1900*

ROBERTS, MRS. MARSHALL O. (CAROLINE D. SMITH) Mrs. Roberts' reception was one of the society affairs of the week in New York. Within, the windows were darkened and the rooms illuminated, while the art gallery was brilliant with a flood of light. At the end of the gallery was the chef-d'oeuvre of Leutze, *Washington Crossing the Delaware*, while hanging in profusion around the room were Bierstadts, Churches, Achenbachs, Gérômes, Troyons, Rosa Bonheurs, and numerous pictures of the Renaissance. *January 18, 1871*

ROBERTSON, MRS. T. MARKOE (CORDELIA DREXEL BIDDLE)—DUKE "I detest resorts," declares the colony's favorite grande dame, "but I adore Southampton. It's so cozy. You can't shoot or buy your way in here. Nobody around here cares a whit about money or social position. After a certain point, you know, one takes all that for granted. If we like you, that's all that matters." *July, 1975*

ROBINSON, ADELINE KING has made a success of her dancing classes for children, held at the Waldorf. Miss Robinson has always been noted for her grace in dancing. As a very young girl, she was one of the remarkable and indefatigable tennis players of Staten Island. But when it became necessary, on the death of her father and mother, for her to add to her income, she promptly chose the art in which she particularly excelled, and the children of fashionable New York flocked to her, their parents delighted to bring them to a teacher who was known so well socially. *May 3, 1902*

ROBINSON, BEVERLY had long been known in the social life of New York. At one time, he was Governor of the Union Club. He was the bearer of a name borne by the men of his family for six generations. He was a descendant

ROCKEFELLER

On their honeymoon: Mr. and Mrs. John D. Rockefeller III in 1933.

The word "billionaire" was coined for John Davison Rockefeller, Sr.: he was America's first and, for decades, only holder of the distinction.

Descended from a German emigrant miller who settled in Somerville, New Jersey, in 1772, John D. was the son of a traveling salesman who hawked patent medicine. A poor boy from a broken family, he was living in Cleveland and working in the produce business when he invested in a small oil refinery. Using strong-arm methods that were bitterly criticized then and later, he consolidated numerous small refineries into the gigantic Standard Oil trust in 1882. Repeatedly broken up by government action, Standard Oil continually reformed itself under new names and grew ever larger.

A pious Baptist, Rockefeller married Laura Spelman, who came from a long line of temperance advocates. No harsh drink was ever served in their home or in that of their only son, John D., Jr. The Rockefellers were not socially conspicuous (nor cared to be) for many years; it was not until they moved to a brownstone on West 54th Street in New York City that the press began to notice the doings of one of America's wealthiest families. *Town & Country* first wrote about the Rockefellers when John D., Sr.'s daughter Elizabeth wed Charles A. Strong, a minister's son, in March 1889.

John D., Jr. married Abby Aldrich, daughter of a U.S. senator and member of a distinguished Rhode Island family, in 1901. Their five sons, John D. III, David, Nelson, Laurance, and Winthrop, were known as "The Brothers," and each was notable in his own right. Nelson became governor of New York and vice president of the United States; Winthrop served as governor of Arkansas; David headed Chase Manhattan Bank —in 1995 *Town & Country* gave him its "Generous American"

award; Laurance was a noted conservationist and philanthropist; John D. III effectively managed the family's funds. Today, their twenty-two children, the fourth generation of Rockefellers, are known collectively as "The Cousins." Included among them are John D. IV, governor of West Virginia, David, Jr., manager of Rockefeller Financial Services, and Laurance, an environmental attorney and preservationist.

Late in life (he lived to be ninety-eight), John D., Sr. succeeded in his greatest accomplishment: he began giving away money. One of the first large gifts was to the Anti-Saloon League. He endowed the University of Chicago in 1892 and the Rockefeller Institute for Medical Research in 1901. In 1913, he established the Rockefeller Foundation, to which he gave $183 million. John D., Jr. continued his father's charities and added many more, such as the restoration of Colonial Williamsburg, Virginia, and the funding of Spelman College, the first institute for the higher education of black women in America. His wife, Abby Aldrich, was herself one of the founders of New York's Museum of Modern Art, and the museum has greatly benefited from the Rockefeller family's personal involvement and financial support throughout its existence. Between them, the two John D.s are calculated to have given away more than $1 billion in their lifetimes. "The Brothers" and "The Cousins" have continued this century-old tradition of philanthropy. In 1995, the Rockefeller Foundation remains a giant, with assets of more than $2 billion.

Less well known are the numerous descendants of John D.'s brother, William Rockefeller. Called the "Greenwich Rockefellers," many have resided through the years in and around Greenwich, Connecticut, often leading more socially prominent lives than their generally staid John D. cousins.

Rockefellers of achievement:
clockwise from below,
Nelson Rockefeller in 1952;
Larry and Wendy Rockefeller, 1994;
Winthrop P. Rockefeller, 1981;
David Rockefeller, 1994.
The family gathers, in the 1930s—
from left, John D. Jr., Abby Aldrich,
Laurance, John D. Sr., Winthrop,
Abby Rockefeller Milton, Nelson.

of a Colonial Lord of the Manor, who received a grant of an estate near the Hudson River from the King of England. *April 1, 1926*

ROBINSON, CALDWELL COLT Scion of both the Colt firearms and du Pont families, he is, at thirty eight, the youngest member of the Palm Beach Town Council. Also the voice of the local Republican Party and a dedicated conservationist, he is former trustee and Vice President of Ducks Unlimited. *March, 1979*

ROBINSON, MRS. DOUGLAS (CORINNE ROOSEVELT) "Henderson Home" is the now cool and inviting summer place of Mrs. Douglas Robinson, of New York. Henderson was erected in 1836 and has descended in the Henderson-Robinson line since the days of good Queen Anne, who issued letters patent to Dr. James Henderson, a surgeon in the Royal Army. The original grant included a forest tract of twenty six thousand acres. *July 1, 1905*

ROBINSON, GWENDOLYN RANDOLPH, daughter of the Marquise de las Claras (Sallie Abell, of Baltimore) married Signor Martino de Alzaga Unzue, famous motor racer and member of an enormously rich Argentine family. The bride's father, the first husband of the Marquise, was the late Moncure Robinson, eldest son of the late very socially important Mr. and Mrs. John Moncure Robinson, of Baltimore. *June 1, 1925*

ROBINSON, MRS. RICHARD HALLETT MEREDITH (ROSALIND WOOD SMITH) is the wife of naval constructor R. H. M. Robinson, and is prominent in the social life of Washington. She is a daughter of Mr. and Mrs. Persifor F. Smith of Pittsburgh, a descendant of Lieutenant-Colonel Persifor Frazier of the Revolution; of Brigadier-General Persifor F. Smith, U.S.A., and of Persifor Frazier, the geologist, who was the first foreigner whom the University of France honored with a degree. *May 4, 1907*

ROBINSON, THEODORE DOUGLAS is the fourth member of the Roosevelt family to occupy the post of Assistant Secretary of the Navy. Mr. Robinson is a son of the late Douglas Robinson and Mrs. Corinne Roosevelt Robinson, sister of the late ex-President. *December 15, 1924*

ROCKEFELLER, DAVID, JR. Great-grandson of John D. Rockefeller and son of the richest and most powerful living Rockefeller, he is studying economics at Trinity College, Cambridge, England, after exceptional performance at Harvard Law School. *June, 1967*

ROCKEFELLER, JOHN D., a magnate of the Standard Oil Company, has in contemplation a project for his own pleasure which promises to result in public benefit. He has purchased five hundred acres of land on the Hudson at Tarrytown, beautifully situated and commanding magnificent views. Setting aside a portion for a palatial residence for himself, he will devote the remainder of his land to the purposes of a park, to which the public will have freedom of access. *October 4, 1893*

ROCKEFELLER, JOHN D., JR., is about thirty years old, a graduate of Brown University, and a young man of much force of character. He has been brought before the public on account of the vast wealth of his father, but he himself is most modest and retiring. He has led a very quiet life, cares little for society, as society is known in New York, belongs to no prominent clubs, takes the most active interest in his Bible class at the Fifth Avenue Baptist Church, and since his graduation from Brown College has devoted himself to acquiring the principles of his father's business. *August 31, 1901*

THE ART OF THE DOLE

"Who is the poorest man in the world today? The poorest man I know is the man who has nothing but money—nothing else in the world—only money," says John D. Rockefeller, the Standard Oil magnate. "My opinion is that no man can trust himself to wait until he has accumulated a great fortune before he is charitable. He must give away some money continually." *March 31, 1897*

ROCKEFELLER, MRS. JOHN D., JR. (ABBY ALDRICH) and Mr. Rockefeller were due at East Hampton, though they did not wish the tradespeople, so it is said, to learn the date of their expected arrival. East Hampton is not at all what the casual observer or visitor imagines. It has a reputation for being rather dull, and while no one there—imported or native—looks gay in the slightest degree, existence is by no means wearisome. *July 13, 1907*

ROCKEFELLER, JOHN D. 3RD has held a $20-a-week job at the League of Nations in Geneva, has visited Japan and China as secretary to James McDonald of the Foreign Policy Association, and has become a trustee of such suitable organizations as the Riverside Church and the Bureau of Social Hygiene. He is a member of the board of Industrial Relations Counselors, Inc., refuses to get excused by any hanky-panky from jury duty, and lives quietly in a Beekman Place duplex with his quite suitable wife, the former Blanchette Hooker of Greenwich, Connecticut, and their three children. *December, 1940*

ROCKEFELLER, MR. AND MRS. LAURANCE (MARY BILLINGS FRENCH) For the last thirty years, a major shaping force in Woodstock, Vermont, has been 82-year-old conservationist and Rockresort founder Laurance Rockefeller. His affection for the town dates back to at least 1934, the year he married Mary Billings French in Woodstock's First Congregational Church. Over the years, he's acquired and protected most of the hills and wooded ridges rimming the town. *October, 1992*

ROCKEFELLER, NELSON, the Phi Beta Kappa of the family, was a Dartmouth man who taught Sunday School in his college years, lived on an allowance of $1,500 a year, and majored in economics. He is the most sociable of the family, President of Rockefeller Center, Inc., a good renting agent, President of the Museum of Modern Art, and a trustee of the Metropolitan Museum. *December, 1940*

ROCKEFELLER, WILLIAM is establishing a "camp" at Bay Pond, some twenty miles from the exclusive settlement on the Upper St. Regis in the Adirondacks. The tract consists of no less than fifty thousand acres, to acquire which Mr. Rockefeller eliminated from the map the little lumbermen's village of Brandon. *August 16, 1902*

ROCKEFELLER, WINTHROP Leaving a trail of business and personal failures back East, Rockefeller decided to settle on a 900-acre spread on rugged Petit Jean Mountain, Arkansas, and create a farm he called "Winrock." He stocked the farm with prize-winning Santa Gertrudis cattle from the King Ranch, and the annual cattle sale at Winrock Farms is still the social event of the year. He was much admired by the people of Little Rock and the state of Arkansas. In 1966, they elected him the first Republican Governor since Reconstruction. *May, 1981*

ROCKHILL, WILLIAM WOODVILLE He studied at the Military Academy of France at St. Cyr and was graduated with honors in ancient and modern European tongues, Oriental languages, history, and international law. Mr. Rockhill was appointed second secretary of legation in Peking in 1884. He then made an exploration of eastern Tibet and Mongolia under the auspices of the Smithsonian, and received for his scientific researches the gold medal and honorary membership of the Royal Geographical Society of Great Britain. Mr. Rockhill was the first American to penetrate the mysterious land of the Lamas. *April 15, 1905*

ROEBLING, PAUL Grandest of all cityscape sculptures, the Brooklyn Bridge, designed by the visionary engineer John Augustus Roebling, will celebrate its 100th anniversary. John A. Roebling died before construction of the bridge had even begun—in 1869, of injuries suffered while making measurements for his great project. So credit for the building of the bridge rightly belongs to his eldest son, Colonel Washington A. Roebling. And the Colonel is survived today by only two direct descendants: the Colonel's sole great-grandson, Paul Roebling, 49, an actor and producer in New York, and Paul's 18-year-old son, Kristian, a senior at New York's Calhoun School. "I observe my class with amused detachment," Paul says. "It's wonderful to be living off this reputation. I couldn't have done anything without the Roeblings' money and their name, and I'm perfectly willing to admit it. But I don't deserve to impose myself on the history of the bridge." *May, 1983*

ROGAN, MR. AND MRS. JOHN (FELICIA WARBURG) Charlottesville, justly regarded as one of the South's most gracious cities, may soon gain equal renown as the center of Virginia's bustling new wine industry, thanks to the efforts of Felicia Warburg Rogan and her husband John, owner of the Boar's Head Inn. Mrs. Rogan is the owner/president of Oakencraft Vineyard & Winery on her husband's "Polled Hereford" farm, which is within view of the Blue Ridge Mountains. *October, 1983*

ROGERS, HENRY HUTTLESTON Most families had just one house at Southampton, but Colonel Henry Huttleston Rogers had two—one on the ocean, the other, a bachelor retreat, "Port o' Missing Men," located inland and today occupied by his grandson Peter Salm. The

Port became famous for shooting parties, and Rogers, a stern taskmaster, ran a tight ship. All the sheets and bedcovers had to be changed daily; and he refused to speak to his footman directly but transmitted instructions through his butler. *July, 1975*

ROGERS, MRS. HUTTLESTON is distinguished for her persevering activities in the development of the American cultural background. Her present cause is the plight of the American Indian. Mrs. Rogers is also distinguished for the relevance, both personal and prophetic, of the clothes she has designed for herself and inspired others to design for her. The first featured event at the Brooklyn Museum's new Edward C. Blum Design Laboratory will be an exhibit of twenty four dresses made for her by Charles James. *July, 1948*

RONALDS, MR. AND MRS. LORILLARD (FANNY CARTER) At a recent dinner at the Tuileries at which the American Minister was present, Mr. Lorillard Ronalds of New York and Mrs. Ronalds were also present. The invitation, which came direct from the palace, was understood to be a compliment to the beauty and accomplishments of Mrs. Ronalds, whom their majesties wished to see more nearly. The Empress Eugénie had already been enchanted with Mrs. Ronalds' remarkable skating on the ice at the Bois de Boulogne; she had there complimented her on her skill. *April 20, 1861*

ROOSEVELT, ALICE A number of Boston people who were at the inauguration in Washington have brought home glowing accounts of the beauty and charm of Miss Alice Roosevelt, daughter of the Vice President. This daughter's mother was Miss Lee, whose parents, Mr. and Mrs. George Cabot Lee of Chestnut Hill, belong on both sides to old and prominent Boston families. Young Roosevelt was engaged while he was a student at Harvard and married directly after his graduation. His wife died soon after the birth of this daughter. *April 13, 1901*

ROOSEVELT, ETHEL is tasting deeper and deeper the delights of being the daughter of the President. A week ago, the table was spread in the great state dining room for Miss Ethel's dinner in honor of the senior class of the National Cathedral School for Girls, to whose junior class the young hostess belongs. After the dinner, an appropriate number of very youthful gallants appeared, and then the young folks had a jolly little dance in the East Room. The affair was so informal that the President and Mrs. Roosevelt went off for dinner, leaving the boys and girls chaperoned by someone else. *April 27, 1907*

ROOSEVELT, FRANKLIN DELANO Since he has been Assistant Secretary of the Navy, he has spent his time going around the country organizing amateur navies, privately owned submarine swatters, and summer resort motor patrol squadrons. Mr. Roosevelt is of Dutch origin. He received his preparatory education at Groton, graduated from Harvard University and Columbia Law School, and practiced law in New York for a time. He is deeply interested in historical research, was one of the orga-

nizers of the Naval History Society, and has for some time been engaged in compiling biographies of the early American naval commanders. *April 1, 1917*

ROOSEVELT, MRS. FRANKLIN D. (ELEANOR ROOSEVELT) It was to take in the hearings on the Edward Bok peace prize that society folk first began to wend their way in appreciable numbers "up on the Hill." Interest centered in the discovery that a former Washingtonian, Mrs. Franklin D. Roosevelt, with Mrs. Frank A. Vanderlip, had been the active agents in shaping the peace prize contest. The hearings brought Mrs. Roosevelt to town again. And so much was clear gain, Mrs. Roosevelt having been exceedingly popular here from the days when her husband was Assistant Secretary of the Navy. *March 1, 1924*

ROOSEVELT, FRANKLIN D., JR. is on the board of several companies, looks after his own portfolio of stocks, and lives an active social life. In Dutchess County, he runs a large farm and raises cattle and horses. His Riverview Terrace town house in Manhattan also serves as his office. It is the springboard to his duties as Chairman of the board of Fiat Roosevelt Motors, Inc., the United States importer and distributor of those popular little Italian cars. *September, 1973*

ROOSEVELT, HELEN ROOSEVELT, in spite of her double share of the name, is only a distant relative of the Chief Executive; but Mr. Theodore Douglas Robinson, whose wife she will be pronounced at Christ Church, in Hyde Park, New York, is a namesake of the President and son of his sister, Mrs. Douglas Robinson (Corinne Roosevelt). The bride's mother was Miss Caroline Astor, who died in 1893, when her husband was attached to the United States Embassy in London. *June 18, 1904*

ROOSEVELT, MRS. HILBORNE (KATE SHIPPEN) A Hawaiian dance was a feature of the clever entertainment at the residence of Mrs. Hilborne Roosevelt. Taking part in it were four graceful, slender girls, all wearing gowns of soft white silk, with accordion-pleated sunburst skirts trimmed with green leaves, and in their hands they carried green leaves that they waved as they swayed to and from. *December 13, 1902*

ROOSEVELT, JAMES has, in some years, been the most conspicuous of the sons of Franklin D. Roosevelt: His divorce from Betsey Cushing as well as repeated rumours of unsavory insurance profits from beneficiaries of the Administration have made this young man unpopular with some voters. America's Prince of Wales still follows the curious Roosevelt practice of stirring up continual tabloid scandals while Father and Mother fill the White House. *December, 1940*

ROOSEVELT, JAMES ALFRED is a young man who has already made an enviable place for himself in the business world. He has just taken an important position with the Third Avenue Railway Company, resuming in New York the work with which he was identified in Tampa, Florida. It is no longer considered prosaic to enter the business world, and the brilliant

businessman of the type which Mr. Roosevelt represents is gradually taking precedence over doctors, lawyers, artists, poets, and even great political chiefs. *May 30, 1908*

ROOSEVELT, KERMIT was always the hunting man of the Roosevelt family. *The Happy Hunting Grounds* is a delightful account of his shooting and hunting exploits with his father, President Theodore Roosevelt. Naturally, he has gone on traveling and has just returned from a big expedition to the lesser-known parts of Asia. In one respect, he does not resemble his father. Apparently he cares nothing for politics. *July 15, 1929*

ROOSEVELT, MRS. KERMIT (BELLE WILLARD) has not been worrying about a new wardrobe but has taken to solving other people's spring problems since she opened up her new service, Your Secretary, Inc. On the second floor of a house on East 69th Street, she and two secretaries are closeted with three telephones all day long. Your Secretary, Inc., was launched by an all-embracing folder—everything from training the children and ordering meals to organizing an African safari is known to Mrs. Roosevelt from her own life with four children and a husband who travels extensively. *May, 1939*

ROOSEVELT, MARCIA Probably no city in the United States has so many beautiful and what club men call "eligible" heiresses as New York. It is not inappropriate to head the list with Miss Marcia Roosevelt. The Roosevelts came of good Knickerbocker stock and were for many years conspicuous among the elite. Mrs. Roosevelt was a Miss Van Ness. At her death, she left her property, valued at $2,000,000, to her only daughter and, it is said, to the exclusion of her sons. *July 26, 1876*

ROOSEVELT, ROBERT B. "We have glorified our ancestors enough," said Robert B. Roosevelt, at the dinner of the Dutchess County Society last week, "and it seems to me it is about time we were doing something to glorify ourselves, so that those who come after us may have reason to feel that we, too, are their worthy ancestors." *March 9, 1898*

ROOSEVELT, THEODORE The Cowboy Regiment or, as it is understood he prefers to have it called, "The Rough Riders' Regiment," organized by Assistant Secretary of the Navy Roosevelt for service in the war with Spain, includes among its members many young men prominent in club and society life. Late recruits are Woodbury Kane, William Tiffany, Craig Wadsworth, Reginald Ronalds, Hamilton Fish, Jr., and Townsend Burden, Jr. All these young men are recent graduates of, or students at, Harvard. *May 11, 1898*

ROOSEVELT, MR. AND MRS. THEODORE, JR. (ELEANOR BUTLER ALEXANDER) Young Theodore Roosevelt's wife, who was well known in Knickerbocker society circles before she married a son of the great Theodore Roosevelt, is also going in for politics. Young Mr. Roosevelt is a member of the Assembly from Nassau County, and his wife is working very hard for the Republican party in Oyster Bay. *October 10, 1920*

ROOSEVELT

Politics and presidents: Theodore Roosevelt in 1910; Franklin D. Roosevelt in 1920.

Long ago, the Roosevelt family split into two American branches—one Republican, the other Democratic, each represented by a U.S. president. All are descended from Claes Martenszen van Rosevelt, a Dutchman (Theodore Roosevelt called him "my very common ancestor") who arrived in Manhattan sometime before 1649. Grandson Johannes Roosevelt founded the Oyster Bay, Long Island, Republican branch of the family, from which Theodore Roosevelt came. His brother Jacobus established his family in Hyde Park, New York, up the Hudson River. In 1933, America inaugurated Theodore's fifth cousin, Franklin D. Roosevelt of Hyde Park, as president.

Both branches of the family were well-to-do. Isaac Roosevelt, of the Hyde Park branch, was a large-scale sugar refiner; his heirs diversified into coal mines and railroads and for generations supported a manorial life with the dividends. Oyster Bay's Cornelius Van Schaaick ("C. V. S.") Roosevelt imported plate glass (then a great luxury) and invested in New York City real estate; by the time of his death in 1871, he was considered one of the five richest men in New York. Investments and trust funds enabled Theodore Roosevelt, C. V. S.'s grandson, to enter politics and his descendants to become diplomats, musicians, and writers.

Theodore was a whirlwind of activity. He began his political career in the New York State Legislature, served as police commissioner of New York City and as New York governor, then moved onto the national scene as vice president. He won renown (and the nation's heart) in the Spanish-American War. With the assassination of William McKinley, he became president himself. In office, T. R. brought about antitrust and civil service reform and strongly supported the conservation of America's natural resources.

The Roosevelt family includes surprising members: Elizabeth Ann (Bayley) Seton became a nun after her husband's death, founded the Sisters of Charity, and eventually was canonized as the first American-born Roman Catholic saint; Hilborne Roosevelt patented the first electric organ; Clinton Roosevelt advocated national socialism.

The Hyde Park Roosevelts married Astors and other New York aristocrats, but it was Franklin Delano Roosevelt who first brought Hyde Park to the public's attention. Like his kinsman Theodore, F. D. R. began his career in New York politics, served as governor of New York and assistant secretary of the Navy. The only man ever elected to serve four terms as president, he led America through World War II, fostered the Social Security and Securities and Exchange acts, and spearheaded other groundbreaking New Deal legislation that altered the lives of every American. His wife, Eleanor, a distant Roosevelt cousin, emerged from a secluded childhood in the Hudson River aristocracy to become an influential international figure.

F. D. R. and Eleanor had four sons and one daughter. Among them, the children married nineteen times and produced twenty children. Five Roosevelts in this century have been assistant secretaries of the Navy; others, including two sons of Franklin, have become congressmen. Current Massachusetts Governor William Weld is married to a great-granddaughter of Theodore Roosevelt.

ROOT, ELIHU In 1899 he became a factor in national politics, when invited to take the war portfolio in McKinley's cabinet. He was called the greatest Secretary of War since Stanton. In 1905, he became Secretary of State. Secretary Root was born on College Hill, Clinton, which is not very far from Utica, New York. His father was for many years a member of the faculty of Hamilton College, and a memorial hall, in his honor, has been erected by Secretary Root. *August 10, 1907*

ROOT, MR. AND MRS. ELIHU, JR. (ALIDA STRYKER) Miss Stryker, to whom Mr. Root was married at Clinton, New York, is the daughter of the Rev. Melancthon Woolsey Stryker, President of Hamilton College. In 1903, Elihu Root, Jr., left college and with another graduate walked from Clinton to New York City—a distance of 273 miles—in two weeks. He has also done a great deal of tramping abroad and has a theory that the rich man should walk to get an idea of what hard work is like and be better able to sympathize with the man with the pickax and with the hoe. *December 14, 1907*

ROSE, ANDREW CARNEGIE Son of Georgia S. Rose, née Rockefeller, he works in thoroughbred and art investments at Boston Safe Deposit & Trust Co., and is on the board of directors of the National Academy of Design. He collects American prints and etchings. *September, 1987*

ROSEKRANS, MR. AND MRS. JOHN N., JR. (GEORGETTE NAIFY)—TOPHAM He is a six-foot-two former varsity football player at Stanford University and Spreckels family patriarch. John's interests include heading a committee that is trying to build English rugby into an American sport on a par with football and baseball. "It saddens me that the last male family member named Spreckels died some years ago and there's no one left to carry on the name," says John Rosekrans. "Nor are any of us left in the sugar industry. My brother Adolph is an architect, and my brother Charles is an opera conductor living in Houston. One of my sons, John, is in real estate, and Peter is a landscape architect." *June, 1988*

ROSENWALD, JULIUS The death of Julius Rosenwald last month deprived Chicago of her greatest philanthropist. Mr. Rosenwald gave to unfortunates of every creed and color. The Negroes particularly aroused his sympathy, and he dispensed millions to build them schools and hospitals. Countless Jewish charities, not only in this country but in Europe, were financed by Mr. Rosenwald. The $30,000,000 Rosenwald Foundation to promote the welfare of mankind, the Industrial Museum now under construction in Grant Park, and the Rosenwald Children's Association Foundation, created just before his death, are only a few of the tablets to the memory of this remarkable man. *February 15, 1932*

ROSENWALD, WILLIAM The sole surviving son of Sears Roebuck patriarch Julius Rosenwald has been one of the outstanding figures in American Jewish philanthropy since the 1930s. He

has also been a generous supporter of the New York Philharmonic, Chicago's Museum of Science and Industry, and Tuskegee Institute. *December, 1983*

ROSPIGLIOSI, PRINCESS (LAURA STALLO) is one of the legendary Stallo sisters of Cincinnati (the other is the late Princess Murat). "Why should I ever leave Palm Beach?" she says. "I have only to stay at home here and the world comes to me." *January, 1950*

ROSS, SIR CHARLES AND LADY (PATRICIA ELLISON), daughter of Mr. Andrew Ellison, of Louisville, Kentucky, entertain largely at their beautiful place in Ross-Shire. "Belnagowan" is one of the largest estates in Scotland, with duck shooting that is famous over the whole kingdom. It is a most interesting place and, as is the case with the majority of such ancient homes, is guardian of a very fine collection of pictures and other treasures, including an old chair once in the possession of Sir William Wallace. *August 31, 1907*

ROUSSEAU, MRS. ENRIQUE (LILLY McKIM)—PULITZER "The old guard is pooped," quips irrepressible Lilly, who started coming down to Palm Beach in 1937 after her mother married Ogden Phipps. Suzy Phipps, owner of the biggest piece of still intact real estate on the island—bigger even than Marjorie Merriweather Post's "Mar-a-Lago"—prides herself in running about town in an old, beat-up Ford van. Lilly herself has moved from her giant mansion, although she is having a new house built, which she claims "keeps getting bigger every day. Life is changing here. There are fewer servants. Everybody building now wants a big live-in kitchen. I entertain quite sloppily." *March, 1983*

ROXBURGHE, DUCHESS OF (MAY GOELET) This summer, it was expected, there would fly from one of the turrets of "Floors Castle" in Scotland the American flag, for the Prince and Princess of Wales were to be the guests of the Duke and Duchess of Roxburghe at the Duke's magnificent ancestral home. The Duchess spent half a million dollars in necessary preparations. Already almost a million dollars has been spent in restoring Floors Castle. The Duchess has adopted the fashion of collecting animals, and she is building a miniature zoo at Floors Castle. The Duchess owns some parrakeets that fly about the castle and, when she whistles for them, light on her shoulder and pick crumbs from her lips. *August 31, 1907*

RUGGLES, SAMUEL BULKLEY laid out New York's Gramercy Park (it was the old Gramercy farm) in 1831 and presented it to the surrounding property-holders. It is hardly just to refer to him always as though giving a park to the rich instead of the poor was his greatest achievement. In fact, he had much to do with the shaping of Union Square, and it was he who selected the name of Lexington Avenue. But he was best known for his office as Commissioner to determine the route of the Erie Canal. He gave it much time and attention as a citizen as well as a Commissioner, and in his day (and now in history) great credit was given him for his zeal. *February 10, 1906*

RUMSEY, CHARLES CARY, who has taken such an active and prominent part in the recent polo tournaments at Coronado Beach, and who is now playing with the Cooperstown team at San Francisco for the Pacific Coast championship, has an interest in the Panama-Pacific Exposition quite apart from the sporting life. He is the sculptor of the heroic statue of Pizarro which stands in the South Gardens of the Exposition grounds—an excellent piece of work, graceful and impressive. *April 1, 1915*

RUSPOLI, PRINCE AND PRINCESS POGGIO SUASA (JOSEPHINE M. CURTIS) The Mayor of Rome, accompanied by his wife, arrived by the *Majestic* on a visit of business and pleasure. Prince Ruspoli has an honorable record as a soldier and is well known in the political affairs of Italy. He was seven times elected a member of the Italian Chamber of Deputies, and is now serving his second term as Mayor, or "Syndic," of Rome. *October 3, 1894*

RUSSELL, MRS. HENRY POTTER (ETHEL M. B. HARRIMAN) In the language of the moderns, the Junior League show this year was a knockout. The Junior Leaguers of New York have always had an idea on which to hang their musical comedy hats, but it seemed that never before has the idea been quite so well etched. Mrs. Henry Russell Potter was the star player among the women in the cast. As "Mommer Lenetsky," she was capital. *February 15, 1922*

RUSSELL, LINDSAY The Pilgrims' Society of London, which has for its object the promotion of friendly relations between the United States and Great Britain, was founded by Mr. Russell at the time of the coronation of King Edward in 1902. A year later, he founded the New York branch of the Pilgrims' Society. For these services, he was entertained at a banquet in London in 1903, the Archdeacon of London presiding. *December 26, 1908*

RUSSELL, SERENA Last season's Ultimate 18-year-old and No. One Deb was, hands down, Serena Russell, daughter of the Edwin F. Russells, of New York and Philadelphia. No girl ever had a more fabulous coming-out party than the one given for Serena at England's Blenheim Palace by her grandfather, the Duke of Marlborough. *June, 1963*

RUTHERFURD, WINTHROP is a graduate of Columbia '84; a member of the Union, Racquet, Meadow Brook, and Westminster Kennel Clubs. He owns the Rutherfurd Kennels at Allamuchy, Hackettstown, one of the most picturesque places in New Jersey. The estate covers several thousand acres, is beautifully laid out, and preserved with many kinds of game. The house itself is long and low in structure, suggestive of the quaintness of the English country house. *January 18, 1902*

RYAN, MRS. JOHN BARRY (MARGARET KAHN) is the daughter of Otto Kahn, German-born Wall Street banker and arts patron who headed the Metropolitan Opera, 1903–1931. Like her father, Margaret was long a Met board member and is still active on the Met's behalf. Her late husband, John Barry Ryan, Jr,. was the grandson of legendary financier Thomas Fortune Ryan. *September, 1988*

RYAN, THOMAS FORTUNE has been a figure in the business and financial world since 1874, when he became a member of the Stock Exchange. From that time, he has gradually made himself felt more and more until in 1905 he acquired control in the Equitable Life Assurance Society. His financial operations include the consolidation and extension of street railways and lighting systems in the different cities and in the reorganization of various railways in the South, coal properties in Ohio and West Virginia, and railways in Ohio. *October 26, 1912*

RYAN, MRS. THOMAS FORTUNE (IDA M. BARRY) She is said to have dispensed over $1,000,000 in charity last year. A unique characteristic in making charitable gifts was that her name be omitted from public lists of acknowledgment. *November 1, 1917*

RYERSON, MR. AND MRS. MARTIN A. The great Chicago collector was a familiar if aloof figure at the Art Institute. In the museum were a number of galleries filled with paintings he had lent—an amazing series which began with Italian panels of the thirteenth century and came to full life with brilliant examples of the Impressionists. To the end, both he and Mrs. Ryerson retained an unconscious elegance, the mark of many Chicagoans of their day. Handsome, dignified, but never stuffy, they moved easily in the salons and gardens of the world. *March, 1951*

S

SAGE, A.G.C., one of the noted Albany family, is a figure constantly seen at all the amateur racing events held on Long Island. Mr. Sage, however, does not confine his interest to racing, for he is especially fond of days with gun and rod. Every winter, he goes south to the big shooting preserves which his father, Mr. W.H. Sage, holds near Thomasville in Georgia. Every Sage is an ardent disciple of Izaak Walton, and they are of that favored coterie who for some time have controlled broad stretches of the famous Restigouche, where there is some of the finest salmon fishing in the world. *October 31, 1914*

SAGE, RUSSELL will be eighty four years old. He arrives at his office every morning at half-past nine. He is a director of thirty eight different companies, from which he draws director's fees ranging from $5 to $20 per meeting and amounting to $20,000 annually. This about covers his whole cost of living expenses, including his stable and his charities. He banks the income that he derives from his $150,000,000 investments, and his wealth is computed at $175,000,000. *March 15, 1899*

SAGE, MRS. RUSSELL (MARGARET OLIVIA SLOCUM) was the widow of the famous financier. On her father's side, she was descended from Miles Standish. She was born in Syracuse, New York, in 1828. At the age of nine, the financial affairs of the family became so involved that she was obliged to go to work to help support her family, little knowing that she would live to become one of the wealthiest women in the United States. Her family valued education and managed to send her to Holyoke Seminary. The turning point of her life came with her romance with Russell Sage. She became his second wife. Her interest in philanthropy awoke about 1890. *November 20, 1918*

SALTONSTALL, G. WEST is the party boy of a distinguished family. He took three years out to serve in the Marine Corps and will graduate Williams next year, likes football but recently has taken to rugby. Very keen on girls, he describes his chief diversion, sailing, as "my madness." *June, 1967*

POOR LITTLE PALM BEACH BABY

Perennial Palm Beacher Stephen "Laddie" Sanford once wrote a song entitled "Poor Little Palm Beach Baby": "Poor little Palm Beach Baby / She leads a sad, sad life; / Nothing to wear but beautiful gowns / Nothing to fear but millionaire's frowns; / She is a perfect lady / Perfect as ladies go; / The season is short, / If she strikes it right / She may become a queen overnight. / Married to millions - maybe - / Poor little Palm Beach baby." *February, 1962*

SALTONSTALL, LEVERETT Sir Richard Saltonstall, nephew of the Lord Mayor of London, began the American line in 1630; his son Henry was graduated from Harvard's first class in 1642. Indeed, the Saltonstalls have sent ten generations of that name to the college—more than any other family. The line has prospered through the years as statesmen, lawyers, East Indian merchants, bankers, and scholars. "Lev," former Governor of Massachusetts, who retired on top as a distinguished United States Senator, is a Boston institution that commands universal respect. *April, 1976*

SALTUS, JOHN SANFORD, patron of the fine arts who, anonymously more times than not, assisted movements of educational value or more possible monuments to artistic achievement all over the world, was a New Yorker of distinguished lineage. *August 15, 1922*

SAMUEL, MRS. FRANK One of the novel events of the season in Philadelphia was a meeting of The Mortals Club, held at the residence of Mrs. Frank Samuel, President of the organization. The club meets at the Merion Cricket Club. There is always a luncheon and a debate, in which some famous man of the past is discussed. He is both praised and criticized. The votes of the members after all arguments have been heard decide the fate of the person discussed, whether he or she shall be elected "an immortal." On Saturday, Thomas Jefferson was the subject. *March 7, 1908*

SAN FAUSTINO, PRINCESS RANIERI BOURBON DEL MONTE (JANE A. CAMPBELL) Imagine the Excelsior Hotel in Venice in the throes of amateur vaudeville produced by the Principessa de San Faustino. Imagine scions of proud, noble Italian houses and British nobility and daughters of American magnates combined in a jazz revue. Think of Lady Wimborne and Lady Northesk and Aileen Flannery and the Marchese di Portago doing a Charleston chorus. Champagne and Lady Diana Cooper dispensing it with Mrs. Cole Porter and Lady Abdy as aides. *October 1, 1926*

SANDS, ANNA Toy dogs were being judged at the Waldorf-Astoria. It was the first of two days devoted to the sixth annual show of the Toy Spaniel Club. Miss Anna Sands won many blue ribbons for her Pomeranians and, perhaps to offset possible envy and enmity caused by her victories, took pains to be particularly nice to everyone and chatted with professional and amateur exhibitors alike. Most democratic is Miss Sands at a dog show! *December 12, 1908*

SANDS, D. C., JR., one of the best known fox-hunting men in the country, has been master of the Middleburg Hunt since 1914. As there exists nowhere that we know of so healthful and robust a young ladies' seminary as has been built up in Middleburg at Foxcroft School, the number of young ladies who have learned about hunting from him must be considerable. *December 1, 1928*

SANDS, FREDERICK P. The members of the Narragansett Gun Club shot for a subscription cup on Thursday at the new grounds on Aquidneck Avenue in Newport. The entrance was five dollars, and the subscription ten dollars. Mr. Frederick P. Sands won the cup, killing ten straight birds. *September 10, 1879*

SANDS, WILLIAM FRANKLIN has been in diplomatic service for the past fifteen years and especially distinguished himself in Korea, where he was the confidential advisor of the Emperor. He was Secretary of the Legation at Guatemala for several years. He is a son of Rear Admiral Sands, and his mother is a niece of the late General George G. Meade. *August 28, 1909*

SANFORD, MR. AND MRS. HENRY (CAROLINE EDGAR) Mr. Samuel L. Sanford, the father of the bridegroom, is a professor of music at Yale, and has been one of the benefactors of the university. The grandfather of the bridegroom was the late Henry Sanford, President of the Adams Express Company, who was a prominent figure in the business world. The family, however, has been identified especially with literature, "learning," and music. Besides the bridegroom's father, there are several Professor Sanfords, each identified with a university. *March 2, 1907*

SANFORD, PROFESSOR SAMUEL SIMONS was the son and heir of Henry Sanford, founder of the Adams Express Company. Professor Sanford was elected to the chair of Applied Music at Yale University in 1894. He did much to develop the Yale Symphony Orchestra and was the most talented pianist of the university, which he served without remuneration. *January 15, 1910*

SANFORD, GENERAL STEPHEN was well known in racing circles. None better. For many years, he campaigned a great stable of horses, virtually all of which he bred himself at his "Hurricane Stock Farm" near Amsterdam in the north of New York State. The General made his home there, and his carpet mills plastered the landscape. In the old days, the Sanford horses were never brought out until the Saratoga meeting. And as Saratoga is not so very far from Amsterdam, the Sanford horses, carrying the famous purple and gold stripes, were supported with undying enthusiasm by all the people in the district. *January 1, 1927*

SANFORD, STEPHEN "LADDIE" plays polo and hunts, and he goes north to shoot. Then he goes over to England to hunt and to enjoy a few more point-to-point races. Afterwards, he dawdles up to Liverpool to see the Grand National and perhaps win it, and then he goes to London to play polo. He has the distinction of being the first American to win the Grand National. This glory fell upon him in 1925. *January 1, 1927*

SARGENT, ALICE, a debutante of last winter, was the victor at the first ping-pong tournament ever given for women. This took place at the Country Club in Boston. Miss Sargent, who is of fine physique—over six feet in height—is one of the finest athletes in the club. *March 8, 1902*

SARGENT, MRS. CHARLES SPRAGUE (MARY ALLEN ROBESON) She married Mr. Sargent, Professor of Botany at Harvard College and long identified with the Arnold Arboretum, whose reputation on the flora of different countries is world-wide, in 1873 and has ever since made her home at their beautiful estate, "Holm Lea" in Jamaica Plain, Massachusetts. She studied the foliage, flowers, and fruit of the trees of North America. Being a painter of much ability, she recorded in permanent form the results of her study in a collection of about four hundred watercolors, illustrating the woods of North America. In the social life of Boston, Mrs. Sargent was a leader. *September 1, 1919*

SATTERLEE, THE RIGHT REV. HENRY YATES was rector of Calvary Church, New York, from 1882 to 1896. In December, 1895 he was chosen bishop of Washington, and consecrated in Calvary Church in March, 1896. His diocese included thirty eight parishes in the District of Columbia and four Maryland counties. *February 29, 1908*

SATTERLEE, MR. AND MRS. HERBERT L. (LOUISA MORGAN) It is a bit unfair to always tag to Mr. Herbert L. Satterlee's name the fact that he had the good fortune to marry one of the attractive daughters of Mr. J. Pierpont Morgan. Mr. Satterlee is a man of much individuality. He has distinguished himself in finance and has become the founder of the Navy League. In the Roosevelt cabinet, he was Assistant Secretary of the Navy. *April 20, 1912*

SATTERLEE, WALTER was a son of George C. Satterlee and Mary Le Roy Livingston Satterlee. Mr. Satterlee was an associate member of the National Academy of Design. In 1886, he received the Clarke prize at the National Academy, and he exhibited many watercolor pictures showing interiors and dainty slender women in Colonial dress. *June 6, 1908*

SAULNIER, HENRY E. The Rose Tree Fox Hunting Club in Philadelphia was established in 1852 and is very vigorous today. The Rose Tree men are not very particular about appointments. Possibly they inherit a prejudice against red coats from their Revolutionary forebears, but they are keen on hunting and they never drop a fox. Some of the oldest fox hunters in the United States are members of the Rose Tree. Mr. Henry E. Saulnier, the venerable President of the Rose Tree, is now in his ninety-third year. *January 3, 1903*

SAUNDERSON, MR. AND MRS. ARMAR DAY-ROLLES (ANNE ARCHBOLD) spent last winter in pursuit of big game in India, and more recently have been in East Africa. With them, they brought some wild animals still in the coquettish infant stage—several lions now said to be gambolling on the lawn at the home at Tarrytown of Mr. John D. Archbold. The marriage of Mr. and Mrs. Saunderson was celebrated at the Cuttyhunk Club, Gosnold, Massachusetts, this place having been chosen for the sake of privacy, as Mrs. Saunderson prefers a panther to the public eye. *May 30, 1908*

SAYRE, FRANCIS BOWES, JR., dean of Washington, D.C.'s National Cathedral, is the second of three Sayre generations to summer at West Chop. His father once recalled that when he was trapped on Corregidor, at the beginning of World War II, "it was to Martha's Vineyard that again and again my thoughts and memories turned." Another member of the family, Woodrow Wilson Sayre, whose mountaineering exploits commanded international attention a few years ago, also summers at West Chop, where he has an A-frame house near the lap of the waves. *August 1971*

SAYRE, ROBERT HEYSHAM was a great civil engineer as well as a railway official. He was one of the pioneers in introducing iron bridges. In Bethlehem, Pennsylvania, he was one of the promoters of the iron industries. He was interested as a philanthropist in the hospitals and was closely allied with all the good works of the Episcopal Church in Pennsylvania's Bethlehem. *July 9, 1910*

SCAIFE, MR. AND MRS. RICHARD MELLON (FRANCES L. GILMORE) "I don't have any great guilt complex about being rich. It's a great advantage if channeled properly," says Dick, president of his late mother's family funds. When the Scaifes are together, they like to summer at the Cape and winter in Florida or California, with an occasional trip to Bermuda and Europe every other year. Two full-time pilots and their own plane help to make traveling easier. *February, 1971*

SCANLON, MRS. JAMES J. (MARY CHRISTY)—CHURCH was the daughter of Samuel Cartmill Christy and a granddaughter of Nicholas Jarrot, who erected in 1796 the first brick mansion on the east side of the Mississippi River near St. Louis. Mrs. Scanlon was one of St. Louis's wealthiest widows. Her residence was one of the handsomest in St. Louis, and she entertained very generously. The stately function that she gave for the descendants of the French officers who had

fought with Rochambeau, Lafayette, and De Grasse is still a pleasant memory to society folk of two decades ago. *July 30, 1904*

SCARBOROUGH, MRS. CHARLES ROGERS (ANNA C. VON BERLAN)—GIBBS is a daughter of Mrs. Seward Coe von Berlan. One of Mrs. Scarborough's ancestors was Roger Coe, whose story is told in *Fox's Book of Martyrs,* and she may also claim descent from the Priscilla whom Miles Standish paid court to. Mrs. Scarborough is especially well known as an earnest worker in the crèche supported by Dr. Parkhurst's Madison Square Church. *May 21, 1904*

SCARRIT, WINTHROP E. was one of the first men in this country to take up motoring and aeronautics. He owned the "House of the White Lions" in Mott Avenue, East Orange, New Jersey, which he recently sold, announcing that he intended leaving a country that did not appreciate Theodore Roosevelt. *December 16, 1911*

SCHELL, F. ROBERT "Birnam House," at Northfield, Massachusetts, the residence of Mr. F. Robert Schell, of New York, is a French château situated on high land in the heart of the historic Connecticut River Valley, commanding views for fifty miles of the Green Mountains of Vermont and the lower White Mountain range in the Granite State. Tall towers flank the entrance hall, which is 80 feet long and 23 feet wide. Mr. Schell's family chapel, cruciform in design, occupies the northeastern corner of the main floor. It is finished in oak, the windows of cathedral glass. Those in the chancel show the Schell family crest, with the rose of England and the blue cornflower of Germany on either side, indicating Mr. Schell's line of descent from those countries. *May 18, 1907*

SCHENCK, NATHALIE PENDLETON CUTTING Her grandfather was the late Rev. Dr. Noah Hunt Schenck, who became rector of St. Ann's Church, Brooklyn, in 1869. Dr. Schenck had a daughter who was the first wife of Mr. R. Fulton Cutting. The mother of Mr. Spotswood D. Schenck (Miss Nathalie's father) was a sister of Senator Pendleton of Ohio. *March 26, 1904*

SCHERMERHORN, F. AUGUSTUS will spend the remainder of the summer on the *Freelance.* Yachting has always been his greatest pleasure. Mr. Schermerhorn will not open his residence, "Pine Croft," at Lenox, Massachusetts, this year. Lenox has always recognized in the Schermerhorns its greatest benefactors. In 1874, Mr. Schermerhorn's mother, Mrs. Adeline E. Schermerhorn, purchased the county courthouse and presented it to the town for a library building. Mr. Schermerhorn added to this building the assembly room, and the campanile of Trinity Church was also a gift from them. *July 26, 1902*

SCHERMERHORN, MRS. WILLIAM C. (ANNIE E. H. COTTENET) The death of Mrs. William C. Schermerhorn may result in some change in old landmarks. The Schermerhorn mansion on Twenty Third Street is the last private residence on the block and stands hemmed in by shops and business buildings. There is a music room, which was also used for dances, and in its day was considered one of the most commodious apartments of its kind. In fact, it was practically the first private ballroom in New York. The Schermerhorn fortune is one of the largest in New York, and its holdings are valuable real estate. Until within a year of the late Mr. Schermerhorn's death, Mrs. Schermerhorn and her daughters each season entertained at the Twenty Third Street house. For many years, these entertainments took the form of musicales with the orchestra of the New York Philharmonic Society or the Opera House. It was the first private residence at which these concerts were ever given, and to be asked there was an absolute cachet of social position. *March 2, 1907*

SCHIEFFELIN, BRADHURST He was associated with Horace Greeley in affairs of public interest and was at one time connected with the People's Party. He believed that no republic can exist where wealth is allowed to accumulate in the hands of a small minority. He favored a law limiting inheritance. Following the Civil War, he turned over his fortune to charity. *March 20, 1909*

SCHIEFFELIN, GEORGE R. The Southampton season will barely last the fortnight. The meets of the Monmouth County hounds prolong it, and they are proving most enjoyable. George R. Schieffelin, Treasurer of the Southampton Horse Show Association, has published a card to the effect that the association will pay any damages to fences or growing crops that may be caused by the hunting under its auspices. *October 4, 1900*

SCHIEFFELIN, WILLIAM JAY is one of the most public-spirited citizens of New York. Mr. Schieffelin is at the head of many excellent reforms and philanthropies and is the moving spirit of all of them. About forty six years of age, he has been for some time the President of Schieffelin & Company, the wholesale druggists, a firm that has existed for more than a century in New York. In 1891, he married Miss Louise Shepard, granddaughter of the late William H. Vanderbilt. Mr. Schieffelin is a grandson of the late John Jay. *August 3, 1912*

SCHIFF, DOROTHY The daughter of Mr. and Mrs. Mortimer L. Schiff, she will be one of an interesting group of girls making her bow this winter. The family's country home is "Northwood," Oyster Bay, Long Island, not far from the Piping Rock Club, with which summer colony the Schiffs have been affiliated for years. *September 20, 1921*

SCHIFF, JOHN M. is undoubtedly the best-mannered polo player extant. You know how difficult it is to be polite during every bruising melee; at Aiken, South Carolina, I saw Mr. Schiff knock a goal post over with his head without uttering an oath. *May, 1939*

SCHIFF, MRS. JOHN M. (EDITH BAKER) shoots skeet at Piping Rock these spring weekends in a tweed suit that is closely akin to Joseph's coat of many colors. Mrs. Schiff spends considerable time on Long Island, coaching her Labrador retrievers, who performed well in the field trials in the autumn, and superin-

tending the planting of innumerable white flowers in the Schiff conservatories. In town, she takes her piano seriously, knits unusual scarfs, dances in the Persian Room in a stunning black dress. *April 1, 1935*

SCHLEY, JESSIE H. is leading propaganda for peace in Europe. As a result of the conference of peace advocates, Miss Schley was appointed a special commissioner to visit Madrid and Washington and lay the protest of two thousand women of all nations before the Queen Regent and President McKinley. *July 17, 1898*

SCHLEY, MR. AND MRS. REEVE III (GEORGIA R. TERRY) both grew up around Far Hills, but they never intended to stay. "We looked all over New Jersey and never found country more beautiful than this spot on the river, and it borders Reeve's father's farm," Georgie says. (The Schleys have been there at least eighty years.) Apart from giving watercolor classes at the National Academy of Design in New York, Reeve shows his paintings at the Graham Modern Gallery. *June, 1986*

SCHLEY, COMMODORE WINFIELD SCOTT "Now, for pity's sake," says Commodore Schley, "don't give my last name with a German accent. It's pronounced Sly—plain, commonplace, Sly. I'm not much on pedigree-searching—too many of my acquaintances have stumbled across horse thieves and pirates to make me desirous for that kind of recreation, but Schley is an old Maryland family, though why they've stuck on all those sloppy Dutch consonants I can't tell. It's Sly I was born, and it's Sly I'll be." *June 15, 1898*

SCHOONMAKER, ALTHEA LIVINGSTON is a member of an old family long identified with Ulster County, New York, and one that has included men of much distinction. Cornelius Schoonmaker, who was born in Ulster County in 1745, sat in the state assembly from the adoption of the Constitution in 1777 till 1790. His grandson, Marius Schoonmaker, was a famous lawyer and a statesman. He was a Congressman and following that, Superintendent of the bank department of the State of New York. *November 6, 1909*

SCHREINER, CHARLES III The most famous of the Hill County, Texas, institutions is the "YO Ranch" owned by the Schreiner family. Run by Charles Schreiner III and his sons, it spreads over more than 100 square miles, covering some 50,000 acres. Charlie, known as Charlie Three, has turned the YO into a Safari Club West. Hunters have come from all over the world to see or shoot exotic game animals. There are some 10,000 animals on the YO, including jack rabbits, javelina, and white-tailed deer. They commingle with zebra, giraffe, ostrich, emu, ibex—exotica from the nether reaches of the globe. *June, 1983*

SCHROEDER, MR. AND MRS. GILLIAT GHEQUIERE (HELEN WHITE STEVENS) She was a descendant of the great Peter Stuyvesant, a granddaughter of the distinguished Dr. Alexander H. Stevens, the founder of the College of Physicians and Surgeons of New York City, and a great-granddaughter of General Ebenezer Stevens of Revolutionary fame. She

was married in old St. Mark's Church, the land on which it stands having been the gift of Peter Stuyvesant, who, from his portrait in a stained-glass window, observed the whole ceremony placidly and watched his pretty little descendant (eighth in line) go up the nave. The bridegroom is a grandson of the late Henry A. Schroeder, the banker and philanthropist of Mobile and Baltimore. *June 10, 1905*

SCHROEDER, HENRY A. of Mobile, Alabama, was one of the most famous financiers of his time and also well known as a host and man of much intellectual attainment. He had traveled over much of the world and in the days when such experiences were rare. He was an authority on all social customs, and "It must be correct, because it was served so at the Schroeders'" was often the defense for some innovation. His "dinings," as they were called in those days, were at his home on Government Street, Mobile's aristocratic thoroughfare. Four o'clock was the time set for dinners, though they were prolonged until late candlelight. *November 23, 1907*

SCHUCHARDT, MARY Her mother, who is of French descent, is a Southerner. On her father's side, she is connected with the Stuyvesants and Remsens. The Schuchardts claim as their native city, however, proud old Frankfort-on-the-Main, and the family is still represented there. Everyone was interested in the treasures in Mrs. Schuchardt's drawing-room in New York, for there are miniatures and also quaint chairs brought over in the famous *Spotted Cow,* a sailing vessel that preceded the *Mayflower. March 12, 1904*

SCHUYLER, J. MONTGOMERY, JR. In appointing Mr. J. Montgomery Schuyler, Jr. second secretary of the Embassy in Russia, President Roosevelt will send from New York one of the most desirable young men in society. He goes to Russia with the goodwill and the regret of not only hosts of pretty girls but also their mothers. Mr. Schuyler, despite his position, belongs to none of the fashionable New York clubs but is a member of the Sons of the Revolution and the Mayflower Descendants. *May 17, 1902*

SCHUYLER, MRS. MONTGOMERY (KATHARINE B. LIVINGSTON) A Martha Washington tea was given, in honor of Washington's birthday, to the Dames of the Revolution by Mrs. Montgomery Schuyler, the society's First Vice President. Mrs. Schuyler's fine collection of Revolutionary relics was greatly admired. Most of them are heirlooms inherited by her husband and herself from Livingston and Schuyler ancestors. The guests were in colonial costume. Mrs. Schuyler personated Martha Washington and received in a rare old cream-colored satin, brocaded with delicate pink roses, shoulder cape of old lace, and little cap of fine muslin. *March 3, 1897*

SCHUYLER, MR. AND MRS. PHILIP VAN RENSSELAER (JEANNIE FLOYD-JONES CARPENDER) He has a name that shows his claim to kinship with the patroons of Rensselaerwyck. Philip John Schuyler, the great soldier who had a home in Albany for forty years, the scene of lavish hospitality, married Catherine Van

Rensselaer. Miss Carpender's name denotes relationship to the Floyd-Jones family that acquired its double patronymic for reasons of inheritance. Judge Davis Jones, having no male heir, deeded his wealth to David Richard Floyd, whose mother was Arabella Jones, on condition that he adopt the hyphenated name Floyd-Jones. Setauket, Long Island, was founded by the Floyds, and Fort Neck, in Queens County, Long Island, belonged to the Jones family. *April 23, 1910*

SCHWAB, CHARLES M. Andrew Carnegie said some years ago he wanted to cross a mountain in Pennsylvania, and a youngster of rather hardy appearance offered to take him over for fifty cents. Carnegie thought the price too great, and told the boy he would pay him only twenty five cents. After a long argument, the youngster won out. "I predicted that the boy would some day make a fortune," said Mr. Carnegie, "and he has." His name was Charles M. Schwab. *April 18, 1903*

SCHWAB, GUSTAV H. was head of the firm of Messrs. Oelrichs & Co., agents for the North German Lloyd Steamship Company. Mr. Schwab, who was for many years a leading figure in the shipping circles of two continents as well as one of New York's most public-spirited citizens, came from illustrious stock. His father was the son of the German poet Gustav Schwab. In 1890, Mr. Schwab was instrumental in forming the People's Municipal League and later the Citizens' Union. He was for fourteen years President of the German Society of the City of New York, which was founded by his great-great-grandfather, Professor John Christopher Kunze. *November 23, 1912*

SCOTT, MR. AND MRS. EDGAR (HELEN HOPE MONTGOMERY) Mrs. Scott is still the same golden girl on whom Philip Barry based the character Tracy Lord in his play *The Philadelphia Story* in 1939. Set on an estate modeled after "Ardrossan," the 750-acre farm on the Main Line where Helen Hope Montgomery Scott still lives, the play was so successful it was made into a movie twice—the second time as the musical *High Society*. *January, 1993*

SCOTT, JEAN BROWNE, of Philadelphia, considered one of the best lady whips in America, took part of her stable to England for the Olympia Horse Show and while there bought Knight Commander at a reported price of $15,000. She won the grand championship at Olympia and the Richmond Horse Show with this horse. *September 15, 1924*

SCOTT, MRS. RANDOLPH (MARION DU PONT) At the foot of the Blue Ridge mountains in Orange Co., Virginia, stands "Montpelier," the impressive home of James Madison, the "Signer" and fourth President of the United States. It is owned by Mrs. Marion du Pont Scott, whose famous stallion Battleship, in the Grand National of 1938, brought her the distinction of being the first American to breed and run the winner of the most difficult and hazardous steeplechase in the world. *September, 1948*

It has taken Columbia University one hundred and sixty one years to find a woman worthy of the degree of LL.D. In conferring the degree upon Miss Louisa Lee Schuyler, President Butler acclaimed her as the "worthy representative of a splendid line of ancestors, great-granddaughter of General Philip Schuyler of the American Revolution and great-granddaughter of Alexander Hamilton of the class of 1777." At the beginning of the Civil War, Miss Schuyler joined the United States Sanitary Commission and was one of its most energetic workers. In 1872, as a result of her visits to the inmates of the poor houses and hospitals supported by the state, she founded the States Charities Aid Association. The first training school for hospital nurses in this country was established by Miss Schuyler at Bellevue Hospital. She would seem to be quite properly entitled to her honorary degree. In fact, it might appear that Columbia has been tardy. *June 10, 1915*

SCOTT, S. BUFORD is Chairman of Scott & Stringfellow, the brokerage founded in Richmond, Virginia, by his grandfather, Frederic Scott, in 1893, now the oldest member organization of the New York Stock Exchange in the South. *August, 1979*

SCOVEL, EDWARD Mr. Edward Scovel, the young American tenor who three or four years ago married Miss Marcia Roosevelt of New York, and has since then been pursuing his musical studies in Italy, appeared as Lohengrin, at the Nice Opera House. His voice is a light tenor of the sweetest quality. The English and American colonies showed their appreciation of his talents by floral offerings so large as to make it doubtful whether the fortunate tenor could take them home. *April 20, 1881*

SCRIBNER, CHARLES was born on Manhattan Island, educated here until he went to Princeton. Princeton runs in the Scribner blood; his father, brother, and son are all alumni, he himself was one of the organizers of the Princeton Club, and for two terms its President. He is now a trustee of the University. He has been head of Scribner's since 1879. *Scribner's Magazine,* in its present form, was started by him in 1887. *October 20, 1916*

SCRIPPS, ELLEN BROWNING, a gentle but tough-minded spinster, had worked beside her brothers in founding the giant Scripps newspaper chain. With her brothers and sisters, but most often alone, she gave the money to build the graceful, simple buildings that today comprise La Jolla, California's town center. She started La Jolla down the road of higher education with the endowment of the Scripps Institution of Oceanography, one of the world's foremost graduate schools in marine studies. *May, 1975*

SCUDDER, RICHARD B. The Publisher of the *Newark News,* he is justly proud of his forebears' importance in the development of the State. A Scudder signed New Jersey into the

---

Union; there is a town called Scudders Falls; his father founded the *Newark News* in 1882; and his aunt, Antoinette Scudder, founded The Paper Mill Playhouse. *March, 1964*

SCULL, DAVID was one of the oldest members of the Society of Friends. He was President of the Board of Trustees of Bryn Mawr College and a member of the Board of Managers of Haverford College. One of his ancestors was Nicholas Scull, who was Surveyor General in Pennsylvania in 1748 and who was a member of Franklin's Junta Club. *November 30, 1907*

SEABURY, LISPENARD The established families of New York filled the Church of the Incarnation on the wedding day of the former Lispenard Seabury and Edward Savage Crocker, 2d. The name Lispenard Seabury means something to those who know their world. Anthony Lispenard, from whom the bride is directly descended, was an early New Yorker. A Seabury ancestor was the first Episcopal bishop in the United States, and she numbers five Colonial governors on her scroll of genealogical history. *June 1, 1923*

SEARS, ELEONORA, great-great-granddaughter of Thomas Jefferson, is a champion athlete: women's squash racquets (1928) and four times tennis doubles title; hiked 75 miles in 16 hours 10 minutes by her log book; often walked 47 miles from Boston to Providence "just for exercise." Has 300 cups for squash, tennis, horse-show jumping. *April, 1962*

SEARS, MRS. JOSHUA MONTGOMERY (SARAH CHOATE) With all Mrs. Sears' wealth and the temptations which come with it for a pleasure-loving life, she is devoted to her painting and has already done some admirable portraits. Her watercolors, too, shown at the last Water Color club exhibition, were pronounced unusually fine. *May 11, 1901*

SEARS, J. MONTGOMERY, JR. The untimely death of J. Montgomery Sears makes his son, who bears his name, the wealthiest young man in Boston. He is very like his father, has good business ability, a thorough education, is something of a linguist, and altogether likable. *June 10, 1905*

SEARS, RUTH AND ESTHER, daughters of Dr. George and Mrs. Sears, of Beacon Street, Boston, and Cohasset, captured the Hodder cup with their *Mighty Mite* seventeen-footer, and brought themselves and the Cohasset Yacht Club much glory. *October 1, 1924*

SEDGWICK, ARTHUR GEORGE He belonged to a family identified with Stockbridge for many generations. He was the son of Theodore Sedgwick, 3d. Arthur George Sedgwick was at one time Editor of the *Evening Post* and also of the *Nation. August 1, 1915*

SEDGWICK, CATHERINE MARIA In Stockbridge, Massachusetts, so the residents all maintain, the crickets chirp "Sedgwick! Sedgwick!" It was the home during the latter part of the eighteenth century of Theodore Sedgwick, the statesman, and the birthplace of his daughter, Miss Catherine Maria Sedgwick, one of the first women in America to gain fame as an author. Never since the statesman made his home there has Stockbridge been without a representative of the Sedgwick family, and no matter how many millionaires might suddenly decide to build show-places in the old town, the crickets would still chirrup, "Sedgwick! Sedgwick!" *September 12, 1908*

SELIGMAN, DE WITT One of the grand events of the season was a wedding at the residence of Mr. Simon Bernheimer. The ceremony was performed by Dr. Gottheil, of the Temple Emmanuel, on Fifth Avenue. The bridegroom was Mr. De Witt Seligman, son of Mr. James Seligman, the banker, and the bride, Addie S., daughter of Mr. and Mrs. Simon Bernheimer. The families on both sides are ranked among our most wealthy Hebrew residents, and they carry their wealth with simplicity. They are well known in social and business circles, the Bernheimers being large real estate owners and the Seligmans being of the firm of J. & W. Seligman & Co., members of the Syndicate. The head of the house, Mr. Joseph Seligman, is a prominent member of the Union League Club. The bridegroom is a brother of Mr. Eugene Seligman, who recently distinguished himself at Columbia College by taking first honors in almost every branch of study at that institution. *June 12, 1878*

SELIGMAN, HENRY was one of eight brothers who founded the banking house that bears the Seligman name. Among his nephews are Albert Joseph Seligman, the banker, who is interested in stock-raising and who has been prominent in the politics of Montana; Edwin R. A. Seligman, who has the McVickar professorship of political economy at Columbia University; and Isaac Newton Seligman, who is one of the most active of the influential New Yorkers interested in charities and good government. *February 27, 1909*

SENFF, CHARLES H., a director of the American Sugar Refining Company and a well-known figure in the sugar trade of this country, died at Whitestone, where his summer home is one of the finest residences on Long Island Sound. Mr. Senff was a relative of the Havemeyer family and was associated with Theodore A., Thomas J., and Henry O. Havemeyer as members of the sugar firm of Havemeyer & Elder. *September 2, 1911*

SETON, MRS. ALFRED, JR. (MARY LORILLARD BARBEY), who is one of the "first ladies" of Tuxedo Park, New York, is a daughter of the late Henry I. Barbey. Her mother, Mrs. Barbey, who is now at her villa in Geneva, Switzerland, is a daughter of the late Peter Lorillard. The Countess de Pourtalès and the Baroness de Neuflize are sisters of Mrs. Seton. *July 27, 1907*

SETON-THOMPSON, MRS. ERNEST (GRACE GALLATIN) first met Ernest Seton-Thompson en route for Europe in 1894. He was then hard at work on his valuable *Art Anatomy of Animals,* and Miss Gallatin, becoming interested in it, rendered invaluable assistance. In the summer of 1896 their marriage took place. Her own new book is called *A Woman Tenderfoot.* In 1899, Mrs. Seton-Thompson with her husband made the famous 10,000 mile

journey through British America, California, and the Rockies; during which, as a result of experience and necessity, she evolved several valuable devices and brought into being practical and suitable costumes and apparatus for riding and for camp life. *November 8, 1900*

SEVERANCE, MR. AND MRS. CORDENIO A. (MARY FRANCES HARRIMAN) He was a law partner of the present Secretary of State, Frank B. Kellogg, was internationally known as a corporation lawyer and as a relief worker during the World War. Both Mr. and Mrs. Severance have been active in the life of the Northwest, their great country home, "Cedarhurst," just outside St. Paul, having been much of a social center. *June 1, 1925*

SEWARD, WILLIAM H. Mr. Seward was there, impassible as ever, with a sandy and tough face, on which the sharp contests of a long life of New York and national politics would seem to have made no impression. *March 8, 1862*

SHATTUCK, ALBERT R. has just purchased "The Mount," the country residence at Lenox, Massachusetts, of Mr. and Mrs. Edward R. Wharton and the place where Mrs. Wharton has written many of her books and stories. One connects Mr. Shattuck with the growth and popularity of motoring as a sport for gentlemen and its proper regulation. As early as 1899, he was one of the incorporators and the first President of the Automobile Club of America. Its object was to record the experieces of members and others using motors, promoting the development of motor contests and good roads, and securing rational legislation. All this has been accomplished. Mr. Shattuck is a man of independent wealth. He married Miss Mary Strong, the daughter of the late Mayor Strong of New York. *September 16, 1911*

SHAW, HOWARD Lake Forest, Illinois, will have another private playhouse. This is to be an open air theater modeled after the Italian amphitheaters of other days and is being built by Mr. Howard Shaw on his grounds in the north shore suburb. The amphitheater has low walls, and it is to have a permanent stage and fittings. Fourteen long brightly-painted poles will support forked pennants, and these will encircle the amphitheater. From pole to pole, Chinese lanterns will be strung. Two roads will lead to the theater—one by the garden for the guests and another by the pergola for the performers. *July 20, 1912*

SHAW, PATRICK is President of the Modern Poetry Association, which publishes *Modern Poetry,* America's oldest poetry magazine. Shaw comes from a family of distinguished Chicagoans: His great-grandfather endowed the Institute's Joseph Winterbotham Collection. A great-aunt, Rue Winterbotham Carpenter, established Chicago as an outpost for contemporary art twenty years before the founding of the Museum of Modern Art. *December, 1988*

SHAW, MR. AND MRS. QUINCY A., SR. (PAULINE AGASSIZ) Mrs. Quincy A. Shaw, Sr., is a distinguished woman of the type that Boston considers peculiar to its city. Plain attire and high culture are qualities which distinguish

the type. Mrs. Shaw is a daughter of the late Professor Louis Agassiz. Like her mother, Mrs. Agassiz, who, though now at a great age, still retains in aristocratic state the homes at Cambridge and Nahant, she has been faithful to the traditions of the family in furthering education. Mr. Quincy A. Shaw, Sr., controls thirty thousand shares of Calumet and Hecla stock. The wealth of this mine was practically established by Professor Agassiz, who not only discovered but developed it. *August 6, 1904*

SHAW, MRS. ROBERT GOULD 2D (NANCY LANGHORNE), who won such fame for her daring riding and hunting at the Myopia Kennels at Hamilton, won new laurels at the horse show at Richmond, Virginia. She rode and drove in the ring, capturing blue ribbons galore. One of Mrs. Shaw's sisters, Mrs. Charles Dana Gibson, was an enthusiastic spectator. *November 1, 1902*

SHELTON, ROBERT His mother's grandfather started the "King Ranch," the largest ranch empire in the world. He learned ranching at the knee of his uncle, Robert Justus Kleberg, Jr., the originator of the Santa Gertrudis breed of cattle and breeder of three Kentucky Derby winners. Shelton stinted nothing that would make his "Comanche Trace" horse breeding farm at Kerrville, Texas, the state of the art. A staff of veterinarians, biologists, computer experts, mechanics, wranglers, and trainers are in-house. At the peak of the season, up to 200 mares may be in foal in the "Mare Motel," their stalls monitored by closed-circuit television. *June, 1983*

SHEPARD, MRS. ELLIOTT F. (MARGARET LOUISA VANDERBILT) gave a pound party in aid of the approaching fair at the Academy of Music for the Young Women's Christian Association. A pound party "is an entertainment to which each person is invited to contribute a pound of such article as he or she may select, which is sold at auction during the evening. Each package remains unopened until purchased." A pound of sausages, with some very witty verses by Miss Milbank, brought $28; a kitten, $6; a mince pie, $7; a pair of boxing gloves marked "good for one pound," $6. *February 2, 1876*

SHEPARD, FINLAY J., whose engagement to Miss Helen Gould, the daughter of the late Jay Gould and the wealthiest unmarried woman in America, has just been announced, is assistant to the President of the Missouri Pacific and other railroads and a bachelor of forty five. Miss Gould's fiancé is interested in the work of the Y.M.C.A., and during a recent trip which she and a party of friends made to inspect her Western railway properties he was almost constantly in her company. Miss Gould, who has never cared for society, has devoted her life and a part of her great fortune to religious and charitable work, particulary to the naval branch of the Y.M.C.A. *December 21, 1912*

SHERIDAN, FRANCIS JOSEPH is a member of the Auchincloss, Fahnestock, and Sheridan clans. He accompanied his two cousins, Bruce and Sheridan Fahnestock, whose findings in their four and a half years of cruising in the

Southwest Pacific in their own schooners proved of great help in the present war, when they were asked by the Army to go to Australia before Pearl Harbor to help form the small-ships branch of transportation. *June, 1945*

SHERMAN, IRENE AND MILDRED, the daughters of Mr. and Mrs. William Watts Sherman, made their formal entry to the social world at a wonderful pink ball. On their mother's side, the Misses Sherman are descended from Chad Brown, who was the first in a long line of distinguished men identified with Providence, Rhode Island. Chad Brown, who came to this country in 1638, was so successful in adjusting the quarrels of the colony that the honorable title of "peacemaker" was accorded him. Nicholas Brown, who died in 1841, was a great philanthropist, and in recognition of his munificent gifts to the Rhode Island College, its name was changed to Brown University. *January 13, 1906*

SHERRILL, GENERAL CHARLES is suddenly interrupted in his reading of old French memoirs in the Library of Congress and ordered to depart for Istanbul as Ambassador to Turkey. One of the most amusing and most amazing of men will step into our Embassy upon the Bosphorus. His work ranges from books about stained glass windows, about the Monroe Doctrine, about kings and presidents he has interviewed, to being Minister to Argentina and heading the American Committee on the Olympic Games. Because he does not have to work for money and because he has a questing mind, he remains eternally busy. *April 1, 1932*

SHEVLIN, MR. AND MRS. THOMAS LEONARD (ELIZABETH SHERLEY) Mr. Shevlin is now President of the Shevlin Lumber Company, commanding a salary as big as that of the President of the United States. Mr. Shevlin graduated from Yale in the class of '05, and that year he was the Captain of the Yale football team. One great secret of his success is that no pastime or amusement, no matter how alluring, can wean his attention from his business. No weather is too cold for him to go off into the far northern part of Minnesota into the lumber districts, to look after his interests. *February 1, 1913*

SHIPMAN, REV. HERBERT is the rector of the Church of the Heavenly Rest, Fifth Avenue, New York. In appearance, he is ascetic and he is high church, but not extreme in his views. Dr. Shipman is a son of the late Jacob S. Shipman, who at one time was rector of Christ Church at Thirty Fifth Street and Fifth Avenue. At Columbia, he was class poet, and he was graduated from there in 1890. For nine years, he was chaplain at the United States Military Academy at West Point. Mrs. Herbert Shipman is the daughter of Mr. and Mrs. Edson Bradley, now of Washington and formerly of Tuxedo. *May 18, 1912*

SHOEMAKER, HENRY WHARTON, JR., began in the banking business. Then he went into diplomacy and was Secretary of the American Legation at Lisbon and the American Embassy at Berlin. He gave up his diplomatic career for practical newspaper work, and he is Editor and owner of the *Altoona Morning Tribune.* He has also published several books. His sister is Mrs. Alfred Wagstaff, the poetess and a part editor of a New York publication devoted to verse and literature. Mr. Henry Francis Shoemaker, the father, was a banker for a number of years and is also interested in coal mining and is a stockholder in many railroads. *May 3, 1913*

SHERMAN'S MARCH FROM WASHINGTON

"I left Washington chiefly because my salary would not support me, and I did not consider the society there a proper place in which to rear a family," said General William Tecumseh Sherman. "Very few cabinet officers are able to live within their salaries. While I was there, the only member of the cabinet who could stand it was Hamilton Fish. With his income of $200,000 a year, he could afford to pay most any price for social pivileges. Nevertheless, it cost him $70,000 a year." *March 8, 1876*

SHORT, CHARLES W., JR. His mother was Miss Mary Dudley of Lexington, granddaughter of Dr. Benjamin W. Dudley, a well-known Kentucky physician and host. The Dudley residence was the scene of many charming entertainments, and it figures in John Fox, Jr.'s, *Little Shepherd of Kingdom Come.* The Dudleys are a most aristocratic family in that little bulwark of aristocracy, Lexington, the pride of the blue grass region. Mr. Short's father was a descendant of John Cleves Symmes, the pioneer of Ohio and former owner of the whole southern part of it, and a descendant of William Short of Virginia, the first Chargé d'Affaires to France, and a cousin of the former Presidents William Henry Harrison and Benjamin Harrison. *September 28, 1912*

SHOTTER, MR. AND MRS. SAMUEL P. The hunt breakfast given by Mr. and Mrs. Samuel P. Shotter of Savannah for the Berkshire Hunt was the most novel event of the season in Lenox, Massachusetts. Everything was Southern, the decorations of Spanish moss and cotton balls having been sent from Savannah for the occasion. There were, among other famous Southern dishes, terrapin, chicken, Virginia ham, beaten biscuits, cornbread, and other delicacies prepared by Mrs. Shotter's cooks, who came from Georgia. Handsome favors were presented, representing cotton pickers carrying baskets of cotton on their heads. *September 30, 1905*

SHOUSE, MRS. JOUETT (CATHERINE FILENE) is the founder and guiding spirit of Wolf Trap Farm Park for the Performing Arts in Virginia. Kay Shouse has had a long career of service. In 1920, she wrote a book on jobs for women. Three years later, she received a master's degree in education from Harvard. Born in Boston, Massachusetts, and heir to the Filene department store fortune, Mrs. Shouse has lived in Washington for fifty four years. Married to Jouett Shouse, a leading Democrat and one-time Assistant Secretary of the Treasury, the Shouses made their headquarters in Georgetown. In 1930, they acquired Wolf Trap Farm. *December, 1976*

SIBLEY, MARGARET of New York is the daughter of Mr. and Mrs. Alfred Brush Sibley and a granddaughter of the late General Henry H. Sibley, who was so prominent in the early history of the Northwest, holding every office of importance that Minnesota as a territory or state could give. The General's home at Mendota, a few miles from St. Paul, was the place where famous men and even Indian chiefs were often welcomed. The house was recently presented to the Minnesota Daughters of the American Revolution by the Catholic Church. *September 3, 1910*

SIBLEY, MRS. RUFUS ADAMS (ELIZABETH SIBLEY CONKEY) will give a dance for her daughter, Miss Elizabeth Sibley. The head of this well-known family in Rochester, New York, was Hiram W. Sibley, who, like his son Mr. Hiram Sibley, was a benefactor of several universities. Mrs. Hiram Sibley is a daughter of the late Fletcher Harper, one of the founders of the Harper Brothers publishing house. *December 28, 1907*

SIDAMON-ERISTOFF, PRINCE AND PRINCESS CONSTANTINE (ANNE PHIPPS) When Prince Eristoff's father and his cousins Pierre and Dimitri escaped to America, "They spoke not a word of English," he recounts. "However the Georgian network had already spread in the U.S., and a man in Newport called Norman Whitehouse, who was married to Princess Tamara Bagration-Moukhransky, had placed each. Father was sent to the Huntington Tracy place to be a chauffeur—which was unfortunate, because he could only ride a horse. He was met at the station by Miss Ann Huntington Tracy, who eventually became his wife." *March, 1984*

SIMMONS, J. EDWARD was the President of the New York Chamber of Commerce. He was President of the Stock Exchange in 1884 and 1885. He served as President of the Board of Education for five years, but several times he declined the nomination for high political offices. *August 13, 1910*

SIMMONS, MR. AND MRS. JOHN (ADELE SMITH) Her great-grandfather Perry Smith ran the Chicago & North Western Railway before the Civil War; another great-grandfather, George Thorne, co-founded Montgomery Ward & Co.; and a great-grandmother Lucy Flower set up Chicago's first juvenile court system. Adele's father, the late Hermon Dunlap Smith, built Marsh & McLennan into a national insurance powerhouse. A former dean at both Tufts and Princeton, she had capped her academic career by becoming, in 1978, President of the iconoclastic Hampshire College in Massachusetts. To the trustees of the equally iconoclastic John D. and Catherine MacArthur Foundation, Chicago's largest, she was the perfect choice to take the helm. *September, 1990*

SIMONDS, MRS. ANDREW (CECILIA BREAUX) is one of the most prominent society women of Charleston, South Carolina. She is well known to New Yorkers, and has spent a great deal of time at Tuxedo, New York. When Mrs. Simonds was unanimously chosen as Chairman of the Board of Entertainment, Ceremonial and Reception Committees for the West Indian Exposition, she invited to serve with her all the representative women of the place—the President of the Colonial Dames and her following to represent the Conservatives, and the "Modernists," the two warring elements in quaint and conservative Charleston. They worked hand in hand for the honor and glory of their town. *April 23, 1904*

SIMPSON, MRS. JAMES, JR. is one of the most talented members of the younger set in Lake Forest, Illinois. She shares the literary tastes of her father, Joseph Medill Patterson, of the *Chicago Tribune*, and is becoming known as a magazine contributor. *September 15, 1928*

SIMPSON, WILLIAM KELLY is professor of Egyptology at Yale and consultative curator of Egyptian and ancient Near Eastern art at Boston's Museum of Fine Arts. Simpson has directed excavations near the pyramids in Egypt, and is also President of the International Association of Egyptologists. Frequently in transit, he maintains residences in Beekman Place, in New Haven, and in upstate New York. *February, 1987*

SINGER, PARIS, youngest son of the sewing-machine millionaire, is preparing to celebrate his approaching coming of age with festivities of unexampled magnificence. The great feature of the festival will be a semi-private performance of Gounod's *Faust*, in which Paris Singer will himself sustain the character of Mephistopheles, while the impersonation of Marguerite will be specially undertaken by Mlle. Marie Van Zandt, who receives two thousand dollars for coming from Paris to take the leading part in the performance. *August 15, 1888*

SLADE, MRS. WILLIAM GERRY (EMMA M. HARDY) The Order of Americans of Armorial Ancestry has issued invitations for a private view of the work of the order. Heraldic illustrations, genealogical records, and book-plates will be shown that are of special interest in connection with the Hudson-Fulton celebration. At four, tea will be served. Mrs. William Gerry Slade is President of the order. *September 25, 1909*

SLATER, ELINOR was born in Norwich, Connecticut, as were her parents and grandparents and great-grandparents. From Norwich, Mr. and Mrs. Slater went to Washington some years ago. They have traveled extensively on Mr. Slater's yacht. Miss Slater's grandfather, Mr. John A. Slater, married Miss Marianna Hubbard of Norwich. The Hubbards and the Slaters were the most influential people of their generation. Both fortunes were made by the aid of the little Shetucket River that runs by Norwich. Too shallow to admit any navigation drawing more water than a row boat, it still poured large fortunes into the busy hands of industrial

New Englanders over one hundred years ago, when the Hubbards established the first paper mill on its banks and the Slaters started a cotton mill. *September 25, 1909*

SLOAN, SAMUEL was born in Lisburn, Ireland, on Christmas Day. He was a graduate of the Columbia College Grammar School of New York and entered on his career as a railroad man in December, 1854, the Christmas month evidently bringing him the good luck for which he was noted in the business world. In 1855, he was appointed President of the Hudson River Railroad; from 1867 to 1899, he was President of the Delaware, Lackawanna and Western, and at one time was also President of the Michigan Central. *September 28, 1907*

THERE ARE MANY GIFTS, II

The Everglades Club, designed by Addison Mizner for Paris Singer, was built in 1919, and the original idea was for it to be a convalescents' home after World War I, for mentally-disturbed servicemen. After the Armistice, Singer invited 300,000 men to come to Palm Beach and enjoy, at his expense, all the facilities of the club. He received just 33 replies. *February, 1962*

SLOANE, EVELYN, on the maternal side, is the granddaughter of the first and only Mayor of Williamsburg, New York, the late Dr. Abram Berry—an aristocrat of the aristocrats who was so particular with his practice, it is said, that unless patients applying were of blue blood, he would turn them over to his assistants. Williamsburg, in the days of the Berrys and before this section of what is now the greater city was swallowed bodily by Brooklyn, had a distinct aristocracy of its own. This element was bitterly opposed to union with Brooklyn, and for a long time after consolidation registered from Williamsburg when traveling, just as some Brooklynites even now refuse to register from New York. *April 27, 1907*

SLOANE, MRS. HENRY Dinner dances are again to be a feature of the winter's gaieties. The first will be given by Mrs. Henry Sloane. The dinner dance is an outcome of the increase of metropolitan society and the impossibility of including the whole of a lady's visiting list in the invitation to one great ball. They have been adopted by the ultra smart set, who thus weed out all those who are uninteresting and uninviting. *December 22, 1897*

SLOANE, JOHN was the son of W. S. Sloane and the nephew of John Sloane, who founded the house of W. & J. Sloane in 1843. He was a director in many companies and an active member of the ·Brick Presbyterian Church. He was a warm personal friend of President McKinley and a stanch Republican. *December 16, 1905*

SLOANE, MRS. JOHN (ADELE VANDERBILT) An inventory of the estate of Mrs. Adele Sloane, widow of John Sloane of Lenox and New York, was filed in the Berkshire Probate Court, Pittsfield, Massachusetts. The inven-

tory shows a total property valuation of $3,247,000. This is the largest inventory ever filed in the Berkshire Probate Court. The bulk of the property is in high-class securities, chief among which is 10,200 shares of Northern Pacific Railway, valued at $1,273,725. *October 7, 1911*

SLOANE, WILLIAM DOUGLAS now owns the finest property in the Berkshires. His "Highlawn Farm" is a notable estate in itself, over one hundred men being employed there in season. His town house receives all of its supplies from this farm—fresh milk, cream, eggs, and fruits such as figs and peaches, which are grown under glass, melons, and flowers. By special arrangement, Mr. Sloane is able to have his farm produce handled by early trains and delivered in New York City daily in time for luncheon. *June 12, 1909*

SMITH, ANITA MERLE is a daughter of the Rev. Wilton Merle Smith. Miss Smith christened the *Robert Fulton* with water from the old well at "Clermont," where once lived Chancellor Robert R. Livingston, the friend of Robert Fulton, whose steamboat the *Clermont* steamed up the Hudson on August 11, 1809. At Miss Smith's side, when she broke the bottle, stood her cousin Miss Katherine L. Olcott. Both young women are granddaughters of Commodore Alfred Van Santvoord, founder of the Hudson River Day Line. *March 27, 1909*

SMITH, CHARLES SPRAGUE He was the founder of the People's Institute, which has as its purpose the education of the masses—lectures, entertainments, and classes in study being held weekly at Cooper Union, New York. He was at one time the Gebhard professor of languages at Columbia University, and later the professor of Romance languages and foreign literature. *April 9, 1910*

SMITH, MR. AND MRS. EDWARD BYRON (LOUISE DEWEY) Mr. Smith, Chairman of the executive committee of the Northern Trust Company, is one of Chicago's social leaders. The Byron Smiths, of all the old Prairie Avenue families, seem to have the largest number of descendants who are socially active today. She is a former President of the Lyric Opera woman's board and of the Antiquarians. *September, 1978*

SMITH, ELIZUR YALE is a scion of staunch old Puritan stock. On both sides, he is a direct descendant of Pilgrims who voyaged here in the *Mayflower* and of whom there were actually but twenty seven families, despite the claims put forth by countless cultivators of family trees. His mother was a Miss Bullard, and his great-grandfather President of Yale. His father, the Hon. Wellington Smith, late member of Congress, is widely known as one of the most extensive paper manufacturers in the East—his great mills as well as his country seat being located at Lee, Massachusetts. *November 10, 1906*

SMITH, MRS. HINKLE Butterflies are symbolical of society the world over, but that is not the reason for Mrs. Hinkle Smith's interest in them. Her collection was gathered in the real ardent zeal of the scientific mind. It is said that she has fixed names of various society folk upon her specimens, but the main thought of the collection is legitimate and far from satire. Mrs. Hinkle Smith gave her last informal at-home of the season. Besides an excellent musical program, she exhibited all her butterflies. *March 3, 1906*

SMITH, J. CLINCH, who is to return to America to live after an absence of some years will, it is rumored, settle near the Meadow Brook Club on Long Island and go in for hunting and sports in the open. He comes from the famous family of Smiths who founded Smithtown, New York, and his mother was a Miss Clinch, one of the heiresses of the A.T. Stewart millions. On his last visit here, he had a most disagreeable experience. He was at the Madison Square Roof Garden on the night when his brother-in-law Stanford White was shot and killed by Harry Thaw, and Thaw stopped and spoke to him a few minutes before the tragedy. *April 29, 1911*

SMITH, MRS. J. CLINCH (BERTHA LUDINGTON BARNES) The largest social function of the season at Newport was the dinner-dance given by Mrs. J. Clinch Smith, of Philadelphia. The table decorations were unique. A square table seating fifty six people was used, and the entire space in the center was made to represent a farmyard scene. The space, twenty feet square, was filled with grass growing on a level with the table, and on the turf were scattered about heaps of all kinds of vegetables. In the center rose a stack of cornstalks, with numerous red-shaded electric lights shining through between the stalks. *August 30, 1902*

SMITH, J. HENRY took charge of the business of two uncles, sturdy Scotchmen, who had come to America just before the Civil War and who had invested heavily in western railroad stocks and in property in the city of Chicago. When the last died, about nine years ago, he had lived in London at a club for a number of years. He knew few people, and no one dreamed that he would leave over thirty millions. This sum was the heritage of Mr. J. Henry Smith, who began immediately to entertain, to go into society, to increase his club membership, to buy a villa at Tuxedo, a box at the opera, and finally to purchase the splendid town house of William C. Whitney, which was easily one of the finest places in the entire city of New York. *July 17, 1909*

SMITH, JOSEPH LINDON laid the magic of his touch on the decorations for the "Submarine Ball." An astonishing array of fishy costumes adorned the dancers, and Horticultural Hall in Boston was transformed into an undersea vista. Gilded fish shed pale illumination over coral grottoes, and on the surface of the sea huge bubbles bobbed softly. Mr. Smith and his two talented daughters, Miss Rebecca and Miss Frances, did a clever frog dance, and everyone was quite delighted with the town's first and only "fish ball." *May 15, 1924*

SMITH, DR. AND MRS. KIRBY FLOWER (CHARLOTTE LAW ROGERS) Dr. Smith was professor of Latin at the Johns Hopkins University and was considered one of the most distinguished of American classical scholars. He was born

in Pawlet, Vermont, but came of distinguished Louisiana ancestry, being a grandson of the late General Kirby Flower Smith of the Southern Confederacy. His wife is a descendant of the Washington and Custis families. *December 20, 1918*

SMITH, PERRY H. was an early head of the Chicago and Northwestern Railroad. His second son, real estate magnate Dunlap Smith, died young, but not before fathering two of the city's most respected figures. As Headmaster of North Shore Country Day School from 1919 to 1954, Perry Dunlap Smith educated generations of Chicago leaders and gained national prominence in progressive education. His brother, Hermon Dunlap ("Dutch") Smith, built Marsh & McLennan into the world's largest insurance brokerage house, then, after retiring in 1971, ran the Field Foundation of Illinois. (A third brother, Elliott Dunlap Smith, was provost of Pittsburgh's Carnegie Institute of Technology.) *September, 1990*

THE WELL-SEASONED GUEST

For nearly fifty of his seventy years, Harry Worcester Smith has been a notable horseman. He began hunting and steeplechasing in 1886. He is ex-Master of the Grafton Hounds, the Piedmont Hunt, and the Loudon Hunt. As master of the Westmeath Hunt (1912–13), he was the first American M. F. H. in the United Kingdom. He has also made a fortune in textile inventions and textile maneuvers, collected a splendid sporting library and picture gallery, insulted scores of people, worn red silk socks with evening clothes, and invented a new way of summoning sleepy butlers. He confesses, "I would throw a salt or pepper cellar at the door with such force that it would wake the dead. They never broke, but marred the doors, but what did it matter? But I will say it was a little disagreeable for the guests sitting at the end of the table, with their backs to the door." *March, 1936*

SMITH, R. PENN In the beautiful Chester Valley, Pennsylvania, lies the running of the Chester Valley Hunt, of which Mr. R. Penn Smith is M. F. H. Mr. Smith's hounds meet at Startford, and they are hunted regularly each season. A day with the Chester Valley hounds is a treat to a man who likes to watch the hounds properly work a scent and not make a steeplechase out of the hunting. *January 3, 1903*

SMITH, ROSAMUND FLOWER, a daughter of Mrs. Wilfred Mustard by her former marriage with the noted scientist, the late Dr. Kirby Flower Smith of the Johns Hopkins, was among the enviable few American girls presented to their Majesties at the First Full Royal Court since the world war. Miss Smith's costume for the occasion was of jade green satin with a court train of chiffon the same color, all embroidered with silver roses and completed by a short tulle veil and three white ostrich feathers in her hair. *August 15, 1922*

SMITH, MR. AND MRS. SYDNEY ANDREW (FLORENCE RICE) One of the most notable of the early summer weddings was theirs in the Byzantine Chapel of St. Bartholomew's in New York. He is the son of Mr. Sydney J. Smith and Mrs. Tailer Carpenter of New York and a nephew of the Countess of Stafford. Mrs. Smith is the daughter of the vivid and popular writer of things sporting, Grantland Rice. *July 15, 1930*

SNOWDEN, CHARLES RANDOLPH was the senior member of the brokerage firm of Snowden, Barclay and Moore. He ranked as about the best polo player in and around Philadelphia, being No. 1 on the Bryn Mawr Club's four. He was also a dashing cross-country rider, taking an active part in all the fox hunts held by the Radnor Hunt Club. *February 15, 1913*

SPALDING, PHILIP E., JR. "In the last ten years business has changed drastically—more mainland money, mainland presidents, and mainland stockholders," notes the President of Hawaiian Western Steel, Ltd. Spalding's roots run deep; his missionary great-grandfather founded the Chief's Children's School, forerunner of Punahou School; his grandmother started Honolulu's Academy of Art. *March, 1971*

SPEARS, GENERAL AND MRS. EDWARD L. (MARY BORDEN) have been in Chicago. Mrs. Spears has advanced greatly in her art since her first book amazed and amused Chicago years ago. Her last book, *Jane Our Stranger,* is highly praised by critics, and her new book, *Three Pilgrims and a Tinker,* is awaited with respectful interest. *October 15, 1924*

SPENCER, LORILLARD, prominent in New York society, was brought up and educated abroad. His sister married into the Cenci family of Rome and became closely attached to the Court of Queen Margherita. Young Lorillard Spencer was not satisfied with life away from his own country. He returned to the United States in 1878 and entered the Columbia Law School. Mr. Spencer was commissioner from Rhode Island to the Chicago World's Fair, and at one time owned and published the illustrated *American Magazine.* He was the owner of "Chastellux" on Halidon Hill, Newport, Rhode Island. *March 23, 1912*

SPENCER, WILLING has been appointed secretary to the American Embassy in Berlin. He comes from a family whose names have long been associated with the law. His mother is one of the leaders in the most exclusive set of the Quaker City society. The Spencers have a large town house on Spruce Street, a charming country house at Devon, and a summer home in Newport. *August 26, 1911*

SPENCER-CHURCHILL, LADY CHARLES (GILLIAN FULLER), a delicious blond sugar-plum, has both maternal and paternal money. Her beautiful mother, Geraldine Spreckels Fuller, comes from a family that was dipped, rather dunked, in sugar. Her father, Andrew Powie Fuller, is a Texas financier and industrialist. Gillian came out a couple of years ago at the Fort Worth Assembly and in New York. The music had hardly died down before Gill was engaged to smashing, dashing Lord Charles

Spencer-Churchill, grandson of the late great American heiress Mme. Jacques Balsan, who was Consuelo Vanderbilt. *May, 1966*

SPERRY, REAR ADMIRAL CHARLES was assigned to the presidency of the United States Naval Academy in 1903. He was ordinance officer at the New York Navy Yard at the beginning of the war with Spain, and after the war was made President of the Naval War College at Newport. His wife is a granddaughter of Governor William L. Marcy of New York. *February 25, 1911*

SPEYER, JAMES is a well-known figure in New York financial circles who has astonished the world of moneyed affairs by successfully financing the new Mexican $40,000,000 gold loan. The deal is regarded as marking a new epoch in international finance. He and his wife have done much to improve the educational facilities of the poor, and they gave $100,000 to the Teachers' College of Columbia University. *January 21, 1905*

SPRECKELS, MR. AND MRS. ADOLPH (ALMA DE BRETTEVILLE) One of San Francisco's finest early mansions is a magnificent white "Parthenon of the West" on Washington Street that was Alma and Adolph's dream home. In this "wedding cake house" (also known as "the sugar palace"), Alma reared three children. The oldest, Adolph junior, was a brawling, irascible man whose sixth wife, Kay Williams, left him to marry Clark Gable. Little Alma and her sister Dorothy had three much-publicized weddings apiece. Dorothy's last, to the multimillionaire Charles Munn of Paris and Palm Beach, was the only one of the twelve marriages that didn't end in divorce. *June, 1988*

SPRECKELS, CLAUS was born in Lamstedt, Hanover. He came to this country in 1846 and was the pioneer in the sugar refining industry of the Pacific Coast. In 1876, he went to the Hawaiian Islands and made himself owner of their product of sugar cane. A fight with the Eastern Sugar Trust and another with the Southern Pacific Railroad made him famous. *January 2, 1909*

SPRECKELS, JOHN D. As early as the Twenties, polo was thriving in California. The sport had been launched there in 1906 by John D. Spreckels—the son of San Francisco "Sugar King" Claus Spreckels—who had moved to San Diego, bought a street-car line, a newspaper, and the Hotel del Coronado. Spreckels sponsored a $5,000 polo cup at his Coronado Country Club. *January, 1987*

SPRECKELS, MR. AND MRS. RUDOLPH (NELLIE JOLLIFFE) of San Francisco are in the East at present, Mr. Spreckels being intent upon bringing about the purchase of the Western Pacific Railroad by the government. Mr. Spreckels is one of the few wealthy Californians who devote their time to the public service. He was prominent in the Woodrow Wilson campaign, and he had the distinction of refusing to be Ambassador to Germany. Mr. Spreckels has repeatedly made the public promise never to take office. Before he became interested in altruistic movements, he

had the finest polo ponies in California at his country home, "Sobre Vista," in Sonoma County. *April 10, 1915*

SPRUANCE, EDIE "You work all year to get to the Garden for the National Horse Show," sighs Pennsylvanian Edie Spruance, who owns hunters and jumpers. "It is a challenge. I guess in the horse business we call it heart. They are tired when they get here. This show doesn't just test their athletic ability; it tests their courage." *October, 1983*

STANFORD, MRS. LELAND (JANE LATHROP), widow of late Senator from California, has executed deeds conveying to Stanford University the bulk of all her wealth, consisting principally of stocks and real estate. Mrs. Stanford's reason for making the conveyance at this time was a desire to have her affairs in such shape that, in case of accident, the university trustees may secure prompt possession of the estate. The total value of Mrs. Stanford's gift to the university is $10,000,000. *June 7, 1899*

STANLEY, JOHN B., an intelligent and wealthy planter residing near Newsmansville, East Florida, is said to be the most successful hunter in the state. Besides his almost daily presence on his plantation during the last twenty five years, he has killed at least ten thousand deer, one hundred wolves, sixty panthers, and twelve bears. *February 28, 1857*

STANTON, MRS. CHESTER (MAUD GURNEY), a lady celebrated for her magnificent social entertainments both in this city and in London, gave a "monogram dinner-party," as it was called, at her handsome Murray Hill residence, which for novelty and elegance has very seldom been surpassed. The invitations, numbering twenty, were gotten up in a beautiful and unique style, a large illuminated monogram covering the entire face of the card and envelope. The object in giving this dinner, we understand, was partly for the purpose of exhibiting a dinner set of china and glass which was made to order at the royal manufactory at Copenhagen, each piece being decorated with the monogram "M. G. S." Much gossip was created in society by the rather odd announcement, and those who were so fortunate as to receive an invitation to the entertainment were objects of envy. *June 3, 1868*

STEARNS, FREDERICK K. The musical event of the season in Detroit was the concert of the New York Symphony Orchestra with Mr. Walter Damrosch as conductor, and this was largely the outcome of the personal efforts and the generosity of Mr. Stearns, who has been much to the fore in the plans for building a spacious and modern music hall in Detroit. After the concert, there was a reception for Mr. Damrosch at "Red Gables," the home of Mr. and Mrs. Stearns on Jefferson Avenue in Detroit. *February 8, 1908*

STEELE, MRS. CHARLES (NANNIE FRENCH), a daughter of Mr. S. Barton French by his first marriage, was one of Southampton's social leaders this summer. A great many matrons in society speak of her as Nannie French, a laughter-loving, curly-headed blonde, who

played tag and hopscotch with her companions in West Thirty Third Street. Mr. Steele is well known as a lawyer and as the legal adviser and partner of Mr. J. Pierpont Morgan. His father was T. Nevitt Steele, the noted lawyer, of Baltimore. *September 26, 1903*

STEELE, FRANKLIN came to St. Anthony, Minnesota, in 1838 and located the first claim in what is now Minneapolis, so that he has been considered the founder of the city. He built the first dam across the Mississippi, the first sawmill and until his death in 1880 was regarded as one of the leading men of the state. He donated to the city the square which bears his name. *December 2, 1911*

STEINWAY, CHARLES H. has his most interesting progenitor in Henry E. Steinway, as the fortune that came later to the family had its basis in his ingenuity, which was demonstrated first when he was a boy at his home in Wolfshagen, Germany. Then his musical constructions were zithers and guitars, made for his amusement. According to Liszt and Rubinstein, Henry Steinway did more to advance the tone quality of pianos than any maker in the world. *July 23, 1904*

STEINWAY, WILLIAM, one of the rapid transit commissioners and a member of the great piano concern, is a guest at Richfield Springs, New York. Mr. Steinway is a genial and versatile conversationalist. His timely generosity toward financially embarrassed, talented young musicians is well known. "Grand, square, and upright," is the sentiment a grateful and enthusiastic admirer expresses toward him. *August 19, 1896*

STEPHENSON, MRS. CHARLES L. (MARTHA WASHBURN) died at her home in Mandan, North Dakota. Mr. Elihu B. Washburn, Minister to France during President Grant's administration; Mr. Israel Washburn, one-time Governor of Maine; General Cadwallader Washburn, Governor of Wisconsin; Mr. Charles A. Washburn, who served as Minister to Paraguay, S.A.; and General William D. Washburn, of Minneapolis, a United States Senator, were her brothers. *May 8, 1909*

STERN, LOUIS, dry goods merchant, of Twenty Third Street in New York, purchased "Graystone" on the Hudson, which the widow of Macy, the banker, found too large for her occupancy. As you drive toward the house from the main entrance and as you come nearer on the road to an immense, new, castle-like three-story stone edifice, the upper windows of which are tastefully draped and curtained, you say to yourself: "What a very large and splendid house Mr. Stern occupies!" So he does, but you are a quarter of a mile distant from it; this is only the stable. *October 26, 1898*

STETTINIUS, MRS. EDWARD R. (JUDITH CARRINGTON) At one of the Bahamas' innumerable flowered-chiffon teas, Mrs. E. R. Stettinius, widow of a Morgan partner, was receiving felicitations on the elevation of her son in U.S. Steel. "You must be very proud to have such a big business in the family," they all cooed. Mrs. Stettinius allowed that she was, but of course she was also proud of her son-in-law, Juan Trippe, head of Pan American. From that moment, she was known to Nassau as the mother of American industry. *June, 1938*

STEVENS, DR. ALEXANDER H. was the first President of the New York Hospital and also President of the College of Physicians and Surgeons. With two other physicians, he shares the honor of having his name encrusted in mosaics in the new Congressional Library at Washington. Dr. Stevens' widow was Miss Phoebe Lloyd, daughter of John Nelson Lloyd of Lloyd's Neck, Lord of the first of the Long Island manors enjoying a charter granted by the King; and this property is still in the family. Mrs. Stevens' mother was a Miss Chanler, whose mother was a Winthrop of the distinguished New England family, and her grandmother was Judith Stuyvesant, a lineal descendant of the great Peter. *November 24, 1906*

STEVENS, MRS. EDWIN A. (EMILY C. LEWIS) gave a Twelfth Night levee at Castle Point, New Jersey, which approached nearer to the spirit and tradition of that good old celebration than anything that has been done in years. About two hundred guests, who were brought from New York by special ferryboats, responded to the quaintly-worded invitations. After a fine show of Mrs. Jarley's wax works, the fun began. There was a King of Misrule, as well as the Yule log and the wassail and a host of traditionary matters. *January 2, 1895*

STEVENS, FREDERICK C. On the outskirts of the village of Attica in Wyoming County, New York, is the stock farm of Senator Frederick C. Stevens, a son of the late Congressman Robert S. Stevens. This is the "Maple Wood Hackney Stud and Stock Farm" and comprises about one thousand acres of the finest land to be found in Western New York. The first foundation stock for The Maplewood Hackney Stud was imported in 1895, to which was added a large importation made in 1896, which latter was probably the largest and most valuable importation ever made of animals of this kind. *November 10, 1906*

STEVENS, FREDERICK W. of 2 West 57th Street, is introducing his daughter, Miss Daisy Stevens. The furnishings and decorations of the ballroom of Mr. Stevens's house, including the oaken floor with its centerpiece of ebony and ivory, were brought from an old château in Flanders and arranged in their original design. The walls present a light neutral tint and are covered with leather and Gobelins tapestry. The ballroom and parlor were both used for dancing, and all the rooms were lighted by wax candles. *January 11, 1882*

STEVENS, MRS. FREDERICK WILLIAM (ADELE LIVINGSTON) The Marquis de Talleyrand-Périgord and Mrs. Stevens were married in Paris. At the instance of the Marquis, settlements were made by which Mrs. Stevens retains the absolute control of her property, and the interests of her children are protected. Judge Pierrepont, of New York, acted as her counsel. The Duc de Dino, father of the Marquis, has conferred upon his son, in honor of the bride, the right to bear the title of Duc. *February 2, 1887*

STEVENS, MR. AND MRS. GEORGE, JR. (ELIZABETH GUEST) They are part of the new generation that's been left with the old family name and the old family money. They are the young affluents. To this select new generation, it's not so much a question of making money as it is a question of what to do with the money they already have. They have been married five "constantly traveling" years, according to George. "We go everywhere together." But all the traveling has a purpose. It's part of George's job as Director of The American Film Institute. *February, 1971*

A MOVEABLE FEAST

Paran Stevens, who is building a private palace for himself at Newport, through some odd notion had his house framed in Boston, the stone prepared there, the joiner work, so far as possible, done, and everything else made ready. The materials are then transferred by railroad, and put together by Boston workmen. He is doing this, probably, because he made most of his money in Boston; but it will not make him many friends among Newporters. *September 9, 1865*

STEVENS, MRS. COMMODORE JOHN COX The Commodore, it will be remembered, took the famous yacht *America* out to England. Mrs. Stevens was one of the most charitable and at the same time most singular of women. Sometimes she promenaded Broadway very carelessly dressed, leading a little poodle dog. At such times, she wished to be incognita, and even her most intimate friends scarcely dared recognize her if they met her. *March 17, 1855*

STEVENS, MRS. JOSEPH SAMPSON (CLARA SHERWOOD)—ROLLINS is prominent in New York, at Newport, and in the Long Island colonies. She is one of the enthusiastic sportswomen who ride to hounds with the Meadowbrook Club. Mr. and Mrs. Stevens make their home at Jericho, Long Island. Mr. Stevens is a son of the Duchess de Dino (Mrs. Sampson) of Paris and a brother of Mrs. Frederick H. Allen of "Bolton Priory," Pelham Manor, New York. His grandparents lived in the old Sampson mansion on Broadway and Bond Street. *November 6, 1909*

STEVENSON, MR. AND MRS. ADLAI (ELLEN BORDEN) A December wedding of interest to those who follow members of the present generation whose forebears formed the nucleus of Chicago society in the past was that of Miss Ellen Borden to Mr. Adlai Stevenson. On her mother's side, she belongs to the Waller tribe who, three generations back, owned most of Chicago's far North Side. Mr. Stevenson is a grandson of a former Vice President of the United States. *January 15, 1929*

STEVENSON, ADLAI III is a former Senator from Illinois. His great-grandfather, the first Adlai Stevenson, was Vice President under Grover Cleveland. His father, Adlai Stevenson II, was one of the century's most respected statesmen, Governor of Illinois, a Presidential candidate, and Ambassador to the U.N. *October, 1986*

STEVENSON, MRS. CORNELIUS, as an archaeologist and an author, is known in the Old World as well as in this country. She is the daughter of Edward Yorke and was born in Paris. In 1897, she went to Rome on a special mission for the department of archaeology and paleontology of the University of Pennsylvania and in 1898 to Egypt for the American Exploration Society in connection with archaeological work on the Nile Valley. Mrs. Stevenson received the first degree ever conferred on a woman by the University of Pennsylvania. *April 4, 1908*

STEVENSON, MRS. DAVID (CHARLOTTE LATROBE) was the daughter of the late Honorable and Mrs. Ferdinand C. Latrobe of Baltimore. Her family connection was one of the most widely known and distinguished in this country. Through her father, who was for many years Democratic Mayor of Baltimore, she belonged to one of the aristocratic old Maryland lines, who were among the earliest settlers of Baltimore. Her mother was Miss Ellen Penrose of Philadelphia. Mrs. Stevenson has been closely identified with the leading social element of several cities. *February 10, 1921*

STEVENSON, MR. AND MRS. JOHN R. (RUTH CARTER)—JOHNSON The Chairman of the Amon Carter Museum board and President of the $120 million Carter Foundation is Amon Carter's daughter, Ruth Carter Stevenson. She now divides her time between Fort Worth, North Carolina, and New York, where her husband, John R. Stevenson, President of the National Gallery, heads the law firm Sullivan & Cromwell. Amon Carter, Sr., died in 1955; his will provided for the founding of a museum in his name. "We would not allow anybody to raise money to build a statue downtown or any of that foolishness," Mrs. Stevenson says. Carter's approximately 350 Russell and fifty Remington oils and bronzes began what his heirs considered a more fitting monument. *November, 1986*

STEVENSON, MALCOLM is chiefly known as one of the great polo players of his day, but as a matter of fact he was equally pre-eminent in the hunting field, and certainly conspicuous on the race course. When still very young, he was elected to the position of Master of the Meadow Brook Hounds, and for some years gave great sport in a country which still remains a shibboleth whenever fast runs and big fences are discussed in America. *April 15, 1928*

STEWART, ALEXANDER TURNEY His picture gallery, in his new Fifth Avenue mansion, was lighted by gas one evening last week for the first time as an experiment. One hundred and twenty five gas burners were brought into use, which shed a brilliant but soft and mellow light on the rare works of art and show them to the best advantage. *September 8, 1869*

STEWART, ANITA is the daughter of Mrs. J. Henry Smith, formerly Mrs. W. Rhinelander Stewart. On the maternal side, she is a niece of Mrs. A. J. Drexel and, on her father's side, a niece of Mr. Lispenard Stewart and a great-granddaughter of the late Philip Rhinelander.

Early in July, announcement was made of Miss Stewart's engagement to Dom Miguel of Braganza. *August 28, 1909*

STEWART, GABRIELLE TOWNSEND has especial prominence as the Secretary of the Municipal Art Society. She was admitted to the New York Bar at the beginning of the present term of court. Miss Stewart was one of the well-known society girls of Cleveland, and began to read law as a diversion but developed such a love for the study that she entered the Law School at the State University at Columbus. She says that her greatest inspiration in her study was the portrait of one of her ancestors, William Murray, Lord Chief Justice of England, the Earl of Mansfield. *March 26, 1904*

STEWART, LISPENARD is a public-spirited citizen of whom New York may well be proud. The Lispenard family is of Huguenot origin, Antoine Lispenard having come to America after the Revocation of the Edict of Nantes. Mrs. Stewart's mother, Mary Rogers Rhinelander, was a member of that well-known German-American family which, for more than a century past, has been so intimately connected with the business growth of New York. He was the only Republican State Senator elected from the city in 1889, and his career in the Senate was most creditable. Among his more notable achievements was his introduction and success in passing through the Legislature the bill creating the Rapid Transit Commission. *August 23, 1900*

STEWART, REDMOND C. As a family, there is precious little they don't know about horses. In 1925, Mr. Redmond C. Stewart beat the best men and the best horses in the county and won with Mrs. Stewart's chestnut mare, Krona. This year, his son Redmond C. Stewart, Jr., did the same, winning the Challenge Cup presented by Mr. Stephen Sanford. Mr. Stewart, although no longer a youngling, remains one of the best across country men going, and for many years was master of the Green Spring Valley Maryland Hounds and hunted them himself, making a reputation which will never fade away. *January 1, 1927*

STEWART, WILLIAM MORRIS He was first District Attorney and then Attorney General of California. He went to Virginia City, in Nevada, in 1860. He became interested in the Comstock Lode and its development. In 1864, he was elected United States Senator and in 1869 re-elected. He owned a residence in Washington called "Stewart Castle," where he entertained lavishly. *May 1, 1909*

STILLMAN, CHAUNCEY The dean of American coaching: A member of both New York's and London's Coaching Club, he has been the champion of historically correct form and elegant equipage in the U.S. Such notables as Princess Anne and Prince Philip have ridden in his George IV phaeton, horsed by a postilion team of Wethersfield Hackneys. *December, 1987*

STILLMAN, THOMAS E. and his two charming daughters, Miss Mary Stillman and Miss Charlotte Stillman, are taking a trip through the South in their private car. Miss Mary Stillman created quite a sensation with her deli-

cate beauty when presented at court several seasons ago. The youngest daughter, Charlotte, is very athletic, and has won some magnificent trophies at golf. *March 15, 1902*

STIMSON, MRS. HENRY A. (JULIA M. ATTERBURY) was the daughter of the late Lewis Boudinot Atterbury of New York. Each of her sons, who survive her, has had unusual success in his profession. Her first son, Mr. Henry A. Stimson, is well known as a Congregational clergyman. Another son is Mr. John Ward Stimson, the artist, who has taught and lectured at Princeton University, while a third son is Dr. Lewis Atterbury Stimson, who has been a professor of surgery at Cornell University. *July 25, 1908*

AND THEY CALLED IT A "COTTAGE"

"Shadow Brook," the home of the Anson Phelps Stokes family at Lenox, Massachussetts, whose hospitality recognizes no limit that numbers can affect, is now open and ready to receive all the sons and daughters of the house with their friends and friends' friends. It is related of Mrs. Stokes that she recently received a telegram from a son in this year's class at Harvard, which read: "Coming tomorrow with a party of '97 men," to which the amiable lady made reply: "Don't make it more than fifty; have friends already here." *June 30, 1897*

STOCKTON, BAYARD The Stocktons are Princeton's one really established, aboriginal, continuously native family. They owned the family house, "Morven," from its building in 1701 until 1945. It was then sold to Governor Edge of New Jersey, who, in turn, gave it to the state for a Governor's mansion. The Stocktons owned land and lived in Princeton in the seventeenth century, before Morven was built. A Stockton signed the Declaration of Independence. There are still Stocktons in Princeton. Most conspicuous of these is Bayard Stockton, who opened and still operates a most successful local liquor store called "Cousins." *September, 1959*

STOCKTON, MR. AND MRS. DAVID (ANNA SCOTT) A noteworthy wedding was that of Miss Anna Scott, daughter of Major Hugh Lenox Scott, U.S.A., to Mr. David Stockton, of the old family which has lived in the Stockton home at Princeton since it was first occupied by Richard Stockton, the signer of the Declaration of Independence. The bride's father is one of the best-known men in the Army. It was he who commanded the Comanche and Apache Indians in 1892 and was in charge of Geronimo's band. *October 27, 1906*

STOKES, MR. AND MRS. ANSON PHELPS (HELEN LOUISA PHELPS) intend to open their new residence at Lenox, Massachusetts, with a house party of seventy people. They can entertain such a number of guests because "Shadow Brook," as their place is called, is probably the largest private house in the

country. To appreciate the size of this house, it may be told that the house is four hundred feet front by one hundred deep, that in walking around it you walk something over a quarter of a mile, that there is an acre of space on each of the four floors. *July 25, 1894*

STOKES, CAROLINE PHELPS always resided with her sister, Miss Olivia E. Phelps Stokes. Together, they gave Woodbridge Hall to Yale University, of which their nephew, the Rev. Anson Phelps Stokes, Jr., is the secretary; St. Paul's Chapel to Columbia University; a training school to Tuskegee Institute, a building to Roberts College in Turkey, and a chapel to Berea College in Kentucky. *May 8, 1909*

STOKES, JAMES His bride, Miss Florence Chatfield, is a daughter of Mr. Henry W. Chatfield, of Brooklyn. The "Homestead," at Brooks Vale, Connecticut, has been in the possession of the Brooks family, to which the late Mrs. Chatfield belonged, for eight generations. On her father's side, Miss Chatfield is descended from George Chatfield, who came to Guilford, Connecticut, in 1630. Miss Chatfield is noted for her harp playing. She has played at many entertainments of the Young Men's Christian Association, branches of which were founded abroad by Mr. Stokes. *April 15, 1905*

STOKES, MR. AND MRS. SYLVANUS, JR. (MARGARET FAHNESTOCK) sailed on the *Aquitania*, intending to spend six weeks abroad. And Mrs. Stokes said frankly that she was going to Paris to buy clothes and to Vienna to buy furniture. Mrs. Stokes was one of the first to introduce the beach frocks of chintz that have been so popular this summer at Bailey's Beach, Newport. They look for all the world as if they were made of furniture covering or wall paper, but they are so undeniably gay and smart. *September 10, 1921*

STOKES, W. E. D. is busy giving personal supervision to his Ansonia Hotel in New York City. In the days of his youth, Mr. Stokes used to say that he couldn't be bothered to take a girl for even a ride behind his fast horses. It was such a bore, he said, that he knew he would tip her out of the carriage before the drive was over. Mr. Stokes had an "old-fashioned mother." It is even said that she could not be induced to go abroad, because the voyage necessitated a Sabbath spent on the water. *June 25, 1904*

STONE, AMASA was the greatest bridge builder of his day. He also built railroads, these including the Chicago & Milwaukee Road, and he was often consulted by Lincoln in regard to army transportation when great war problems presented themselves. Mr. Stone gave $600,000 to Adelbert College of Western Reserve University, he endowed a home for aged women and an industrial school for children in Cleveland. *August 15, 1914*

STONE, MRS. HORATIO O. (SARA L. CLARKE) of Chicago, who is one of the three or four society leaders of that city, has established herself for the summer in a cottage at Beach Bluff, Swampscott, two or more hours' steam ride from Boston. It has been and is rather of an enigma as to why Mrs. Stone, with her social ambitions and her position, should elect to light year after year upon such an inconsequential resort as the Bluff, not at all choice or fashionable. *July 19, 1902*

STONE, ISABEL is the daughter of former Governor William Alexis Stone of Pennsylvania. Her mother comes from two of the oldest and most distinguished families of the Keystone State. One grandfather was a descendant of William Penn, being a Page, from whom Thomas Nelson Page, the Southern writer, is also descended. Her grandfather Bache came to this country when a young man to visit his cousin, Richard Bache, who married Sallie Franklin, daughter of Benjamin Franklin. *September 2, 1905*

STORER, BELLAMY, one-time American Minister to Belgium and to Spain and Ambassador to Austria-Hungary, died at the Hotel Plaza Athenée, Paris. He is survived by his wife, formerly Maria Longworth, of Cincinnati, Ohio, who was the recipient of the famous "Maria" letters brought out when Mr. Storer was summarily removed from his post as Ambassador to Vienna by the late Theodore Roosevelt. *December 15, 1922*

STORER, MRS. BELLAMY (MARIA LONGWORTH NICHOLS) It is gratifying to Cincinnatians that the name of Longworth, especially identified since the founding of the Miami Valley more than one hundred years ago with all movements of art and chivalry, is to be prominent in society events in Washington. One of the well-known members of the family is Mrs. Maria Longworth Nichols Storer, who gave Rookwood pottery to the art world. One woman of the Longworth family married the Marquis de Chambrun, and another became the wife of Count Albert de Chambrun. *November 21, 1903*

STOTESBURY, MR. AND MRS. EDWARD T. (EVA ROBERTS)—CROMWELL The marriage surpassed in general interest any wedding of the present season. The Bishop of Washington officiated, the bride's gown was worthy of a princess, and a rope of pearls, the bridegroom's gift, the most valuable necklace in America. In addition to a fortune in jewels, Mr. Stotesbury is said to have presented his bride with securities representing a quarter million dollars. In addition to the string of matched pearls which the bride wrapped seven times around her neck, her necklaces included four strands of diamonds. Mrs. Stotesbury's engagement ring was a ruby of ten carats worth $50,000. There is a $500,000 diamond and pearl tiara, a bandeau of large oriental pearls and diamonds worth $750,000, and a diamond tiara with big pear-shaped pearls worth $100,000. *January 27, 1912*

STOW, MARGARET belongs to one of the oldest California families. She is one of the heirs of her father, the late Sherman Stow, and with her mother makes her home at "La Patera," a ranch of many hundreds of acres about eleven miles from Santa Barbara. *October 2, 1909*

STRAIGHT, WHITNEY WILLARD The Drexels and the Whitneys have formed so many ties in England that it is no surprise to find them now about to unite. The engaged couple are Whitney Willard Straight and Lady Daphne Finch-Hatton. A young automobile racer, Mr. Straight is the son of Mrs. Leonard K. Elmhirst, who runs a modern school at her home "Dartington Hall," in Devonshire. As a grandson of Cleveland's Secretary of the Navy, William Collins Whitney, he is a nephew of the late Payne and Harry Payne Whitney. His father was the late Major Willard D. Straight. Lady Daphne is the elder daughter of the fourteenth Earl of Winchilsea and his Countess, who was Margaretta Drexel. *May 15, 1935*

STRAIGHT, MR. AND MRS. WILLARD (DOROTHY WHITNEY) Major Straight was born in Oswego, New York, in 1880. His father was the late Professor Henry H. Straight. Young Straight accompanied his parents to Japan and, later, to China. He learned to speak the languages of both countries like a native. In 1902, he was appointed to the Chinese Imperial Maritime Customs Service and went to Nanking and Peking, where he was for two years. Later, he became associated with J. P. Morgan & Co. *December 10, 1918*

STRAUS, ISIDORE, who lost his life in such an heroic manner on the *Titanic,* was one of three brothers who have been notable figures in the diplomatic and mercantile worlds and who have all been famous philanthropists. In the mercantile world, he was a member of the firms of L. Straus & Sons, R. H. Macy & Co., New York, and Abraham & Straus, Brooklyn. He married Miss Ida Blun in 1871, and she elected to die with him on the *Titanic.* *May 11, 1912*

STRAWBRIDGE, ANITA Now comes the announcement from Newport, where the Strawbridges have been spending the summer, that Miss Strawbridge has made a record in swimming at the famous resort. She swam from Bailey's to Hazard's Beach at Newport in thirty six minutes, beating the record of thirty eight made a number of years ago by the Countess Guy de Lasteyrie. *September 20, 1920*

STRAWBRIDGE, ROBERT The re-election of Mr. Robert Strawbridge as M.F.H. Cottesmore Hunt, in England, is remarkable for the reason that it is seldom that an American has been chosen for such a position. Mr. Strawbridge has been active for some years in polo and field sports, and he is a member of a well-known Philadelphia family. His father was Justus C. Strawbridge, a Quaker who established a large retail business in Philadelphia. Mr. Robert Strawbridge and his brothers, Messrs. Frederick H. Strawbridge and Francis R. Strawbridge, represent the interests of their father. For several years, Mr. Strawbridge has been following the Quorn Hunt, and he has a hunting box at Melton Mowbray. *March 22, 1913*

STREETT, W. B. He rode in the hurdle race at Aqueduct, jumped aboard a waiting plane, and, flying across the Sound to Rye, arrived to ride Falmouth in the Gold Cup. Young Mr. Streett comes by his enthusiasm and his skill and courage naturally, for all Streetts love horses. From time immemorial, the Streetts have been concerned with horses in Maryland and elsewhere. *November 1, 1930*

STRONG, CORNELIA LIVINGSTON VAN RENSSELAER probably has one of the most impeccable bloodlines in America. Her distinguished Strong forefathers arrived in New England in 1630. Among them were three Colonial governors, the founder of Rutgers University, famous lawyers, mathematicians, jurists, and scientists. There is little she doesn't know about New York social history. She has no kind words for the jet set: "It's the tinsel set, my dear. The mud-bottom of society. The thing to do now when you get divorced is to fly to California and run around with the Hollywood crowd." *September, 1973*

STRONG, WILLIAM, a tenth-generation Livingston descendant, is highly verbal, introspective, and creative. He is of particular interest in that the cumulative qualities of his ancestors merge in him. He was educated at Exeter and at Harvard, where he wrote book and lyrics to this year's Hasty Pudding theatricals. He has obviously given a lot of thought to why the Livingston family is not in the news today: "People who are proud of their ancestors' political achievements nonetheless find it distasteful to enter politics themselves. Modern politics seems to have forgotten the word honor." *September, 1973*

STURGES, BETTY, daughter of Mr. and Mrs. Hollister Sturges, is engaged to Henry Field. Although the young people have spent most of their lives in England, they both inherit a Chicago background. Miss Sturges was presented at the Court of St. James's last spring by her uncle and aunt, the Earl and Countess of Sandwich. Mr. Field is a grandson of Mrs. Thomas Nelson Page and a great-nephew of Marshall Field. He recently returned from Mesopotamia, where he did valuable work for the Field Museum. *January 15, 1929*

STURGIS, FRANK is a New Yorker and a member of a large banking firm. It is through his efforts that Lenox, where he has a country seat, has established a yearly horse show. He is also one of the founders of the show at Newport, and he acts there each year as a judge. *November 11, 1905*

STURGIS, RUSSELL was Professor of Architecture at the College of the City of New York from 1878 to 1880. His chief work as a practical architect was done between the years of 1863 and 1880. The houses of the late James Alfred Roosevelt and of the late Theodore Roosevelt, the President's father, both of which are in West Fifty Seventh Street, are regarded as his best work as an architect. *February 20, 1909*

STUYVESANT, MRS. JOHN At the Grand Opera (formerly Pike's), Mrs. John Stuyvesant of Gramercy Park wore an entire suit of dark blue velvet, richly trimmed with satin folds of the same color, the skirt being looped up *en panier,* and the sacque made with a deep Spanish hood, lined with blue satin, and trimmed with lace. With this toilette was worn a delicate and exquisitely beautiful bonnet, of blue velvet and black lace, just small enough to be very expensive. *January 27, 1869*

STUYVESANT, MRS. LEWIS RUTHERFURD (ROS- ALIE STUYVESANT PILLOT) In the chantry of St. Thomas's Church in New York, Miss Pillot became the bride of Mr. Lewis Rutherfurd Stuyvesant. Two old families of New York are reunited, as the principals in this nuptial event are distant cousins. *May 1, 1925*

STUYVESANT, RUTHERFURD is now creating on his large estate at Allamuchy, New Jersey, the largest game preserve in the East, if not in the United States. He now owns the old Stuyvesant property, which is widely distributed over Warren County. The Rutherfurd tract has always been noted as a natural harbor for all kinds of American game. Mr. Stuyvesant purchased a large farm in Allamuchy Mountain, which he is now fencing in with the view of making it a deer park. Since the opening of the season, he has had a dozen or more gamekeepers patrolling these new grounds. New dog kennels have just been completed, and they now contain more than one hundred fox terriers, pointers, and setters. *December 28, 1887*

STUYVESANT, MRS. RUTHERFURD (COUNTESS MATHILDE E. DE WASSENAER) has presided over the old Stuyvesant home in New York and also at "Tranquility Farms," the estate in New Jersey, but since their marriage, Mr. and Mrs. Stuyvesant have spent much time abroad. Mr. Stuyvesant is a son of the late Lewis Morris Rutherfurd; he changed his name to conform to the desire of his grand-uncle, Nicholas William Stuyvesant, from whom he inherited a great fortune. *January 19, 1907*

SUFFOLK AND BERKSHIRE, COUNTESS OF (MARGUERITE HYDE "DAISY" LEITER) is expected shortly to spend some time in Chicago in connection with the subdividing of the Lake Geneva estate of her late father, Levi Z. Leiter. The estate was for years the rendezvous of Chicago's most distinguished businessmen on weekend hunting parties. *October 15, 1926*

SULLIVAN, MRS. CORNELIUS J. (MARY JOSEPHINE QUINN) Without Mary Sullivan, there might never have been any Museum of Modern Art. The widow of Cornelius J. Sullivan, with whom she brought together one of America's best collections of modern art, is one of those vital individuals with enough enthusiasm to wear out all the junior committees assisting her enterprises. Aside from her duties as Trustee of the Museum of Modern Art, Mrs. Sullivan finds time to get good pictures for out-of-town galleries and encourage art in the colleges. A tall, athletic figure, Mrs. Sullivan is a great walker, loves police dogs and riding, is often to be seen lunching at the Cosmopolitan Club. *May 1, 1934*

SULLIVAN, MRS. JAMES F. (LULUE R. NICHOLS) is one of the young matrons of Philadelphia, now prominent at Bar Harbor. She is a member of the Indoor Tennis Club and one of the governors of the Sedgeley Club, an organization devoted to aquatic sports, with the best names of the Quaker City enrolled on its membership. Recently, Mrs. Sullivan joined the Society of Colonial Dames of America. She can claim descent from King Robert Bruce; she is a direct descendant of Sergeant Francis Nichols, who was a grandson of Sir Edward Bruce. *August 13, 1904*

SUTRO, ADOLPH, who has just been elected Mayor of San Francisco, is said to own a tenth of the city, and he turns his large income to good account. He is a philanthropist, among his works being the famous Sutro free baths on the Pacific ocean. His magnificent park-like grounds are open to all visitors. *September 28, 1894*

SWAN, DONNELL, who is now approaching middle age, has been for years the most conspicuous figure in Baltimore society. He is an expert whip, an experienced huntsman, and altogether a man of most fascinating qualities. He is of distinguished lineage, his mother having belonged to one of the First Families of Virginia. *March 15, 1902*

SWIFT, E. C., the Chicago millionaire, and Mrs. Swift, who have been living in Boston for the last two years, have been at Beverly Farms all summer. Lately Mr. Swift has been busy superintending his new villa. There is to be a stable to accommodate thirty horses. Miss Mabel Swift married Clarence Moore, M. F. H. of the fashionable Chevy Chase in Washington. Miss Swift was a Myopia huntswoman, and carried to her new home a half dozen or more of her best hunters. *December 6, 1900*

SWIFT, HENRY WOODRUFF Swift's grandfather, George Parker Swift, came to Columbus, Georgia, from the Connecticut textile country in 1867. In 100 years, the Swifts have become related to nearly everyone with money in Columbus, which is one of the biggest textile towns in the South. One of the Swifts married a Jordan of the Jordan mills, and Swifts married Woodruffs. Swift had a grandfather who was a brother of Ernest Woodruff, the Coca-Cola man. *May, 1969*

SWIGERT, DANIEL was one of the great horsemen of all time. Owner of the original Elmendorf tract in Kentucky, named in honor of his wife's grandmother, Blandina Elmendorf, of Dutch descent, he bred four Kentucky Derby winners as well as Spendthrift, progenitor of Man O' War. Spendthrift was named in honor of Mrs. Swigert, who returned her husband's compliment by christening another yearling Miser. *May, 1950*

SWOPE, MR. AND MRS. HERBERT BAYARD (MARGARET HONEYMAN POWELL) By 1920, he was *The New York World*'s Executive Editor, the only man ever elevated from city room to editor's chair by a New York paper. Meanwhile, the lady of his choice had become the presiding spirit of one of the maddest, most exciting, and cosmopolitan ménages found anywhere. Today, although the Swopes perch securely on the social ladder, comfortably buttressed by millions of Swope's own making, the stamp of their early life in semi-Bohemia is clear. Principally, they divide their time between a Park Avenue apartment and a huge, comfortable home built by Stanford White at Sands Point. No other host and hostess in America can quite keep pace with the Swopes in providing hospitality which is so consistently alluring to so many oddly assorted people. *March, 1938*

SYMINGTON, JAMES WADSWORTH recently took time off between a season of singing at the Sherry-Netherland's Carnaval Room and returning to law classes at Columbia to fly to St. Louis and get married. Jim is credited with an assist in the successful campaign his father, Senator Stuart Symington, fought in Missouri last fall. Public service and a good voice seem to run in the family, for his mother Eve is remembered as the first socially-registered singer to take the limelight in a night club, and her father, the late James Wadsworth, served New York in the House and Senate for more than a quarter of a century. *March, 1953*

SYMINGTON, MRS. STUART (NANCY HEMINGWAY)—WATSON Nancy Watson Symington's family gathered to christen not one but four new babies at the outdoor Children's Chapel in the woods on Rockport's Vesper Hill. For Mrs. Symington, widow of Arthur Kittredge Watson (a former board chairman of IBM World Trade Corporation and Ambassador to France) and Senator Stuart Symington, Camden, Maine, provides a summer respite. Camden is "the definition of peace and serenity." *July, 1991*

SYPHAX, WILLIAM T. The first Syphax, William, was an itinerant minister who arrived in Washington from Canada in the early part of the nineteenth century. He prospered sufficiently to be able to buy freedom for his wife and three daughters. His son Charles, however, worked as a slave on the Virginia plantation of George Washington Parke Custis, grandson of Martha Washington, who had a daughter by Arianna Carter, one of his house slaves. Charles Syphax and daughter Maria fell in love. Her father, Mr. Custis, was delighted and gave the pair a fancy wedding in the parlor of the great house. Custis freed both. William T. is probably the richest Syphax. In 1954, he and his wife, Marguerite, started Syphax Enterprises, Inc., a construction and management firm that today earns $8,000,000 annually and is one of the twenty leading black firms in the United States. *September, 1975*

SZÉCHÉNYI, COUNTESS LASZLO (GLADYS MOORE VANDERBILT) On the morning of her first wedding day when the bride arose to look through the three-inch and five-inch openings in the Venetian lace stretched across every window of the Vanderbilt palace, there was the full glory of a golden day. Perhaps when she took her first peep through the lace, the police had already surrounded her home. Women down at the heel—dragging babies with them—who looked as though they might better be at home attending to the Monday washing, arrived as early as half-past nine, hoping to press close to the high iron fence that surrounds the Vanderbilt residence. They soon learned from the bluecoats, however, that it is against the law to loiter. *February 1, 1908*

T

TAFT, CHARLES P. The Tafts have produced not only a United States President but a current Senator, Robert Taft, Jr., and a number of prominent Cincinnati lawyers and businessmen. Taft Broadcasting Inc. is a powerful force in the city, and the firm of Taft, Stettinius & Hollister is Cincinnati's most prestigious law firm. The Tafts, too, have been enormously generous to the city. And even though William Howard Taft could legitimately trace his ancestry back to a *Mayflower* arrival, it is typical of Cincinnati's lack of ostentation that the late President's son, Charles P. Taft, drives around town in an ancient Volkswagen with a canoe strapped on the roof. *October, 1975*

TAFT, MR. AND MRS. CHARLES PHELPS (ANNE SINTON) Mrs. Taft is the only child of the late David Sinton, a great ironmaster in his day who possessed the wonderful faculty of transmuting the base metal into gold. He left a great fortune. Mr. and Mrs. Taft are enthusiastic collectors of pictures and *objets d'art*. Their paintings are valued at one million dollars, and they are still collecting. *November 6, 1909*

TAFT, HELEN had been the guest of honor at more than thirty dinner parties since December first. In addition, several notable luncheons were given in her honor, although as a rule Miss Taft does not go to luncheons. Dances have also been given for the President's daughter, and she has been the guest at private balls. And the end is not in sight, for Miss Taft has engagements to dine or to dance five nights out of each remaining week of the season. Happily, she shows no sign of fatigue. *January 21, 1911*

TAFT, ROBERT A. II, a former Ohio State Representative, is the fifth successive public servant in a line established by his great-great-grandfather Alphonso Taft, who settled the family in Cincinnati in the 1830s and eventually became Secretary of War, U.S. Attorney General, and Minister to both Austria-Hungary and Russia. Another notable member of the family is William Howard Taft IV, current Deputy Secretary of Defense. *October, 1986*

TAFT, MR. AND MRS. WILLIAM HOWARD (HELEN HERRON) were in the vanguard of those who have sailed for Europe. They are spending five or six weeks in England, where the Chief Justice is making a study of the British judicial system and where honors of all sorts are being showered upon them. The Chief Justice received an honorary degree from Oxford University. It would seem that they'll have little time to spend this year at their summer home at Murray Bay, Canada. *July 15, 1922*

TAILER, EDWARD N. recently celebrated his eighty-second birthday. Possessed of ample fortune, Mr. Tailer has of recent years devoted himself to the chronicling of social and local history. In his home on Washington Square North in New York City, he has a collection of bound diaries and scrapbooks in which are given the details of what society has been doing for the past fifty years. Mr. Tailer was one of the committee which welcomed the late Edward VII when he visited New York as Prince of Wales and was also on the committee for the ball given at the Academy of Music. The Tailer fortune comes from an established wholesale mercantile business of many years' standing. *August 3, 1912*

TAILER, MR. AND MRS. T. SUFFERN have praise from all classes in Newport, which is something seldom achieved. A child was hurt by their motor-car, but not seriously. Father and mother tell, however, of the big sums of money they received, but the chief point is that Mr. Tailer went to call on the little boy every day. This sounds trite, perhaps, outside of Newport. But to be in Newport, it is a rather refreshing story, where every move of the rich is watched with aggressive eye and gladly misconstrued. *September 14, 1912*

NEVER HOT TO TROT

So long as Mr. H. A. C. Taylor is one of the governors of the Newport Casino, the turkey-trot will meet with disapproval from a powerful source. Mr. Taylor has much to say at the Metropolitan Opera House in regard to the comfort of the box-holders, and at Newport both he and Mrs. Taylor are avowed enemies of the trot, the snapshot, and the suffragist. On Saturday morning at the Casino, Mr. Conrad played popular dance music in response to the young people's good spirits and agility on the tennis courts. But Mr. Taylor soon ran up the steps of the veranda, where the orchestra is stationed, and in quick, decided tones gave the command for something classical. From *The Sunshine Girl* the musicians changed obediently to *Samson et Dalila*. *July 26, 1913*

TAILER, T. SUFFERN, JR., is a son of the internationally famous sportsman, Mr. T. Suffern Tailer, the owner of the famous private links at Newport. Young Master Tailer, though only fourteen, has excited wide comment by his aptitude for golf and has played the Piping Rock course in the seventies. No young player has ever showed greater promise. *January 1, 1927*

TALBOT, GRACE HELEN, who is engaged to Mr. Robert Ingersoll Brown, is the granddaughter of the late Thomas Talbot, Governor of Massachusetts. Her work in sculpture has attracted the attention of the artistic world here and abroad, and she has exhibited frequently in New York. Mr. Ingersoll Brown is a direct descendant of Richard Brown, a founder of Newburyport, Massachusetts, and of Thomas Dudley, first Governor of Massachusetts; of Rev. John Woodbridge, first minister ordained in New England; and of General James Cudworth, the first to stand for religious toleration in the Plymouth Colony. *June 15, 1924*

TALBOTT, NELSON S. was a distinguished athlete at Yale. He was in the Class of 1915, and in his last year was tackle and Captain of the Varsity Football Team. He was also on the Yale track team, where he indulged in the gentle pastime of hurtling the hammer around the lot, and he brightened up his idle hours with wrestling. At its last meeting, the United States Polo Association elected Mr. Talbott a member of the Executive Committee. *April 1, 1927*

TALLEYRAND, MARQUIS AND MARQUISE DE (ELIZABETH CURTIS) Five miles from Jacksonville, Florida, are the beautiful grounds which once belonged to the Marquis de Talleyrand. A few years after the Civil War, this French nobleman came to Florida with his rich American wife, Miss Curtis of New York, and purchased a large tract of land, beautifying it until it blossomed like a rose. When the Marquis and Marquise appeared on horseback, she with a bright-colored costume and tall hat with waving plumes, and the Marquis in knee-breeches and silk stockings, the people looked, admired, and wondered; but they wondered still more when the titled gentleman brought garden truck and sold it, reckoning his gains and haggling for pence like common men. *January 30, 1884*

TALLMADGE, FREDERICK S. was a prominent member of the Society of the Sons of the Revolution and was the President of that organization for many years. His last official act as President was the signing of the contract for the purchase of Fraunces Tavern in New York City. *July 2, 1904*

TANDY, MRS. CHARLES (ANNE BURNETT)— WAGGONER—HALL—WINDFOHR is a striking woman who wears Western clothes, buys her own art, possesses the 48-carat Vargas diamond, has been married four times, and owns outright four ranches totaling more than half a million acres. According to legend, her grandfather Samuel Burk Burnett won one of the ranches (known as "The Four 6's") in a poker game, but the legend is apocryphal. *September, 1979*

TARKINGTON, BOOTH The announcement of the engagement of Mr. Booth Tarkington and Miss Louise Fletcher, daughter of the Indianapolis banker Mr. Stoughton Fletcher, has been received with much interest. Miss Fletcher is reputed to be a beauty as well as an heiress, and has figured in several of Mr. Tarkington's novels. "Old Tark," as the Princeton boys call him, was one of the most popular men at college. His talents were not confined to literature, for he possesses much histrionic and vocal ability, and with his rich baritone voice used to sing "Danny Deever" on the campus in the most thrilling and dramatic fashion. *March 29, 1902*

TAYLOR, BAYARD, the author, was born in Kennett Square, which is in Chester County, Pennsylvania. In 1858, after long travels abroad, during which he wrote many of his best poems and books about foreign lands, Mr. Taylor returned to Kennett Square, bringing with him his wife (who was the daughter of Professor Peter A. Hansen, founder of the Erfurt Observatory). Near Kennett Square, he purchased a large tract of land, and in 1861 the house that became his residence was completed there. In 1877, he was appointed Minister to Germany by President Hayes. *September 26, 1908*

TEVIS, LANSING is one of the sons of Mr. and Mrs. William S. Tevis. The Tevis boys have always gone in for the most perilous sports. Each has had his own racing car since childhood. Young Lloyd Tevis, who married Miss Lee Girvin of Menlo Park, spent part of his honeymoon in an airship, to the consternation of the conservative Menlo Park set, among whom has always been regret that the telephone was ever invented. *April 10, 1915*

TEVIS, WILLIAM The Burlingame set were treated to a glimpse of old California when Willie Tevis, scion of the Pacheco family, undertook to hold a private bronco busting. Forty guests were summoned to witness the fray. Willie suffered no wounds, though his riding suit was nothing more durable than his ordinary sport costume of flannel trousers and silk shirt. Willie Tevis has since taken himself to the Atlantic Coast, where he will compete in a series of polo tournaments, at which sport he is an expert. *July 1, 1919*

THAW, MRS. BENJAMIN is one of the matrons of Pittsburgh best known to New Yorkers, as she spends several months each year at Newport. Mr. and Mrs. Thaw have a summer residence, "Beach Mound," on Bellevue Avenue. They are also well known at Palm Beach. Mr. Thaw, at his Pittsburgh home, recently entertained the local branch of the Y.M.C.A. (of which he is the highest official), one of the oldest branches in the country. *December 10, 1904*

THAYER, EUGENE VAN RENSSELAER was the son of Nathaniel Thayer, who erected Thayer Hall at Harvard University in memory to his father, the Rev. Nathaniel Thayer, and who bore the expenses of Professor Louis Agassiz's expedition to South America. Mr. Eugene Van Rensselaer Thayer was prominent in both the social and the financial worlds of Boston and for about five years was President of the Somerset Club. *December 28, 1907*

THAYER, EVELYN The Vincent Club in Boston held its yearly election. Miss Evelyn Thayer was elected President. She had charge of the drill in the last club show, *Rouge et Noir,* and took the part of Captain, leading her shapely company of "soldiers" through the intricacies of the various manoeuvres with much grace and skill. Last year, Miss Thayer also took part in the dance of the Bashi-Bazooks, a prominent feature of *Harum-Scarum,* the club success of that season. *June 11, 1910*

THAYER, MARY DIXON It has not been many years ago that the daughter of General and Mrs. Russell Thayer was introduced to Philadelphia Society. While in the glory of her first year out, she commercialized her experiences and published a clever book on "don't" for debutantes. Miss Thayer is also the Molly Thayer of tennis fame, and her literary work in no way interferes with her practice for the tournaments. *April 15, 1923*

THAYER, NATHANIEL possessed fine artistic taste, and was a director of the Museum of Fine Arts in Boston, to which he contributed generously. On his father's side of the house, he came of an old Massachusetts family, and his mother was the daughter of Mr. and Mrs. Stephen Van Rensselaer of New York. His sec-

ond wife was Miss Pauline Revere, a lineal descendant of Paul Revere of Revolutionary fame. *April 1, 1911*

THAYER, PEGGY is the daughter of Mrs. John B. Thayer of "Redwood," in Haverford, Pennsylvania. Shortly following on her debut, not many years ago, Miss Thayer went into business, and although woolen sweaters, gowns, hats, etc., were the drawing cards, everything from Swiss cheese to imported perfumes could be purchased from her. Last November, she startled society by announcing that she was leaving for a projected big game hunting trip in British East Africa. She only traveled as far as Cairo, where she was stricken with typhoid fever. *September 1, 1925*

THELIN, MR. AND MRS. ELIAS GRISWOLD (MARIAN GOUVERNEUR HEISKELL)—EMORY Through her father, the late James Monroe Heiskell of Virginia, she is a descendant of President James Monroe, her great-grandmother Maria Monroe having been the first White House bride. On the maternal side, she "belongs" to the Deringer family, famous as the inventors of the Deringer pistol. Mr. Thelin also comes of a connection rich in historic associations. Among his paternal ancestors was Charles Thelin, prominent at the court of both the first and third Napoleons. His mother was a Miss Griswold, member of a prominent Colonial New England line. *April 10, 1915*

THOMAS, MRS. WILLIAM BAILEY (HELEN MOORE) was a Southern belle of much prominence. Since her widowhood, though she has spent much of her time at her old home in Mobile she has frequently visited Palm Beach and Virginia Hot Springs. Mrs. Thomas is a sister of Miss Amanda Moore, the clever young woman who in Mobile edits (and owns), during several months of each year, a bright little society journal called *Chat.* *December 3, 1904*

THOMPSON, FREDERICK DIODATI was a descendant of Lion Gardiner and of Count Jules Diodati. He was Turkish commissioner to the World's Colombian Exposition in 1893 and was made a Roman Count in 1902. He was a member of the Society of Colonial Wars, grand officer of the Order of Osmaine and of the Medjide, Turkey. He was a chevalier of the Order of St. Maurice and St. Lazarus and of the Holy Sepulchre, Jerusalem. *October 20, 1906*

THOMPSON, MRS. FREDERICK From the shores of the Hudson River to Niagara Falls, there is an almost unbroken chain of these large estates. One of the handsomest of these is "Sonnenberg," the home of Mrs. Frederick Thompson, the wife of the former President of the First National Bank. There is a remarkable Japanese garden, designed by one of the best landscape gardeners of Japan and now under the care of several Japanese gardeners. Mrs. Thompson's philanthropies are seemingly unbounded. Her native town, Canandaigua, shows many evidences of her generosity. The new chapel that she gave to Williams is considered one of the handsomest ever presented to a college. *September 25, 1909*

THOMPSON, MR. AND MRS. L. S. (BETTY CRAIGHEAD WATSON) An interesting young couple who are spending their honeymoon at Del Monte Lodge, Pebble Beach, are Mr. and Mrs. L. S. Thompson, Jr., of New Orleans. Before her marriage, Mrs. Thompson had the distinction of being Queen of the Mardi Gras in New Orleans last year. Young Mr. Thompson's grandfather was one of the founders of the Standard Oil Company. *January 1, 1929*

THOMPSON, COLONEL ROBERT M. was born in Corsica, Jefferson County, Pennsylvania, in 1849. He went into the U.S. Navy and was graduated from Annapolis in 1868. Then he studied law and was admitted to the Bar. He was elected President of the New York Metal Exchange, became interested in naval athletics, and was the donor of the Thompson Cup played for in football contests between the United States Military and Naval Academies. Colonel Thompson has his summer home at Southampton, Long Island, and in the winter he usually goes to Palm Beach, where his houseboat, *The Everglades,* is in commission. *September 7, 1912*

THORN, LEONARD MORTIMER Early in life, Mr. Thorn spent much time in Texas, made a study of the Indians of the region, and learned to speak the languages of several tribes. He was a partner in the manufacturing business of the late Commodore William T. Garner. Mr. Thorn was a brother of William K. Thorn, who married Emily Vanderbilt, the fourth child of Commodore Cornelius Vanderbilt. *August 28, 1909*

THORNE, MRS. JAMES W. (NARCISSA NIBLACK) She's the great Narcissa Thorne, the creator of "the little rooms" which are reproduced with such wonderful accuracy and charm that they have easily rivaled any doll's house or other miniature exhibition in the world. Mrs. Thorne is a very rich woman as well as a great artist. She does this entirely as a hobby and has kept the same staff of wood-carvers and workmen for the last twenty years. The exhibition of thirty of these rooms in the Fine Arts Building will prove to be one of the most fascinating exhibits in the San Francisco World's Fair. *March, 1939*

THORNE, OAKLEIGH It remained this season for an Aiken, South Carolina, habitué who had been absent for several winters to give the most successful "dove drive" pulled off, or shot off, in Aiken in many a long day. "Dove driving" is one of the great pastimes of the South Carolina resort, and Oakleigh Thorne gave one that will probably not only be the record of the season but for some time to come. Sixteen shooters brought down two hundred and sixteen birds. Within a radius of fifteen miles, there are several open fields surrounded by underbrush and pines. For a week or more before a "drive," a field is bated with corn by the caretakers. By the time the day has arrived for the sport, hundreds of the pretty gray wild birds that have found the promised land and the great feast have become so used to the field that the shots do not alarm them for some time. *March 10, 1916*

THORNTON, ALBERT EDWARD As a capitalist, banker, manufacturer, and public spirited citizen, Mr. Thornton filled a prominent place in the development of the New South. He was Vice President of the Atlanta National Bank, President of the Elberton Cotton Oil Mills, and at the head of many important corporations. He was a leader in the social as well as the business world of Atlanta. *April 20, 1907*

THORNTON, MRS. ALBERT, one of Atlanta's grandes dames, patroness of the arts, and the only woman trustee of the city's children's hospital, regards Atlanta's boom with a jaundiced eye: "Having been born here," she says, "I don't like it." *May, 1969*

TIFFANY, REV. CHARLES COMFORT He had been rector of Trinity Church, Boston; of the Church of Atonement, New York, and of Zion Church, New York, before, in 1893, he became Archdeacon of New York. *August 31, 1907*

TIFFANY, CHARLES LEWIS, founder of the jewelry house of Tiffany & Co., celebrated the anniversary of his eighty-fifth birthday. He came to New York in 1837, and he opened a bric-a-brac store at Broadway and Chambers Street. Mr. Tiffany has been decorated by the French government and by the Emperor of Russia. *February 17, 1897*

TIFFANY, LOUIS COMFORT A Japanese chrysanthemum festival was held in his studio for the benefit of the New York Infirmary for Women and Children. The central room was converted into a great conservatory, in which there were no flowers save chrysanthemums. Along the south end of the room were terraces covered with yellow blossoms and presided over by young women in Japanese gowns. The most valuable chrysanthemum was the "Mrs. Alpheus Hardy," valued at fifteen hundred dollars. *November 13, 1889*

TILFORD, FRANK is President and Director of the Lincoln Trust Company, which, in a brief period, has grown to be one of the foremost financial institutions of New York. He is a member of the well-known wholesale grocery house of Park & Tilford. His graceful white yacht *Norman,* with its nose pointed up the Hudson or along the Sound, is one of the craft familiar to all yachtsmen. *December 15, 1906*

TILTON, MRS. WEBSTER (ALICE BUSCH) In 1922, the Veiled Prophet Ball in St. Louis kept pace with the opulence of the twenties. Queen Alice Busch wore a five-thousand-dollar coronation dress solidly hand-embroidered in rhinestones and pearls. *September, 1952*

TIPPETT, MR. AND MRS. CLOYCE J. (ELIZABETH ALTEMUS) — WHITNEY Whether she is in the paddock at Hialeah, the winner's circle at Santa Anita, or the sales ring at Saratoga, Liz Whitney Tippett is the cynosure of excitement. She can't be missed, dressed as she always is in purple and fuchsia, her racing hues. She is the consummate horsewoman, proprietress of three top-rate thoroughbred stables (Llangollen of Virginia, Llangollen of Ocala, Florida, and Llangollen of California, near San Diego). She and her handsome Colonel husband commute between farms in their purple and fuchsia helicopter. *May, 1971*

A TIFFANY JEWEL

The structure now being erected by the Tiffanys on Madison Avenue and Seventy Second Street is to be occupied by Charles Tiffany, the jeweler, and his son, Louis C., the decorator. It will be five stories high to the coping, its style of architecture French, based on the Renaissance. The walls are of brick of a peculiar form, manufactured specially for the purpose at Perth Amboy. The ground floor has twenty two rooms, and these, excepting the large billiard room, are all assigned to the servants and to storage. The first and second floors up will be occupied by Mr. Charles Tiffany and his family (twenty rooms). The fourth floor and attic will be the home of Louis C. Tiffany. The attic will be wholly appropriated by Mr. Tiffany for his studio, and a royal room it will be — fifty feet square and fifty feet high. *December 19, 1883*

TOBIN, MRS. EDGAR (MARGARET BATTS), of San Antonio, is the widow of oil entrepreneur Edgar Tobin and one of the most powerful patrons of the arts in America. A prolific collector of art — including a famous water lily painting, *Nymphéas,* by Monet — and an avid supporter of opera nationwide, she is board Chairman of the city's McNay Art Institute as well as of the family business enterprise, Tobin Surveys. *September, 1979*

TOBIN, RICHARD M. No one on this side of the Atlantic will miss the genial and hospitable Richard M. Tobin when he leaves to take up his new duties as American Minister to the Netherlands more than the polo enthusiasts of San Mateo on San Francisco Bay. Mr. Tobin's magnificent home of old English architecture overlooks the San Mateo polo field and has always been a rendezvous for players and spectators throughout the California season. He is a native of San Francisco and one of the leading bankers and lawyers of California. *April 15, 1923*

TODD, MR. AND MRS. WEBSTER B. (ELEANOR SCHLEY) Webster B. Todd was a contractor whose family firm was responsible for the reconstruction of Williamsburg, Virginia, and the construction of Rockefeller Center in New York. In 1950, he retired and turned to his lifelong passion, Republican politics. Mrs. Todd was Chairman of the board of Foxcroft, the boarding school in Middleburg, Virginia, where students wore military uniforms, often arrived accompanied by their own horse, and slept on unheated porches. *March, 1995*

TORLONIA, DON AND DONNA MARINO (ELSIE MOORE) The majority of dukes and other foreigners of title who have married our American girls have been disappointing in physique, if not in pedigree. We are accustomed to, and rather expect, "the Duke" to look like the bride's little brother. Every one, therefore, who knows Miss Elsie Moore, the bright daughter of Mr. and Mrs. Charles A. Moore, was delighted to find her duke so tall, attractive, and manly. Don Marino Torlonia, to whom Miss Moore was married, is a member of one of Italy's noblest families. Mr. Moore, the bride's father, has an important place in the business world of New York, but besides being the President and a director of many companies, one finds him enrolled as a Chevalier of the Legion of Honor in France. *August 24, 1907*

TORREY, FRANKLIN As a young man, Mr. Torrey was associated with Bowker, Torrey & Co. of Boston in the Carrara marble business, but retired about sixty years ago and had lived almost continuously in Italy ever since. Mr. Torrey was a prominent member of the American colony in Florence and was identified with all its interests. He was the moving spirit in building the beautiful Episcopal Church in Florence, which he just lived to see dedicated. *November 23, 1912*

TOWER, CHARLEMAGNE American official relations in Berlin have undoubtedly taken on new importance since the advent of Ambassador Charlemagne Tower. The palace in which Ambassador and Mrs. Tower have their official residence in the Koenigs-Platz easily ranks among the finest embassies in Europe. Mr. Tower pays several thousand dollars a year more rent for his house than his entire annual salary as Ambassador — a striking illustration of the necessity of filling our ambassadorial posts with rich men, if the country wishes representation in keeping with its wealth and on a par with that afforded by all the other great powers. *December 17, 1904*

TOWER, MR. AND MRS. WHITNEY Houses are very special in Aiken, South Carolina. Most impressive is Mr. and Mrs. Whitney Tower's "Joye Cottage." It was once owned by Whitney Tower's great-grandfather, William C. Whitney, and is a many-roomed white Victorian marvel that takes up a solid block and sports the amusing address of Whiskey Road and Easy Street. Whitney Tower, 1976 Eclipse Award-winning racing editor, is now busy restoring the historical showplace to its former dignity. *March, 1977*

TOWNSEND, MRS. HOWARD (JUSTINE VAN RENSSELAER) The Colonial Dames of Virginia celebrated the two-hundred-and-eighty-fourth anniversary of the marriage of Pocahontas and John Rolfe at Richmond. Mrs. Howard Townsend, of New York, the national President, was present and was the guest of the Dames during the sojourn in Richmond. *May 4, 1898*

TOWNSEND, MRS. JOHN D. is assisted in receiving this winter by her daughter, Mrs. Frank P. Fremont, who, with her husband, has passed the last two years at Fort Shaw, Montana Territory. Mrs. Fremont is gifted with a remarkably fine soprano voice which her Western life has only served to strengthen and improve. Lieutenant Fremont is a son of General and Jessie Benton Fremont. *January 20, 1886*

TOWNSEND, THOMAS SEAMAN was the oldest of the five children of the late John R. Townsend, the first President of the New York Life Insurance and Trust Company, and Caroline Drake. He was a writer on historical subjects, his chief work being *The Record of the Great Rebellion. December 5, 1908*

TRACY, GENERAL BENJAMIN F. Oswego is his birthplace, and he was the original member of the Republican party in Tioga County, having organized the party there. General Tracy owes his military title to the Civil War, when he raised two companies of volunteers. The Congressional Medal of Honor was given him in 1895 for gallant behavior in the Battle of the Wilderness. In the cabinet of the late President Harrison, General Tracy was Secretary of the Navy. He resides with his daughter, Mrs. Ferdinand Wilmerding. Mrs. Frederick R. Coudert is General Tracy's granddaughter. *May 4, 1912*

TRAIN, CUTHBERT and his two brothers, Middleton and Russell, are Cave Dwellers from both sides of the family. Their mother, Errol Cuthbert Brown, was a descendant of Obadiah Bruen Brown, a Baptist minister who came to Washington in 1807. "He was quite a fellow, quite a citizen," says Middleton Train. "He was pals with Dolley Madison and the President; he and his wife and Dolley started the first orphan asylum in Washington, and his daughter-in-law started the first children's hospital." Since its founding, there has always been a Train on the board of Children's Hospital. *September, 1975*

TRAIN, MR. AND MRS. RUSSELL E. (AILEEN BOWMAN)—TRAVERS Russell Train, chairman of the World Wildlife Fund, is a sixth-generation Washingtonian, the descendant of Obadiah Bruen Brown, once chaplain to Congress. Russell and Aileen Train, tireless workers on behalf of worldwide conservation efforts, travel frequently to remote project sites. *February, 1988*

TRASK, MRS. SPENCER (KATRINA NICHOLS), who has been at her home at "Yaddo," Saratoga, is before the public again as an author. She has written a Christmastide play called *The Little Town of Bethlehem,* which will be presented by the Ben Greet players. The wonderful gardens at Yaddo are expressive of Mrs. Trask's understanding of what is truly beautiful. In a little niche of a green wall made by evergreen, there is a statue by William Ordway Partridge representing Christolan, the hero of one of Mrs. Trask's novels. *December 26, 1908*

TRAVERS, MRS. WILLIAM R. (LILLIE HARRIMAN) Everything is in readiness for the opening of her tea house in Newport. It is furnished in true Japanese style. Tapestries, with quaint Japanese figures, hang on the walls, and parasols and lanterns are suspended from the ceilings. Mrs. Travers will maintain Japanese servants throughout the summer, and guests will be requested on some occasions to attend in Japanese costume. A great many American women are just learning, however, that the kimono is an article of apparel never worn by the high-born ladies of Japan, but the distinctive garb of the Geisha girls. Perhaps there will be more careful study of Eastern manners and customs. *June 25, 1904*

TRIPP, BARTLETT made his home in South Dakota many years ago and was President of its first Constitutional Convention in 1883, Chief Justice of the Supreme Court of the Dakota Territory in 1885–89, and United States Minister to Austria 1893–97. *December 16, 1911*

TROBRIAND, COMTESSE DE (MARY JONES) A conspicuous member of the American colony in Paris is Comtesse de Trobriand, the wife of General de Trobriand, who won a distinguished reputation in the Union Army during the Civil War. She was a Miss Mary Jones of New York, the daughter of the founder and President of the Chemical Bank. Her salon in Paris has been for many years the resort of distinguished Americans, French, Russians, Germans, and Italians. Representatives of the literary, artistic, and diplomatic worlds are to be found always at her Monday receptions. The Countess gathers around her more people of distinction than any other lady who receives in Paris. *February 1, 1882*

TRUESDALE, ROBERT SOULE, a descendant of George Soule, who came here on the *Mayflower,* is a graduate of nearby Harvard. He likes to ski in Utah, shoot quail in Georgia, and hunt pheasant in the New England woods. He owns a farm in Westport, Massachusetts. "It is less sophisticated and more rural than the North Shore," he says, "and is located in the area the Plymouth settlers farmed. Reclaiming fields from woodland, I feel I am returning to my family heritage." *February, 1987*

TUCKER, MRS. NION R. (PHYLLIS DE YOUNG) When San Franciscans are asked if there is a *Grande Dame,* the name mentioned most often is that of Mrs. Nion R. Tucker, who has probably served on more boards and been active in more civic activities than any other resident of the city. She is the founder of the San Francisco Debutante Cotillion, one of the most selective gatherings of 18-year-old females and their carefully chosen escorts in the country. *February, 1973*

TUCKERMAN, MR. AND MRS. BAYARD (COTTON SMITH) are now at "Sunswick," one of the residences on the estate at Ipswich, Massachusetts, that has been named "Spider Nest." The houses on the property belong to people who are kin to the Appleton family. The central residence was at one time the home of the late Daniel Fuller Appleton of New York. This house was built by the great-grandfather of Mr. Tuckerman in 1795. Mr. and Mrs. Gerald Hoyt of New York and Mr. Randolph M. Appleton are others who have homes in Spider Nest, which is approached by twelve roads. *August 27, 1910*

TUCKERMAN, BAYARD, JR. is one of the leading spirits of the Eastern Horse Club at Brookline, Massachusetts, being chairman of the race committee. He not only takes an active part in the management of the affairs of this body but personally participates with great enthusiasm in the steeplechases. *July 15, 1926*

TUDOR, WILLIAM, JR. All the men of the Tudor family have been allied with Harvard. The first William Tudor, who was on General Washington's staff as Judge Advocate, was a member of the class of 1769, while his son, the second William, graduated in 1796. It was this second William Tudor—he was the author of much that was published in *The North American Review*—who, with his brother Frederic Tudor, founded the ice trade with tropical countries. *November 16, 1907*

TUFTS, RICHARD Until his death in 1980, the number-one resident of Pinehurst, North Carolina, was Richard Tufts, whose family had owned Pinehurst from 1895 to 1971. Tufts was called simply "Mr. Golf." He served on and headed more committees of the U.S.G.A. than any other man, and was its President in 1956 and 1957. A few of his contributions included standardizing course conditions for the U.S.G.A. national championships, helping to start junior and senior U.S.G.A. championships, and being the leading architect of the U.S.G.A.'s handicap system. *October, 1982*

TULLY, ALICE BIGELOW, granddaughter of Corning Glass founder Amory Houghton (1837–1909), is a leading patroness of the performing arts and countless other causes. But aside from Tully Hall at New York's Lincoln Center—for which she provided a good part of the construction money—she keeps a low profile philanthropically. *December, 1983*

TWEED, CHARLES HARRISON was admitted to the New York Bar in 1868. He became later the general counsel for the Central Pacific Railroad. In 1903, he entered the banking firm of Speyer & Company. *November 1, 1917*

TWIGG-SMITH, THURSTON As Publisher of *The Honolulu Advertiser,* Twigg-Smith gives the capital city its morning news, occasionally spiked with ambitious features like the paper's recent "Hawaii in the year 2000" series, a penetrating glimpse into the state's future. A fifth-generation descendant of missionaries, he's into a clutch of activities—a trustee of Punahou School, the city's Academy of Arts, and the Honolulu Symphony Society. *March, 1971*

TWOMBLY, MRS. HAMILTON MCK. (FLORENCE ADELE VANDERBILT) The costume dinner given at the Morristown, New Jersey, golf club was a brilliant affair. Mrs. Twombly's dress was a perfect copy of the one worn by Marie Antoinette when her portrait was painted by Madame Le Brun. With the costume, she wore the pearls purchased at the recent sale of the jewels of the Empress Eugénie. *November 8, 1900*

TWOMBLY, RUTH The clever driving of Miss Ruth Twombly was by far the most interesting feature of the Morristown Horse Show. On two days, she drove a coach and four and on both occasions captured the blue ribbon. In fact, Miss Twombly and her sister, Miss Florence Twombly, are the best whips in Northern New Jersey, and whenever either young woman appeared in the ring there was round after round of applause. *October 18, 1902*

TYLER, MRS. AUGUSTUS CLEVELAND, of New London, Connecticut, has finished the libretto of Frederick Coit Wright's new comedy opera, *A Venetian Romance,* which will be produced at the Knickerbocker Theater. Mrs. Tyler is a very wealthy and clever woman and has written the libretto for her own amusement. She is most generous with her millions, acquired through her father, Dr. Charles S. Osgood, of Norwich, Connecticut, the patentee of the famous "Cholygogue." *March 19, 1904*

TYLER, HARRISON RUFFIN, JR. "Sherwood Forest," a national landmark house in Charles City County, Virginia, is the home of Mr. and Mrs. Harrison R. Tyler, Jr. The Regency-style 32-room clapboard mansion was built in 1790 and eventually restored in 1841 by John Tyler, tenth President of the United States and the grandfather of Harrison R. Tyler. Today's Harrison Tyler is only 46—handsome, athletic, an avid tennis player, and President of Chemical Treatment Co. Yet his father was born in 1853, and his grandfather in 1790. His father was 75 in 1928, when Tyler was born. Sherwood Forest is in the throes of another restoration, under the guidance of Mrs. Tyler, who has "given up all outside activities for the next year except hunting." *December, 1975*

TYNG, LUCIEN HAMILTON This studio, this theatre, this concert hall, this gallery for the exhibition of works of art: What can one call it? A "pleasure dome," perhaps; for, as Kubla Khan decreed at Xanadu, so did Mr. and Mrs. Lucien Hamilton Tyng decree at Southampton, Long Island. Mr. and Mrs. Tyng are real patrons of the arts. That's why they built what they did. They wanted to lend the place to struggling artists for exhibitions. They wanted it used for the production of plays. *July 1, 1931*

U

UIHLEIN, ROBERT A., JR., the tall, barrel-shouldered Board Chairman and President of the Jos. Schlitz Brewing Company, has not only been playing polo regularly for the past thirty years but has also pretty much subsidized the sport in Milwaukee. *March, 1975*

UNDERWOOD, DAVID Houstonian, 27, a young conservative, son of investment banker Milton Underwood. His family endows libraries, hospitals, other civic institutions. David is a member of the exclusive Allegro, Treasurer of the Bachelors Club. Will inherit awesome fortune. Spends weekends at the family Texas ranch, where he keeps five horses. *June, 1964*

UNTERMYER, SAMUEL "Greystone," at Yonkers, now owned by Mr. Samuel Untermyer, was the residence of the great Samuel J. Tilden, who died at Greystone in 1886. Mr. Untermyer is a half-brother of Randolph Guggenheimer, who has done much for the public schools and who built the New York Commercial Building. With his brother, Mr. Untermyer formed a partnership in the practice of law twenty five years ago. Both Mr. and Mrs. Untermyer are well known as patrons of art and music, and many men and women of literary fame are among their friends. *May 4, 1907*

V

VAIL, MR. AND MRS. THOMAS VAN HUSEN (IRIS JENNINGS) One great-grandfather was Thomas Howard White (White Sewing Machine). One grandfather was Windsor T. White (White Motor Company). And another great-grandfather, Liberty E. Holden, acquired the *Cleveland Plain Dealer* in 1885. Vail is married to the former Iris Jennings, a Standard Oil heiress, and their estate, "L'Ecurie," is one of the city's most lavish. "I have known Tom forever, and I simply do not believe," protests another Old Clevelander with a wicked smile, "that he calls his place 'The Stable' because he thinks he's the Baby Jesus." *October, 1981*

VALENTINE, MRS. E. MILES (JOY DREW-BEAR)—LANDRETH Probably the most famous of the Philadelphia Valentines, Mrs. E. Miles Valentine, lives in Unionville, Pennsylvania. Chairman of the board of stewards of the American Steeplechase Association, she is one of America's foremost horsewomen. She keeps a stable in Ireland, and few meets occur on the East Coast without the participation of one of her splendid horses, ridden by jockeys sporting the famous Valentine silks—candybox pink patterned all over with red hearts. *February, 1993*

VALENTINE, HARRY, JR. is 47 years old and in his first year at Yale Divinity School. Ten years ago, he founded The Churchill School in New York for special and gifted children. He professes: "It is the Christian responsibility of families such as the Valentines not to bask in the many advantages we have realized. What we have received from our forefathers is a glorious heritage, but we must be eternally aware that God created everything which exists and he demands that we love and share with others." *February, 1983*

VALENTINE, J. ALFRED On three occasions, the Valentines of Long Island have married into the equally socially registered Hewlett family, most recently when the late J. Alfred Valentine married the former Gulielma Robbins, a direct descendant of Richard Hewlett. Back in 1939, J. Alfred Valentine, who was heavily into real estate investment, was one of the founders of Roosevelt Raceway in Hempstead. He was Chairman of the board and Executive Vice President of the track until his retirement in 1962, and it is said he ruled with such an iron hand that "no one lifted a horseshoe without his approval." *February, 1983*

VALENTINE, COLONEL JOHN R. showed a taste for sport from his youth, and his career as a hunting man is well known to sportsmen wherever they hunt. Living in the country hunted by the Radnor Hounds, he hunted with that pack for a number of years, and in 1901 he was elected Master. During his mastership, the Radnor Hunt attained its zenith, and sportsmen came from all over the land to hunt there. *September 1, 1921*

VALENTINE, MASSIE, JR. Tall, ruggedly good-looking young Massie Valentine, Jr., was for long one of the coveted eligibles of Richmond. Last November, Massie married Margaret Izard, a direct descendant of Pocahontas. Marvin Bush, son of Vice President George Bush, was among the fourteen groomsmen. During the reception of 600, Bush surveyed the roomful of elegantly turned-out guests and mused: "You know, the Valentines are the ideal American family. The American family at its very best." *February, 1983*

VAN ALEN, JAMES J. A gentleman of the old school, and seemingly at odds with some of the new customs of Newport, within recent years Mr. Van Alen has spent little time in Newport. He has always been glad, so it appeared, to get away to his Canadian river for fishing or to England, where he was once Ambassador at the Court of St. James—a social environment of which he was so fond that he retained the ambassadorial trappings on his carriage, for use at Newport and New York. *August 10, 1915*

VAN ALEN, MRS. JAMES J. At her stately stone mansion, "Ochre Point," in Newport, all is in keeping with the times of "Good Queen Bess." The house is an exact copy of an old mansion in the reign of Elizabeth. No gas pipes are allowed within or about the place. Glittering wax candles illuminate the interior. The outside is imposing rather than picturesque. Time may perhaps soften the effect of the extreme regularity of the architecture. *July 24, 1889*

VAN ALYEA, MR. AND MRS. THOMAS STEVENS own one of Milwaukee's most fascinating houses. Built in 1890 by the present owner's grandfather, it is built into a cliff overlooking Lake Michigan. Below the part the Van Alyeas use are a large caretaker's apartment and a two-story tavern, the latter entirely below street level. Mr. Van Alyea is a grandson of Mrs. Walter Drake, who was decorated by the French government after World War I for her relief efforts. *October, 1965*

VAN BEUREN, ELIZABETH SPINGLER was a granddaughter of Henry Spingler, who in 1788 bought the land on Union Square in New York where the original Spingler farm was situated. The estate on Fourteenth Street was selected as a home by the grandmother of Miss Elizabeth Spingler Van Beuren. *August 1, 1908*

VAN BUREN, EDITH was married to Genna Baron Vessichio de Castelmenardo, of Naples. She is a great-grandniece of President Van Buren. Her father, for many years, was United States Minister to Japan. About four years ago, she won the prize of honor in the carnival at Nice for her flower-decked carriage. Several years ago, accompanied by Mrs. Roswell D. Hitchcock, the Baroness visited the Klondike, roughing it, as told in Mrs. Hitchcock's book of her travels, *Two Women in the Klondike. July 19, 1900*

VAN CORTLANDT, AUGUSTUS BIBBY The first Van Cortlandt arrived from Holland in 1638. Van Cortlandt Manor, in the midst of Van Cortlandt Park, was the family home for generations, until it was recently sold to the city. It passed into the ownership of a son of Henry White, who married Anne Van Cortlandt early in the last century. When he succeeded to the estate, he dropped his father's name because there were no male Van Cortlandt heirs. Mr. Robert Van Cortlandt has been a most successful financier and has a handsome fortune of his own. *August 9, 1913*

VANDERBILT, ALFRED GWYNNE Newport was the scene of the marriage of Mr. Alfred Gwynne Vanderbilt and Miss Ellen French, the daughter of Mrs. Francis Ormonde French. The

VANDERBILT

In 1909, the beautiful Consuelo,
Duchess of Marlborough, born Vanderbilt.

The Vanderbilts were builders, above all else. Cornelius Vanderbilt constructed the greatest rail empire in nineteenth-century America, 20,000 miles of the New York Central Railroad. His children and grandchildren built houses that still stand as America's most opulent. At "The Breakers" in Newport, heated salt water was piped to bathrooms; at "Eagle's Nest" at Northport, Long Island, each hole on the golf course was named after a Vanderbilt yacht. "Biltmore," in Asheville, North Carolina, was the largest house ever constructed in America, with 245 rooms and 45 bathrooms. The Vanderbilt scale was invariably palatial.

At his death in 1877, Cornelius Vanderbilt (called "the Commodore," though he held no naval rank) was the richest American who had ever lived, with an estate of more than $100 million. But he began humbly. Born in 1794, he started his empire by hauling freight on a little boat between Staten Island and Manhattan. From sailboats, he progressed to ocean-going steamships; he made his first fortune carrying passengers bound for California during the Gold Rush. When he was past sixty, he began to invest in railroads; by 1873, his rails linked New York and Chicago.

The Commodore believed in primogeniture: his eldest son, William Henry, received a full $90 million of the estate. When he died only seven years after his father, he had doubled the fortune.

Within six years of the Commodore's death, his grandson's wife, Mrs. William K. Vanderbilt, was showing off her new house on Fifth Avenue with the grandest ball seen in this country. The 1883 party marked the Vanderbilts' final acceptance by the New York City Old Guard. Vanderbilt children played out lives at Society's forefront.

Son Harold Stirling Vanderbilt, a yachtsman, successfully defended the America's Cup three times and was the inventor of contract bridge. Son William K. Vanderbilt II sponsored the first official automobile race in the United States in 1904 and awarded the Vanderbilt Cup trophy. Their sister, Consuelo, became Duchess of Marlborough in 1895 in the grandest of all marriages between an American heiress and European nobility. Cousin Alfred Gwynne Vanderbilt, a horse breeder and leading figure in coaching, went down on the Lusitania in 1915. His brother Reginald, also a sportsman, was the father of Gloria Vanderbilt, actress, artist, and clothing designer.

Alfred Gwynne Vanderbilt (II), present head of the family, is a great name in American racing, owner of Hall of Fame horses Discovery and Native Dancer, and the man who has kept the Vanderbilt silks in the public eye for more than fifty years. In 1994, several hundred descendants of the Commodore gathered at St. Bartholomew's Episcopal Church in New York City (long known as "the Vanderbilt church") to celebrate the 200th anniversary of Cornelius' birth.

The builders, the shippers, the movers: *clockwise from top left,* Alfred G. Vanderbilt, 1904; Harold S. Vanderbilt at the helm; William K., in 1922; little Gloria, snow-covered and playing in Central Park, in 1929; Mr. and Mrs. Alfred G., Jr., 1938; Mrs. Cornelius Vanderbilt and children, 1905; Mrs. Alfred G. in 1915.

wedding of a Vanderbilt always excites much interest. In the language of the daily newspaper editor, it was "the story of the day." It is true that the daily newspapers have been filled with very exaggerated accounts of the wedding, and for days beforehand stories of the extraordinary splendor with which it would be celebrated were current. In fact, it was an extremely simple affair. The guests for the wedding were brought from New York by rail, and accommodations were provided for them. To the church, Mrs. French had sent cards to many of the citizens of Newport who had known the family, irrespective of caste. *January 17, 1901*

VANDERBILT, ALFRED GWYNNE, JR. He has made a notable success of breeding race horses, and in 1935 he even made his stables pay. Last year, his "Sagamore Farm" stable suffered the nominal loss of $40,000. He once owned the largest string of race horses in the country and the most elaborate training farm. His prize money amounted to over $300,000 in 1935, and he is the youngest President the Jockey Club has ever had. He is also President of Belmont and Pimlico racetracks. *December, 1940*

VANDERBILT, MRS. ALFRED GWYNNE, JR. (JEANNE MURRAY) is one of the most distinguished hostesses of New York. At one of her parties, she might mix the cream of the theatre, the liveliest of the social set, prominent television personalities, as well as members of the top echelon in Washington's political circles. She is working toward a degree from Columbia University. She guest-acted at the Cleveland Playhouse in *Blithe Spirit*, Dos Passos' *U.S.A.*, while her daughter Heidi acted in repertory there. *January, 1969*

VANDERBILT, COMMODORE CORNELIUS remarked: "The old days, when men made fortunes by putting one penny on the top of another, are gone. The man who makes money nowadays is the quick thinker. While the old-fashioned plodder is scheming how to save a cent on this week's board bill, the new man, who doesn't seem to work half as hard, and is always reading, evolves a scheme by which he makes a million cents." *October 3, 1894*

VANDERBILT, MRS. CORNELIUS II (ALICE GWYNNE) The elaborate and sumptuous musicale given at "The Breakers" in Newport was one of the events of the season. All Newport was present—that is, all its wealth, fashion, and fame. The Casino Orchestra, hidden behind a bank of flowers in the billiard-room, played during the supper. In the dining room were seen some unique table decorations, one of the most conspicuous being a large parrot made of seven hundred pieces of candied sugar and almonds. A chain of silver almonds hung around the neck and fastened one foot to the solid candy pedestal below. *August 31, 1887*

VANDERBILT, MRS. CORNELIUS III (GRACE WILSON) The dinner to be given by Mrs. Cornelius Vanderbilt in honor of Prince Henry of Prussia will be the most elaborate banquet that has ever taken place at a private residence in this country, and doubtless there will be many heart burnings after the invitations are out. The distinction of entertaining the Prince establishes Mrs. Vanderbilt's position beyond doubt. It is curious to note that a short visit from royalty can radically alter the face of New York society. *March 8, 1902*

VANDERBILT, FLORENCE ADELE The marriage to Mr. Hamilton McK. Twombly is arranged for eight o'clock this evening in St. Bartholomew's Church in New York. Of the bride's wedding dress, a correspondent writes from Paris: "American women are noted in Paris for the costliness of their dress, but the preparations for the forthcoming wedding of Miss Vanderbilt exceed the extravagance usual on similar occasions. For the bridal dress, the *modiste* drew her own design for the brocaded satin and, taking it to a Lyons manufactory, had it woven in the looms according to her fancy. Even the bridal hosiery is made to order, and in the gauziest white silk stockings are introduced long medallions of Valenciennes lace covering the instep, in patterns to match the brocade of the dress." *November 21, 1877*

THE HOUSE THAT VANDERBILT BUILT

In Mr. and Mrs. William Vanderbilt's new house at 640 Fifth Avenue, the ceiling of the central vestibule is of bronze and stained glass. The walls are of light African marble, surmounted by a frieze containing figures in mosaic. The drawing room walls are covered with carved woodwork inlaid with mother-of-pearl. At the side of each door are columns of onyx with bronze capitals, bearing vases of stained glass and clusters of light. Mr. Vanderbilt's dressing room is wainscotted eight feet high in glass and opalescent tiles of blue, gold, and silver tints. Between six hundred and seven hundred men were employed for a year and a half on the interior decorations. Sixty stone cutters and carvers were brought here from Europe and kept at work for two years. The total cost, including the furniture, is said to have been three million dollars. *January 25, 1882*

VANDERBILT, MR. AND MRS. FREDERICK W. (LOUISE ANTHONY) The Adirondack camp of Mr. and Mrs. Frederick W. Vanderbilt, on the Upper St. Regis Lake, is of Japanese architecture. He went to the expense of having it designed by Japanese architects and built by skilled Japanese workmen, who came to this country expressly for that purpose. The Oriental effect of the spires and minarets, and peculiar upturned roofs of the exterior of the building further emphasized by the Oriental scheme of interior decoration, contrast strongly with the rugged setting of mountain and lake scenery amid which the luxurious camp is located. *July 23, 1910*

VANDERBILT, GEORGE W. His enormous estate in North Carolina, "Biltmore," compares favorably in size with some of the English landed properties. It is in fact a park of one hundred and eighty square miles in extent. Many of the large ducal estates in Great Britain have an extended acreage, but they are taken up by villages and towns, so that the proprietor is narrowed down to a park only a few miles in area. Mr. Vanderbilt's one hundred thousand acres are entirely for his own use. *February 14, 1894*

VANDERBILT, GLADYS MOORE At the opera, she has seldom been seen with even a flower or a bit of ribbon in her dark hair, and a tiara and ropes of pearl seem too ponderous for her small, well-poised head and for her slim throat. When she was in this country, one would often see her walking briskly down Fifth Avenue in her plain tailored suit with one of her old school friends beside her. Everywhere among the young people she was hailed as "Gladys." Not even the girl who was of the "newly rich," or the girl who had only pedigree to give her prestige, ever thought of her as "a Vanderbilt." *October 22, 1907*

VANDERBILT, HAROLD STIRLING, the skipper of the *Enterprise,* is one of the syndicate to build the boat, and he has been sailing her in the preliminary races to determine the defender of the *America*'s Cup. All his life, he has been passionately fond of the sea, all his life he has sailed boats, and, like his older brother, Mr. W. K. Vanderbilt, he is a skilled navigator. *August 1, 1930*

VANDERBILT, MURIEL was a flower in one of the dancing groups of the "Mah-Jongg Fete," the most original entertainment of its kind since the Oriental game captured the modern hearts of western hemispherites. It was held under the generation direction of Miss Vanderbilt's mother, Mrs. W. K. Vanderbilt, 2d, the proceeds going to the protective work indicated by the name of The Big Sisters. *January 15, 1924*

VANDERBILT, REGINALD CLAYPOOLE On Tuesday came the all-important event—the wedding of Cathleen Gebhard Neilson and Mr. Reginald Claypoole Vanderbilt at "Arleigh," the large stone house on Bellevue Avenue, at Newport. A terrace of from ten to fifteen thousand lilies was used. On Monday, when the special trains arrived, traps of every description were seen on the wharf, while the horses were decked with red and white roses. After the breakfast, all the young people had a straw ride around the city in a large lumber wagon hired for the occasion. Mr. Vanderbilt gave the owner of the cart thirty dollars to buy white ribbon for decorating the vehicle. There was a very bride-like though eccentric effect. *April 18, 1903*

VANDERBILT, WILLIAM HENRY A special train from Saratoga arrived at the Union Depot in Troy, consisting of three special horse-cars containing the horses and equipages of William H. Vanderbilt and the private drawing-room car of that gentleman. This superb coach is called the "Vanderbilt." On the sides are four scenes panelled in oil colors, one representing the Grand Central Depot; another depicting the Falls of Niagara; another the great Fourth Avenue Tunnel; and the other the massive river bridge between Greenbush and Albany. *September 18, 1878*

VANDERBILT, WILLIAM K., SR. A fete for Venetian poor at the W. K. Vanderbilt house, 660 Fifth Avenue, was a perfect Fete de Luxe, consisting of tableaux of Venetian pictures from quatro-cento to now, done by society men and women and arranged by Baron de Meyer, who knows his Venice *con amore,* and M. Diaghileff of the Ballet Russe. Tickets will be twenty five dollars; but remember how poor the Venetians are without tourists and how gladly you'd pay twenty five dollars to be floating out past San Giorgio on the wide Lagoon in a gondola! *April 20, 1916*

VANDERBILT, WILLIAM K., JR. Two years ago, the first company was organized for the purpose of holding automobile races under recognized official rules. Foremost among the advocates, enthusiastic in his belief in its future, and consistent in the desire for the development of its interests, both as a healthful, pleasurable sport and a new field for the American manufacturer, was Mr. W. K. Vanderbilt, Jr. Himself an ardent devotee of the sport and an expert chauffeur, he energetically backed up every movement that tended to advance its interests. *September 27, 1902*

VAN DER KEMP, MR. AND MRS. GERALD (FLORENCE HARRIS) Mrs. Gerald van der Kemp sees that 85 candles are lighted in her dining room every evening. It's a task she takes on gladly, for the candles give the perfect ceremonial touch to an apartment set in the midst of the opulent Palace of Versailles. Gerald van der Kemp has been curator at Versailles for twenty years, and his American-born wife has a natural affinity for a life spent among such extraordinary treasures. Her father, Rear Admiral Frederick R. Harris, was a collector of French furniture, snuffboxes, Renaissance jewels, and jades and was a benefactor of the Metropolitan Museum of Art in New York. *June, 1972*

VANDERLIP, FRANK A. More than usual interest attached this year to the annual garden party which Mr. Frank A. Vanderlip, President of the National City Bank, gave to the employees of that institution at his country home, near Scarboro-on-Hudson, New York, because it is the centennial of the existence of the bank. At the age of thirty seven, he resigned his Assistant Secretaryship of the Treasury to become a Vice President of the institution of which he is now the active head. *June 29, 1912*

VANDERPOEL, AARON J. A Democrat by birth and education, Aaron J. Vanderpoel was trusted and consulted by President Lincoln during the war, and was one of the private counsel of President Johnson during the impeachment proceedings. His election to the Presidency of the Manhattan Club was a frank acknowledgment of his political as well as his social supremacy among the city Democracy. *June 4, 1884*

VANDERPOEL, MARY VAN BUREN has reopened her old home at One Hundred and Fortieth Street and Seventh Avenue in New York City. June fourth will bring the formal dedicating of a tablet at the old fort at One Hundred and Twenty Third Street and Amsterdam Avenue, marking the line of defense of the American troops during the War of 1812. This is an enterprise of the Women's Auxiliary of the American Scenic and Historic Preservation Society, of which Miss Vanderpoel is President. *June 4, 1904*

VANDERPOEL, DR. ROBERT, one of the oldest medical practitioners in the city and an offshoot of the genuine Knickerbocker stock, recently gave his annual soiree to the friends of the family, commemorating the miraculous escape of his son Edward from death at the hands of the July rioters in 1863. The Muggins Association, so called from a fond appellative given to his son in infancy, together with friends and invited guests, some seventy or eighty persons in all, assembled to make the occasion a pleasant one. *February 8, 1871*

HIS SPEECH-WRITER WAS ECSTATIC

Robert A. Van Wyck, former Mayor of New York, died in Paris at his home. He entered Columbia University at the age of nineteen and graduated at the head of his class in 1897. He was named the Democratic candidate for Mayor. Contrary to the custom of some of our leading Democrats, he made just one speech during the campaign, composed of 187 words! *December 1, 1918*

VAN DYKE, ELLEN "When I won the amteur owner hunter championship at the National Horse Show, I thought, 'Well, now I don't have to prove anything,'" says Ellen Van Dyke, who rode Ruxton to victory in 1982. "If you win here, it's more than just winning against twenty horses. You are up there with the top horses of all time." *October, 1983*

VAN ETTEN, MRS. EDWARD (LILLIAN FRANCES CRAMBLETT), the next Vice President General D.A.R. for Massachusetts, is the wife of Edward Van Etten, Vice President of the New York Central lines. Her father, the Rev. Ezra Cramblett, was formerly of Cleveland, Ohio, and she has seven uncles who are clergymen. Mrs. Van Etten is writing a book in defense of Lord Byron. Lord Byron was one of her ancestors, as she descended through her mother from George Gordon, the sixth Lord. Mrs. Van Etten thinks Lord Byron has been maligned, and from evidence she has been able to procure, and from other papers in the possession of the British Museum, she hopes to prove this to the satisfaction of the public. *February 10, 1906*

VAN LENNEP, DR. WILLIAM B. is noted as a surgeon. He was born in Constantinople, Turkey, where his parents, the Rev. Henry John Van Lennep, and Mary Elizabeth Lennep were missionaries. Henry John van Lennep, who descended from an eminent line of Dutch scholars and writers, was born in Smyrna, Asia Minor. He was sent to this country for his education, but returned to Asia Minor as a missionary. *March 30, 1907*

VAN METER, SOLOMON L., JR. In the heart of the Blue Grass section of Kentucky, one of the richest, most thickly sodded, and best grassed tracts of land in the state is reserved as a grazing ground for shorthorn cattle. The Van Meters were the earliest importers of fine cattle to America. They were also among the first settlers of the New World, landing at New Amsterdam when that village belonged to the Dutch. Mr. Solomon Van Meter, Jr., though sportsman, successful financier, and politician serving his second term in the Kentucky Legislature, with all the alluring possibilities of racehorse development constantly before him, remains true to the interests of his fathers. *September 12, 1903*

VAN PELT, MR. AND MRS. WILLIAM There is a Van Pelt Library at the University of Pennsylvania, and there's a Van Pelt Street in the city, in concrete testimony to the Glories of The Family. Mainliners Billy and Alida Van Pelt (8th generation) pay lip service to their inherited place. Alida, who was *not* born in Philadelphia, takes an irreverent attitude toward Philadelphia tradition: "The best thing that happened to the Van Pelts recently was me, bringing new blood." And Billy himself says: "One of the things that is holding Philadelphia back from being the dynamic and vital city it could be is the old guard. And my family is definitely part of that. It's very nice socially to be a member. But it is these same people who are keeping the city on dead center." *October, 1970*

VAN RENSSELAER, ELIZABETH, as the daughter of Mr. and Mrs. Kilaen Van Rensselaer, has the most desirable sort of an ancestor at the base of her family tree, for as the name of her father indicates, she is a descendant of the great patroon Kilaen Van Rensselaer, who had a great deal to do with the bringing over and afterward the governing of many other good Dutch families who crossed the ocean in the stout craft *Rensselaerwyck. November 7, 1903*

VAN RENSSELAER, MRS. JOHN KING (MAY KING) gave a reception recently for the purpose of letting people know that her two sons, John and Harold, had reached the age when they were ready to enter society. There was a five o'clock tea party, the invitations to which were issued in Mrs. Van Rensselaer's name alone. This social function has been for some time in vogue in Boston, but tried only on rare occasions before in New York. *November 22, 1893*

VAN RENSSELAER, MRS. SCHUYLER (MARIANA GRISWOLD) is best known as an art critic and author. She has written much about English cathedrals, and to her credit as an author there is a history of the city of New York in the seventeenth century. However—and very unfortunately—Mrs. Van Rensselaer gives all her sympathy to women who are content; those who most need the vote they don't want. Her book, *Should We Ask for the Suffrage?* is strongly "anti" in argument. *September 20, 1913*

VAN RENSSELAER, STEPHEN H., the son of Mrs. Van Rensselaer (née Heckscher), has an interesting personality, and his hobbies have made him well known. He is as much devoted to Indian research as Mr. Robb de Peyster Tytus is to archaeological work in Egypt. His part in the Spanish-American war as a Rough Rider resulted in great expertness as an equestrian, and at private charitable affairs he has given exhibitions on horseback. *July 29, 1905*

VAN RENSSELAER, MRS. SUSAN DE LANCEY has secured an option on the historic Greenbush manor house on the Hudson River, opposite Albany. The manor house, which was built in 1642, is famous for being one of the oldest habitable houses in the United States and the place where "Yankee Doodle" was composed. *February 8, 1899*

VARNUM, GENERAL JAMES MITCHEL, one of the most prominent lawyers, was born in New York in 1848, the great-grandson of Senator Joseph Bradley Varnum (brother of General James Mitchel Varnum, who was President *pro tempore* of the Senate and Acting Vice President of the United States from 1813 to 1814). General James Mitchel Varnum was of course one of the great soldiers of the Revolution. At his instance, the legislature passed an act offering freedom to all slaves who should enlist in the army. Mr. Varnum met his death in an automobile accident. *April 6, 1907*

VAUGHAN, HENRY GOODWIN When the Masters of Foxhounds Association of America holds its thirtieth annual meeting in New York, the man in the chair will be Henry Goodwin Vaughan. From 1934 through 1936, he represented South Berwick, Maine, in the state legislature. During term, he lived at the family seat, "The Homestead," in Hallowell, the first American home of the Vaughans. Dr. Benjamin Vaughan, an Englishman who had been active in arranging the Peace of Paris, built it in 1796. The doctor experimented with fruits and cereals, designed the state seal, and entertained lavishly. *February, 1937*

VAUX, ROBERT, the jurist and author, was one of the originators of the public school system in Philadelphia and zealous in the cause of prison reform. Richard Vaux, the son of Robert Vaux, as Mayor effected a complete reorganization of the city government. He was even more earnest and untiring than his father in his work for prison reform, and wrote voluminously on the subject. He had one distinction that Philadelphia is apt to refer to— the honor of dancing with Queen Victoria. *September 30, 1905*

VIELE, HERMAN KNICKERBOCKER, who was born in New York in 1856, was a civil engineer, an artist, and an author. He is survived by his wife, who was Miss Mary Wharton of Philadelphia; and by a brother, Egbert L. Viele, a poet, known as Francis Viele Griffin. His father was Egbert Ludovickus Viele, also known in three walks of life, as a soldier, an engineer, and an author. (He, the father, was appointed chief engineer of Central Park in 1856 and prepared the original plan which was adopted for the park.) Herman K. Viele, the son, studied engineering in his father's office and was associated with him in the extension of the city of Washington. *December 26, 1908*

VIETOR, GEORGE FREDERICK was senior member of the firm of Frederick Vietor & Achelis, and President of the New Jersey Iron Mining Company. The Vietor & Achelis firm was established in 1825. His wife was, before his marriage, Annie M. Achelis. *February 5, 1910*

VIETOR, JOHN A., a grandson of Orator Woodward, Jell-O manufacturer, bought his oceanfront four-story Mediterranean-style villa on Camino de la Costa in La Jolla sight-unseen from an advertisement he spotted in *Town & Country* in 1947. So Vietor, then 33, migrated to La Jolla. A writer, columnist, and ex-State Department official with a mild reputation as an eastern seaboard playboy, Vietor had been a Lieutenant Colonel in the Air Force and a prisoner of war in Germany. Tall, slim, dashing, he cut quite a figure in his new hometown. *May, 1975*

EVERY GENTLEMAN NEEDS ONE

The private railroad cars of Mr. Jewett, President of the Erie Railway, Henry Villard of the Oregon Railway and Navigation Company, and Mr. Pullman, the car builder, are nearly alike in construction and appointment. The first room is walled with Irish bog oak, carved and ceiled with light wood, stenciled ornately. A hallway wide enough for two to pass in leads to the main saloon. Two doors open from this passage-way, one leading to a bathroom whose walls are of polished mahogany and the other to a private bedroom containing wine and linen lockers and a full-sized bed that shuts up and becomes an imitation wardrobe of mahogany, rich in carving. Under the car are refrigerator lockers for wine, meat, milk, ice, and so on. *August 16, 1882*

VILLARD, MRS. HENRY (FANNY GARRISON) The name of William Lloyd Garrison, "the Great Emancipator," has been given to one of the many clubs devoted to "Equal Rights." Mrs. Henry Villard, a daughter of Mr. Garrison, is a member of this association and gave a reception for its members. Mrs. Villard has all of her father's interest in the betterment of the human race, but unlike many of the present-day suffragists she believes in the peaceful outcome of all the twentieth-century pother about the feminine vote. *March 6, 1909*

VITETTI, COUNTESS LEONARDO (NATHALIE COE) is the daughter of William Robertson Coe of Oyster Bay. Her husband, successor to Count Ciano, is the new head of the Prime Minister's Cabinet. Countess Vitetti and Countess Ciano are great friends. Both are in their early twenties, both fond of riding, skiing, and dancing; and they are equally allergic to bridge, the scourge of Rome. In preparation for entertaining, the Vitettis have redecorated their Orsini Palace apartment. *April, 1937*

VON BERNSTORFF, COUNTESS JOHANN (MARY KNOWLTON) Americans are beginning to discover the unique charms of Garmisch-Partenkirchen, the twin villages nestling in the very heart of the Bavarian Alps. Many American-born women have homes around the picturesque Lake of Starnberg: Count Johann von Bernstorff, erstwhile German Ambassador to Washington, and the Countess, who was Miss Mary Knowlton, of Brooklyn; Prince and Princess Karl Ysenburg

(formerly Miss Bertha Lewis of Detroit), who have recently renovated a picturesque old castle; and Count Lerchenfels, former Prime Minister of Bavaria, whose wife was Miss Ethel Newman, also of Detroit. Here, too, Mrs. Franz Hanfstaengel, of the well-known New England family of Sedgwicks, is running a model farm, and one of the show places of the region is the magnificent home owned by Consul and Mrs. Scharrer (née Minnie Busch, of St. Louis). *September 1, 1925*

VON BREDOW, LIEUTENANT AND MRS. (FRANCES NEWLANDS) The latest international marriage sensation in Washington came to pass almost surreptitiously. Miss Frances Newlands, the youngest daughter of Senator Newlands, married Lieutenant von Bredow of the Cuirassier Guards, in Berlin. This latest American wife of a German lord is a young woman of much character and, moreover, immense wealth by right of inheritance from her mother, Senator Newlands' first wife, a daughter of Senator Sharon of California. Lieutenant von Bredow is of distinguished lineage, but untitled. *May 13, 1905*

VON FURSTENBERG, PRINCE AND PRINCESS TASSILO (CECIL AMELIA BLAFFER)—HUDSON The daughter of Houston oilman Robert Lee Blaffer, "Titi," divides her time between Monte Carlo, the family hunting lodge near Salzburg, and her world travels. Her elder son, Edward Joseph Hudson, Jr., heads the family firm, the R. L. Blaffer Company. Her younger son, Robert Lee Blaffer Hudson, is a viticulturist in Napa Valley. *December, 1981*

VON GONTARD, ADALBERT "It used to be the guy who bought the most expensive horse won the class at the National Horse Show," laughs Mr. Adalbert von Gontard, who wears the red tails and royal blue-and-gold collar of the Fairfield Hunt. "Now everyone has the most expensive horse." *October, 1983*

VON HILLER, BARON AND BARONESS FRIEDRICH (EMILY D. BARNEY) The marriage was celebrated at St. Paul's Church in Ogontz, Pennsylvania, which was founded by the bride's grandfather, the late Jay Cooke. The bride's great-grandfather, Eleuthoras Cooke, was one of the pioneers in the railroad enterprises of the West; her grandfather, Jay Cooke, was at the head of the firm which became the government agent for the placing of war loans; and her great-uncle, Henry D. Cooke, was at one time the owner of daily papers in Ohio, the first Governor of the District of Columbia, and the founder of a mission church in Georgetown. *June 13, 1908*

VON KETTELER, BARON AND BARONESS (MATILDE CASS LEDYARD) The daughter of Mr. Henry B. Ledyard was married to the Baron von Ketteler in Detroit. Because of the services to the Church by the von Kettelers, a special dispensation for a church wedding was granted. It was attended by the German Ambassador to the United States and was a noted social event. The tragic death of Baron von Ketteler, who was Ambassador to China from Germany at the date of the Boxer uprising, is a matter of history. The Baroness is very high in favor at the German Court, and a palace was presented her in Berlin, where she spends her winters, returning to her father's home in Detroit yearly. *September 25, 1909*

VON LIMBURG, BARON AND BARONESS THEODORE MARINNS ROEST (BELLE CASS) Miss Belle Cass, daughter of General Lewis Cass, the prominent statesman, was one of the first of the daughters of Detroit to marry a title. Her marriage to Baron von Limburg, who was connected with the German Legation in Washington, took place in that city and was a brilliant affair. Belle Isle, the garden river park of Detroit, was named in honor of Miss Belle Cass. *September 25, 1909*

VON ROMBERG, BARONESS MAXIMILIAN HUGO CONVERSE WILHELM (EMILY HALL) was formerly Miss Emily Hall, of Santa Barbara, California. Her marriage to Baron Maximilian Hugo Converse Wilhelm von Romberg, of Wiesbaden, took place in New York. Baron von Romberg is related on his mother's side to Mrs. Converse Strong of New York and Santa Barbara, and to Mr. Edmund C. Converse of Santa Paula, California. *May 15, 1928*

VON STADE, F. SKIDDY is one of the best-known and most experienced horsemen in the country. He has hunted a great deal in America and a great deal in England also, where he spent several seasons with the Midland packs. He has ridden the winner of the Meadow Brook Cup on two occasions, and Mr. von Stade comes by his love of racing and steeplechasing very naturally. His great-grandfather, Mr. Francis Skiddy, was one of the early supporters of the sport in this country. Mr. von Stade's father, Mr. F. H. von Stade, has for years been a keen supporter of racing, and in particular was interested in the sport at Saratoga. *February 1, 1927*

VON STEINWEHR, FLORENCE is one of the most prominent among Cincinnati's brides-to-be. She is a granddaughter of Baroness von Steinwehr, who resides at her estate at Launeau, near Hanover. Mr. William Whiting Andrews, her fiancé, is a resident of Cleveland and a grandson of Judge Sherlock Andrews, who, with Thomas Corwin, shared the leadership of the Ohio Bar. He is also a kinsman of the Gwynnes, the family of which Mrs. Cornelius Vanderbilt is a member. *December 3, 1904*

VON WALDERSEE, COUNTESS ALFRED (MARY ESTHER LEE)—VON NOER was the third daughter of the late David Lee, a New York merchant. Her first husband was Prince Frederick of Schleswig-Holstein, a brother of the Queen of Denmark, who gave up his title in order to marry her and who was known as Count von Noer. At his death eight months later, the Countess was made a Princess by the Emperor of Austria. Eight years after the death of her first husband, the Princess married Count von Waldersee, the General who was later created Field Marshall. *July 11, 1914*

VREELAND, MARJORIE A. The engagement of Miss Marjorie A. Vreeland and Mr. George von Gal was announced at a dinner. After dinner, all the young people were assembled in the hall to witness a little ceremony that has been a custom in the Vreeland family for generations. Miss Vreeland, standing in front of the old grandfather's clock, pulled a ribbon that hung below the pendulum and from the little door below fell a shower of gold coins. They had been placed there by her father, Mr. H. H. Vreeland, on different anniversaries and on red-letter days in her life. The gold will buy her trousseau. *February 10, 1915*

VREELAND, MRS. T. REED (DIANA DALZIEL) When she arrived in Palm Beach early in the season, she brought plenty of color with her to wear against the white sands. Her heavy linen shorts were bright emerald-green, with red zippers; her jerseys (cut like a concierge's jacket) were lemon-yellow or scarlet; and an orange tweed skirt was topped by Patou's turquoise-blue cardigan. At night, her little tweed jackets in lovely colors went with her everywhere. Mrs. Vreeland has her own special head covering against the Southern sun—squares of heavy chiffon, like old-fashioned motoring veils, that follow her hairline, are fastened low on the back of her head, and fall in soft folds to her shoulders. *February, 1937*

W

WADSWORTH, MR. AND MRS. ADRIAN R. (CECIL DWIGHT) will live in Farmington in the old Wadsworth homestead, which has been occupied by succeeding generations of the family since 1682. This marriage united descendants of Colonial Connecticut families. Mr. Wadsworth's ancestor, Sergeant John, was present with his brother, Captain Joseph Wadsworth, on the historic occasion when the latter seized the State Charter and secreted it in the Oak. Mrs. Wadsworth is descended from the founders of Hartford, Windsor, and Middletown, Connecticut. *May 10, 1921*

WADSWORTH, ALICE TILTON Another entry for the family Bible of the Wadsworth clan, who have pursued dual careers as public servants and country squires in the Genesee Valley of New York since 1790, was the marriage of Trowbridge Strong and Alice Tilton Wadsworth, the daughter of James Jeremiah Wadsworth, former New York State Assemblyman. The wedding took place in "Hartford House," the home of her grandfather, James W. Wadsworth, onetime Senator, now Representative, which was built by her great-great-grandfather, James S. Wadsworth, in 1835. *August, 1948*

WADSWORTH, EVELYN This charming daughter of Senator and Mrs. James W. Wadsworth is a granddaughter of the late John Hay, who was Lincoln's secretary and served as Secretary of State. The Wadsworth family has been identified with the Genesee Valley since Colonial days. She is engaged to Mr. W. Stuart Symington 3rd of Baltimore. The family belongs to what the Baltimore correspondent of a certain scandalous weekly is wont to call "the gold spoon set" and is allied with several of Maryland's finest lines. *October 1, 1923*

WADSWORTH, JAMES W. Fox hunting, which has so recently come into prominence in this country, bids fair to get a permanent hold here. Several runs have been successfully made in Livingston County, New York, under the patronage of James W. Wadsworth of Genesee. One of these was at Mr. Wadsworth's "Oneida Farm." The fox was unable to elude the keen scent of the hounds and came to a violent death. Miss Ella Youngs took the brush. *November 7, 1877*

WADSWORTH, JAMES W., JR. Eastertide brought with it the announcement of the engagement of Miss Alice Hay, the second daughter of Secretary of State and Mrs. John Hay, to Mr. James W. Wadsworth, Jr. Mr. Wadsworth, known to his friends as Jimmie, has been called "the most popular man who ever went to Yale," from which university he graduated in '97. He was one of the best character singers in the Glee Club, and was especially good in his comic German Schneider songs. When the war with Spain broke out, he enlisted with the famous Philadelphia "Battery A." He belongs to the Geneseo Wadsworths and is one of the best riders in the Geneseo Hunt Club. His father is Representative Wadsworth, and his grandfather was the late William R. Travers. *April 5, 1902*

WADSWORTH, DR. SARAH JOSEPHINE for many years was one of the foremost women physicians of New Jersey. Following her graduation in 1876 from the New York Medical College for Women, she practised medicine in New York, later removing to Morristown, New Jersey, where she opened a private sanitarium for the treatment of brain and nervous diseases. Mrs. Wadsworth was related on her father's side to Major André, the English spy of Revolutionary fame, and on her mother's side to the American spy Nathan Hale. *March 1, 1913*

WAGSTAFF, MR. AND MRS. ALFRED (MARY ANDERSON BARNARD) are brave and venturesome, and aerial flights will probably succeed the long motor-journeys they made abroad. They have journeyed by automobile to the Sahara and have lived under tents in the desert. Mrs. Wagstaff has genius as a poet, so new adventures all add to the color and life of her verses. *August 13, 1910*

WALDO, RHINELANDER belongs to a small group of well-born young men who took up politics about twelve years ago and went into the active service of the Democratic Party. He was an only son, and his mother, a rich woman, was a Miss Rhinelander. Mr. Waldo was a student of police regulations in Paris and London and also of traffic regulations. He early in the service of the New York police demonstrated that he was not a dude but a man of brains and determination and ideas. Whatever may be said of him, the fact remains that he is a man of inherited wealth and education and that the possibilities of graft could not apply to him. *August 10, 1912*

WALKER, MR. AND MRS. JOHN III (LADY MARGARET DRUMMOND) John Walker III has been the chief Curator at the Mellon-founded National Gallery of Art since that fabulous opening night eleven years ago when Mr. Roosevelt was there in person to describe it as "a symbol of the human spirit." Mr. Walker's wife is the daughter of the Earl of Perth.

Besides themselves, their household includes their two children and a huge black and immensely aristocratic French poodle named Cognac, who is descended from a show dog bred by Walter Lippmann. *February, 1952*

WALKER, MR. AND MRS. THOMAS BARLOW (HARRIET C. HULET) have returned to Minneapolis after a stay of many months in New York. Mr. Walker brought with him many new treasures for his art gallery, which already contains one of the most interesting private collections in the United States. Among the new pictures is Rembrandt's *Christ and the Erring Woman,* which was but recently brought to America. The jade collection has also been greatly enriched, so that it is now one of the finest in the world. Mr. Walker is one of those great capitalists of the Northwest who have made fortunes in the lumber industry. He owns great pine land and milling interests in Minnesota. *July 13, 1912*

WALLACE, MRS. DEWITT (LILA ACHESON) She and her late husband, DeWitt Wallace, co-founded the *Readers Digest* in 1922; individually and with her husband, she has made countless major donations before and after his death in 1981. Two foundations funded by Lila—the L.A.W. Fund and the High Winds Fund—both dispense annual grants totaling in the millions of dollars. *December, 1983*

WALLACE, MR. AND MRS. JOHN (GLENN WALKER) Both the Utah Symphony and Ballet West owe their existence largely to the efforts of one energetic and determined woman: Glenn Walker Wallace, Salt Lake City's undisputed grande dame. Mrs. Wallace is the daughter of Matthew Henry Walker, the youngest of four English brothers who came to Salt Lake in 1852 and founded the first bank between the Missouri River and the Pacific Coast. She is one of four U.S. women declared a Grande Dame by the Knightly Order of St. Brigitte. She and banker-husband John entertain in their château-like home, filled with French antiques. *August, 1983*

WALLACE, MRS. SALLY (STETSON)—WINSLOW Mrs. Wallace is one of the most unfortunate persons, matrimonially, that San Francisco has ever seen. Her husbands never appreciate her. Yet she is one of the most domestic women imaginable. Her defect is that she is too fond of her husbands. She was devoted to the handsome Chauncey Winslow, who went away to Portland to escape her devotion. After a few years, Mrs. Winslow married Colonel Wallace, Quartermaster in the United States Army. This marriage was even more unsuccessful than the Winslow marriage. Mrs. Winslow has a large fortune of her own inherited by her from her father, J. B. Stetson. *January 1, 1917*

WALSH, THOMAS F. He developed, equipped, and became the sole owner and operator of the Camp Bird mines at Ouray, Colorado. During the years he devoted to mining, he was a close student of geology and all the sciences a knowledge of which aids in finding ore bodies and the development and treatment of ores. Mr. Walsh's only son, Vincent Walsh, was killed in a motor accident in Newport in 1905. His daughter Evelyn was married in 1908 to Mr. Edward McLean. *April 16, 1910*

WALTERS, WILLIAM THOMPSON, who has an art gallery in Baltimore valued at one million dollars, is a Pennsylvanian of Scotch-Irish ancestry. His love for art has been the ruling passion of his life. The first five dollars he ever spent was for a picture. Every year he put aside a part of his income for art purchases. The result has been a private art gallery which many critics consider the most harmonious and beautiful in the world. *May 25, 1887*

WALTON, JAMES MELLON had his choice of remaining in the family's petro-world of Gulf oil or coming back to Pittsburgh. He had traveled the former for ten years, but in 1968 he settled in Pittsburgh as President of the board of the venerable Carnegie Institute, which for generations has benefited mightily from the strong Mellon feeling for cultural leadership and responsibility. From his office in the doughty, soot-crusted library, he presides over all three entities that comprise the Institute: the Art Museum, the Natural History Museum, and the Library and its branches. *February, 1975*

WANAMAKER, JOHN is probably as well known as a man of strong religious convictions and practices as he is as a merchant. In 1857, he was secretary of the Philadelphia Y.M.C.A. The Bethany Sunday School of which he was superintendent in 1858 began with twenty seven scholars but became one of the largest in the country, claiming 2,600 students. Under President Harrison's administration, he was Postmaster General. From Tuesday until Friday of every week, Mr. Wanamaker lives at New York's Plaza Hotel, and often as late as seven in the evening he is still at the office in his great emporium on Broadway and Ninth Street. *July 31, 1909*

WANAMAKER, CAPTAIN JOHN, JR., is the grandson of the merchant who became Postmaster General. With his bride, Wanamaker sailed on the *Conte de Savoia* to take part in last month's motor boat regatta on the waters of Lake Garda. The object was sport for sport's sake, and the hope of encouraging Italian racers to come over for next winter's events in Florida. *June 1, 1933*

WANAMAKER, RODMAN gave a dinner in Paris which will be talked of for many a day. That the dinner was served in questionable taste, to say the least, is not perhaps to the point. There were twenty two guests. The decorations of the dining room were marvelously beautiful. Luminous fountains planted upon great blocks of ice kept the air cool. It is said that the dinner cost twenty thousand dollars. It was not one dinner, but twenty two independent dinners, separately served, one to each guest. Each guest had before him a whole leg of mutton, a whole salmon, and a double magnum of champagne, besides bottles of wine of sacred vintage and fabulous cost. *July 31, 1895*

WANAMAKER, RODMAN II, who won the "free for all" race at Miami with his speed boat, *Little Old Man,* returned that evening to Palm Beach by airplane from Miami, in the record time of forty two minutes. *April 15, 1923*

WANAMAKER, THOMAS B. was the eldest son of the former Postmaster General John Wanamaker. He was graduated from Princeton in 1883. His marriage to Miss Mary Lowber Welsh, a granddaughter of the late John Welsh, Ambassador to the Court of St. James, took place in 1887. Mr. Wanamaker was much interested in art, and at his country home at Meadowbrook, Pennsylvania, which was destroyed by fire, he had a collection of paintings considered one of the finest in the country. *March 14, 1908*

WARBURG, MR. AND MRS. GERALD (NATICA NAST) When they decided to build a house, they knew exactly what they wanted. They saw no good reason why, since the site was on Long Island, at Brookville, they could not have a patio. As Gerald Warburg, Vice President of New York City's City Center of Music and Drama, is a concert cellist and a conductor, a main consideration was a good-sized music room which would do the right thing by acoustics, provide an attractive center for musical evenings and a quiet room for work and study. *August, 1945*

WARBURTON, MR. AND MRS. BARCLAY (MARY B. WANAMAKER) Mrs. Warburton is the oldest daughter of Mr. John Wanamaker of Philadelphia, former Postmaster General of the United States. Mr. Warburton succeeded his father, Charles E. Warburton, as the publisher of one of the daily papers in Philadelphia; he was the organizer and captain of Light Battery A, formed during the Spanish-American War, and he served in the Puerto Rico campaign in command of the battalion of Pennsylvania artillery. *December 7, 1907*

WARD, THE HON. MRS. JOHN HUBERT (JEAN REID) The daughter of Ambassador Reid, when a girl, annually spent her summers at camp "Wildair," her father's beautiful camp on the Upper St. Regis Lake, in the Adirondacks. And with her brother, Mr. Ogden Mills Reid, she delighted to take part in the exciting sailing races under the direction of the St. Regis Yacht Club. Somewhere at the bottom of the Upper St. Regis Lake there is said to be a diamond-studded bracelet that slipped from the arm of the young girl as she was guiding her brother's yacht over the course in a high wind a few seasons ago. *August 20, 1910*

WARD, DR. LESLIE DODD He practised medicine in Newark, New Jersey, taking high rank in his profession. In 1874, with John F. Dryden, he founded the Prudential Life Insurance Company. He was president of the commission in charge of the $2,000,000 Essex County Court House in Newark. The beauty of the interior and exterior were chiefly the result of his discrimination and work. He had made valuable collections of pictures for his home in Newark and his country estate at Brooklake Farms, near Madison, New Jersey, and his libraries contain thousands of rare volumes. *July 23, 1910*

WARDWELL, WILLIAM T. was one of the organizers of the Standard Oil Company. He was at one time President of the New York Red Cross Hospital and was prominent in politics as a Prohibitionist. He was a candidate for Mayor on the Prohibition ticket in 1886 and later for Governor. *January 14, 1911*

WARFIELD, WALLIS Of considerable general interest is the recent announcement of the engagement of pretty little Wallis Warfield to Lieutenant E. Winfield Spencer, U.S.N. Miss Warfield is called for her father, the late Wallis Warfield, a member of the old Maryland family. The wedding will take place in Baltimore at Christ Church and will be among the most brilliant social affairs of the autumn in that city. *October 1, 1916*

WARNER, HENRY LUKE III An outstanding golfer, he has won several championships, including the Middle Atlantic. Excellent basketball player. Resort: Palm Beach, where he is a frequent guest of his aunt and uncle, Mary and "Laddie" Sanford. *June, 1968*

WARREN, BAYARD has owned various notable steeplechasers, and he was the moving spirit in making the Grand National Steeplechase, run at Belmont Park in the autumn, the immensely valuable stake it has since become. *July 15, 1931*

WARREN, LLOYD Following Mrs. Ogden Mills' dignified dinner last week, the guests repaired to the studio of Mr. Lloyd Warren for a dance, and really "played"—for at a studio, austerity can unbend. At this studio-dance the favors included mechanical toys. These started on their trips by the dancers and made their way in the zig-zag fashion of the contrivances one sees on the sidewalks of the shopping district. The person before whom they stopped was forced to accept the sender as a partner. *January 27, 1906*

WARREN, WHITNEY is an exponent of the French school of architecture in this country. In this, he is a true disciple of the Ecole des Beaux Arts, where he distinguished himself. There are many monuments of Mr. Warren's creation in New York: the New York Yacht Club, the Ritz-Carlton, and the new Grand Central terminus. Mr. Warren comes from the old New York state family related to the Phoenixes and others notable in the history of society. The Warrens originally derived their fortune in Troy. *December 7, 1912*

WARREN, WHITNEY, JR., is another of the San Francisco bachelors. He adores California, and has a wonderful farm up in Merced County, where he has actually managed to make peaches pay. He cleared $20,000 last year. He has a lovely apartment up on Russian Hill, which has a view second to none. *March, 1939*

WASHBURN, GENERAL WILLIAM DREW was the seventh son of Israel and Martha Washburn, the youngest of a group of brothers known for many years in American public life. Israel Washburn, the eldest and of the eighth generation to bear that name, was a Congressman from Maine for five years and was the war Governor of Maine. Elihu Benjamin Washburn was a Congressman from Illinois for eight terms, an intimate friend of President Lincoln, Secretary of State under President Grant, and Minister to France. Cadwallader Washburn was a Congressman from Wisconsin for four terms, a Major General in the Civil War, and Governor of Wisconsin. Charles A. Washburn was United States Minister to Paraguay. William Drew Washburn was in Congress from Minnesota three terms and United States Senator for six years. He was in Congress while his three brothers were there, an unusual record for an American family. The American family is descended from John Washburn, who was one of the first secretaries of the Plymouth colony. *August 17, 1912*

WASHINGTON, REV. RICHARD BLACKBURN is a popular figure at Hot Springs, Virginia, recently appointed by the Bishop of Richmond as pastor of the little Catholic church on the side of the mountain and in the heart of the cottage colony, where the residents are helping him to build a rectory. He is a son of the late George Washington, who was born in "Mount Vernon" and who is a direct descendant of Lawrence Washington, eldest brother of George Washington and of Mrs. Washington, who was Serena Porterfield, daughter of the famous Southern general. *May 1, 1923*

WASHINGTON, COLONEL WILLIAM DE HERTBERN The most artistic ball on record in the capital city social annals was the dance given by the Daughters of the American Revolution. The function celebrated the anniversary of Washington's wedding day. The ball was opened by the grand march, led by Mrs. Charlotte Emerson Main, in the character of Martha Washington, escorted by Colonel William De Hertbern Washington, directly descended from the brother of George Washington. Colonel Washington, who came from Detroit to attend the ball, has the distinction of being the nearest living relative of the first President of the United States, in addition to bearing a strong personal resemblance to his distinguished ancestor. *January 30, 1904*

WATERBURY, ELSIE, daughter of Mr. and Mrs. James M. Waterbury and a sister of the famous polo players Mr. Lawrence Waterbury and Mr. "Monty" Waterbury, is now among the brides-to-be. She has been prominent in the life of the Westchester Country Club, and Mr. Gouverneur Morris is also identified with this locality. Mr. Morris, who wrote his first successful book when twenty one years of age, is a grandson of Gouverneur Morris, who was Minister to France during the French Revolution. *December 24, 1904*

WATERBURY, JAMES M. Mr. Waterbury's amateur circus at Pelham, New York, seems to have aroused as much interest in a limited circle as the Centennial ball. About three hundred and fifty guests drove from the station through torch-lighted roads to Mr. Waterbury's country house at Baychester. There was a genuine sawdust ring, and galleries were arranged on two sides for the Hungarian band and Lander's orchestra. The grand entrée was made at half-past nine o'clock. Four gentlemen and four ladies mounted on matched thoroughbreds dashed from the anteroom and began to dance the grand quadrille on horseback. Supper and dancng concluded the unique entertainment. *May 8, 1889*

WATERBURY, LAWRENCE Among the young men there are a number, associated usually with sports or more frivolous pastimes, who are accomplished and studious. The Waterbury brothers, for instance, have interests other than polo, are fine linguists, and still devote a great deal of time to the study of French. Even "Larry" Waterbury, the jovial owner of "Stumpy," has certain hours which he sets aside for mental improvement. *April 5, 1902*

WATERBURY, MRS. LAWRENCE From the New York Yacht Club station at the foot of East Twenty Third Street during the Hudson-Fulton celebration, one could see the yachts lying at anchor, each dress ship with little flags of vivid color strung from bow to stern. Mrs. Lawrence Waterbury was one of the animated young women who set out to sea on one of the yachts. She wore one of the new beaver turbans, but it had a long white aigrette at the side. And with her bright blue suit, she wore a wide scarf of fur, and she carried an enormous tail-trimmed muff. *October 2, 1909*

WAUD, MR. AND MRS. REEVE (MELISSA ANN WHEELER) "In almost any business in Chicago, I could find a cousin who's involved," laughs 26-year-old private equity investor Reeve Waud. Reeve's great-great-grandfather, Byron Laflin Smith, founded the Northern Trust Bank and Illinois Tool Works, of which Reeve's great-grandfather Harold Cornelius Smith was first President and director. Reeve's mother is a great-granddaughter of legendary Chicago meat packer Gustavus Swift (as well as a relative of the Lowells of Massachusetts and the Roosevelts of Oyster Bay, New York). And the prolific Swifts are related to Cudahys, Blocks, and Woods, among other prominent old Chicago family names. *September, 1990*

WEAR, JOSEPH WALKER is a native of St. Louis, a graduate of Yale, and a partner of Messrs. Cassatt and Co. of Philadelphia. When he left college and returned to St. Louis, he took up racquets and partnered with the Honorable Dwight Davis; they became the doubles champions. When he came East to live near Philadelphia, he paired a great many times both in racquets and court tennis with Jay Gould; and this famous combination won several national tournaments. He is a fine lawn tennis player; and it is a fine tribute that he was made Captain of the Davis Cup team of 1929, though not playing actively himself. *September 1, 1931*

WEATHERBEE, HENRIETTA CONSTABLE has no small claim to the interest of New Yorkers, being the granddaughter of a merchant who held such a prominent and such an enviable place in the business world. The house of Arnold, Constable & Co. was founded by A. Arnold in 1827. It is one of the oldest and best-known in the United States, and also in France. After the death of A. Arnold, James Constable became the head of the firm. "Waytes Court," the residence of Mr. and Mrs. Weatherbee, at Mamaroneck, is one of the largest country estates of the vicinity. *February 10, 1906*

WEAVER, WILLIAM C., JR. "Although Nashville is an unusual town from many standpoints," he says, "one thing I find most impressive about it is that there is probably no other city in the U.S. where the old families are still so active in the community." Weaver himself is archetypal of this tradition. "I was born and raised right here on the Murfreesboro Road," he says. "I was the fifth generation to be born on the same land, and I lived there until I was 27 years old." *June, 1971*

WEBB, GENERAL ALEXANDER STEWART received medals for bravery in the Civil War, combining military with literary ability, as he is the author of *The Peninsula: McClellan's Campaign of 1862,* and has written a great deal about the strife between the States. His bravery in wartime may be traced—as an inheritance—to his grandfather, Samuel Blatchley Webb, who fought in the Revolution, and his aptitude for writing to his father, Mr. James Watson Webb, the journalist and author. *November 21, 1903*

WEBB, FREDERICA The announcement of the engagement of Miss Frederica Webb, the daughter of Dr. and Mrs. W. Seward Webb, to Mr. Ralph Pulitzer is the chief bit of social news of the sort that is pleasant, yet desirably exciting. Mr. Pulitzer is a son of Mr. Joseph Pulitzer, the editor and publisher and one of our national characters, while on his mother's side he is a grandson of the late John Davis, of the family of authors and statesmen, and Mrs. Davis, who is a Frelinghuysen by birth. Miss Webb, on the maternal side, is a great-granddaughter of Cornelius Vanderbilt the first. *June 24, 1905·*

WEBB, JAMES WATSON is a grandson of the late William H. Vanderbilt and of General James Watson Webb, who was Minister and Envoy-extraordinary to Brazil during the sixties and Editor and Proprietor of the *Morning Courier and New York Enquirer* for thirty years. The ancestral home of the Webb family is in Wethersfield, Connecticut. On a tombstone in the graveyard at Wethersfield, one may read: "To the memory of Joseph Webb, late an eminent Merch't in Wethersfield, Whose Applycation and Industry were equal'd only by his ability and integrity in business." This Joseph Webb was the great-great-grandfather of James Watson Webb. *February 12, 1910*

WEBB, DR. WILLIAM SEWARD, President of the Wagner Palace Car Company, left by special train last week for California and Vancouver. He was accompanied by his wife and children. The train consists of six cars, sumptuously fitted and appointed, including a dining car, observation car, compartment car, baggage car, and a car fitted up as a playroom for the children. They will be gone three months. *April 5, 1893*

WEBER, MR. AND MRS. JOHN C. (CHARLOTTE D. COLKET) She is the Philadelphia-born granddaughter of John Dorrance, Sr., who invented condensed soup in 1899, founded Campbell Soup Co., and left a $129 million estate at his death in 1930. She and her husband, a professor of cell biology and anatomy at Cornell Medical College, are avid collectors of ancient Chinese arts; they funded and stocked the Weber Galleries, which opened this year at the Metropolitan Museum of Art and display one of the Western world's largest and finest collections of ancient Chinese art. *September, 1988*

WEBSTER, SIDNEY From 1853 to 1857, he was the secretary of President Pierce. In 1860, he married Miss Sarah Fish, daughter of Senator Hamilton Fish. As a lawyer, he made a specialty of corporation and international questions. In 1883, he became one of the directors of the Illinois Central Railway. *June 4, 1910*

WEEKES, ARTHUR DELANO was an authority on real estate law and values, an enthusiastic sportsman, and a member of many clubs. He was Vice President of the Union Club and in the club when it was attacked by a mob because, in commemoration of the Landing of the Pilgrims in 1920, it flew the Union Jack. The flag was kept flying. *June 15, 1925*

WEEKS, SINCLAIR has already followed his father into the mayor's office of Newton, Boston suburban source of more Harvard athletes than most of the church schools put together. Sinclair Weeks was born forty-two years ago in Newton, during the early days of his father's banking partnership in Hornblower & Weeks. He was sent to Harvard, where he admits "squeaking through with the reputation of a good golfer" in the class of '14. The next step took him into the flat-silver business, and now he is President of the firm of Reed & Barton. He is a regular ringside fan at boxing and wrestling matches, favors the outdoor life, goes to church on Sundays, and has a dozen hobbies, half of which are his six children. *March, 1936*

WEEMS, MR. AND MRS. FONTAINE CARRINGTON (MARY ANN SLEDGE) The Weems name is well known not only to Houstonians but to children across America: Ancestor Parson Weems originated the tale of George Washington and the cherry tree. Today, the family head is Fontaine Carrington Weems, a commercial real estate brokerage firm owner. Wife Mary Ann is a member of Alabama's Sledge family and descendant of Virginia's Seabury clan. *September, 1991*

WEIGHTMAN, WILLIAM By the will of William Weightman, head of the firm of Powers & Weightman, manufacturing chemists, who died in Philadelphia at the age of ninety-one years, his entire estate, valued at more than $50,000,000, is left to his daughter, Mrs. Anne M. Walker, widow of Congressman Robert J. C. Walker, of Williamsport, Pennsylvania. Mrs. Walker, who is the only surviving child, becomes sole proprietor of the extensive chemical works, which makes her one of the richest women in the world. She will assume active management of the drug business, besides looking after the real estate left her by her father, who was one of the largest holders of real estate in the country. *September 3, 1904*

WELCH, SOHIER, the elder son of one of Boston's most respected and affluent estate lawyers, is a considerable figure in the community, given slightly to preciosity in his viticultural jargon but the possessor of a vast oenophilic fund of information and an enthusiast of the first order. He is, too, the brilliant skipper of a sailboat in the Marblehead-Buzzards Bay Class, and he and Mrs. Welch give monthly waltzing parties in their Louisburg Square, Boston, home. *December, 1938*

WELD, PHILIP SALTONSTALL In 1963 Weld introduced the catamaran to the North Shore of Boston. Not just any catamaran—this was the largest and fastest cat on the East Coast. He sailed it through the entire fleet during Race Week at Marblehead. It was ten years before Weld was invited back to Marblehead to compete. *June, 1974*

WELD, RODMAN The Welds do not believe in idle hands. The first ancestor in the new world, Captain Joseph, was the richest man in the Massachusetts Bay Colony. The family declined in importance somewhat, until William Fletcher Weld founded the fleet of sailing ships that made the family a power in India and the China trade. "A Boston gentleman," said Rodman Weld, "never takes a drink before three o'clock or east of Park Street." *April, 1976*

WELLDON, MRS. SAMUEL A. (JULIA M. HOYT) New York is a city of so few surviving traditions that a select circle regretted the departure of Mrs. Samuel A. Welldon from the grand old house in which she was born, on 36th Street, opposite the Morgan Library. The house, home of her family, the Hoyts, figured fictionally in *Twenty-Four Hours* by her cousin-in-law Louis Bromfield and socially as the center of pleasant gatherings of the more amusing and better-mannered members of international society and the arts. *January, 1942*

WELLES, SUMNER is a "graduate" of the American diplomatic service, but since his resignation several years ago, he has been kept busy almost continuously on special missions for the State Department. As American High Commissioner, he had a hand in the pacification of Santo Domingo and more recently he was sent to Honduras. Mr. Welles' first wife was Miss Esther Slater, daughter of Mrs. Horatio Nelson Slater and heiress to a considerable share of the Slater millions made in the cotton mills of Massachusetts. *August 1, 1925*

WELLES, MRS. SUMNER (MATHILDE TOWNSEND) is not a city girl, and her happiest days are spent at "Oxon Hill Manor," her place in Maryland. Since her husband is Under-Secretary of State, she must whisk into town occasionally for official doings, but she manages all her own entertaining in the country. Mathilde Welles prefers simple tailored clothes for daytime wanderings around the Maryland house, and sleek Chanel dinner dresses first, last, and always are her fashion-wise choice for dining by candlelight. *January, 1939*

WENDELL, EVERT JANSEN is greatly interested in the coming production of the Comedy Club's latest venture, *The Jilt,* in which his brother, Mr. Jacob Wendell, will take the leading role. The latter is without doubt the finest amateur actor in the country, and Mr. Evert J. Wendell, who will be remembered for his clever personation of the English detective in *Jim the Penman,* is noted for his philanthropy and charity, especially toward working boys. Another brother of this interesting family is Mr. Barrett Wendell, professor of English at Harvard University. *November 23, 1901*

WENDELL, MRS. TEN EYCK (MAY D. FOOTE), whose home is now in Cazenovia, New York, has just had published a little song to the words of a poem written by Mrs. Payne Whitney, daughter of Secretary Hay. In singing the song to her little son as a "nightcap," the suggestion came that it might give pleasure to other children. The late Mme. Benjamin Wendell, the *grande dame* of Cazenovia, was Mr. Ten Eyck Wendell's mother. *September 3, 1904*

WENTWORTH, JOHN One of the most eligible of Chicago's bachelors was conspicuous by his absence. John Wentworth was in Baltimore, from which place had come the announcement of his engagement to Mrs. Theodore Marburg, Jr., niece of those three delightful Baltimore ladies who, a generation ago, married Chicago men—Mrs. Stanley Field, Mrs. Honoré Palmer, and Mrs. Walter Keith. John Wentworth is the son of Mrs. Moses Wentworth. The name is connected with Chicago's earliest history, his granduncle, "Long" John Wentworth, having had a great part in laying the foundations of the young city. *January 1, 1925*

WERNER, MR. AND MRS. LOUIS II (ANNE DESLOGE) She was the most memorable Veiled Prophet Queen and graced the throne in 1946. She delights in sports: riding, hunting, skiing, hare-coursing in Portugal, and shooting ducks from her private club on the Mississippi Flyway. *March, 1970*

WEST, AUGUSTA TWIGGS SHIPPEN Her engagement to Mr. Roland Sletor Morris is announced. It is a curious coincidence that Miss West is a direct descendant of Mr. Edward Shippen, the first Mayor of Philadelphia, and Mr. Morris a direct descendant of Anthony Morris, the city's second Mayor. Since those early days, both families have been closely identified with history and the social life of the place, but curiously enough this is the first intermarriage that has taken place. Also among Miss West's ancestors was the famous beauty, Peggy Shippen, the wife of Benedict Arnold. *April 5, 1902*

WESTINGHOUSE, MR. AND MRS. GEORGE (MARGUERITE E. WALKER) held an elaborate flag-raising at Erskine Park in Lenox, Massachusetts. The pole, 125 feet above ground, was brought by trucks from Troy, New York. It is of Nova Scotia pine and a perfect taper. The flag-raising was augmented by an electrical display and fireworks, of a magnitude which had never been known in Lenox before. Mr. Westinghouse has one of the most complete electrical plants in the western part of the state, and from the plant is lighted the entire town of Lenox. *July 13, 1898*

WETHERILL, MRS. CORTRIGHT (ELLA WIDENER) After being graduated from Shipley School, the vivacious and pretty heiress to one of America's most famous racing names made her debut at the Bellevue-Stratford Hotel in Philadelphia. She chose to maintain the traditions of her great family name and plunged enthusiastically into charity work. She owns the incredibly perfect emeralds of the Romanoff collection, which were smuggled out of Russia in 1917 and were purchased in two parts by her grandfather, Joseph P. Widener. An inveterate traveler, she spends several months abroad each year and keeps a sharp eye on fashion trends. *August, 1962*

THERE ARE PRIORITIES

George A. "Frolic" Weymouth, who chairs the Brandywine Conservancy, took his coach-and-four abroad for three months to traverse over 1,000 miles in England and France. His luggage was limited to a mere ten sets of harness, eighteen trunks, eighteen hats for all occasions and, to control the horses' manes, a case of Dippity-Do. *December, 1987*

WETHERILL, COLONEL FRANKLYN has a catboat at Newport that will never be overlooked, though it may be outraced. Miss Wetherill, in order to tell when her father is on the homestretch, has painted the sail of the boat in the most glowing shades of orange and yellow. This is to represent a Venetian boat, but, candidly, one must admit that at a distance the little "cat" resembles a flaming Indian wigwam more than any Venetian boat ever seen in a painting or on the water around Venice, possibly because the waters in which it sails and the surrounding scenery are not at all Venetian. *July 18, 1903*

WETHERILL, MR. AND MRS. JOHN PRICE (ALICE D. CORTRIGHT) Their new houseboat, *Savanilla,* was launched recently at Greenwich, New Jersey. The guests who attended the function were entertained at dinner on the craft, which is one of the most comfortable and modern ever built on the Delaware's banks. As the boat was christened, the pretty Japanese custom of liberating pigeons from a large net was carried out. *November 28, 1903*

WETMORE, GEORGE PEABODY The Wetmores have taken a prominent part in the gaiety in London. Later, they will be in Newport, which is in reality their home, and where Miss Maude K. Wetmore, the champion golf player, is considered indispensable in awakening interest in outdoor sports. Mrs. George Peabody Wetmore is a member of the Keteltas family, her sister being Miss Alice Keteltas, who still resides at the Keteltas residence in St. Mark's Place, one of the old houses representative of aristocratic New York of a generation ago. *June 28, 1902*

WETZEL, HERVEY was the only son of Harry Wetzel, a founder of Parke-Davis Pharmaceuticals in Detroit. Young Hervey was Harvard class of 1902 and something of a protégé of Isabella Gardner of Boston. He began collecting Oriental art and eventually went to Paris, where he became head of the American Red Cross office. Jane Valentine Noble of Chicago, the daughter of Albertine Flershem Valentine, recalls: "Hervey Wetzel's collection of Oriental art was superior. When he died, he left everything to my mother, his cousin. She in turn gave a third of his Oriental collection to the Fogg Museum at Harvard and much of the rest to the Boston Museum of Fine Arts. She also donated a significant portion of what remained to The Chicago Art Institute." *February, 1983*

WEYERHAUSER, MRS. FREDERICK (ELIZABETH BLOEDEL) was born in Niedersaulheim, Germany, and she came to the United States with her father while still an infant. Her marriage to Mr. Weyerhauser took place in Rock Island, Illinois, in 1857, five years after he had come to this country. They lived in Rock Island for many years, and Mr. L. Weyerhauser amassed a huge fortune in the lumber business. For about ten years, they have made their home in St. Paul. *December 9, 1911*

WHARTON, BROMLEY, who, it has just been announced, will be associated with Governor Pennypacker of Pennsylvania, is a descendant of Thomas Wharton, Jr., President of the Supreme Executive Council of Pennsylvania in 1777 and 1778. Another ancestor was Samuel Carpenter, Treasurer of Pennsylvania Province under William Penn. Mr. Wharton's home is "Sunbury" house near Croyden, but he also has a city residence. *January 24, 1903*

WHARTON, EDWARD R., who, with Mrs. Wharton, is at "The Mount," in Lenox, was suddenly seized with the automobile fever on the morning of the Fourth of July. His order was placed, the machine purchased, and made ready for delivery on the seventh, when Mr. Wharton went to Hartford and returned with his new car. *July 16, 1904*

WHARTON, MRS. EDWARD (EDITH NEWBOLD JONES), the writer of so many entertaining novels of life in society, will go to Lenox, Massachusetts, in July. There Mr. and Mrs. Wharton have built on a slight eminence looking out on Laurel Lake a beautiful country place which they call "The Mount." Here, while not among her flowers, Mrs. Wharton does the greater share of her year's literary work. She finds Lenox and its environments conducive to her best efforts. *June 10, 1905*

WHARTON, MR. AND MRS. JOHN F. (CAROLIN "CARLY" BUMILLER) lead double lives. A prominent corporation lawyer, he is also author of several down-to-earth books on economic and political subjects, a director of the Playwrights Company, and the leading authority on legal matters pertaining to show business. Carly Wharton has been a commercial artist, sculpts and paints, wrote and produced *La Cucaracha,* the first technicolor movie, and is an outstanding Broadway manager. *January, 1947*

WHARTON, JOSEPH A hefty percentage of the bluest blood on Philadelphia's Main Line assembled some fifty miles outside of their native city to celebrate Joseph Wharton Day. "Batsto," the beloved country home of brilliant financier and industrialist Joseph Wharton, fairly groaned with Biddles, Lippincotts, O'Neils, and Wrights. Wharton bought this land in 1876, for $14,000. He owned Bethlehem Steel, founded the nation's metallic zinc and nickel industries and the Wharton School of Finance and Commerce at the University of Pennsylvania. *January, 1981*

WHITNEY

Beagler Harry Payne Whitney in 1901.

"In banking and baseball, fine art and films, magazines and medicine, theater and thoroughbred racing," *Town & Country* proclaimed in 1981, "you'll always find a star Whitney." Few American dynasties have been busier.

All descend from John Whitney, who emigrated from England to Massachusetts in 1635. The family tree includes inventor Eli Whitney and the geologist for whom California's Mount Whitney is named; but the best-known—and richest—family members sprang from the 1836 marriage of James Scollay Whitney, president of Boston Water Power, and Laurinda Collins, a descendant of Governor William Bradford of the Plymouth Colony.

Their son, William Collins Whitney, was both political kingmaker for Grover Cleveland, who appointed him secretary of the Navy, and a financier on a grand scale. He built an immense fortune investing in New York City street railways. Clubman and sportsman, he owned ten houses in New York, Long Island, the Berkshires, New York's Adirondack Mountains (100,000 acres there), and Aiken, South Carolina. A multimillionaire in his own right, he married Flora Payne, a Standard Oil heiress.

Their children included Payne Whitney, a famous figure in horse racing, and his confusingly named brother Harry Payne Whitney, a polo player and all-around sportsman. Payne was also an astute businessman, who, at his death in 1927, left the largest estate ever probated in the United States: $178 million. Incredibly, despite the Great Depression, when the estate was finally distributed in 1931 it had increased to $230 million. Charities and educational institutions received

$67 million. In 1930, brother Harry died (while playing tennis), leaving only $63 million; but his wife, Gertrude Vanderbilt, was an heiress in her own right. A sculptor of note, she founded the Whitney Museum of American Art in New York City.

The next generation of Whitneys was famous for the dizzying variety of their activities: John Hay ("Jock") Whitney, Payne's son, was a producer of *Gone With the Wind,* owned the *New York Herald-Tribune,* was ambassador to Great Britain, and was the backer of *Life with Father, A Streetcar Named Desire,* and other Broadway successes. His sister Joan (Mrs. Charles Shipman Payson) owned the New York Mets baseball team, a children's bookstore, and her own venture capital company. Both were famous collectors of Impressionist and Post-Impressionist art, both were trustees of the Museum of Modern Art, and both were beneficent supporters of New York Hospital, where Whitneys have been on the governing board for more than a century. Their enormous homes at Manhasset, Long Island, complete with polo fields and helicopter landing pads, adjoined that of Jock's brother-in-law, William Paley of CBS.

Cousin Cornelius Vanderbilt ("Sonny") Whitney was equally active: He was cofounder of Pan American Airways, owner of the controlling interest in Hudson Bay Mining and Smelting Company, and, like his cousins, a motion picture investor (*Rebecca, A Star is Born*). At his death in 1992, Sonny still owned 52,000 acres (about 81 square miles) in the Adirondacks. His fourth wife, Mary Lou (Horsford), is famous both for her Saratoga parties and her entrances at them: she once descended in a balloon to her August gala.

The Whitneys of New York:
clockwise from top left, Flora
Payne Whitney, 1915; Mrs. Harry
Payne Whitney in 1925 fancy dress;
William C. and son Harry Payne,
1904; John Hay Whitney at polo,
in 1928; young H. P. Whitney III,
1933; Barbara and Joan in 1913;
at center, Sonny and Mary Lou
(Mr. and Mrs. C. V.) Whitney in 1965.

WHEELER, FROST, second secretary to the American Embassy, left Tokyo on January seventh. To quote from a Tokyo newspaper: "No more popular or capable man has filled the post in the American Embassy here." The Kokumin Shimbun presented Mr. Wheeler with a Japanese sword of sixteenth-century workmanship, with the hope that he would take with him "The Soul of the Samurai." Mr. Wheeler was well known in this country as an author, and it will be recalled that he was Tissot's model for the Christ. Mrs. Wheeler writes her novels over her maiden name, Hallie Erminie Rives. *February 12, 1910*

WHEELER, MRS. THOMAS M. (CANDACE THURBER) was the author of fairy tales and books on domestic subjects, founder of the first Society of Decorative Arts and the Associated Artists, director of the Woman's Building at the Chicago Exposition in 1893. *September 1, 1923*

WHELEN, ELSIE Quaker City society was well mingled with that of New York at the marriage of Miss Elsie Whelen, of Philadelphia, to Mr. Robert Goelet, son of Mrs. Ogden Goelet of New York. In Philadelphia, no wedding can take place without serious discussion of pedigree, and Quaker City papers have been delighted to call attention to the fact that Miss Whelan is a direct descendant of the fourth Earl of Wemyss, who was forced to flee from England during a Jacobin [sic] uprising. With his family, he came to America and settled in Chester Valley. *June 18, 1904*

WHITE, ERNEST is a member of the distinguished family from Syracuse, New York. He and his brother, Mr. Horace White, the latter at one time the Lieutenant Governor of the state, have always been greatly interested in trotting horses, and owned many good ones. In many places, with horses of all kinds, Mr. Ernest White has had his fun. *January 1, 1929*

WHITE, HENRY, the indefatigable United States Secretary of Legation in London, has endeavored to rescue American society from the position into which it had been lowered in English eyes by the general behavior of Americans in England. Mr. Henry White has come in for some pretty rough language in the American press for what it has pleased his enemies to call his "Anglomania." Their howls have gone forth because Mr. White, as an American gentleman, and in the interests of American society, decided to discriminate when Americans asked to be presented at court under the authority of the American minister. *September 19, 1888*

WHITE, MRS. HENRY (EMILY VANDERBILT) —SLOANE After W. D. Sloane's death, his widow married Henry White, onetime Ambassador to France and to Italy. It was 1920, and she was 68, but the couple departed on a honeymoon to Europe and had lunch in London with the King and Queen. White died some years later, and thereafter his widow lived in solitary splendor in "Elm Court" in Lenox, Massachusetts, coming downstairs for each meal and never retiring until the footmen were relieved at 10 P.M. She

played bridge at a dollar a point—and there were few takers—virtually to the day she died in August, 1946, at ninety four. *August, 1949*

WHITE, REV. AND MRS. LUKE MATTHEWS (JANE ELLIS TUCKER) St. Paul's Church, Norfolk, Virginia, was the scene of an important wedding when Miss Jane Ellis Tucker, daughter of the Rev. and Mrs. Beverly Dandridge Tucker and granddaughter of Colonel John Augustus Washington, the last owner of "Mount Vernon," was married to the Rev. Luke Matthews White, lineal descendant of Alexander Spotswood, the Colonial governor of Virginia. *July 8, 1905*

OH, SAY, CAN YOU SEE?

At the debutante ball given by Alice Whitehouse's parents, the J. Norman de R. Whitehouses, in Newport, the United States Navy, as a favor to the hostess, anchored a number of warships offshore and provided spectacular lighting with their searchlights. *November, 1958*

WHITEHOUSE, F. COPE has been lately devoting much time, energy, and money to a scheme for the irrigation of the Egyptian desert. The Khedive of Egypt has conferred a decoration of honor upon the American gentleman, who is endeavoring to confer such a benefit upon his majesty's country. *September 19, 1888*

WHITEHOUSE, FITZHUGH, of Madison Avenue, New York, and Mrs. Whitehouse (nee Miss Sheldon) resided during the season months in Wilton Crescent, near Belgrave Square, London, where they kept up quite a grand establishment. Mr. Whitehouse and family after the season took a most charming country house in Kent. One night lately, he had a fine display of fireworks for the amusement of the villagers. He also reads the lessons in the village church on Sundays. *September 19, 1888*

WHITEHOUSE, J. NORMAN DE R. has been in the diplomatic service since 1882. He has a residence at Irvington, New York, but his favorite home is the "Villa Denanton" in Ouchy, Switzerland. He is the author of many books on Italian subjects, is a member of the Dante Alighieri Society, and was decorated by King Humbert. His interests are largely abroad, because he delights in historical research in the Old World cities. *July 20, 1912*

WHITEHOUSE, WILLIAM FITZHUGH is the young explorer who, in 1899, when only twenty-two years old, started on his journey to Abyssinia and East Africa. At Yale, this dauntless traveler was a roommate of Mr. Alfred G. Vanderbilt. Lord Hindlip was with Mr. Whitehouse when he explored Abyssinia. They were prisoners together once in savage domain, but made a great friend of the Emperor Menelik. *July 20, 1907*

WHITING, MR. AND MRS. JASPER, whose travels are always far from the beaten paths, are embarked for the romantic coast of South America and the storied Caribbean, having abandoned their original plan of a jaunt into Mexico, where revolutions do not add to the joys of traveling. *February 15, 1924*

WHITING, WILLIAM F. News that Mr. Hoover's place as Secretary of Commerce is taken by Mr. William F. Whiting, of Holyoke, Massachusetts, is received with great joy in Washington. "Whiting" means a descendant of the yeoman of Oxford, Thomas Whyton, whose son, James, landed in Massachusetts in 1660 and settled in Hingham. Mrs. Whiting's family is equally a part of old New England history. She is the daughter of Judge Edward Whitman Chapin, the most eminent lawyer of his community before he went on the bench. Her brother had been six times Mayor of Holyoke. Their only daughter, Ruth, was married a short time ago to her distant cousin, Mr. Neil Chapin. *September 15, 1928*

WHITMAN, MRS. AND MRS. JOHN R. (CHRISTINE T. TODD) Christine Todd Whitman was elected the first woman Governor of New Jersey in 1993. Less than a year after she took office, politicians and the press latched onto her as a prospect to become the first woman Vice President of the United States. Even the first woman President. She said, "I am not interested in being Governor of New Jersey. I am interested in governing New Jersey." *March, 1995*

WHITMAN, MRS. MALCOLM (JENNIE A. CROCKER) The Crocker family are holding a reunion in Burlingame and San Mateo. Mrs. Whitman is at her home; her brother and his wife, the Templeton Crockers, are in San Mateo; and "New Place" in Burlingame (the William Crocker home) is harboring at the present Princess André Poniatowski and Comte and Comtesse André de Limur of Paris, the latter of whom was Miss Ethel Crocker. *August 15, 1922*

WHITNEY, ALFRED RUTGERS was at one time a partner in the Carnegie Steel Company. During the Sixties, he obtained the contract for the iron used in the construction of the Grand Central Station and, during the Civil War, closed a contract with the government to supply the nation with all the material used in the construction of ironclads. *November 6, 1909*

WHITNEY, ARTHUR has been nominated for Governor of New Jersey on the Republican ticket. He is connected by marriage with the family of Stevens, who, at Castle Point and Bernardsville, are part and parcel of New Jersey life. Some years ago, Mr. H. Otto Wittpenn also received the nomination. Mr. Wittpenn married Miss Caroline B. Stevens, a sister of the late and greatly loved Mr. Robert L. Stevens, who married Mr. Whitney's sister, Miss Mary Stuart Whitney. *September 15, 1925*

WHITNEY, ASA, the originator of the great Pacific Railroad scheme, is extensively engaged in the milk business in Washington. He lives a few miles out, keeps about fifty cows, and supplies Washington people with milk. He looks like a plain farmer and talks like a statesman, especially on the Pacific Railroad question. *December 20, 1856*

WHITNEY, CHARLES W. was one of the famous warship builders of this country. He designed and built the *Keokuk,* which was launched at East River and Eleventh Street in December, 1862, and in April of the next year, it figured in the attack on Fort Sumter. After the war,

Mr. Whitney took up the study of Herbert Spencer's philosophy. When Herbert Spencer visited New York in 1882, and Henry Ward Beecher welcomed him at a banquet at Delmonico's, Mr. Whitney was a member of the reception committee. *January 2, 1909*

WHITNEY, CORNELIUS VANDERBILT, known to every newspaper reader as "Sonny," has perhaps done as much for the progress of aviation in America as anyone alive, with the exception of Colonel Lindbergh. After graduation from Yale in the class of 1922, he exposed his parents, the Harry Payne Whitneys, to that nightmare of prominent families: a breach-of-promise suit. The courts were enlivened for several years in the '20s by the case of Evan Burrows Fontaine, who demanded a cool million on the plea of having secretly married Mr. Whitney while he was still an undergraduate at Yale. The case was later dropped, and Miss Fontaine was found guilty of fraud and perjury. *December, 1940*

WHITNEY, EDWARD and Mr. William Hunnewell, of Boston, have been to "Sandringham," seat of the Prince of Wales, to inspect the method of raising pheasants. Thirty compartments were occupied by twelve hen-pheasants and one cock. Eggs were gathered every morning and put under domestic hens, twelve under each hen. When hatched, the hen and young pheasants are taken to coops, each with a little yard; when old enough, these young pheasants are turned out into the preserves. In one spring, three thousand are raised in this manner. *May 23, 1883*

WHITNEY, EDWIN BALDWIN was a son of the late William Dwight Whitney, who was Editor-in-chief of the Century Dictionary. Governor White appointed Mr. Whitney to the New York State Supreme Court. As a lawyer, Mr. Whitney worked to bring about reforms that would benefit the masses in the city. His uncle, the Honorable Simeon E. Baldwin, is Governor of Connecticut. His wife is a daughter of the late Professor Simon Newcomb, U.S.N., the famous astronomer. *January 14, 1911*

WHITNEY, HARRY PAYNE He plays polo and he hunts. He is a capital shot and a good fisherman. He plays golf and tennis, drives a four, and he is a seasoned and excellent skipper. His horses have won stakes in all parts of the country, and there is hardly a classic which has not been won at some time or another by a thoroughbred bred at Brookdale or in Kentucky, bearing the famous colors, Eton blue with brown cap, which Mr. Whitney inherited from his father. *August 1, 1926*

WHITNEY, MRS. HARRY PAYNE (GERTRUDE VANDERBILT) The announcement that she has taken a studio in the Bryant Park Building in New York and will devote herself seriously to art is not a surprise to her intimate friends. Mrs. Whitney has never cared for society, and being of a serious turn of mind has tried to develop her artistic talent, so now the results of years of study justify her in making art the real aim of her existence. *April 5, 1902*

WHITNEY, JOAN The announcement by her parents, Mr. and Mrs. Payne Whitney, of the engagement of Miss Joan Whitney to Mr. Charles Shipman Payson, of Portland, Maine,

has been the subject of pleasant comment. Miss Whitney's grandfather, on her mother's side, was John Hay, formerly Ambassador to England and Secretary of State. On her father's side, the bride-to-be is a granddaughter of William C. Whitney, Secretary of the Navy. Mr. Payson is a son of Mr. Herbert Payson, member of the firm of H. M. Payson & Co., bankers, of Portland, Maine. *March 1, 1924*

TO REGISTER OR NOT TO REGISTER: THAT IS THE QUESTION

The attack on the *Social Register* comes from many quarters. Jock Whitney, who asked to be removed from its pages, calls it "a travesty of democracy." He charges the book "has absurd notions of who is and who isn't socially acceptable." *August, 1966*

WHITNEY, JOHN HAY "JOCK" "Wouldn't it be wonderful if I could somehow manage to give away more than the Rockefellers," said "Jock" Whitney some years ago. Whether he succeeds or not, he's already left an indelible mark on New York City as philanthropist, civic leader, publisher, and financier. "Whitney," says a close friend, "combines the manners of an aristocrat with the soul of a democrat." *September, 1967*

WHITNEY, MRS. PAYNE (HELEN HAY) bought her first horse because she was just a bit bored. Since then (it was twenty four years ago) her keenest interest, outside her family, has been her stable. She has become the owner of the largest racing establishment in America. She has won the Belmont Stakes, the Kentucky Derby, and so many other sweepstakes she has lost count. She has been awarded a gold medal "for her steadfast loyalty to racing." *August 15, 1934*

WHITNEY, WILLIAM C. The gift by Mr. W. C. Whitney to the State of New York of twenty elk and the offer of twenty more from his large herd at Lenox, for the purpose of helping to restock the game-ravaged forests of the Adirondacks, is another evidence of the growing realization of the importance of preventing the extinction of American game. *July 6, 1901*

WHITRIDGE, ARNOLD He was at Oxford when the war broke out, taking a postgraduate course. He had already graduated from Yale, with the class of '13. He left Oxford and joined the Royal Field Artillery, fighting in the great Somme push. In the spring of 1916, he received the Military Cross. When America actively threw in her fortunes with the Allies, he joined the home army and sailed for France. *April 10, 1918*

WHITRIDGE, FREDERICK W. was elected President of the Automobile Club of America. Mr. Whitridge is the President of the Third Avenue Railway Company. Mr. Whitridge is what one might call a many-sided man, as he is a member of the Bar, a director in railroads and construction companies, one of the pro-

moters of the rubber industry in South America, and a contributor to leading reviews and magazines. *June 15, 1912*

WHITRIDGE, MRS. FREDERICK W. (LUCY C. ARNOLD) It has frequently been asserted that New York has no salon, but such a salon has existed for years in that particularly fascinating old-fashioned double house at 16 East Eleventh Street. The mistress of this salon is Mrs. Frederick W. Whitridge, a daughter of Matthew Arnold. To Mrs. Whitridge the older and more conservative element of New York is attached—gentle folk, averse to newspaper notoriety. Mrs. Whitridge is at home between five and seven every evening of the week, and in her house at that time of the day there will always be found a number of interesting men and women, who drop in for English afternoon tea and to exchange and discuss the news of the day. *May 4, 1912*

WHITRIDGE, JOAN, one of this season's debutantes in New York, is a daughter of Mr. Frederick W. Whitridge, the official representative of the United States at the wedding of Princess Ena to the King of Spain. On the maternal side, she is a granddaughter of the late Matthew Arnold, the English scholar, and a relative of Mrs. Humphrey Ward. *December 28, 1907*

WHITTEN, MRS. FRANCIS S. (MARY K. LEWIS), who comes every year to Miami, is considered one of the best dressed women at that resort and always wears orchids. Mr. and Mrs. Whitten have a beautiful place right on Biscayne Bay, with a well on it which tradition says was used by pirates to hide their booty. *April 15, 1922*

WHITTIER, GENERAL CHARLES A. was formerly a resident of Boston. In 1898, he was appointed a Lieutenant Colonel in the volunteer army. In the Orient, he became interested in railroads in China and was made President of the American-China Development Company, which owned and operated the Hankow-Canton Railroad. In 1905, with Mr. J. Pierpont Morgan, he negotiated the sale of the road to the Chinese Government for $6,700,000. General Whittier is survived by two daughters, the Princess Belosselsky-Belozersky of Russia and Mrs. Ernest Iselin of New York. *May 23, 1908*

WHYTE, SENATOR WILLIAM PINKNEY was born in Baltimore in 1829. His mother was the daughter of William Pinkney, Minister to Russia and Special Envoy to Naples during the administration of President Monroe. He was appointed to the United States Senate in 1868. He was also at one time Mayor of Baltimore. *March 28, 1908*

WIBORG, MARY HOYT Notable among the debutantes in Cincinnati is Miss Mary Hoyt Wiborg. Miss Wiborg is a grandniece of that great statesman, John Sherman, and that incomparable warlord, General Tecumseh Sherman. She is very pretty and fascinating and was educated in Europe by masters under her mother's chaperonage. *November 3, 1906*

WIDENER, MISS JOSEPHINE P. "FIFI" The sensational elopement of Miss "Fifi" Widener and young Carter Randolph Leidy is still the subject of conversation among exclusive circles in Philadelphia. The very day on which her parents were giving a large dinner-dance in her honor at their home, "Lynwood Hall," in Elkins Park, a sudden recall to the invitations was issued—owing to the fact that there was no debutante to be introduced. The young people slipped quietly away to Knoxville and cheated society from witnessing a most interesting wedding. The bride, although but seventeen years of age, has been a prominent figure in Philadelphia society. She is an heiress to the Widener fortunes, being a granddaughter of the late P. A.B. Widener. *February 20, 1920*

WIDENER, P. A. B., of Philadelphia, is noted for the splendor of his entertainments and the comprehensiveness of his art collection. In his superb home at Ogontz, one of the Quaker City's prettiest suburbs, where last year he gave a dinner to Mr. J. Pierpont Morgan to which more than thirty millionaires were invited, he has a gallery containing works of most of the leading masters. Principal among them are pictures illustrating sacred themes. *March 7, 1903*

WIDENER, MR. AND MRS. P. A.B. II are the inheritors of one of the legendary patronymics of the American turf. Mr. Widener is a director of Hialeah Park and grandson of its founder, Joseph Widener, who imported the first flock of flamingos to grace the track's grounds. The Wideners live most of the year at their quarter-horse ranch in Wyoming. *January, 1983*

WIEN, LAWRENCE A lawyer and real estate syndication pioneer, Wien is one of New York's leading civic philanthropists. Just as notable as his giving is the creativity of his philanthropy. Wien bought 100 shares of stock in each of nearly 500 major corporations. Then, as a shareholder, he filed proxy proposals to increase each company's charitable giving. As a result, at least 450 of the companies increased their philanthropic donations; the increase involved ran into millions. *December, 1983*

WILDE, COLONEL AND MRS. H. GEORGE (MAR-JORIE FIELD) Their farm, "High Lawn," Lenox, Massachusetts, is now the largest Jersey-breeding enterprise in the Northeast. High Lawn's main house, in which the Wildes live, is a Georgian mansion of some fifty rooms. The walls inside are lined with heads of mountain sheep and caribou, shot in Alaska by adventurous relatives. High Lawn's outdoor swimming pool, not to be confused with Lake Erie, measures 180 feet by 80. *August, 1949*

WILLARD, JOSEPH EDWARD, former United States Ambassador to Spain and father of Mrs. Kermit Roosevelt, was born in Washington and graduated from Virginia Military Institute in 1886. He entered on a political career in Virginia. In 1913, he was appointed Minister to Spain. *May 1, 1924*

WILLETS, WALTER R., of "Waverly Lawn," in Long Island, during the last few years has traveled to the Canadian forests to spend one or two months at the Caughnawa Camp, which is more than two hundred miles distant from Ottawa. He is one of the charter-members of the hunting and fishing club that owns this camp, and at his Roslyn home has some fine trophies showing his success in the hunt. Mr. Willets is a good marksman, and when at Roslyn keeps in practice at the rifle range on his farm. *August 8, 1908*

WILLIAMS, ELOISE, a debutante who is being much feted in Detroit, made her debut in a snow festival. Great showers of confettti were sent down from cones by electric fans. There was a log cabin, a painted snow scene on a large curtain, and also a "man in the moon," who, propelled by electricity, made a journey across the ballroom on a wire, an owl being perched on the crescent. *December 31, 1904*

OSCAR WILDE ON THE BEACH

Oscar Wilde arrived in Newport in company with Mr. Sam Ward, and a reception was given in his honor by Mrs. Julia Ward Howe, at her cottage in Lawson Valley. Mr. Wilde breakfasted with Mr. and Mrs. George E. Waring. Later in the day, he enjoyed a pleasant sail around the harbor and in the evening dined with Chaplain Hayward of the United States Navy, on board the man-of-war *Minnesota*. Mr. Wilde attended the dance at the Casino. He was dressed in a suit of velvet, with knee breeches, light kid gloves, and a ruffled shirt front. *July 19, 1882*

WILLIAMS, MR. AND MRS. JOHN SKELTON (LILA LEBVRE ISAACS) As Comptroller of the Currency, he has undoubtedly enforced the banking regulations with exceeding strictness, if not harshness; and, coming atop a period where regulations were lax, this has been a bit hard on the bankers. As a youngster, John Skelton Williams was considered one of the handsomest men in Virginia. He is an F. F. V. of the first water. On his father's side, he is descended from Judge Bartholomew Dandridge, brother of Martha Washington, and on his mother's side from the Skeltons and the Randolphs. *March 1, 1917*

WILLIAMS, MR. AND MRS. JOHN W. (LANI SEWALL) Lani Williams made her first appearance in Honolulu when her father was Minister to Hawaii. This mahogany-haired offspring of the shipbuilding Sewalls from Bath, Maine, was named after Princess Kaiulani, who left her a spectacular collection of china and glass. High moments in the Williams life are spent at the Sewall camp at Small Point, Maine. From Maine, the Williams family drifts back to Maryland for the hunting, then on to Thomasville for shooting. *June, 1939*

WILLIAMS, SUSAN She resided at "The Hermitage," Queen Anne's County, Maryland, one of the finest original Colonial estates still existent, and which she inherited through direct female descent from Dr. Richard Tilghman, an eminent surgeon of London who settled in Maryland in 1660. During her ownership of The Hermitage, Miss Williams devoted a considerable portion of the property to the raising of thoroughbred stock and built up one of the most valuable registered Jersey herds in Maryland. *June 20, 1919*

WILLING, REBECCA The most noteworthy engagement that has recently been announced is that of Miss Rebecca Willing, of Chestnut Hill, and Mr. Benjamin Franklin Pepper, of Philadelphia. This will unite two families that have been closely connected with the history of this city since its earliest days. Through her mother, Miss Willing is descended from Edward Shippen, the first Mayor of Philadelphia under the charter of 1701. Her grandmother was Miss Paul, and she is a cousin of the late Mrs. William Waldorf Astor. She is nearly related also to Mrs. John Jacob Astor, who was formerly Miss Ava Willing. Mr. Pepper is a descendant of both Benjamin Franklin and Commodore Perry. *March 2, 1901*

WILLING, RICHARD LLOYD, a member of one of Philadelphia's oldest and best-known families, was a great-grandson of Thomas Willing, financier and banker of Revolutionary times. Mr. Willing was educated in Europe and returned to America shortly before the outbreak of the Civil War. He enlisted, with many other well-known Philadelphians, in Landis's battery and was in active service throughout the war. Mr. Willing married Miss Elizabeth Kent Ashhurst, great-granddaughter of Chancellor James Kent, the author of *Kent's Commentaries*. *April 19, 1913*

WILLOUGHBY, MR. AND MRS. HUGH LAUSSAT (M. ANTOINETTE SHERMAN)—ABD-EL MESSIH The winter months Mr. and Mrs. Willoughby always spend in Florida. Their preference for both Florida and Newport has a reason more interesting than simply the usual attraction that results from climate and social conditions. In Florida, Mr. Willoughby is a friend of the Seminole Indians and is the author of *Across the Everglades*. In 1894, he organized the Naval Reserve Torpedo Company, being ranking officer of the Rhode Island Naval Reserves. *April 2, 1904*

WILMERDING, LUCIUS The students of Columbia College had their annual presentation of the "Goodwood Cup" to the most popular gentleman in the class. The evening being fine, the attendance was large, comprising as on all occasions of similar interest a goodly number of beautiful women. The college buildings and grounds were brilliantly illuminated, a lantern being suspended from each window and strings of blue, red, violet, and white were stretched across the lawn, from Madison to Fourth Avenue. Mr. J. W. Arnold presented the "Goodwood Cup" to Mr. Lucius Wilmerding. *June 19, 1867*

WILSON, MRS. GEORGE B. An exquisite collection of orchids has been gathered very carefully by Mrs. George B. Wilson, whose home is in Philadelphia. Eleven large buildings on the Wilson property are devoted to this wonderful collection of flowers. One house is devoted entirely to white orchids, all of which are worth five hundred dollars apiece. *October 18, 1902*

WILSON, GENERAL JAMES GRANT His mother was a niece of James Sibbald, the literary antiquary of Scotland who was a friend of Bobbie Burns. His father came to this country and founded a publishing house at Poughkeepsie.

General Wilson's career is well known. His patriotism and his love for literature are both shown in the statues he was active in erecting in Central Park. It was largely due to his efforts that the statue of Columbus was erected in Central Park, and for this achievement he was knighted by the Queen Regent of Spain. *May 25, 1907*

WILSON, MR. AND MRS. MARSHALL ORME (CAROLINE ASTOR) The headdress dinner given by Mr. and Mrs. M. Orme Wilson was even more surprisingly beautiful than Mr. James H. Hyde's ball. Or, rather, it should be said that the costumes were more striking, because less attention was given to the background. On Mrs. Edmund L. Baylies's head there rested a basket of flowers which in no way impeded the quick movements that accompany her vivacious manner. Mrs. John R. Drexel was thought to be "Night" by her admirers, her attire being raven-like and a blackbird surmounting her head. The hostess, in a pansy-colored gown, had a headdress suggesting the flower that signifies thought. Crystals sparkled on the petals, each painted in yellow and purple like those in nature. *February 18, 1905*

WILSON, MRS. RICHARD T. (MELISSA C. JOHNSTON), who is the prettiest little great-grandmother in society, is not so active as she was. She was missed last winter at the opera, for in previous seasons, with her tall white-haired husband, she faithfully attended even the matinees. During the dainty little lady's last visits to the opera, however, the attendants would meet her at the foot of the crimson stairway, and the heavy mantle of chinchilla fur would be removed, so that ascent was less tedious. *July 6, 1907*

WILSON, MRS. WOODROW (EDITH BOLLING)— GALT Pocahontas, the Indian maid who married John Rolfe, an Englishman, and went to London to be a court lady, is an interesting and romantic figure. It is the proudest boast of the Bolling family of Virginia that they are descended from this union. When Pocahontas died in England, she left one son, Thomas Rolfe, who returned to Virginia and married Jane Proytheress. Their daugher, Jane Rolfe, became the wife of Colonel Robert Bolling, who arrived in the colonies in 1660 and settled in Virginia. Mrs. Galt's father was Judge William H. Bolling of Wytheville, Virginia. Until the announcement of her engagement to the President, little was known of her, for she is one of those women who believe that a woman's name should appear in the papers only three times—at her birth, marriage, and death. *October 20, 1913*

WIMAN, CHARLES DEERE, brother of Dwight Wiman, the producer, inherited the family plowshares in Moline, Illinois. Passing through Moline, you would observe just such a quiet Middle Western town as used to bemuse Sherwood Anderson and make "Red" Lewis see that way. But neither of them would ever have known it on one of the annual winter houseparties that Charlie Wiman takes down in private Pullmans from Chicago. Usually coinciding with the hangover from the Twelfth Night Ball, these occasions are remembered and talked over for weeks by the lucky many. *February 1, 1932*

WINANS, BEATRICE The engagement of Miss Beatrice Winans, daughter of Mr. and Mrs. Ross Winans, to Prince Henri de Galard et de Chalais, has been announced. Miss Winans has been in England with her parents for two years. Here Miss Winans was introduced, and she never has had a part in the social life of her native city, Baltimore. The Prince is secretary to the French embassy in St. Petersburg. *May 27, 1905*

BALTIMORE WAS SHOCKED

Around the grounds of the Winans mansion in Baltimore is a high stone wall erected by Mr. Ross Winans because, many years ago, when the garden was first built, he filled it with statues copied from the antique and opened it to the public. The nude in art was not regarded with as liberal and artistic an eye in those days as it is today, and the people of Baltimore applied to the City Council to have the statues removed. The Council paid no attention to this petition, but Mr. Winans was so enraged by it that he surrounded his garden with a wall so high that no one could see over it. *September 21, 1887*

WINANS, ROSS The first Ross Winans prominent in the United States was a resident of Baltimore, where he died in 1877, at the age of eighty one. He was an inventor who turned his genius toward everything connected with railroads. His son, Thomas de Kay Winans, who for some years lived in Newport, Rhode Island, was a famous engineer, and he, too, had important work in connection with the railroad between Moscow and St. Petersburg. As a boy, he experimented with mechanical toys. He invented a tubular adjustment by which young trout are fed, and Maryland people still remember the chimney, one hundred feet high, that he built to ventilate his residence. *September 3, 1910*

WINCHESTER, LYCURGUS is a member of an old Maryland family. Even when in knickerbockers, Mr. Winchester was noted for being a Chesterfield, his exquisite manners winning firm friends among people of all ages. When a small boy, he was known as the "Beau Brummel of Baltimore," not so much for sartorial perfection as for his manners. "If your grandmother had a splinter in her finger or some member of the family a slight cold," said a Baltimore woman, "he would even as a child be quite sure to remember and make solicitous inquiries thereto the next time he met you." *May 7, 1904*

WING, JOHN D. At Millbrook, in Dutchess County, the late Mr. Wing built his country home. The estate is called "Sandanona," which is the Indian word for sunshine. On the grounds of his own place, he built a house for each of his sons. He was one of the first New York men with great country estates to establish farms near their property. Sandanona has always been noted for its fine black sheep. The wool is woven into cloth, which the late Mr. Wing always gave away to his sons and daughters. *June 4, 1910*

WING, S. BRYCE is not one of the lightweights of the hunting field, nor is he one of the lightweights in the council rooms where affairs of hunts and the United Hunts are discussed. He is indeed one of the leading officials in the affairs of the United Hunts. At one time, he used to confine his hunting to the Millbrook country, but he has now thrown in his lot with the Harford County Hounds. *March 1, 1927*

WINGATE, GENERAL GEORGE WOOD The colony at Twilight Park in the Catskills is interesting in the same way that Onteora appeals to New Yorkers who dislike those resorts given over to any parade of fashion. General George Wood Wingate is a central figure in the colony at Twilight Park. Instead of competition at sports, in Twilight Park there seems to be rivalry in "good deeds" such as the work of the Woman's Improvement League and the sales for the benefit of the industries of the Little Italy Settlement in Brooklyn. In regard to many of these projects, General Wingate is often consulted. But he takes interest in sports, for is he not called "the Father of Rifle Practice in America"? *July 27, 1912*

WINMILL, MRS. ROBERT C. is one of Virginia's best-known and best-loved horsewomen. Although now over sixty and a grandmother fourteen times, Mrs. Winmill still rides to hounds regularly with the Warrenton Hunt, where she served as Master of Foxhounds from 1925 to 1933. Earlier this year, she spent two months in Ireland, riding in twenty five hunts with thirteen different packs of hounds. Her Warrenton house, "Whiffle-Tree Manor," is one of the show places of the Virginia hunt country and reflects her lifelong love of horses. *October, 1952*

WINTERSTEEN, MRS. JOHN (BERNICE MCILHENNY) is a forthright Philadelphian who fits into the grande dame category. Her home, "Stoke Poges," in Villanova, houses a magnificent collection of French Impressionist paintings. It also houses a spectacular potpourri of French, English, and American antique furniture and porcelains. Bernice "Bonnie" Wintersteen was the first woman to become President of a major museum in the United States, the august Philadelphia Museum of Art, a position held previously by both her father and her brother. Currently, she is President of the Board of Directors at The Moore College of Art, where she takes student strikes in stride. *October, 1970*

WINTHROP, EGERTON LEIGH matriculated from Eton in 1881 and came to America to enter Harvard. He became partner in the law firm of Winthrop and Stimson. Mr. Winthrop was for many years President of the Board of Education of New York, and later under his indefatigable guidance the Legal Aid Society grew to its present proportions. Because John Jacob Astor, son of Colonel John Jacob Astor, who went down on the *Titanic*, was born after his father's death, it became necessary to reopen the will of Colonel Astor. Mr. Winthrop represented the child in these proceedings and was appointed his guardian in August 1912. *February 15, 1926*

WINTHROP, FREDERIC John Winthrop was the original Governor of Massachusetts, coming to America in 1630. His family, along with the Adamses and the Saltonstalls, represents the true royalty of Boston. The family genealogy includes two Senators, physicists, the first officer on the Union side killed in the Civil War, authors, and historians. The annual Thanksgiving Hunt at Myopia begins at "Groton House Farm," the working farm home of Frederic Winthrop. *April, 1976*

WINTHROP, MARGARET Boston society worked indefatigably last week at the Sharon Sanatorium bazaar. Handsome Miss Margaret Winthrop, the accomplished young society dancer who gave the "can-can" at the Vincent Club show, did some Spanish dances in a decidedly finished manner. No one even among the straight-laced folks seemed a bit shocked to note that she smoked a cigarette while dancing. *May 13, 1905*

WINTHROP, ROBERT DUDLEY "Westbury Ranch," Long Island, is a beautiful American country home with all the dignity of an English one both in the architecture of the house and the simplicity of the grounds surrounding it. Walking on a little further, one comes to a thick woods, and here are the elk of which Mr. Winthrop owns a large herd that roam at will. *December 20, 1902*

WINTHROP, ROGERS just recently had a good old-fashioned "down East" housewarming at his country place at Newport. The invitations were written on torn bits of brown paper, and in bucolic style; clever imitations of the labored chirography and unconventional spelling of a farmer who "hadn't no book larnin' to speak of." They also delicately made known the fact that it was to be a donation party. Mr. Winthrop's friends took the hint, and on the evening of the housewarming the lawn resembled a live-stock fair. Mr. Alfred G. Vanderbilt contributed a frisky heifer, and the approach of Mr. James Hyde was announced by the cackling of a flock of geese. *June 20, 1903*

WISTAR, DR. CASPAR The Wistar Club is one of Philadelphia's oldest social organizations for men, and its fortnightly receptions are among the most popular events of the season. It was founded many years ago by old Dr. Caspar Wistar, who, as a young man living in Paris, gathered around him the most prominent Americans visiting the city until he unexpectedly found himself at the head of a circle composed of Philadelphians resident in Paris. Upon his return to Philadelphia—many of the older members having returned also—the club was regularly organized, and is now one of the leading societies here. *March 22, 1902*

WISTAR, GENERAL GEORGE The manner in which the Dutch Reformed Church of Tulpehocken, Pennsylvania, held land belonging to the Wistar family is an interesting survival of a medieval custom. The Wistars deeded one hundred acres of land along Tulpehocken Creek to the church, and exacted the yearly

payment of one red rose. This payment has never been made, and at a recent conference with the Wistar family it was suggested and decided that at a special service in the church full payment for the past years (one hundred and fifty-seven roses) should be made. Most of the members of the Wistar family now living in Philadelphia, will be present—among them being General George Wistar. *May 31, 1902*

WISTER, MRS. OWEN JONES (SARAH BUTLER) was the widow of Owen Jones Wister, the daughter of Pierce Butler and Fanny Kemble, a granddaughter of Charles Kemble, and a great-niece of Mrs. Sarah Siddons. Mrs. Wister, by her marriage into one of the historic Philadelphia families, had additional prestige. Her son, Owen Wister, the author of *The Virginian,* was born in Philadelphia in 1860. *June 20, 1908*

WOLFE, CATHERINE LORILLARD, one of the richest unmarried women in America, and not less eminent for her many charities, died at her home, 13 Madison Avenue. Since inheriting her father's fortune, Miss Wolfe has been known as an indulgent patroness of art and literature. Among the most prominent of her charities were the building of the Newsboys' Lodging House, Grace House, and the American Chapel at Rome. *April 6, 1887*

WOOD, MARION H. Another Philadelphia girl has determined to "seek the bubble reputation" on the stage. Although descended from a long line of Quaker ancestry, Miss Wood has always taken a keen interest in the theater and its people, and her decision to work for histrionic laurels was not made without forethought. *March 12, 1904*

WOODRUFF, ROBERT The Coca-Cola patriarch has channeled $215 million to Emory University in Atlanta since 1937—most of it through a foundation established by his banker father Ernest Woodruff, but much of it from his own Trebor Foundation (that's Robert spelled backwards) or from his own pocket. The $105 million gift to Emory from the Emily and Ernest Woodruff Foundation in 1979 was at that time the largest single gift by a living individual in the history of American philanthropy. Woodruff's personal creed: "There is no limit to what a man can do or where he can go if he doesn't mind who gets the credit." *December, 1983*

WOODWARD, JAMES T. was born in Anne Arundell County, not far from Annapolis, Maryland. Soon after the Civil War, he came to New York City. Early in the Seventies, he became a director in the Hanover National Bank. In 1877, he was elected President. In politics as well as in finance, he figured prominently. He was a close friend of President Cleveland. He had a residence at Newport, and a country home near Bowie, Prince George County, Maryland. *April 23, 1910*

WOODWARD, STANLEY, JR., son of the distinguished former U.S. Chief of Protocol, has lived in Mallorca for almost 26 years. A man of many talents, Woodward now has a 12-acre finca dedicated to breeding Arabian horses. There are some 30 breeders in Spain, according to Woodward, whose own horse, Dalilah,

was the Spanish National Champion mare. "Arabitis—love of the Arabian horse—is a disease which gets you," he said. "I love their noblesse, beauty, strength, and stamina. It's the hardiest horse in the world, and the most beautiful Arabians are found in Spain." *July, 1977*

WOODWARD, WILLIAM The chairman of the Jockey Club, one of the most responsible and honorable positions in the world of sport, Mr. Woodward has an establishment at Belair, Maryland. He races under the *nom de course* of Belair Stud, with animals of his own breeding, the most sensational of which was Gallant Fox. *May 15, 1933*

WOODWARD, MRS. WILLIAM (ELSIE CRYDER) Raised on the strict formality of the past, Elsie Woodward's society was literally the Four Hundred, and the only people she met at parties were those with family backgrounds similar to her own—those she knew already. "You never met anyone new," laments Mrs. Woodward, who looks back on the days of the Four Hundred as the dullest period in society's history. *May, 1965*

WOODWARD, WILLIAM III Third-generation Harvard, where he served on *Crimson*, he skis, likes English racing cars, but of course horse racing is in the blood (Woodward Stable, one of greatest in the U.S.). His grandfather, Board Chairman of Hanover Bank, owned Gallant Fox; his father owned Nashua. Bill now presents the Woodward classic every year. *June, 1967*

WOOLSEY, MARGARET ELLINWOOD is a granddaughter of the late Theodore Dwight Woolsey, President of Yale and a niece of Professor Theodore S. Woolsey of Yale. Miss Woolsey is also a relative of Sarah Chauncey, who, under the pen-name of Susan Coolidge, wrote some of the children's books that were best sellers during the Eighties. *December 20, 1913*

WRIGHT, COBINA, JR., is the daughter of a flamboyant stock broker who had gone busted in the crash and an indomitable, extravagant mother who always seemed to get what she wanted. Cobina Jr. developed into a blonde beauty, and at fifteen appeared in the Trianon Room of the Hotel Ambassador as a "mystery singer." She also saw Europe, where she had a whirlwind romance with Prince Philip of Greece. When she was 17, mamma decided against a formal debut and launched her child on the waves of what Cleveland Amory calls "Publi-ciety." When Cobina married wealthy auto heir Palmer Beaudette, writer Kyle Crichton credited her new husband with having brought an era to an end by taking her out of circulation. "With one stroke he has killed the age of glamour." *June, 1962*

WRIGHT, J. DUNBAR has long had a reputation for his many accomplishments. On his motor tours, he has made wonderful photographs, has shot big game, and has written much of his travels that is valuable and interesting. This last motor-tour was in Egypt. When he reaches this country, a new 45 horsepower Oldsmobile will be in readiness for Mr. Wright, but this summer he will rest at the Wright camp in the Adirondacks. *June 1, 1907*

WRIGHT, MRS. J. HOOD (MARY A. MOORE)—ROBINSON is always mindful of the welfare of the hospital named after her husband, the late J. Hood Wright. Often she gives entertainments (the proceeds of which are devoted to the hospital) at her summerhome, "The Folly," at Fort Washington, New York, once a house considered far out in the country and the first private residence in the United States to have an electric lighting plant installed. *December 28, 1907*

WRIGHT, WARREN His "Calumet Farm" in Kentucky, with its white buildings trimmed in devil's red, the racing colors of the Calumet Stable, its twenty one miles of white plank fences and its twelve hundred acres of rolling bluegrass pastures, has developed into a small city within itself. Here were bred the four Calumet Derby winners. *May, 1950*

WRIGHT, MR. AND MRS. WILLIAM MAY (SALLY D. DIXON) A Bakst party at their home in New York left one in a dazed aftermath of sumptuous memories. A great many of the costumes were designed by the artist, who was present. Wonderful to behold and keeping all admirers at a distance, by reason of its feather reach, was the Bird of Fire costume of Mrs. Wright. Her skirt, of ballet length, was a creation of unfurled ostrich, outstanding from her body ballet width, the fabric that held it of cloth of gold. *May 1, 1923*

WRIGHTSMAN, MR. AND MRS. CHARLES (JAYNE LARKIN) spend every winter in Palm Beach in a house filled with museum pieces to match the museum pieces in their New York apartment. The Wrightsmans, knowledgeable collectors both, are part of the Jackie Kennedy set as well as the Duke and Duchess of Windsor set—a double bull's eye. Jayne Wrightsman is one of the best-dressed women, and little pale linen dresses and well-cut pants are her Palm Beach trademarks. *January, 1966*

WRIGLEY, PHILIP K. Philadelphian William Wrigley, Jr., arrived in Chicago in 1891 with $32 in his pocket to run the Chicago branch of his father's soap business. The chewing gum given away to attract customers proved more popular than the products. Within a year, he had switched to producing chewing gum, and the rest is history. The company's greatest expansion came under the founder's modest son, Philip K. Wrigley. Asked how he'd like to be remembered, P. K. replied simply: "For being honest and fair." More likely, he'll be remembered as the long-suffering owner of baseball's lowly Chicago Cubs, who haven't won a pennant since 1945. *September, 1990*

WYNKOOP, ELIZABETH HILLES The wedding of Miss Wynkoop, the daughter of Dr. Gerardus H. Wynkoop, to Stuyvesant Fish Morris, Jr., will be a union of two old Knickerbocker families, descendants of the original Dutch settlers in New Amsterdam. The old Knickerbocker families have adopted Calvary Church as their place of worship, and at Calvary Church will be held the ceremony. *December 27, 1900*

XYZ

YATES, MR. AND MRS. ARTHUR GOULD (VIRGINIA L. HOLDEN) gave a tea at Palm Beach that was different from the majority of five o'clock gatherings. Its novelty depended neither upon the sun nor the moon, for they entertained their guests in their private car *Virginia*. Mr. Yates is the well-known railroad president of Rochester, New York, so the private car, it goes without saying, made an attractive setting for the tea. *March 28, 1908*

YERKES, CHARLES TYSON At the age of twenty one, he opened a stockbroker's office in Philadelphia. He failed, in 1871, for a large amount. With the year 1886 began his work in Chicago. He was for a long time at the head of the North and West Side Railway Corporations. He gave to the University of Chicago a telescope said to be the finest in the world. His Fifth Avenue residence is a veritable museum of art. Much of the furniture once belonged to the "Mad King Ludwig." The dining room is a replica of a room in Warwick Castle. *January 6, 1900*

YLVISAKER, MR. AND MRS. WILLIAM T. (JANE P. MITCHELL) "Bill" Ylvisaker is both a leader in U.S. industry and one of the world's most enthusiastic players and promoters of the bruising game of polo. Chairman of the board and chief executive officer of Gould Inc., one of America's largest manufacturing concerns, Bill still finds time to play polo in national and occasionally international competitions. Tirelessly promoting his sport, Bill has founded an impressive polo showcase, the Gould World Polo Championship. The total prize money of $150,000—far the largest purse in polo history—has attracted crack teams from all over the polo-playing world. *August, 1977*

YOUNG, MRS. ROBERT (ANITA O'KEEFFE) is the widow of the railroad tycoon and sister of painter Georgia O'Keeffe. The Youngs owned the "Towers," an Addison Mizner house. After Mr. Young's death, she tore the Towers down and built, in the same spot, the largest and most lavish house since "Mar-a-Lago"— complete with self-washing windows, two bowling alleys, and rooms filled with early O'Keeffes. *March, 1979*

YOUNG, STANLEY C. K. is one of the active members of the Greenbrier Amateur Movie Club, which has a membership of fifty and a considerable waiting list, and recently started to film a new amateur motion picture for production in The Little Theatre of The Greenbrier, White Sulphur Springs. All scenes are being photographed in and about The Greenbrier and grounds. The informal group which made and showed very successfully pictures last fall has been organized into a club which is attracting much attention here. *April 1, 1932*

YZNAGA DEL VALLE, MRS. ANTONIO (ELLEN CLEMENTS) died at her home, "Ravenswood Plantation," Lake St. John Concordia, near Natchez, Mississippi. She was the mother of Consuelo, Duchess of Manchester, of Lady Lister-Kaye, and of the late Fernando Yznaga, whose first wife was a sister of Mrs. Oliver H. P. Belmont. The present Duke of Manchester, who married Miss Helen Zimmerman, is her grandson. When little Lord Eugene Montagu was christened, she was determined that the waters of the Mississippi should be used. The Mississippi not only flows along the shores of Vicksburg, where Mr. Zimmerman was born, but past the Yznaga home in the South. *February 1, 1908*

ZABRISKIE, REV. DR. JEREMIAH LOTT was a member of a notable family identified with the history of Flatbush, New York, since the day of the first Dutch settlers. He was a graduate of Columbia University, class of '58. He held the pastorate of several churches, but in 1883 retired from the ministry and devoted himself to microscopical research. *April 9, 1910*

ZABRISKIE, MRS. TITUS Sarah T. Zabriskie's musicale and tea brought together all the members of the older cottage colony—people who were identified with Newport long before it became the "Queen City." The Zabriskie house is in the more conservative part of town, where comfort takes precedence over show. Catharine Street has many residents who, like Mrs. Zabriskie, are old Newporters. Another interesting part of Newport claims Mrs. Zabriskie, for down on the Point, the old-time court end of town, is the Zabriskie Memorial Church, which she built especially for the benefit of the mixed population of that part of town. *August 5, 1905*

ZIMBALIST, MRS. EFREM (MARY LOUISE CURTIS)—BOK After the death of her first husband, Edward Bok, Editor of the *Ladies' Home Journal,* she married violin virtuoso Efrem Zimbalist. She not only purchased the site for Camden, Maine's, public library but also endowed an outdoor amphitheater landscaped by the renowned Fletcher Steele. She and others donated the land for the village green and brought in Frederick Law Omsted, Jr., from Boston to landscape it. During the Depression, she bought and renovated a dozen Rockport houses, providing work for the townspeople and residences for faculty and students enrolled in another of her creations: a summer program of the Philadelphia-based Curtis Institute of Music, which she founded. *July, 1991*

ZU HOHENLOHE-SCHILLINGFURST, PRINCE AND PRINCESS ALFRED (CATHERINE BRITTON) "Will Catherine marry her Prince?" has been a pressing question in Washington for nearly a year and one productive of much discussion on the side as to whether the Emperor of Austria would consent and the Prince's family remove their objections. Although the consent of the Prince's family was not forthcoming, the marriage had the sanction of the embassy, presumably by order of the new Emperor, and all went merrily. It will be interesting to see the position this young couple will hold in Austria after the war, for we all know the rigid etiquette of the aristocracy of that country. *January 1, 1917*

ACKNOWLEDGMENTS

For 150 years, essayists and reporters, social observers and crusty commentators have provided the wit and wonderful detail that has made up *Town & Country*. It is impossible to thank each one of them by name; listed here are just some of the authors and staff members whose wise words I've gratefully cited, in small detail, in this volume: Cleveland Amory, Jobie Arnold, Linda Ashland, Bettina Ballard, Michael Ballentine, Caroline Bancroft, William J. Barker, Betty Grove Barnes, Hope Batey, Patricia Beard, David Bertigli, Hugh Best, Nan Tillson Birmingham, Stephen Birmingham, Earl Blackwell, Don Blanding, Ralph D. Blumenfeld, Lucyann Mueller Boston, Gloria Braggiotti Etting, Vinton P. Breese, James Brown, J. Bryan III, Harry Adsit Bull, Ted Burke, Sophy Burnham, Nathaniel Burt, Niven Busch, Catherine Calvert, John Cantrell, Igor Cassini, George Christy, Elizabeth Churchill, Hyde Clement, Elizabeth Cobb, Bruce David Colen, Stephen R. Conn, J.C. Cooley, M. Phillip Copp, Bernice Pons Cullen, Matthew J. Culligan, John T. Cunningham, Charlotte Curtis, William Curtis, Martha Axley de Bonneville, Jacques de Paris, Brenda de Suze, Landt Dennis, Anthony Del Balso, Roger Dove, M. Stannard Doyle, Peter Dragadze, Mrs. Hammond Dugan, Morgan Farrell, Athlyn Deshais Faulkner, Martin Filler, Myrna Firestone, Mildred Fitz-Hugh, Cynthia Frank, Jill Gerston, William Gildea, Burt Glinn, Kathy Gogick, Arturo Gonzalez, Janeann Gonzalez, Nancy Grace, Gloria Greer, Gene Grove, Sherwood Hall, Anne Hard, Taylor Scott Hardin, Leon Harris, Catherine Healy, Anne Randolph Hearst, Christopher Hemphill, A. Henry Higginson, Lafe Hill, Ron Hollander, Kent Hollingsworth, Nancy Holmes, A.E. Hotchner, Henry Beetle Hough, Wendy Insinger, Louise Ireland, Sally Iselin, Hillary Johnson, Marguerite Johnston, Richard A. Kagan, Ellen Kaye, Foxhall Keene, Barbara King, Suzy Knickerbocker, Oliver La Farge, Nelson Lansdale, La Roche, Merrie A. Leeds, Therese Lewis, Patricia Linden, Kathryn Livingston, Lorna Livingston, Elizabeth L.F. Locke, Nancy Love, Elizabeth Lounsbery, Elsa Maxwell, James A. Maxwell, Winzola McLendon, Monica Meenan, Peter D. Meltzer, Richard Miller, Alice-Leone Moats, Charles Monaghan, Wendy Lyon Moonan, Roberta Nederhoed, Tom O'Reilly, Eleanor Page, Gretta Palmer, Augusta Owen Patterson, John Pekkanen, Nina Phillips, Rhinelander Phillips, Christina Pittel, W.A. Powers, John Randolph, Ruth Randolph, Basil Rauch, Harris Walter Reynolds, Daniel Catton Rich, Selwa Roosevelt, Dan Rottenberg, Margaret Allen Ruhl, G.F.T. Ryall, Hubert Saal, Robert L. Sammons, Edwin F. Self, Sandy Granville Sheehy, Eugenia Sheppard, Elizabeth Simpson, Betty Grove Smith, Liz Smith, Louis Sobol, John D. Spooner, William Stadiem, Kay Sullivan, Horace Sutton, Jean Tailer, Barry Tarshis, Murray Tynan, Lindsy Van Gelder, Henry Van Horn, J.B. Van Urk, Kim Waller, Lee Walsch, Rita Wellman, Suzy Whitehouse, Howard Whitman, Suzanne Wilding, Julie S. Wilson, Reginald A. Wilson, Marion G.C. Wood, Thomas Wood, William Wright, Kathryn Zahony, Merla Zellerbach.

Opposite page: Mrs. William K. Vanderbilt, Jr., decked out for the sands of Palm Beach in 1914.

PICTURE CREDITS

Opposite: In 1915, the handler was Master Ogden Phipps. The equally well-bred beagle was Wheatley Frantic. *Overleaf:* A winter 1906 houseparty at Sagamore, Alfred Vanderbilt's Adirondack camp. *Left to right, top row:* Monson Morris, Worthington Whitehouse, Willing Spencer, Austen Gray, Alfred Vanderbilt, Fred Davies, Arthur Iselin, William Whitehouse, Fred Kernochan, Clinton Gray. *Second row:* Miss Edith Colford, Mrs. William G. Loew, Mrs. Alfred Vanderbilt, Mrs. August Belmont, Jr., Thomas Clarke, William G. Loew, Peter Goelet Gerry, DeLancey Kountze. *Front row:* Winthrop Burden, Mrs. Arthur Scott Burden, Miss Natica Rives, Mrs. Austen Gray, Mrs. Arthur Iselin, Miss Evelyn Parsons, Arthur Burden.